KEN Narzi Kuh
1 - 1   2009.

D1327287

MODERN ADVANCED
ACCOUNTING

McGRAW-HILL BOOK COMPANY

New York   St. Louis   San Francisco   Auckland   Düsseldorf
Johannesburg   Kuala Lumpur   London   Mexico   Montreal   New Delhi
Panama   Paris   São Paulo   Singapore   Sydney   Tokyo   Toronto

WALTER B. MEIGS
PH.D., C.P.A.

A. N. MOSICH
PH.D., C.P.A.

E. JOHN LARSEN
D.B.A., C.P.A.

Professors of Accounting
University of Southern California

MODERN ADVANCED ACCOUNTING

MODERN ADVANCED ACCOUNTING

2 3 4 5 6 7 8 9 0   KPKP   7 9 8 7 6 5

This book was set in Vega by York Graphic Services, Inc.
The editors were J. S. Dietrich, Sonia Sheldon, and Edwin Hanson;
the designer was Anne Canevari Green;
the production supervisor was Joe Campanella.
Kingsport Press, Inc., was printer and binder.

Library of Congress Cataloging in Publication Data
Meigs, Walter B
  Modern advanced accounting.

  Includes index.
    1. Accounting.   I. Mosich, A. N., joint author.
II. Larsen, E. John, joint author.   III. Title.
HF5635 M494   657′.046   75-5601
ISBN 0-07-041390-8

Contents

1

Organization. Characteristics of the partnership. Ease of formation. Limited life. Mutual agency. Unlimited liability. Co-ownership of partnership property and profits. Deciding between a partnership and a corporation. Is the partnership a separate entity? The partnership contract. Owners' equity accounts for partners. Loans to and from partners. Valuation of investments by partners. Profit-sharing arrangements. The partner's equity in assets versus his share in profits. Dividing profits and losses. Equal division of profits and losses or in some other agreed ratio. Division of profits and losses in the ratio of partners' capitals. Interest on partners' capitals with remaining profit or loss divided in an agreed ratio. Salary allowances with remaining profit or loss divided in an agreed ratio. Bonus to managing partner based on income. Salaries to partners combined with interest on capitals. Income statement presentation. Statement of partners' capitals. Adjustment of net income of prior years. Changes in personnel. Accounting for changes in partnership personnel. Accounting and managerial issues. Admission of a new partner. Purchase of an interest by direct payment to one or more partners. Acquisition of an interest by investment. Bonus or goodwill allowed to old partners. Bonus to old partners. Recognition of goodwill. Evaluation of bonus and goodwill methods. Fairness of asset valuation. Bonus or goodwill allowed to new partner. Bonus to new partner. Goodwill to new partner. Retirement of a partner. Computing the settlement price. Payment of bonus to retiring partner. Settlement with retiring partner for less than carrying value. Death of a partner.

Liquidation. The meaning of liquidation. Distribution of loss or gain. Distribution of cash. Determining the settlement with each partner. Division of losses and gains during liquidation. Equity of each partner sufficient to absorb loss from liquidation. Equity of one partner not sufficient to absorb his share of loss from liquidation. Equities of two partners not sufficient to absorb their shares of loss from liquidation. Partnership insolvent but partners personally solvent. Partnership insolvent and partners personally insolvent. Installment payments to partners. General principles guiding installment payment procedures. Advance planning for installment payments to partners. Withholding of cash for unpaid liabilities and liquidation expenses. Incorporation of a partnership. Joint ventures, Present-day ventures. Accounting for a joint venture. Separate set of accounting records. No separate set of accounting records.

Establishment of branches and divisions. Sales agency contrasted with branch. Accounting system for a sales agency. Illustrative entries for operation of a sales agency. Accounting system for a branch. Reciprocal accounts. Expenses incurred by home office and charged to branches. Alternative methods of billing merchandise shipments to branch. Separate financial statements for branch and home office. Combined financial statements for home office and branch. Illustrative entries for operation of a branch. Working paper for combined financial statements. Combined financial statements illustrated. Billings to branch in excess of cost. Working paper when billings to branch are in excess of cost. Treatment of beginning inventory priced above cost. Closing entries. Perpetual inventories. Reconciliation of reciprocal accounts. Transactions between branches. Start-up costs of opening new branches.

4   **BUSINESS COMBINATIONS**   **126**

Business combinations: why and how? Antitrust considerations. Methods for arranging business combinations. Statutory mergers. Statutory consolidation. Acquisition of stock. Acquisition of assets. Establishing the price for a business combination. Illustration of exchange ratio. Methods of accounting for business combinations. Purchase accounting. Determination of cost of an acquired company. Amount of consideration. Out-of-pocket costs. Contingent consideration. Allocation of cost of an acquired company. "Negative goodwill." Illustration of purchase accounting. Pooling-of-interests accounting. Illustration of pooling-of-interests accounting. Popularity of pooling-of-interests accounting. Differences in net assets. Differences in total paid-in capital. Impact of divergent price-earnings ratios. Abuses of pooling-of-interests accounting. Retroactive poolings. Retrospective poolings. Part-pooling, part-purchase accounting. Treasury stock issuances. Issuances of unusual securities. Creation of "instant earnings." Contingent payouts. "Burying" the costs of pooling combinations. The Westec Corporation scandal. Abuses of purchase accounting. Action by the AICPA. Conditions requiring pooling-of-interests accounting. Independence of combining companies. Substantially all voting common stock. Restrictions on treasury stock. No pending provisions. Presentation and disclosure of business combinations in financial statements. Purchase. Pooling of interests. Footnote disclosure of business combinations. Appraisal of accounting methods for business combinations. Criticism of purchase accounting. Criticism of pooling-of-interests accounting. Appendix: Specified conditions for pooling-of-interests accounting.

5   **CONSOLIDATED FINANCIAL STATEMENTS: AT DATE OF
        BUSINESS COMBINATION**   **164**

Nature of consolidated financial statements. Should all subsidiaries be consolidated? The meaning of "controlling financial interest." Criticism of traditional concept of control. Unconsolidated subsidiaries in consolidated financial statements. Consolidation of wholly owned subsidiaries at date of business combination. Purchase: wholly owned subsidiary. Consolidating balance sheet. Consolidated balance sheet. Pooling of interests: wholly owned subsidiary. Consolidating financial statements. Consolidated financial statements. Consolidation of partially owned subsidiaries at date of business combination. Purchase: partially owned subsidiary. Consolidating balance sheet. Pooling of interests: partially owned subsidiary. Consolidating financial statements. Consolidated financial statements. Nature of minority interest. Footnote disclosure of consolidation policy. Advantages and shortcomings of consolidated financial statements.

Intercompany transactions and balances. Loans on notes or open account. Discounting of intercompany notes. Leases of real or personal property. Rendering of professional services. Income taxes applicable to intercompany transactions. Summary: intercompany transactions and balances. Accounting for operating results of subsidiaries. Choosing between equity method and cost method. Illustration of equity method of accounting. Equity method: wholly owned pooled subsidiary. Consolidating financial statements. Closing entries. Equity method: partially owned purchased subsidiary. Consolidating financial statements. Closing entries. Illustration of cost method of accounting. Cost method: partially owned purchased subsidiary. Consolidating financial statements. Concluding comments on equity method and cost method.

Importance of eliminating intercompany profits and losses. Intercompany sales of merchandise (inventory). Intercompany sales of merchandise at cost. Intercompany profit in ending inventory. Intercompany profit in beginning and ending inventory. Intercompany profit in inventory and minority interest. Elimination of net profit versus elimination of gross profit. Intercompany sales of property and equipment and intangible assets. Intercompany profit on sale of land. Intercompany profit on sale of depreciable asset. Intercompany profit at date of sale of depreciable asset. Intercompany profit subsequent to date of sale of depreciable asset. Intercompany profit in depreciation and minority interest. Intercompany profit in later years. Intercompany profit on sale of intangible asset. Purchases of affiliate's bonds. Illustration of purchase of affiliate's bonds. Disposition of gain on reacquisition. Minority interest in gain on reacquisition of debentures. Accounting for imputed gain in subsequent years. Working paper consolidation elimination at April 30, Year 9. Working paper consolidation elimination at April 30, Year 10. Reissuance of intercompany debentures. Comprehensive illustration of consolidating financial statements working papers. Concluding comments.

installments. The installment method of accounting. Single sale of real estate on the installment plan. Sales of merchandise on the installment plan by a dealer. Data for illustration. Recording transactions. Adjusting entries. Defaults and repossessions. Other accounting issues relating to installment sales. Trade-ins. Interest on installment contracts receivable. Installment method for income tax purposes only. Accounting for retail land sales. Financial statement presentation. Income statement. Balance sheet. Consignments. The meaning of consignments. Distinguishing between a consignment and a sale. Rights and duties of the consignee. The account sales. Accounting methods for consignee. Accounting methods for consignor. Should gross profits on consignments be determined separately? Illustration of accounting methods for consignor. Accounting for partial sale of consigned goods. Return of unsold goods by consignee. Advances from consignees. Nature of the Consignment Out account.

13 PRESENT VALUE: CONCEPTS AND APPLICATIONS 479

Amount of $1 formula. Summary. Present value of $1 formula. Summary. Annuities—a series of equal receipts or payments. Amount of ordinary annuity of $1 formula. Summary. Amount of an annuity due. Amount of deferred annuity. Present value of ordinary annuity of $1 formula. Summary. Present value of annuity due. Present value of deferred annuity. Compound interest methods of depreciation. Annuity method. Sinking fund method. Refunding a bond issue. Direct valuation by discounting future cash flows. Can greater use be made of direct valuation in financial reporting? Use of direct valuation in current value accounting. Proposed current value reporting model. Personal financial statements. Appendix: Personal financial statements.

14 GOVERNMENT ENTITIES: FUNDS AND PROGRAMS 519

Nature of government entities. Theory of accounting for government entities. The governmental accounting entity. The modified accrual basis of accounting. Recording of expenditures rather than expenses. Recording of purchase orders for goods and services. Recording the budget. Types of operating budgets. Journal entries for a general fund budget. Illustrations of accounting for government entities. Accounting for the general fund. Illustration of accounting for a general fund. Closing entries for a general fund. Financial statements for a general fund. Concluding comments on accounting for a general fund. Accounting for special revenue funds. Accounting for debt service funds. Journal entries for a debt service fund. Financial statements for a debt service fund. Accounting for capital projects funds. Journal entries for a capital projects fund. Financial statements for a capital projects fund. Accounting for enterprise funds. Financial statements for an enterprise fund. Accounting for trust and agency funds. Accounting for intragovernmental service funds. Accounting for special assessment funds. Journal entries for a special assessment fund. Financial statements for a special assessment fund. The general fixed assets and general long-term debt account groups. Combined financial statements for governmental units. Checklist for governmental entity accounting.

15 NOT-FOR-PROFIT ENTITIES 565

Characteristics of not-for-profit entities. Characteristics comparable to those of governmental entities. Characteristics comparable to those of commercial enterprises. Accounting for not-for-profit entities. Unrestricted fund. Designated fund balance of unrestricted fund. Revenue of unrestricted fund. Revenue for services. Donated goods and services. Pledges. Revenue from pooled investments. Expenses of unrestricted fund. Assets and liabilities of unrestricted fund. Restricted fund. Endowment fund. Agency fund. Annuity and life income funds. Annuity fund. Life income fund. Loan fund. Plant fund. Financial statements for not-for-profit entities. Illustrative financial statements of a not-for-profit entity. Appendix: Civic Welfare Organization.

16 ACCOUNTING FOR ESTATES AND TRUSTS 597

Legal and accounting aspects of estates. Provisions of Uniform Probate Code governing estates. Wills. Probate of wills. Appointment of personal representative. Powers and duties of personal representative. Exempt property and allowances. Claims of creditors against the estate. Distributions to devisees. Estate and inheritance taxes. Closing estates. Provisions of Revised Uniform Principal and Income Act governing estates. Illustration of accounting for an estate. Trial balance of estate accounts. Charge and discharge statement. Closing entry for estate. Concluding comments on accounting for estates. Legal and accounting aspects of trusts. Provisions of Uniform Probate Code affecting trusts. Provisions of Revised Uniform Principal and Income Act governing trusts. Illustration of accounting for a trust. Trial balance of trust accounts. Charge and discharge statement for trust. Closing entry for trust.

Preface

Modern Advanced Accounting is not a revision but a new book in the Meigs and Mosich coordinated accounting series, which includes volumes at both the introductory and intermediate accounting levels. In recognition of the fact that the time allotted to the advanced accounting course is now seldom more than one semester or two quarters, the number of chapters has been held to sixteen, and the overall length is clearly much less than for most earlier textbooks in advanced accounting.

New challenging topics characterize *Modern Advanced Accounting* despite its compact size. The coverage includes many of the current controversial topics which have stirred the accounting profession and the entire financial community in recent years. Focusing on these currently debated issues are chapters dealing with pooling-of-interests accounting for business combinations, interim financial statements, forecasts, segment reporting, and financial reporting by multinational companies, including new approaches to foreign currency translation. The problem of changes in asset values is discussed in Chapter 13, "Present Value: Concepts and Applications," in which direct valuation techniques and fair-value accounting are illustrated.

The traditional topics of advanced accounting are presented in concise fashion. Thus, partnerships and joint ventures are covered in Chapters 1 and 2, which carry the student from the basic concepts often summarized in introductory accounting to the CPA examination level, with its more complex problems of profit-sharing, realignment of ownership, and liquidation. Chapter 3, "Accounting for Branches," provides a logical stepping-stone to the larger area of business combinations (Chapter 4). This chapter sets the stage for the various phases of consolidated financial statements, which comprise a major portion of the book and are presented in a carefully coordinated format in Chapters 5 through 8.

In the continuing effort to avoid bulk and procedural details, the traditional topics of installment sales and consignments are covered in a single chapter. Individual streamlined chapters are also devoted to government entities: funds and programs, to not-for-profit entities, to bankruptcy and corporate reorganization, and to accounting for estates and trusts. In older advanced accounting textbooks, each of these topics often occupied two or more chapters.

Carefully selected financial statements recently published by a large CPA firm and by two leading corporations are presented in an appendix, so that many of the theoretical concepts in the text may be conveniently traced into real-world situations. Compound interest tables are also presented in an appendix.

The authoritative pronouncements of the Financial Accounting Standards Board and of its predecessor, the Accounting Principles Board, are interwoven into the discussion and in problem material throughout the book. We believe, however, that accounting education should encourage students to participate in a critical evaluation of accounting concepts and should make students aware of the conflicts and shortcomings that exist within the traditional structure of accounting theory. We have therefore tried to provide students with an analytical basis for making this evaluation, to help them see that most of the controversial areas of accounting ultimately center on underlying issues and questions to which there are no neat and simple answers.

Review Questions, Exercises, Short Cases for Analysis and Decision, and Problems

In providing four levels of problem material at the end of each chapter, this book goes well beyond the conventional range of textbooks in advanced accounting.

The review questions are intended for use by students as a self-testing and review device to measure their comprehension of key points in each chapter. Many of the questions are also of a provocative nature, which makes them suitable for written assignments and engenders lively class discussion.

The exercises included at the end of each chapter typically cover a specific important point or topic and generally do not require extensive computations. Many instructors may wish to use the exercises to supplement problem assignments, for class discussion, and for examination purposes.

The short cases for analysis and decision, which follow the exercises at the end of each chapter, are essentially problems that require analytical reasoning but involve little or no quantitative data. In this category of problem material, students are called upon to analyze business situations, to apply accounting principles, and to propose a course of action. They are not required, however, to prepare lengthy working papers or otherwise to manipulate accounting data on an extensive scale. These short cases have all been class-tested and have proved their worth as a means of encouraging students to take clear-cut positions in the argument of controversial accounting issues. A number of short cases for analysis and decision have been adapted from CPA examination material. The cases are especially recommended if the instructor wishes students to develop skill in communicating accounting concepts and to weigh the merits of opposing arguments.

The problems range in difficulty from simple to complex and in the length of time required for solution—from 15 minutes to more than an hour. Many of the problems are adapted from the Accounting Theory and Accounting Practice sections of recent Uniform CPA Examinations. Others have been designed especially to demonstrate the concepts presented in the theoretical discussion. Probably no more than a quarter of the total case and problem material would be used in a single offering of the course; consequently ample opportunity exists to vary problem assignments from year to year.

Partially Filled-in Working Papers (Accounting Work Sheets)

A set of partially filled-in working papers for all problems is published separately from the textbook. On these work sheets, the company names the problem numbers, numerous headings, and some preliminary data (such as trial balances) have been entered to save student time and to facilitate rapid review by the instructor.

Checklist of Key Figures

In this checklist, key figures are provided for all but the shortest problems. It is available, free, in quantity to instructors who wish to distribute key figures to students. The purpose of the checklist is to aid students in verifying their problem solutions.

Other Supplementary Materials

Another important supplement accompanying this book is a *Study Guide* prepared by the authors of the textbook and designed to help students measure their progress by immediate feedback. The *Study Guide* contains for each chapter an outline of the most important points in the textbook plus a variety of objective questions and short exercises. Answers to the questions and exercises appear in the back of the *Study Guide* to help students in a prompt self-evaluation of their understanding of each chapter. Experience indicates that the use of a well-organized *Study Guide* as a supplement to the textbook increases student understanding of the subject matter with a minimum of additional effort.

Also provided with the textbook is a series of objective tests closely correlated with the text. Each of the four achievement tests is intended for use in a 50-minute class period. A comprehensive examination covering the entire book and requiring about 100 minutes is also provided. The increased use of objective questions on recent Uniform CPA Examinations has provided an extensive source of this type of test material. The use of these tests should aid students interested in preparing for the Accounting Theory and Accounting Practice sections of the Uniform CPA Examination, as well as providing comprehensive testing over all chapters in the book.

Contributions by Others

Our sincere thanks go to the many faculty members from whom we received valuable suggestions. Especially helpful was the advice received from Professors W. W. Harned and Allen R. Bailey, California State University, San Diego; L. Vann Seawell, Indiana University; L. C. Jurgensen, University of South Florida; Robert W. Hill, California State University, Hayward; R. E. Curtis, University of Minnesota, Duluth; Robert W. Vanasse, California State University, Fullerton; James W. Pratt, University of Houston; Joseph O'Rourke, Portland State University; Edwin Pinto, California State University, San Jose; and William K. Harper, University of Southern California. Important assistance in the preparation of problems and manuscript was provided by Jane Iizuka, Martin Kubota, and Mel Woods of the University of Southern California.

We also acknowledge with appreciation permission from the American Institute of Certified Public Accountants to quote from many of its pronouncements and to utilize materials adapted from the Uniform CPA Examinations. Finally, we express our appreciation to the Financial Accounting Standards Board for permission to quote from its pronouncements.

Walter B. Meigs
A. N. Mosich
E. John Larsen

1

30 pgs.

Partnership organization and operation

Much of our discussion of partnerships will be based on the Uniform Partnership Act which has been adopted by many of the states. This act defines a **partnership** (often referred to as a **firm**) as "an association of two or more persons to carry on, as co-owners, a business for profit." Although the word **persons** suggests living individuals, a partnership can also include other partnerships among its members; in some states a corporation can become a partner. The creation of a partnership requires no approval by the state; in fact, a partnership may be formed without a written contract or documents of any type, although a carefully formulated written contract is highly desirable.

Partnerships are traditionally associated with the practice of law, medicine, public accounting, and other professions, and also with small business concerns. In some states the licensed professional person such as the CPA is forbidden to incorporate on the grounds that the creation of a corporate entity might weaken the personal relationship of the practitioner to his client. In recent years, however, a number of states have approved legislation designed to permit **professional corporations**. A few large industrial and merchandising enterprises also use the partnership form of organization.

ORGANIZATION

Characteristics of the partnership

The basic characteristics of a partnership are briefly summarized below:

Ease of Formation In contrast to a corporation, a partnership may be created by oral or written agreement between two or more persons or may be implied by their conduct. This advantage of convenience and minimum expense in the formation of a partnership may in some cases be offset by certain difficulties inherent in such an informal and loosely designed organizational structure.

Limited Life A partnership may be ended by the death, retirement, bankruptcy, or incapacity of a partner. The admission of a new member to the firm legally ends the existing partnership.

Mutual Agency Each partner has the authority to act for the partnership and to enter into contracts binding upon it. Acts beyond the normal scope of business operations, however, such as the borrowing of funds by a partner, generally do not bind the partnership unless specific authority has been given to the partner to enter into such transactions.

Unlimited Liability The term *general partnership* refers to a firm in which all the partners are personally responsible for debts of the firm and all have authority to act for the firm. Each partner in a general partnership is personally responsible for the liabilities of the firm. Creditors who are having difficulty in collecting from the partnership will be likely to turn to those individual members of the firm who have other financial resources. In a *limited partnership* one (or more) of the partners has no personal liability for debts of the partnership. The activities of a limited partner are somewhat restricted, and he must maintain an agreed investment in the firm. Statutes providing for limited partnerships require that the firm identify itself publicly as a limited partnership and that at least one member be a general partner.

Co-ownership of Partnership Property and Profits When an individual invests assets in a partnership, he retains no claim to those specific properties but merely acquires an *equity* in all assets of the firm. Every member of a partnership has an ownership interest in the profits; in fact, participation in profits and losses is one of the tests of the existence of a partnership.

Deciding between a partnership and a corporation

One of the most important considerations in choosing between a partnership and the corporate form of organization is the income tax status of the business and of its owners. A partnership pays no income tax but is required to file an information return showing its revenue and expenses, the amount of its net income, and the division of that income among the partners. The partners in turn include their respective shares of the *ordinary net income* from the partnership and such items as dividends, capital gains and losses, and charitable contributions on their individual income tax returns, regardless of whether they received more or less than this amount of cash from the partnership during the year.

The corporation is a separate legal entity subject to a corporate income tax. The net income, when and if distributed to stockholders in the form of dividends, is also taxable income to stockholders. Certain corporations with not more than ten stockholders are eligible to avoid being taxed as corporations provided their income or loss is fully assumed by their stockholders. These "tax-option corporations" file information returns as do partnerships, and their stockholders report on individual tax returns their respective shares of the year's profit or loss. Some partnerships have chosen to incorporate but elect to be taxed as partnerships. A partnership may also elect to be taxed as a corporation. Income tax rates and regulations are subject to frequent change, and new interpretations of the rules often arise. The tax status of the owners is also likely to change from year to year. For all these reasons, management should regularly review the tax implications of the partnership and corporate forms of organization so that the business entity may adapt most successfully to the tax environment.

The burden of taxation is not the only factor in making a choice between the partnership and the corporate form of organization. Perhaps the factor which most often tips the scales in favor of incorporation is the opportunity of obtaining greater amounts of capital when ownership can be divided into shares of stock, readily transferable and offering the advantages inherent in the separation of ownership and management.

Is the partnership a separate entity?

In accounting literature, the legal aspects of partnerships have generally received more emphasis than the managerial and financial issues. It has been common practice to distinguish a partnership from a corporation by saying that the former was an association of persons and the latter a separate entity. Such a distinction unfortunately stresses the legal form rather than the economic substance of the business organization. In terms of managerial policy and business objectives, many a partnership is as truly a business entity as if it were incorporated. Such partnerships typically are guided by long-range plans not likely to be affected by the admission or withdrawal of a single member. In these firms the accounting policies logically should carry out the concept of the partnership as an entity apart from its individual owners.

Viewing the partnership as a business entity will often aid in developing financial statements that provide the most meaningful picture of financial position and results of operations. Among the accounting policies to be stressed is continuity in asset valuation, despite changes in the ratio of profit sharing and changes in personnel. Another helpful step may be recognition in expense accounts of the value of personal services rendered by partners who also hold managerial positions. In theoretical discussions considerable support is found for viewing every business as an entity, apart from its owners, regardless of the form of legal organization. A managing partner under this view plays two roles: one as an employee of the entity, and the other as an owner. The value of the personal services rendered by the partner is an expense of managing the business entity. Unless this operating expense is deducted from revenue, the measurement of income is to a considerable extent invalid.

The inclusion of partners' salaries among expenses has been opposed by some accountants on grounds that partners' salaries may be set at unrealistic levels unrelated to the value of the services rendered and that the partnership is merely an association of individuals in which the partner is an owner and not an employee.

In practice many accountants are accustomed to viewing partnerships as separate entities with continuity of accounting policies and asset valuations not broken by changes in partnership personnel. However, much work must yet be done before generally accepted standards are adequate to guide the accountant in determining the impact on accounting policies when a partner retires or a new member is admitted to the firm.

The partnership also has the characteristics of a separate entity in that it may hold title to property in its own name, may enter into contracts, and in some states may sue or be sued as an entity.

The partnership contract

Although a partnership may exist on the basis of an oral agreement or be implied by the actions of its members, good business practice demands that the partnership contract be clearly stated in writing. Among the more important points to be covered by the partnership contract are:

1 The date of formation of the partnership, the duration of the contract, the names of the partners, and the name and nature of the partnership.
2 The assets to be invested by each partner, the procedure for valuing non-cash investments, and the penalties for failure to invest and maintain the agreed amount of capital.
3 The authority to be vested in each partner and the rights and duties of each.
4 The accounting period to be used, the nature of accounting records, financial statements, and audits by certified public accountants.
5 The plan for sharing profits and losses, including the frequency of income measurement and the distribution to partners.

6 The salaries and drawings allowed to partners and the penalties, if any, for excessive withdrawals.

7 Insurance on the lives of partners, with the partnership or surviving partners named as beneficiaries.

8 Provision for the arbitration of disputes and the liquidation of the partnership at the end of the specified term of the contract or at the death or withdrawal of a partner. Especially important in avoiding disputes is agreement upon procedures for valuation of the business and the method of settlement with the estate of a deceased partner.

One advantage of developing an adequate partnership contract with the aid of attorneys and accountants is that the process of reaching agreement on specific issues will develop a better understanding among the partners on many issues which might be highly controversial if not settled at the outset. Of course, it is seldom possible to cover specifically in a partnership contract every issue which may later arise. Revision of the partnership contract generally requires the agreement of all partners.

Disputes arising among partners which cannot be resolved by reference to the partnership agreement may be settled by arbitration or in the courts. The partner who is not satisfied with the handling of disputed issues always has the right to withdraw from the firm. The relationship of partners is a voluntary one; no one can be forced against his will to continue as a partner, regardless of the agreed term of operations.

Owners' equity accounts for partners

Accounting for a partnership differs from accounting for a single proprietorship or a corporation chiefly with respect to the sharing of profits and losses and the maintenance of the owners' equity accounts. Although it would be possible to operate a set of partnership records with only one equity account for each partner, the usual practice is to maintain three types of accounts. These equity accounts consist of (1) *capital* accounts, (2) *drawing* or *personal* accounts, and (3) accounts for *loans to or from partners*.

The original investment by each partner in the firm is recorded by debiting the assets invested, crediting any liabilities being assumed by the firm, and crediting the partner's capital account with the fair value of the net assets invested. Subsequent to the original investment, the partner's equity may be *increased* by additional investment of cash or other property and by a share of the partnership income. The partner's equity in the firm may be *decreased* by withdrawal of cash or other assets and by sharing losses incurred by the firm.

Another possible source of increase or decrease in partners' equity arises from changes in partnership personnel, as discussed on pages 19–31.

The original investment of assets by a partner is recorded by credit to his capital account. Drawings by a partner in anticipation of profits or drawings which are considered as the equivalent of a salary are recorded by debit to his drawing account. However, a large withdrawal which is viewed as a permanent reduction in the equity of a partner should be charged directly to the partner's capital account.

At the end of the accounting period the income or loss shown by the Income Summary account is transferred to the partners' capital accounts in accordance with the profit-sharing agreement. The debit balances in the drawing accounts at the end of the year are also closed into the partners' capital accounts. Since the accounting procedures for partners' equity accounts are not subject to state regulations as in the case of capital stock and other stockholders' equity accounts of a corporation, many deviations from the procedures described here are possible.

Loans to and from partners

Occasionally a partner may withdraw a substantial sum from the partnership with the intention of repaying this amount. Such a transaction may be debited to the Notes Receivable from Partners account rather than to the partner's drawing account.

On the other hand, a partner may make an advance to the partnership which is viewed as a loan rather than an increase in his capital account. This type of transaction is recorded by a credit to Loans Payable to Partners and is desirably accompanied by the issuance of a note payable. Amounts due from partners may be reflected as assets in the balance sheet and amounts owing to partners shown as liabilities. The classification of these items as current or long-term would, of course, depend upon the maturity date specified in the loan agreement. As for all transactions not consummated at arm's length, a greater weight of evidence is needed to support the prospects for completion of the transaction according to the agreed terms.

If a substantial unsecured loan has been made by a partnership to one of the partners and repayment appears doubtful, the better financial statement presentation may be to offset the receivable against the partner's capital account. If this is not done, assets and the owners' equity may be inflated to the point of being misleading. In any event, adequate disclosure calls for separate listing of any receivables from partners.

Valuation of investments by partners

The investment in the firm by a partner often includes assets other than cash. It is imperative that the partners agree upon the fair value of these assets at the time of their investment and that the assets be recorded at their fair values at this time. Any gain or loss resulting from the disposal of such assets during the operation of the partnership or at the time of liquidation will be divided according to the agreement for sharing profits and losses. Equitable treatment of the individual partners, therefore, requires a starting point of fair values recorded for all assets invested in the firm. It will then follow that partnership gains or losses upon disposal of non-cash assets invested by the partners will be limited to the difference between the disposal price and the fair value of the assets when invested by the partners, adjusted for depreciation or amortization to date of disposal.

PROFIT-SHARING ARRANGEMENTS

The partner's equity in assets versus his share in profits

The equity of a partner in the assets of the firm should be clearly distinguished from his share of profits and losses. Thus, to say that X is a one-third partner is not a clear statement. He may have a one-third claim on the net assets of the firm but have a share in profits greater or smaller than this proportion. Such a statement might also be interpreted to mean that X was entitled to one-third of the profits or losses, although his capital account represented much more or much less than one-third of the total ownership equity. To state the matter concisely, the partners may agree upon any type of profit-sharing plan, regardless of the amount of their respective capital accounts. The Uniform Partnership Act states, however, that *if partners fail to specify a plan for sharing profits and losses, it shall be assumed that they intended to share equally.*

Dividing profits and losses

The many possible arrangements for sharing of profits and losses among partners may be summarized into the following four categories:

1 Dividing profits and losses equally or in some other agreed ratio
2 Dividing profits and losses in the ratio of partners' capitals as of a particular date, or in the ratio of average capitals during the year
3 Allowing salaries to partners and dividing the remaining profit or loss in an agreed ratio
4 Allowing salaries to partners, allowing interest on capitals, and dividing the remaining profit or loss in an agreed ratio

These variations in profit-sharing plans emphasize that the value of personal services rendered by individual partners may vary widely, as may the amounts of capital invested by each. The amount and quality of managerial services rendered and the amount of capital invested are important factors in the success or failure of the business. Therefore it is often logical to provide for salaries to partners and interest on their respective capitals as a preliminary step in dividing the profits of the business. Residual profits or losses may then be divided equally.

Another factor affecting the success of the firm may be that one of the partners has very large personal financial resources, which cause the partnership to have a high credit rating merely because of his membership in it. Similarly, a partner with a name widely known in a professional field or even in industry may contribute importantly to the success of the firm even though he may not actively participate in management of the business. These two factors may be taken into account in devising the profit-sharing plan by judicious selection of the ratio in which any residual profits or losses are divided.

We shall now illustrate how each of the methods of dividing net income (profits) or loss may be applied. This series of illustrations is based on the partnership of A and B, which is assumed to earn net income of $30,000 during the first year of operation. The partnership agreement provides that each partner may withdraw $500 on the last day of each month. These drawings are not a factor in dividing net income; they are recorded by debits to the partners' drawing accounts and are not to be regarded as salaries. All other withdrawals, investments, and income or losses will be entered in the partners' capital accounts.

Partner A's original investment on January 1 was $40,000 and he invested an additional $10,000 on April 1. Partner B's investment on January 1 was $80,000 and he withdrew $5,000 on July 1. These transactions are illustrated in the following capital and drawing accounts for the two partners and by the Income Summary account showing a net income of $30,000 to be divided.

A, Capital			B, Capital		
	Jan. 1 40,000	July 1 5,000	Jan. 1 80,000		
	Apr. 1 10,000				

A, Drawing		B, Drawing	
Jan.–Dec., inclusive 6,000		Jan.–Dec., inclusive 6,000	

Income Summary	
	Dec. 31 30,000

Equal Division of Profits and Losses or in Some Other Agreed Ratio Many partnership agreements provide that net income or loss will be divided equally. Also, if the partners have made no specific agreement for sharing profits, the Uniform Partnership Act provides that an intent of equal division will be assumed. The net income of $30,000 for partnership A and B will therefore be transferred from the Income Summary account to the partners' capital accounts by the following journal entry:

```
Income Summary. . . . . . . . . . . . . . . . . . . . . . . . . . . . . . . . . . . .   30,000
        A, Capital  . . . . . . . . . . . . . . . . . . . . . . . . . . . . . . .                 15,000
        B, Capital  . . . . .  . . . . . . . . . . . . . . . . . . . . . . . .                 15,000
To divide the net income equally between A and B.
```

The drawing accounts will now be closed to the partners' capital accounts so that each partner's capital account at the end of the year will show the equity resulting from combining the positive factors of beginning capital, subsequent investments, and share of net income with the negative factors of monthly drawings and any other withdrawals of capital.

If the business owned by A and B had operated at a loss of, say, $20,000 during the first year, the Income Summary account would show a debit balance of $20,000. This loss would be transferred to the capital accounts by debiting each capital account for $10,000 and crediting Income Summary for $20,000.

Assuming that A and B agree to share profits and losses in the ratio of 60% to A and 40% to B and that net income amounts to $30,000, the net income would be divided $18,000 to A and $12,000 to B. The agreement that A should receive 60% of the net income (perhaps because of his greater experience and personal contacts) would cause him to suffer a larger share of the loss if the business operated unprofitably. Some partnership agreements provide that profits will be divided in a certain ratio such as 60% to A and 40% to B, but that losses will be divided equally or in some other ratio. Another variation intended to compensate for unequal contributions by the partners provides that the agreed ratio (60% and 40% in our example) shall be applicable to a given amount of earnings, but that additional earnings shall be shared in some other ratio. A profit-sharing agreement of this type places extreme importance on the *timing* of partnership income. Close decisions are often necessary in determining whether a given expenditure shall be treated as expense immediately or as a prepayment. Similar difficult decisions may be necessary in deciding whether certain revenue items belong in the current year or in the following year.

Division of Profits and Losses in the Ratio of Partners' Capitals Division of partnership earnings in proportion to the capital provided by each member of the firm is most likely to be found in the type of business in which substantial investment is the principal ingredient for success. For example, a partnership engaged in purchasing land and holding it for higher prices might select this method of dividing profits and losses. To avoid controversy, it is essential that the agreement specify whether the profit-sharing ratio is based on the original capital investments, the capitals at the beginning of each year, the capitals at the end of each year (before the distribution of net income or loss), or the average capitals during each year.

Continuing our illustration of the partnership of A and B, assume that the agreement calls for division of net income in the ratio of the **original capitals.** The first year's net income will be divided as follows:

$$A, \$30,000 \times \$40,000/\$120,000 = \$10,000$$
$$B, \$30,000 \times \$80,000/\$120,000 = \$20,000$$

The entry to close the Income Summary account would be similar to the entry illustrated on page 9.

Assuming that the net income was to be divided in the ratio of capitals at the **end of the year** (before drawings and the distribution of net income), the net income for the first year would be divided as follows:

$$A, \$30,000 \times \$50,000/\$125,000 = \$12,000$$
$$B, \$30,000 \times \$75,000/\$125,000 = \$18,000$$

Dividing net income on the basis of (1) original capitals, (2) yearly beginning capitals, or (3) yearly ending capitals may prove inequitable if there are significant changes in capital during the period because of withdrawals or added investments by partners. Using average capitals as a basis is preferable in that it reflects the capital actually available for use by the business during the year.

If the partnership agreement provides for sharing net income in the ratio of average capitals during the year, it should also state the amount of drawings each partner may make without affecting his capital account. In our continuing example of the firm of A and B, the partners are entitled to withdraw $500 monthly, and these drawings are recorded in the drawing accounts. Any additional withdrawals and any investments are entered in the partners' capital accounts and therefore influence the computation of the average capital ratio. The partnership agreement should also state whether capital balances are to be computed in terms of dollar-months, dollar-weeks, or dollar-days.

In our example, ratio of average capitals in dollar-months for A and B and division of net income are computed at the top of page 11.

In making these calculations we could have computed the average capital for each partner by dividing his dollar-months by 12. Thus, average capital for A was $570,000 ÷ 12, or $47,500; and average capital for B was $930,000 ÷ 12, or $77,500. The ratio between these average capitals is the same as the ratio of dollar-months in the schedule on page 11.

It is worth repeating that partners may divide profits and losses in any manner they wish; variations from the methods illustrated are virtually unlimited.

A & B PARTNERSHIP
Computation of Average Capitals
Current Year

Partner	Date	Decrease in capital	Increase in capital	Capital balance	Months unchanged	Dollar-months
A	Jan. 1		$40,000	$40,000	3	$ 120,000
	Apr. 1		10,000	50,000	9	450,000
					12	$ 570,000
B	Jan. 1		80,000	80,000	6	$ 480,000
	July 1	$5,000		75,000	6	450,000
					12	$ 930,000

Total dollar-months for A and B combined $1,500,000

Division of net income:

To A: $30,000 × $570,000/$1,500,000 . . . . $ 11,400

To B: $30,000 × $930,000/$1,500,000 18,600

Total net income . . . . $ 30,000

Interest on Partners' Capitals with Remaining Profit or Loss Divided in an Agreed Ratio In the preceding section the plan for dividing the entire net income in the ratio of partners' capital was based on the assumption that invested capital was the dominant factor in profitable operation of the business. In most lines of business, however, the amount of invested capital is only one of several factors which are significant in achieving profitable operation. Consequently, many partnerships choose to divide only a portion of net income in the capital ratio, and to divide the remainder equally or in some other agreed ratio.

To allow interest on capitals at an agreed rate of, say, 6% is essentially the same thing as dividing a *limited portion* of net income in the ratio of partners' capitals.

If the partners agree to allow interest on capital as a first step in dividing net income, they should of course specify the interest rate to be used and also state whether the calculation is to be based on capital accounts at specific dates or on average capitals during the year.

Let us use again our basic illustration of the firm of A and B with a net income of $30,000 during the first year and capital accounts as shown on page 8. Assume that the partnership agreement allows interest on partners' average capitals at 6% with any remaining income or loss to be divided equally. The net income would be divided as follows:

	A	B	Combined
Interest on average capitals:			
A: 6% of $47,500	$ 2,850		$ 2,850
B: 6% of $77,500		$ 4,650	4,650
Subtotal			$ 7,500
Balance ($30,000 − $7,500) divided equally	11,250	11,250	22,500
Total	$14,100	$15,900	$30,000

The entry to close the Income Summary account follows:

Income Summary.	30,000	
A, Capital		14,100
B, Capital		15,900
To divide the net income for the year.		

As a separate case, assume that the partnership of A and B was unsuccessful in its first year and sustained a net loss of $1,000. If the partnership agreement provides for allowing interest on capitals, this provision *must be enforced regardless of whether operations are profitable or unprofitable*. The only justification for omitting the allowance of interest on partners' capitals during a loss year would be in the case of a partnership agreement containing a specific clause requiring such omission. Note in the following schedule that the $1,000 debit balance in the Income Summary account resulting from the operating loss is increased by allowance of interest to a debit total of $8,500, which is then divided equally between the partners.

	A	B	Combined
Interest on average capitals:			
A: 6% of $47,500	$ 2,850		$ 2,850
B: 6% of $77,500		$ 4,650	4,650
Subtotal			$ 7,500
Resulting deficiency ($1,000 + $7,500)			
divided equally	(4,250)	(4,250)	(8,500)
Total	$(1,400)	$ 400	$(1,000)

The entry to close the Income Summary account is shown below:

A, Capital   1,400
        Income Summary   1,000
        B, Capital   400
To divide the net loss for the year.

At first thought, the idea of a net loss of $1,000 causing one partner's capital to increase and the other partner's capital to decrease may appear unreasonable, but there is sound logic to support this result. Partner B did invest substantially more capital to the firm than did A; this capital was used to carry on operations, and the fact that a net loss was incurred in the first year is no reason to deny recognition of B's greater capital investment.

A significant contrast between two of the profit-sharing plans we have discussed (the capital ratio plan versus the interest on partners' capitals plan) is apparent if we consider the case of a business operating at a loss. Under the capital ratio plan, the partner who has invested more capital will be required to bear a larger share of the net loss. This result may be considered unreasonable, because the investment of capital is presumably not the cause of a net loss. Under the interest on capitals plan of sharing profit and loss, the partner who has invested more capital will receive credit for this factor and thereby be charged with a lesser share of the net loss or may even be credited with a "gain."

We have thus far considered interest allowances on partners' capitals as a technique for sharing partnership profits and losses equitably but as having no effect on determining the net income or loss of the business as an entity. Interest on partners' capitals is not an expense of the business, but interest on loans from partners to the firm is regarded as interest expense and a factor in determining net income or loss for the period. Similarly, interest earned on loans by the firm to partners represents an element of revenue. This treatment is consistent with the point made earlier in this chapter that loans to and from partners are assets and liabilities of the partnership. It follows that interest on such loans should be accrued in the usual manner.

Another item of expense arising from dealings between a partnership and one of its partners is commonly encountered when the partnership rents property from a landlord who is a partner in the firm. Rent expense and a liability for rent payable should be recognized in such situations. The landlord, although a partner, is also a creditor of the partnership.

Salary Allowances with Remaining Profit or Loss Divided in an Agreed Ratio
In discussing salaries to partners, a first essential is to distinguish clearly

between salaries and drawings. Since the word *salary* has a connotation to many people of weekly or monthly cash payments for personal services, the accountant should be quite specific in suggesting and defining the terminology used in accounting for a partnership. We have used the term *drawings* in only one sense: a withdrawal of assets which reduces the partner's equity but plays no part in the division of net income. We shall limit the word *salaries* in partnership accounting to mean a device for sharing net income. When salaries is used with this meaning, the division of net income is the same regardless of whether salaries have been paid in cash or merely used in a year-end computation.

A partnership agreement which permits partners to make regular withdrawals of specific amounts should clearly state whether such withdrawals are intended to be a factor in the division of profit and loss. Assume, for example, that the agreement merely says that Partner A may make drawings of $300 monthly and Partner B $800. If the intent is not clearly stated to include or exclude these drawings as an element in the division of net income, controversy is probable because one interpretation will favor A and the opposing interpretation will favor B.

Let us assume that Partner A has greater experience and ability than Partner B and also devotes more time to the partnership. It seems reasonable that the partners will want to recognize the greater contribution of personal services by A in choosing a plan for division of profits. One approach to this objective would be to adopt an unequal ratio: for example, 70% of net income to A and 30% to B. Use of an arbitrary ratio is usually not a satisfactory solution, however, for the same two reasons mentioned in criticizing the capital ratio as a profit-sharing plan. An arbitrary ratio based on the greater contribution of personal services by A may not reflect the fact that other factors apart from personal services of partners are important in determining the profitability of the business. A second significant point is that if the business sustains a loss, the partner rendering the larger amount of personal services will be charged with the larger portion of that loss.

A simple solution to the problem of recognizing unequal personal services by partners is to provide in the partnership agreement for varying salary allowances to partners, with the remaining profit or loss divided equally or in some other agreed ratio.

Let us apply this reasoning to our continuing illustration of the firm of A and B, and assume that the partnership agreement provides for an annual salary of $10,000 to A and $6,000 to B with any remaining profit or loss to be divided equally. The salaries are not actually paid during the year. The first year's net income of $30,000 would be divided as follows:

	A	B	Combined
Salaries	$10,000	$ 6,000	$16,000
Balance ($30,000 − $16,000) divided equally.	7,000	7,000	14,000
Total	$17,000	$13,000	$30,000

If the partners should choose to take their authorized salaries in cash on a monthly basis, these payments should be debited to partners' drawing accounts.

Bonus to Managing Partner Based on Income When one partner serves as a manager of the business, he is sometimes entitled by contract to receive a bonus equal to a given percentage of income. The partnership agreement should state whether the basis of the bonus is income before deduction of the bonus or income minus the bonus. For example, assume that the firm of A and B provides for a bonus to B, the managing partner, of 25% of income **before** deduction of the bonus and that the remaining income is to be divided equally. As in the preceding examples, the income before the bonus is assumed to be $30,000. After the bonus of $7,500 to B, the remaining $22,500 of income would be divided $11,250 to A and $11,250 to B. Thus A would receive $11,250 of the income and B would receive $18,750.

On the other hand, if the partnership agreement provides that the basis of the bonus is income **after** a 25% bonus, the bonus may be computed as follows:

Bonus + income after the bonus = $30,000

Let X = income after the bonus

$.25X$ = bonus

Then $1.25X$ = income before bonus of $30,000

$X = \$30,000 \div 1.25$

$X = \$24,000$

$.25X = \$6,000$ bonus to B[1]

The net income of $30,000 in this case would be divided as follows: A, $12,000; B, $18,000.

---

[1] An alternative computation consists of converting the bonus percentage to a fraction. The bonus can then be computed by adding the numerator to the denominator and applying the resulting fraction to the income before the bonus. In the preceding example, 25% is converted to $\frac{1}{4}$, and by adding the numerator to the denominator, the $\frac{1}{4}$ becomes $\frac{1}{5}$. One-fifth of $30,000 equals $6,000.

The concept of a bonus is not applicable to a loss; in other words, if the partnership operates at a loss, the bonus provision becomes non-operative. The partnership agreement may also specify that extraordinary items or other unusual gains and losses be excluded from the basis for the bonus.

Salaries to Partners Combined with Interest on Capitals Many partnerships find it reasonable to divide net income by allowing salaries to partners and also interest on their respective capital accounts. Any remaining profit or loss is divided equally or in some other agreed ratio. Such plans have the merit of recognizing that the value of personal services rendered by different partners may vary greatly, and that differences in amounts of invested capital also warrant recognition in devising an equitable plan for sharing profits. The procedures for carrying out this type of agreement are the same as illustrated in earlier sections.

Income statement presentation

Explanations of the division of net income between partners may be included in the income statement. This information is sometimes referred to as the distribution section of the income statement. The following illustration shows the division of net income among partners in a highly condensed income statement.

A & B PARTNERSHIP
Income Statement
Current Year

Sales		$300,000
Cost of goods sold		180,000
Gross profit on sales		$120,000
Operating expenses		90,000
Net income		$ 30,000
Distribution of net income:		
Partner A	$14,100	
Partner B	15,900	
Total	$30,000	

If salaries paid to partners are included in operating expenses, the amount of such salaries should be disclosed.

Internal reports for use by management in appraising the performance of individual profit centers may call for different accounting concepts and classifications from those generally used for the financial statements prepared for outsiders. To develop the most meaningful cost data for internal use, it may be helpful to treat partners' salaries as expense rather than as a device for dividing profits and losses. This approach is particularly appropriate if one profit center (for example, a branch) has a partner as active manager and another profit center is managed by a salaried employee. The partners must, of course, include the salaries in their individual income tax returns. In large organizations with a number of partners of whom only one or two are active in the management of the business, partners' salaries may realistically be viewed as operating expenses similar to payments to employees. This approach follows the view that the partnership is an entity and that all management expenses must be deducted from revenue to measure the net income of the entity.

Statement of partners' capitals

Each partner will naturally want a complete explanation of the change in his capital account each year. To meet this need, a *statement of partners' capitals* is prepared as a basic financial statement. The following illustrative statement of partners' capitals is based on the accounts presented on page 8 and also uses the division of net income illustrated on page 16.

A & B PARTNERSHIP
Statement of Partners' Capitals
Current Year

	A	B	Combined
Partners' capitals, Jan. 1	$40,000	$80,000	$120,000
Additional investment (or withdrawal) of capital	10,000	(5,000)	5,000
Balance before net income and drawings .	$50,000	$75,000	$125,000
Net income	14,100	15,900	30,000
Subtotal	$64,100	$90,900	$155,000
Less: Drawings	(6,000)	(6,000)	(12,000)
Partners' capitals, Dec. 31	$58,100	$84,900	$143,000

Adjustment of net income of prior years

Any business, whether it be organized as a single proprietorship, partnership, or corporation, will from time to time discover errors made in the measurement of net income in prior years. Examples include errors in computing prior years' depreciation, errors in inventory valuation, and omission of accruals of revenue or expense.When such errors come to light, the question arises as to whether the corrections should be treated as part of the determination of net income for the current period or as *prior period adjustments* and entered directly to partners' capitals.

The correction of prior years' net income becomes particularly important when the profit-sharing ratio has been changed. For example, assume that in Year 1 the reported net income for A and B was $50,000 and that the partners shared profits equally, but in Year 2 they changed the ratio to 60% for A and 40% for B. During Year 2, it was discovered that the ending inventory for Year 1 had been overstated by $10,000 because of a clerical error. The $10,000 reduction in the net income for Year 1 should be divided $5,000 to each partner, in accordance with the profit and loss ratio which prevailed in the *year in which the error occurred.*

Somewhat related to the correction of errors of prior years is the treatment of nonoperating gains and losses. When the income-sharing ratio of a partnership is changed, the partners should consider the differences which exist between the carrying value of assets and their current fair value. As a somewhat extreme example, assume that the partnership of A and B owns marketable securities acquired for $20,000 which have risen in value to $50,000 at the date when the profit-sharing ratio is changed from 50% for each to 60% for A and 40% for B. If the securities were sold for $50,000 just prior to changing the profit-sharing ratio, the $30,000 gain would cause each partner's capital account to rise by $15,000. If the securities were sold for $50,000 immediately after establishment of the 60:40 profit-sharing ratio, the $30,000 gain would be divided $18,000 to A and only $12,000 to B.

A solution sometimes suggested for such partnership problems is to revalue the assets to fair value when the profit-sharing ratio is changed or when a new partner is added or an old one retires. Under certain circumstances, the revaluation of assets may be justified, but in general the continuity of cost valuations in a partnership is desirable, for the same reasons that support the use of the cost principle in a corporation. A secondary objection to revaluation of assets is that, with a few exceptions such as marketable securities, satisfactory evidence of current fair value is seldom available. A better solution to the problem of change in the ratio of profit sharing may usually be achieved by making appropriate adjustments between partners' capitals rather than by restating asset values up or down.

When the accountant acts in the role of management consultant to a partnership, he should bring to the attention of the partners any significant differences between carrying value and fair value of assets, and make them aware of the implications of a change in the profit-sharing ratio.

CHANGES IN PERSONNEL

Accounting for changes in partnership personnel

Most changes in partnership personnel are accomplished without interrupting the regular operation of the business. For example, when a large and well-established partnership promotes one of its employees to partnership status, there is usually no significant change in the financial condition, the accounting policies, or the operating routines of the business. From a legal viewpoint, however, a partnership is dissolved by the retirement or death of a partner or by the admission of a new partner to the firm.

Dissolution of a partnership may also result from such causes as the bankruptcy of the firm or of any single partner, the expiration of a time period stated in the partnership agreement, or the mutual agreement of the partners to end their association.[2]

Before trying to summarize accounting principles applicable to dissolution of a partnership, we must consider the tremendous range of business events to which the term *dissolution* may be applied. These events include, on the one hand, a minor change of ownership interest not affecting operation of the business; on the other hand, a joint decision of all members of a firm to end entirely their business relationships. In the one type of event the going-concern assumption, which is so fundamental to accounting policies, is left undisturbed; in the more serious example of dissolution, the going-concern assumption must be abandoned. Consequently, it is difficult to formulate a single set of accounting rules to be applied universally to all changes in partnership personnel.

The professional accountant is concerned with the economic substance of a transaction rather than with its legal form. Therefore, he must evaluate all the circumstances of the individual case in determining how a change in partnership personnel can most effectively be reflected in the accounting records and in the financial statements. In the remaining pages of this chapter, we shall consider the principal kinds of changes in partnership personnel and illustrate one or more acceptable accounting treatments for each type of change.

Accounting and managerial issues

Although a partnership association is ended in a legal sense when a partner withdraws or a new partner is added, the business as a going concern often continues with little outward evidence of change. In current accounting practice, a partner's interest is often viewed as a share in a continuing business which may be transferred, much as shares of stock

[2] The dissolution of a partnership is defined by the Uniform Partnership Act as "the change in the relation of the partners caused by any partner ceasing to be associated in the carrying on as distinguished from the winding up of the business."

are transferred between stockholders, without disturbing the continuity of the enterprise. For example, in a successful firm of certified public accountants, if a partner wishes to retire or a new partner enters the firm, the agreement for the change in ownership is usually carefully planned to avoid disturbing client relationships.

In a very large CPA firm with hundreds of partners scattered throughout the country, the decision to promote an employee to the rank of partner may often be made by a committee rather than by the action of all partners.

Changes in partnership personnel in any line of business raise a number of complex accounting and managerial issues upon which the professional accountant can serve as consultant. Among these issues are the determination of the amount to be paid to a retiring partner, the setting of terms for admission of a new partner, the possible revaluation of assets, and the development of a new basis for division of profits and losses.

Of particular importance is the establishment of a new plan for sharing profits or losses. Since a change in partnership personnel changes the relationship of partners, it wipes out the former profit-sharing agreement.

Admission of a new partner

When a new partner is admitted to a small firm of perhaps two or three partners, it is particularly appropriate to consider the fairness and adequacy of past accounting policies and the need for correction of errors in prior years' accounting data. The terms of admission of a new partner are often influenced by the level and trend of past earnings, because they may be indicative of future earnings. Sometimes specific accounting policies, such as the completed-contract method of recognizing profits on long-term construction contracts, may cause the records to convey a misleading impression of operating results in the periods preceding the admission of a new partner.

Adjustments of the records may be necessary to provide an equitable statement of partners' capitals and other elements of financial position before the change in membership of the firm is carried out. Carrying values and fair (or market) values of assets are often far apart.

As an alternative to revaluing the assets, it may be preferable to evaluate the dollar significance of any discrepancies between the accounts and current economic values and to make appropriate adjustment in the terms set for admission of the new partner. In other words, the amount invested or price paid by the incoming partner can be set at a level which reflects the current fair value of the business even though the carrying value of assets remains unchanged in the accounting records. Consideration must be given to the fact that if assets have appreciated in value but such appreciation is ignored, the subsequent disposal of the assets after admission of a new partner will cause him to share in profits which existed prior to his joining the firm.

The admission of a new partner to a firm may occur in either of two ways: (1) through the *purchase* of all or part of the interest of one or more of the existing partners, or (2) through the *investment* of assets in the firm by the new partner, thus increasing the resources of the partnership.

Purchase of an interest by direct payment to one or more partners

If the incoming partner purchases his interest from one or more of the original partners, the transaction is recorded by opening a capital account for the new partner and decreasing the capital accounts of the selling partners by the same amount. No assets are received by the partnership; the transfer of assets is between two or more individuals.

As a very simple illustration of this situation, assume that L and M are partners sharing profits equally and each having a capital of $60,000. Partner L (with the consent of M) sells half of his interest to a new partner, N. The entry to record this change in ownership is:

L, Capital	30,000	
N, Capital		30,000
To record the transfer of one-half of L's capital to N.		

The price paid by N in buying half of L's interest may have been the carrying value of $30,000 or it may have been more or less than carrying value. Possibly no price was established; L may have made a gift to N of one-half of his interest in the partnership, or perhaps N won it in a poker game. Regardless of the terms of the transaction between L and N, the entry illustrated above is all that is required on the partnership's records. No change has occurred in the assets, the liabilities, or the total of the owners' equity.

To explore further some of the implications involved in the purchase of an interest by an incoming partner, assume that N paid $40,000 to L for one-half of his $60,000 equity in the business. Some accountants have suggested that the willingness of the new partner to pay $10,000 in excess of carrying value for a one-fourth interest in the total capital of the partnership indicates that the total capital should be valued at $40,000 more than presently shown in the accounting records. From this assumption they reason that the assets of the old firm should be written up by $40,000, or goodwill of $40,000 should be recorded as an asset with offsetting credits of $20,000 each to the capital accounts of the old partners, L and M. Most accountants, however, take the position that the payment by N to L is a personal transaction between them and that the partnership, which has neither received nor distributed any assets, should make no accounting entry except to transfer one-half of L's capital to N, the new partner.

What are the arguments for these two opposing views of the purchase of an interest by a new partner? Those who advocate a write-up of assets stress the legal concept of dissolution of the old firm and formation of a new partnership. This change in identity of owners, it is argued, justifies departure from the going-concern assumption and the revaluation of assets at fair value in order to achieve an accurate measurement of the capital invested by each member to the new partnership.

The opposing argument, that the purchase of an interest by an incoming partner requires only a transfer from the capital account of the selling partner to the capital account of the new partner, is based on several points. First, the partnership as an entity did not participate in negotiating the price paid by N to L for one-half of his interest in the firm. Many factors other than the valuation of assets may have been involved in the negotiations between the two individuals. Perhaps N paid more than carrying value because he was allowed very generous credit terms or received more than a one-fourth share in profits as part of the purchase agreement. Perhaps the new partner was very anxious to join the firm because of his confidence in the personal abilities of L and M or because he anticipated great growth in the particular industry.

Because of these and other similar reasons, we may conclude that the purchase price of an interest transferred from one of the old partners to a new partner is not highly dependable or objectively verifiable evidence to support extensive changes in the carrying value of the partnership's assets. This conclusion is just as applicable when the new partner pays less than carrying value for his interest as when he pays a price in excess of carrying value.

Acquisition of an interest by investment

An incoming partner may gain admission to the firm by investing assets directly in the partnership. The assets which he invests are recorded in the firm's accounting records, and consequently the total assets of the firm and its total capital are increased.

As an example, assume that X and Y are partners operating an automobile rental business. They share profits equally and each has a capital account of $60,000. Assume also that the carrying value of the partnership assets is approximately the same as current fair value. Adjacent to the business is a tract of land owned by Z which could be used for expansion of operations. X and Y agree to admit Z to the partnership upon his investment of the land; profits and losses of the new firm are to be shared equally. Cost of the land to Z was $50,000, but a current appraisal indicates it is now worth $80,000.

The admission of Z to the partnership is recorded by the following entry:

Land	80,000	
Z, Capital		80,000
To record admission of Z.		

The new partner has a capital account $20,000 larger than the capitals of his partners. In other words he owns a 40% (or $80,000/$200,000) interest in the firm. The fact that the three partners share profits and losses equally does not require that their capital accounts be equal.

Bonus or goodwill allowed to old partners

In a profitable, well-established firm, the partners may insist that a portion of the investment by a new member be allowed to them as a bonus or that goodwill be recognized and credited to the original partners. The incoming partner may reasonably agree to such terms because of the benefits to be gained by becoming a member of a firm with high earning power.

Bonus to Old Partners   Assume that A and B are partners who share profits equally and have capitals of $45,000 each. Asset valuations are assumed to approximate fair value. The partners agree to admit C to a one-third interest in assets and a one-third share in profits upon investment of $60,000 in the firm. The total assets of the new firm will therefore amount to $150,000 (or $45,000 + $45,000 + $60,000). The following entry to record the investment by C will give him the agreed one-third interest and will divide the $10,000 bonus equally between A and B in accordance with their prior agreement to share profits and losses equally.

Cash	60,000	
A, Capital		5,000
B, Capital		5,000
C, Capital		50,000
To record investment by C for a one-third interest with bonus		
of $10,000 divided equally between old partners.		

Recognition of Goodwill   In the preceding illustration, C invested $60,000 but received a capital account of only $50,000, representing a one-third interest in the firm. He might prefer that his capital account show the full amount of his investment. This could be done while still allotting him a one-third interest if goodwill is recorded in the accounts with the offsetting credit divided equally between the two original partners. If C is to be given a one-third interest represented by a capital account of $60,000, the total indicated capital is $180,000, and the capitals of A and B together must total $120,000. Since their present combined capitals amount to $90,000, a write-up of $30,000 in net assets would be recorded as follows:

Cash	60,000	
Goodwill	30,000	
A, Capital		15,000
B, Capital		15,000
C, Capital		60,000
To record investment by C for a one-third interest with good-		
will of $30,000 divided equally between old partners.		

Evaluation of Bonus and Goodwill Methods   When the incoming partner invests an amount greater than the book value of the interest he acquires, the transaction should usually be handled by allowing a bonus to the old partners. The bonus method has the advantage of adhering to the cost principle of asset valuation and is in accord with the concept of a partnership as a continuing business entity. The alternative method of recording the goodwill *implied* by the purchase price is not considered acceptable by the authors. Use of the goodwill method signifies the substitution of estimated fair value of an asset rather than valuation on a cost basis. The goodwill of $30,000 shown in the preceding example was not purchased. Its existence is merely implied by the price the incoming partner paid for a one-third interest in the firm. As previously pointed out, the price paid by the incoming partner may have been influenced by many factors, some of which may be personal rather than economic in nature. To attribute the excess of the purchase price over carrying value of net assets to goodwill is an assumption which is usually difficult to support with objective evidence.

Apart from the questionable theoretical basis for such recognition of goodwill, there are other practical difficulties. The presence of goodwill created in this manner is likely to evoke criticism of the firm's financial statements, and such criticism may lead the partnership to amortize or to write off the goodwill.[3] Also, if the business should be liquidated, the

[3] According to *APB Opinion No. 17,* "Intangible Assets," issued by the AICPA in 1970, only purchased goodwill should be recorded in the financial records, and it must be amortized over a period of 40 years or less.

goodwill would probably have to be written off as a loss. Will the recording of goodwill and its subsequent write-off injure one partner and benefit another? The net results to the individual partners will be the same under the bonus and goodwill methods only if two specific conditions are met: (1) the incoming partner's share of profits must be equal to his percentage equity in assets at the time of his admission, and (2) the original partners must continue to share income between themselves in the same ratio as in the original partnership. Both these conditions were met in our example; that is, the new partner, C, received a one-third interest in the assets and a one-third share of profits and losses. Secondly, the original partners shared profits and losses equally both before and after the admission of C.

Assume, however, that the three partners agreed on a profit and loss ratio of A 40%, B 40%, and C 20%; the goodwill method would then benefit C and injure A and B as compared with the bonus method. This is demonstrated below:

	A	B	C	Combined
Capitals if bonus method is used	$50,000	$50,000	$50,000	$150,000
Capitals if goodwill method is used	$60,000	$60,000	$60,000	$180,000
Write-off of goodwill (40%, 40%, 20%) . . .	12,000	12,000	6,000	30,000
Capitals after write-off of goodwill	$48,000	$48,000	$54,000	$150,000

The first of the two necessary conditions for equivalent results from the bonus method and goodwill method is no longer met. The incoming partner's share of profit and loss is not equal to his share in assets. C is now assumed to have a 20% share in profit and loss, although as in the preceding example he has a one-third interest in assets. The use of the goodwill method in admitting C and the subsequent write-off of the goodwill would cause a $4,000 shift of capital from Partners A and B to Partner C.

Fairness of Asset Valuation In the preceding examples of bonus or goodwill allowed to the original partners, it was assumed that the carrying values of assets on the records of the old partnership approximated fair value. If such assets as land and buildings have been owned by the partnership for many years, it is probable that carrying value and fair value are quite far apart. Inventory priced on the lifo basis may also differ substantially from its current replacement cost.

To bring this problem into focus, let us assume that the assets of the partnership of A and B carried at $90,000 were estimated to have a current fair value of $120,000 at the time of admitting C as a partner.

Our previous example called for C to receive a one-third interest upon investment of $60,000. Why not write up the assets from $90,000 to $120,000, with a corresponding increase in the capitals of the original partners? Neither a bonus nor the recognition of goodwill would then be necessary to record the admission of C to a one-third interest upon investment of $60,000 because his investment would now be equal to the carrying value of his equity.

Such restatement of asset values would not be acceptable practice in a corporation merely because the corporation's stock had risen in price. If we assume the existence of certain conditions in a partnership, then adherence to cost as a basis for asset valuation is as appropriate a policy as for a corporation. These specific conditions are that the ratio for sharing profit and loss should correspond to the share of equity held by each partner, and that the profit and loss ratio should continue unchanged. When these conditions do not exist, a restatement of assets from cost to current fair value may be the most convenient method of achieving equity among the partners.

One objection to substitution of fair values for assets in any type of organization is that such estimates are subject to a wide range of opinion. They are less objective in nature than are cost data. Furthermore, the function of independent verification by a certified public accountant becomes almost meaningless if financial statements are presented in terms of estimated fair values. Public confidence in financial statements would probably be lessened by a significant degree if accounting practice condoned the substitution of estimates of fair values for the cost basis of valuation.

Bonus or goodwill allowed to new partner

An existing partnership may be very anxious to bring a new member into the firm, because the business is desperately in need of cash or because the prospective new member has unusual ability or extraordinary business contacts. To ensure the admission of the new partner, the present firm may offer him a capital account larger than the amount he invests.

Bonus to New Partner Assume that F and G, who have capitals of $35,000 each and share profit and loss equally, offer to admit H to a one-third interest in assets and a one-third share of income upon his investment of $20,000. Their offer is based on a desperate need for more cash and upon the conviction that H's personal abilities and business contacts will be of great value to the business. The investment of $20,000 cash in the firm by the new partner, when added to the existing capital of $70,000, gives a total capital of $90,000 of which H is entitled to one-third, or $30,000. The excess of H's capital account over his investment represents a $10,000 bonus allowed him by the old partners. Since F and G share profits and losses equally, the $10,000 bonus will be deducted from their capital accounts in equal amounts, as shown by the following entry to record admission of the new partner H.

Cash	20,000	
F, Capital.	5,000	
G, Capital	5,000	
H, Capital		30,000
To record admission of H with bonus of $10,000 from F and G.		

In outlining this method of accounting for the admission of H, we have assumed that the assets of the old partnership were properly valued. On the contrary, if the admission of the new partner to a one-third interest upon investment of $20,000 was based upon recognition that the assets owned by the old partnership were worth only $40,000, consideration should be given to writing down assets by $30,000. Such write-downs would be proper if accounts receivable, for example, included doubtful accounts, or if inventory were obsolete.

Goodwill to New Partner   Assume that the incoming partner is the owner of a successful business which he invests in the partnership rather than making his investment in cash. Using the same data as in the preceding example, assume that F and G with capitals of $35,000 each admit H to a one-third interest in assets and in profits. The identifiable tangible and intangible assets comprising the business owned by H are worth $20,000, but, because of its superior earnings record, a fair value for his going business is agreed to be $35,000. The admission of H as a partner is then recorded as follows:

Identifiable Tangible and Intangible Assets	20,000	
Goodwill	15,000	
H, Capital		35,000
To record admission of H; goodwill is assigned to going busi-		
ness invested by H.		

The point to be stressed here is that generally goodwill is recognized as part of the investment of a new partner only when he contributes a going business of superior earning power. If H is admitted by reason of a cash investment and is credited with a capital larger than the cash invested, the proper accounting for the transaction is to subtract this differential from the capitals of the old partners or to write down any overvalued assets. Goodwill should be recognized in the accounts only when substantiated by objective evidence; it should not be recorded to avoid recognition of a loss or merely as a convenient balancing device.

Retirement of a partner

When a partner retires, he usually receives a settlement representing the amount of his equity paid from partnership assets. It is also possible that he might arrange for the sale of his equity to one or more of the continuing partners as individuals, or that he might sell his interest in the firm to an outsider. Since we have already considered the accounting principles applicable to the purchase of an interest by an incoming or continuing partner, our discussion of the retirement of a partner is limited to the situation in which the partner receives settlement from the assets of the partnership.

An assumption underlying this discussion is that the partner has a right to withdraw under the terms of the partnership agreement. A partner always has the **power** to withdraw, as distinguished from the **right** to withdraw. If a partner withdraws in violation of the terms agreed upon in the partnership contract and without the consent of his partners, he may be liable for damages caused his partners by his violation of the contract.

Computing the Settlement Price   What is a fair measurement of the equity of a retiring partner? A first indication is the amount of his capital account, but this amount may require various adjustments before it represents an equitable settlement. These adjustments may include the correction of errors in accounting data and the recognition of differences between carrying values of assets and current fair values. In approaching these adjustments, the accountant will first refer to the partnership agreement, which may contain specific instructions for computing the amount to be paid a retiring partner. These instructions, for example, might provide for the appraisal of assets, might call for an audit by independent certified public accountants, and might prescribe a formula to be used in determining goodwill. If the business has not maintained good accounting records or has not been regularly audited, it is possible that the capital accounts are grossly misstated because of improper depreciation charges, failure to provide for uncollectible accounts, and other deficiencies in accounting.

If the partnership contract does not contain provisions for computing the equity of a retiring partner, the accountant may be able to obtain joint authorization from the partners to follow a specific approach to determining an equitable settlement amount.

In most cases the equity of the retiring partner is computed on the basis of current fair values for all assets. The gain or loss indicated by the difference between the carrying value of assets and their fair values is divided in the profit and loss ratio. After the equity of the retiring partner has been computed in terms of current fair values for assets, the partners may agree to settle by payment of this amount or they may agree upon a higher or lower amount. The computation of an estimated current value for the partner's equity is a necessary step in reaching a settlement; an independent decision should be made as to whether the fair values and the related changes in partners' capitals should be recorded in the accounting records.

Payment of Bonus to Retiring Partner   The partnership agreement may provide for recognition of goodwill at the time of a partner's retirement and may specify the methods of computing it. Usually the amount of the computed goodwill will be attributable to the partners in the profit and loss ratio. For example, assume that C is to retire from the firm of A, B, and C. Each partner has a capital of $60,000 and profits and losses are shared equally. The partnership agreement states that a retiring partner is entitled to receive the balance shown by his capital account plus his share of goodwill. At the time of C's retirement, goodwill in the amount of $30,000 is computed to the mutual satisfaction of the partners. In the opinion of the authors this goodwill should not be entered in the records of the partnership.

Serious objections exist to recording goodwill as determined in this fashion. Since only $10,000 of the goodwill is included in the payment for C's equity, the remaining $20,000 of goodwill *has not* been purchased by the continuing partnership. Its inclusion in the balance sheet of the partnership is not supported by the cost principle nor by any verifiable evidence. The fact that the partners "voted" for $30,000 of goodwill does not meet our need for objective evidence of asset value. As an alternative, it would be possible to record only $10,000 of goodwill and credit C's capital for the same amount, since this amount was "paid for" by the continuing partnership in acquiring C's interest. This method is perhaps more justifiable but objective evidence is still lacking that goodwill exists. The most satisfactory method of accounting for the retirement of Partner C is to treat the amount paid to C for goodwill as a $10,000 bonus. Since the settlement with C is for the amount of his capital account ($60,000) plus estimated goodwill of $10,000, the following entry could be made to record the amount to be paid to C:

C, Capital	60,000	
A, Capital	5,000	
B, Capital	5,000	
Liability to C		70,000

To record the obligation to retiring Partner C, including a bonus of $10,000.

The bonus method illustrated here is appropriate whenever the settlement with the retiring partner exceeds the carrying value of his capital. The agreement for settlement may or may not use the term *goodwill;* the essence of the matter is determining the amount to be paid to the retiring partner.

Settlement with Retiring Partner for Less than Carrying Value A partner may be so anxious to escape from an unsatisfactory business situation that he surrenders his equity for less than carrying value. In other cases, willingness by the retiring partner to accept a settlement below carrying value may reflect personal problems entirely apart from the business. Another possible explanation is that the retiring partner considers the assets overvalued, or that he anticipates declining profits or even operating losses in future years.

In brief, there are many subjective and unmeasurable factors which may induce a partner to accept less than carrying value in settlement for his equity in the business. Since a settlement below carrying value is seldom supported by objective evidence of overvaluation of assets, the preferred accounting treatment is to leave asset valuations undisturbed unless a large amount of goodwill is carried in the accounting records. The difference between the retiring partner's capital account and the amount he accepts in settlement should be credited as a bonus to the continuing partners in the profit and loss ratio.

For example, assume that in the firm of A, B, and C with capitals of $60,000 each, Partner B retires upon payment of $50,000. Assuming that profit and loss is shared equally, the entry is:

B, Capital	60,000	
Cash		50,000
A, Capital		5,000
C, Capital		5,000

To record the retirement of B for an amount below the carrying value of his equity.

The final settlement with a retiring partner is often deferred for some time after his withdrawal to permit the accumulation of cash, the determination of profit or loss to date of withdrawal, the obtaining of bank loans, or other steps needed to complete the transaction. The retirement of a partner does not terminate his personal responsibility for partnership debts existing at the date of his retirement unless the creditors agree to release him.

Death of a Partner The partnership agreement often provides that partners shall purchase life insurance policies on each others' lives so that funds will be available for settlement with the estate of a deceased partner. A buy and sell agreement may be formed by the partners with a trustee appointed to carry out the plan. Under a buy and sell agreement, the partners commit their estates to sell their interests in the business and the surviving partners to buy such interests. Another form of such an agreement gives the surviving partners an option to buy or "first refusal" rather than imposing an obligation to buy.

REVIEW QUESTIONS

1 In the formation of a partnership, partners often invest in the firm such assets as land, buildings, and machinery as well as cash. Should these non-cash assets be recorded by the partnership at appraised value, at cost to the partners, or on some other basis of valuation? Give reasons for your answer.

2 Some CPA firms have thousands of staff members, and hundreds of partners, and operate on a national or international basis. Would the corporate form of organization not be more appropriate than the partnership form for such large organizations? Explain.

3 Explain the proper presentation in the balance sheet of loans to and from partners, and the treatment of interest on such loans.

4 Explain how partners' salaries should be shown in the income statement, if at all.

5 List at least six items that should be covered in a partnership agreement.

6 List at least five methods by which partnership income may be divided.

7 The partnership of Adams and Barnes offered to admit Crawford to a one-third interest in the firm upon his investment of $50,000. Does this offer mean that Crawford would be entitled to one-third of the partnership profits and losses?

8 Davis and Estes are negotiating a partnership agreement, with Davis investing $60,000 and Estes $20,000. Davis suggests that interest be allowed on average capitals at 8% and that any remaining profit or loss be divided in the ratio of average capitals. Estes prefers that the entire profit or loss be divided in the ratio of average capitals. Comment on these proposals.

9 The partnership agreement of Farmer and Goss is very brief on the subject of profit sharing. It says: "Profits are to be divided 70% to Farmer and 30% to Goss and each partner is entitled to draw $800 a month." What difficulties do you see in carrying out this agreement? Illustrate possible difficulties under the assumption that the firm earned an income of $40,000 in the first year.

10 Muir and Miller operated a partnership for several years, sharing profits and losses equally. On January 1 of the current year, they agreed to revise the profit-sharing ratio to 70% for Muir and 30% for Miller because of Miller's desire for semiretirement. On March 1 the partnership received $10,000 in settlement of a lawsuit initiated two years previously. Since the outcome of the litigation had been considered highly uncertain, no receivable had ever been entered in the accounts. Explain the accounting treatment you would recommend for the $10,000 cash receipt.

11 Should the valuation of assets as shown by the accounting records of a partnership be changed to correspond to current fair value whenever a partner withdraws or a new partner is admitted to the firm? Explain fully and give specific examples.

12 When a new partner is admitted to an established firm, he is often required to invest an amount larger than the carrying value of the interest in net assets he acquires. In what ways can such a transaction be recorded? What is the principal argument for each method?

13 Bennett, Cross, and Dirks have operated a partnership business for many years and have shared profits equally. The partners now agree that Gray, a key employee of the firm who is an able manager but has limited financial resources, should become a partner with a one-sixth interest in capital. It is further agreed that the four partners will share profits equally in the future. Bennett suggests that the assets in the records of the old partnership should be restated at current fair value at the time of admitting Gray, but Cross and Dirks advocate that the accounts be left undisturbed in order to have a consistent accounting record. What is the argument for restating assets at the time of Gray's admission? What alternative, if any, would you suggest for such restatement of asset values?

14 The partnership of James, Wylie, and Martin has operated successfully for many years but Martin has now reached retirement age. In discussions of the settlement to be made with Martin, the point was made that the inventories of the firm had consistently been valued on a lifo basis for many years. Martin suggested that the current replacement value of the inventory be determined and the excess of this sum over the carrying value be regarded as a gain in which he would share. James objected to this suggestion on the grounds that any method of inventory valuation would give reasonably accurate results provided it were followed consistently and that a departure from the long-established method used by the partnership would produce an erroneous picture of the profits realized over the life of the firm. Evaluate the objections raised by James.

15 Lewis and Marlin are partners who share profits equally. They offer to admit Naylor to a one-third interest in assets and in profits upon his investment of $50,000 cash. The total capital of the partnership prior to the admission of Naylor was $110,000. Naylor makes a counteroffer of $40,000, explaining that his investigation of the business indicates that many receivables are past due and that a significant amount of obsolescence exists in the inventory. Lewis and Marlin deny both these points. They contend that inventory is valued in accordance with generally accepted accounting standards and that the receivables are fully collectible. However, after prolonged negotiation, the admission price of $40,000 proposed by Naylor is agreed upon. Explain two ways in which the admission of Naylor *could* be recorded and indicate which method is more justifiable. Comment on the possibility of recording goodwill.

EXERCISES

Ex. 1-1 In the firm of Drew, Long, and Blue, the partnership agreement provided that Drew as managing partner should receive a bonus equal to 20% of the annual net income and that the remaining net income should be divided 40% each to Drew and Long and 20% to Blue. Net income for the first year amounted to $63,600.

Explain two alternative ways in which the bonus provision could be interpreted. Compute the division of the year's net income under each of these interpretations.

Ex. 1-2 John Bell and Ray Jones are partners sharing profits equally; each has a capital account of $100,000. Jones (with the consent of Bell) sells one-fifth of his interest to his son, Arthur, for a price of $25,000, with payment to be made in five annual installments without any interest charge.

Give the entry to record the change in ownership, and explain why you would or would not recommend a change in the valuation of assets on the accounting records of the partnership.

Ex. 1-3 L and M are partners with capital accounts of $70,000 each who share profits equally. The partners agree to admit N to a one-third interest in assets and a one-third share in profits upon investment by him in the firm of $100,000. Assume that the assets are fairly valued and that N's admission is recorded by allowing a bonus to the old partners.

Prepare a journal entry to record the admission of N to the firm.

Ex. 1-4 Assume that A and B are partners in a successful business, sharing profits in a 60:40 ratio. Their capital accounts are A, $60,000 and B, $40,000. They agree to admit C to a 30% interest in assets and a 20% interest in profits upon his investment of $50,000. The new profit-sharing ratio is to be 48:32:20 for A, B, and C, respectively. The partners are discussing whether to record the admission of C by a bonus to A and B or by recording goodwill.

What would be the amount of the bonus to A and B, respectively? What would be the total goodwill implied by C's investment? Would the goodwill method be more advantageous to C if we assume the goodwill were written off in full two years later? What would be the dollar amount of the advantage or disadvantage to C from use of the goodwill method?

Ex. 1-5 The partnership of Fain and Green was formed on March 1. At that date the following assets were invested:

	Fain	Green
Cash	$ 25,000	$35,000
Inventory	-0-	55,000
Land	-0-	25,000
Building	-0-	75,000
Furniture and equipment	115,000	-0-

The building is subject to a mortgage loan of $30,000, which is to be assumed by the partnership. The partnership agreement provides that Fain and Green share profits or losses 40% and 60%, respectively.

a Compute the amount of Green's capital account at March 1, assuming that each partner is credited for the full amount of net assets invested.

b If the partnership agreement provides that the partners initially should have an equal interest in partnership capital with no contribution of intangible assets, what would be the balance in Fain's capital account at March 1?

Ex. 1-6 Lewis and Mason have capitals at the beginning of the year of $40,000 and $45,000, respectively. They share profits as follows: (1) 8% interest on beginning capitals, (2) salary allowance of $15,000 to Lewis and $7,500 to Mason, and (3) balance in 3:2 ratio. They earn only $10,000 during the current year before interest and salary allowances.

a Show how the net income of $10,000 should be distributed between Lewis and Mason.

b Assuming that Lewis and Mason simply agree to share profits in a 3:2 ratio with a minimum of $12,000 guaranteed to Mason, show how the partnership income of $10,000 should be distributed.

Ex. 1-7 Activity in the capital accounts for Rees and Sims for Year 10 follows:

	Rees	Sims
Balances at Jan. 1	$20,000	$40,000
Investment on Mar. 1	10,000	
Withdrawal on Nov. 30		20,000

Income for the year amounts to $24,000 before interest or salary allowances. Determine the division of the income under each of the following assumptions:

a The partnership contract is silent as to sharing of profits and losses.

b Income or loss is divided on the basis of the weighted-average capitals (not including the income or loss for the current year).

c Income or loss is divided on the basis of beginning capitals.

d Income or loss is divided on the basis of ending capitals (not including the income or loss for the current year).

Ex. 1-8 Austin and Bradford are partners who share profits equally and have equal capital accounts. The net assets of the firm have a carrying value of $40,000. Crane is admitted to the partnership with a one-third interest in profits and net assets. To acquire his interest, Crane pays $18,000 cash into the partnership.

Prepare journal entries to show three possible methods of recording the admission of Crane in the partnership accounts. State the conditions (if any) under which each method would be appropriate.

Ex. 1-9 A and B have capitals of $15,000 and $10,000, respectively. They share profits and losses in a 3:1 ratio. What entries would be made to record the admission of C to the partnership under each of the following conditions?

a C invests $15,000 for a one-fourth interest in net assets; the total firm capital after C's admission is to be $40,000.

b C invests $15,000, of which $5,000 is considered a bonus to A and B. In conjunction with the admission of C, the carrying value of the inventory is increased by $8,000. C's capital is recorded at $10,000.

SHORT CASES FOR ANALYSIS AND DECISION

Case 1-1 X, Y, and Z, who share profits equally, earned an operating profit of $30,000 during their first year in business. However, near the end of the year, they learned of two unfavorable developments: (a) the bankruptcy of Jones, maker of a two-year promissory note for $20,000 which had been contributed to the firm by Partner X at face value as his original investment; and (b) the appearance on the market of new competing patented devices which rendered worthless a patent contributed to the firm by Partner Y at a valuation of $10,000 as part of his original investment.

The partnership had retained the promissory note with the expectation of discounting it when cash was needed for operating purposes. Quarterly interest payments had been received regularly prior to the bankruptcy of Jones, but present prospects were for no further collections of either interest or principal.

Partner Z states that the $30,000 profit from operations should be divided $10,000 to each partner, with the $20,000 loss on the note charged against the capital account of Partner X and the $10,000 loss on the patent charged against the capital account of Partner Y.

Instructions Do you agree with Partner Z? Should the apparent loss on the note and the patent be handled in the same manner? Explain.

Case 1-2 When asked how the organizers of a business might choose between a partnership and a corporation in order to minimize the burden of taxation, an accounting student made the following statement:

"The choice is very simple. Organization as a partnership will result in only one income tax, that is, the tax on individual income. If the business is incorporated, it must pay the corporation income tax and in addition the owners must pay individual income taxes as the income of the corporation is distributed to them. Consequently, the partnership form of organization always provides a lesser burden of taxation."

Instructions Do you agree with the student? Explain.

Case 1-3 Doyle and Williams formed a partnership on January 1, Doyle contributing cash of $50,000 and Williams contributing cash of $20,000 and marketable securities worth $80,000. A portion of the securities were sold at carrying value in January to provide funds for business operations.

The agreement stated that "profits were to be divided in the capital ratio and that each partner was entitled to withdraw $1,000 monthly." Doyle withdrew $1,000 on the last day of each month, but Williams made no withdrawals until July 1, when he withdrew all the securities which had not been sold by the partnership. The securities which Williams took had a market value of $46,000 when contributed to the partnership on January 1 and a market value of $62,000 on July 1 when he withdrew them. He instructed the firm's accountant to record the transaction by reducing his capital account by $46,000, which was done. Income from operations for the first year amounted to $24,000. Income tax issues may be ignored.

Instructions You are asked to determine the proper division of net income for the first year. If the profit-sharing agreement is unsatisfactory in any respect, state the assumptions you would make in order to arrive at an equitable interpretation of the partners' intentions. Also indicate what adjustments, if any, you believe should be made in the accounts.

Case 1-4 Blake and Carter have been in business for many years and have shared profits equally. They own and operate a resort hotel which includes a golf course and other recreational facilities. Blake has maintained a larger capital investment than Carter, but Carter has devoted much more time to the management of the business.

The business is located in one of the fastest-growing areas in the country and has been expanding rapidly. To help meet the problems of this expansion, the partners decide to admit Dunn as a partner with a one-third interest in the firm and a one-third share in profits. Dunn is known as an excellent administrator and has ample cash to invest for his share in the firm. You are retained by the partnership to give advice upon any accounting issues created by the admission of Dunn as a partner.

Instructions List the factors that you believe deserve consideration and prepare a brief set of recommendations to guide the partners in dealing with these issues.

PROBLEMS

1-5 Long and Moore formed a partnership at the beginning of Year 6. Their capital accounts show the following changes during Year 6:

	Long	Moore
Original investment, Jan. 7, Year 6	$120,000	$180,000
Investments: May 1	15,000	
July 1		15,000
Withdrawals: Nov. 1	30,000	75,000
Capital accounts, Dec. 31, Year 6	105,000	120,000

The net income before allowances for salary or interest was $63,600. The net income included an extraordinary gain of $12,000.

Instructions Determine each partner's share of net income to the nearest dollar, assuming the following alternative profit-sharing arrangements:
a The agreement is silent as to division of net income.
b Income before extraordinary items is shared equally after allowing 8% interest on average capitals (computed to the nearest month) and after allowing $20,000 to Long and $30,000 to Moore as salaries. Extraordinary items are shared in the ratio of original investments.
c Income before extraordinary items is shared on the basis of average capitals, and extraordinary items are shared on the basis of original investments.
d Income before extraordinary items is shared equally between Long and Moore after allowing a 25% bonus to Moore based on income before extraordinary items after the bonus. Extraordinary items are shared on the basis of original investments.

1-6 Barr and Carr wish to purchase the partnership interest of their partner Dorn at June 30, Year 5. The balance sheet for the partnership on this date shows the following:

BARR, CARR, AND DORN

Balance Sheet

June 30, Year 5

Assets		Liabilities & Partners' Capital	
Cash	$18,000	Liabilities	$15,000
Receivables	12,000	Barr, capital	40,000
Equipment (net)	45,000	Carr, capital	20,000
Goodwill	10,000	Dorn, capital	10,000
Total	$85,000	Total	$85,000

The partners share profits in the ratio of 3:2:1.

Instructions Record the withdrawal of Dorn under each of the following four assumptions:
a Dorn is paid $11,000 and the excess paid to Dorn over the amount in his capital account is viewed as a bonus to Dorn.
b Dorn is paid $9,000 and the difference is viewed as a bonus to Barr and Carr.

  c Dorn is paid $9,000 and goodwill currently on the records of the partnership is reduced by the total amount implicit in the transaction.
  d Dorn accepts cash of $6,500 and equipment with a current fair value of $4,000. The equipment cost $10,000 and was 90% depreciated.

1-7 Nolan and Obers started a partnership in Year 1, each investing $10,000 in cash and agreeing to share all profits and losses equally. At the beginning of Year 3, Petrie was admitted to the partnership upon an investment of $12,500. Petrie's admission to the partnership was recorded by a debit to Cash and a credit to Petrie, Capital for $12,500. The profit and loss ratio for the new partnership was set at 3:2:1 for Nolan, Obers, and Petrie.
  Additional information is given below:

	Year 1	Year 2	Year 3	Year 4	Total
Net income as reported. . . .	$18,000	$27,500	$36,000	$44,700	$126,200
Drawings (equal amounts					
for each partner)	15,000	22,000	27,000	15,600	79,600
Accounts receivable not					
recorded at year-end	5,000	8,000	15,000	18,000	46,000
Inventory not counted at					
year-end	3,000	4,500	6,600	9,000	23,100
Accounts payable not					
recorded at year-end	6,000	4,000	10,000	12,500	32,500
Capital balances:					
Nolan	11,500	14,250	23,250	40,400	
Obers	11,500	14,250	17,250	26,950	
Petrie			9,250	11,750	

  Each year the income statement was prepared on the cash basis, that is, accounts receivable were not recorded and payments for merchandise were treated as cost of goods sold.

Instructions
a Prepare a statement of partners' capitals covering the four-year period based on the accrual basis of accounting. Combine net income and drawings for Years 1 and 2 and for Years 3 and 4. Prepare a supporting schedule to restate net income from the cash to the accrual basis for the first two-year period (Years 1 and 2) and for the second two-year period (Years 3 and 4).
b Prepare a balance sheet for the partnership at the end of Year 4. Prepare a separate schedule to determine the cash figure appearing in the balance sheet at the end of Year 4. Assume that the only assets and liabilities are: Cash, accounts receivable, inventory, and accounts payable.
c Using the information given in the problem and the partners' capital balances at the end of Year 4 determined in **a,** prepare a journal entry to restate the accounts of the partnership to the accrual basis of accounting.

1-8 Xavier, Yary, and Zimmer are partners sharing profits in a 3:2:1 ratio. The business has been successful, as indicated by the following data concerning the partners' capital accounts:

	Original investments	Retained earnings	Present balances
Xavier, capital.	$33,000	$42,000	$ 75,000
Yary, capital	22,400	28,000	50,400
Zimmer, capital	11,500	12,500	24,000
Totals	$66,900	$82,500	$149,400

At this time Zimmer becomes ill and retires from the partnership, receiving $30,000 in full payment for his equity. Xavier and Yary decide to continue in partnership and to share profits equally. However, as a condition of this change in profit sharing, Yary agrees to invest an additional $12,000 cash in the firm. The investment is made but the partners have difficulty in agreeing on the method to be used in recording Zimmer's withdrawal from the firm. Xavier wants to record the entire goodwill of the partnership as implied by the amount paid for Zimmer's interest. Yary argues that the amount of goodwill to be recorded should not be greater than the amount paid for Zimmer's share of the partnership goodwill. The accountant for the firm points out that the profit-sharing ratio is being changed and suggests that this is a reason for recognizing the goodwill of the business prior to Zimmer's withdrawal. Zimmer suggests that the entire controversy over goodwill can be avoided by treating the amount paid to him in excess of his capital account as a bonus from Xavier and Yary.

Instructions

a Give the entries in the accounts of the partnership required by the recommendation of each of the three partners (three independent sets of entries).

b Assume that the business is sold for $167,400 in cash shortly after the withdrawal of Zimmer, with the buyer assuming the liabilities. Prepare orderly schedules showing how the cash would be divided between Xavier and Yary under each of the three alternative methods for handling the withdrawal of Zimmer as previously described.

c For this portion of the problem, assume the same data as to original investments and retained earnings by Xavier, Yary, and Zimmer. However, rather than having Zimmer withdraw from the partnership, assume that the three partners agree to admit Newman as a fourth partner for an investment of $41,000 cash in the firm. Newman is given a 25% interest in the partnership net assets and a 25% share in profits. Xavier, Yary, and Zimmer will share the remaining 75% of partnership profits in the same original ratio existing among them prior to admission of Newman to the firm. Xavier, Yary, and Zimmer each withdraw $10,000 cash from the business. Prepare the journal entries needed to record the withdrawals of cash and the admission of Newman into the partnership using (1) the goodwill method and (2) the bonus method.

d Assume the same facts presented in *c* above, and further that the business is sold for $172,000 shortly after the admission of Newman to the firm. The buyer assumes the liabilities. Prepare a schedule showing how the cash would be distributed among the four partners if the admission of Newman had been recorded by using (1) the goodwill method and (2) the bonus method.

1-9 The partnership of Mock and Newberg has maintained accounting records on the accrual basis except for the method of handling credit losses. Uncollectible accounts have been recognized by a direct charge-off to expense at the time individual accounts receivable were determined to be uncollectible.

The partners are anticipating the admission of a third member, Olson, to the firm and they retain you as an accountant to review the records before this action is taken. You suggest that the firm change retroactively to the allowance method of accounting for uncollectible accounts so that the planning for admission of

Olson to partnership can be based upon a full accrual system. The following information is available:

Year accounts receivable originated	Year accounts were written off			Additional estimated uncollectibles
	2	*3*	*4*	
1	$1,200	$ 200		
2	1,500	1,300	$ 600	$ 450
3		1,800	1,400	1,250
4			2,200	3,800
	$2,700	$3,300	$4,200	$5,500

The partners shared profits equally until Year 4. In Year 4 the profit-sharing plan was changed as follows: salaries of $8,000 and $6,000 to be allowed Mock and Newberg, respectively, any balance to be divided 60% to Mock and 40% to Newberg. Net income of the partnership for Year 4 according to the accounting records was $28,000.

Instructions
a Prepare a journal entry giving effect to the change in accounting method for uncollectible accounts. Support your entry with a carefully prepared schedule showing changes in net income for the year.
b Assume that after you prepared the entry in *a* above, Mock's capital is reported at $48,000 and Newberg's capital is reported at $22,000. If Olson invests $30,000 for a 20% interest in total assets of the partnership and a 25% share in net income, illustrate by journal entries two methods that may be used to record his admission into the partnership. Any increment in capital of old partners is to be divided 60% and 40%. Which method would be more advantageous to Olson if the goodwill is later substantiated through a profitable sale of the business? Which method would be more advantageous to Olson if we assume that the goodwill is written off in the year following his admission to the firm?

1-10 The retail business operated as a partnership by Dee, Elm, and Fry was completely destroyed by fire on December 31, Year 2. The only assets remaining were the bank account with a balance of $26,100 and a claim against the insurance company which was settled for $220,000 early in Year 3. All accounting records were destroyed in the fire. The company had only a few creditors and all of these have presented their claims, which amounted in total to $32,000 at December 31, Year 2.

The present three-man partnership had been formed on January 1, Year 1. Prior to that time Dee and Elm had been partners for several years and had shared profits equally. No written contract of partnership was prepared for the new firm, and a dispute has now arisen as to the terms of the partners' oral agreement for sharing profits. The business had not utilized the services of independent accountants, except for some assistance with the information return required for income tax purposes at December 31, Year 1.

You are retained by the partnership to determine the profit-sharing plan which was followed for Year 1 and to apply this same plan to the events of Year 2, thus determining the present equity of each partner. The partners agree in writing that the profit-sharing plan used in Year 1 was correct and should be applied in an identical manner to the net income or loss for Year 2. The information available to you consists of the following: a copy of the information tax return of the partnership for Year 1, and a statement of the withdrawals made by the partners during Year 2. This latter statement has been agreed to in writing by all three partners and appears as follows:

	Dee	Elm	Fry	Combined
Inventory	$ 1,500	$850	$2,300	$ 4,650
Salary	8,000		6,000	14,000
Other cash withdrawals	750			750
Totals	$10,250	$850	$8,300	$19,400

Partner Dee explains to you that the $750 in "other cash withdrawals" resulted from the accidental payment by the firm of a personal debt of his when the invoice was sent to the partnership address.

From the information tax return for the preceding year, you obtain the following information:

	Dee	Elm	Fry	Combined
Capitals, Jan. 1, Year 1	$40,000	$50,000	$92,500	$182,500
Capitals, Dec. 31, Year 1	$51,000	$61,000	$85,300	$197,300
Net income for Year 1				$ 87,600
Division of net income:				
Salaries	$12,000	$15,000	$ 6,000	$ 33,000
Interest on capitals	2,000	2,500	4,625	9,125
Remainder (15%:30%:55%)	6,821	13,643	25,011	45,475
Totals	$20,821	$31,143	$35,636	$ 87,600

Instructions
a Prepare a statement of partners' capitals for Year 2, supported by a schedule showing the computation of net income or loss for Year 2 and the division of the net income or loss among the partners in accordance with the profit-sharing plan followed in the preceding year. Round computations to nearest dollar.
b How much cash will each partner receive if the partnership is terminated early in Year 3?

1-11 The law firm of Long, Morse, and Nagy was organized on January 1, Year 1, when the three attorneys decided to consolidate their individual law practices. The partners reached agreement on the following matters:
(1) Each partner would contribute to the firm the assets and liabilities of his individual practice and would be credited with a capital contribution equal to the net assets taken over by the partnership. The receivables contributed by each partner were personally guaranteed by him to be collectible. The assets and liabilities acquired by the partnership in this manner were as follows:

	Long	Morse	Nagy
Cash	$10,000	$10,000	$10,000
Accounts receivable	28,000	12,000	32,000
Law library and furniture	8,600	5,000	12,400
Accumulated depreciation	(4,800)	(3,000)	(9,400)
Total assets	$41,800	$24,000	$45,000
Less: Accounts payable	600	2,800	1,400
Net assets (capital invested)	$41,200	$21,200	$43,600

(2) The partnership decided to occupy Nagy's office space until his lease expired on June 30, Year 1. The monthly rental was $1,200 but the partners agreed that this was an excessive rate for the space provided and that $900 monthly would be reasonable. They therefore agreed that the excess rent would be charged to Nagy at the end of the year. When the lease expired on June 30, Year 1, the partners moved to a new office with a monthly rental of $1,000.

(3) The profit-sharing agreement did not provide for salaries to the partners but specified that individual partners should receive 20% of the gross fees billed to their respective clients during the first year of the partnership. The balance of the fees after deduction of operating expenses was to be credited to the partners' capital accounts in the following proportions: Long, 40%; Morse, 40%; Nagy, 20%.

A new partner, Orr, was admitted to the partnership on April 1, Year 1; he was to receive 20% of the fees from new business obtained after April 1 after deducting expenses applicable to that new business. Expenses were to be apportioned to the new business in the same ratio that total expenses, other than uncollectible accounts expense, bore to total gross fees.

(4) Fees were billed during Year 1 as follows:

Long's clients	$ 44,000
Morse's clients	24,000
Nagy's clients	22,000
New business:	
Prior to April 1	6,000
After April 1	24,000
Total	$120,000

(5) Total expenses for Year 1, excluding depreciation and uncollectible accounts expense but including the total amount paid for rent, were $38,700. Depreciation was to be computed at the rate of 10% on original cost to individual partners. Depreciable assets purchased during Year 1, on which one-half year's depreciation was to be taken, totaled $10,000.

(6) Cash charges to the partners' drawing accounts during Year 1 were:

Long	$10,400
Morse	8,800
Nagy	11,600
Orr	5,000
Total	$35,800

(7) Accounts receivable acquired from Long in the amount of $2,400 and from

Morse in the amount of $900 proved to be uncollectible. Also, a new client billed in March for $3,000 had been adjudged bankrupt and a settlement of 40 cents on the dollar was made.

Instructions Prepare a statement of the partners' capitals for the year ended December 31, Year 1. All supporting computations should be carefully organized and presented in good form. Income taxes are to be disregarded.

1-12 The partnership of King, Gill, and Fisher engaged you to adjust its accounting records and convert the records uniformly to the accrual basis in anticipation of admitting Wagner as a new partner. Some accounts are on the accrual basis and others are on the cash basis. The partnership's accounts were closed at December 31, Year 5, by the accountant, who prepared the following general ledger trial balance:

KING, GILL, AND FISHER
Trial Balance
December 31, Year 5

Cash	$ 14,000	
Accounts receivable	40,000	
Inventory	26,000	
Land	9,000	
Buildings	50,000	
Accumulated depreciation: buildings		$ 2,000
Equipment	56,000	
Accumulated depreciation: equipment		6,000
Goodwill	5,000	
Accounts payable		59,000
Reserve for future inventory losses		3,000
King, capital		40,000
Gill, capital		60,000
Fisher, capital		30,000
Totals	$200,000	$200,000

Your inquiries disclosed the following:
(1) The partnership was organized on January 1, Year 4, with no provision in the partnership agreement for the distribution of profits and losses. During Year 4 profits were distributed equally among the partners. The partnership agreement was amended effective January 1, Year 5, to provide for the following profit and loss ratio: King, 50%; Gill, 30%; and Fisher, 20%. The amended partnership agreement also stated that the accounting records were to be maintained on the accrual basis and that any adjustments necessary for Year 5 should be allocated according to the Year 4 distribution of profits.
(2) The following amounts were not recorded as prepayments or accruals:

	December 31	
	Year 5	**Year 4**
Unexpired insurance	$700	$ 650
Advances from customers	200	1,100
Accrued interest payable		450

The advances from customers were recorded as sales in the year the cash was received.

(3) In Year 5 a provision of $3,000 was recorded (by a debit to expense) for anticipated declines in inventory prices. You convinced the partners that the provision was unnecessary and should be removed from the accounts.

(4) Equipment purchased for $4,400 on January 3, Year 5, was charged to expense. This equipment has an estimated life of 10 years and an estimated salvage value of $400. The partnership depreciates its equipment under the income tax declining-balance method at twice the straight-line depreciation rate.

(5) The partners agreed to establish an allowance for uncollectible accounts at 2% of current accounts receivable and 5% of past due accounts. At December 31, Year 4, the partnership had $54,000 of accounts receivable, of which only $4,000 was past due. At December 31, Year 5, 15% of accounts receivable was past due, of which $4,000 represented sales made in Year 4, and was generally considered collectible. The partnership had written off uncollectible accounts in the year the accounts became worthless as follows:

	Account written off in	
	Year 5	Year 4
Year 5 accounts	$ 800	
Year 4 accounts	1,000	$250

(6) Goodwill was improperly recorded in Year 5 and credited to the partners' capital accounts in the profit and loss ratio in recognition of an increase in the value of the business resulting from improved sales volume. The partners agreed to write off the goodwill before admitting Wagner.

Instructions

a Prepare an adjusted trial balance for the partnership on the accrual basis at December 31, Year 5. All adjustments affecting income should be made directly to partners' capital accounts. Number your adjusting entries. Supporting computations should be in good form. (Do not prepare formal financial statements or formal journal entries. The working paper should have pairs of columns for Unadjusted Trial Balance, Adjustments, and Adjusted Trial Balance.)

b Without prejudice to your solution to *a* above, assume that the assets were properly valued and that the adjusted total of the partners' capital account balances at December 31, Year 5, was $140,000 and on that date Wagner invested $55,000 in the partnership. Compute the amount of goodwill that might be recorded on the partnership records under each of the following alternative agreements and allocate the goodwill to the partners:

(1) Wagner is to be granted a one-fourth interest in the partnership. The other partners will retain their 50 : 30 : 20 profit- and loss-sharing ratio for the remaining three-fourths interest.

(2) The partnership has been earning and expects to continue to earn an annual return of 15% on invested capital. The normal rate of return for comparable partnerships is 10%. The superior earnings (expected earnings of the new partnership in excess of the normal rate of return) are to be capitalized as goodwill at the rate of 20%. The partners are to share profits and losses in the ratio: King, 40%; Gill, 30%; Wagner, 20%; Fisher, 10%.

2

Partnership liquidation; joint ventures

LIQUIDATION

The meaning of liquidation

The liquidation of a partnership means winding up the business, usually by selling the assets, paying the liabilities, and distributing the remaining cash to the partners. In some cases, the business may be sold as a unit, possibly with the purchaser agreeing to assume the liabilities; in other cases, particularly for unsuccessful firms, the assets are sold on a piece-meal basis and most or all of the cash received must be used to pay creditors. A business which has ended normal operations and is in the process of converting its assets into cash and making settlement with its creditors is said to be *in liquidation* or in the process of being liquidated. This process of liquidation may be completed quickly or it may require several months or years.

The term *liquidation* is also used in a narrower sense to mean the payment of liabilities; in this chapter, however, we shall use it only in the broader sense of bringing to a close the business of a partnership. Another term commonly used by a business in process of liquidation is *realization,* which means the conversion of assets into cash.

When the decision is made that a partnership is to be liquidated, the accounts should be adjusted and closed, and the net income or loss for the final period of operations entered in the capital accounts of the partners.

The liquidation process usually begins with the sale (realization) of assets. The gains or losses from realization of assets should be divided among the partners in the profit and loss ratio and entered in their capital accounts. The amounts shown as their respective equities at this point are the basis for settlement. However, before any payment to partners, all outside creditors must be paid in full. If the cash obtained through realization of assets is insufficient to pay liabilities in full, any unpaid creditor may act to enforce collection from the personal assets of any partner, regardless of whether that partner has a debit or credit balance in his capital account. As pointed out in the preceding chapter, the partnership is viewed as an entity for many purposes such as changes in partnership personnel, but it cannot use the shield of a separate entity to protect partners personally against the claims of partnership creditors.

Distribution of loss or gain

The underlying theme in accounting for the liquidation of a partnership may be briefly stated: *Distribute the loss or gain from the realization of assets before distributing the cash.* As assets are sold, any loss or gain is apportioned among the partners' capital accounts in the established ratio for sharing profit or loss. The amount of cash, if any, which a partner is entitled to receive in liquidation cannot be determined until his capital account has been adjusted for his share of any loss or gain on the realization of the assets. Strictly interpreted, this reasoning might indicate that no cash can be distributed to a partner until after all the assets have been sold, since the net loss or gain will not be known until the sale of all assets has been completed. In this chapter we shall first illustrate a series of liquidations in which the realization of assets is completed before any payments are made to partners. We shall then consider liquidation in installments; that is, payments to partners after some of the assets have been sold and the liabilities paid but with the final loss or gain from sale of the remaining assets not yet known. The installment payments to partners are computed by a method which provides a safeguard against overpayment.

An important service by the accountant to a partnership in liquidation is to determine proper distribution of cash or other assets to individual partners after the liabilities have been paid. The partners may of course choose to receive certain assets, such as automobiles or furniture, *in kind* rather than to convert such property into cash. Regardless of whether cash or other assets are being distributed to partners, it is imperative to follow the basic rule that no distribution of assets be made to partners until after all possible losses and liquidation expenses have been taken into account. Failure to follow the basic rule may result in overpayment of a partner. If the partner is unable to return the excess payment, the person who authorized the improper distribution may become personally liable for the loss forced on the other partners by his error.

Distribution of cash

The Uniform Partnership Act lists the order for distribution of cash as (1) payment of creditors in full, (2) payment of partners' loan accounts, and (3) payment of partners' capital accounts. The indicated priority of partners' loans over partners' capitals appears to be a legal fiction. This rule is nullified for all practical purposes by an established legal doctrine called the **right of offset**. If a partner has a debit balance in his capital account (or even a potential debit balance depending on possible future losses), any credit balance in his loan account must be offset against the deficiency (or potential deficiency) in his capital account. Because of the right of offset, the total amount of cash received by a partner during the liquidation process will always be the same as if his loan to the partnership had been recorded in his capital account. Furthermore, the existence of a partner's loan account will not advance the time of payment to any partner during the liquidation. Consequently, in preparing a statement of realization and liquidation, the accountant may prefer to reduce the number of columns and simplify the statement by combining the amount of a partner's loan with the amount shown in his capital account. The statement of realization and liquidation will then include only one column for each partner; the top figure in the column will be the total equity (including any loans) of the partner at the beginning of the liquidation.

Combining the capital and loan accounts of a partner in the statement of realization and liquidation does not imply merging these accounts in the ledger. Separate ledger accounts for a partner's capital and for his loan to the firm should be maintained to provide a clear record of the terms under which funds were invested by the partners.

Determining the settlement with each partner

The amount which each partner receives from the liquidation of a partnership will be equal to (1) the capital he invested in the business, whether recorded in a capital account or in a loan account; (2) his share of operating net income or loss minus his drawings; and (3) his share of loss or gain from the realization of assets in the course of liquidation. In other words, each partner will receive in the settlement the amount of his equity in the partnership. The amount of a partner's equity is increased by the positive factors of investing capital and sharing in profits; it is decreased by the negative factors of drawings and sharing in losses. If the negative factors are the greater, the partner will have a capital deficiency (a debit balance in his capital account), and he must pay in to the partnership the amount of such deficiency. Failure to make good a capital deficiency by payment to the partnership would mean that the partner had not lived up to the partnership agreement for sharing profit and loss. This would cause his fellow partners to bear more than their contractual share of losses, or, stated conversely, to receive less in settlement than their equities in the business.

Division of losses and gains during liquidation

The profit or loss ratio used during the operation of the partnership is also applicable to the losses and gains during liquidation, unless the partners have made a specific agreement to the contrary. A partnership agreement is not superseded because of the decision to cease operations; the agreement for division of profit or loss therefore continues in force.

Accountants generally agree that the annual or quarterly determinations of net income or loss are approximations because of the estimates involved on such matters as the useful life of plant assets and the collectibility of receivables. Errors in these estimates affect the periodic net income or loss allocated to the partners. Consequently, the net loss or gain resulting from the liquidation of a partnership should logically be divided among the partners in the same ratio used in dividing income or loss from normal activities.

When the net loss or gain from liquidation is divided among the partners in accordance with the profit and loss ratio, the final balances in the partners' capital and loan accounts will be equal to the cash available for distribution to them. *Payments are then made in the amounts of the partners' respective equities in the business.*

Equity of each partner sufficient to absorb loss from liquidation

Assume that A and B, who share profit and loss equally, decide to liquidate. A condensed balance sheet prepared just prior to liquidation is as follows:

A & B PARTNERSHIP
Balance Sheet
June 30, 19___

Assets		Liabilities & Partners' Capitals	
Cash	$10,000	Liabilities	$20,000
Other assets	75,000	B, loan	20,000
		A, capital	40,000
		B, capital	5,000
Total	$85,000	Total	$85,000

As a first step in the liquidation, the non-cash assets with a carrying value of $75,000 are sold for cash of $35,000, thus resulting in a loss of $40,000 to be shared equally by A and B. Since B's capital account is only $5,000, it will be necessary to exercise the right of offset by transferring $15,000 from his loan account to his capital account. The following statement of partnership realization and liquidation, covering the period July 1–15, 19___, shows the division of the loss between the partners, the payment of creditors, and the distribution of the remaining cash to the partners. (The profit and loss ratio appears next to each partner's name.)

A & B PARTNERSHIP
Statement of Realization and Liquidation
July 1–15, 19___

	Assets		Liabilities	B, loan	Partners' capitals	
	Cash	Other			A(50%)	B(50%)
Balances before liquidation	$10,000	$75,000	$20,000	$20,000	$40,000	$ 5,000
Sale of assets at a loss of $40,000 . .	35,000	(75,000)			(20,000)	(20,000)
Balances	$45,000		$20,000	$20,000	$20,000	$(15,000)
Payment to creditors	(20,000)		(20,000)			
Balances	$25,000			$20,000	$20,000	$(15,000)
Offset capital deficit of B against his loan account . . .				(15,000)		15,000
Balances	$25,000			$ 5,000	$20,000	
Payment to partners	(25,000)			(5,000)	(20,000)	

In the statement of realization and liquidation, B's loan account of $20,000 and his capital account of $5,000 may be combined into a single equity figure of $25,000 for B. As stated earlier, such a procedure would be appropriate because the statutory priority of a partner's loan account has no significance in determining either the total amount of cash paid to a partner or the timing of the payments in the course of liquidation.

In the preceding illustration, Partner A received a settlement of $20,000 and Partner B a settlement of $5,000. Neither partner received payment until after creditors had been paid in full. Since assets consist entirely of cash of $25,000 at this point, it is reasonable to assume that checks to A and B for $20,000 and $5,000, respectively, were written and delivered to the partners at the same time. It is apparent that a partner's loan account has no special significance in the liquidation process. Therefore, in succeeding illustrations we shall not show a partner's loan account in a separate column of the statement of realization and liquidation. Whenever a partner's loan account is encountered, it may be combined with the partner's capital account in preparing the statement of realization and liquidation.

Equity of one partner not sufficient to absorb his share of loss from liquidation

In this case, the loss on realization of assets when distributed in the profit and loss ratio results in a debit balance in the capital account of one of the partners. It may be assumed that the partner with a debit balance has no loan account, or that the total of his capital account and loan account combined is less than his share of the loss on realization. To fulfill his agreement to share a given percentage of partnership profit and loss, the partner must pay in to the partnership sufficient cash to eliminate his capital deficiency. If he is unable to do so, his deficiency must be absorbed by the other partners as an additional loss to be shared in the same proportion as they have previously shared profit and loss among themselves. Assume the following balance sheet for D, E, and F just prior to liquidation.

D, E, & F PARTNERSHIP

Balance Sheet

May 20, 19___

Assets		Liabilities & Partners' Capitals	
Cash	$ 20,000	Liabilities	$ 30,000
Other assets	80,000	D, capital	40,000
		E, capital	21,000
		F, capital	9,000
Total	$100,000	Total	$100,000

The profit and loss ratio is D 20%, E 40%, and F 40%. The other assets with a carrying value of $80,000 are sold for $50,000 cash, resulting in a loss of $30,000 to be divided among the partners. Partner F is charged with 40% of this loss, or $12,000, which creates a debit balance of $3,000 in his capital account. In the following statement of realization and liquidation, it is assumed that F pays the $3,000 to the partnership:

D, E, & F PARTNERSHIP
Statement of Realization and Liquidation
May 21–31, 19__

	Assets		Liabilities	Partners' capitals		
	Cash	Other		D(20%)	E(40%)	F(40%)
Balances before liquidation	$20,000	$80,000	$30,000	$40,000	$21,000	$ 9,000
Sale of assets at a loss of $30,000 . .	50,000	(80,000)		(6,000)	(12,000)	(12,000)
Balances	$70,000		$30,000	$34,000	$ 9,000	$(3,000)
Payment to creditors	(30,000)		(30,000)			
Balances	$40,000			$34,000	$ 9,000	$(3,000)
Cash paid in by F .	3,000					3,000
Balances	$43,000			$34,000	$ 9,000	
Payments to partners	(43,000)			(34,000)	(9,000)	

Next let us change one condition of the preceding illustration by assuming that Partner F was not immediately able to pay in his $3,000 debt to the partnership. If the cash on hand after payment of creditors is to be distributed to D and E without waiting to determine the collectibility of the $3,000 claim against F, the statement of realization and liquidation will appear as follows:

D, E, & F PARTNERSHIP
Statement of Realization and Liquidation
May 21–31, 19__

	Assets		Liabilities	Partners' capitals		
	Cash	Other		D(20%)	E(40%)	F(40%)
Balances before liquidation	$20,000	$80,000	$30,000	$40,000	$21,000	$ 9,000
Sale of assets at a loss of $30,000 . .	50,000	(80,000)		(6,000)	(12,000)	(12,000)
Balances	$70,000		$30,000	$34,000	$ 9,000	$(3,000)
Payment to creditors	(30,000)		(30,000)			
Balances	$40,000			$34,000	$ 9,000	$(3,000)
Payment to partners	(40,000)			(33,000)	(7,000)	
Balances				$ 1,000	$ 2,000	$(3,000)

The cash payments of $33,000 to D and $7,000 to E leave each partner with a sufficient credit balance to absorb his share of the additional loss if F fails to make good the $3,000 debit balance in his capital account. The profit and loss shares were 20% for D and 40% for E; consequently, the possible additional loss of $3,000 would be charged to them in the proportion of $\frac{2}{6}$ or $1,000 to D, and $\frac{4}{6}$ or $2,000 to E. The payment of the $40,000 cash available to partners is therefore divided between them in a manner that pays D down to a balance of $1,000 in his capital account and pays E down to a balance of $2,000.

If F later pays in the $3,000 he owes to the partnership, this amount will be divided by paying $1,000 to D and $2,000 to E. The preceding statement of realization and liquidation could be completed as follows:

	Cash	D(20%)	E(40%)	F(40%)
Balances from schedule above		$1,000	$2,000	$(3,000)
Cash paid in by F	$3,000			3,000
Payments to partners	(3,000)	(1,000)	(2,000)	

On the other hand, if the $3,000 due from F is determined to be uncollectible, the statement of realization and liquidation would be completed by showing the write-off of F's debit balance as an additional loss borne by D and E as follows:

	Cash	D(20%)	E(20%)	F(40%)
Balances from schedule above		$1,000	$2,000	$(3,000)
Additional loss from inability to				
collect deficiency from F		(1,000)	(2,000)	3,000

Equities of two partners not sufficient to absorb their shares of loss from liquidation

We have already observed that inability of a partner to make good a deficiency in his capital account causes an additional loss to the other partners. A partner may have sufficient capital or combination of capital and loan accounts to absorb his direct share of loss on the realization of assets, but not a sufficient equity to absorb his share of the additional actual or potential loss caused by inability to collect the deficiency in another partner's capital account. In brief, one capital deficiency if not collectible may cause a second capital deficiency, which may or may not be collectible.

Assume that J, K, L, and M are partners sharing profit and loss in the ratio of 10%, 20%, 30%, and 40%. Their capital accounts are as shown in the statement of realization and liquidation on page 53. The assets are realized at a loss of $80,000, and creditors are paid in full. Cash of $20,000 is available for distribution to the partners. In making this distribution, the guiding principle is to pay each partner an amount equal to the excess of his capital account over any additional possible losses which may be charged against him. In other words, pay a partner's capital account down to the level necessary to absorb any additional losses which may be charged against him because of the uncollectibility of deficiencies owed by other partners.

The statement of realization and liquidation on page 53, along with Schedule A on page 54, show that the $20,000 of cash in hand can safely be distributed $16,000 to J and $4,000 to K. If the $24,000 deficiency in M's capital proves uncollectible, the additional loss to be divided among the other three partners will cause L's capital account to change from a $6,000 credit balance to a $6,000 debit balance (deficiency). He is therefore not eligible to receive a cash payment. If this deficiency in L's account proves uncollectible, the balances remaining in the capital accounts of J and K, after the cash payment indicated above, will be equal to the amounts needed to absorb the additional loss shifted from L's account.

Partnership insolvent but partners personally solvent

If a partnership is insolvent, at least one and perhaps all of the partners will have deficiencies in their capital accounts. In any event the total amount of the deficiencies will exceed the total of the credit balances. If the partner or partners with a capital deficiency pay in the required amount, the partnership will have cash to pay its liabilities in full. However, the creditors may demand payment from *any* partner individually, regardless of whether his capital account shows a deficiency or a credit balance. In terms of relationships with creditors, the partnership is not a separate entity. A partner who personally makes payment to partnership creditors of course receives a credit to his capital account. As an illustration of an insolvent partnership with partners personally solvent, assume that N, O, and P, who share profit and loss equally, present the condensed balance sheet on page 54 just prior to liquidation:

J, K, L, & M PARTNERSHIP
Statement of Realization and Liquidation
August 1–15, 19___

	Assets		Liabilities	Partners' capitals			
	Cash	Other		J(10%)	K(20%)	L(30%)	M(40%)
Balances before liquidation	$ 20,000	$200,000	$120,000	$30,000	$32,000	$30,000	$ 8,000
Sale of assets at a loss of $80,000	120,000	(200,000)		(8,000)	(16,000)	(24,000)	(32,000)
Balances	$140,000		$120,000	$22,000	$16,000	$ 6,000	$(24,000)
Payment to creditors	(120,000)		(120,000)				
Balances	$ 20,000			$22,000	$16,000	$ 6,000	$(24,000)
Payment to partners (Schedule A on page 54) . .	(20,000)			(16,000)	(4,000)		
Balances				$ 6,000	$12,000	$ 6,000	$(24,000)

Schedule A: Computation of Cash Payments to Partners

	Partners' capitals			
	J(10%)	K(20%)	L(30%)	M(40%)
Capital balance before distributing cash to partners	$22,000	$16,000	$ 6,000	$(24,000)
Additional loss to J, K, and L if M's deficiency is uncollectible (ratio of 10:20:30) .	(4,000)	(8,000)	(12,000)	24,000
Balances	$18,000	$ 8,000	$(6,000)	
Additional loss to J and K if L's deficiency is uncollectible (ratio of 10:20)	(2,000)	(4,000)	6,000	
Amounts which may safely be paid to partners	$16,000	$ 4,000		

N, O, & P PARTNERSHIP
Balance Sheet
September 5, 19___

Assets		Liabilities & Partners' Capitals	
Cash	$ 15,000	Liabilities.	$ 65,000
Other assets	85,000	N, capital	18,000
		O, capital	10,000
		P, capital	7,000
Total	$100,000	Total	$100,000

The other assets with a carrying value of $85,000 are sold for $40,000 cash, which causes a loss of $45,000 to be divided equally among the partners. The total cash of $55,000 is paid to the creditors, which leaves unpaid liabilities of $10,000. Partner N has a credit balance of $3,000 after absorbing his one-third share of the loss on realization. Partners O and P owe the partnership $5,000 and $8,000, respectively. If O and P pay in the amounts of their deficiencies, the partnership will use $10,000 of the $13,000 to pay the remaining liabilities and will distribute $3,000 to N in settlement of his equity. These events are portrayed in the statement of realization and liquidation at the top of page 55.

Assume that there was some delay in collecting the deficiencies from O and P and during this period the creditors demanded and received payment of their $10,000 in claims from Partner N. This payment by N would cause his equity to increase from $3,000 to $13,000. When O and P paid in their deficiencies totaling $13,000, this amount of cash would then go to N in settlement of the credit balance in his capital account.

Another alternative is that creditors might collect the final $10,000 due

N, O, & P PARTNERSHIP
Statement of Realization and Liquidation
September 5–28, 19__

	Assets		Liabilities	Partners' capitals		
	Cash	Other		N(⅓)	O(⅓)	P(⅓)
Balance before liquidation .	$15,000	$85,000	$65,000	$18,000	$10,000	$ 7,000
Sale of assets at a loss . . .	40,000	(85,000)		(15,000)	(15,000)	(15,000)
Balances	$55,000		$65,000	$ 3,000	$(5,000)	$(8,000)
Partial payment to creditors	(55,000)		(55,000)			
Balances	$ –0–		$10,000	$ 3,000	$(5,000)	$(8,000)
Cash paid in by O and P . .	13,000				5,000	8,000
Balances	$13,000		$10,000	$ 3,000		
Final payment to creditors .	(10,000)		(10,000)			
Balances	$ 3,000			$ 3,000		
Payment to N	(3,000)			(3,000)		

them directly from O or P. Payments by these partners to creditors would increase their equities and eliminate or reduce their indebtedness to the firm. So long as we assume that the partners with deficiencies make payment to the partnership or directly to partnership creditors, the results are the same. Creditors will be paid in full and partners will share losses on liquidation as provided in the partnership agreement.

Partnership insolvent and partners personally insolvent

In the preceding illustration of an insolvent partnership, we assumed that the partners were personally solvent and therefore able to make good their capital deficiencies. We shall now consider an insolvent partnership in which one or more of the partners are personally insolvent. This situation raises a question as to the relative rights of two groups of creditors (1) those persons who extended credit to the partnership, and (2) those persons who extended credit to the partners as individuals. The relative rights of these two groups of creditors are governed by the legal rules of *marshaling of assets.* These legal rules provide that assets of the partnership are first available to creditors of the partnership, and that assets owned individually by a partner are first available to his personal creditors. After the debts of the partnership have been paid in full, if any assets remain in the partnership, the creditors of an individual partner have a claim against the assets of the partnership to the extent of the partner's equity in the partnership.

After the personal creditors of a partner have been paid in full from his personal assets, any remaining assets are available to creditors of the partnership regardless of whether the partner's capital account shows a credit or debit balance. Such claims by creditors of the partnership are permitted only when these creditors are unable to obtain payment from the partnership.

To illustrate the relative rights of creditors of an insolvent partnership and personal creditors of an insolvent partner, assume that R, S, and T, who share profits and losses equally, have the following balance sheet just prior to liquidation:

R, S, & T PARTNERSHIP
Balance Sheet
November 30, 19__

Assets		Liabilities & Partners' Capitals	
Cash	$ 10,000	Liabilities	$ 60,000
Other assets	100,000	R, capital	5,000
		S, capital	15,000
		T, capital	30,000
Total	$110,000	Total	$110,000

Assume also that the partners as individuals have the following personal assets and liabilities apart from the equities they have in the partnership:

Partner	Personal assets	Personal liabilities
R	$100,000	$25,000
S	50,000	50,000
T	5,000	60,000

The realization of partnership assets results in a loss of $60,000, as shown in the statement of realization and liquidation at the top of page 57.

The creditors of the partnership have received all the assets of the partnership and still have unpaid claims of $10,000. They cannot collect from S or T personally because the personal assets of these two partners are just sufficient or insufficient to meet their personal liabilities. However, the partnership creditors can collect the $10,000 in full from R, who is personally solvent. By chance, R has a deficiency of $15,000 in his capital, but this is of no concern to the creditors. They could collect in full from

R, S, & T PARTNERSHIP
Statement of Realization and Liquidation
December 1–12, 19__

	Assets		Liabilities	Partners' capitals		
	Cash	Other		R(⅓)	S(⅓)	T(⅓)
Balances before liquidation	$10,000	$100,000	$60,000	$ 5,000	$15,000	$30,000
Sale of assets at a loss . . .	40,000	(100,000)		(20,000)	(20,000)	(20,000)
Balances	$50,000		$60,000	$(15,000)	$ (5,000)	$10,000
Payment to creditors	(50,000)		(50,000)			
Balances			$10,000	$(15,000)	$ (5,000)	$10,000

any partner who had sufficient personal assets regardless of whether his capital account showed a debit or credit balance. The statement of realization and liquidation shown above is now continued to show the payment by R personally of the final $10,000 due to partnership creditors. Since our assumptions about R's personal finances showed that he had $100,000 of assets and only $25,000 in liabilities, he is also able to pay into the firm the additional $5,000 needed to make good his capital deficiency. This $5,000 of cash is promptly paid to Partner T, the only partner with a credit balance.

	Cash	Liabilities	Partners' capitals		
			R(⅓)	S(⅓)	T(⅓)
Balances as above		$10,000	$(15,000)	$(5,000)	$10,000
Payment by R to partnership creditors		(10,000)	10,000		
Balances			$ (5,000)	$(5,000)	$10,000
Additional investment by R . .	$5,000		5,000		
Balances	$5,000			$(5,000)	$10,000
Payment to T	(5,000)				(5,000)
Balances				$(5,000)	$ 5,000

The continued statement of realization and liquidation now shows that S owes $5,000 to the firm; however, his personal assets of $50,000 are exactly equal to his personal liabilities of $50,000. Under the Uniform Partnership Act, all the personal assets of S will go to his personal creditors; therefore the $5,000 deficiency in his capital account represents an additional loss to be shared equally between R and T. To conclude the liquidation, R, who is personally solvent, will be required to pay $2,500 to the partnership and the amount will go to T or to his personal creditors, since T is hopelessly insolvent. These payments are shown below in the completed statement of realization and liquidation.

	Cash	Partners' capitals		
		R(⅓)	S(⅓)	T(⅓)
Balances carried forward			$(5,000)	$5,000
Write off S's deficiency as uncol-				
lectible		$(2,500)	5,000	(2,500)
Balances		$(2,500)		$2,500
Cash paid in by R	$2,500	2,500		
Balances	$2,500			$2,500
Payment to T	(2,500)			(2,500)

The final results of the liquidation show that the partnership creditors received payment in full because of the personal financial strength of Partner R. Since R was personally solvent, his personal creditors could also collect in full. The personal creditors of S were paid in full, thereby exhausting his personal assets; however, he failed to make good the $5,000 deficiency in his capital, thus shifting an additional loss to his partners. The personal creditors of T received all his personal assets and also $7,500 from the partnership, representing T's equity in the firm. However, T's personal creditors were able to collect a total of only $12,500 on their claims of $60,000.

INSTALLMENT PAYMENTS TO PARTNERS

In the illustrations of partnership liquidation in the preceding sections, all the firm's assets were sold and the total loss from liquidation was divided among the partners before any payments were made to them. The liquidation of some businesses, however, may extend over several months; in these extended liquidations the partners will usually want to receive cash as it becomes available rather than waiting until the last asset has been converted into cash. Installment payments to partners are quite proper so long as the necessary safeguards are used to ensure that all creditors are paid in full and that no partner is paid more than the amount to which he is ultimately entitled after all losses on realization of assets have become known.

Liquidation in installments may be regarded as a process of selling some of the assets, paying creditors, paying the remaining available cash to partners, selling additional assets, and making further payments to partners. The liquidation continues until all assets have been sold and all cash distributed to creditors and partners.

The circumstances of installment liquidation are likely to vary; consequently, our approach is to emphasize the general principles guiding liquidation in installments rather than to provide illustrative models of all possible liquidation situations. Among the variables which cause partnership liquidations to differ are the sufficiency of each partner's capital to absorb his share of the possible losses remaining after each installment, the shifting of losses from one partner to another because of inability to collect a capital deficiency, the offsetting of loan accounts against capital deficiencies, and the possible need for setting aside cash to meet future liquidation expenses or unpaid liabilities.

General principles guiding installment payment procedures

The critical element in installment liquidations is that the liquidator authorizes cash payments to partners before he knows what losses will be incurred and charged against the partners. If a payment is made to a partner and later losses cause a deficiency to develop in his capital account, the liquidator will have to ask for the return of the payment. If he cannot recover the payment, he may be personally liable to the other partners for the loss caused them by his unwise distribution of cash. Because of this danger, the only safe policy for determining installment cash payments to partners is summarized as follows:

1 Assume a total loss on all remaining assets and provide for all possible losses, including potential expenses of realization and liquidation.

2 Assume that any partner with a capital deficiency will be unable to pay anything to the firm; in other words, distribute each installment of cash as if no more cash would be forthcoming either from sale of assets or from collection of deficiencies from partners.

Under these assumptions the liquidator will authorize a payment to a partner only if he has a credit balance in his capital account (or in his capital and loan account combined) in excess of the amount required to absorb his share of the maximum possible loss which may be incurred. A partner's "share of the maximum possible loss" would include any loss that may be shifted to him because of the inability of his partners to make good any capital deficiencies which may arise in their capital accounts.

When installment payments are made according to these rules, the effect will be to bring the equities of the partners into the profit and loss ratio as quickly as possible. *When installment payments have proceeded to the point that the partners' capitals correspond to the profit and loss ratio, all subsequent payments can be divided in that ratio,* because each partner's capital will be sufficient to absorb his share of the maximum possible remaining loss.

Advance planning for installment payments to partners

The amounts of cash which could safely be distributed to the partners each month (or at any other point in time) may be determined by calculating the impact on partners' equities (capital and loan balances) of the maximum possible remaining loss. Although this method is sound, it is somewhat cumbersome. Furthermore, it does not show at the beginning of the liquidation how cash will be divided among the partners as it may become available. For these reasons, it is more efficient to prepare a complete cash distribution program in advance to show how cash will be divided in the course of liquidation. If such a program of cash distribution is prepared, any amounts of cash received from disposal of partnership assets can be paid immediately to the partners as specified in this program.

Assume that X, Y, and Z, who share profits and losses in a 4:3:2 ratio, decide to liquidate their business and want a complete cash distribution program prepared in advance. The balance sheet just prior to liquidation on July 5, 19___, is as follows:

X, Y, & Z PARTNERSHIP
Balance Sheet
July 5, 19___

Assets		Liabilities & Partners' Capitals	
Cash	$ 8,000	Liabilities	$ 61,000
Other assets	192,000	X, capital	40,000
		Y, capital	45,000
		Z, capital	54,000
Total	$200,000	Total	$200,000

The first $61,000 of available cash must, of course, be paid to creditors and any additional amount can be paid to partners. The amount of cash to be paid to partners during liquidation may be developed as illustrated on page 61.

The procedures followed in the development of the cash distribution program are explained below:

1 The net capital balances before liquidation represent the **equities** of the partners in the partnership, that is, the balance in a partner's capital account, plus or minus the balance (if any) of a loan made by a partner to the partnership or a loan made by the partnership to a partner.

2 The net capital balance before liquidation for each partner is divided by his profit and loss ratio in order to determine the amount of net capital per unit of profit and loss for each partner. This step is critical because it (**a**) identifies the partner with the largest net capital per unit of profit and loss who will

X, Y, & Z PARTNERSHIP
Cash Distributions to Partners during Liquidation
July 5, 19___

	X	Y	Z
Net capital balances before liquidation . . .	$40,000	$45,000	$54,000
Profit and loss ratio	4	3	2
Divide net capital balances before liquidation by profit and loss ratio to obtain net capital per unit of profit and loss for each partner	$10,000	$15,000	$27,000
Required reduction in capital per unit of profit and loss for Z to bring his balance down to the next highest balance (for partner Y). This is the amount of the first cash distribution to a partner **per unit** of his profit and loss. Since Z has 2 units of profit and loss, he will receive the first $24,000 ($12,000 × 2 = $24,000)			(12,000)
Balances per unit of profit and loss	$10,000	$15,000	$15,000
Required reduction in capital per unit of profit and loss for Y and Z to bring their balances down to X's balance which is the lowest capital per unit of profit and loss. The required reduction is multiplied by each partner's profit and loss ratio to determine the amount of cash to be paid. Thus Y receives $15,000 ($5,000 × 3 = $15,000) and Z receives $10,000 ($5,000 × 2 = $10,000)		(5,000)	(5,000)
Balances per unit of profit and loss after payment of $15,000 to Y and $34,000 to Z. **Remaining cash can now be distributed in the profit and loss ratio**	$10,000	$10,000	$10,000

Summary of cash distribution program:

	Total	X	Y	Z
To creditors before partners receive anything	$ 61,000			
To partners:				
First distribution, to Z ($12,000 × 2)	24,000			$ 24,000
Second distribution, to Y ($5,000 × 3), and Z ($5,000 × 2)	25,000		$15,000	10,000
	$110,000			
Any amount in excess of $110,000 to X, Y, and Z in profit and loss ratio.		$\frac{4}{9}$	$\frac{3}{9}$	$\frac{2}{9}$

therefore be the first to receive cash, (**b**) facilitates the ranking of partners in the order in which they will be entitled to receive cash, and (**c**) provides the basis for determining the amount of cash each partner should receive at various stages of the liquidation process. Since Z's net capital per unit of profit and loss is largest, he will be the first to receive cash, followed by Y, and finally by X.

3 Z should receive enough cash to bring his net capital balance of $27,000 per unit of profit and loss down to $15,000 so that it will be equal to the balance for Y, the second ranking partner. In order to accomplish this, Z's balance must be reduced by $12,000 per unit of profit and loss, and since he has 2 units of profit and loss, he must receive $24,000 ($12,000 × 2 = $24,000) before Y can receive any cash.

4 At this point the net capital balances per unit of profit and loss for Y and Z are equal at $15,000, indicating that they are entitled to receive cash until their balances are reduced by $5,000 in order to bring them down to the $10,000 balance for X, the lowest ranking partner. Since Y has 3 units and Z has 2 units of profit and loss, Y is entitled to receive $15,000 ($5,000 × 3 = $15,000) and Z is entitled to receive $10,000 ($5,000 × 2 = $10,000) before X can receive any cash. After Z receives $24,000, Y and Z would share any amount of cash available up to $25,000 in a 3:2 ratio.

5 After Y has received $15,000 and Z has received $34,000 ($24,000 + $10,000 = $34,000), the net capital balances per unit of profit and loss are $10,000 for each of the three partners, and any additional cash can be paid to the partners in the profit and loss ratio (4:3:2) because their capitals have been brought down to the profit and loss ratio as illustrated below:

	X (4)	Y (3)	Z (2)
Net capital balances before liquidation . . .	$40,000	$45,000	$54,000
First payment of cash to Z			(24,000)
Second payment of cash to Y and Z in 3:2 ratio		(15,000)	(10,000)
Net capital balances (in profit and loss ratio of 4:3:2) after payment of $49,000 to Y and Z	$40,000	$30,000	$20,000

Only when installment payments reach the point at which partners' net capital balances correspond to the profit and loss ratio can subsequent payments be made in that ratio.[1]

We should point out that a cash distribution program, such as the one developed above, should also be used to ascertain an equitable distribution of non-cash assets to the partners. The agreed fair value of non-cash

[1]The procedure for preparing a cash distribution program illustrated above can be used regardless of the number of partners involved and the complexity of the profit and loss ratio. For example, assume that partners share profits as follows: A 41.2%, B 32.3%, C 26.5%. We can view the profit and loss ratio as 412 for A, 323 for B, and 265 for C and apply the same technique illustrated above.

assets such as securities, inventory, or equipment distributed to partners should be treated as equivalent to cash payments. If a distribution of non-cash assets departs from the cash distribution program by giving one of the partners a larger distribution than he is entitled to receive, subsequent distributions should be adjusted to allow the remaining partners to "make up" the distribution prematurely made to one of the partners. In such cases it would be desirable to prepare a new cash distribution program because the original relationship between the partners' capital accounts has been disrupted. To safeguard himself, the liquidator may also choose to require a bond from the partner receiving the premature distribution or may arrange for such non-cash assets to be placed in trust temporarily.

To illustrate how the cash distribution program can be used, assume that the realization of assets by the partnership of X, Y, and Z is as follows:

X, Y, & Z PARTNERSHIP
Realization of Assets
July 5 to September 30, 19__

Month	Carrying value of assets sold	Loss on sale	Cash received
July	$ 62,000	$13,500	$ 48,500
August	66,000	36,000	30,000
September	64,000	31,500	32,500
	$192,000	$81,000	$111,000

The cash available each month should be paid to creditors and partners according to the summary of cash distribution program on page 61 as follows:

X, Y, & Z PARTNERSHIP
Distribution of Cash to Creditors and Partners
July 5 to September 30, 19__

Month	Cash	Liabilities	Partners' capitals X	Y	Z
July (including $8,000 on hand at July 5)	$ 56,500	$56,500			
August	30,000	4,500			$24,000 ⎫
				$ 900	600 ⎭
September	32,500			14,100	9,400 ⎫
			$4,000	3,000	2,000 ⎭
	$119,000	$61,000	$4,000	$18,000	$36,000

The entire cash balance of $56,500 available in July is paid to creditors, leaving $4,500 in unpaid liabilities. When $30,000 becomes available in August, $4,500 should be paid to creditors, thus leaving $25,500 to be paid to the partners according to the cash distribution program developed earlier. The program calls for Z to receive the first $24,000 available for distribution to partners and for Y and Z to share the next $25,000 in a 3:2 ratio. In August only $1,500 ($30,000 − $4,500 − $24,000 = $1,500) is available for payment to Y and Z; thus Y and Z receive $900 and $600, respectively. Of the $32,500 available in September, the first $23,500 is paid to Y and Z in a 3:2 ratio, or $14,100 and $9,400, respectively, in order to complete the distribution of $25,000 to Y and Z before X participates; this leaves $9,000 ($32,500 − $23,500 = $9,000) to be distributed to X, Y, and Z in a profit and loss ratio of 4:3:2.

A statement of realization and liquidation is presented below:

X, Y, & Z PARTNERSHIP
Statement of Realization and Liquidation
July 5 to September 30, 19___

	Assets		Liabilities	Partners' capitals		
	Cash	Other		X(4)	Y(3)	Z(2)
Balances before liquidation	$ 8,000	$192,000	$61,000	$40,000	$45,000	$54,000
July installment:						
Sale of assets at a loss of $13,500	48,500	(62,000)		(6,000)	(4,500)	(3,000)
Balances	$56,500	$130,000	$61,000	$34,000	$40,500	$51,000
Payment of creditors	(56,500)		(56,500)			
Balances		$130,000	$ 4,500	$34,000	$40,500	$51,000
August installment:						
Sale of assets at a loss of $36,000	30,000	(66,000)		(16,000)	(12,000)	(8,000)
Balances	$30,000	$ 64,000	$ 4,500	$18,000	$28,500	$43,000
Payment of creditors	(4,500)		(4,500)			
Balances before paying partners	$25,500	$ 64,000		$18,000	$28,500	$43,000
Payment to partners	(25,500)				(900)	(24,600)
Balances		$ 64,000		$18,000	$27,600	$18,400
September installment:						
Sale of assets at a loss of $31,500	32,500	(64,000)		(14,000)	(10,500)	(7,000)
Balances	$32,500			$ 4,000	$17,100	$11,400
Payment to partners	(32,500)			(4,000)	(17,100)	(11,400)

The journal entries required to record the realization of assets and to complete the liquidation of the partnership appear on page 65.

19__

July

Cash	48,500	
X, Capital	6,000	
Y, Capital	4,500	
Z, Capital	3,000	
Other Assets		62,000

To record sale of assets and division of loss of $13,500 among partners.

| Liabilities | 56,500 | |
| Cash | | 56,500 |

Partial payment to creditors.

Aug.

Cash	30,000	
X, Capital	16,000	
Y, Capital	12,000	
Z, Capital	8,000	
Other Assets		66,000

To record sale of assets and division of loss of $36,000 among partners.

Liabilities	4,500	
Y, Capital	900	
Z, Capital	24,600	
Cash		30,000

Paid balance due to creditors and first installment to partners.

Sept.

Cash	32,500	
X, Capital	14,000	
Y, Capital	10,500	
Z, Capital	7,000	
Other Assets		64,000

To record sale of remaining assets and division of loss of $31,500 among partners.

X, Capital	4,000	
Y, Capital	17,100	
Z, Capital	11,400	
Cash		32,500

Paid final installment to partners.

Withholding of cash for unpaid liabilities and liquidation expenses

As previously emphasized, creditors are entitled to payment in full before anything is paid to partners. In some cases, however, the liquidator may find it more convenient merely to set aside in a separate fund the cash required to pay certain liabilities, and to distribute the remaining cash to the partners. The withholding of cash for payment of recorded liabilities is appropriate when for any reason it is not practicable or advisable (if the amount of the claim is in dispute) to pay an obligation before distributing cash to partners. An amount of cash equal to recorded unpaid liabilities which is set aside in a fund is not a factor in computing possible future losses; the possible future loss is measured by the amount of non-cash assets, any *unrecorded* liabilities, and potential expenses which may be incurred in the course of liquidation.

Any expenses incurred during the liquidation should be deducted in determining the cash available for distribution to partners. Expenses of liquidation are thereby treated as part of the total loss from liquidation. However, in some cases, the liquidator may wish to withhold cash in anticipation of future liquidation expenses. The amount of cash withheld or set aside for future liquidation expenses or for payment of liabilities not recorded in the accounts should be combined with the non-cash assets in computing the maximum possible loss in the remainder of the liquidation.

INCORPORATION OF A PARTNERSHIP

Most successful partnerships give consideration at times to the possible advantages to be gained by incorporating. Among the advantages are limited liability, ease of attracting outside capital without loss of control, and possible tax savings.

A new corporation formed to take over the assets and liabilities of a partnership will usually sell stock to outsiders for cash either at the time of incorporation or at a later date. To assure that the former partners receive an equitable portion of the total capital stock, the assets of the partnership must be adjusted to current fair value before being transferred to the corporation. Any identifiable intangible assets or goodwill developed by the partnership should be included among the assets transferred.

The accounting records of a partnership may be modified and continued in use when the firm changes to the corporate form. As an alternative, the partnership accounts may be closed and a new set of accounting records established for the corporation. The latter alternative is generally followed and is illustrated in the *Intermediate Accounting* text of this series.

If new accounting records are to be opened for the corporation, entries should first be made in the partnership accounts for revaluation of assets, liabilities, and partners' capitals. The next step is to transfer the assets and liabilities to the corporation, setting up a special receivable for the net amount due. This receivable is collected through receipt by the partnership of capital stock. The final entry to close the partnership accounts is based on distribution of the shares of stock to the partners by debiting their capital accounts and crediting the asset account representing capital stock of the new corporation held by the partnership.

The entries in the records of the corporation consist of recording the net assets acquired from the partnership at the adjusted valuations, with an offsetting liability for the amount owed to the partnership. This liability is discharged by the issuance of shares of capital stock to the partnership, accompanied by credits to the Capital Stock and Paid-in Capital in Excess of Par (or Stated) Value accounts.

JOINT VENTURES

A *joint venture* differs from a partnership in that it is limited to carrying out a single project, such as the sale of a lot of merchandise or construction of a building. Historically, joint ventures were used to finance the sale or exchange of a cargo of merchandise in a foreign country. In an era when marine transportation and foreign trade involved many hazards, individuals would band together to undertake a venture of this type. The capital required was usually larger than one person could provide, and the risks were too great to be borne singlehanded. Because of the risks involved and the relatively short duration of the project, no profit was recognized until the venture had been completed. At the end of the voyage, the profit or loss was divided among the participants and their association was ended. A joint venture may therefore be regarded as a type of partnership which comes to an end with the attainment of a specific business objective.

In its traditional form, the accounting for a venture did not follow the accrual concept. The assumption of continuity was not appropriate; instead of the determination of income at regular intervals, the measurement and reporting of profit or loss awaited the completion of the venture.

Present-day ventures

In today's business community, joint ventures are less common but are still employed for many projects such as (1) the purchase, development, and sale of a specific tract of real estate; (2) the sale of agricultural products; (3) exploration for oil and gas; or (4) the construction of a bridge, building, or dam. Since these associations are formed to carry out a specific project, they may be called joint ventures.

The term **corporate joint venture** is also used at present by many large American corporations to describe overseas operations by a company whose ownership is divided between the American corporation and a foreign company. Many examples of jointly owned companies also are found in some domestic industries. A corporate joint venture and the accounting for such a venture are described in **APB Opinion No. 18** as follows:

> "Corporate joint venture" refers to a corporation owned and operated by a small group of businesses (the "joint venturers") as a separate and specific business or project for the mutual benefit of the members of the group. A government may also be a member of the group. The purpose of a corporate joint venture frequently is to share risks and rewards in developing a new market, product or technology; to combine complementary technological knowledge; or to pool resources in developing production or other facilities. A corporate joint venture also usually provides an arrangement under which each joint venturer may participate, directly or indirectly, in the overall management of the joint venture. Joint venturers thus have an interest or relationship other than as passive investors. An entity which is a subsidiary of one of the "joint venturers" is not a corporate joint venture. The ownership of a corporate joint venture seldom changes, and its stock is usually not traded publicly. A minority public ownership, however, does not preclude a corporation from being a corporate joint venture.[2]
>
> . . . .
>
> The Board concludes that the equity method best enables investors in corporate joint ventures to reflect the underlying nature of their investment in those ventures. Therefore, investors should account for investments in common stock of corporate joint ventures by the equity method, both in consolidated financial statements and in parent-company financial statements prepared for issuance to stockholders as the financial statements of the primary reporting entity.[3]
>
> . . . .
>
> When investments in common stock of corporate joint ventures or other investments of 50% or less accounted for under the equity method are, in the aggregate, material in relation to the financial position or results of operations of an investor, it may be necessary for summarized information as to assets, liabilities, and results of operations of the investees to be presented in the notes or in separate statements, either individually or in groups, as appropriate.[4]

Our use of the term **joint venture** in this chapter is in the traditional meaning of a partnership limited to carrying out a single project.

Accounting for a joint venture

The key issue in accounting for a joint venture is whether to establish a separate set of accounting records for the venture. If a separate set

[2] APB Opinion No. 18, "The Equity Method of Accounting for Investments in Common Stock," AICPA (New York: 1971), pp. 348–349.
[3] Ibid., p. 355.
[4] Ibid., p. 361.

of records is not established, two alternative methods are commonly used. One of these two methods calls for each participant (partner) to record all transactions of the venture in his own accounting records. He will open a Joint Venture account and also a receivable or payable with each other participant. The other commonly used procedure calls for each participant to record in his own accounts only those transactions in which he participates directly.

Separate Set of Accounting Records The complexity of modern business, the emphasis upon good organization and strong internal control, the importance of income taxes, the extent of government regulation, and the need for preparation and retention of adequate records are strong arguments for establishing a complete separate set of records for every joint venture of large size and long duration. This approach views the joint venture as a separate accounting entity. Each participant is credited for the amount of cash or for the fair value of non-cash assets which he invests. The fiscal year of the joint venture may or may not coincide with the fiscal years of the participants, but the use of accrual accounting and periodic financial statements for the venture permit regular reporting of the share of profit or loss allocable to each participant.

The accounting records of such a joint venture will include all usual accounts for assets, liabilities, owners' equity, revenue, and expenses. The entire accounting process will conform to generally accepted accounting practices customarily followed in a partnership or corporate organization, from the recording of transactions to the preparation of financial statements.

Each participant in the venture will open an account in his general ledger entitled Investment in Joint Venture. This account is debited for capital invested in the venture, for any services billed to the venture, and for the proper share of any venture net income. The Investment in Joint Venture account is credited for any amounts received from the venture and for a proper share of any venture losses. The account will normally have a debit balance, representing the net investment in the venture. A participant does not make any accounting entry in his records for transactions between the venture and the other participants. The account Investment in Joint Venture will appear in the balance sheet as an asset, either current or noncurrent, depending upon the expected completion date for the venture.

No Separate Set of Accounting Records If a separate set of records is not maintained by the venture as an accounting entity, there are, as previously explained, two common alternative methods available. Each participant may record in his own accounts all transactions entered into by the venture, or each participant may record only those transactions to which he is a party. Let us assume the first method is in use. Thus, if Participant

A contributes merchandise to the venture, he debits Joint Venture and credits Inventory. Each of the other participants makes an entry debiting Joint Venture and crediting Participant A. When sales are made, the participant handling the transaction debits Cash or Accounts Receivable and credits Joint Venture. The other participants debit the participant who executed the sale and credit Joint Venture. In brief, each participant maintains in his own accounts a complete record of all transactions by the joint venture and of the equities of the other participants in the venture.

Upon completion of the venture, the net profit or loss is shown by the balance in the Joint Venture account. Assuming that a profit has been realized, the entry to divide the profit and to close the Joint Venture account will be to debit Joint Venture for the balance, credit each other participant for his share of the profit, and credit Income Summary for the participant's own share. Each participant will then have an account with each of the other participants; the final step is to make payment or collection of these accounts.

If a venture has not been completed at the date one of the participants prepares a balance sheet, only the equity of that participant should be presented as an asset. Since the ledger account Joint Venture shows the total investment by all participants, the balance of this account less the equities of the other participants should be listed as an asset in the balance sheet.

The operation of a joint venture without a separate set of records is appropriate when the venture is expected to be of short duration and not to require complex transactions. If prompt communication among participants in the joint venture is not practicable, convenience may dictate that each participant record only transactions of the venture for which he is personally responsible.

REVIEW QUESTIONS

1 Adams and Barnes have capital accounts of $60,000 and $80,000, respectively. In addition, Adams has made a non-interest-bearing loan of $20,000 to the firm. Adams and Barnes now decide to liquidate their partnership. What priority or advantage, if any, will Adams enjoy in the liquidation with respect to his loan account?

2 State briefly the procedure to be followed in a partnership liquidation when a debit balance arises in the capital account of one of the partners.

3 In the liquidation of the partnership of Baynes, Cross, and David, the sale of the assets resulted in a loss which produced the following balances in the capital accounts: Baynes, $25,000 credit; Cross, $12,500 credit; and David, $5,000 debit. The partners shared profits and losses in a 5:3:2 ratio. All liabilities have been paid and $32,500 of cash is available for distribution to partners. However, it is not possible to determine at present whether David, who is ill, will be able to make good his $5,000 capital deficiency. Can the cash on hand be distributed without waiting to determine the collectibility of the amount due from David? Explain.

4 After disposing of all assets and distributing all cash to creditors, the partnership of A, B, and C still had accounts payable of $12,000. The capital account of Partner A showed a credit balance of $16,000 and that of B a credit balance of $2,000. Creditors of the firm demanded payment from A personally, but he replied that the three partners shared profits and losses equally and had begun operations with equal capital investments. A, therefore, offered to pay the creditors one-third of their claims and no more. What is your opinion of the position taken by A? What is the balance in C's capital account? What entry, if any, should be made in the partnership records for a payment by A personally to the partnership creditors?

5 In the partnership of Jones, Kendall, and Littrell, Jones serves as general manager. The partnership agreement provides that Jones is entitled to an annual salary of $12,000, payable in 12 equal monthly installments, and that remaining profits or losses shall be divided equally. On June 30, the firm suspended operations and began liquidation. Because of a shortage of working capital, Jones had not drawn his salary for the last two months of operation. How should his claim for $2,000 of "unpaid wages" be handled in the liquidation of the partnership?

6 M and N are partners and have agreed to share profits and losses equally. State your reasons in support of dividing losses incurred in liquidation in the profit and loss ratio or in the ratio of capital balances.

7 State briefly the basic rule or principle to be observed in distributing cash to partners when the liquidation of a partnership business extends over several months.

8 During the installment liquidation of a partnership, it is necessary to determine the possible future loss from sale of the remaining assets. What entries, if any, should be made to reflect in the partners' capital accounts their respective shares of the maximum possible loss which may be incurred during the remaining stages of dissolution?

9 The XYZ Partnership is liquidated over a period of several months with several distributions of cash to the partners. Will the total amount of cash received by each partner under these circumstances be more, less, or the same amount as if the liquidator had retained all cash until all assets had been sold and had then made a single payment to the partners?

10 Under what circumstances, if any, is it sound practice for a partnership undergoing installment liquidation to distribute cash to partners in the profit and loss ratio?

11 Judd, Klein, and Lund, who share profits equally, have capital balances of $30,000, $25,000, and $21,000, respectively, when the firm begins the process of liquidation. Among the assets is a note receivable from Klein in the amount of $7,000. All liabilities have been paid. The first assets sold during the liquidation are some marketable securities carried in the accounts at $15,000; cash of $18,000 is received from their sale. How should this $18,000 of cash be divided among the partners?

12 When the partnership of R, S, and T began the process of liquidation, the capital accounts were R $38,000, S $35,000, and T $32,000. When the liquidation was complete, R had received less cash than either of his partners. List several factors which might explain why the partner with the largest capital account might receive the smallest amount of cash in liquidation.

13 How does a *joint venture* differ from a partnership?

14 When the concept of the joint venture is considered from the historical viewpoint, how has the process of income determination differed from that of a partnership or corporation? Does this difference prevail in present practice?

15 What are **corporate joint ventures?** What accounting procedures for such ventures were recommended by the Accounting Principles Board in **Opinion No. 18?**

EXERCISES

Ex. 2-1 Grant and Hall are partners who share profits and losses in a 60:40 ratio. They have decided to liquidate their partnership. A portion of the assets has been sold but other assets with a carrying value of $32,000 must still be realized. All liabilities have been paid, and cash of $20,000 is available for distribution to partners. The capital accounts show balances of $30,000 for Grant and $22,000 for Hall. How should the cash be divided?

Ex. 2-2 Kramer and Lamden started in business some years ago and managed to operate profitably for several years. Recently, however, they lost a substantial legal suit and incurred unexpected losses on accounts receivable and inventories. As a result they decided to liquidate. They sold all assets and only $18,000 was available to pay liabilities, which amounted to $30,000. Their capital accounts before the start of liquidation and their profit and loss ratios are shown below:

	Capital balances	Profit and loss ratio
Kramer	$20,000	60%
Lamden	11,500	40%

a Compute the total loss incurred on the liquidation of the partnership.
b Show how the final settlement should be made between the partners, after Kramer pays $12,000 to creditors. Kramer is personally insolvent after paying the creditors, but Lamden has personal net assets in excess of $100,000.

Ex. 2-3 The balance sheet of the A-B Partnership prior to liquidation follows:

Assets		Liabilities & Partners' Capitals	
Cash	$ 5,000	Liabilities	$ 25,000
Investments	20,000	A, capital	72,000
Other assets	100,000	B, capital	28,000
Total	$125,000	Total	$125,000

Partners A and B share operating profits in a 2·1 ratio and capital gains and losses in a 3:1 ratio.

Partner A takes over the portfolio of investments at an agreed value of $45,000; the rest of the assets (except cash) and the trade name are sold to Rupp Company for $200,000 face amount of bonds having a fair market value of $180,000.

Prepare appropriate journal entries in the accounts of the partnership to record the liquidation. Assume that (1) Partner A takes $100,000 face value of bonds, (2) Partner B takes $60,000 face value of bonds, (3) the remaining bonds are sold for $35,600 net of commissions, (4) all liabilities are paid, and (5) any available cash is distributed to the partners.

Ex. 2-4 After sale of a portion of the assets of the XYZ Partnership, which is being liquidated, the capital accounts are X $35,000; Y $40,000; and Z $43,000. Cash of $42,000 and other assets with a carrying value of $78,000 are on hand. Creditors' claims total $2,000. X, Y, and Z share profits equally. What cash payments can be made to the partners at this time?

Ex. 2-5 Landon and Hayes, partners who shared profits equally, were both incapacitated in an airplane accident and a liquidator was appointed to wind up their business. The accounts showed cash, $30,000; other assets, $100,000; liabilities, $20,000; Landon, capital, $61,000; and Hayes, capital, $49,000. Because of the highly specialized nature of the non-cash assets, the liquidator anticipated that considerable time would be required to dispose of them. He estimated that the expenses of liquidating the business (advertising, rent, travel, etc.), might approximate $7,000. How much cash can safely be distributed to each partner at this point?

Ex. 2-6 The following balance sheet was prepared for the partnership of Able, Boyer, and Cain:

Assets		*Liabilities & Partners' Capitals*	
Cash	$ 20,000	Liabilities	$ 50,000
Other assets	180,000	Able, capital (40%)	37,000
		Boyer, capital (40%)	65,000
		Cain, capital (20%)	48,000
Total	$200,000	Total	$200,000

Figures shown parenthetically reflect agreed profit- and loss-sharing percentages.

a The partnership is being liquidated by selling assets in installments. The first sale of non-cash assets having a carrying value of $90,000 realizes $50,000 and all cash available after settlement with creditors is distributed. Compute the amount of cash each partner should receive in the first installment.

b If the facts are as in *a* above except that $3,000 cash is to be withheld, how much cash should each partner receive?

c As a separate case, assume that each partner properly received some cash in the distribution after the second sale of assets. The cash to be distributed amounts to $12,000 from the third sale of assets, and unsold assets with an $8,000 carrying value remain. How should the $12,000 be distributed?

Ex. 2-7 D, E, and F have capital balances of $20,000, $25,000, and $9,000, respectively, and share profits and losses in a ratio of 4:2:1.
a Prepare an advance program for cash distributions.
b How much will be paid to all partners if D receives only $4,000 on his equity?
c If D received $13,000 as his share of the cash paid pursuant to liquidation, how much did F receive?
d If E received only $11,000 as a result of the liquidation, how much did the partnership lose on the sale of assets? No partner invested additional amounts in the partnership.

Ex. 2-8 The balance sheet for P and Q Partnership at June 1 of Year 10 follows:

Assets		Liabilities & Partners' Capitals	
Cash	$ 5,000	Liabilities	$20,000
Other assets	55,000	P, capital	22,500
		Q, capital	17,500
Total	$60,000	Total	$60,000

Partners share profits as follows: P 60%; Q 40%. In June, assets with a carrying value of $22,000 are sold for $18,000, creditors are paid in full, and $2,000 is paid to partners in such a way as to bring their capital accounts down to the profit-sharing ratio. In July, assets with a carrying value of $10,000 are sold for $12,000, liquidation expenses of $500 are paid, and cash of $12,500 is distributed to partners. In August, the remaining assets are sold for $22,500 and final settlement is made between the partners.
Compute the amount of cash each partner should receive in June, in July, and in August.

Ex. 2-9 The net equities and profit and loss ratios for A, B, C, and D before liquidation are as follows:

	A (6)	B (4)	C (2)	D (1)
Net equity in partnership	$36,000	$32,400	$8,000	$(1,500)

Assets will be sold at amounts significantly in excess of carrying values.
Prepare an orderly program showing how cash should be distributed as it becomes available in the course of liquidation.

Ex. 2-10 Wagman and Berman enter into an agreement to speculate on the American Stock Exchange, each using approximately $5,000 of his own capital. The profits and losses are to be divided equally and settlement is to be made at the end of the year after all securities have been liquidated. A summary of the monthly brokerage statements for the year follows:

	Wagman	Berman
Total of all purchase confirmations	$45,000	$20,000
Total of all sales confirmations	48,700	16,800
Interest charged on margin accounts	80	50
Dividends credited to accounts	40	100

How should settlement be made between Wagman and Berman at the end of the year?

SHORT CASES FOR ANALYSIS AND DECISION

Case 2-1 Allen and Brett formed a partnership and agreed to share profits and losses equally. Although they began business with equal capitals, Allen made more frequent withdrawals than Brett, with the result that his capital account became the smaller of the two. The partners have now decided to liquidate their business at June 30; on that date the accounts were closed and financial statements prepared. The balance sheet showed a capital account for Allen of $40,000 and Brett's capital as $60,000. In addition the balance sheet showed that Brett had made a $10,000 loan to the partnership.

The liquidation of the partnership was managed by Allen because Brett was hospitalized by an auto accident on July 1, the day after regular operations were suspended. The procedures followed by Allen were as follows: First, to sell all the assets at the best prices obtainable; second, to pay the creditors in full; third, to pay Brett's loan account; and fourth, to divide all remaining cash between Brett and himself in the 40:60 ratio represented by their capital accounts.

When Brett was released from the hospital on July 5, Allen met him and informed him that through good luck and hard work, he had been able to find buyers for the assets and complete the liquidation during the five days of Brett's hospitalization. As the first step in the liquidation, Allen delivered two cashier's checks to Brett at the moment of his release from the hospital. One check was for $10,000 in payment of the loan account; the other was in settlement of Brett's capital account.

Instructions
a Do you approve the procedures followed in the liquidation? Explain fully.
b Assume that the liquidation procedures followed resulted in the payment of $24,000 to Brett in addition to the payment of his loan account in full. What was the amount of gain or loss on the liquidation? If you believe that other methods should have been followed in the liquidation, explain how much more or less Brett would have received under the procedure you recommend.

Case 2-2 In reply to a question as to how settlement with partners should be made during liquidation of a partnership, Student A made the following statement:

"Accounting records are usually based on cost and reflect the going-concern concept. When a business is broken up, it is often necessary to sell the assets for a fraction of their carrying value. Consequently, a partner usually receives in liquidation a settlement far below the amount of his equity in the business."

Student B offered the following comment:

"I agree fully with what A has said, but he might have gone further and added that no payment should ever be made to any partner until all the assets of the partnership have been sold and all creditors have been paid in full. Until these steps have been completed, the residual amount available for distribution to partners is unknown, and therefore any earlier payment to a partner might have to be returned. If the partner were unable to return such amount, the person who authorized the payment might be held personally responsible."

Student C made the following statement:

"In the liquidation of a partnership, each partner receives the amount of his equity in the business; no more and no less. As to timing of payments, it is often helpful to a partner to receive a partial payment before the assets are sold and creditors are paid. If proper precautions are taken, such early partial payments are quite satisfactory."

Instructions Evaluate the statements made by each student.

Case 2-3 The partnership of Coe, Dell, and Earp is insolvent and in process of liquidation under the Uniform Partnership Act. After conversion of the assets into cash and distribution of the loss equally among the three partners, their positions are as follows:

	Equity in partnership	Personal financial position other than equity in partnership	
		Assets	Liabilities
Coe	$20,000	$110,000	$45,000
Dell	(21,000)	20,000	40,000
Earp	(55,000)	55,000	35,000

Instructions Explain the prospects for collection by
a The creditors of the partnership.
b The personal creditors of each partner.
c Partner Coe from his copartners. Starting from the assumption that Coe has a $20,000 equity in the firm, what is the amount of loss he should sustain?

Case 2-4 On November 15, in beginning the liquidation of the XYZ Partnership, the liquidator found that an 8% note payable for $100,000 issued by the firm had six months remaining until maturity on May 15 of next year. Interest had been paid to November 15. Terms of the note provided that interest at 8% to the due date must be paid in full even though the note was paid prior to maturity. The liquidator had paid all other liabilities and had on hand cash of $150,000. The remaining non-cash assets had a carrying value of $200,000, and the liquidator believed that six months would be required to dispose of them. He estimated that the realization of the non-cash assets over this period would produce cash at least 25% in excess of the carrying values of the assets.
   Partner X made the following statement to the liquidator: "I realize you can't pay the partners until creditors have been paid in full, but I need cash for another business I'm starting. So I'd like for you to immediately pay off the note and interest to May 15 of next year and distribute the remaining available cash to the partners." Partner Y objected to this proposal for immediate cash payments on the ground that it would entail a loss of $4,000. He argued that if such action were taken, the interest cost of $4,000 be charged entirely against X's capital account. Partner Z said that he had no particular concern about the matter but as a convenience to his partners he would personally assume the note liability, if $102,000 in cash were paid to him immediately. To insure the noteholder against loss, he would deposit collateral of $104,000 in government bonds. The noteholder expressed his willingness to accept this arrangement. Partner Z specified that the proposed payment of $102,000 to him would be in his new role as a creditor and that it would not affect his right to share in any cash distributions to the three partners.

Instructions Evaluate the proposal by each partner. What action should be taken by the liquidator? Would your answer differ if the assumptions were changed to indicate a probable loss on the realization of the remaining non-cash assets?

PROBLEMS

2-5 Following is the balance sheet of a partnership prior to liquidation:

ROSS, SNEAD, AND TODD
Balance Sheet
June 15, Year 1

Assets		Liabilities & Partners' Capitals	
Cash	$ 1,500	Liabilities	$15,500
Other assets	64,000	Snead, loan	4,000
		Ross, capital	17,000
		Snead, capital	23,000
		Todd, capital	6,000
Total	$65,500	Total	$65,500

The partners share profits as follows: Ross 40%; Snead 40%; Todd 20%. On June 15, Year 1, other assets were sold for $30,500 and $16,000 had to be paid to liquidate the liabilities because of unrecorded claims amounting to $500. Snead and Ross are personally solvent, but Todd's personal liabilities exceed his personal assets by $4,000.

Instructions
a Prepare a statement of realization and liquidation. Combine Snead's loan account with his capital account.
b Prepare journal entries required to record the liquidation.
c How much cash would other assets have to bring in liquidation in order that Todd would take enough out of the partnership to pay his personal creditors? Assume that it takes $16,000 to pay off the partnership liabilities.

2-6 The accounts of Udall, Young, and Wade, who share profits in a 5:3:2 ratio, are as follows on December 31, Year 5:

Udall, drawing (debit balance)	$(16,000)
Wade, drawing (debit balance)	(4,000)
Young, loan	20,000
Udall, capital	82,000
Young, capital	67,000
Wade, capital	63,000

Total assets amount to $308,000, including $85,000 in cash, and liabilities total $96,000. The partnership is liquidated and Wade ultimately receives $46,000 cash for his equity in the partnership.

Instructions
a Compute the total loss from the liquidation of the partnership.
b Prepare a statement of realization and liquidation.
c Prepare journal entries for the records of the partnership to account for the liquidation.

2-7 Johns, Keeler, and Lindsey decide to form a partnership early in Year 6. Their capital investments and profit-sharing ratio are listed below:

Johns: *$15,000—50%*

Keeler: *$10,000—30%, with a salary allowance of $6,000 per year or a proportionate amount*
for a period less than a year

Lindsey: *$8,000—20%*

During the first six months of Year 6, the partners were not particularly concerned over the poor volume of business and the loss of $14,000 reported by their accountant, since they had been told that it would take at least six months to establish their business and to achieve profitable operations. Business during the second half of the year did not improve and the partners decided to go out of business before additional losses were incurred. The decision to liquidate was hastened when two major customers filed bankruptcy proceedings.

The sale of assets was completed during October and all available cash was paid to creditors. Suppliers' invoices of $1,800 remained unpaid at this time. The personal financial status of each partner on October 31, Year 6, was as follows:

	Personal assets	*Personal liabilities*
Johns	$10,000	$ 8,500
Keeler	20,000	5,000
Lindsey	25,000	14,000

The partners had made no cash withdrawals during Year 6; however, in August Lindsey had withdrawn merchandise with a cost of $400 and Keeler had taken title to some equipment at an agreed consideration of $250.

The partners have decided to end the partnership immediately and to arrive at a settlement among themselves in accordance with the provisions of the Uniform Partnership Act.

Instructions Prepare a four-column statement of partners' capitals (including liquidation) as of October 31, Year 6. You need not show the changes in liabilities, cash, or non-cash assets, merely the changes in the total capital and individual capitals of the three partners.

2-8 A partnership doing business as Royalty Hacienda was formed on January 2, Year 5, by equal contributions from Jim Colson and Bob Means. Colson, who was in the toy business, contributed $20,000 of inventory for his 50% interest and Means, who was a distributor of appliances, contributed inventory valued at $16,000 plus $4,000 in cash for his 50% interest. The partners agreed to share profits and losses equally.

The operation of Royalty Hacienda did not prove profitable, and after the Christmas shopping season of Year 5, Colson and Means decided to dissolve the partnership. They retained you at this time to assist in the termination of the business. Your investigation reveals the following information:

(1) The part-time accountant employed by Royalty Hacienda was also the accountant for Means' appliance business. The condition of the records indicated a lack of competence on his part. He had discarded all cash register tapes and invoices for expenses and purchases.

(2) The partners assure you in writing that the only liabilities are to the two firms which they own as single proprietorships. The amounts are $19,480 owing to Colson's Toys and $10,520 owing to Means' Appliance Shop.

(3) Through an analysis of bank statements and paid checks you are able to construct the following summary of cash transactions:

Opening cash balance		$ 4,000
Receipts:		
Sales	$140,000	
Inventory liquidation	14,000	154,000
		$158,000
Disbursements:		
Purchases	$ 72,000	
Operating expenses	52,000	
Leasehold improvements (five-year lease)	12,000	
Liquidation expenses	8,000	144,000
Balance, Dec. 31, Year 5		$ 14,000

(4) Payments of $7,000 were made to each of the partners on December 31, Year 5, in partial settlement of the firm's liabilities.
(5) You are informed by the partners that the dollar amounts of regular sales during the year were divided approximately equally between toys and appliances and that the dollar amounts of liquidation sales of toys and appliances were also approximately equal. The markup was uniformly 40% of cost on toys and 25% of cost on appliances. All sales were for cash. The ending inventory of shopworn merchandise was liquidated on December 31, Year 5, for 50% of the retail sales price. The partners believe that some appliances may have been returned to Means' Appliance Shop, but the accountant failed to enter any such returns in the records of either organization.

Instructions
a Prepare a schedule showing the computation of unrecorded returns of merchandise by Royalty Hacienda. Assume that no theft of merchandise had occurred.
b Prepare an income statement for Royalty Hacienda for the period from January 2 to December 31, Year 5.
c Prepare a statement of partners' capitals for the year ended December 31, Year 5.

2-9 Murdock and Newhouse were attorneys and automobile fanciers who became acquainted because of their interest in imported automobiles. They decided to become partners in a law firm and persuaded a third attorney, Oldfield, to join with them. The partnership maintained only meager accounting records, but a secretary in the firm did maintain a careful daily record of cash receipts, which were almost entirely in the form of checks received through the mail. The only other systematically maintained record was the checkbook used for all disbursements by the partnership. Some miscellaneous working papers were on file relating to income tax returns of prior years but these were not very informative.

Early in Year 7 the partners quarreled over the use of partnership funds to buy expensive automobiles; this quarrel led to a decision to liquidate the firm as of June 30, Year 7. You were retained to assemble the financial data needed for an equitable distribution of assets. You learn that the partnership was formed four years ago with equal capital investments and an agreement to share profits equally. By inspection of the income tax return for the calendar year ended December 31, Year 6, you determine that the amounts of depreciable assets and accumulated depreciation were as follows at December 31, Year 6:

	Depreciable assets (cost)	Accumulated depreciation, Dec. 31, Year 6
Office equipment	$ 7,500	$ 2,250
Library	4,500	900
Automobiles:		
Bentley—assigned to Murdock	10,000	3,000
Buick—assigned to Newhouse	5,000	1,000
Rolls-Royce—assigned to Oldfield . .	15,000	3,000
Totals	$42,000	$10,150

By reference to the cash records, you find that cash receipts for the first six months of Year 7 amounted to $300,000. The cash disbursements were summarized as follows:

Automobile and miscellaneous expenses	$ 7,490
Entertainment expense	20,000
Wages and salaries expense	70,510
Rent expense	7,000
Drawings: Murdock	45,000
Drawings: Newhouse	50,000
Drawings: Oldfield	60,000
Total cash disbursements	$260,000

The automobiles were depreciated on a straight-line basis over a five-year life and depreciation was treated as a charge against partnership revenue. A 10-year life was used for depreciation of office equipment and the library. As one step in the liquidation, the partners agree that the automobiles which were purchased from partnership funds should be retained by the partners to whom assigned. They also agree upon equal distribution of the office equipment among them in kind. The entire library will be distributed to Murdock. All assets distributed are assigned a fair value equal to carrying value.

Cash on hand and in bank at June 30, Year 7, amounted to $100,010. The capital accounts of the partners were equal at December 31, Year 6. Assume that the partnership had no other assets or liabilities, either at the beginning or the end of the six-month period ended June 30, Year 7.

Instructions Prepare a statement of partners' capitals for the period January 1 to June 30, Year 7, including the final distribution of cash and other assets to partners. To support this statement, prepare an income statement for the six months ended June 30, Year 7.

2-10 Farmer, Garrison, and Harris present the following balance sheet on April 30, Year 3, just prior to liquidation of the partnership.

FARMER, GARRISON, AND HARRIS
Balance Sheet
April 30, Year 3

Assets		Liabilities & Partners' Capitals	
Cash	$ 20,000	Liabilities	$ 80,000
Other assets	280,000	Farmer, capital	60,000
		Garrison, capital	70,000
		Harris, capital	90,000
Total	$300,000	Total	$300,000

During May, assets with a carrying value of $105,000 were sold for $75,000 cash. During June, assets with a carrying value of $61,000 were sold for $25,000 cash, and in July the remaining assets with a carrying value of $114,000 were sold for $87,000 cash. The cash which became available each month was promptly distributed. The partners shared profits equally.

Instructions
a Prepare a statement of realization and liquidation covering the entire period of liquidation, and a supporting schedule showing the computation of install- ment payments to partners as cash becomes available.
b At what point in the liquidation did the partners' capital accounts have balances corresponding to the profit and loss ratio? Of what significance is this rela- tionship with respect to subsequent cash distributions to partners?

2-11 Partners S, T, and U share profits and losses in a ratio of $5:3:2$. At the end of a very unprofitable year, they decided to liquidate the firm. The partners' capital accounts at this date were as follows: S, Capital, $22,000; T, Capital, $27,000; U, Capital, $14,000. The liabilities shown in the balance sheet amounted to $28,000, including a loan of $8,000 from S. The cash balance was only $3,280.
   The partners plan to sell the non-cash assets on a piecemeal basis and to distribute cash as rapidly as it becomes available. So far as is known, all three partners are personally solvent.

Instructions Answer each of the following questions and show how you reached your conclusions. (Each question is independent of the others. An advance program for cash distributions to partners would be helpful.)
a If T received $5,000 on the first distribution of cash, how much did S and U each receive at that time?
b If S received a total of $25,000 as a result of the liquidation, what was the total amount realized on the sale of the non-cash assets?
c If U received $4,000 on the first distribution of cash, how much did S receive at that time?

2-12 On August 25, Year 4, Nye, Olds, and Parr entered into a partnership agreement to acquire a speculative second mortgage on undeveloped real estate. They invested $55,000, $32,000, and $12,500, respectively. They agreed on a profit and loss ratio of $4:2:1$, respectively.
   On September 1, Year 4, they purchased for $99,500 a mortgage note with an unpaid balance of $120,000. The amount paid included interest accrued from June 30, Year 4. The note principal matures at the rate of $2,000 each quarter. Interest at the annual rate of 8% computed on the unpaid balance is also due quarterly.

Regular interest and principal payments were received on September 30 and December 31, Year 4. A petty cash fund of $100 was established, and collection expenses of $20 were paid in December.

In addition to the regular payment on September 30, the mortgagor made a lump-sum principal reduction payment of $10,000 plus a penalty of 2% (on $10,000) for prepayment.

Because of the speculative nature of the note, the partners agree to defer recognition of the discount until their cost has been fully recovered.

Instructions

a Assuming that no cash distributions were made to the partners, prepare a schedule computing the cash balance available for distribution to the partners on December 31, Year 4.

b After payment of collection expenses, the partners expect to have cash in the total amount of $173,000 available for distribution to themselves for interest and return of principal. They plan to distribute the cash as soon as possible so that they can individually reinvest the cash. Prepare a schedule showing how the total cash of $173,000 should be distributed to the individual partners by installments as it becomes available.

2-13 A, B, C, and D have decided to dissolve their partnership. They plan to sell the assets gradually in order to minimize losses. They share profits and losses as follows: A 40%; B 35%; C 15%; and D 10%. Presented below is the partnership's trial balance as of October 1, Year 8, the date on which liquidation begins.

	Debit	Credit
Cash	$ 400	
Receivables	51,800	
Inventory, Oct. 1, Year 8	85,200	
Equipment (net)	39,600	
Accounts payable		$ 6,000
A, loan		12,000
B, loan		20,000
A, capital		40,000
B, capital		43,000
C, capital		36,000
D, capital		20,000
Totals	$177,000	$177,000

Instructions

a Prepare a statement as of October 1, Year 8, showing how cash will be distributed among partners by installments as it becomes available. In order to simplify computations, restate the profit and loss ratio to 8:7:3:2.

b On October 31, Year 8, cash of $25,400 became available to creditors and partners. How should it be distributed?

c If, instead of being dissolved, the partnership continued operations and earned $47,250, how should this income be distributed if, in addition to the afore-mentioned profit-sharing arrangement, it was provided that D receive a bonus of 5% of the income after treating such bonus as an expense? The income of $47,250 is before deducting the bonus.

2-14 The partnership of D, E, and F has called upon you to assist in winding up the affairs of the partnership.

You are able to gather the following information:

(1) The trial balance of the partnership at March 1, Year 3, is as follows:

	Debit	Credit
Cash	$ 6,000	
Accounts receivable	22,000	
Inventory	14,000	
Plant and equipment (net)	99,000	
D, loan receivable	12,000	
F, loan receivable	7,500	
Accounts payable		$ 17,000
D, capital		67,000
E, capital		45,000
F, capital		31,500
Totals	$160,500	$160,500

(2) The partners share profits and losses as follows: D 50%; E 30%; and F 20%.
(3) The partners are considering an offer of $100,000 for the accounts receivable, inventory, and plant and equipment at March 1. The $100,000 would be paid to the partners in installments, the number of installments and amounts of which are to be negotiated.

Instructions
a Prepare a cash distribution schedule as of March 1, Year 3, showing how the total available cash of $106,000 would be distributed as it becomes available.
b Assume the same facts as in **a**, except that the partners have decided to liquidate their partnership instead of accepting the offer of $100,000. Cash is distributed to the partners at the end of each month.

A summary of the liquidation transactions follows:

March: *$16,500—collected on accounts receivable, balance is uncollectible.*
    $10,000—received for the entire inventory.
    $1,000—liquidation expenses paid.
    $8,000—cash retained in the business at end of the month.
April: *$1,500—liquidation expenses paid.*
    As part payment of his capital, F accepted a piece of equipment that he had developed which had a carrying value of $4,000. The partners agreed that a fair value of $10,000 should be placed on the equipment for liquidation purposes.
    $2,500—cash retained in the business at end of the month.
May: *$72,000—received on sale of remaining plant and equipment.*
    $1,000—liquidation expenses paid.
    No cash retained in the business.

Prepare a schedule of cash payments as of May 31, Year 3, showing how the cash was actually distributed.

3

Accounting for branches

Establishment of branches and divisions

As a business grows it often establishes branches in order to market its products over a larger territory. The term *branch* has been used to describe a company unit located at some distance from the home office which carries a stock of merchandise, makes sales in its local area, approves customers' credit, and makes collection of its own receivables.

The merchandise handled by a branch may be obtained solely from the home office or a portion may be purchased from outside suppliers. The cash receipts of the branch are often deposited in a bank account belonging to the home office; the expenses are then paid from an imprest fund provided by the home office. As the fund is depleted, the branch submits a list of disbursements supported by vouchers and receives a check from the home office to replenish the fund.

The use of an imprest fund gives the home office strong control over the cash receipts and disbursements of the branch. However, in larger branches it is common practice for the branch to maintain its own bank accounts; that is, to deposit its cash receipts and issue its own checks. In summary, we may say that the extent of independence and responsibility given to a branch will vary greatly in different companies and even among different branches within the same company.

A segment of a business may also be operated as a *division.* The accounting procedures for a division which is not organized as a separate corporation are similar to those used to account for branch operations.

When a segment of a business is operated as a separate corporate entity (subsidiary), consolidated financial statements would generally be required. Consolidated financial statements are described in detail in Chapters 5 to 8; accounting and reporting problems for divisions of a business entity are included in Chapter 9.

Sales agency contrasted with branch

The term *sales agency* is sometimes applied to a company unit which performs only a small portion of the functions traditionally associated with a branch. For example, a sales agency usually carries samples of company products but does not have a stock of merchandise. Orders are taken from customers and transmitted to the home office, which approves the customers' credit and ships the merchandise directly to them. The accounts receivable are maintained at the home office, which also performs the collection function. An imprest fund is maintained at the sales agency to permit payment of its operating expenses.

Accounting system for a sales agency

A sales agency which does not carry a stock of merchandise, maintain receivables, or make collections has no need for a complete set of accounting records. All that is needed is a record of sales to customers and a listing of cash payments supported by vouchers.

If the home office wants to measure the profitability of each sales agency separately, it will establish in the general ledger special revenue and expense accounts in the name of the agency, for example, Sales: Lakeview Agency; Rent Expense: Lakeview Agency. The cost of goods sold by each agency must also be determined. If perpetual inventories are maintained, shipments to customers of the Lakeview Agency would be debited to Cost of Goods Sold: Lakeview Agency.

If a periodic inventory system is in use, a shipment of goods sold by an agency may be recorded by debiting Cost of Goods Sold: Lakeview Agency and crediting Shipments of Merchandise: Agencies. This entry will be necessary only at the end of the accounting period if a memorandum record is maintained during the period listing the cost of goods shipped to fill sales orders received from agencies. At the end of the period the account Shipments of Merchandise: Agencies will be offset against the total of beginning inventory and purchases to determine the cost of goods available for sale by the home office in its own operations.

Office furniture or other assets located at a sales agency may be carried in a separate account in the general ledger of the home office, or control over such assets may be achieved by use of a subsidiary ledger with a detail record for each item showing location as well as cost and other data.

Illustrative Entries for Operation of a Sales Agency The accounting entries made by the home office in connection with operation of a sales agency are illustrated below, based on the assumption of a periodic inventory system:

Home Office Records

Inventory of Samples: Lakeview Agency	*1,500*	
Shipments of Merchandise: Lakeview Agency		*1,500*
Shipped merchandise to agency for use as samples.		
Imprest Fund: Lakeview Agency	*1,000*	
Cash		*1,000*
To establish agency imprest fund.		
Accounts Receivable	*50,000*	
Sales: Lakeview Agency		*50,000*
To record filling of sales orders received through Lakeview Agency.		
Various Expense Accounts: Lakeview Agency	*10,000*	
Cash		*10,000*
To replenish imprest fund. (This entry represents several checks sent to the agency during the period.)		
Cost of Goods Sold: Lakeview Agency	*35,000*	
Shipments of Merchandise: Lakeview Agency		*35,000*
To summarize memorandum record of cost of goods sold during period to fill orders received through agency.		
Sales: Lakeview Agency	*50,000*	
Cost of Goods Sold: Lakeview Agency		*35,000*
Various Expense Accounts: Lakeview Agency		*10,000*
Income Summary: Lakeview Agency		*5,000*
To close revenue and expense accounts into a separate Income Summary account for sales agency.		
Income Summary: Lakeview Agency	*5,000*	
Income Summary		*5,000*
To close the agency Income Summary account to the home office Income Summary account.		

Accounting system for a branch

The extent of the accounting activity at a branch depends upon company policy. The policies of one company may provide for a complete accounting structure at each branch; the policies of another company may call for concentration of all accounting records in the home office. In some of the drug and grocery chain stores, for example, the branches submit daily reports and documents to the home office, which enters all transactions by branches in accounting records kept in one central location. The home office may not even conduct operations on its own but merely serve as an accounting and control headquarters for the branches.

In many fields of business, however, the branch maintains a complete, self-balancing set of records with journals, ledgers, and a chart of accounts similar to those of an independent business. Financial statements are prepared at regular intervals by the branch and forwarded to the home office. The number and type of accounts, the internal control practices, the form and content of financial statements, and the accounting policies generally are prescribed by the home office. Internal auditors may perform examinations to determine whether branch personnel carry out these policies and procedures in a uniform and consistent manner.

In the remainder of this chapter we shall be concerned with a branch operation that includes a complete set of accounting records. The range of transactions to be accounted for by the branch should ordinarily include all controllable expenses and revenue for which the branch manager is held responsible. If his responsibility includes all assets and all expenditures, then the accounts should reflect this responsibility. More commonly, expenses such as depreciation are regarded as not subject to control by the branch manager, and both the asset and related depreciation accounts are maintained by the home office.

Reciprocal accounts

The records maintained by the branch will include a Home Office account which will be credited for all merchandise, cash, or other resources provided by the home office; it will be debited for all cash, merchandise, or other resources sent by the branch to the home office or to other branches. The Home Office account is an ownership equity account which shows the investment made in the branch. At the end of the accounting period when the branch closes its accounts, the Income Summary account is closed into the Home Office account. A net income increases the credit balance of the Home Office account; a net loss decreases this balance.

In the home office records a reciprocal account with a title such as Investment in Branch is maintained. This account is debited for the cash, merchandise, and services provided to the branch, and for net income earned by the branch. It is credited for the cash or other assets received from the branch, and for any net loss incurred by the branch. A separate investment account is generally maintained by the home office for each branch. If there is only one branch, the account title is likely to be Investment in Branch; if there are numerous branches, each account title will include a name or number to identify the individual branch.

Expenses incurred by home office and charged to branches

Some companies follow a policy of notifying branches of expenses incurred by the home office in their behalf. As previously mentioned, plant and equipment located at branches are commonly carried on the home office accounting records. This practice facilitates the use of standard depreciation procedures throughout the company. If an asset is purchased by the home office for the branch, the entry for the acquisition is the usual one of debiting an asset account and crediting Cash or Accounts Payable. If the branch makes the purchase of an asset, it will debit the Home Office account and credit Cash or Accounts Payable. The home office will then make an entry debiting an asset account such as Plant and Equipment: Branch Z and crediting the reciprocal account Investment in Branch Z.

The home office also usually purchases insurance, pays property and other taxes, and places some advertising which benefits all branches. Clearly such expenses as depreciation, taxes, insurance, and advertising must be considered in determining the profitability of a branch. A policy decision must be made as to whether these expense data are to be retained at the home office or are to be reported to the branches so that the income statement prepared by each branch will give a complete picture of operations.

If the home office does not make sales itself but functions only as a control center, most or all of its expenses may be allocated to the branches. In order to facilitate comparison of the operating results achieved by the various branches, the home office may charge each branch interest on the capital invested in that branch. Such interest expense recorded by the branches would be offset by interest revenue to the home office and would not appear in the combined income statement of the company as a whole.

In some companies the expenses incurred by the home office relating to branch operations are not transmitted to the branches but are used in the home office in restating and analyzing the financial statements prepared by the branches.

Alternative methods of billing merchandise shipments to branch

Three alternative methods are available to the home office in pricing merchandise shipped to a branch. The merchandise shipped may be billed (1) at cost, (2) at cost plus an arbitrary percentage, or (3) at retail sales price. Of course the shipment of merchandise to a branch does not constitute a sale because ownership of the goods does not change.

Billing at cost is the simplest procedure and is widely used. It avoids the complication of unrealized profit in inventories and permits the financial statements of the branch to give a meaningful picture of operations. However, billing goods to branches at cost attributes all profits of the organization to the branches, even though some of the goods may be manufactured by the home office. Under these circumstances cost may not be the most realistic basis for pricing shipments of goods to branches.

Billing shipments to the branch at an arbitrary percentage above cost (such as 110% of cost) may be intended to allocate a reasonable profit to home office operations or may be used merely to prevent branch personnel from knowing the full profits earned by the branch. This latter reason is a dubious one because a competent branch manager will necessarily be well aware of the cost of merchandise in his own store and also the costs of competing lines. Moreover, the internal process of arbitrarily writing up merchandise shipped to branches is necessarily known by some employees.

When goods are billed to the branch at a price in excess of cost, the profits reported by the branch will of course be understated and the ending inventory will be overstated. Adjustments must be made by the home office to compensate for the excess of inventory pricing above cost before completing the financial statements at the end of each period.

Billing shipments to a branch at retail sales price may be based on a desire to conceal profit information from branch personnel and also to strengthen internal control over inventories. The inventory accounts of the branch show the merchandise received at retail sales prices and show units sold at the same prices. Consequently, the accounts will show the ending inventory which *should* be on hand priced at retail. The home office record of shipments to a branch, when considered along with sales reported by the branch, provides a perpetual inventory stated at sales price. If the physical inventory taken periodically at the branch does not agree with the amounts thus determined, some type of error or theft is indicated and can be promptly investigated.

Separate financial statements for branch and home office

A separate income statement and balance sheet should be prepared by the branch so that management can review the operating results and financial position of the branch. The income statement has no unusual features if merchandise is billed to the branch at cost. However, if merchandise is billed to the branch at retail sales price, the income statement will necessarily show a net loss approximating the amount of operating expenses. The only unusual aspect of the balance sheet for a branch is the use of the Home Office account in lieu of the ownership equity accounts used by a separate business entity. The separate financial statements prepared by a branch may be revised in the home office to include expenses incurred by the home office allocable to the branch, and also to show branch operations after elimination of any interoffice profits.

Separate financial statements are also usually prepared for the home office so that management will be able to appraise the results of its operations and its financial position. It is important to emphasize, however, that separate financial statements of the home office and of the branch are for internal use only. They do not meet the needs of investors, bankers, or other outside users of financial statements.

Combined financial statements for home office and branch

A balance sheet for distribution to bankers, creditors, stockholders, and government agencies must show the financial position of the business as a *single unit.* A convenient starting point in preparing a combined balance sheet consists of the adjusted trial balances of the home office and of the branch. A working paper for the combination of these trial balances is illustrated on pages 94 to 95.

The assets and liabilities of the branch are substituted for the Investment in Branch account shown on the home office trial balance. Like accounts are combined to produce one amount for the total cash of the business, one amount for accounts receivable, and similarly for other assets and liabilities.

In the preparation of a combined balance sheet, reciprocal accounts are eliminated because they lose all significance when one views the branch and home office as one entity. The Home Office account is offset against the Investment in Branch account; also any receivables and payables between two branches or between the home office and a branch are eliminated.

The operating results of the entire business are shown by an income statement in which the revenue and expenses of the branch are combined with corresponding revenue and expense accounts for the home office. Interoffice profits must be eliminated. The stockholders, creditors, and other outsiders interested in the company naturally want to see an income statement which reveals the earnings for the business as a whole.

In the preparation of a combined income statement, the two accounts showing transfer of merchandise between home office and branch must be eliminated. The account on the branch accounting records called Shipments from Home Office is eliminated by offsetting it against Shipments to Branch on the home office records.

Illustrative Entries for Operation of a Branch   Assume that Ryan Company bills merchandise to Branch X at cost, and that the branch maintains complete accounting records and prepares monthly financial statements. Both the home office and the branch use the periodic inventory system. Equipment used at the branch is carried in the home office records. Certain expenses, such as advertising and insurance, are incurred by the home office on behalf of the branch and are billed to the branch so that its records will give a realistic picture of operating results. Transactions during the first year (Year 1) of operation of the branch are summarized below:

(1) Cash of $1,000 sent to branch
(2) Merchandise with a cost of $60,000 shipped to branch
(3) Equipment purchased by branch for $500, to be carried in home office records (Other assets for branch normally purchased by home office)
(4) Sales by branch on credit, $80,000
(5) Collections of accounts receivable by branch, $62,000
(6) Payment of operating expenses by branch, $20,000
(7) Cash remittance to home office, $37,500
(8) Operating expenses incurred by home office charged to branch, $3,000

These transactions are recorded by the home office and by the branch with the following journal entries.

Home Office Records		Branch Records	
(1) Investment in Branch X 1,000		Cash 1,000	
Cash	1,000	Home Office	1,000
(2) Investment in Branch X 60,000		Shipments from Home	
Shipments to		Office. 60,000	
Branch X	60,000	Home Office	60,000
(3) Equipment: Branch X 500		Home Office 500	
Investment in		Cash	500
Branch X	500		
(4) None		Accounts Receivable 80,000	
		Sales	80,000
(5) None		Cash 62,000	
		Accounts Receivable	62,000
(6) None		Operating Expenses 20,000	
		Cash	20,000
(7) Cash 37,500		Home Office 37,500	
Investment in		Cash	37,500
Branch X	37,500		
(8) Investment in Branch X 3,000		Operating Expenses 3,000	
Operating Expenses	3,000	Home Office	3,000

In the home office accounts, the ledger account Investment in Branch X has a debit balance of $26,000 before the accounts are closed and the branch net income of $12,000 is debited to Investment in Branch X:

Investment in Branch X

Explanation of transactions	Debit	Credit	Balance
Cash sent to branch	1,000		1,000
Merchandise billed to branch at cost	60,000		61,000
Equipment purchased by branch, recorded on			
home office accounts		500	60,500
Cash received from branch		37,500	23,000
Operating expenses billed to branch	3,000		26,000

In the branch records, the ledger account Home Office has a credit balance of $26,000 before the accounts are closed and the net income of $12,000 is credited to Home Office:

Home Office

Explanation of transactions	Debit	Credit	Balance
Cash received from home office		1,000	1,000
Merchandise received from home office		60,000	61,000
Equipment purchased by branch	500		60,500
Cash sent to home office	37,500		23,000
Operating expenses billed by home office		3,000	26,000

Assume that the inventory at the end of Year 1 amounts to $15,000 for the branch. The adjusting and closing entries relating to the branch are given on page 93.

In the home office records, the Shipments to Branch account will be closed to the Income Summary along with the closing of the other revenue and expense accounts.

Home Office Records			Branch Records		
None			Inventory	15,000	
			Sales	80,000	
			Shipments from		
			Home Office . .		60,000
			Operating Expenses		23,000
			Income Summary .		12,000
Investment in Branch X .	12,000		Income Summary	12,000	
Income: Branch X		12,000	Home Office		12,000
Income: Branch X	12,000				
Income Summary .		12,000	None		

Working paper for combined financial statements

A working paper for combined financial statements has three purposes: (1) to combine accounts for like assets and like liabilities, (2) to eliminate any intracompany profits, and (3) to eliminate the reciprocal accounts. The working paper on pages 94 to 95 for the Ryan Company is based on the branch transactions illustrated on page 91 and additional assumed data for the home office trial balance. All the routine year-end adjusting entries are assumed to have been made and the working paper is begun with the adjusted trial balances of the home office and the branch. Income taxes are ignored in this illustration.

Note that the $26,000 debit amount in the Investment in Branch X account and the $26,000 credit amount in the Home Office account are the balances before the accounts are closed, that is, before the $12,000 net income of the branch is entered in these two reciprocal accounts. In the Combination Eliminations columns, entry (a) offsets the Shipment to Branch X account against the Shipments from Home Office account. Entry (b) offsets the Investment in Branch X account against the Home Office account. These eliminations appear in the working paper only. They are not recorded in the accounts of either the home office or branch, because their only purpose is to aid in the preparation of the combined financial statements.

RYAN COMPANY
Working Paper for Combined Financial Statements of Home Office and Branch X
For Year Ended December 31, Year 1
(First year: Billings to branch at cost)

| | Adjusted trial balances | | | | Combination eliminations | | Home office and branch combined | |
| | Home office | | Branch | | | | | |
	Debit	Credit	Debit	Credit	Debit	Credit	Debit	Credit
Income statement:								
Sales		400,000		80,000				480,000
Inventory, Dec. 31, Year 0	40,000						40,000	
Purchases	300,000						300,000	
Shipments to Branch X		60,000			(a) 60,000			
Shipments from Home Office			60,000			(a) 60,000		
Inventory, Dec. 31, Year 1		45,000		15,000				60,000
Operating expenses	90,000		23,000				113,000	
Subtotals	430,000	505,000	83,000	95,000				
Net income (to statement of retained earnings below)	75,000		12,000				87,000	
Totals	505,000	505,000	95,000	95,000			540,000	540,000
Statement of retained earnings:								
Retained earnings, Dec. 31, Year 0		70,000						70,000
Net income (as above)		75,000		12,000				87,000
Dividends	40,000						40,000	
Retained earnings, Dec. 31, Year 1 (to balance sheet, on page 95)							117,000	
Totals							157,000	157,000

Balance sheet:	Home office Dr	Home office Cr	Branch Dr	Branch Cr	Eliminations Dr	Eliminations Cr	Combined Dr	Combined Cr
Cash	24,000		5,000				29,000	
Accounts receivable	40,000		18,000				58,000	
Inventory, Dec. 31, Year 1	45,000		15,000				60,000	
Investment in Branch X	26,000					(b) 26,000		
Plant and equipment	150,000						150,000	
Accumulated depreciation: plant and equipment		10,000						10,000
Accounts payable		20,000						20,000
Home office				26,000	(b) 26,000			
Capital stock, $5 par value		150,000						150,000
Retained earnings (from page 94)				38,000				117,000
Totals	325,000	325,000	38,000	38,000	86,000	86,000	297,000	297,000

(a) To eliminate reciprocal accounts for merchandise shipments.
(b) To eliminate reciprocal accounts for branch and home office.

Combined Financial Statements Illustrated The working paper provides the information for the combined financial statements of Ryan Company given below and on page 97.

RYAN COMPANY

Income Statement

For Year Ended December 31, Year 1

Sales		$480,000
Cost of goods sold:		
Inventory, Dec. 31, Year 0	$ 40,000	
Add: Purchases	300,000	
Cost of goods available for sale	$340,000	
Less: Inventory, Dec. 31, Year 1	60,000	280,000
Gross profit on sales		$200,000
Operating expenses		113,000
Net income		$ 87,000
Earnings per share		$ 2.90

RYAN COMPANY

Balance Sheet

December 31, Year 1

Assets

Cash		$ 29,000
Accounts receivable		58,000
Inventory		60,000
Plant and equipment	$150,000	
Less: Accumulated depreciation	10,000	140,000
Total assets		$287,000

Liabilities & Stockholders' Equity

Liabilities:		
Accounts payable		$ 20,000
Stockholders' equity:		
Capital stock, $5 par value	$150,000	
Retained earnings	117,000	267,000
Total liabilities & stockholders' equity		$287,000

RYAN COMPANY
Statement of Retained Earnings
For Year Ended December 31, Year 1

Retained earnings, Dec. 31, Year 0	$ 70,000
Net income	87,000
Subtotal	$157,000
Less: Dividends	40,000
Retained earnings, Dec. 31, Year 1	$117,000

Billings to branch in excess of cost

As explained earlier, some companies prefer to bill merchandise to branches at cost plus an arbitrary percentage, or at retail sales price. Since both these methods involve similar modifications of accounting procedures, a single example will illustrate the key points involved. We shall now repeat the Ryan Company illustration with one changed assumption: the home office bills merchandise to the branch at 50% above cost.

Under this assumption the entries for the first year's transactions by the home office and the branch will be the same as those previously presented on page 91, except for the entries showing shipment of merchandise from the home office to the branch. These shipments ($60,000 + 50% markup = $90,000) will be recorded as follows:

Home Office Records			**Branch Records**		
(2) Investment in			Shipments from Home		
Branch X. 90,000			Office 90,000		
Shipments to			Home Office		90,000
Branch X	60,000				
Allowance for					
Overvaluation of					
Inventory:					
Branch X	30,000				

In the home office records the Investment in Branch X now has a debit balance of $56,000 before the accounts are closed and the branch net income or loss is entered in the Investment in Branch X account. This amount is $30,000 higher than the $26,000 balance in our prior illustration; the increase represents the increase over cost of the merchandise shipped to the branch:

Investment in Branch X

Explanation of transactions	Debit	Credit	Balance
Cash sent to branch	1,000		1,000
Merchandise billed to branch at 50% above cost	90,000		91,000
Equipment purchased by branch, recorded in			
home office accounts		500	90,500
Cash received from branch		37,500	53,000
Operating expenses billed to branch	3,000		56,000

In the branch records the ledger account entitled Home Office now has a credit balance of $56,000 before the accounts are closed and the branch net income or loss is entered in the Home Office account:

Home Office

Explanation of transactions	Debit	Credit	Balance
Cash received from home office		1,000	1,000
Merchandise received from home office		90,000	91,000
Equipment purchased by branch	500		90,500
Cash sent to home office	37,500		53,000
Operating expenses billed by home office		3,000	56,000

The branch recorded the merchandise received from the home office at the invoiced amount of $90,000. The $90,000 debit balance in the account Shipments from Home Office is reciprocal to two accounts in the home office records. These two accounts are Shipments to Branch X with a credit balance of $60,000 and Allowance for Overvaluation of Inventory: Branch X with a credit balance of $30,000.

The use of two reciprocal accounts rather than one enables the home office to maintain a record of the *cost* of goods shipped to the branch, as well as the amount of the unrealized "write-up" on the shipments. The home office will deduct the Shipments to Branch X account, which is stated at cost, from the total of the beginning inventory and purchases to determine the cost of the goods that are available for sale by the home office.

At the end of the period the branch will report its inventory (based on invoice prices) at $22,500. The cost of this inventory is $15,000 (computed as follows: $22,500 ÷ 1.50). In the home office records the required balance in the account entitled Allowance for Overvaluation of Inventory: Branch X is therefore only $7,500 and the account should be reduced from its present balance of $30,000 to $7,500. The reason for this reduction is that the 50% write-up of merchandise over cost has become realized profit with respect to the goods sold by the branch. Consequently, at the end of the year the home office should reduce its allowance for overvaluation of the branch inventory to the $7,500 excess valuation contained in the ending inventory. This adjustment of $22,500 in the allowance account is transferred as a credit to Income Summary: Branch X, because it represents additional profit on branch operations over that reported by the branch. (An alternative interpretation under certain circumstances would be to regard the $22,500 portion of the year's income as realized profit attributable to the operations of the home office.)

Of course the actual net income earned through operation of the branch will be the same amount of $12,000 as shown in our prior illustration when merchandise was billed to the branch at cost. Under the present assumptions, however, the branch will *report* a net loss of $10,500. This amount will be picked up by the home office and adjusted to a net income of $12,000, as shown by the following entries at the end of Year 1 relating to branch operations.

Home Office Records

Income: Branch X	10,500	
Investment in Branch X		10,500
To record net loss reported by branch.		
Allowance for Overvaluation of Inventory: Branch X	22,500	
Income: Branch X		22,500
To reduce allowance to amount by which ending inventory exceeds cost.		
Income: Branch X	12,000	
Income Summary		12,000
To close branch net income (as adjusted) to Income Summary.		

After these entries have been recorded, the accounts in the home office records used to portray branch operations will be as shown on page 100.

A separate balance sheet prepared for the home office alone would show the $7,500 credit balance in Allowance for Overvaluation of Inventory: Branch X as a deduction from the $45,500 debit balance in the Investment in Branch X account. As an alternative the net amount of $38,000 could be shown as Investment in Branch X.

Investment in Branch X

Explanation of transactions	Debit	Credit	Balance
Cash sent to branch	1,000		1,000
Merchandise billed to branch at 50% above cost	90,000		91,000
Equipment purchased by branch, recorded in home office accounts		500	90,500
Cash received from branch		37,500	53,000
Operating expenses billed to branch	3,000		56,000
Net loss reported by branch		10,500	45,500

Allowance for Overvaluation of Inventory: Branch X

Explanation of transactions	Debit	Credit	Balance
Write-up of merchandise shipped to branch by 50% of cost		30,000	30,000
Realization of 50% write-up on merchandise sold by branch	22,500		7,500

Income: Branch X

Explanation of transactions	Debit	Credit	Balance
Net loss reported by branch	10,500		10,500
Realization of 50% write-up on merchandise sold by branch		22,500	12,000(cr)
Net income of branch (as adjusted) closed to Income Summary account	12,000		–0–

The closing entries by the branch at the end of Year 1 are as follows:

Branch Records

Inventory	22,500	
Sales	80,000	
Income Summary	10,500	
Shipments from Home Office		90,000
Operating Expenses		23,000
To record the ending inventory and to close the nominal accounts.		
Home Office	10,500	
Income Summary		10,500
To close the net loss in the Income Summary account to the		
Home Office account.		

After these closing entries have been posted by the branch, the Home Office account will show a credit balance of $45,500, the same as the debit balance in the Investment in Branch X account on the records of the home office.

Home Office

Explanation of transactions	Debit	Credit	Balance
Cash received from home office		1,000	1,000
Merchandise received from home office		90,000	91,000
Equipment purchased by branch	500		90,500
Cash sent to home office	37,500		53,000
Operating expenses billed by home office		3,000	56,000
Net loss for the year	10,500		45,500

Working paper when billings to branch are in excess of cost

The working paper to develop combined financial statements when billings to the branch are in excess of cost is shown on pages 102–103. It differs from the previously illustrated working paper by the inclusion of entries to adjust the ending inventory of the branch to a cost basis. Also the net loss reported by the branch is adjusted by the $22,500 of merchandise "write-up" which has become realized profit through the sale of the goods by the branch. Bear in mind that the entries in the Combination Eliminations columns appear only in the working paper. They repre-

RYAN COMPANY
Working Paper for Combined Financial Statements of Home Office and Branch X
For Year Ended December 31, Year 1
(First year: Billings to branch above cost)

	Adjusted trial balances				Combination eliminations		Home office and branch combined	
	Home office		Branch					
	Debit	Credit	Debit	Credit	Debit	Credit	Debit	Credit
Income statement:								
Sales		400,000		80,000				480,000
Inventory, Dec. 31, Year 0	40,000						40,000	
Purchases	300,000						300,000	
Shipments to Branch X		60,000			(a) 60,000			
Shipments from Home Office			90,000			(a) 90,000		
Inventory, Dec. 31, Year 1		45,000		22,500	(b) 7,500			60,000
Operating expenses	90,000		23,000				113,000	
Subtotals	430,000	505,000	113,000	102,500			453,000	540,000
Net income (to statement of retained earnings below)	75,000		10,500		(c) 22,500		87,000	
Totals	505,000	505,000	113,000	113,000			540,000	540,000
Statement of retained earnings:								
Retained earnings, Dec. 31, Year 0		70,000						70,000
Net income (as above)		75,000				(c) 22,500		87,000
Dividends	40,000						40,000	
Retained earnings, Dec. 31, Year 1 (to balance sheet on page 103)							117,000	
Totals							157,000	157,000

Balance sheet:

	Home Office	Branch X	Eliminations Dr	Eliminations Cr	Combined
Cash	24,000	5,000			29,000
Accounts receivable	40,000	18,000			58,000
Inventory, Dec. 31, Year 1	45,000	22,500		(b) 7,500	60,000
Allowance for overvaluation of inventory: Branch X	30,000		(a) 30,000		
Investment in Branch X	56,000			(d) 56,000	
Plant and equipment	150,000				150,000
Accumulated depreciation: plant and equipment	10,000				10,000
Accounts payable	20,000				20,000
Home office		56,000	(d) 56,000		
Capital stock, $5 par value	150,000				150,000
Retained earnings (from page 102)					117,000
Totals	355,000	56,000	176,000	176,000	297,000

(a) To eliminate reciprocal accounts for merchandise shipments.

(b) To reduce ending inventory of branch to a cost basis.

(c) To increase reported net income of branch by the portion of merchandise write-up which has become realized profit.

(d) To eliminate reciprocal accounts for branch and home office.

sent a mechanical step to aid in the preparation of combined financial statements and are not entered in the accounting records of the home office or the branch.

Note that the amounts in the Home Office and Branch Combined columns of this working paper are exactly the same as in the working paper prepared when the shipments to the branch were billed at cost. Consequently, the financial statements would be identical with those presented on pages 96 to 97.

Treatment of beginning inventory priced above cost

The working paper on pages 102 to 103 shows how the ending inventory and the related allowance for overvaluation of inventory were handled. However, since this was the first year of operation for the branch, no beginning inventory was involved.

We shall now continue the illustration of the Ryan Company into a second year of operations (Year 2) in order to demonstrate the handling of a beginning inventory carried by the branch at a value in excess of cost. The beginning inventory for Year 2 was carried by the branch at $22,500, or 150% of the cost of $15,000. Assume that during the second year the home office shipped to the branch goods which cost $80,000 and were billed at $120,000. The branch inventory at the end of Year 2 amounted to $30,000 at billed prices, representing cost of $20,000 plus a 50% markup by the home office at time of shipment to the branch.

The flow of merchandise at the branch during Year 2 may be summarized as follows:

	Cost	Markup	Billed price
Beginning inventory	$15,000	$ 7,500	$ 22,500
Add: Shipments from home office	80,000	40,000	120,000
Available for sale	$95,000	$47,500	$142,500
Less: Ending inventory	(20,000)	(10,000)	(30,000)
Goods sold	$75,000	$37,500	$112,500

The activities of the branch during Year 2, as shown by the home office records, are reflected in the ledger accounts on page 105.

On the home office records at the end of the second year, the balance required in the account Allowance for Overvaluation of Inventory: Branch X is $10,000, that is, the billed price of $30,000 less cost of $20,000 for goods in the ending inventory. The account should therefore be reduced from its present balance of $47,500 to $10,000. This reduction of $37,500 represents the 50% write-up of merchandise in excess of cost which has

Investment in Branch X

Explanation of transactions	Debit	Credit	Balance
Balance, Dec. 31, Year 1			45,500(dr)
Merchandise billed to branch at 50% above			
cost	120,000		165,500
Cash received from branch		113,000	52,500
Operating expenses billed to branch	4,500		57,000
Net income reported by branch	10,000		67,000

Allowances for Overvaluation of Inventory: Branch X

Explanation of transactions	Debit	Credit	Balance
Balance, Dec. 31, Year 1 (see page 100)			7,500(cr)
Write-up of merchandise shipped to branch			
during Year 2 (50% of cost)		40,000	47,500
Realization of 50% write-up on merchandise			
sold by branch during Year 2	37,500		10,000

Income: Branch X

Explanation of transactions	Debit	Credit	Balance
Net income reported by branch		10,000	10,000(cr)
Realization of 50% write-up on merchandise			
sold by branch during Year 2		37,500	47,500
To close branch net income (as adjusted) to			
Income Summary account	47,500		–0–

become realized profit on goods sold by the branch during Year 2 and is credited to Income Summary: Branch X.

On the branch records the account with the home office showed the following activity for Year 2:

Home Office

Explanation of transactions	Debit	Credit	Balance
Balance, Dec. 31, Year 1			45,500(cr)
Merchandise received from home office		120,000	165,500
Cash remitted to home office	113,000		52,500
Operating expenses billed by home office		4,500	57,000
Net income reported by branch		10,000	67,000

RYAN COMPANY
Working Paper for Combined Financial Statements of Home Office and Branch X
For Year Ended December 31, Year 2
(Second year: Billings to branch above cost)

	Adjusted trial balances				Combination eliminations		Home office and branch combined	
	Home office		Branch					
	Debit	Credit	Debit	Credit	Debit	Credit	Debit	Credit
Income statement:								
Sales		500,000		150,000				650,000
Inventory, Dec. 31, Year 1	45,000		22,500			(b) 7,500	60,000	
Purchases	400,000						400,000	
Shipments to Branch X		80,000			(a) 80,000			
Shipments from Home Office			120,000			(a) 120,000		
Inventory, Dec. 31, Year 2		70,000		30,000	(c) 10,000			90,000
Operating expenses	120,000		27,500				147,500	
Subtotal	565,000	650,000	170,000	180,000			607,500	740,000
Net income (to statement of retained earnings below)	85,000		10,000		(d) 37,500		132,500	
Totals	650,000	650,000	180,000	180,000			740,000	740,000
Statement of retained earnings:								
Retained earnings, Dec. 31, Year 1		117,000						117,000
Net income (as above)		85,000		10,000		(d) 37,500		132,500
Dividends	60,000						60,000	
Retained earnings, Dec. 31, Year 2 (to balance sheet on page 107)							189,500	
Totals							249,500	249,500

Balance sheet:	Home Office	Branch	Eliminations Dr	Eliminations Cr	Combined
Cash	30,000	9,000			39,000
Accounts receivable	64,000	28,000			92,000
Inventory, Dec. 31, Year 2	70,000	30,000		(c) 10,000	90,000
Allowance for overvaluation of inventory: Branch X	47,500		(a) 40,000 (b) 7,500		
Investment in Branch X	57,000			(e) 57,000	
Plant and equipment	158,000				158,000
Accumulated depreciation: plant and equipment	15,000				15,000
Accounts payable	24,500				24,500
Home office		57,000	(e) 57,000		
Capital stock, $5 par value	150,000				150,000
Retained earnings (from page 106)					189,500
Totals	439,000	67,000	232,000	232,000	379,000

(a) To eliminate reciprocal accounts for merchandise shipments.
(b) To reduce beginning inventory of branch to a cost basis.
(c) To reduce ending inventory of branch to a cost basis.
(d) To increase reported net income of branch by portion of merchandise write-up which has become realized profit.
(e) To eliminate reciprocal accounts for branch and home office.

The working paper for Year 2 (pages 106 to 107) is very similar to that of Year 1 (pages 102 to 103), except for one additional entry in the pair of columns for Combination Eliminations. Entry (*b*) reduces the beginning inventory of the branch by the $7,500 of unrealized profit contained therein, with an offsetting debit to the Allowance for Overvaluation of Inventory: Branch X. All the other elimination entries follow the pattern previously shown in the working paper for the first year.

Closing Entries In the branch records, the closing entries at the end of Year 2 are as follows:

Branch Records

Inventory, Dec. 31, Year 2	30,000	
Sales	150,000	
Inventory, Dec. 31, Year 1		22,500
Shipments from Home Office		120,000
Operating Expenses		27,500
Income Summary		10,000

To record the ending inventory and to close the beginning inventory and the nominal accounts.

Income Summary	10,000	
Home Office		10,000

To close net income to the Home Office account.

In the home office records, the closing entries at the end of Year 2 will be as illustrated below and on page 109.

Home Office Records

Investment in Branch X	10,000	
Income: Branch X		10,000

To record the net income reported by the branch.

Allowance for Overvaluation of Inventory: Branch X	37,500	
Income: Branch X		37,500

To recognize as realized income the write-up of merchandise applicable to goods sold by the branch during the year.

Income: Branch X	47,500	
Income Summary		47,500

To close branch income to Income Summary account.

Inventory, Dec. 31, Year 2	70,000	
Sales	500,000	
Shipments to Branch X	80,000	
Inventory, Dec. 31, Year 1		45,000
Purchases		400,000
Operating Expenses		120,000
Income Summary		85,000

To record ending inventory and to close beginning inventory
and nominal accounts.

Income Summary	132,500	
Retained Earnings		132,500

To close Income Summary account.

Retained Earnings	60,000	
Dividends		60,000

To close Dividends account.

Perpetual inventories

If the home office and branch maintain perpetual inventory records, the ledger accounts, Shipments to Branch X and Shipments from Home Office, shown in the preceding illustrations, will be unnecessary. The home office debits Investment in Branch X for the billed price of the merchandise shipped to the branch, credits the Inventory account for the actual cost of goods shipped to the branch, and credits any excess of billed price over actual cost to Allowance for Overvaluation of Inventory: Branch X. Upon receipt of the merchandise, the branch will debit Inventory from Home Office and credit Home Office at the billed price. When the branch makes sales, the Cost of Goods Sold account is debited and the Inventory account is credited. At the end of the period the home office will reduce its Allowance for Overvaluation of Inventory: Branch X to the amount of overvaluation existing in the ending inventory. The offsetting credit will be to Income: Branch X.

Reconciliation of reciprocal accounts

At the end of an accounting period, the Investment in Branch account in the home office records may not agree with the Home Office account in the branch records because certain transactions may have been recorded by one office but not by the other. The situation is comparable to that of reconciling the ledger account for Cash in Bank with the balance shown by the bank statement. The lack of agreement between the reciprocal accounts causes no difficulty during the accounting period, but at the end of the accounting period the reciprocal accounts must be brought into agreement before combined financial statements are prepared.

As an illustration of the procedure for reconciling reciprocal accounts at the year-end, assume that the branch and home office records contain the following data:

In Records of Home Office:

Investment in Branch A				
Nov. 30	Balance	45,000	Dec. 10 Cash received from	
Dec. 29	Merchandise shipped		branch	20,000
	to branch	10,000	Dec. 27 Collection of branch	
	(Balance, $34,000)		account receivable	1,000

In Records of Branch A:

Home Office				
Dec. 7	Cash sent to home		Nov. 30 Balance	45,000
	office	20,000	Dec. 30 Collection of home	
Dec. 28	Purchased office		office account receivable	2,000
	equipment	3,000	(Balance, $24,000)	

Comparison of these accounts shows the existence of four reconciling items, which are described below:

1 A debit of $10,000 in the Investment in Branch A account without a related credit in the Home Office account.

On December 29 the home office shipped merchandise to the branch in the amount of $10,000. The home office will normally debit its account with the branch on the date of shipping merchandise, but the branch will not credit its account with the home office until the merchandise is received, perhaps several days later. The required adjustment at year-end for this type of reconciling item will be an entry in the branch records as follows:

Shipments from Home Office—In Transit	. . . .	10,000
Home Office		10,000

In preparing the income statement for the branch, the accountant will combine the $10,000 balance in the account Shipments from Home Office—In Transit with the account Shipments from Home Office. The total will be equal to the amount shown in the home office records for Shipments to Branch; therefore these two reciprocal accounts can be eliminated for the purpose of preparing a combined income statement.

In determining its ending inventory, the branch must also add to the inventory on hand the $10,000 of merchandise in transit. This lot of merchandise will therefore appear on the branch balance sheet and also as part of the total inventory in the combined financial statements.

2 A credit of $1,000 in the Investment in Branch A account without a related debit in the Home Office account.

On December 27 an account receivable of the branch was collected directly from the branch's customer by the home office. The collection was recorded by the home office by debiting Cash and crediting Investment in Branch A. No entry has been made by the branch; therefore, the following entry is needed in the branch records:

Home Office	1,000	
Accounts Receivable		1,000

3 A debit of $3,000 in the Home Office account without a related credit in the Investment in Branch A account.

On December 28 the branch purchased some office equipment at a cost of $3,000. Since the assets in use at the branch are carried in the home office records, the entry made by the branch was to debit Home Office and credit Cash. No entry has yet been made by the home office; therefore, the following entry will be made at December 31 in the home office records:

Office Equipment	3,000	
Investment in Branch A		3,000

4 A credit of $2,000 in the Home Office account without a related debit in the Investment in Branch A account.

On December 30 an account receivable of the home office was collected directly from the home office's customer by the branch. The collection was recorded by the branch by debiting Cash and crediting Home Office. No entry has been made by the home office; therefore, the following entry is needed in the home office records:

Investment in Branch A	2,000	
Accounts Receivable		2,000

The effect of these four end-of-period entries is to bring the reciprocal accounts into agreement, as shown by the reconciliation on page 112.

	Investment in Branch A account (In home office records)	Home Office account (In branch records)
Balances prior to adjustment	$34,000 (dr)	$24,000 (cr)
Increases by adjusting entries:		
(1) Merchandise shipped to branch		10,000
(4) Receivable owned by home office, collected by branch	2,000	
Subtotals	$36,000 (dr)	$34,000 (cr)
Decreases by adjusting entries:		
(2) Receivable owned by branch, collected by home office		1,000
(3) Office equipment purchased by branch . .	3,000	
Adjusted balances	$33,000 (dr)	$33,000 (cr)

Transactions between branches

Efficient operations may on occasion require that merchandise or equipment be transferred from one branch to another. A branch should not carry an account with another branch but should clear the transfer through its account with the home office. For example, if Branch A ships merchandise to Branch B, Branch A will debit Home Office and credit Shipments from Home Office. Upon receipt of the goods, Branch B will debit Shipments from Home Office and credit Home Office. The home office will record the transfer between branches by debiting Investment in Branch B and crediting Investment in Branch A.

The transfer of merchandise from one branch to another does not justify increasing the inventory value by the additional freight costs incurred because of the indirect routing. The amount of freight costs properly included in inventory at a branch is limited to the cost of shipping the merchandise directly from the home office to their present location. Excess freight costs should be treated as an operating expense of the current period by the home office.

To illustrate the accounting for excess freight costs on interbranch transfers of merchandise, assume the following data. The home office shipped merchandise costing $6,000 to Branch D and paid freight of $400. Shortly afterward, the home office instructed Branch D to transfer this merchandise to Branch E. Freight costs of $300 were paid by Branch D to carry out this order. If the merchandise had been shipped directly from the home office to Branch E, the freight cost would have been $500. The entries to be made in the three sets of accounting records are as follows:

In Records of Home Office:

Investment in Branch D	6,400	
Shipments to Branch D		6,000
Cash		400

To record shipment of merchandise and payment of freight costs of $400.

Investment in Branch E	6,500	
Shipments to Branch D	6,000	
Excess Freight Expense—Interbranch Transfers	200	
Shipments to Branch E		6,000
Investment in Branch D		6,700

To record transfer of merchandise from Branch D to Branch E. Interbranch freight of $300 paid by Branch D caused total freight costs on this merchandise to exceed direct shipment costs by $200.

In Records of Branch D:

Shipments from Home Office	6,000	
Freight Expense	400	
Home Office		6,400

Received merchandise from home office with freight paid in advance by the home office.

Home Office	6,700	
Shipments from Home Office		6,000
Freight Expense		400
Cash		300

Transferred merchandise to Branch E at instruction of home office; paid freight of $300.

In Records of Branch E:

Shipments from Home Office	6,000	
Freight Expense	500	
Home Office		6,500

Received merchandise from Branch D transferred by order of home office; recorded normal freight cost billed by home office.

The practice of treating excess freight costs on merchandise transferred from one branch to another as an expense of the current period is a specific example of the accounting principle that losses should be given prompt recognition rather than being concealed by inflating the carrying value of assets. The excess freight costs from cross-shipment of goods between branches are in most cases the result of inefficient planning of original shipments. The expense arising from such errors does not add to the utility of the merchandise and should not be included in inventory cost.

In treating excess cost of interbranch transfers as an expense attributable to the home office, we have assumed that the home office makes the decisions directing all shipments. If the branch offices are given authority to order shipments, then the excess freight costs from errors in such orders should be borne by the branches.

Start-up costs of opening new branches

The establishment of a new branch often requires the incurring of considerable cost before a significant flow of revenue has been generated. Operating losses in the first few months are very likely. Some companies have made a practice of capitalizing these start-up losses on the grounds that such unprofitable operation is a necessary prelude to successful operation at a new location. However, most companies write off start-up costs in connection with the opening of a new branch in the period the costs are incurred.

The decision should be based on the familiar concept that net income is measured by matching costs against related revenue. If a given cost can clearly be shown to benefit future periods, it should be deferred and assigned to those periods. Seldom is there any positive assurance that a new branch will achieve a profitable level of operations in later years.

REVIEW QUESTIONS

1 Explain briefly the usual distinctions between a *sales agency* and a *branch.*

2 The Sprouse Company has several sales agencies and wishes to determine the profitability of each. Describe briefly the principal accounting procedures that you would recommend be performed by the home office and by the individual sales agencies to achieve this goal.

3 Some branches maintain complete accounting records and prepare financial statements in much the same way as an autonomous business. Other branches perform only limited accounting functions, with most accounting activity concentrated in the home office. Assuming that a branch has a fairly complete set of accounting records, what criterion or principle would you suggest be used in deciding whether various types of expenses applicable to the branch should be accounted for in the home office or in the branch?

4 Explain the use of *reciprocal accounts* in home office and branch accounting systems.

5 The branch and home office reciprocal accounts of the Kirk Company are out of balance at the year-end by a substantial amount. What factors might have caused this lack of agreement?

6 Sapiro Company operates a number of branches but centralizes its accounting activities in the home office and maintains rigorous control of branch operations. The home office finds that Branch D has ample stock of a certain type of merchandise but that Branch E is almost out of this item. The home office therefore instructs Branch D to ship merchandise with a cost of $5,000 to Branch E. What entry should Branch D make, and what principle should guide the treatment of freight costs?

7 The president of Schuetze Company informs you that a branch store is being opened and requests your advice in the following words: "I have been told that we can bill goods to the branch at cost, at selling price, or anywhere in between. Do you as an independent public accountant really have that much latitude in your definition of generally accepted accounting principles?"

8 The policies of the Frank Company provide that equipment in use by its branches shall be carried in the records of the home office. The purchase of new equipment may be carried out either by the home office, or by a branch with the approval of the home office. Branch X, with the approval of the home office, purchases new equipment at a cost of $8,000. Give the entries to be made by the branch and by the home office for acquisition of this equipment.

9 The Armstrong Company operates ten branches in addition to its main store, and bills merchandise to the branches at 10% above cost. The plant assets for the entire company are carried in the home office records. The home office also conducts a regular advertising program which benefits all the branches. Each branch maintains its own accounting records and prepares separate financial statements. In the home office, the accounting department prepares (a) financial statements for the main store; (b) revised financial statements for each branch; and (c) combined financial statements for the company as a whole.

Explain briefly the purpose of the financial statements prepared by the branches, the home office financial statements, the revised financial statements for the branches, and the combined financial statements.

EXERCISES

Ex. 3-1 Prepare journal entries in the records of the home office and in the records of Branch P for each of the following transactions:

a Home office transferred cash of $5,000 and merchandise (at cost) of $10,000 to Branch P. Both the home office and the branch use a perpetual inventory system.

b Home office allocated operating expenses of $1,500 to Branch P.

c Branch P informed the home office that it had collected $416 on a note payable to the home office. Face value of the note was $400.

d Branch P made sales of $12,500, terms 2/10, n/30, and incurred operating expenses of $2,500. The cost of goods sold was $8,000 and the operating expenses were paid in cash.

e Branch P reported a net income of $500. (Debit Income Summary in branch records.)

Ex. 3-2 The Hard Goods Company has a single branch in Exeter. On March 1, Year 1, the records of the company contain an account, Allowance for Overvaluation of Branch Inventory, with a balance of $32,000. During March, merchandise costing $36,000 was shipped to the Exeter branch and billed at a price representing a 40% markup on the billed price. At March 31, the branch prepared a report indicating a loss of $11,500 for March, with an ending inventory at billed prices of $25,000.

a What was the cost of the branch inventory on March 1, assuming a uniform markup on all shipments to the branch?

b Prepare the journal entry to adjust the Allowance for Overvaluation of Branch Inventory account at March 31.

c What is the correct net income or net loss for the Exeter Branch for the month of March as reflected by the above information?

Ex. 3-3 A home office bills its only branch at 25% above cost for all merchandise shipped to the branch. During Year 5, the home office shipped merchandise to the branch at a billed price of $30,000. Branch inventories for Year 5 are as follows:

	Jan. 1	Dec. 31
Acquired from home office (at billed price).	$15,000	$19,500
Acquired from outsiders	6,800	8,670

a Prepare the journal entries (including adjusting entries) that should appear in the records of the home office for Year 5 to reflect the foregoing information.

b Assuming that the home office holds merchandise costing $29,500, including $2,500 held on consignment from the Loker Art Corporation, show how the inventories should be reported on a combined balance sheet for the home office and the branch at the end of Year 5.

Ex. 3-4 The Shane Company bills its only branch for merchandise at 30% above cost. The branch sells the merchandise at 10% above billed price. Shortly after the close of business on January 28, some of the branch merchandise was destroyed by fire. The following additional information is available:

Inventory on Jan. 1 (at billed price from home office)	$19,500
Inventory on Jan. 28 of merchandise not destroyed (at selling price)	7,150
Shipments from home office from Jan. 1 to Jan. 28 (at billed price)	71,500
Sales from Jan. 1 to Jan. 28	51,840
Sales returns from Jan. 1 to Jan. 28 (goods actually returned)	3,220
Sales allowances from Jan. 1 to Jan. 28 (price adjustments)	300

a Compute the estimated cost (to the home office) of the merchandise destroyed by fire.

b Prepare the journal entry in the records of the branch to recognize the fire loss.

Ex. 3-5 The following accounts appear in the records of the Novess Branch on December 31:

Home Office

Cash remitted directly to		Balance, Jan. 1	22,180
home office	8 100	Merchandise from home office	18,300
Merchandise returned to home		Supplies from home office	610
office	630		
Purchase of fixtures	3,000		

Income Summary

Expenses	19,040	Revenue	21,900

Home Office Notes

Cash deposited in		Balance, Jan. 1	1,350
home office		Notes collected	800
bank account	1,550		

The branch collects non-interest-bearing notes receivable as an accommodation to the home office and periodically deposits the proceeds in a home office bank account.

a Reproduce the Investment in Novess Branch account in the home office records, assuming that all interoffice transactions are recorded in a single reciprocal account by the home office.

b Prepare the entries required to bring the branch records up to date, assuming that the branch also wants to use a single reciprocal account to record subsequent interoffice transactions.

SHORT CASES FOR ANALYSIS AND DECISION

Case 3-1 You are engaged in the audit of Canyon Corporation, which opened its first branch office in Year 10. During the audit the president of Canyon Corporation raises the question of the accounting treatment of the branch office operating loss for its first year, which is material in amount.

The president proposes to capitalize the operating loss as a start-up cost to be amortized over a five-year period. He states that branch offices of other firms engaged in the same field generally suffer a first-year operating loss which is invariably capitalized, and you are aware of this practice. He argues, therefore, that the loss should be capitalized so that the accounting will be conservative; further, he argues that the accounting must be consistent with established industry practice.

Instructions

a Discuss the president's use of the words ***conservative*** and ***consistent*** from the standpoint of accounting terminology. Discuss the accounting treatment you would recommend.

b What disclosure, if any, would be required in the financial statements?

Case 3-2 The Snowpeak Company operates a number of branches as well as a main store. Each branch carries in stock a complete line of merchandise which is obtained almost entirely from the home office. The branches also handle their own billing, approve customer credit, and make collections. Each branch has its own bank account and each maintains complete accounting records. All noncurrent assets at the branches, consisting chiefly of furniture and office equipment, are carried in the home office records and depreciated by the straight-line method at 10% a year.

On July 1, Year 1, the Bishop Branch purchased some office equipment on the orders of the newly appointed branch manager. The equipment had a list price of $2,400 but was acquired on the installment payment plan with no down payment and 24 monthly payments of $110 beginning August 1, Year 1. No entry was made for this transaction by the branch until August 1, when the first monthly payment was recorded by debiting Miscellaneous Expense. The same entry was made for the next four monthly payments made during Year 1. On December 2 the branch manager became aware during a meeting at the home office that equipment could be purchased by the branches only with prior approval by the home office. Regardless of whether the home office or the branches purchased assets, such assets were to be carried on the home office records. In an effort to avoid criticism, the Bishop Branch manager immediately disposed of the office equipment acquired July 1 by sale for $1,500 cash to an independent store in a nearby town. The manager then paid off the balance due on the installment contract using his own funds (a personal check) and the $1,500 check he had received from sale of the equipment. In consideration of the advance payment of the remaining installments on December 3, the equipment dealer agreed to a $100 reduction in the total of the contract. No entry was made for the disposal of the equipment or the settlement of the liability.

Assume that you are a CPA engaged to perform a year-end audit of the Snowpeak Company. During your visit to the Bishop Branch you analyze the Miscellaneous Expense account and investigate the five monthly debits of $110. This investigation discloses the acquisition and subsequent disposal of the office equipment. After some hesitation the branch manager gives you a full account of the events.

Instructions

a Would you, as an independent auditor, take any action on this matter? Indicate the major issues involved rather than the accounting details. Give reasons for your answers.

b Draft the entries which should have been made for the entire series of events in the records of the branch. Assume that the company accepts responsibility for the branch manager's actions.

c Draft the entries which should have been made on the home office records for the entire series of events, assuming that the home office was currently informed of each event and accepts responsibility for all actions by the branch manager.

d As an independent situation from *b* and *c,* draft the entries which could best be made at the time of your audit to correct the accounts with a minimum of work. One compound entry in each set of accounting records is suggested. Assume that interest expense belongs in the branch records. Also assume that the company wishes to show on the branch records a liability to the manager for his personal "loans," if any, and will consider later any disciplinary action to be taken. The accounts have not been closed for Year 1.

PROBLEMS

3-3 The Hankin Company, which uses the periodic inventory system, established the Moro Bay Branch on January 1. During the first year of operation, Hankin Company shipped to the branch merchandise which cost $200,000. Billings were made at prices 20% in excess of cost. Freight charges amounted to $7,000 and were paid by the home office. Sales by the branch were $300,000 and operating expenses were $64,000, all on the cash basis. At the end of the year the branch took a physical inventory which showed goods on hand of $48,000 at billed prices.

Instructions Prepare entries to record (in the home office and branch accounts) the shipment of merchandise, payment of freight charges, setting up of the ending inventory, and other related adjustments at year-end. (Allocate a proportional amount of freight charges to the ending inventory of the branch.)

3-4 On December 31, the Investment in Cole Branch account in the ledger of the Lefand Company shows a debit balance of $13,220. The following facts are ascertained in analyzing this account:

(1) On December 31 merchandise billed at $3,200 was in transit from the home office to the branch. Assume that a periodic inventory system is used by both the home office and the branch.

(2) The branch collected a home office account receivable for $180; the home office was not notified.

(3) On December 29, the home office mailed a check for $2,000 to the branch but the accountant for the home office recorded the check in the Charitable Contributions account; the branch had not received the check as of December 31.

(4) Branch net income for December was erroneously recorded by the home office at $840 instead of $480. The credit was entered in the Income: Cole Branch account.

(5) The branch returned supplies costing $80 to the home office; the home office had not recorded the receipt of the supplies.

Instructions

a Assuming that all other transactions have been properly recorded, prepare a schedule to determine the **unadjusted** balance of the Home Office account in the ledger of the branch.

b Prepare the journal entries for the home office to bring its records up to date. Closing entries have not been made.

c Prepare the journal entries for the Cole Branch to bring its records up to date.

d Prepare a reconciliation of the Investment in Cole Branch account in the records of the home office and the Home Office account in the records of the branch. Use a column for each account and start with the unadjusted balances.

3-5 The Red River Corporation operates a branch in Pueblo to which it bills merchandise at prices 30% above cost. The branch obtains goods only from the home office and sells the merchandise at prices averaging 15% above the prices billed by the home office. Both the home office and the branch maintain perpetual inventory records and both close their accounts on December 31.

On March 10, Year 1, a fire at the branch destroyed a part of the inventory. Immediately after the fire, a physical inventory taken of the stock of merchandise on hand and not damaged showed it to have a selling price of $5,980. On January 1, Year 1, the inventory of the branch at billed price had been $15,600. Shipments from the home office during the period January 1 to March 10 were billed to the Pueblo branch in the amount of $57,200. The branch records show that sales during this period were $41,472, less sales returns of $808.

Instructions Prepare the journal entries necessary to record the loss from the fire on (1) the branch records, and (2) the home office records. Show how all amounts were determined. You need not prepare closing entries.

3-6 On January 1 of Year 5, the Stine Company opened its first branch with instructions to the branch manager that he should, among other duties, perform the functions of granting credit, billing customers, accounting for receivables, and making collections. The branch paid its operating expenses by checks drawn on its bank account. The branch obtained merchandise solely from the home office; billings for these shipments were on the basis of cost to the home office. The trial balances for the home office and for the branch after one year were as shown below:

STINE COMPANY

Trial Balances

December 31, Year 5

	Home Office		Branch	
	Debit	*Credit*	*Debit*	*Credit*
Cash	$ 42,000		$ 8,600	
Notes receivable	7,000			
Accounts receivable (net) . . .	120,400		37,300	
Inventory, Dec. 31, Year 4 . . .	90,500			
Furniture & equipment (net) . .	48,100			
Accounts payable		$ 41,000		
Capital stock		200,000		
Retained earnings		25,000		
Sales		400,000		$ 95,100
Purchases	315,800			
Operating expenses	69,500		21,900	
Shipments to branch		110,000		
Shipments from home office . .			110,000	
Investment in branch	82,700			
Home office				82,700
	$776,000	$776,000	$177,800	$177,800

The physical inventories taken on December 31, Year 5, amounted to $95,800 for the home office and $24,200 for the branch.

Instructions
a In the branch records, prepare the closing entries needed at December 31, Year 5.
b In the home office records, prepare the adjusting entries pertaining to the branch and also all closing entries for the home office.
c Prepare an eight-column working paper for combined financial statements of home office and branch.

3-7 You are engaged to make an audit for the year ended December 31, Year 1, of Gulf Supply Co. which carries on merchandising operations at both a home office and a branch location. The trial balances of the home office and of the branch are given on page 121.

GULF SUPPLY CO.

Trial Balances

For the Year Ended December 31, Year 1

Debits	Home Office	Branch
Cash	$ 20,000	$ 5,200
Inventory—home office	23,000	
Inventory—branch		11,550
Sundry assets	200,000	48,450
Investment in branch	60,000	
Purchases	190,000	
Purchases from home office		105,000
Freight-in from home office		5,500
Sundry expenses	42,000	24,300
Totals	$535,000	$200,000

Credits

	Home Office	Branch
Sundry liabilities	$ 35,000	$ 8,500
Home office		51,500
Sales	155,000	140,000
Sales to branch	110,000	
Allowance for overvaluation of branch inventory	1,000	
Capital stock	200,000	
Retained earnings	34,000	
Totals	$535,000	$200,000

The audit at December 31, Year 1, disclosed the following:

(1) The branch office deposits all cash receipts in a local bank for the account of the home office. The audit working paper for the cash cutoff revealed:

Amount	Date deposited by branch	Date recorded by home office
$1,050	Dec. 27, Year 1	Dec. 31, Year 1
1,100	Dec. 30, Year 1	Jan. 2, Year 2
600	Dec. 31, Year 1	Jan. 3, Year 2
300	Jan. 2, Year 2	Jan. 6, Year 2

(2) The branch office pays expenses incurred locally from an imprest bank account that is maintained with a balance of $2,000. Checks are drawn once a week on this imprest account and the home office is notified of the amount needed to replenish the account. At December 31, an $1,800 reimbursement check was mailed to the branch office.

(3) The branch office receives all its goods from the home office. The home office bills the goods at cost plus a markup of 10% of cost. At December 31 a shipment with a billing value of $5,000 was in transit to the branch. Freight costs are typically 5% of billed values. Freight costs are considered to be inventoriable costs.

(4) The trial balance opening inventories are shown at their respective costs to the home office and to the branch office. The inventories at December 31, excluding the shipment in transit, are:

Home office, at cost $30,000

Branch office, at billing value 10,400

Instructions Prepare a working paper for Gulf Supply Co. and its branch with columns for Trial Balance (one column for the home office and one for the branch), Combination Adjustments and Eliminations, Home Office Income Statement, Branch Income Statement, and Combined Balance Sheet. The adjustments should include the determination of cost of goods sold both for the branch and the home office. The branch income statement should be prepared on the basis of home office cost. Disregard income taxes. (Formal journal entries are not required. Supporting computations must be in good form.) Number the working paper adjustments and elimination entries.

3-8 The Chamber Music Studios, a single proprietorship owned by Peter Chamber, operates two retail music stores, one located in Seattle and the other in Tacoma. Each store maintains a complete and independent set of accounting records including a capital account. Neither store is regarded as a home office and no Home Office account is used. However, since both stores are owned and controlled by Peter Chamber, they engage in intercompany transactions whenever such actions are beneficial. Intercompany transfers or transactions are recorded by the Seattle store in an account entitled "Intercompany Account—Tacoma"; the Tacoma store maintains a similar account entitled "Intercompany Account—Seattle."

Purchases of major items of inventory such as organs or pianos are charged to Organ Purchases or Piano Purchases. Perpetual inventories are not maintained. Purchases are usually made under a financial arrangement with a local bank advancing 90% of the invoice price and the store paying 10%. If the bank note remains unpaid at the end of 90 days, the store is required to pay an additional 10% of the invoice price as a payment on the note.

In August of Year 3, the Seattle store purchased an organ for which the seller's draft in the amount of $6,300 was sent to The First National Bank of Seattle, which refused to finance the purchase of the instrument. Because of the refusal by the bank, the Seattle store made no entry to record the purchase. Instead arrangements were made through the Tacoma store with The Citizens Bank of Tacoma to provide the financing. The bank loaned Tacoma 90% of the invoice price, or $5,670, which Tacoma deposited and credited to Notes Payable. The Seattle store drew a check payable to the Tacoma store for $630, or 10% of the invoice price, charging Tacoma intercompany account in its records. Tacoma took up the deposit, crediting the intercompany account carried with Seattle.

Tacoma, using the 10% received from Seattle and the 90% advanced by the bank, drew a check payable to The First National Bank of Seattle in full payment of the draft, charging Notes Payable.

In November, Seattle made the second payment of $630 directly to the Tacoma bank, charging the Tacoma intercompany account, and also notified the Tacoma accountant that the payment had been made. Tacoma recorded the transaction, charging Organ Purchases and crediting Seattle. In December, Seattle paid off the balance on the note charging Organ Purchases. Interest charges may be disregarded.

Instructions
a What amount has been recorded in the Organ Purchases account of the Seattle store with respect to the purchase of the organ?
b Prepare a journal entry, with detailed explanation, to be entered in the records of the Seattle store to correct the account balances.
c Prepare a journal entry, with detailed explanation, to be entered on the records of the Tacoma store to correct the account balances.

3-9 The following reciprocal accounts are found in the records of the home office and the branch of the Hermosa Company:

Investment in Branch

Feb. 1	Balance	122,408	Mar. 31	Cash received	2,000
Feb. 6	Shipment of merchan-		Apr. 2	Merchandise returned	450
	dise, 160 cases @ $49	7,840	Apr. 29	Corrected loss on disposal	
Feb. 17	Note receivable collected			of branch equipment	
	by branch	2,500		from $780 to $250	530
Apr. 26	Loss on disposal of				
	branch equipment	780			
Apr. 28	Operating expenses				
	chargeable to branch	1,200			

Home Office

Mar. 30	Deposited cash in bank		Feb. 1	Balance	122,408
	account of home office	2,000	Feb. 8	Merchandise from home	
Mar. 31	Returned merchandise	450		office, 160 cases	7,480
Mar. 31	Paid a repair bill for the		Feb. 14	Received shipment di-	
	home office	375		rectly from supplier,	
Mar. 31	Excess merchandise re-			invoice to be paid by	
	turned to home office	4,100		home office	2,750
			Feb. 15	Note receivable collected	
				for home office	2,500
			Apr. 30	Net income for quarter	
				(tentative)	9,210

You have been called in by the company to assist it with some accounting work preliminary to the preparation of financial statements for the quarter ended April 30. Your first task is to prepare a reconciliation of the reciprocal accounts. Additional information available to you follows:

(1) Branch equipment is carried in the records of the home office; the home office notifies the branch periodically as to the amount of depreciation applicable to equipment used by the branch. Gains or losses on disposal of branch equipment are reported to the branch and included in the branch income statement.

(2) Because of the error in recording the shipment from the home office on February 8, the sale of this merchandise has been improperly charged to cost of goods sold at $46.75 per case.

(3) The branch frequently makes collection in home office accounts receivable and the home office also collects receivables belonging to the branch. On April 30, the branch collected a receivable of $350 belonging to the home office but the branch employee who recorded the collection mistakenly treated the receivable as belonging to the branch.

(4) The branch recorded the tentative profit of $9,210 by a debit to Income Summary and a credit to Home Office, although the revenue and expense accounts had not been closed.

Instructions

a Reconcile the interbranch accounts to the correct total as of April 30. Use a four-column schedule (debit and credit columns for the Investment in Branch account in the home office records and debit and credit columns for the Home

Office account in the branch records). Start with the unadjusted balances at April 30 and work to corrected balances, inserting full explanations of all adjusting or correcting items.

b Prepare individual entries in the records of the branch to bring the records up to date, assuming that corrections can still be made to revenue and expense accounts. The branch uses a periodic inventory system.

c Prepare required correcting entries in the records of the home office. The home office uses a periodic inventory system.

3-10 The preclosing general ledger trial balances at December 31, Year 3, for the Burlap Wholesalers, Inc., and its Waco Branch are shown below.

BURLAP WHOLESALERS, INC.

General Ledger Trial Balances

December 31, Year 3

Accounts	Home Office Dr (Cr)	Branch Office Dr (Cr)
Cash	$ 36,000	$ 8,000
Accounts receivable	35,000	12,000
Inventory—home office, Jan. 1, Year 3	70,000	
Inventory—branch, Jan. 1, Year 3		15,000
Equipment, net	90,000	
Investment in Waco Branch	20,000	
Accounts payable	(36,000)	(13,500)
Accrued liabilities	(14,000)	(2,500)
Home office		(9,000)
Capital stock, $10 par value	(50,000)	
Retained earnings, Jan. 1, Year 3	(45,000)	
Home office:		
Sales	(440,000)	
Purchases	290,000	
Operating expenses	44,000	
Branch:		
Sales		(95,000)
Purchases		24,000
Purchases from home office		45,000
Operating expenses		16,000
	$ –0–	$ –0–

Your audit disclosed the following:

(1) On December 23 the branch manager purchased $4,000 of equipment but failed to notify the home office. The branch accountant, knowing that equipment is carried in the home office accounts, recorded the proper entry in the branch records. It is the company's policy not to take any depreciation on equipment acquired in the last half of a year.

(2) On December 27 a branch customer erroneously paid his account of $2,000 to the home office. The accountant made the correct entry in the home office accounts but did not notify the branch.

(3) On December 30 the branch remitted cash of $5,000 which was received by the home office in January, Year 4.

(4) On December 31 the branch erroneously recorded the December allocated expenses from the home office as $500 instead of $1,500.

(5) On December 31 the home office shipped merchandise billed at $3,000 to the branch, which was received in January, Year 4.

(6) The entire beginning inventory of the branch had been purchased from the home office. Home office Year 3 shipments to the branch were purchased by the home office in Year 3. The physical inventories at December 31, Year 3, excluding the shipment in transit, are home office—$55,000 (at cost); branch—$20,000 (comprised of $18,000 from home office and $2,000 from outside vendors).

(7) The home office consistently bills shipments to the branch at 20% above cost. The Sales account is credited for the invoice price.

Instructions Prepare a working paper with two columns each for Trial Balances (one column for the home office and one column for the branch), Combination Adjustments and Eliminations, Home Office Income Statement, Branch Income Statement, and Combined Balance Sheet. The branch income data should be on the basis of home office cost. Number your working paper adjustments and eliminations. The adjustments should include the determination of cost of goods sold both for the branch and the home office. (Formal journal entries are not required. Supporting computations, including the computation of the ending inventories, should be in good form. Disregard income taxes.)

CHAPTER

4

Business combinations

Business combinations—the bringing together into one accounting entity of a corporation and one or more incorporated or unincorporated businesses[1]—have been consummated in substantial numbers in recent years. Statistics issued by W. T. Grimm & Co., a financial consulting firm which compiles data on business combinations, show that as many as 4,000 or more business combinations have been completed in some recent years.

In the first section of this chapter we shall discuss reasons for the popularity of business combinations and methods of arranging them. Then, the two generally accepted methods of accounting for business combinations—*purchase* and *pooling of interests*—will be explained and illustrated, followed by an appraisal of the two methods.

BUSINESS COMBINATIONS: WHY AND HOW?

Why does a corporation enter into a business combination? Although a number of reasons have been cited, probably the overriding one in recent years has been *growth*. Business enterprises should have—and do have—major operating objectives other than growth, but that goal has increasingly motivated corporation managements to arrange business combinations. Advocates of this *external* method of achieving growth point out that it is much more rapid than growth through *internal* means. There is no question that expansion and diversification of product lines,

[1] *APB Opinion No. 16,* "Business Combinations," AICPA (New York: 1970), p. 281.

or enlarging the market share for current products, is readily achieved through a business combination with a successful enterprise. However, the disappointing experiences of many corporations engaging in business combinations suggest that much can be said in favor of more gradual and reasoned growth through internal means, utilizing available management, employees, and financial resources.

Other reasons often advanced in support of business combinations are obtaining new management strength or better utilization of existing management, and achieving manufacturing or other operating economies. In addition, a business combination may be undertaken for the income tax advantages available to one or more parties to the combination.

Antitrust considerations

One danger faced by large corporations which undertake business combinations is the possibility of antitrust litigation. The U.S. government has often expressed opposition to unwarranted concentration of economic power in very large business enterprises. In consequence, business combinations have frequently been attacked by the Federal Trade Commission or the Antitrust Division of the Department of Justice, under the provisions of Section 7 of the Clayton Act, which reads in part as follows:

> . . . no corporation engaged in commerce shall acquire, directly or indirectly, the whole or any part of the stock or other share capital and no corporation subject to the jurisdiction of the Federal Trade Commission shall acquire the whole or any part of the assets of another corporation engaged also in commerce, where in any line of commerce in any section of the country the effect of such acquisition may be substantially to lessen competition or to tend to create a monopoly.

The breadth of the above legislation has led to federal antitrust action against all types of business combinations: *horizontal* (combinations involving companies in the same industry), *vertical* (combinations between a company and its customers or suppliers), and *conglomerate* (combinations between companies in unrelated industries or markets).

Methods for arranging business combinations

The four most common methods for carrying out a business combination are statutory merger, statutory consolidation, acquisition of stock, and acquisition of assets.

Statutory Merger As its name implies, a statutory merger is executed under provisions of applicable state laws. In a statutory merger, the boards of directors of the two or more corporations involved approve a plan for the exchange of voting stock (and perhaps some preferred stock, cash, or debt) of one of the corporations (the "survivor") for all the voting stock of the other corporations. Shareholders of all involved corporations must approve the terms of the merger; some states require approval of a two-thirds majority of shareholders. The surviving corporation issues its stock for the stock owned by the shareholders of the other corporations, thus acquiring those companies' assets and liabilities. The other corporations then cease to exist as separate legal entities. The business operations of the defunct corporations often are continued as *divisions* of the survivor.

Statutory Consolidation Like a statutory merger, a statutory consolidation is consummated in accordance with state law. However, in a consolidation a *new* corporation is formed to issue its stock for the stock of two or more existing corporations, which then go out of existence. The new corporation thus acquires the assets and liabilities of the defunct corporations, whose business operations may be continued as divisions of the new corporation.

Acquisition of Stock One corporation (the *investor*) may issue stock, cash, debt, or a combination thereof to acquire all or part of the voting stock of another corporation (the *investee*). This stock acquisition program may function through direct purchase in the stock market, through negotiations with the principal shareholders of a closely held company, or through a *tender offer.* A tender offer is a publicly announced agreement by the offering corporation to acquire, for a stated amount of cash or stock per share, a maximum number of shares "tendered" by holders thereof to an agent, usually a commercial bank. The price per share stated in the tender offer is usually well above the prevailing market price. If more than 50% of a corporation's voting stock is acquired, that corporation becomes affiliated with the acquiring corporation as a *subsidiary* but remains a separate legal entity. Business combinations arranged through stock acquisitions require authorization by the acquiring corporation's board of directors, and ratification by the acquirer's shareholders is sometimes required. Accounting for business combinations involving the acquisition of stock is discussed in Chapter 5.

Acquisition of Assets A company may buy all or most of the assets of another corporation for cash, debt, the acquirer's stock, or a combination thereof. The transaction must be approved by the boards of directors and stockholders of both companies. The selling corporation continues its existence as a separate legal entity or it may be liquidated; it does not become an affiliate of the acquiring corporation.

Establishing the price for a business combination

An important early step in planning the acquisition of another business entity is deciding upon an appropriate price to pay. The amount of cash or debt securities, or the number of shares of stock, to be issued in a business combination is usually determined by one or both of the following methods:

1. Capitalization of expected average earnings of the acquired company at a desired rate of return
2. Determination of fair value of the acquired company's tangible and intangible assets (including goodwill) less liabilities

The price for a business combination consummated for cash or debt is usually expressed in terms of the aggregate dollar amount of the consideration issued. When stock is issued in exchange for shares of the acquired company, the price is expressed as a ratio of the number of shares of the issuing company's stock to be exchanged for each share of the acquired company's stock.

Illustration of Exchange Ratio   The negotiating officers of Palmer Corporation have agreed with J. R. Simpson, sole shareholder of Simpson Company, to acquire all 20,000 outstanding shares of Simpson Company stock for an aggregate price of $1,800,000. Palmer Corporation's common stock is presently trading on a national exchange at $61 per share. Mr. Simpson agrees to accept 30,000 shares of Palmer Corporation's common stock at a value of $60 per share in exchange for his stock in Simpson Company. The exchange ratio will be expressed as $1\frac{1}{2}$ shares of Palmer Corporation common stock for each share of Simpson Company stock, in accordance with the following computation:

Number of Palmer Corporation shares to be issued	30,000
Number of Simpson Company shares to be exchanged	20,000
Exchange ratio—30,000 ÷ 20,000	$1\frac{1}{2}$:1

METHODS OF ACCOUNTING FOR BUSINESS COMBINATIONS

Purchase accounting

Since the majority of business combinations involve an identified *acquiring* corporation and one or more *acquired* companies, it is logical to account for business combinations, regardless of how consummated, as the acquisition of assets. Thus, assets (including goodwill) acquired in a business combination for cash would be recorded at the amount of cash disbursed, while assets acquired in a business combination involving the issuance of stock would be recorded at the fair values of the assets or of the stock, whichever was more readily determinable. This approach is known as *purchase accounting* for business combinations, and was widely applied prior to the 1950s.

APB Opinion No. 16, "Business Combinations," set forth the concept of purchase accounting as follows:

> Accounting for a business combination by the purchase method follows principles normally applicable under historical-cost accounting to record acquisitions of assets and issuances of stock and to accounting for assets and liabilities after acquisition.[2]

Determination of cost of an acquired company

The cost at date of acquisition of a company acquired and accounted for by the purchase method is the total of the consideration paid by the acquiring corporation, the acquirer's direct "out-of-pocket" costs of the acquisition, and any *contingent consideration* which is determinable at the date of acquisition.

Amount of Consideration This is the aggregate of the amount of cash paid, the fair value of other assets distributed, the present value of debt securities issued, and the fair value of equity securities issued by the acquiring corporation.

Out-of-pocket Costs Included in this category are legal fees and "finder's fees." Costs of registering and issuing equity securities are a reduction in the fair value of the securities, not direct costs of the acquisition.

Contingent Consideration Contingent consideration is additional cash, other assets, or securities which may be issuable in the future, contingent upon future events, such as a specified level of earnings or a designated market price for a security issued to carry out the business combination. Contingent consideration which is *determinable* at the consummation date of a business combination is recorded as part of the cost of the acquisition. Contingent consideration *not determinable* at the date of the combination should be recorded when the contingency is resolved and the additional consideration is issued or becomes issuable.

Allocation of cost of an acquired company

APB Opinion No. 16 provided the following principles for allocating cost of an acquired company in a business combination accounted for as a purchase:

> First, all identifiable assets acquired . . . and liabilities assumed in a business combination . . . should be assigned a portion of the cost of the acquired company, normally equal to their fair values at date of acquisition.

> Second, the excess of the cost of the acquired company over the sum of the amounts assigned to identifiable assets acquired less liabilities assumed should be recorded as goodwill.[3]

[2] *Ibid.,* p. 311.
[3] *Ibid.,* p. 318.

The recognition of goodwill is quite common in business combinations, because the total price paid tends to exceed the fair value of identifiable assets acquired. However, in a few business combinations (known as *bargain purchases*), fair values assigned to the assets acquired will exceed the total cost of the acquired company. A bargain purchase is most likely to occur in acquiring a company with a history of net losses. The excess of fair values over total cost is applied pro rata to reduce the values initially assigned to noncurrent assets other than long-term investments in corporate securities. In assigning fair values to assets acquired, it is essential not to overstate the worth of the assets in terms of their ability to generate net income for the acquiring company.

"Negative Goodwill" If the proration described in the preceding paragraph does not extinguish the bargain purchase excess, a deferred credit, sometimes termed *negative goodwill,* is established. Negative goodwill means an excess of fair value of assets acquired over their cost. It is amortized over the period benefited, not to exceed 40 years. This amortization offsets subsequent losses of the acquired company.

Illustration of Purchase Accounting On April 30, Year 6, Mason Company merged with Saxon Corporation in a business combination. Both companies used the same accounting principles for assets, liabilities, revenue, and expenses. Saxon Corporation exchanged 150,000 shares of its $10 par value common stock (market value $25 per share) for all 100,000 issued and outstanding shares of Mason Company's no-par value, $10 stated value capital stock. In addition, Saxon Corporation made the following expenditures associated with the business combination:

CPA audit fees for SEC registration statement	$ 60,000
Legal fees:	
For the business combination	10,000
For SEC registration statement	50,000
Finder's fee	56,250
Printer's charges for printing securities and SEC registra-	
tion statement	23,000
SEC registration statement fee	750
Total expenditures	$200,000

Immediately prior to the merger, Mason Company's condensed balance sheet was as follows:

MASON COMPANY
Balance Sheet
April 30, Year 6

Assets

Current assets	$1,000,000
Property, plant, and equipment (net)	3,000,000
Other assets	600,000
Total assets	$4,600,000

Liabilities & Stockholders' Equity

Current liabilities	$ 500,000
Long-term debt	1,000,000
Capital stock, $10 stated value	1,000,000
Paid-in capital in excess of stated value	700,000
Retained earnings	1,400,000
Total liabilities & stockholders' equity	$4,600,000

The board of directors of Saxon Corporation adjudged the fair values of Mason Company's identifiable assets and liabilities to be: Current assets—$1,150,000; property, plant, and equipment—$3,400,000; other assets—$600,000; current liabilities—$500,000; long-term debt (present value)—$950,000.

The following condensed entries would be made in the general journal of Saxon Corporation to record the merger with Mason Company on April 30, Year 6, as a purchase:

Investment in Mason Company (150,000 shares × $25) .	3,750,000	
Common Stock		1,500,000
Paid-in Capital in Excess of Par		2,250,000
To record merger with Mason Company as a purchase.		

Investment in Mason Company ($10,000 + $56,250) . . .	66,250	
Paid-in Capital in Excess of Par	133,750	
Cash		200,000
To record payment of costs incurred in merger with Mason Company. Legal and finder's fees in connection with the merger are recorded as an acquisition cost; other out-of-pocket costs are recorded as a reduction in the proceeds received from issuance of common stock.		

Current Assets	1,150,000	
Property, Plant, and Equipment	3,400,000	
Other Assets	600,000	
Goodwill	116,250	
Discount on Long-term Debt	50,000	
Current Liabilities		500,000
Long-term Debt		1,000,000
Investment in Mason Company		3,816,250

To allocate cost of Mason Company acquisition to identifiable assets and liabilities, with the remainder to goodwill.

Mason Company would make the following condensed entry at April 30, Year 6:

Current Liabilities	500,000	
Long-term Debt	1,000,000	
Capital Stock	1,000,000	
Paid-in Capital in Excess of Stated Value	700,000	
Retained Earnings	1,400,000	
Current Assets		1,000,000
Property, Plant, and Equipment (net)		3,000,000
Other Assets		600,000

To record liquidation of company in conjunction with merger with Saxon Corporation.

Pooling-of-interests accounting

In the late 1940s, the pooling-of-interests method of accounting for business combinations received increasing attention from accountants. The major premise of this method was that certain business combinations involving the issuance of stock were more in the nature of a *combining of stockholder interests* than an *acquisition of assets.* Combining of stockholder interests was evidenced by combinations involving common stock exchanges between corporations of relatively the same size. The shareholders and managements of these companies continued their relative interests and activities in the combined corporation as they previously did in the separate corporations. Since neither of the like-size combining corporations could be considered the *acquirer,* the pooling-of-interests method of accounting provided for carrying forward the combined assets, liabilities, and retained earnings of the combining companies at their *recorded amounts* in the accounting records of the companies. The fair value of the stock issued to effect the business combination was disregarded.

Illustration of Pooling-of-Interests Accounting The Saxon Corporation–Mason Company business combination described on page 131 would be accounted for as a pooling of interests by the following condensed entries in Saxon Corporation's general journal at April 30, Year 6:

Current Assets	1,000,000	
Property, Plant, and Equipment	3,000,000	
Other Assets	600,000	
Current Liabilities		500,000
Long-term Debt		1,000,000
Common Stock		1,500,000
Paid-in Capital in Excess of Par		200,000
Retained Earnings		1,400,000
To record merger with Mason Company as a pooling of interests.		
Expenses of Business Combination	200,000	
Cash		200,000
Payment of costs incurred in merger with Mason Company.		

The expenses of business combination are not deductible for income tax purposes; thus Saxon Corporation should not adjust its income taxes expense & liability accounts.

Mason Company's journal entry at April 30, Year 6, would be identical to the entry illustrated on page 133.

In the first of the preceding entries, Mason's assets, liabilities, and retained earnings are assigned their values in Mason's premerger balance sheet (see page 132). Since the common stock issued by Saxon Corporation must be recorded at *par value* (150,000 shares × $10 = $1,500,000), the $200,000 credit to paid-in capital in excess of par is a *balancing figure* for the journal entry. It can be verified as follows:

Total paid-in capital of Mason Company prior to merger	$1,700,000
Par value of Saxon Corporation common stock issued in merger . . .	1,500,000
Amount credited to Saxon Corporation paid-in capital in excess of par	$ 200,000

If the par value of common stock issued by Saxon Corporation had *exceeded* the total paid-in capital of Mason Company, Saxon's account for Paid-in Capital in Excess of Par would have been *debited* in the illustrated entry. If the balance of the Paid-in Capital in Excess of Par account were insufficient to absorb the debit, the Retained Earnings account would be reduced.

Popularity of pooling-of-interests accounting

The pooling-of-interests method of accounting for business combinations was first sanctioned by the AICPA in *Accounting Research Bulletin No. 40,* "Business Combinations," issued in 1950. *ARB No. 40* provided very few criteria for identifying those business combinations which qualified for pooling-of-interests accounting, and was therefore unsatisfactory as a guide for this accounting method. Consequently, in 1957 *Accounting Research Bulletin No. 48,* also entitled "Business Combinations," superseded the previous pronouncement with an expanded discussion of the pooling-of-interests concept. *ARB No. 48* continued to sanction pooling accounting for certain business combinations.

ARB No. 48 failed to provide definitive guidelines for identifying those business combinations which qualified for pooling-of-interests accounting. As a result, an increasing number of business combinations arranged during the 1950s and 1960s were accounted for as poolings of interests, despite the fact that the "combining of stockholder interests" aspect was often nonexistent.

Why had pooling accounting become so popular? Some of the reasons are apparent from a comparison of the combined Saxon Corporation journal entries illustrated previously for the merger with Mason Company.

	Purchase accounting		*Pooling accounting*	
Current Assets	1,150,000		1,000,000	
Property, Plant, and Equipment	3,400,000		3,000,000	
Other Assets	600,000		600,000	
Goodwill	116,250		–0–	
Discount on Long-term Debt	50,000		–0–	
Expenses of Business Combination	–0–		200,000	
Current Liabilities		500,000		500,000
Long-term Debt		1,000,000		1,000,000
Common Stock		1,500,000		1,500,000
Paid-in Capital in Excess of Par		2,116,250		200,000
Retained Earnings		–0–		1,400,000
Cash		200,000		200,000

Differences in Net Assets The first difference to consider in comparing the preceding entries is that the net assets recorded by the purchase method ($3,616,250) exceed the pooling method net assets ($2,900,000) by $716,250. The composition of the $716,250 is as follows:

Excess of purchase asset values over pooling asset values:	
Current assets	$150,000
Property, plant, and equipment	400,000
Goodwill	116,250
Excess of pooling liability values over purchase liability values:	
Long-term debt	50,000
Total	$716,250

If we assume that the $400,000 difference in property, plant, and equipment is attributable to depreciable assets rather than to land, operating expenses of Saxon Corporation in years subsequent to April 30, Year 6, will be $716,250 greater under purchase accounting than would be the case in pooling accounting. Assume, for example, that the $150,000 difference in current assets is attributable to inventory which will be allocated to revenue on a fifo basis; the average life of plant and equipment is 10 years; the goodwill is to be amortized over a 40-year period; and the long-term debt has a remaining five-year term to maturity. Saxon Corporation's income before income taxes for the year ending April 30, Year 7, would be nearly $203,000 less in purchase accounting than in pooling accounting, due to the following greater expenses in purchase accounting:

Cost of goods sold	$150,000
Depreciation ($\frac{1}{10} \times$ $400,000)	40,000
Amortization of goodwill ($\frac{1}{40} \times$ $116,250)	2,906
Interest expense ($\frac{1}{5} \times$ $50,000)	10,000[4]
Excess of Year 7 pre-tax income using pooling accounting rather	
than purchase accounting	$202,906

It is true that pre-tax income for the year ended April 30, Year 6 (the year of the merger) is $200,000 less in pooling accounting than in purchase accounting, because the pooling method included the immediate *expensing* of the out-of-pocket costs of the business combination. How-

[4]For the sake of simplicity, the discount on long-term debt is amortized by the straight-line method. Theoretically, and in actual practice, the *effective interest* method described in *Intermediate Accounting* of this series should be used.

ever, this situation tends to be obscured by the fact that the income statements of Saxon Corporation and Mason Company would be combined in pooling accounting for the *entire* year ended April 30, Year 6 (as described in a subsequent section of this chapter).

In summary, the favorable effect of pooling accounting on post-combination earnings has been a popular feature of this accounting method.

Differences in Total Paid-in Capital The increase in Saxon Corporation's total paid-in capital is $1,916,250 smaller ($3,616,250 − $1,700,000) in pooling-of-interests accounting than in purchase accounting. Of this difference, $1,200,000 ($1,400,000 − $200,000) is attributable to a net increase in Saxon Corporation's retained earnings in the pooling accounting method. If state laws make this $1,200,000 available for ordinary dividends, the advantage of using the pooling method of accounting is obvious.

Impact of Divergent Price-earnings Ratios Even more dramatic than the preceding advantages inherent in pooling-of-interests accounting is the potential impact on the market value of Saxon Corporation's common stock if the price-earnings ratios for Saxon's and Mason's stock differed significantly prior to the merger. Suppose, for example, that Saxon Corporation and Mason Company had the following financial measurements prior to the business combination:

	Saxon Corporation	Mason Company
Year ended Apr. 30, Year 6:		
Net income	$500,000*	$375,000
Earnings per share	$0.50	$3.75
At Apr. 30, Year 6:		
Number of shares outstanding	1,000,000†	100,000†
Market price per share	$25	$30
Price-earnings ratio	50	8

*Net of $200,000 expenses of business combination
†Outstanding during entire year

After consummation of the business combination, Saxon Corporation's income statement for the year ended April 30, Year 6, would report the combined corporation's net income as $875,000—the total of the separate net incomes of the two merged companies. "Pooled" earnings per share for Saxon Corporation would thus be increased to approximately $0.76. This increased amount of earnings per share is computed by dividing combined earnings of $875,000 by 1,150,000, the *effective* number of Saxon Corporation shares outstanding during the year ended April 30, Year

6. If the price-earnings ratio for Saxon's common stock continued unchanged, the stock's market price would increase after the merger to $38 per share ($0.76 × 50)—a 52% increment. As a consequence, Saxon Corporation would probably attain the reputation of an "exciting growth company" in investing circles; and Saxon's directors would likely seek out another merger prospect like Mason Company.

Less spectacular advantages attributed to the pooling-of-interests method of accounting for business combinations result from the fact that asset values are not restated. Pooling-of-interests accounting thus parallels income tax accounting if the business combination qualifies as a "tax-free corporate reorganization." Further, goodwill amortization (not deductible in computing taxable income) is not required in the pooling method. Finally, the Securities and Exchange Commission has allegedly favored pooling accounting for business combinations, because pooling does not require valuing assets at appraisal amounts.

Abuses of pooling-of-interests accounting

The attractive features of pooling-of-interests accounting described in the preceding section, together with the absence of firm guidelines for poolings in *Accounting Research Bulletin No. 48,* led to a number of serious abuses of the method during the 1960s. Among these abuses were *retroactive poolings; retrospective poolings; part-pooling, part-purchase accounting; treasury stock issuances; issuances of unusual securities; creation of "instant earnings"; contingent payouts;* and *"burying" the costs of pooling combinations.*

Retroactive Poolings After *Accounting Research Bulletin No. 48* was issued in 1957, some accountants interpreted its provisions as permitting pooling-of-interests accounting for many business combinations which had already been accounted for as *purchases* under *Accounting Research Bulletin No. 40.* Accordingly, a significant number of business combinations treated as purchases in the late 1950s and early 1960s were *retroactively restated* as poolings in subsequent years. The obvious question was: When are accounting transactions really *finalized?*

Retrospective Poolings The theory that the combining companies in a pooling of interests were *effectively combined* in accounting periods preceding the actual business combination led to the practice of *retrospective poolings.* This technique involved the consummation of pooling business combinations shortly after the close of a corporation's fiscal year but prior to the issuance of its annual financial statements. The income statement which was ultimately issued included the operating results of the subsequently pooled company on a retrospective basis. As a consequence, a desired earnings per share figure might be attained merely by a working-paper adjustment.

Part-pooling, Part-purchase Accounting Some business combinations involving the issuance of common stock as well as cash and debt were accounted for as *poolings* to the extent of the stock issuance, and as *purchases* for the remainder of the consideration. This hybrid method seemed inconsistent with any orderly structure of accounting theory.

Treasury Stock Issuances Pooling accounting required the exchange of common stock between the combining corporations. One method devised to avoid the potential dilution of earnings per share resulting from common stock issuances was the cash acquisition of treasury stock, and its subsequent reissuance in a pooling business combination. If substance is emphasized over form, such a combination is effected for *cash,* not for *previously unissued stock.*

Issuances of Unusual Securities As another means of minimizing the dilutive effects of common stock issuances in poolings, many unusual securities were devised to consummate business combinations. These securities, usually in the form of either preferred stock or a second or third class of common stock, were in most cases convertible into the issuing corporation's conventional common stock. In substance, therefore, these unusual securities may or may not have been equivalent to voting common stock, yet the business combinations involving these securities were treated as poolings.

Creation of "Instant Earnings" The discussion on pages 135 to 137 comparing the purchase and pooling-of-interests accounting entries for Saxon Corporation, pointed out how pooling accounting could *instantly enhance earnings per share* for the year of a business combination. Another technique for creating instant earnings was the sale of a combining company's assets shortly after the pooling combination. Since the sales price generally exceeded the recorded asset values by a substantial amount, a one-time gain was created. Yet the sales price usually paralleled the market value of the stock issued in the business combination; thus in substance the instant earnings were fictitious. The gain in effect represented proceeds from issuance of stock.

Contingent Payouts If the "combining of stockholder interests" feature of a pooling combination were genuine, there would be no unresolved contingencies with respect to the number of shares to be issued in the combination. Nevertheless, a large number of business combinations involving contingent issuances of additional shares were accounted for as poolings of interests.

"Burying" the Costs of Pooling Combinations The out-of-pocket costs of pooling combinations effected before 1970 were charged to paid-in capital in excess of par rather than to expenses of the combined corporation. This accounting method ignored the assumption that a pooling is not in substance an *acquisition* of one company by another or an *obtaining of capital.*

The Westec Corporation scandal

Perhaps the most spectacular example of pooling accounting abuse was revealed in the Westec Corporation scandal. Westec was a rapidly growing, diversified company whose stock increased from a market price low of $2 per share in 1964 to more than $67 per share early in 1966. Thereafter, the stock's price began to decline. In August 1966, trading in the stock was suspended when it was learned that approximately 160,000 shares of Westec common stock, purchased by or on behalf of the president of the company, had not been paid for.

The trend in Westec's reported earnings had been as follows:

Period	Net income	Earnings per share
Year ended Dec. 31,		
1963	$ 270,000	(not available)
1964	1,332,000	$0.43
1965	4,869,000	1.10
Six months ended June 30, 1966 (unaudited)	5,346,000	1.15

The 1965 net income included the operating results of five companies acquired in pooling business combinations *early in 1966.* The amount of the retrospectively pooled income was not disclosed but was variously estimated at $1.5 million to $2.5 million.

Westec subsequently entered into bankruptcy proceedings, and audited financial statements for the eight months ended August 31, 1966, showed a net loss of $2,576,000. The former president of Westec pleaded guilty to charges of stock price manipulation and false earnings statements, and the former board chairman was convicted of the same charges as well as of mail fraud.

Abuses of purchase accounting

Purchase accounting was not free of improprieties during the 1950s and 1960s. The principal abuse of purchase accounting was the failure to allocate the cost of an acquired company to the identifiable assets acquired and to goodwill. Instead, an "Excess of Cost over Book Value of Purchased Company" account was created and presented in the post-combination balance sheet as an intangible asset—usually not subject to amortization. Consequently, reported earnings subsequent to these purchase combinations were the same as though pooling-of-interests accounting had been applied.

Action by the AICPA

In 1970 the AICPA's Accounting Principles Board reacted to the abuses of pooling-of-interests and purchase accounting by tightening the rules permitting pooling to be used and by limiting drastically the range of situations in which pooling would be allowed. The Board's action is summarized in the following paragraph of *APB Opinion No. 16,* ''Business Combinations'':

> The Board concludes that the purchase method and the pooling of interests method are both acceptable in accounting for business combinations, although not as alternatives in accounting for the same business combination. A business combination which meets specified conditions requires accounting by the pooling of interests method. A new basis of accounting is not permitted for a combination that meets the specified conditions, and the assets and liabilities of the combining companies are combined at their recorded amounts. All other business combinations should be accounted for as an acquisition of one or more companies by a corporation. The cost to an acquiring corporation of an entire acquired company should be determined by the principles of accounting for the acquisition of an asset. That cost should then be allocated to the identifiable individual assets acquired and liabilities assumed based on their fair values; the unallocated cost should be recorded as goodwill.[5]

By this action the Accounting Principles Board effectively thwarted most of the abuses of pooling-of-interests and purchase accounting described on pages 138 to 141. Retrospective poolings and part-pooling, part-purchase accounting were expressly prohibited. Substantial restrictions were placed upon the use of treasury stock and unusual securities to consummate pooling combinations. Pooling accounting was forbidden for a business combination containing any contingent payout provisions or plans to shortly dispose of assets acquired in the combination. Out-of-pocket costs of business combinations were required to be expensed, even though these costs are not deductible for income tax purposes.

Conditions requiring pooling-of-interests accounting

The Board provided a number of specified conditions for business combinations that were to be accounted for as poolings of interests. The conditions, *all* of which were to be satisfied for pooling to be appropriate, were divided into the three following groups:

1 Attributes of the combining companies. The conditions in this group were designed to assure that the pooling combination was truly a combining of two or more companies whose common stockholder interests were previously *independent* of each other.

[5]*APB Opinion No. 16,* ''Business Combinations,'' AICPA (New York: 1970), p. 283.

2 Manner of combining interests. The conditions in this group supported the requirement for pooling that an exchange of stock to combine *existing* voting common stock interests actually took place, in substance as well as in form.

3 Absence of planned transactions. The planned transactions prohibited by this group of conditions were those which would be inconsistent with the combining of entire existing interests of common stockholders.

The appendix on pages 148 to 149 includes in their entirety the specified conditions outlined by the Accounting Principles Board for pooling-of-interests accounting. Many of the conditions are self-explanatory. However, four of them warrant further discussion.

Independence of Combining Companies At the dates of initiation and consummation of a business combination, no combining company may have more than a 10% ownership of the outstanding voting common stock of another combining company. Otherwise, the companies could not be considered independent of each other.

Substantially All Voting Common Stock This condition requires that at least 90% of one combining company's outstanding voting common stock be exchanged for the issuing corporation's majority voting common stock. The following are excluded in computing the number of shares exchanged:

1 Shares acquired before the date the combination is initiated and held by the issuing corporation or its subsidiaries at that date.

2 Shares acquired by the issuing corporation or its subsidiaries after the combination is initiated, other than in exchange for the issuing corporation's voting common stock.

3 Shares of the combining company still outstanding at the date the combination is consummated.

In addition, any voting common stock of the issuing corporation owned or acquired by the combining company before the combination is effected must be considered. These issuing corporation shares are converted into equivalent shares of the combining company for the 90% test.

To illustrate, assume that on March 13, Year 2, Patton Corporation and Sherman Company initiated a plan of business combination. Under the plan, $1\frac{1}{2}$ shares of Patton Corporation voting common stock (1,000,000 shares issued at March 13, Year 2) were to be exchanged for each outstanding share of Sherman Company capital stock (100,000 shares issued at March 13, Year 2).

At this time, Patton Corporation owned 7,500 shares of Sherman Company capital stock, and Sherman Company owned 6,000 shares of Patton Corporation voting common stock; in addition, 500 shares of Sherman Company stock were in Sherman's treasury. On March 26, Year 2, Patton Corporation purchased in the stock market for cash 1,000 shares of Sherman Company capital stock; and on June 30, Year 2, Patton Corporation issued 136,500 shares of its voting common stock in exchange for 91,000 outstanding shares of Sherman Company capital stock, to complete the business combination.

Computation of the 90% requirement follows:

Total Sherman Company shares issued as of June 30, Year 2		100,000
Less: Shares in Sherman Company's treasury		500
Total Sherman Company shares outstanding as of June 30, Year 2 . .		99,500
Less:		
Sherman Company shares owned by Patton Corporation Mar. 13, Year 2	7,500	
Sherman Company shares acquired by Patton Corporation for cash Mar. 26, Year 2	1,000	
Equivalent number of Sherman Company shares represented by Patton Corporation stock owned by Sherman Company at Mar. 13, Year 2 (6,000 ÷ 1½)	4,000	12,500
Effective number of Sherman Company shares acquired June 30, Year 2 in exchange for Patton Corporation stock		87,000
Application of 90% requirement (90% × 99,500)		89,550

Thus, the 91,000 shares of Sherman Company stock actually exchanged on June 30, Year 2, are in effect restated to 87,000 shares. Since the restated amount is less than 90% of Sherman Company's 99,500 shares of capital stock outstanding, the business combination does not qualify for pooling-of-interests accounting.

Restrictions on Treasury Stock To preclude the treasury stock abuses described on page 139, the Accounting Principles Board provided that any treasury stock acquisitions by the issuing corporation in a business combination qualifying for pooling accounting must be in accordance with a systematic plan of acquisitions. The systematic pattern of acquisitions must have been established for at least two years prior to the initiation of a business combination; and the stock acquisitions must be required for stock option and compensation plans, or for other recurring stock distributions. Any "untainted" treasury stock issued to effect a pooling business combination should be accounted for as though retired and then issued as previously unissued stock.

No Pending Provisions For pooling-of-interests accounting to be appropriate for a business combination, no additional stock must be contingently issuable to former shareholders of a combining company after a combination has been initiated. In addition, no stock must have been issued to an escrow agent pending the resolution of a contingency.

A business combination which meets the Board's specified conditions is accounted for as a pooling of interests regardless of the legal form of the combination (statutory merger, statutory consolidation, acquisition of stock, acquisition of assets). An acquisition of assets may be construed as an "exchange of voting common stock interests" if all the specified conditions for a pooling are met.

Presentation and disclosure of business combinations in financial statements

Under both purchase and pooling-of-interests accounting, a balance sheet issued as of the date of a business combination accomplished through a statutory merger, statutory consolidation, or acquisition of assets includes all the assets and liabilities of the companies involved in the combination. (The *consolidated* balance sheet issued following a business combination which results in a parent-subsidiary relationship is described in Chapter 5.) The income statement for the period in which a business combination is carried out will differ depending on whether purchase or pooling accounting is applied to record the combination.

Purchase The income statement of the acquiring corporation for the period in which a purchase occurred includes the operating results of the acquired company *after the date of acquisition only.*

For example, under purchase accounting, Saxon Corporation's post-merger income statement for the year ended April 30, Year 6, would be identical to Saxon's premerger income statement using pooling accounting illustrated on page 145, except that net income would be $700,000 and selling, general, and administrative expenses would be $1,400,000. (The $200,000 out-of-pocket costs of the business combination are not charged to *expense* in purchase accounting; $66,250 is part of the cost to Saxon Corporation of Mason Company's net assets, and $133,750 is a reduction in Saxon's paid-in capital in excess of par.)

Pooling of Interests The income statement of the combined corporation for the period in which a pooling of interests took place includes the results of operations of the constituent companies *as though the combination had been completed as of the beginning of the period.* Comparative income statements or balance sheets for preceding periods must be restated in a comparable fashion. Intercompany transactions prior to the business combination must be eliminated from the combined income statements in a manner comparable to that described in Chapter 3 for branches.

This presentation stems from the concept that a business combination accounted for as a pooling of interests is a *combining of stockholder interests* rather than an *acquisition of assets.* Since stockholder interests are combined, previous financial statements showing changes in those interests are also combined.

To illustrate, assume that the income statements of Saxon Corporation and Mason Company for the year ended April 30, Year 6 (prior to their merger described earlier in this chapter), were as follows:

	Saxon Corporation	Mason Company
Revenue	$10,000,000	$5,000,000
Costs and expenses:		
Cost of goods sold	$ 7,000,000	$3,000,000
Selling, general, and administrative expenses	1,600,000*	962,000
Interest expense	150,000	100,500
Income taxes expense	750,000	562,500
	$ 9,500,000	$4,625,000
Net income	$ 500,000	$ 375,000

* Includes $200,000 expenses of business combination

Assume also that Mason Company's interest expense included $25,000 attributable to a loan from Saxon Corporation which had been repaid prior to April 30, Year 6.

The working paper for the postmerger income statement of Saxon Corporation under pooling-of-interests accounting is illustrated below. The amounts in the Combined column would appear in Saxon Corporation's published postmerger income statement for the year ended April 30, Year 6.

SAXON CORPORATION
Combining Income Statement (Pooling of Interests)
Year Ended April 30, Year 6

	Saxon Corporation	Mason Company	Combination eliminations	Combined
Revenue	$10,000,000	$5,000,000	(a) $(25,000)	$14,975,000
Costs and expenses:				
Cost of goods sold	$ 7,000,000	$3,000,000		$10,000,000
Selling, general, and administrative exp.	1,600,000	962,000		2,562,000
Interest expense	150,000	100,500	(a) $(25,000)	225,500
Income taxes expense	750,000	562,500		1,312,500
	$ 9,500,000	$4,625,000	$(25,000)	$14,100,000
Net income	$ 500,000	$ 375,000	$-0-	$ 875,000

Explanation of elimination entry:
(a) To eliminate intercompany interest received by Saxon Corporation from Mason Company.

Footnote disclosure of business combinations

Because of the complex nature of business combinations and their effects on the financial position and operating results of the reporting entity, extensive footnote disclosure is required for the periods in which they occur. The following footnotes, from recent annual reports of Cutler-Hammer, Inc., and General Signal Corporation, respectively, illustrate the required disclosures for purchases and poolings of interests.

Purchase In October 1971, Cutler-Hammer, Inc., through a newly organized, wholly owned, subsidiary, acquired all the outstanding stock of Brookhirst Igranic Limited of Bedford, England and Donovan Electrical Company Limited of Birmingham, England which are engaged in the manufacture and sale of electrical control devices.

The acquisitions are being accounted for using the purchase method and, accordingly, the results of operations since October 1, 1971, attributable to these companies, have been included in the financial statements.

The cost of the acquisitions required an initial payment of $16,269,000, which includes a repayment of amounts advanced to the companies by their parent of $8,075,000. The purchase agreement also includes an arrangement under which the price may be incrementally increased by an additional $3,200,000 for achievement of a given cumulative level of sales within the next five years. Goodwill, amounting to $1,949,842 based on the initial purchase price, has been recognized in the transactions and is amortized to earnings using the straight line method over a 40 year period. Any additional goodwill which may result from an increase in the purchase price will be similarly amortized.

The following supplemental information summarizes the combined results of operations on a pro forma basis as though the companies had been combined as of January 1, 1970.

	Year Ended December 31,	
	1971	*1970*
Net sales	$253,400,000	$259,800,000
Net income	$ 7,525,000	$ 7,250,000
Net income per share	$ 2.23	$ 2.15

Pooling of Interests During 1971 the company acquired The Cincinnati Time Recorder Company, a manufacturer of time recorders and automatic parking systems, and The Perolin Company, Inc., a supplier of specialty chemicals and services, for 257,468 and 94,990 shares of common stock, respectively. Each transaction has been accounted for as a pooling of interests. The consolidated financial statements for the year ended December 31, 1970 have been restated to reflect the operating results of these companies.

Net sales and net earnings before and after pooling of interests are summarized as follows:

	1971	1970
Net sales:		
Before 1971 poolings	$202,472,436	$193,187,013
1971 poolings	14,003,930	12,998,793
After 1971 poolings	$216,476,366	$206,185,806
Net earnings:		
Before 1971 poolings	$ 9,729,663	$ 8,907,621
1971 poolings	723,588	470,145
After 1971 poolings	$ 10,453,251	$ 9,377,766

APPRAISAL OF ACCOUNTING METHODS FOR BUSINESS COMBINATIONS

Earlier in this chapter, we stressed that logic suggests that business combinations be accounted for as the acquisition of assets; that is, by the *purchase* method of accounting. Despite the elaborate framework for pooling-of-interests accounting established by the AICPA, pooling accounting is founded upon a delicate assumption. This assumption—that some business combinations involving exchanges of voting common stock result in a combining of stockholder interests rather than an acquisition of assets—is difficult to support in accounting theory. Two *Accounting Research Studies* recommended abolishing the pooling-of-interests accounting method for business combinations between independent companies.[6]

Criticism of purchase accounting

The principal theoretical arguments against purchase accounting center on its recognition of *goodwill.* First, the goodwill in a purchase business combination is valued on a *residual* basis, rather than at *fair value,* as are the other assets acquired and liabilities assumed. Some accountants have contended that part of the amounts thus assigned to goodwill probably apply to other *identifiable* intangible assets. Second, only the goodwill of the *acquired* company is recorded in purchase accounting; yet the bargaining parties also considered goodwill of the *acquiring* corporation in negotiating the exchange price for the business combination. Third, the mandatory amortization of goodwill, established by *APB Opinion No. 17,* is difficult to defend for goodwill having an indeterminate useful life.

[6] *Accounting Research Study No. 5,* "A Critical Study of Accounting for Business Combinations," AICPA (New York: 1963), p. 105; *Accounting Research Study No. 10,* "Accounting for Goodwill," AICPA (New York: 1968), pp. 106, 109.

Criticism of pooling-of-interests accounting

The principal objections to pooling-of-interests accounting are as follows:

1 There is no explicit disclosure of the aggregate value of the issuing company's common stock exchanged in a business combination accounted for as a pooling of interests. The disclosure required by **APB Opinion No. 16** is limited to stating the number and type of shares of stock issued in a pooling business combination. Thus, there is no accurate way of ascertaining the agreed-upon value of the consideration issued in the combination.

2 The assets of the acquired company in a pooling business combination are not accounted for at their **cost** when acquired. In the illustrated pooling-of-interests accounting for the merger of Saxon Corporation and Mason Company (see page 134), the net assets of Mason Company were recorded in Saxon Corporation's accounts at the values recorded in Mason's accounts—$3,100,000. This amount is $716,250 less than the **cost** of Mason's net assets—$3,816,250—reflected in the purchase accounting illustration.

3 As a consequence of the misstatement of asset values, earnings for periods subsequent to a pooling of interests are misstated.

Because of these alleged defects in purchase and pooling-of-interests accounting, it is realistic to state that the current accounting standards for business combinations are less than satisfactory. As long as this situation exists, critics of accounting practices will continue to stress the lack of a sound basis for this body of accounting theory.

APPENDIX: SPECIFIED CONDITIONS FOR POOLING-OF-INTERESTS ACCOUNTING

1 Attributes of the combining companies.
  a Each of the combining companies is autonomous and has not been a subsidiary or division of another corporation within two years before the plan of combination is initiated.
  b Each of the combining companies is independent of the other companies.
2 Manner of combining interests.
  a The combination is effected in a single transaction or is completed in accordance with a specific plan within one year after the plan is initiated.
  b A corporation offers and issues only common stock with rights identical to those of the majority of its outstanding voting common stock in exchange for substantially all of the voting common stock interest of another company at the date the plan of combination is consummated.
  c None of the combining companies changes the equity interest of the voting common stock in contemplation of effecting the combination either within two years before the plan of combination is initiated or between the dates the combination is initiated and consummated; changes in contemplation of effecting the combination may include distributions to stockholders and additional issuances, exchanges, and retirements of securities.
  d Each of the combining companies reacquires shares of voting common stock only for purposes other than business combinations, and no company reacquires more than a normal number of shares between the dates the plan of combination is initiated and consummated.
  e The ratio of the interest of an individual common stockholder to those of other common stockholders in a combining company remains the same as a result of the exchange of stock to effect the combination.

f The voting rights to which the common stock ownership interests in the resulting combined corporation are entitled are exercisable by the stockholders; the stockholders are neither deprived of nor restricted in exercising those rights for a period.

g The combination is resolved at the date the plan is consummated and no provisions of the plan relating to the issue of securities or other consideration are pending.

3 Absence of planned transactions.

a The combined corporation does not agree directly or indirectly to retire or reacquire all or part of the common stock issued to effect the combination.

b The combined corporation does not enter into other financial arrangements for the benefit of the former stockholders of a combining company, such as a guaranty of loans secured by stock issued in the combination, which in effect negates the exchange of equity securities.

c The combined corporation does not intend or plan to dispose of a significant part of the assets of the combining companies within two years after the combination other than disposals in the ordinary course of business of the former separate companies and to eliminate duplicate facilities or excess capacity.

SOURCE: *APB Opinion No. 16*, "Business Combinations," AICPA (New York: 1970), pp. 295–304.

REVIEW QUESTIONS

1 Distinguish between a **purchase** and a **pooling of interests** in terms of the entity relationships between the combining and the continuing units. (Ignore accounting differences.)

2 The term **goodwill** often appears in connection with business combinations.
a What is goodwill? Explain.
b What is negative goodwill? Explain.

3 If a business combination meets the specified conditions requiring treatment as a pooling of interests, what is the accounting effect as compared with a purchase interpretation?

4 Comment on the following quotation:

It is our judgment that the weight of logic and consistency supports the conclusion that business combinations between independent entities are exchange transactions involving a transfer of assets and that the accounting action to account for an exchange transaction is necessary to reflect properly the results of the business transaction.

5 Compare and contrast a **statutory merger** and a **statutory consolidation.**

6 What two methods are generally used, individually or jointly, to determine an appropriate price to pay in a business combination?

7 Identify five abuses of pooling-of-interests accounting during the 1960s.

8 State how each of the following out-of-pocket costs of a merger business combination treated as a purchase should be accounted for:

a Printing costs for proxy statement mailed to shareholders in advance of special meeting to ratify terms of the merger

b Legal fees for negotiating the merger

c CPA fees for auditing SEC registration statement covering shares of stock issued in the merger

d Printing costs for securities issued in the merger

e Legal fees for SEC registration statement covering shares of stock issued in the merger

f CPA fees for advice on income tax aspects of the merger

9 Discuss some of the reasons for the popularity of pooling-of-interests accounting for business combinations during the 1950s and 1960s.

10 *a* What is **contingent consideration** in a business combination?

  b If a plan of business combination includes a provision for contingent consideration, is pooling-of-interests accounting appropriate for the combination? Explain.

11 How is the cost of an acquired company allocated in a business combination treated as a purchase?

12 How do the journal entries to the Paid-in Capital in Excess of Par account differ in purchase and pooling-of-interests accounting?

13 What are **retrospective poolings?** How were they used in the Westec Corporation scandal?

14 Critics have charged that pooling-of-interests accounting creates "instant earnings." How is this accomplished?

EXERCISES

Ex. 4-1 Select the best answer for each of the following multiple-choice questions:

  1 Shares of treasury stock delivered to effect a business combination that is properly accounted for by the pooling-of-interests method should be accounted for as being:

  a A reissue of treasury shares.

  b A reissue of treasury shares at fair market value.

  c Retired and then newly issued.

  d Retired and then newly issued at fair market value.

  2 Out-of-pocket costs related to effecting a business combination accounted for by the pooling-of-interests method should be:

  a Deducted in determining the net income of the resulting combined corporation for the period in which the costs are incurred.

  b Capitalized and amortized over a discretionary period elected by management.

  c Charged to Retained Earnings when incurred.

  d Treated as a prior period adjustment.

  3 Two companies which have merged in Year 3 in accordance with pooling-of-interests accounting are contemplating the preparation of financial statements at the end of Year 3. It has been proposed to present Year 2 statements also on a comparative basis.

  a The Year 2 statements must remain as they were prepared originally.

  b The Year 2 statements must be restated to reflect what the results would have been had the merger occurred then or earlier.

c The Year 2 statements must be dropped from consideration, as it is not possible to prepare statements to reflect a relationship which did not in fact exist in Year 2.

d The Year 3 statements must be so prepared as not to reflect the combination.

4 Meredith Company and Kyle Company were combined in a purchase transaction. Meredith was able to acquire Kyle at a bargain price. The sum of the market or appraised values of identifiable assets acquired less the fair value of liabilities assumed exceeded the cost to Meredith. After revaluing noncurrent assets to zero, there was still some negative goodwill. Proper accounting treatment by Meredith is to report the amount as:

a An extraordinary item.

b Part of current income in the year of combination.

c A deferred credit and amortize it.

d Paid-in capital in excess of par.

5 Ecol Corporation issued voting preferred stock with a fair value of $1,000,000 in exchange for all the outstanding common stock of Ogee Service Company. Ogee has tangible net assets with a carrying value of $500,000 and a fair value of $600,000. In addition, Ecol Corporation issued stock valued at $100,000 to an investment banker as a finder's fee for arranging the combination. As a result of this combination, Ecol Corporation should record an increase in net assets of:

a $500,000.   *b* $700,000.   *c* $600,000.   *d* $1,100,000.

6 The business combination of James Company—the issuing company—and Brighton Corporation was consummated on March 14, Year 8. At the initiation date, James held 1,000 shares of Brighton. If the combination were accounted for as a pooling of interests, the 1,000 shares of Brighton held by James would be accounted for as:

a Retired stock.

b 1,000 shares of treasury stock.

c (1,000 ÷ the exchange rate) shares of treasury stock.

d (1,000 × the exchange rate) shares of treasury stock.

Ex. 4-2 Dillon Corporation offered to exchange two shares of Dillon common stock for each share of Butler Company common stock. On the date of the offer Dillon held 3,000 shares of Butler common and Butler held 500 shares of Dillon common. In later cash transactions, Dillon purchased 2,000 shares of Butler common and Butler purchased 2,500 shares of Dillon common. At all times the number of common shares outstanding was 1,000,000 for Dillon and 100,000 for Butler. After consummation of the business combination, Dillon held 100,000 Butler common shares. The number of shares considered exchanged in determining whether this combination should be accounted for by the pooling-of-interests method is:

a 190,000.   *b* 95,000.   *c* 93,500.   *d* 89,000.

e None of the above or not determinable from the above facts.

Ex. 4-3 Farmer Corporation paid $50,000 cash for the net assets of Anselm Company, which consisted of the following:

	Carrying value	Fair value
Current assets	$10,000	$14,000
Plant and equipment	40,000	55,000
Liabilities assumed	(10,000)	(9,000)
	$40,000	$60,000

The plant and equipment acquired in this business combination should be recorded at

a $55,000.   *b* $50,000.   *c* $45,833.   *d* $40,000.
e None of the above or not determinable from the above facts.

Ex. 4-4 Condensed balance sheets of Starling Corporation and Sampson Corporation at July 31, Year 9, appear below.

	Starling Corporation	Sampson Corporation
Total assets	$700,000	$670,000
Total liabilities	$300,000	$300,000
Capital stock ($25 par value)	200,000	250,000
Paid-in capital in excess of par	80,000	130,000
Retained earnings (deficit)	120,000	(10,000)
	$700,000	$670,000

On that date, Starling Corporation and Sampson Corporation entered into a statutory consolidation. The new company, Starson Corporation, issued 75,000 shares of $10 par value capital stock for all the outstanding stock of Starling and Sampson. Out-of-pocket costs of the combination were immaterial.

a Prepare a journal entry to record the consolidation in the accounts of Starson Corporation as a pooling of interests.

b Prepare a journal entry to record the consolidation in the accounts of Starson Corporation as a purchase. Assume that fair values of identifiable assets are $800,000 for Starling Corporation and $700,000 for Sampson Corporation; that each company's liabilities are fairly valued at $300,000; and that the market value of Starson Corporation stock is $12 per share.

Ex. 4-5 The net earnings of Skiles Corporation and Myers Company during Year 4 were as follows:

	Jan. 1–Oct. 31	Nov. 1–Dec. 31
Skiles Corporation	$420,000	$80,000
Myers Company	350,000	50,000

Condensed balance sheet and other data for Year 4 follow:

	Skiles Corporation Oct. 31	Skiles Corporation Dec. 31	Myers Company Oct. 31	Myers Company Dec. 31
Assets	$3,500,000	$4,080,000	$4,000,000	$4,150,000
Liabilities	500,000	500,000	1,000,000	1,100,000
Capital stock, $10 par value	2,000,000	2,500,000	2,000,000	–0–
Retained earnings	1,000,000	1,080,000	1,000,000	–0–
Market price per share of capital stock	100	130	20	–0–

Neither company paid dividends during Year 4. In recent months, Skiles Corporation stock has been selling at about 40 times earnings; prior to November 1, Year 4, Myers Company stock had been selling at 10 times earnings.

On November 1, Year 4, Skiles Corporation issued 50,000 shares of its stock in exchange for all the stock of Myers Company. Out-of-pocket costs of the combination were negligible. Skiles Corporation tentatively recorded the additional shares issued at par value and debited Investment in Myers Company for $500,000. Myers Company thereupon liquidated and became a division of Skiles Corporation.

Answer the following questions (Supporting computations must be in good form.):

a Assuming that the merger is accounted for as a pooling of interests, what is Skiles Corporation's net income for Year 4?

b What is the amount of the Year 4 earnings per share for Skiles Corporation on a pooling basis?

c If the merger had been accounted for as a purchase, what would Skiles Corporation's net income have been for Year 4?

d What is Skiles Corporation's earnings per share for Year 4 on a purchase basis?

e What is the amount of retained earnings on a pooling basis at the end of Year 4?

f What is the amount of retained earnings on a purchase basis at the end of Year 4?

g Why did Skiles Corporation issue stock having a market value of $5,000,000 in exchange for Myers Company stock which had a market value of only $4,000,000 (200,000 shares at $20 per share = $4,000,000) at the date of the business combination?

SHORT CASES FOR ANALYSIS AND DECISION

Case 4-1 After extended negotiations Stamm Corporation bought from Moore Company most of the latter's assets on June 30, Year 3. At the time of the sale Moore's accounts (adjusted to June 30, Year 3) reflected the following descriptions and amounts for the assets transferred:

	Cost	Contra accounts	Carrying value
Receivables	$ 83,600	$ 3,000	$ 80,600
Inventories	107,000	5,200	101,800
Land	20,000	–0–	20,000
Buildings	207,500	73,000	134,500
Fixtures and equipment	205,000	41,700	163,300
Goodwill	50,000	–0–	50,000
	$673,100	$122,900	$550,200

You ascertain that the contra accounts were allowance for doubtful accounts, allowance to reduce inventory to market, and accumulated depreciation.

During the extended negotiations Moore held out for a consideration of approximately $600,000 (depending upon the level of the receivables and inventories). However, as of June 30, Year 3, Moore agreed to accept Stamm's offer of $450,000 cash plus 1% of the net sales (as defined in the contract) of the next five years, with payments at the end of each year. Moore expects that Stamm's total net sales during this period will exceed $15,000,000.

Instructions
a How should Stamm Corporation record this transaction? Explain.
b Discuss the propriety of recording goodwill in the accounts of Stamm Corporation for this transaction.

Case 4-2 The boards of directors of Quinton Corporation, Fulton Company, Russell, Inc., and Towne Corporation are meeting jointly to discuss plans for a merger. Each of the corporations has one class of common stock outstanding; Fulton also has one class of preferred stock outstanding. Although terms have not as yet been settled, Quinton will be the surviving corporation. Because the directors want to conform to generally accepted accounting standards, they have asked you to attend the meeting as an advisor.

Instructions Consider each of the following questions independently of the others and answer each in accordance with generally accepted accounting standards. Explain your answers.
a Assume that the merger will be consummated August 31, Year 5. Explain the philosophy underlying the accounting and how the balance sheet accounts of each of the four corporations will appear on Quinton's balance sheet on September 1, Year 5, if the merger is accounted for as a
  (1) Pooling of interests
  (2) Purchase
b Assume that the merger will be consummated August 31, Year 5. Explain how the income statement accounts of each of the four corporations will be accounted for in the preparation of Quinton's income statement for the year ended December 31, Year 5, if the combination is accounted for as a
  (1) Pooling of interests
  (2) Purchase
c Some of the directors believe that the terms of the merger should be agreed upon immediately and that the method of accounting to be used may be chosen at some later date. Others believe that the terms of the merger and the accounting method to be used are very closely related. Which position is correct?
d Quinton and Towne are comparable in size; Russell and Fulton are much smaller. How do these facts affect the choice of accounting method for the merger?
e Fulton was formerly a subsidiary of Garson Corporation, which has no other relationship to any of the four companies discussing combination. Garson voluntarily spun off Fulton 18 months ago. What effect, if any, do these facts have on the choice of accounting method for the merger?
f Quinton holds 2,000 of Fulton's 10,000 outstanding shares of preferred stock and 15,000 of Russell's 100,000 outstanding shares of common stock. All of Quinton's holdings were acquired during the first three months of Year 5. What effect, if any, do these facts have on the choice of accounting method?
g Since the directors feel that one of Towne's major divisions will not be compatible with the operations of the combined company, they anticipate that it will be sold as soon as possible after the combination is consummated. They expect to have no trouble in finding a buyer. What effect, if any, do these facts have on the choice of accounting method?

Case 4-3 On February 15, Year 6, the negotiating officers of Shane Corporation agreed with G. W. Miles, sole shareholder of Miles Company and Miles Industries, Inc., to acquire all of Miles's stock ownership in the two companies in the following manner:

10,000 shares of Shane Corporation $1 par value common stock (market value $25 per share) would be issued to Miles on February 28, Year 6, for his 1,000 shares of $10 par value capital stock of Miles Company. In addition, 10,000 shares of Shane common would be issued to Miles February 28, Year 11, if aggregate earnings of Miles Company for the five-year period then ended exceeded $150,000.

$250,000 cash would be paid to Miles on February 28, Year 6, for his 10,000 shares of $1 par value capital stock of Miles Industries, Inc. In addition, $250,000 in cash would be paid to Miles February 28, Year 11, if aggregate earnings of Miles Industries, Inc., for the five-year period then ended exceeded $150,000.

Both Miles Company and Miles Industries, Inc., are to be merged into Shane Corporation as of February 28, Year 6, and are to continue operations after that date as divisions of Shane Corporation. Miles also agreed not to compete with Shane Corporation for the period March 1, Year 6, through February 28, Year 11. Because the merger was negotiated privately and Miles signed a "letter agreement" not to dispose of the Shane Corporation stock he received, the business combination was not subject to the jurisdiction of the SEC, and out-of-pocket costs of the combination were negligible.

Key financial statements measures of the three combining companies as of February 28, Year 6 (prior to the merger), were as follows:

	Shane Corporation	Miles Company	Miles Industries, Inc.
Total assets	$25,000,000	$ 500,000	$ 600,000
Stockholders' equity	10,000,000	200,000	300,000
Net sales	50,000,000	1,500,000	2,500,000
Earnings per share	5	30	3

The controller of Shane Corporation drafted the following condensed journal entries to record the merger as of February 28, Year 6:

Assets	500,000	
Liabilities		300,000
Common Stock		10,000
Common Stock to Be Issued		10,000
Paid-in Capital in Excess of Par		180,000

To record merger with Miles Company on a pooling-of-interests basis.

Assets	650,000	
Goodwill	150,000	
Liabilities		300,000
Due to G. W. Miles		250,000
Cash		250,000

To record merger with Miles Industries, Inc., on a purchase basis, with assets and liabilities of Miles recorded at fair values, and goodwill to be amortized over a 40-year period.

Instructions Do you concur with the controller's journal entries? Discuss.

PROBLEMS

4-4 Car-Mart Company (a partnership) was organized on July 1, Year 1. Under the partnership agreement $900,000 was invested by Carson and $600,000 by Martin as initial capital; income and losses were to be shared in the same ratio as the initial capital investments. No additional capital investments have been made. The June 30, Year 6, balance sheet of Car-Mart Company follows.

Assets	
Cash	$ 500,500
Accounts receivable (net)	950,000
Inventory (lifo basis)	1,500,000
Prepaid insurance	18,000
Land	58,000
Building, machinery, and equipment (net)	1,473,500
	$4,500,000

Liabilities & Partners' Capitals	
Current liabilities	$1,475,000
Carson, capital	1,815,000
Martin, capital	1,210,000
	$4,500,000

Carson and Martin have engaged in lengthy discussions with the directors and executives of Prince Corporation during the past few months. With the permission of Carson and Martin, the independent auditors of Prince Corporation conducted an examination of and expressed an unqualified opinion on the financial statements of Car-Mart Company as of June 30, Year 6.

Carson agrees to accept 8,700 shares and Martin agrees to accept 5,800 shares of Prince Corporation common stock in exchange for all partnership interests. During the month of June, Year 6, the per-share market price of Prince Corporation common stock was $265. The stockholders' equity account balances of Prince Corporation as of June 30, Year 6, follow:

Common stock, $100 par value	$2,000,000
Paid-in capital in excess of par	580,000
Retained earnings	2,496,400
	$5,076,400

Instructions
a Prepare the necessary journal entry or entries in the accounts of Prince Corporation to record the business combination as a pooling of interests on July 1, Year 6.
b Prepare the necessary journal entry or entries in the accounts of Car-Mart Company to record the liquidation of the partnership.

4-5 A condensed balance sheet at March 31, Year 7, and related fair value data for Maine Company are presented on page 157.

	Historical cost	Fair value
Assets		
Current assets	$ 500,000	$ 575,000
Property, plant, and equipment (net)	1,000,000	1,200,000
Patent (net)	100,000	50,000
	$1,600,000	
Liabilities & Stockholders' Equity		
Current liabilities.	$ 300,000	$ 300,000
Long-term debt	400,000	450,000
Capital stock, $10 par value	100,000	
Retained earnings	800,000	
	$1,600,000	

On April 1, Year 7, Singer Corporation issued 50,000 shares of its $5 par value common stock (market value $14 per share) and $250,000 cash for the net assets of Maine Company, in a business combination qualifying for purchase account-ing. Of the $125,000 out-of-pocket costs paid by Singer on April 1, Year 7, $50,000 were legal fees and finders' fees related to the combination.

Instructions Prepare the necessary journal entry or entries to record the busi-ness combination in the accounting records of Singer Corporation.

4-6 As of the close of business August 31, Year 2, Miller Company merged into Selby Corporation in a business combination meeting the specified conditions for pooling-of-interests accounting. Premerger income statements of the two com-panies for the year ended August 31, Year 2, were as follows:

	Selby Corporation	Miller Company
Revenue:		
Net sales	$800,000	$550,000
Rent	–0–	50,000
	$800,000	$600,000
Costs and expenses:		
Cost of goods sold	$480,000	$300,000
Selling, general, and administrative expenses	55,000	50,000
Interest expense	15,000	10,000
Income taxes expense	150,000	144,000
	$700,000	$504,000
Net income	$100,000	$ 96,000

During the year prior to the merger, Miller Company had obtained from and repaid to Selby Corporation a $100,000, 9%, 90-day loan; Selby Corporation had rented for the entire year a sales office owned by Miller Company, with a monthly rental of $500 plus 1% of net sales; and Selby Corporation had sold to Miller Company, at Selby's regular markup, goods costing $120,000, all of which were resold during the year to outside customers at Miller's regular markup.

Instructions Prepare in general journal form working-paper combination eliminations for Selby Corporation's postmerger income statement for the year ended August 31, Year 2.

4-7 On June 30, Year 2, Millard Company and Manion Company entered into a statutory consolidation. A new company, Millman Corporation, issued 100,000 shares of its 500,000 authorized shares of no-par, $3 stated value common stock as follows:

60,000 shares for all 10,000 outstanding shares of Millard Company's $2 par value capital stock

40,000 shares for all 15,000 outstanding shares of Manion Company's $1 par value capital stock

Costs associated with the statutory consolidation (legal and audit fees, printing charges, SEC fees, etc.) aggregating $50,000 were paid in cash June 30, Year 2 (prior to the consolidation), by Millard Company on behalf of Millman Corporation. There were no other intercompany transactions.

Following are condensed financial statements of Millard Company and Manion Company for the year ended June 30, Year 2, prior to the consolidation.

Balance Sheets	Millard Company	Manion Company
Assets		
Current assets	$ 200,000	$300,000
Due from Millman Corporation	50,000	–0–
Property, plant, and equipment (net)	700,000	500,000
Other assets	60,000	10,000
	$1,010,000	$810,000
Liabilities & Stockholders' Equity		
Current liabilities	$ 160,000	$ 80,000
Long-term debt	200,000	90,000
Capital stock	20,000	15,000
Paid-in capital in excess of par	80,000	150,000
Retained earnings	550,000	475,000
	$1,010,000	$810,000

Statements of Income and Retained Earnings		
Net sales	$2,000,000	$3,000,000
Costs and expenses:		
Cost of goods sold	$1,200,000	$2,000,000
Selling, general, and administrative expenses	400,000	500,000
Interest expense	15,000	10,000
Income taxes expense	231,000	294,000
	$1,846,000	$2,804,000
Net income	$ 154,000	$ 196,000
Retained earnings, July 1, Year 1	396,000	279,000
Retained earnings, June 30, Year 2	$ 550,000	$ 475,000

Millard Company costs its inventory on the fifo basis; Manion Company uses lifo cost for inventory. As part of the consolidation agreement, Manion Company agreed to change its inventory valuation method from lifo to fifo. Relevant inventory data for Manion Company are as follows:

	Lifo cost	Fifo cost
Inventory, June 30, Year 2	$100,000	$150,000
Inventory, June 30, Year 1	90,000	130,000

Instructions

a Prepare the adjusting journal entry at June 30, Year 2, to change Manion Company's inventory from lifo cost to fifo cost. Manion Company's combined federal and state income tax rate is 60%. (***Note:*** In accordance with ***APB Opinion No. 20,*** "Accounting Changes," a change from lifo to another inventory costing method requires the retroactive adjustment of retained earnings.)

b Prepare the June 30, Year 2, journal entry or entries for Millman Corporation to record the statutory consolidation as a pooling of interests.

c Prepare a working paper computing pooled net income of Millman Corporation for the year ended June 30, Year 2.

4-8 Wilson Corporation agreed to pay $750,000 cash and issue 50,000 shares of its $10 par value ($20 market price per share) common stock on September 30, Year 4, for all the net assets of Harding Company except cash. In addition, Wilson Corporation agreed that if the market price of its common stock was not $20 per share or higher on September 30, Year 5, a sufficient number of additional shares of common stock would be issued to the former shareholders of Harding Company on that date to make the aggregate market value of their Wilson common shareholdings equal to $1,000,000.

The balance sheet of Harding Company at September 30, Year 4, with related fair values of assets and liabilities, appears below.

	Historical cost	Fair value
Assets		
Cash	$ 100,000	$ 100,000
Accounts receivable (net)	300,000	300,000
Inventories	600,000	680,000
Short-term prepayments	20,000	20,000
10% investment in common stock of Coolidge Company .	100,000	80,000
Land	500,000	650,000
Other plant and equipment (net)	1,000,000	1,250,000
Patent	80,000	100,000
	$2,700,000	
Liabilities & Stockholders' Equity		
Current liabilities	$ 700,000	$ 700,000
Long-term debt	500,000	480,000
Capital stock	600,000	
Paid-in capital in excess of par	400,000	
Retained earnings	500,000	
	$2,700,000	

Out-of-pocket costs of the business combination paid by Wilson Corporation on September 30, Year 4, were as follows:

Audit fees—SEC registration statement	$ 30,000
Finder's fee (2% of aggregate consideration)	35,000
Legal fees—business combination	15,000
Legal fees—SEC registration statement	20,000
Printing costs—securities and SEC registration statement	25,000
SEC registration fee	350
Total out-of-pocket costs of business combination	$125,350

Instructions
a Prepare as of September 30, Year 4, journal entries for the accounts of Wilson Corporation to reflect the above transactions.
b Assume that on September 30, Year 5, the market price of Wilson Corporation's common stock was $18 per share. Prepare a journal entry to reflect the issuance of additional Wilson Corporation common shares to former shareholders of Harding Company on that date and the payment of cash in lieu of fractional shares.

4-9 The board of directors of Pullman Corporation is considering a merger with Raymond Company. Presented below and on page 161 are the most recent financial statements (condensed) and other financial data for the two companies, both of which use the same accounting standards and practices.

Balance Sheets October 31, Year 8	Pullman Corporation	Raymond Company
Assets		
Current assets	$ 500,000	$200,000
Property, plant, and equipment (net)	1,000,000	500,000
Other assets	300,000	100,000
	$1,800,000	$800,000
Liabilities & Stockholders' Equity		
Current liabilities	$ 400,000	$100,000
Long-term debt	500,000	300,000
Capital stock, $10 par value	600,000	100,000
Paid-in capital in excess of par	100,000	100,000
Retained earnings	200,000	200,000
	$1,800,000	$800,000

Statements of Income and Retained Earnings
Year Ended October 31, Year 8

Net sales.	$5,000,000	$1,000,000
Costs and expenses:		
Cost of goods sold	$3,500,000	$ 600,000
Selling, general, and administrative expenses	1,000,000	200,000
Interest expense	200,000	50,000
Income taxes expense	180,000	90,000
	$4,880,000	$ 940,000
Net income	$ 120,000	$ 60,000
Retained earnings, Nov. 1, Year 7	80,000	140,000
Retained earnings, Oct. 31, Year 8	$ 200,000	$ 200,000
Earnings per share.	$2.00	$6.00
Price-earnings ratio	10	5

    Pullman Corporation's directors estimate that the out-of-pocket costs of the merger will be as follows:

Finder's fee and legal fees for the merger	$ 5,000
Costs associated with SEC registration statement.	7,000
Total out-of-pocket costs of merger	$12,000

    The fair values of Raymond Company's liabilities at October 31, Year 8, are equal to their balance sheet amounts. Fair values of Raymond's assets at that date are as follows:

Current assets (difference from balance sheet amount attributable to	
inventories)	$230,000
Property, plant, and equipment (difference from balance sheet amount	
attributable to land—$60,000 and to depreciable assets with a five-	
year remaining useful life—$40,000)	600,000
Other assets (difference from balance sheet amount attributable to	
leasehold with a remaining term of four years)	120,000

    Pullman Corporation's board of directors is considering two alternative plans for effecting the merger, as follows:

    Plan 1 Issue 30,000 shares of capital stock for all the outstanding capital stock of Raymond Company in a business combination meeting the specified conditions for pooling-of-interests accounting.

    Plan 2 Issue 15,000 shares of capital stock, $100,000 cash, and an 8%, three-year note for $200,000 for all the outstanding capital stock of Raymond Company.

    Under either plan, Raymond Company would continue operations as a division of Pullman Corporation.

Instructions To assist Pullman Corporation's board of directors in their evaluation of the two plans, prepare a working paper computing the following for each plan as though the merger had been effected as of October 31, Year 8:
a Net income and earnings per share of Pullman Corporation for the year ended October 31, Year 8.

b Net income and earnings per share of Pullman Corporation for the year ending October 31, Year 9, assuming the same basic sales and cost patterns for the year ended October 31, Year 8.
Ignore income taxes in your computations.

4-10 Financial statements of Grant Corporation and Dale Corporation appear below.

Balance Sheets June 30, Year 7	Grant Corporation	Dale Corporation
Assets		
Cash	$ 25,500	$ 1,500
Notes and accounts receivable (net)	24,500	7,500
Inventories, at fifo cost	42,000	8,800
Due from Dale Corporation	7,600	–0–
Property and equipment (net)	59,500	35,800
Other assets	4,500	200
	$163,600	$53,800
Liabilities & Stockholders' Equity		
Notes and accounts payable	$ 20,700	$39,920
Due to Grant Corporation	–0–	7,600
Income taxes payable	11,400	–0–
Other liabilities	1,500	2,200
Capital stock, $10 par value	50,000	–0–
Capital stock, $100 par value	–0–	25,000
Paid-in capital in excess of par	30,000	32,000
Retained earnings (deficit)	50,000	(52,920)
	$163,600	$53,800

Statements of Income and Retained Earnings (Deficit)
Six Months Ended June 30, Year 7

Revenue:		
Net sales	$150,000	$ 60,000
Other revenue	5,000	–0–
	$155,000	$ 60,000
Costs and expenses:		
Cost of goods sold	$105,000	$ 54,000
Selling, general, and administrative expenses	31,000	12,100
Income taxes expense	11,400	–0–
	$147,400	$ 66,100
Net income (loss)	$ 7,600	$ (6,100)
Retained earnings (deficit), Jan. 1, Year 7	44,900	(46,820)
	$ 52,500	$(52,920)
Dividends	2,500	–0–
Retained earnings (deficit), June 30, Year 7	$ 50,000	$(52,920)

The pre-tax accounting income (loss) of the two corporations for the last six years is as follows (pre-tax accounting income and taxable income are the same):

	Grant Corporation	Dale Corporation
Year 1	$18,000	$(10,000)
Year 2	(7,500)	4,000
Year 3	12,600	(15,000)
Year 4	14,900	(6,000)
Year 5	31,200	(7,000)
Year 6	28,900	(11,100)

On July 1, Year 7, Dale Corporation transferred to Grant Corporation all its assets net of all liabilities, in exchange for unissued Grant Corporation capital stock. The terms of the merger provided that the fair value of the stock in each corporation is to be its net assets value, except that an allowance is to be made for the value of any net operating loss carryforward. Obtaining the benefit of the loss carryforward deduction was not the principal purpose of the merger. (Assume a combined federal and state income tax rate of 60% and that the state net operating loss carryover rules are the same as the federal rules, which require that an operating loss of the current year first be carried back three years and then forward five years.)

Instructions
a Compute (1) the total number of shares of Grant Corporation capital stock to be distributed to shareholders of Dale Corporation, and (2) the exchange ratio of Grant Corporation stock for Dale Corporation stock.
b Prepare the general journal entry for Grant Corporation to record the merger with Dale Corporation as a pooling of interests.
c Prepare a compound journal entry for Dale Corporation to record the merger with Grant Corporation. Assume that Dale Corporation does not record in its accounts the potential income tax benefit of its operating loss carryforward.

CHAPTER

5

Consolidated financial statements: at date of business combination

In our discussion of business combinations in Chapter 4, we used the terms *investor* and *investee.* If Corporation A (the investor) acquires more than 50% of the voting common stock of Corporation B (the investee), a parent-subsidiary relationship is established. Corporation B becomes a *subsidiary* of the acquiring *parent* but remains a separate legal entity.

Strict adherence to the legal aspects of such a business combination would require the issuance of separate financial statements for the parent and the subsidiary at the date of the business combination, and also for all subsequent periods of the affiliation. However, such strict adherence to legal form would ignore the *substance* of most parent-subsidiary relationships: a parent and its subsidiary are usually a single *economic entity.* In recognition of this fact, *consolidated financial statements* are issued to report the financial position and operating results of a parent and its subsidiaries as a single *accounting entity.*

Nature of consolidated financial statements

Consolidated financial statements are similar to the *combined* financial statements described in Chapter 3. Assets, liabilities, revenue, and expenses of the parent and its subsidiaries are aggregated; intercompany transactions and balances are eliminated; and the final consolidated amounts are reported in the consolidated balance sheet, statements of income and retained earnings, and statement of changes in financial position.

However, the separate *legal entity* status of parent and subsidiary corporations necessitates working-paper consolidation eliminations which are generally more complex than the eliminations described in Chapter 3. Before illustrating consolidation eliminations, however, it is desirable to examine some basic principles of consolidation.

Should all subsidiaries be consolidated?

A wide range of consolidation practices exists among major companies in the United States.[1] For example, a recent edition of *Accounting Trends & Techniques,* the AICPA's annual survey of accounting practices in the published financial statements of 600 companies, reported the following:

1 A total of 398 companies consolidated all domestic and Canadian subsidiaries, while 191 companies excluded some domestic and Canadian subsidiaries from the consolidated financial statements. (The remaining 11 companies surveyed either did not issue consolidated financial statements or had no indication of domestic or foreign subsidiaries.)

2 Of 390 companies reporting policies for consolidation of foreign subsidiaries, 248 consolidated all such subsidiaries, 122 consolidated some foreign subsidiaries, and 20 excluded all foreign subsidiaries from consolidation.

3 The principal types of subsidiaries (other than foreign affiliates) excluded from consolidation were finance-related subsidiaries and insignificant or inactive subsidiaries. "Finance-related subsidiaries" include finance companies, insurance companies, banks, and leasing companies.

In the authors' opinion, such wide variations in consolidation policy are undesirable and difficult to justify from a theoretical point of view. The purpose of consolidated financial statements is to present in one accounting entity the combined resources, obligations, and operating results of a family of related corporations; consequently, there is no theoretical reason for excluding from consolidation any subsidiary which is genuinely *controlled.* The argument that finance-related subsidiaries should not be consolidated with parent manufacturing or retailing companies because of their unique features is hardly supportable when one considers the wide variety of production, marketing, and service companies that are consolidated in a *conglomerate* or highly diversified family of corporations.

The meaning of "controlling financial interest"

Traditionally, one corporation's direct or indirect ownership of more than 50% of an affiliate's voting common stock has been required to evidence

[1] Adequate guidelines for consolidation policies have not been provided by the AICPA; a limited step in this direction was contained in the following excerpt from *Accounting Research Bulletin No. 51:* "There is a presumption that consolidated statements are more meaningful than separate statements and that they are usually necessary for a fair presentation when one of the companies in the group directly or indirectly has a controlling financial interest in the other companies." *ARB No. 51,* "Consolidated Financial Statements," AICPA (New York: 1959), p. 41.

the controlling financial interest underlying a parent-subsidiary relationship. However, even though such a stock ownership exists, other circumstances may negate the parent's *actual* control of the subsidiary. For example, a subsidiary which is bankrupt or in court-supervised reorganization is not really controlled by its parent. Also, a foreign subsidiary in a country having severe production, monetary, or income tax restrictions may in reality be subject to the authority of the foreign country rather than to its parent.

It is important to recognize that a parent's control of a subsidiary may be achieved *indirectly.* For example, if Plymouth Corporation owns 85% of the outstanding voting common stock of Selwyn Company and 45% of Talbot Company's common stock, while Selwyn Company also owns 45% of Talbot's common, both Selwyn and Talbot are controlled by Plymouth, because it effectively owns 90% of Talbot. This effective ownership consists of 45% held directly and 45% indirectly.

Criticism of traditional concept of control

Some accountants have challenged the conventional definition of *control* described in the preceding section. These accountants maintain that a corporation owning less than 50% of another company's voting common stock may effectively control the affiliate, especially if the remaining stock is widely scattered among a number of individual shareholders who do not attend shareholder meetings or give proxies. Effective control of an investee is also possible if the individuals comprising management of the investor corporation own a substantial number of shares of the investee or successfully solicit proxies from the investee's other shareholders. These arguments merit further study in the search for a less arbitrary definition of *control* than the one outlined in the preceding section.

Unconsolidated subsidiaries in consolidated financial statements

Current accounting standards[2] require the *equity method* of accounting for unconsolidated subsidiaries in consolidated financial statements. The equity method of accounting, which is discussed in depth in Chapter 6, reflects the parent's share of the earnings of an unconsolidated subsidiary on a single line in the consolidated statement of income. Use of the equity method of accounting in this manner results in a figure for consolidated net income identical to that which would have resulted from consolidating the subsidiary.

[2] *APB Opinion No. 18,* "The Equity Method of Accounting for Investments in Common Stock," AICPA (New York: 1971), pp. 353–354.

CONSOLIDATION OF WHOLLY OWNED SUBSIDIARIES AT DATE OF BUSINESS COMBINATION

Purchase: wholly owned subsidiary

To illustrate consolidated financial statements for a parent and a purchased wholly owned subsidiary, assume that as of the close of business December 31, Year 10, Palm Corporation issued 10,000 shares of its common stock (market value $45 per share) for all the outstanding capital stock of Starr Company. Out-of-pocket costs of the combination paid by Palm Corporation on that date consisted of the following:

Finder's fee and legal fees relating to the combination	$50,000
Costs associated with SEC registration statement.	35,000
Total out-of-pocket costs	$85,000

The business combination qualified for purchase accounting; Starr Company is to continue its corporate existence as a wholly owned subsidiary of Palm Corporation. Both companies use the same accounting standards, and no adjusting journal entry is required for either company prior to the business combination. The combined federal and state income tax rates for each company total 60%.

Financial statements of Palm Corporation and Starr Company for the year ended December 31, Year 10, prior to consummation of the business combination, are presented below and on page 168.

	Palm Corporation	Starr Company
Income Statements, Year Ended December 31, Year 10		
Revenue		
Net sales	$ 990,000	$600,000
Interest revenue	10,000	–0–
	$1,000,000	$600,000
Costs and expenses		
Cost of goods sold	$ 635,000	$410,000
Selling, general, and administrative expenses . . .	80,000	30,000
Interest expense	50,000	30,000
Income taxes expense	141,000	78,000
	$ 906,000	$548,000
Net income	$ 94,000	$ 52,000

	Palm Corporation	Starr Company
Statements of Retained Earnings, Year Ended December 31, Year 10		
Retained earnings, Jan. 1, Year 10	$65,000	$100,000
Net income	94,000	52,000
	$159,000	$152,000
Dividends	25,000	20,000
Retained earnings, Dec. 31, Year 10	$134,000	$132,000
Balance Sheets, December 31, Year 10		
Assets		
Cash	$100,000	$ 40,000
Inventories	150,000	110,000
Other current assets	110,000	70,000
Due from Starr Company	25,000	–0–
Property, plant, and equipment (net)	450,000	300,000
Patent	–0–	20,000
	$835,000	$540,000
Liabilities & Stockholders' Equity		
Due to Palm Corporation	$ –0–	$ 25,000
Income taxes payable	66,000	10,000
Other liabilities	285,000	115,000
Common stock, $10 par value	300,000	–0–
Capital stock, $5 par value	–0–	200,000
Paid-in capital in excess of par	50,000	58,000
Retained earnings	134,000	132,000
	$835,000	$540,000

The December 31, Year 10, fair values of Starr Company's identifiable assets and liabilities were the same as their financial statement values, except for the following assets:

	Fair value, Dec. 31, Year 10
Inventories	$135,000
Property, plant, and equipment	365,000
Patent	25,000

Since Starr Company is continuing as a separate corporation and current accounting standards do not sanction write-ups of assets of a going concern, Starr would make no journal entries associated with the business combination. Palm Corporation would record the combination as a purchase at December 31, Year 10, with the following entries:

Investment in Subsidiary (10,000 shares × $45).........	450,000	
Common Stock (10,000 shares × $10)		100,000
Paid-in Capital in Excess of Par		350,000
To record issuance of 10,000 shares of common stock for all the outstanding capital stock of Starr Company in a business combination accounted for as a purchase.		
Investment in Subsidiary	50,000	
Paid-in Capital in Excess of Par...............	35,000	
Cash		85,000
To record payment of out-of-pocket costs of business combination with Starr Company. Finder's and legal fees relating to the combination are recorded as additional costs of the investment; costs associated with the SEC registration statement are recorded as an offset to the previously recorded proceeds from the issuance of common stock.		

The first entry above is similar to the entry illustrated in Chapter 4 (page 132) for a merger accounted for as a purchase. An Investment in Subsidiary account is charged with the fair value of the common stock issued to effect the business combination, and the paid-in capital accounts are credited in the usual manner for any stock issuance. In the second entry, the direct out-of-pocket costs of the combination are also charged to the Investment in Subsidiary account, while the costs associated with the SEC registration statement, being costs of issuing stock, are applied to reduce the gross proceeds of the stock issuance.

Unlike the journal entries for a purchase illustrated in Chapter 4, the above entries do not include any debits or credits to record individual assets and liabilities of Starr Company in the accounts of Palm Corporation. The reason is that Starr Company was not *liquidated* as in a merger; it remains a separate legal entity.

After the preceding journal entries have been posted, the affected financial statement items for Palm Corporation have the following balances:

Cash	$ 15,000
Investment in subsidiary	500,000
Common stock, $10 par value...........................	400,000
Paid-in capital in excess of par	365,000

Consolidating Balance Sheet Purchase accounting for the business combination of Palm Corporation and Starr Company requires a fresh start for the consolidated entity. This reflects the theory that a business combination which meets the requirements for purchase accounting is an *acquisition* of one company's assets (less liabilities) by another company. The operating results of Palm Corporation and Starr Company prior to the date of their business combination are those of two separate *economic*—as well as *legal*—entities. Accordingly, a consolidated balance sheet is the only financial statement issued at December 31, Year 10—the date of the business combination of Palm Corporation and Starr Company.

The consolidating balance sheet working paper and the related working paper showing the consolidation elimination appear below and on page 171.

Purchase: wholly owned subsidiary

PALM CORPORATION AND SUBSIDIARY
Consolidating Balance Sheet
December 31, Year 10

	Palm Corporation	Starr Company	Consolidation eliminations Increase(Decrease)		Consolidated
Assets					
Cash	$ 15,000	$ 40,000			$ 55,000
Inventories	150,000	110,000	(a)	$ 25,000	285,000
Other current assets	110,000	70,000			180,000
Intercompany receivable (payable)	25,000	(25,000)			–0–
Investment in subsidiary	500,000	–0–	(a)	(500,000)	–0–
Property, plant, and equipment	450,000	300,000	(a)	65,000	815,000
Patent	–0–	20,000	(a)	5,000	25,000
Goodwill	–0–	–0–	(a)	15,000	15,000
	$1,250,000	$515,000		$(390,000)	$1,375,000
Liabilities & Stockholders' Equity					
Income taxes payable	$ 66,000	$ 10,000			$ 76,000
Other liabilities	285,000	115,000			400,000
Common stock, $10 par value	400,000	–0–			400,000
Capital stock, $5 par value . .	–0–	200,000	(a)	$(200,000)	–0–
Paid-in capital in excess of par	365,000	58,000	(a)	(58,000)	365,000
Retained earnings	134,000	132,000	(a)	(132,000)	134,000
	$1,250,000	$515,000		$(390,000)	$1,375,000

Purchase: wholly owned subsidiary

PALM CORPORATION AND SUBSIDIARY
Consolidation Elimination
December 31, Year 10

(a) Capital Stock—Starr	200,000	
Paid-in Capital in Excess of Par—Starr	58,000	
Retained Earnings—Starr	132,000	
Inventories—Starr ($135,000 − $110,000)	25,000	
Property, Plant, and Equipment—Starr ($365,000 − $300,000)	65,000	
Patent—Starr ($25,000 − $20,000)	5,000	
Goodwill—Starr ($500,000 − $485,000)	15,000	
Investment in Subsidiary—Palm		500,000

To eliminate intercompany investment and equity accounts of subsidiary at date of business combination; and to allocate excess of
cost over carrying values of identifiable assets acquired, with remainder to goodwill.

The following features of the consolidating balance sheet working
paper at the date of the combination should be emphasized:

1 The consolidating balance sheet and consolidation elimination are working
papers only. The consolidation elimination is not posted to either company's
accounting records.

2 The consolidation elimination is used to reflect differences between fair values
and carrying values of the subsidiary's assets, because the subsidiary does
not write up its assets to fair values.

3 The Consolidation Eliminations column in the consolidating balance sheet
working paper reflects *increases* and *decreases,* rather than *debits* and
credits.

4 Intercompany receivables and payables are placed on the same line of the
consolidating balance sheet working paper and combined to produce consolidated amounts of zero.

5 The respective corporations are clearly identified in the consolidation elimination. The reason for precise identification will be clarified in Chapter 6.

6 The consolidated paid-in capital accounts are those of the parent company
only. Subsidiaries' paid-in capital accounts are *always* eliminated in consolidation.

7 Consolidated retained earnings at the date of the business combination includes only the retained earnings of the parent. This treatment is consistent
with the theory that purchase accounting reflects a fresh start in an acquisition
of assets (less liabilities), not a combining of existing stockholder interests.

Consolidated Balance Sheet The amounts in the Consolidated column of
the consolidating balance sheet working paper are presented in the
customary fashion in the formal consolidated balance sheet of Palm
Corporation and subsidiary.

Pooling of interests: wholly owned subsidiary

For the business combination of Palm Corporation and Starr Company described in preceding pages of this chapter, the following journal entries would be made by Palm Corporation as of December 31, Year 10, to record the combination as a pooling of interests:

Investment in Subsidiary	*390,000*	
Common Stock (10,000 shares × $10)		*100,000*
Paid-in Capital in Excess of Par ($258,000 –		
$100,000)		*158,000*
Retained Earnings of Subsidiary		*132,000*
To record issuance of 10,000 shares of common stock for all the outstanding capital stock of Starr Company in a business combination accounted for as a pooling of interests.		
Selling, General, and Administrative Expenses	*85,000*	
Cash		*85,000*
To record payment of out-of-pocket costs of business combination with Starr Company.		

The first of the preceding entries records Palm Corporation's investment in Starr Company's capital stock at the *carrying value* of Starr's stock on December 31, Year 10 ($200,000 + $58,000 + $132,000 = $390,000). In addition, a Retained Earnings of Subsidiary account is established to record the amount of Starr Company's retained earnings at December 31, Year 10. This separate account emphasizes that Starr Company's retained earnings are not a source of dividends to Palm Corporation shareholders, as is often true in a statutory merger. The first entry thus reflects the underlying theory of pooling accounting—the *combining of stockholder interests* concept—while recognizing the separate corporate identity of the pooled subsidiary.

In the second entry shown above, all out-of-pocket costs of the business combination are recorded as expenses. As explained in Chapter 4, this procedure is required in a pooling of interests.

Although Palm Corporation's expenses are increased in the second entry above, there is no adjustment of Palm's income taxes expense or liability accounts. Costs of a pooling business combination expensed for financial accounting are not deductible for tax purposes. The U.S. Treasury Department considers such costs to be capital expenditures, rather than expenditures which may be deducted when incurred or amortized over a period of years. The Treasury Department's position is contained in regulations for amortizable organizational expenditures.[3]

---

[3] U.S. Treasury Regulations, Section 1.248-1 (b).

After the journal entries on page 172 have been posted, the affected financial statement items for Palm Corporation have the following balances:

Selling, general, and administrative expenses ($80,000 + $85,000) . . .	$165,000
Net Income ($94,000 − $85,000)	9,000
Cash ($100,000 − $85,000)	15,000
Investment in subsidiary	390,000
Common stock, $10 par value ($300,000 + $100,000)	400,000
Paid-in capital in excess of par ($50,000 + $158,000)	208,000
Retained earnings ($134,000 − $85,000)	49,000
Retained earnings of subsidiary	132,000

In a pooling business combination involving a wholly owned subsidiary, the Investment in Subsidiary account is similar to the Branch account illustrated in Chapter 3. However, the subsidiary's three stockholders' equity accounts (which total $390,000), rather than a single Home Office (or Parent Company) account, offset Palm Corporation's Investment in Subsidiary account.

Consolidating Financial Statements When a business combination qualifies for pooling-of-interests accounting, all four basic financial statements are consolidated for the period ended on the date of the combination. This is consistent with the assumption that a pooling is a combining of stockholder interests, rather than an acquisition of assets.

Consolidating financial statements working papers and the related consolidation elimination for Palm Corporation and subsidiary for the year ended December 31, Year 10, are presented below and on pages 174 to 175. All intercompany transactions and balances, including $10,000 interest received during Year 10 by Palm Corporation on its advances to Starr Company, are eliminated in consolidation.

PALM CORPORATION AND SUBSIDIARY
Consolidation Elimination
December 31, Year 10

(a) Capital Stock—Starr	200,000	
Paid-in Capital in Excess of Par—Starr	58,000	
Retained Earnings of Subsidiary—Palm	132,000	
Investment in Subsidiary—Palm		390,000

To eliminate intercompany investment and related accounts for stockholders' equity of subsidiary at date of business combination.

Pooling of interests: wholly owned subsidiary

PALM CORPORATION AND SUBSIDIARY
Consolidating Financial Statements
Year Ended December 31, Year 10

	Palm Corporation	Starr Company	Consolidation eliminations Increase (Decrease)	Consolidated
Income Statement				
Revenue				
Net sales	$ 990,000	$600,000		$1,590,000
Intercompany revenue (expense)	10,000	(10,000)		–0–
	$1,000,000	$590,000		$1,590,000
Cost and expenses				
Cost of goods sold	$ 635,000	$410,000		$1,045,000
Selling, general, and administrative expenses .	165,000	30,000		195,000
Interest expense	50,000	20,000		70,000
Income taxes expense . .	141,000	78,000		219,000
	$ 991,000	$538,000		$1,529,000
Net income	$ 9,000	$ 52,000		$ 61,000
Statement of Retained Earnings				
Retained earnings, Jan. 1, Year 10	$ 65,000	$100,000		$ 165,000
Net income	9,000	52,000		61,000
	$ 74,000	$152,000		$ 226,000
Dividends	25,000	20,000		45,000
Retained earnings, Dec. 31, Year 10	$ 49,000	$132,000		$ 181,000
Balance Sheet				
Assets				
Cash	$ 15,000	$ 40,000		$ 55,000
Inventories	150,000	110,000		260,000
Other current assets	110,000	70,000		180,000
Intercompany receivable (payable)	25,000	(25,000)		–0–
Investment in subsidiary .	390,000	–0–	(a) $(390,000)	–0–
Property, plant, and equipment	450,000	300,000		750,000
Patent	–0–	20,000		20,000
	$1,140,000	$515,000	$(390,000)	$1,265,000

Pooling of interests: wholly owned subsidiary

PALM CORPORATION AND SUBSIDIARY (Continued)
Consolidating Financial Statements
Year Ended December 31, Year 10

	Palm Corporation	Starr Company	Consolidation eliminations Increase (Decrease)	Consolidated
Liabilities & Stockholders' Equity				
Income taxes payable . . .	$ 66,000	$ 10,000		$ 76,000
Other liabilities	285,000	115,000		400,000
Common stock, $10 par				
value	400,000	–0–		400,000
Capital stock, $5 par				
value	–0–	200,000	(a) $(200,000)	–0–
Paid-in capital in excess of				
par	208,000	58,000	(a) (58,000)	208,000
Retained earnings	49,000	132,000		181,000
Retained earnings of sub-				
sidiary	132,000	–0–	(a) (132,000)	–0–
	$1,140,000	$515,000	$(390,000)	$1,265,000

In reviewing the consolidating financial statements working papers for a pooling business combination, the following points should be noted:

1 A separate consolidating statement of changes in financial position is not illustrated at this point in order to focus attention on more fundamental issues. Once the consolidated balance sheet, income statement, and statement of retained earnings are available, a consolidated statement of changes in financial position can be conveniently prepared from comparative consolidated statements and supplementary data relating to depreciation, exchange transactions, etc.

2 Intercompany revenue and expenses are placed on the same line in the consolidating income statement, so that they are automatically eliminated without a formal consolidation elimination. There are no other intercompany items that require use of the Consolidation Eliminations column in the consolidating income statement.

3 Each pair of financial statements is consolidated in turn, in the sequence of the conventional accounting cycle. Thus, consolidated net income is carried forward to the consolidating statement of retained earnings, and consolidated retained earnings is carried forward to the consolidating balance sheet.

4 Dividends declared by Starr Company are not eliminated in the consolidating statement of retained earnings, because the dividends were paid to the former shareholders of Starr Company, not to Palm Corporation.

5 Consolidated retained earnings includes the retained earnings of both Palm Corporation and Starr Company, in accordance with pooling-of-interests accounting theory.

Consolidated Financial Statements   The formal consolidated financial statements for Palm Corporation and subsidiary consist of the amounts in the Consolidated columns of the consolidating financial statements working papers. Since all intercompany transactions and balances have been eliminated in the computation of the consolidated amounts, these balances reflect only the transactions of Palm Corporation and Starr Company with **outside parties.**

There are no unusual features of a consolidated income statement or a consolidated balance sheet in a pooling combination involving a wholly owned subsidiary. However, since a pooling of interests represents an accounting change of the type classified as a **change in the reporting entity,**[4] the consolidated statement of retained earnings of Palm Corporation and subsidiary for the year ended December 31, Year 10, would be as follows:

PALM CORPORATION AND SUBSIDIARY
Consolidated Statement of Retained Earnings
Year Ended December 31, Year 10

Retained earnings, Jan. 1, Year 10		
As previously reported		$ 65,000
Adjustment to reflect pooling of interests with Starr Company		100,000
As restated		$165,000
Net income		61,000
Subtotal		$226,000
Dividends		
Palm Corporation ($0.83⅓ per share)	$25,000	
Starr Company, prior to business combination	20,000	45,000
Retained earnings, Dec. 31, Year 10		$181,000

The "adjustment to reflect pooling of interests with Starr Company" in the preceding statement represents the retroactive application of the pooling-of-interests accounting method to include Starr Company's beginning-of-year retained earnings of $100,000 with the retained earnings of Palm Corporation at the beginning of the year.

CONSOLIDATION OF PARTIALLY OWNED SUBSIDIARIES AT DATE OF BUSINESS COMBINATION

The consolidation of a parent and its partially owned subsidiary differs from the consolidation of a wholly owned subsidiary in one major respect—the recognition of minority interest. **Minority interest** is a term

[4]*APB Opinion No. 20,* "Accounting Changes," AICPA (New York: 1971), p. 388.

applied to the claims of shareholders other than the parent against the net income and net assets of the subsidiary. The minority interest in the subsidiary's net income is reported in the consolidated income statement, while the minority interest in the subsidiary's net assets is reported in the consolidated balance sheet.

Purchase: partially owned subsidiary

To illustrate the consolidation techniques for a purchase business combination involving a partially owned subsidiary, assume the following facts. At the close of business April 30, Year 6, Post Corporation issued 57,000 shares of its common stock (market value $20 per share) in exchange for 38,000 of the 40,000 outstanding shares of Sage Company's capital stock. Thus, Post acquired a 95% interest in Sage. Out-of-pocket costs of the business combination, paid in cash by Post Corporation April 30, Year 6, were as follows:

Finder's fee and legal fees relating to the combination	$ 52,250
Costs associated with SEC registration statement	72,750
Total out-of-pocket costs	$125,000

Financial statements of Post Corporation and Sage Company for the year ended April 30, Year 6, prior to consummation of the business combination, are presented on page 178. There were no intercompany transactions prior to the combination.

The April 30, Year 6, fair values of Sage Company's identifiable assets and liabilities were the same as their financial statement values except for the following assets:

	Fair value, Apr. 30, Year 6
Inventories	$ 526,000
Property, plant, and equipment	1,290,000
Leasehold	30,000

Post Corporation would record the business combination with Sage Company at April 30, Year 6, as a purchase by means of the two journal entries shown at the top of page 179.

Posting the entries shown at the top of page 179 yields the following new balances for Post Corporation:

Cash ($200,000 − $125,000)	$ 75,000
Investment in subsidiary ($1,140,000 + $52,250)	1,192,250
Common stock, $1 par value ($1,000,000 + $57,000)	1,057,000
Paid-in capital in excess of par ($550,000 + $1,083,000 − $72,750) . .	1,560,250

	Post Corporation	Sage Company
Income Statements, Year Ended April 30, Year 6		
Net sales	$5,500,000	$1,000,000
Costs and expenses		
Cost of goods sold	$3,850,000	$ 650,000
Selling, general, and administrative expenses	600,000	100,000
Interest expense	75,000	40,000
Income taxes expense	585,000	126,000
	$5,110,000	$ 916,000
Net income	$ 390,000	$ 84,000
Statements of Retained Earnings, Year Ended April 30, Year 6		
Retained earnings, May 1, Year 5	$ 810,000	$ 250,000
Net income	390,000	84,000
	$1,200,000	$ 334,000
Dividends	150,000	–0–
Retained earnings, Apr. 30, Year 6	$1,050,000	$ 334,000
Balance Sheets, April 30, Year 6		
Assets		
Cash	$ 200,000	$ 100,000
Inventories	800,000	500,000
Other current assets	550,000	215,000
Property, plant, and equipment (net)	3,500,000	1,100,000
Goodwill	100,000	–0–
	$5,150,000	$1,915,000
Liabilities & Stockholders' Equity		
Income taxes payable	$ 100,000	$ 76,000
Other liabilities	2,450,000	870,000
Common stock, $1 par value	1,000,000	–0–
Capital stock, $10 par value	–0–	400,000
Paid-in capital in excess of par	550,000	235,000
Retained earnings	1,050,000	334,000
	$5,150,000	$1,915,000

Investment in Subsidiary (57,000 shares × $20)	1,140,000	
Common Stock (57,000 shares × $1)		57,000
Paid-in Capital in Excess of Par		1,083,000

To record issuance of 57,000 shares of common stock for 38,000 of the 40,000 outstanding shares of Sage Company in a business combination accounted for as a purchase.

Investment in Subsidiary	52,250	
Paid-in Capital in Excess of Par	72,750	
Cash		125,000

To record payment of out-of-pocket costs of business combination with Sage Company.

Consolidating Balance Sheet The consolidation elimination is presented below and the consolidating balance sheet working paper at April 30, Year 6, for Post Corporation and subsidiary appears on page 180.

POST CORPORATION AND SUBSIDIARY
Consolidation Elimination
April 30, Year 6

(a) Capital Stock—Sage	400,000	
Paid-in Capital in Excess of Par—Sage	235,000	
Retained Earnings—Sage	334,000	
Inventories—Sage ($526,000 − $500,000)	26,000	
Property, Plant, and Equipment—Sage ($1,290,000 − $1,100,000)	190,000	
Leasehold—Sage ($30,000 − $0)	30,000	
Goodwill—Sage ($1,255,000 − $1,215,000)	40,000	
Investment in Subsidiary—Post		1,192,250
Minority Interest in Subsidiary		62,750

To eliminate intercompany investment and equity accounts of subsidiary at date of business combination; to allocate excess of cost over carrying values of identifiable assets acquired, with remainder to goodwill; and to establish minority interest in subsidiary at date of business combination (5% × $1,255,000 = $62,750).

Purchase: partially owned subsidiary

POST CORPORATION AND SUBSIDIARY
Consolidating Balance Sheet
April 30, Year 6

	Post Corporation	Sage Company	Consolidation eliminations Increase (Decrease)	Consolidated
Assets				
Cash	$ 75,000	$ 100,000		$ 175,000
Inventories	800,000	500,000	(a)$ 26,000	1,326,000
Other current assets	550,000	215,000		765,000
Investment in subsidiary	1,192,250	–0–	(a)(1,192,250)	–0–
Property, plant, and equip-				
ment	3,500,000	1,100,000	(a) 190,000	4,790,000
Leasehold	–0–	–0–	(a) 30,000	30,000
Goodwill	100,000	–0–	(a) 40,000	140,000
	$6,217,250	$1,915,000	$ (906,250)	$7,226,000
Liabilities & Stockholders' Equity				
Income taxes payable	$ 100,000	$ 76,000		$ 176,000
Other liabilities	2,450,000	870,000		3,320,000
Minority interest in subsidiary	–0–	–0–	(a)$ 62,750	62,750
Common stock, $1 par value	1,057,000	–0–		1,057,000
Capital stock, $10 par value	–0–	400,000	(a) (400,000)	–0–
Paid-in capital in excess of				
par	1,560,250	235,000	(a) (235,000)	1,560,250
Retained earnings	1,050,000	334,000	(a) (334,000)	1,050,000
	$6,217,250	$1,915,000	$ (906,250)	$7,226,000

The April 30, Year 6, consolidation elimination for Post Corporation and subsidiary reflects a computational technique inherent in the *entity theory* of consolidated financial statements (discussed in a subsequent section of this chapter). This technique is founded on the premise that the cost of an investment in a partially owned subsidiary *implies* a fair value for the total net assets of the subsidiary. Thus, dividing the $1,192,250 total cost of Post Corporation's investment in Sage Company by Post's 95% ownership of Sage's stock yields an implied value of $1,255,000 for Sage's total net assets. The minority shareholders' 5% interest in the $1,255,000 implied value is $62,750. The $1,255,000 implied value of Sage Company's total net assets, reduced by the $1,215,000 aggregate fair value of Sage Company's identifiable net assets, yields a $40,000 imputed valuation for goodwill of Sage.

An alternative position, taken by proponents of the *parent company theory* of consolidated financial statements (also discussed in a subsequent section of this chapter), is that goodwill in a business combination involving a partially owned subsidiary should be valued at the difference between the parent company's investment in subsidiary and the parent's share of the aggregate fair values of the subsidiary's identifiable net assets. Applying this technique to the Post Corporation–Sage Company business combination would yield the following:

Cost of Post Corporation's 95% interest in Sage Company	*$1,192,250*
95% of $1,215,000 aggregate fair values of Sage Company's net assets	*1,154,250*
Goodwill	*$ 38,000*

Under this parent company approach, the goodwill is an asset of the parent company rather than of the subsidiary; and the minority interest is computed as the appropriate percentage of the fair values of the subsidiary's identifiable net assets. Thus Sage Company's minority interest would be computed as 5% of $1,215,000, or $60,750, under the parent company theory.

The differences between the two approaches are not usually significant, as indicated by the following amounts for the Post Corporation–Sage Company business combination:

	Entity theory	Parent company theory
Goodwill	$40,000	$38,000
Minority interest	62,750	60,750

In the opinion of the authors, the entity theory approach illustrated in the consolidation elimination on page 179 is the more defensible of the two methods. This approach recognizes the implied *total* fair value of the *acquired subsidiary's* goodwill—a position consistent with purchase accounting's requirement for a determination of fair values for the subsidiary's *identifiable* net assets. The attribution of computed goodwill to the parent company—inherent in the parent company theory—is difficult to reconcile with the overall framework of purchase accounting theory. Accordingly, the entity theory approach for valuing goodwill and minority interest in a partially owned subsidiary will be stressed throughout this book.

Pooling of interests: partially owned subsidiary

Post Corporation's April 30, Year 6, journal entries to record the business combination with Sage Company as a pooling of interests are presented below:

Investment in Subsidiary (95% × $969,000)	920,550	
Common Stock		57,000
Paid-in Capital in Excess of Par		
[(95% × $635,000) − $57,000]		546,250
Retained Earnings of Subsidiary (95% × $334,000) . .		317,300
To record issuance of 57,000 shares of common stock for 38,000 of the 40,000 outstanding shares of Sage Company in a business combination accounted for as a pooling of interests.		
Selling, General, and Administrative Expenses	125,000	
Cash		125,000
To record payment of out-of-pocket costs of business combination with Sage Company.		

Note that the first of the above entries records Post Corporation's **95% share** of the net assets and retained earnings of Sage Company.

As pointed out on page 172, costs of a business combination expensed for financial accounting are not deductible or amortizable for income taxes. Thus, although the second of the above entries increases Post Corporation's expenses, Post's income taxes expense and liability accounts are not adjusted. The costs of the business combination represent a **permanent difference,** rather than a **timing difference,** between Post's pretax accounting income and taxable income. There is no income tax advantage to a pooling corporation for costs of the business combination, just as a purchasing corporation receives no tax benefits from the amortization of purchased goodwill.

After the preceding entries have been posted, Post Corporation's relevant financial statement items have the following balances:

Selling, general, and administrative expenses ($600,000 + $125,000)	$ 725,000
Net income ($390,000 − $125,000)	265,000
Cash ($200,000 − $125,000)	75,000
Investment in subsidiary	920,550
Common stock ($1,000,000 + $57,000)	1,057,000
Paid-in capital in excess of par ($550,000 + $546,250)	1,096,250
Retained earnings ($1,050,000 − $125,000)	925,000
Retained earnings of subsidiary	317,300

Consolidating Financial Statements Fiscal Year 6 consolidating financial statements working papers and related consolidation eliminations for Post Corporation and subsidiary are set forth below and on page 184.

Pooling of interests: partially owned subsidiary

POST CORPORATION AND SUBSIDIARY
Consolidating Financial Statements
Year Ended April 30, Year 6

	Post Corporation	Sage Company	Consolidation eliminations Increase (Decrease)	Consolidated
Income Statement				
Net sales	$5,500,000	$1,000,000		$6,500,000
Costs and expenses				
Cost of goods sold	$3,850,000	$ 650,000		$4,500,000
Selling, general, and administrative expenses .	725,000	100,000		825,000
Interest expense	75,000	40,000		115,000
Income taxes expense . .	585,000	126,000		711,000
Minority interest in net income of subsidiary . . .	–0–	–0–	(b)$ 4,200	4,200
	$5,235,000	$ 916,000	$ 4,200	$6,155,200
Net income	$ 265,000	$ 84,000	$(4,200)	$ 344,800
Statement of Retained Earnings				
Retained earnings, May 1, Year 5	$ 810,000	$ 250,000	(a) $(12,500)	$1,047,500
Net income	265,000	84,000	(4,200)	344,800
	$1,075,000	$ 334,000	$(16,700)	$1,392,300
Dividends	150,000	–0–		150,000
Retained earnings, Apr. 30, Year 6	$ 925,000	$ 334,000	$(16,700)	$1,242,300
Balance Sheet				
Assets				
Cash	$ 75,000	$ 100,000		$ 175,000
Inventories	800,000	500,000		1,300,000
Other current assets	550,000	215,000		765,000
Investment in subsidiary .	920,550	–0–	(a) $(920,550)	–0–
Property, plant, and equipment	3,500,000	1,100,000		4,600,000
Goodwill	100,000	–0–		100,000
	$5,945,550	$1,915,000	$(920,550)	$6,940,000

Pooling of interests: partially owned subsidiary

POST CORPORATION AND SUBSIDIARY (Continued)
Consolidating Financial Statements
Year Ended April 30, Year 6

	Post Corporation	Sage Company	Consolidation eliminations Increase (Decrease)	Consolidated
Liabilities & Stockholders' Equity				
Income taxes payable . . .	$ 100,000	$ 76,000		$ 176,000
Other liabilities	2,450,000	870,000		3,320,000
Minority interest in subsidiary	–0–	–0–	(a) $ 44,250 (b) 4,200	48,450
Common stock, $1 par value	1,057,000	–0–	–0–	1,057,000
Capital stock, $10 par value	–0–	400,000	(a) (400,000)	–0–
Paid-in capital in excess of par	1,096,250	235,000	(a) (235,000)	1,096,250
Retained earnings	925,000	334,000	(16,700)	1,242,300
Retained earnings of subsidiary	317,300	–0–	(a) (317,300)	–0–
	$5,945,550	$1,915,000	$(920,550)	$6,940,000

POST CORPORATION AND SUBSIDIARY
Consolidation Eliminations
April 30, Year 6

(a) Capital Stock—Sage	400,000	
Paid-in Capital in Excess of Par—Sage	235,000	
Retained Earnings—Sage (5% × $250,000)	12,500	
Retained Earnings of Subsidiary—Post	317,300	
Investment in Subsidiary—Post		920,550
Minority Interest in Subsidiary		44,250

To eliminate intercompany investment and establish
minority interest in subsidiary at beginning of year
[5% × ($400,000 + $235,000 + $250,000) = $44,250].

(b) Minority Interest in Net Income of Subsidiary	4,200	
Minority Interest in Subsidiary		4,200

To establish minority interest in net income of subsidiary
(5% × $84,000 = $4,200).

The following should be stressed in review of the consolidating financial statements working papers of Post Corporation and subsidiary under the pooling theory:

1 The $4,200 charge (debit) to Minority Interest in Net Income of Subsidiary—consolidation elimination (*b*)—is posted to the consolidating income statement; the $12,500 debit to Retained Earnings of Sage Company is posted to the **beginning-of-year** line in the consolidating statement of retained earnings. All consolidation eliminations which affect consolidating statements other than the consolidating balance sheet are posted directly to the appropriate consolidating statements.

2 As in the previously illustrated consolidating financial statements working papers in this chapter, the net income totals of the consolidating income statement are brought forward intact to the consolidating statement of retained earnings, while the end-of-year retained earnings balances in the latter statement are forwarded to the consolidating balance sheet.

3 The combined effect of the $12,500 and $4,200 debit entries of consolidation eliminations (*a*) and (*b*) is to include in consolidated retained earnings only Post Corporation's 95% interest in the end-of-year retained earnings of Sage Company. Thus, total consolidated retained earnings at April 30, Year 6, is composed of the following:

Retained earnings of Post Corporation	$ 925,000
Retained earnings of Sage Company (95% × $334,000)	317,300
Consolidated retained earnings	$1,242,300

4 The combined effect of the $44,250 and $4,200 credit entries of consolidation eliminations (*a*) and (*b*) is to reflect the minority interest in subsidiary at April 30, Year 6, ($48,450) at its correct amount of 5% of Sage Company's total stockholders' equity ($400,000 + $235,000 + $334,000 = $969,000) at that date.

Consolidated Financial Statements   The consolidated financial statements for Post Corporation and subsidiary incorporate the amounts in the Consolidated columns of the consolidating financial statements working papers. The consolidated statement of retained earnings would be in the form illustrated on page 176 for Palm Corporation and Subsidiary.

Nature of Minority Interest   The appropriate classification and presentation of minority interest in the consolidated income statement and balance sheet has been a perplexing problem for accountants. Over the years, two theories for consolidated financial statements have been developed to account for minority interest—the **parent company theory** and the **entity theory.** One authority has described these two theories as follows:

> The "parent company" concept views consolidated statements as an extension of parent company statements, in which the investment account of the parent is replaced by the individual assets and liabilities underlying the parent's investment, and subsidiaries are viewed as almost the equivalent of

branches. When subsidiary ownership is not complete, the consolidation process segregates the minority interest in the partially owned subsidiary. The *minority interest is considered to be an outside group and a liability as far as the parent shareholder group is concerned.*

. . . .

In contrast to the parent company concept, the "entity" concept views consolidated statements as those of an economic entity with *two classes of proprietary interest*—the major or dominant interest and the minority interest. It holds that in consolidation these interests should be treated consistently. The consolidated statements are not viewed as an extension of parent company statements; rather, they are viewed as an expression of the financial position and operating results of a distinct "consolidated entity" consisting of a number of related companies whose relationship arises from common control (based on powers conferred by share ownership). When related companies are viewed as parts of such an entity, the minority interest, instead of representing an accountability to an outside group by the parent, represents *"a part of capital"*.[5]

As indicated in the preceding quotation, the parent company theory of consolidated financial statements treats the minority interest in net assets of a subsidiary as a **liability.** *This liability is increased each accounting period by an expense representing the minority's share of the subsidiary's net income* (or decreased by the minority's share of the subsidiary's net loss). *Dividends paid by the subsidiary to minority shareholders decrease the liability to them. Consolidated net income is* **net** *of the minority's share of the subsidiary's net income.*

In the entity theory, the minority interest in the subsidiary's net assets is included in the stockholders' equity section of the consolidated balance sheet. *The consolidated income statement presents the minority interest in the subsidiary's net income as a subdivision of total consolidated* net income. Thus, for Post Corporation and subsidiary, a condensed consolidated income statement for the year ended April 30, Year 6, would appear as follows *under the entity theory:*

Net sales	$6,500,000
Costs and expenses	6,151,000
Net income	$ 349,000
Distribution of net income	
To majority interest	$ 344,800
To minority interest in subsidiary (5% × $84,000)	4,200
Total net income	$ 349,000

In the authors' opinion, the entity theory of consolidated financial statements overemphasizes the **legal aspects** of the separate corporate

[5] *Consolidated Financial Statements,* Accountants International Study Group (Plaistow, England: 1973), p. 7.

organizations comprising a parent-subsidiary relationship. In substance, minority shareholders are a special class of creditors of the consolidated entity, for in the usual case they exercise *no ownership control whatsoever* over the operations of either parent or subsidiary. If consolidated financial statements are to present clearly the operating results and financial position of a single economic entity, the niceties of minority shareholders' nominal ownership of a part of the subsidiary should be ignored. Consequently, the parent company theory of accounting for minority interest in subsidiary will be stressed throughout this book.

Footnote disclosure of consolidation policy

The "Summary of Significant Accounting Policies" footnote required by *APB Opinion No. 22,* "Disclosure of Accounting Policies," should include a description of consolidation policy reflected in consolidated financial statements. The following excerpt from a recent annual report of Eastman Kodak Company is typical:

> *Basis of Consolidation*—The consolidated financial statements include the accounts of all subsidiary companies. Intercompany transactions are eliminated and net earnings are reduced by the portion of the earnings of subsidiaries applicable to minority share owners. The excess of the cost of investments in subsidiaries acquired since 1965, over the value ascribed to the company's equity in such subsidiaries at the time of acquisition, is amortized over the succeeding 15-year period.

Advantages and shortcomings of consolidated financial statements

Consolidated financial statements are useful principally to stockholders and prospective investors of the parent. These users of consolidated financial statements are provided with comprehensive financial information concerning the economic unit represented by the parent corporation and its subsidiaries, without regard for legal separateness of the affiliates.

Creditors of all consolidated corporations and minority shareholders of subsidiaries find only limited use for consolidated financial statements, because such statements do not show the financial position or operating results of the individual companies comprising the consolidated group. In addition, creditors of the constituent companies cannot ascertain the asset coverages for their respective claims. But perhaps the most telling criticism of consolidated financial statements in recent years has come from financial analysts. These critics have pointed out that consolidated financial statements of a highly diversified corporate group are impossible to categorize into a single industry or product classification. Thus, say the financial analysts, consolidated financial statements of a conglomerate cannot be used for comparative purposes. The problem of financial reporting by diversified organizations will be considered further in Chapter 9.

REVIEW QUESTIONS

1 The use of consolidated financial statements for reporting to stockholders is common. Under some conditions, however, it is the practice to exclude a subsidiary from consolidation. List the conditions under which a subsidiary is often excluded from consolidated financial statements.

2 Early in Year 1, Lindley Corporation exchanged 10,000 shares of its own $20 par value common stock for 90% of the outstanding capital stock of Jubilee Company.
  a The principal limitation of consolidated financial statements is their lack of separate information about the assets, liabilities, revenue, and expenses of the individual companies included in the consolidation. List the problems which the reader of consolidated financial statements encounters as a result of this limitation.
  b Depending upon the accompanying circumstances, the combination of Lindley Corporation and Jubilee Company may be accounted for as a purchase or as a pooling of interests. Discuss the differences between (1) a consolidated balance sheet prepared for a *purchase* and (2) a consolidated balance sheet prepared for a *pooling of interests.*

3 What criteria could influence a parent in its decision to include or exclude, a subsidiary in consolidated financial statements? Explain.

4 Discuss the similarities and dissimilarities between:
  a Consolidated financial statements for parent and subsidiary corporations, and
  b Combined financial statements for segments of a single legal entity.

5 Compare the *parent company theory* and the *entity theory* of consolidated financial statements as they relate to the classification of minority interest in the consolidated income statement and the consolidated balance sheet.

6 Explain the purpose of the account entitled Retained Earnings of Subsidiary.

7 For the year ended October 31, Year 2, Staley Company had net income of $60,000. As of the close of business that date, Pryor Corporation acquired most of the outstanding capital stock of Staley Company in exchange for Pryor's previously unissued common stock.
  Consolidation eliminations for the year ended October 31, Year 2, included the following:

Minority Interest in Net Income of Subsidiary   1,200
  Minority Interest in Subsidiary   1,200

  a Was the business combination of Pryor Corporation and Staley Company accounted for as a purchase or as a pooling of interests? Explain.
  b What percentage of Staley Company's outstanding capital stock was exchanged for Pryor Corporation common stock? Explain.

8 Are consolidation eliminations recorded in the accounting records of the parent company or of the subsidiary? Explain.

9 If a business combination resulting in a parent-subsidiary relationship is accounted for as a purchase, the identifiable net assets of the subsidiary must be reflected at their fair values in the consolidated balance sheet at the date of the business combination. Does this require the subsidiary to record the fair values in its accounting records? Explain.

10 The retained earnings balances of Pelham Corporation and Skeene Company at September 30, Year 5, were $1,000,000 and $800,000, respectively. At the close of business that date Skeene Company became a subsidiary of Pelham Corporation when Pelham acquired 96% of Skeene's outstanding capital stock.

What is the amount of consolidated retained earnings in the consolidated balance sheet of Pelham Corporation and subsidiary at September 30, Year 5, if the business combination is accounted for as:

a A purchase? Explain.
b A pooling of interests? Explain.

11 The controller of Premier Corporation, which has just become the parent of Screed Company in a purchase-type business combination, inquires if a consolidated statement of changes in financial position is required for the year ended on the date of the combination. What is your reply? Explain.

EXERCISES

Ex. 5-1 Select the best answer for each of the following multiple-choice questions.

1 Consolidated financial statements are used to present the results of operations and the financial position of:
a A company and its branches.
b A company and its subcontractors.
c A company and its subsidiaries.
d Any group of companies with related interests.
e None of the above.

2 Consolidated financial statements are intended primarily for the benefit of:
a Stockholders of the parent company.
b Taxing authorities.
c Management of the parent company.
d Creditors of the parent company.
e None of the above.

3 Consolidated financial statements for X, Y, and Z are proper if:
a X owns 100% of the outstanding common stock of Y and 49% of Z; Q owns 51% of Z.
b X owns 100% of the outstanding common stock of Y; Y owns 75% of Z.
c X owns 100% of the outstanding common stock of Y and 75% of Z; X bought the stock of Z one month before the statement date and sold it six weeks later.
d There is no interrelation of financial control among X, Y, and Z. However, they are contemplating the joint purchase of 100% of the outstanding common stock of W.
e X owns 100% of the outstanding common stock of Y and Z. Z is in bankruptcy.

4 P's cost of investment in M exceeded its equity in the fair values of M's identifiable net assets at the business combination date. The excess is not attributable to specific assets. In the consolidated balance sheet, this excess should be:
a Eliminated.
b Allocated proportionately to M's plant and equipment.
c Shown on the balance sheet as a deferred charge.
d Shown on the balance sheet as goodwill.
e None of the above.

5 P's cost of investment in J was less than its equity in the fair values of J's identifiable net assets at the acquisition date. The difference is related to the

decline in productivity of J's machinery. In the consolidated balance sheet, this difference should be shown as:
a A reduction in machinery.
b Part of consolidated paid-in capital in excess of par.
c Part of consolidated retained earnings.
d Negative goodwill.
e None of the above.

6 Negative goodwill is:
a Acceptable terminology for financial statement purposes.
b Subtracted from goodwill, if any, for financial reporting purposes.
c A deferred credit which should be amortized.
d Also known as "excess of cost over fair values of identifiable net assets."
e None of the above.

Ex. 5-2 Presented below are the January 1, Year 3, balance sheets of two companies prior to their business combination:

	Palace Corporation	Slayton Company
Assets		
Cash	$ 3,000	$ 100
Inventory (at fifo cost, which approximates fair value)	2,000	200
Property, plant, and equipment (net)	5,000	700*
	$10,000	$1,000
Liabilities & Stockholders' Equity		
Current liabilities	$ 600	$ 100
Common stock, $1 par value	1,000	100
Paid-in capital in excess of par	3,000	200
Retained earnings	5,400	600
	$10,000	$1,000

*Fair value at Jan. 1, Year 3, is $1,500.

1 On January 1, Year 3, Palace Corporation acquires all the outstanding common stock of Slayton Company by issuing 200 shares of Palace Corporation common stock (market value $10 per share) in a business combination qualifying for pooling-of-interests accounting. In the January 1, Year 3, consolidated balance sheet for Palace Corporation and subsidiary, paid-in capital in excess of par is:
a $3,000.   b $3,100.   c $3,200.   d $3,900.

2 On January 1, Year 3, Palace Corporation acquires all the outstanding common stock of Slayton Company by paying $2,000 cash in a business combination qualifying for purchase accounting. In the January 1, Year 3, consolidated balance sheet for Palace Corporation and subsidiary, goodwill is:
a $200.   b $900.   c $1,100.   d $300.

3 On January 1, Year 3, Palace Corporation acquires all the outstanding common stock of Slayton Company by paying $1,500 cash in a business combination qualifying for purchase accounting. In the January 1, Year 3, consolidated balance sheet for Palace Corporation and subsidiary, the carrying value of property, plant, and equipment is:
a $5,700.   b $6,500.   c $6,300.   d $6,700.

Ex. 5-3 On December 31, Year 4, the balance sheet of Sears Company included stock-holders' equity of $1,000,000. As of the close of business that date, Pierce Corporation obtained for cash a controlling financial interest in the outstanding capital stock of Sears Company. If the December 31, Year 4, fair values of Sears Company's identifiable net assets totaled $1,200,000 and goodwill under the entity theory of consolidated financial statements was correctly computed as $90,000, how much cash did Pierce Corporation pay for its interest in Sears Company if it owns:

a 100% of Sears capital stock? *1,290,000 = 1,290,000 + 90,000*
b 90% of Sears capital stock? *1,170,000*
c 80% of Sears capital stock? *1,050,000*

Ex. 5-4 The working paper consolidation elimination at August 31, Year 5, for the consolidating balance sheet of Pacer Corporation and Sensor Company is set forth below. As of the close of business that date, Pacer Corporation acquired most of the outstanding capital stock of Sensor Company for cash.

PACER CORPORATION AND SUBSIDIARY
Consolidation Elimination
August 31, Year 5

Capital Stock—Sensor	60,000	
Paid-in Capital in Excess of Par—Sensor	35,250	
Retained Earnings—Sensor	50,100	
Inventories—Sensor	3,900	
Property, Plant, and Equipment—Sensor	28,500	
Patent—Sensor	4,500	
Goodwill—Sensor	6,000	
Investment in Subsidiary—Pacer		165,660
Minority Interest in Subsidiary		22,590

To eliminate intercompany investment and equity accounts of subsidiary at date of business combination; to allocate excess of cost over fair values of identifiable net assets acquired to goodwill; and to establish minority interest in subsidiary at date of business combination—all in accordance with entity theory of consolidated financial statements.

    Answer the following questions (supporting computations should be in good form):

a What percentage of the outstanding capital stock of the subsidiary was acquired by the parent company?
b What was the aggregate fair value of the subsidiary's identifiable net assets at August 31, Year 5?
c What value would be assigned to goodwill under the parent company theory of consolidated financial statements?
d What value would be assigned to minority interest in subsidiary under the parent company theory of consolidated financial statements?

Ex. 5-5 The condensed individual and consolidated balance sheets of Parish Corporation and its subsidiary, Spartan Company, as of the date of their business combination appear on page 192.

PARISH CORPORATION AND SUBSIDIARY
Individual and Consolidated Balance Sheets
June 30, Year 3

	Parish Corporation	Spartan Company	Consolidated
Assets			
Cash	$ 100,000	$ 40,000	$ 140,000
Inventories	500,000	90,000	610,000
Other current assets	250,000	60,000	310,000
Investment in subsidiary	390,600	–0–	–0–
Property, plant, and equipment (net) . .	1,000,000	360,000	1,440,000
Goodwill	100,000	–0–	100,000
	$2,340,600	$550,000	$2,600,000
Liabilities & Stockholders' Equity			
Income taxes payable	$ 40,000	$ 35,000	$ 75,000
Other liabilities	580,600	195,000	775,600
Minority interest in subsidiary	–0–	–0–	29,400
Common or capital stock	1,000,000	200,000	1,000,000
Paid-in capital in excess of par	400,000	210,000	400,000
Retained earnings (deficit)	320,000	(90,000)	320,000
	$2,340,600	$550,000	$2,600,000

a Was the business combination of Parish Corporation and Spartan Company accounted for as a purchase or as a pooling of interests? Explain.

b Reconstruct in good form, including a complete explanation, the June 30, Year 3, working paper consolidation elimination indicated by the above data.

Ex. 5-6 Select the best answer for each of the following multiple-choice questions.

1 On the consolidated balance sheet of a parent company and its only subsidiary two different types of goodwill may be reflected: (1) ordinary goodwill and (2) goodwill from consolidation. The second type:

a Should be combined with the first type and both should be eliminated.

b Reflects the fact that the subsidiary was acquired at a price in excess of the fair value of its identifiable net assets.

c Reflects the fact that the subsidiary already had goodwill in the accounts.

d Reflects the fact that the subsidiary was acquired at a bargain price.

2 Consolidated financial statements are **not** appropriate if:

a The subsidiary is in legal reorganization.

b The minority interest is small.

c The subsidiary has a large bonded indebtedness to outsiders.

d The parent company buys nothing from the subsidiary.

3 Arkin, Inc., owns 90% of the outstanding stock of Baldwin Company. Curtis, Inc., owns 10% of the outstanding stock of Baldwin Company. On the consolidated financial statements of Arkin, Inc., Curtis, Inc., should be considered as:

a A holding company.

b A subsidiary not to be consolidated.

c An affiliate.

d A minority interest.

4 Consolidated financial statements are proper for Neely, Inc., Randle, Inc., and Walker, Inc., if:

a Neely owns 80% of the outstanding common stock of Randle and 40% of Walker; Randle owns 30% of Walker.

b Neely owns 100% of the outstanding common stock of Randle and 90% of Walker; Neely bought the stock of Walker one month before the balance sheet date and sold it seven weeks later.

c Neely owns 100% of the outstanding common stock of Randle and Walker; Walker is in legal reorganization.

d Neely owns 80% of the outstanding common stock of Randle and 40% of Walker; Reeves, Inc., owns 55% of Walker.

SHORT CASES FOR ANALYSIS AND DECISION

Case 5-1 The minority interest in a subsidiary might be presented several ways on the consolidated balance sheet. Discuss the propriety of reporting the minority interest on the consolidated balance sheet:

a As a liability.

b As a part of stockholders' equity.

c In a separate classification between liabilities and stockholders' equity.

Case 5-2 Because of irreconcilable differences of opinion, a dissenting group within the board of directors and management of Ames Company resigned and formed Blake Corporation to purchase a manufacturing division of Ames Company. After negotiation of the agreement but just before the closing and actual transfer of the property, a minority shareholder of Ames notified Blake that a prior stockholders' agreement with Ames empowered him to prevent the sale. The minority shareholder's claim was acknowledged by Blake's board of directors. Blake's board then organized Cane, Inc., to acquire the minority shareholder's interest in Ames for $75,000, and Blake advanced the cash to Cane. Blake exercised control over Cane as a subsidiary corporation with common directors and officers. Cane paid the minority shareholder $75,000 (about twice the market value of his Ames stock) for his interest in Ames. Blake then purchased the manufacturing division from Ames.

Instructions

a Should the financial statements of Blake Corporation and Cane, Inc., be consolidated? Discuss.

b Assume that unconsolidated financial statements are prepared. Discuss the propriety of treating the $75,000 expenditure in the financial statements of Blake Corporation as:

(1) An account receivable from Cane, Inc.

(2) An investment in Cane, Inc.

(3) Part of the cost of property, plant, and equipment

(4) A loss

Case 5-3 In Year 6 Pasadena Corporation, a chain of discount stores, embarked upon a program of business combinations with its suppliers. On May 31, Year 6, the close of its fiscal year, Pasadena Corporation paid $8,500,000 cash and issued 100,000 shares of its common stock (market value $20 per share) for all 10,000 outstanding shares of capital stock of Sylmar Company. Sylmar Company was a furniture manufacturer whose products were featured in Pasadena Corporation's stores. Total stockholders' equity of Sylmar Company on May 31, Year 6, was $9,000,000. Out-of-pocket costs attributable to the business combination itself (as opposed to the SEC registration statement for the 100,000 shares of Pasadena Corporation common stock) paid by Pasadena Corporation May 31, Year 6, totaled $100,000.

In the consolidated balance sheet of Pasadena Corporation and subsidiary at May 31, Year 6, the $1,600,000 difference between the parent's cost and the subsidiary's net assets was allocated in accordance with purchase accounting as follows:

Inventory	$ 250,000
Property, plant, and equipment	850,000
Patents	300,000
Goodwill	200,000
Excess of cost over subsidiary's net assets	$1,600,000

Under terms of the indenture for a $1,000,000 debenture liability of Sylmar Company, Pasadena Corporation is obligated to maintain Sylmar Company as a separate corporation and to issue a separate balance sheet for Sylmar each May 31. Pasadena Corporation's controller contends that Sylmar Company's balance sheet for May 31, Year 6, should show net assets of $10,600,000—their cost to Pasadena Corporation. Sylmar Company's controller disputes this valuation, claiming that generally accepted accounting standards require issuance of a *historical cost* balance sheet for Sylmar Company at May 31, Year 6.

Instructions
a Present arguments in favor of the Pasadena controller's position.
b Present arguments in favor of the Sylmar controller's position.
c Which position do you approve? Explain.

PROBLEMS

5-4 Presented below is the consolidating statement of retained earnings working paper for Plane Corporation and subsidiary for the year ended the date Plane Corporation exchanged its common stock for 92% of the outstanding capital stock of Steele Company in a pooling business combination.

PLANE CORPORATION AND SUBSIDIARY
Consolidating Statement of Retained Earnings
Year Ended March 31, Year 7

	Plane Corporation	Steele Company		Consolidation eliminations Increase (Decrease)	Consolidated
Retained earnings,					
Apr. 1, Year 6 .	$100,000	$50,000	(a)	$(4,000)	$146,000
Net income	60,000	40,000		(3,200)	96,800
	$160,000	$90,000		$(7,200)	$242,800
Dividends	20,000	–0–			20,000
Retained earnings,					
Mar. 31, Year 7	$140,000	$90,000		$(7,200)	$222,800

Prior to the business combination with Steele Company, Plane Corporation had 100,000 shares of common stock outstanding for many years.

Instructions Prepare in good form a consolidated statement of retained earnings for Plane Corporation and subsidiary for the year ended March 31, Year 7.

5-5 As of the close of business September 30, Year 1, Pyne Corporation issued 100,000 shares of its $5 par value common stock (market value $12 per share) for 18,800 shares of the outstanding $20 par value capital stock of Seine Company. The $150,000 out-of-pocket costs of the business combination paid by Pyne Corporation on September 30, Year 1, were allocable as follows: 60% to legal fees and finder's fee directly related to the combination, and 40% to the SEC registration statement for Pyne Corporation common stock issued in the business combination.

Immediately prior to the business combination, stockholders' equity accounts of the two companies were as follows:

	Pyne Corporation	Seine Company
Common stock or capital stock	$4,000,000	$ 400,000
Paid-in capital in excess of par	1,500,000	–0–
Retained earnings	3,000,000	700,000
Total stockholders' equity	$8,500,000	$1,100,000

Income tax effects, if any, may be ignored.

Instructions Prepare in good form Pyne Corporation's journal entries to record the business combination with Seine Company:
a As a purchase
b As a pooling of interests

5-6 Individual statements of retained earnings for Prosser Corporation and Starrett Company for the year ended May 31, Year 2 (prior to their business combination), are set forth below.

PROSSER CORPORATION AND STARRETT COMPANY
Statements of Retained Earnings
Year Ended May 31, Year 2

	Prosser Corporation	Starrett Company
Retained earnings, June 1, Year 1	$500,000	$290,000
Net income	100,000	80,000
Subtotal	$600,000	$370,000
Dividends	40,000	25,000
Retained earnings, May 31, Year 2	$560,000	$345,000

As of the close of business May 31, Year 2, Prosser Corporation issued 50,000 shares of its $1 par value common stock for 54,600 of the 60,000 outstanding shares of $3 par value capital stock of Starrett Company. Total paid-in capital attributable to Starrett's stock was $7 per share. The $80,000 out-of-pocket costs of the business combination, which qualified for pooling-of-interests accounting, were paid by Prosser Corporation on May 31, Year 2. Each company had an effective combined federal and state income tax rate of 60%. There were no intercompany transactions prior to the date of the business combination.

Instructions Compute the following in good form:
a Minority interest in net income of Starrett Company for the year ended May 31, Year 2.
b Consolidated net income for Prosser Corporation and subsidiary for the year ended May 31, Year 2.
c Minority interest in net assets of Starrett Company at May 31, Year 2.
d Consolidated retained earnings for Prosser Corporation and subsidiary at May 31, Year 2.

5-7 The chief accountant of Pollard Corporation prepared the following general journal entries as of March 31, Year 8:

Investment in Subsidiary	783,000	
Minority Interest in Subsidiary	16,000	
Common Stock		49,000
Paid-in Capital in Excess of Par of Subsidiary		300,000
Retained Earnings of Subsidiary		450,000

To record issuance of 4,900 shares of $10 par value common stock for 9,800 of 10,000 outstanding shares of Stark Company $5 par value capital stock in a business combination qualifying for pooling-of-interests accounting; to bring forward Stark Company's Paid-in Capital in Excess of Par and Retained Earnings accounts at their balances in Stark's accounting records; and to provide for minority interest in Stark Company's net assets ($800,000) on March 31, Year 8.

Investment in Subsidiary	80,000	
Paid-in Capital in Excess of Par	70,000	
Cash		150,000

To record payment of out-of-pocket costs of business combination with Stark Company, as follows:

Finder's fee and legal fees relating to the combination	$80,000
Costs associated with SEC registration statement . .	70,000
Total out-of-pocket cost	$150,000

Instructions Prepare adjusting journal entries, in good form, to correct Pollard Corporation's accounting for its business combination with Stark Company on March 31, Year 8. Ignore income taxes.

5-8 On July 31, Year 10, Poole Corporation issued 20,000 shares of its $2 par value common stock (market value $10 per share) for all 5,000 shares of outstanding $5 par value capital stock of Sharpe Company, which is to remain a separate corporation. Out-of-pocket costs of the business combination, paid by Poole Corporation on July 31, Year 10, are shown on page 197.

Finder's fee and legal fees relating to the business combination	$20,000
Costs associated with SEC registration statement for Poole Corporation	
stock	10,000
Total out-of-pocket costs of business combination	$30,000

Sharpe Company's condensed balance sheet at July 31, Year 10, prior to the business combination, follows:

SHARPE COMPANY

Balance Sheet

July 31, Year 10

Assets

Current assets	$150,000
Property, plant, and equipment (net)	300,000
Goodwill	20,000
	$470,000

Liabilities & Stockholders' Equity

Current liabilities	$120,000
Long-term debt	200,000
Capital stock, $5 par value	25,000
Paid-in capital in excess of par...................	50,000
Retained earnings	75,000
	$470,000

Sharpe Company's goodwill arose in Sharpe's July 31, Year 4, purchase of the net assets of Thorpe Company.

Sharpe Company's assets and liabilities having July 31, Year 10, fair values different from their balance sheet values were as follows:

	Fair value	Balance sheet value
Inventories	$ 65,000	$ 60,000
Property, plant, and equipment	340,000	300,000
Long-term debt	190,000	200,000

There were no intercompany transactions prior to the business combination.

Instructions

a Prepare Poole Corporation's general journal entries at July 31, Year 10, in good form, to record the business combination with Sharpe Company as a:
(1) Purchase
(2) Pooling of interests (Disregard income tax considerations.)

b Prepare the consolidation eliminations, in good form, for consolidating financial statements working papers of Poole Corporation and subsidiary at July 31, Year 10, assuming the business combination was accounted for as a:
(1) Purchase
(2) Pooling of interests

H-23-7

5-9 On October 31, Year 4, Portsmouth Corporation acquired 93% of the outstanding capital stock of Stillwater Company in exchange for 50,000 shares of Portsmouth's $2 par value ($10 market value per share) common stock. Out-of-pocket costs of the business combination paid by Portsmouth Corporation on October 31, Year 4, were as follows:

Legal fees and finder's fee relating to the business combination	$34,750
Costs associated with SEC registration statement for Portsmouth Corporation stock	55,250
Total out-of-pocket costs of business combination	$90,000

There were no intercompany transactions between the two companies prior to the business combination. Stillwater Company is to be a subsidiary of Portsmouth Corporation.

Individual financial statements of the two companies prior to the business combination are presented below and at the top of page 199.

	Portsmouth Corporation	Stillwater Company
Income Statements, Year Ended October 31, Year 4		
Net sales	$1,500,000	$ 800,000
Costs and expenses		
Cost of goods sold	$1,000,000	$ 480,000
Selling, general, and administrative expenses	150,000	80,000
Interest expense	50,000	25,000
Income taxes expense	180,000	129,000
	$1,380,000	$ 714,000
Net income	$ 120,000	$ 86,000
Statements of Retained Earnings, Year Ended October 31, Year 4		
Retained earnings, Nov. 1, Year 3	$ 560,000	$ 250,000
Net income	120,000	86,000
	$ 680,000	$ 336,000
Dividends	50,000	–0–
Retained earnings, Oct. 31, Year 4	$ 630,000	$ 336,000
Balance Sheets, October 31, Year 4		
Assets		
Cash	$ 250,000	$ 150,000
Inventories	860,000	600,000
Other current assets	500,000	260,000
Property, plant, and equipment (net)	3,400,000	1,500,000
Patents	–0–	80,000
	$5,010,000	$2,590,000

Liabilities & Stockholders' Equity

Income taxes payable	$ 40,000	$ 60,000
Other current liabilities	390,000	854,000
Long-term debt	950,000	1,240,000
Common stock, $2 par value	1,500,000	–0–
Capital stock, $10 par value	–0–	100,000
Paid-in capital in excess of par	1,500,000	–0–
Retained earnings	630,000	336,000
	$5,010,000	$2,590,000

Other information

(1) Fair values of Stillwater Company's identifiable net assets were the same as their carrying values at October 31, Year 4, except for the following:

Inventories	$ 620,000
Property, plant, and equipment	1,550,000
Patents	95,000
Long-term debt	1,225,000

(2) Income taxes, if any, may be ignored.

Instructions

a Prepare Portsmouth Corporation's general journal entries at October 31, Year 4, in good form, to record the business combination with Stillwater Company as a:
(1) Purchase
(2) Pooling of interests

b Prepare the working paper consolidation eliminations, in good form, for October 31, Year 4, consolidating financial statements of Portsmouth Corporation and subsidiary, assuming the business combination was accounted for as a:
(1) Purchase
(2) Pooling of interests

6

Consolidated financial statements: subsequent to date of business combination

Subsequent to the date of a business combination, a parent and its subsidiaries may enter into a number of business transactions with each other. In addition, the parent must account for the operating results and dividend declarations of its subsidiaries. Both parent and subsidiary companies should account for these intercompany transactions in a manner which facilitates the consolidation process. To this end, separate ledger accounts should be established for all intercompany assets, liabilities, revenue, and expenses. These separate accounts clearly identify those intercompany items which must be eliminated for consolidated financial statements. Finally, the parent company should adopt either the *equity method* or the *cost method* of accounting for the subsidiary's operating results.

The accounting techniques described above are designed to assure that consolidated financial statements include only those balances and transactions resulting from the consolidated group's dealings with *outsiders.* In this chapter we shall deal with these issues of accounting for intercompany transactions.

INTERCOMPANY TRANSACTIONS AND BALANCES

Among the numerous types of transactions (other than dividends) consummated between a parent and its subsidiaries are the following:

Sales of merchandise (inventory)
Sales of land or depreciable assets
Sales of intangible assets
Loans on notes or open account
Leases of real or personal property
Rendering of professional services

The first three types of transactions listed above usually involve an element of profit or loss, which complicates the preparation of consolidated financial statements. Discussion of these intercompany transactions is deferred until Chapter 7.

Loans on notes or open account

Parent corporations generally have more extensive financial resources or bank lines of credit than do their subsidiaries. Also, it may be more economical in terms of favorable interest rates for the parent to carry out *all* of the affiliated group's borrowings from financial institutions. Under these circumstances, the parent will make loans to its subsidiaries for their working capital or other needs. Generally, the rate of interest on such loans exceeds the parent's borrowing rate.

To illustrate, assume that during the year ended December 31, Year 11, Palm Corporation (see Chapter 5, pages 167–168) made the following cash loans to its wholly owned subsidiary, Starr Company, on formal promissory notes:

Date of note	Term of note, months	Interest rate, %	Amount
Feb. 1, Year 11	6	10	$10,000
Apr. 1, Year 11	6	10	15,000
Sept. 1, Year 11	6	10	21,000
Nov. 1, Year 11	6	10	24,000

To properly differentiate between intercompany loans and loans with outsiders, Palm Corporation and Starr Company would use the accounts shown on page 202 to record the above note transactions (assuming all notes were paid when due).

In consolidating financial statements working papers for Palm Corporation and subsidiary for the year ended December 31, Year 11, the

Palm Corporation				Starr Company		
Intercompany Notes Receivable				**Intercompany Notes Payable**		
Feb. 1	10,000	Aug. 1	10,000	Aug. 1	10,000	Feb. 1	10,000
Apr. 1	15,000	Oct. 1	15,000	Oct. 1	15,000	Apr. 1	15,000
Sept. 1	21,000					Sept. 1	21,000
Nov. 1	24,000					Nov. 1	24,000

Intercompany Interest Receivable				**Intercompany Interest Payable**		
Dec. 31	1,100					Dec. 31	1,100

Intercompany Interest Revenue				**Intercompany Interest Expense**		
		Aug. 1	500	Aug. 1	500		
		Oct. 1	750	Oct. 1	750		
		Dec. 31	1,100	Dec. 31	1,100		

accounts illustrated above would appear as follows:

	Palm Corporation	Starr Company	Consolidation eliminations	Consolidated
Income Statement				
Revenue				
Intercompany revenue				
(expenses)	$ 2,350	$ (2,350)		$ –0–
Balance Sheet				
Assets				
Intercompany receiv-				
ables (payables) . .	$46,100	$(46,100)		$ –0–

It is apparent from the above illustration that careful identification of intercompany transactions and balances in the accounting records of the affiliated companies is essential for correct elimination of the intercompany items in the consolidating financial statements working papers.

Discounting of Intercompany Notes If an intercompany note receivable is discounted by the holder, the note in effect is payable to an *outsider*—the discounting bank. Consequently, discounted intercompany notes are *not eliminated* in consolidating financial statements working papers.

Suppose, for example, that on December 1, Year 11, Palm Corporation had discounted the $24,000 note receivable from Starr Company at a 12% discount rate. Palm would make the following general journal entry:

Cash	23,940	
Interest Expense	260	
Intercompany Notes Receivable		24,000
Intercompany Interest Revenue		200

To record discounting of 10%, six-month note receivable from Starr Company dated Nov. 1, Year 11 at a discount rate of 12%. Cash proceeds computed as $25,200 maturity value of note, less $1,260 discount ($25,200 × 12% × 5 months).

The above entry records intercompany interest revenue for the one month the note was held by Palm Corporation. This approach is required because Starr Company will reflect in its accounts one month of intercompany interest expense on the note.

To assure proper accountability for the $24,000 note, Palm Corporation should notify Starr Company of the discounting. Starr Company would then record the following general journal entry at December 1, Year 11:

Intercompany Notes Payable	24,000	
Intercompany Interest Expense	200	
Notes Payable		24,000
Interest Payable		200

To transfer 10%, six-month note payable to Palm Corporation dated Nov. 1, Year 11, from intercompany notes to outsider notes. Action is necessary because Palm Corporation discounted the note on this date.

In the preceding entry, Starr Company credited Interest Payable rather than Intercompany Interest Payable for the $200 accrued interest on the note. This approach is required because the *discounting bank,* not Palm Corporation, is now the payee for the *total maturity value* of the note.

Under the note discounting assumption, the accounts related to intercompany notes would appear in the December 31, Year 11, consolidating financial statements working papers as follows:

	Palm Corporation	Starr Company	Consolidation eliminations	Consolidated
Income Statement				
Revenue				
Intercompany revenue				
(expenses)	$ 2,150*	$ (2,150)*		$ –0–
Balance Sheet				
Assets				
Intercompany receivables				
(payables)	$21,700†	$(21,700)†		$ –0–

*$200 less than in illustration on page 202 because $24,000 discounted note earned interest for one month rather than two months.
†$21,000 note dated Sept. 1, Year 11, plus $700 accrued interest thereon.

Leases of real or personal property

If a parent leases real or personal property to a subsidiary, or vice versa, it is essential that both affiliates use the same accounting principles for the lease. If the lease is an *operating lease*,[1] the lessor affiliate should account for rental payments as revenue, and the lessee affiliate should record the payments as expense. For a *financing lease*,[1] the lessor affiliate should record a sale of the real or personal property, and the lessee affiliate should account for the lease as an installment purchase of the property. Accounting for a financing lease often involves intercompany profits or losses, which are discussed in Chapter 7.

To illustrate consolidation techniques for an intercompany *operating lease,* assume that Palm Corporation leases space for a sales office to Starr Company under a 10-year lease dated February 1, Year 11. The lease requires monthly rentals of $2,500 payable in advance the first day of each month beginning February 1, Year 11.

In the consolidating income statement working papers for the year ended December 31, Year 11, Palm Corporation's $27,500 rent revenue would be offset against Starr Company's rent expense in a manner similar to the offset of intercompany interest illustrated previously. There are no intercompany assets or liabilities to be offset in an operating lease with rent payable in advance.

Rendering of professional services

One affiliate may render various professional services to another, with resultant intercompany fee revenue and expenses. A common example is the *management fee* charged by a parent company to its subsidiaries.

[1] The accounting for operating leases and financing leases is included in *Intermediate Accounting* of this series.

The object of this fee is to reimburse the parent company for managerial advice and supervision rendered to the subsidiaries.

Management fees are often billed monthly by the parent, computed as a percentage of the subsidiary's net sales, number of employees, total assets, or some other measure. No new consolidation problems are introduced by intercompany fee revenue and expenses. However, care must be taken that both the parent and the subsidiary record the fee billings in the same accounting period, since the billings are issued typically a few days after the end of the month.

Income taxes applicable to intercompany transactions

The intercompany revenue and expense transactions illustrated in this chapter do not include an element of intercompany profit or loss for the consolidated entity. This is true because the revenue of one affiliate exactly offsets the expense of the other affiliate in the consolidating income statement working papers. As a consequence, there are no income tax effects associated with the elimination of the intercompany revenue and expenses, whether the parent and its subsidiaries file separate income tax returns or a consolidated return.

Summary: Intercompany transactions and balances

The preceding sections have emphasized the necessity of clearly identifying intercompany transactions and balances in the accounting records of both parent and subsidiary. This careful identification facilitates the elimination of intercompany items for consolidated financial statements. Sometimes, the separate financial statements of parent and subsidiary companies include differing balances for intercompany items which should offset. Before preparing consolidating financial statements working papers, the accountant should make any necessary adjusting journal entries to correct intercompany balances.

ACCOUNTING FOR OPERATING RESULTS
OF SUBSIDIARIES

In accounting for the operating results of subsidiaries, a parent company may select one of two methods—the *equity method* or the *cost method.*[2] In the equity method, the parent company reflects in its accounting records its share of the subsidiary's net income or net loss, as well as dividends declared by the subsidiary. In the cost method, the parent accounts for the operations of the subsidiary only to the extent dividends are declared by the subsidiary. Net income or net loss of the subsidiary

---

[2] *Intermediate Accounting* of this series contains an extended discussion of the equity method and the cost method.

is *not* recognized in the accounting records of a parent using the cost method. Thus, the equity method stresses the *economic substance* of the parent and subsidiary relationship; the two companies constitute a single economic entity for accounting purposes. The cost method, however, emphasizes the *legal form* of the relationship between parent and subsidiary, that is, that the two companies are separate legal entities.

Choosing between equity method and cost method

Consolidated financial statement balances will be the same, regardless of whether a parent company uses the equity method or the cost method to account for a subsidiary's operations. However, the consolidation eliminations used in the two methods are different, as illustrated in subsequent sections of this chapter.

It should be pointed out, however, that the equity method of accounting is appropriate for both *pooled* subsidiaries and *purchased* subsidiaries. The cost method, on the other hand, is compatible with *purchase accounting* only. In purchase accounting, the parent's original investment in the subsidiary is recorded at *cost.* Hence, accounting for operating results of purchased subsidiaries by the cost method may be considered a logical extension of purchase accounting. In pooling accounting, however, the parent company's investment at the date of the combination is recorded at the carrying value of the subsidiary's net assets. As a result, the parent's investment account reflects the parent's equity in the subsidiary's net assets at the date of the combination. The equity method of accounting for a pooled subsidiary's operations is thus consistent with pooling accounting.

Illustration of equity method of accounting

In the remainder of this chapter, we shall first illustrate the equity method of accounting and consolidating financial statements working papers for a wholly owned *pooled* subsidiary. Then we shall illustrate both the equity method and the cost method of accounting for a partially owned *purchased* subsidiary, together with the related consolidating financial statements working papers.

Equity Method: Wholly Owned Pooled Subsidiary Assume that Palm Corporation's wholly owned pooled subsidiary, Starr Company (see Chapter 5, pages 172–175), reported net income of $60,000 for the year ended December 31, Year 11. Assume further that Starr's board of directors on December 20, Year 11, declared a cash dividend of $0.60 per share on the 40,000 outstanding shares of Starr Company capital stock. The dividend was payable January 8, Year 12, to stockholders of record December 29, Year 11.

Under the equity method of accounting, Palm Corporation would make the following general journal entries to record the operating results of Starr Company for the year ended December 31, Year 11:

Intercompany Dividends Receivable (40,000 shares × $0.60). .	24,000	
Investment in Subsidiary		24,000
To record dividend declared by Starr Company, payable Jan. 8, Year 12 to stockholders of record Dec. 29, Year 11.		
Investment in Subsidiary	60,000	
Intercompany Investment Income		60,000
To record 100% of Starr Company's net income for the year ended Dec. 31, Year 11.		

The income tax effects of Palm Corporation's accrual of its share of Starr Company's net income are not dealt with at this time. Income tax allocation problems associated with all aspects of parent and subsidiary accounting are considered in Chapter 8.

After the preceding entries are posted, Palm Corporation's Investment in Subsidiary account appears as follows:

Investment in Subsidiary			
Dec. 31, Year 10	390,000	Dec. 29, Year 11	24,000
Dec. 31, Year 11	60,000		

The $426,000 balance of Palm Corporation's Investment in Subsidiary account at December 31, Year 11, exactly offsets the stockholder's equity accounts of Starr Company at that date (see Starr Company's December 31, Year 11, balance sheet on page 209), as follows:

Starr Company's stockholder's equity accounts:	
Capital stock, $5 par value	$200,000
Paid-in capital in excess of par	58,000
Retained earnings	168,000
Total stockholder's equity of Starr Company	$426,000

The Investment in Subsidiary account thus reflects Palm Corporation's 100% interest in the net assets of Starr Company at Starr's carrying value.

In this way, the equity method of accounting is consistent with pooling-of-interests accounting theory.

Consolidating financial statements Condensed consolidating financial statements working papers and the related consolidation elimination for Palm Corporation and subsidiary for the year ended December 31, Year 11, are presented below and on page 209. The intercompany receivables and payables and intercompany revenue and expenses include those illustrated earlier in this chapter for intercompany loans (pages 201–202) and intercompany leases (page 204). (The advances by Palm Corporation to Starr Company which were outstanding at December 31, Year 10, were repaid by Starr January 2, Year 11.) Also included in intercompany receivables and payables is the $24,000 dividend payable by Starr Company to Palm Corporation at December 31, Year 11.

PALM CORPORATION AND SUBSIDIARY
Consolidation Elimination
December 31, Year 11

(a) Capital Stock—Starr	200,000	
Paid-in Capital in Excess of Par—Starr	58,000	
Retained Earnings of Subsidiary—Palm	132,000	
Intercompany Investment Income—Palm	60,000	
Investment in Subsidiary—Palm		426,000
Dividends—Starr		24,000

To eliminate intercompany investment related accounts for stockholders' equity of subsidiary, and investment income from subsidiary.

In reviewing the consolidating financial statements working papers for Palm Corporation and subsidiary, these points should be observed:

1 The following intercompany revenue and expenses are placed on the same line of the consolidating income statement so that they automatically eliminate:

Intercompany interest (page 202)	$ 2,350
Intercompany rent (page 204)	27,500
Total intercompany revenue and expenses	$29,850

2 The intercompany receivables and payables at the top of page 210 also automatically eliminate.

Equity method: wholly owned pooled subsidiary

PALM CORPORATION AND SUBSIDIARY
Consolidating Financial Statements
Year Ended December 31, Year 11

	Palm Corporation	Starr Company	Consolidation Eliminations Increase (Decrease)	Consolidated
Income Statement				
Revenue				
Net sales	$1,100,000	$680,000		$1,780,000
Intercompany investment income	60,000	–0–	(a) $ (60,000)	–0–
Intercompany revenue (expenses)	29,850	(29,850)		–0–
	$1,189,850	$650,150	$ (60,000)	$1,780,000
Costs and expenses				
Cost of goods sold	$ 700,000	$450,000		$1,150,000
Selling, general, and administrative	180,850	50,150		231,000
Interest expense	49,000	–0–		49,000
Income taxes	120,000	90,000		210,000
	$1,049,850	$590,150		$1,640,000
Net income	$ 140,000	$ 60,000	$ (60,000)	$ 140,000
Statement of Retained Earnings				
Retained earnings, Jan. 1, Year 11	$ 49,000	$132,000		$ 181,000
Net income	140,000	60,000	$ (60,000)	140,000
	$ 189,000	$192,000	$ (60,000)	$ 321,000
Dividends	30,000	24,000	(a) (24,000)	30,000
Retained earnings, Dec. 31, Year 11	$ 159,000	$168,000	$ (36,000)	$ 291,000
Balance Sheet				
Assets				
Intercompany receivables (payables)	$ 70,100	$(70,100)		$ –0–
Investment in subsidiary	426,000	–0–	(a) $(426,000)	–0–
Other assets	703,900	650,100		1,354,000
	$1,200,000	$580,000	$(426,000)	$1,354,000
Liabilities & Stockholders' Equity				
Liabilities	$ 301,000	$154,000		$ 455,000
Common stock, $10 par value	400,000	–0–		400,000
Capital stock, $5 par value	–0–	200,000	(a) $(200,000)	–0–
Paid-in capital in excess of par	208,000	58,000	(a) (58,000)	208,000
Retained earnings	159,000	168,000	(36,000)	291,000
Retained earnings of subsidiary	132,000	–0–	(a) (132,000)	–0–
	$1,200,000	$580,000	$(426,000)	$1,354,000

Intercompany loans and accrued interest (page 202)	$46,100
Intercompany dividend	24,000
Total intercompany receivables and payables	$70,100

3 The consolidation elimination cancels *all* intercompany transactions and balances not dealt with by the two offsets described above.

4 *Consolidated net income* is the same as the *parent company's net income.* Also, *consolidated retained earnings* is equal to the total of the *parent company's* two retained earnings accounts, as demonstrated below:

Palm Corporation's accounts:	
Retained earnings	$159,000
Retained earnings of subsidiary	132,000
Total (equal to consolidated retained earnings)	$291,000

This equality is a direct result of Palm Corporation's use of the equity method of accounting for Palm's investment in Starr Company.

5 Despite the equalities indicated above, *consolidated financial statements* are superior to *parent company financial statements* in presenting financial position and operating results of parent and subsidiary companies. The effect of the consolidating income statement for Palm Corporation and subsidiary is to reclassify Palm's $60,000 share of its subsidiary's net income into the revenue and expense components of that net income. Similarly, Palm's $426,000 investment in the subsidiary is reclassified by the consolidating balance sheet into the assets and liabilities comprising the subsidiary's net assets.

6 The consolidation elimination cancels the parent's Retained Earnings of Subsidiary account, because it carries a balance equal to the subsidiary's retained earnings *at the beginning of the year.* Only in this manner can each of the three sets of financial statements (income statement, statement of retained earnings, and balance sheet) be consolidated in turn.

Closing entries The equity method of accounting ignores legal form in favor of the economic substance of the relationship between a parent and its subsidiary. However, state corporation laws necessitate a careful accounting for retained earnings available for dividends. Accordingly, Palm Corporation should make the following condensed closing entry at December 31, Year 11:

Net Sales	1,100,000	
Intercompany Investment Income	60,000	
Intercompany Revenue	29,850	
Costs and Expenses		1,049,850
Retained Earnings of Subsidiary		36,000
Retained Earnings ($140,000 − $36,000)		104,000

To close revenue and expense accounts; to transfer net income legally available for dividends to retained earnings; and to segregate 100% share of net income of subsidiary not distributed as dividends by subsidiary.

The above entry excludes from Palm Corporation's retained earnings the amount of Palm's recorded net income not available for dividends to Palm's shareholders—$36,000. This amount is computed as follows:

Net income of Starr Company recorded by Palm Corporation	$60,000
Less: Dividends paid by Starr Company to Palm Corporation	24,000
Amount of Starr Company's net income not distributed to Palm Corporation	$36,000

In addition, the closing entry illustrated above increases Palm's Retained Earnings of Subsidiary account as follows:

Balance before closing entry	$132,000
Amount of closing entry	36,000
Balance after closing entry (agrees with Starr Company's ending retained earnings)	$168,000

Equity Method: Partially Owned Purchased Subsidiary The Post Corporation–Sage Company consolidated entity described in Chapter 5 (pages 177–180) will be used to illustrate the equity method of accounting for the operating results of a partially owned purchased subsidiary.

Assume that during the year ended April 30, Year 7, Post Corporation and Sage Company had no intercompany loans or leases, but that Sage Company agreed to pay Post Corporation a management fee of 1% of annual net sales. Assume further that Sage Company on March 24, Year 7, declared a $1 per share dividend payable April 16, Year 7, to common shareholders of record April 1, Year 7; and that Sage Company reported net income of $90,000 for the year ended April 30, Year 7.

The following general journal entries would record the above transactions in Sage Company's accounts:

Dividends (40,000 shares × $1).	40,000	
Dividends Payable		2,000
Intercompany Dividends Payable		38,000

To record declaration of dividend payable Apr. 16, Year 7 to stockholders of record Apr. 1, Year 7. Dividend to minority stockholders: $40,000 × 5% = $2,000; dividend to parent company = $40,000 × 95% = $38,000.

Dividends Payable	2,000	
Intercompany Dividends Payable	38,000	
Cash		40,000

To record payment of dividend declared Mar. 24, Year 7 to stockholders of record Apr. 1, Year 7.

Intercompany Management Fee Expense	11,000	
Intercompany Accounts Payable		11,000

To accrue management fee to Post Corporation for year ended Apr. 30, Year 7: 1% × $1,100,000 net sales = $11,000.

Post Corporation would make the following entries:

Intercompany Dividends Receivable	38,000	
Investment in Subsidiary		38,000

To record dividend declared by Sage Company, payable Apr. 16, Year 7 to stockholders of record Apr. 1, Year 7.

Cash	38,000	
Intercompany Dividends Receivable		38,000

To record receipt of dividend from Sage Company.

Intercompany Accounts Receivable	11,000	
Intercompany Management Fee Revenue		11,000

To accrue management fee from Sage Company for year ended Apr. 30, Year 7.

Investment in Subsidiary	85,500	
Intercompany Investment Income		85,500

To record 95% of net income of Sage Company for the year ended Apr. 30, Year 7: $90,000 × 95% = $85,500. (Income tax consequences are ignored.)

The above entries are similar to those of the pooled subsidiary illustrated in a preceding section of this chapter. However, a *purchase* business combination involves a restatement of net asset values of the subsidiary, as illustrated in Chapter 5. Sage Company's reported net income of $90,000 does not reflect cost expirations attributable to Sage's restated asset values, *because the restatements were not reflected in Sage's accounts.*

As a consequence, the $286,000 difference between the implied value of 100% of Sage Company's net assets at date of the business combination ($1,255,000—see page 180) and the $969,000 carrying value of those net assets must be accounted for by Post Corporation. Assume, as in Chapter 5, that the $286,000 difference was allocable to Sage's assets as follows:

Inventories		$ 26,000
Property, plant, and equipment:		
Land	$60,000	
Building (20-year remaining useful life)	80,000	
Machinery and equipment (5-year remaining useful life) . .	50,000	190,000
Leasehold (6-year remaining useful life)		30,000
Goodwill (40-year useful life)		40,000
Total		$286,000

Post Corporation would make the following additional entry to reflect the effects of the above on Sage Company's reported net income for the year ended April 30, Year 7:

Intercompany Investment Income	43,700	
Investment in Subsidiary		43,700
To amortize differences between Sage Company's assets' fair		
values and carrying values at Apr. 30, Year 6:		
Inventory—to cost of good sold	$26,000	
Building—depreciation $\frac{1}{20}$ × $80,000	4,000	
Machinery and equipment—depreciation $\frac{1}{5}$ ×		
$50,000	10,000	
Leasehold—amortization $\frac{1}{6}$ × $30,000	5,000	
Goodwill—amortization $\frac{1}{40}$ × $40,000	1,000	
Total difference applicable to Year 7	$46,000	
Amortization for Year 7: $46,000 × 95%	$43,700	

The income tax effects of Post Corporation's entries to the Intercompany Investment Income account are discussed in Chapter 8.

After the preceding entries are posted, Post Corporation's Investment in Subsidiary and Intercompany Investment Income accounts appear as follows:

Investment in Subsidiary

Apr. 30, Year 6	*1,192,250*	*Mar. 24, Year 7*	*38,000*
Apr. 30, Year 7	*85,500*	*Apr. 30, Year 7*	*43,700*

Intercompany Investment Income

Apr. 30, Year 7	*43,700*	*Apr. 30, Year 7*	*85,500*

The $41,800 balance in Post Corporation's Intercompany Investment Income account represents 95% of the $44,000 adjusted net income ($90,000 − $46,000) of Sage Company for the year ended April 30, Year 7. The $1,196,050 balance in Post's Investment in Subsidiary account may be analyzed as follows:

95% × $1,255,000 implied value of Sage Company's net assets at date of business combination, Apr. 30, Year 6	*$1,192,250*
95% × $44,000 adjusted net income of Sage Company for year ended Apr. 30, Year 7	*41,800*
Subtotal	*$1,234,050*
Less: Dividend received from Sage Company Apr. 16, Year 7: 95% × $40,000	*38,000*
Balance at Apr. 30, Year 7	*$1,196,050*

Consolidating financial statements   Condensed consolidating financial statements working papers and the related consolidation eliminations for Post Corporation and subsidiary for the year ended April 30, Year 7, are presented on pages 215–217.

The following aspects of the consolidating financial statements and consolidation eliminations should be emphasized:

1 Three assumptions underlie the first consolidation elimination. First, the fifo method of inventory accounting is used by Sage Company. Thus, the $26,000 difference attributable to Sage's beginning inventory is allocable to cost of good sold. Second, Sage's building depreciation and goodwill amortization are allocable equally to cost of good sold and to selling, general, and administrative expenses. Third, Sage's machinery and equipment depreciation and leasehold amortization are allocable solely to cost of goods sold.

2 Income tax effects of the first consolidation elimination's increase of Sage Company's expenses are not included in the elimination. In Chapter 8, all aspects of income tax accounting in consolidated financial statements will be considered.

Equity method: partially owned purchased subsidiary

POST CORPORATION AND SUBSIDIARY
Consolidating Financial Statements
Year Ended April 30, Year 7

	Post Corporation	Sage Company	Consolidation Eliminations Increase (Decrease)		Consolidated
Income Statement					
Revenue					
Net sales	$5,600,000	$1,100,000			$6,700,000
Intercompany investment income	41,800	-0-	(a) $	(41,800)	-0-
Intercompany revenue (expenses)	11,000	(11,000)			-0-
	$5,652,800	$1,089,000	$	(41,800)	$6,700,000
Costs and expenses					
Cost of goods sold	$3,925,000	$ 700,000	(a) $	43,500	$4,668,500
Selling, general, and adminis-					
trative expenses	556,000	129,000	(a)	2,500	687,500
Interest and income taxes	710,000	170,000			880,000
Minority interest in net income					
of subsidiary	-0-	-0-	(b)	2,200	2,200
	$5,191,000	$ 999,000	$	48,200	$6,238,200
Net income	$ 461,800	$ 90,000	$	(90,000)	$ 461,800
Statement of Retained Earnings					
Retained earnings, May 1, Year 6	$1,050,000	$ 334,000	(a) $	(334,000)	$1,050,000
Net income	461,800	90,000		(90,000)	461,800
	$1,511,800	$ 424,000	$	(424,000)	$1,511,800
Dividends	158,550	40,000	(a)	(40,000)	158,550
Retained earnings, Apr. 30, Year 7	$1,353,250	$ 384,000	$	(384,000)	$1,353,250
Balance Sheet					
Assets					
Intercompany receivables (payables)	$ 11,000	$ (11,000)			$ -0-
Inventories	850,000	450,000			1,300,000
Other current assets	639,000	371,000			1,010,000
Investment in subsidiary	1,196,050	-0-	(a)	$(1,196,050)	-0-
Property, plant, and equipment	3,600,000	1,150,000	(a)	176,000	4,926,000
Leasehold	-0-	-0-	(a)	25,000	25,000
Goodwill	95,000	-0-	(a)	39,000	134,000
	$6,391,050	$1,960,000	$	(956,050)	$7,395,000
Liabilities & Stockholders' Equity					
Liabilities	$2,420,550	$ 941,000			$3,361,550
Minority interest in subsidiary	-0-	-0-	(a) $	60,750	
			(b)	2,200	62,950
Common stock, $1 par value	1,057,000	-0-			1,057,000
Capital stock, $10 par value	-0-	400,000	(a)	(400,000)	-0-
Paid-in capital in excess of par	1,560,250	235,000	(a)	(235,000)	1,560,250
Retained earnings	1,353,250	384,000		(384,000)	1,353,250
	$6,391,050	$1,960,000	$	(956,050)	$7,395,000

POST CORPORATION AND SUBSIDIARY
Consolidation Eliminations
April 30, Year 7

(a) Capital Stock—Sage 400,000

Paid-in Capital in Excess of Par—Sage 235,000

Retained Earnings—Sage 334,000

Intercompany Investment Income—Post 41,800

Property, Plant, and Equipment—Sage ($190,000 –
$14,000) 176,000

Leasehold—Sage ($30,000 – $5,000) 25,000

Goodwill—Sage ($40,000 – $1,000) 39,000

Cost of Goods Sold—Sage 43,500

Selling, General, and Administrative Expenses—Sage . . 2,500

    Investment in Subsidiary—Post   1,196,050

    Dividends—Sage   40,000

    Minority Interest in Subsidiary   60,750

To carry out the following:

(1) Eliminate intercompany investment and equity accounts of subsidiary at beginning of year, and subsidiary dividend.

(2) Provide for Year 7 depreciation and amortization on
differences between combination date fair values
and carrying values of Sage's assets, as follows:

	To cost of goods sold	To selling, general, and administrative expenses
Inventories sold	$26,000	$ –0–
Building depreciation .	2,000	2,000
Machinery and equip- ment depreciation . .	10,000	–0–
Leasehold amortization	5,000	–0–
Goodwill amortization	500	500
Totals.	$43,500	$2,500

(Income tax effects are ignored.)

(3) Allocate remaining unamortized differences between
combination date fair values and carrying values to
appropriate assets.

(4) Establish minority interest in subsidiary at beginning
of year ($62,750), less minority share of dividends
declared by subsidiary during year (5% × $40,000 =
$2,000).

(b) Minority Interest in Net Income of Subsidiary	2,200	
Minority Interest in Subsidiary		2,200

To establish minority interest in subsidiary's adjusted net income for Year 7, as follows:

Net income reported by subsidiary	$90,000
Net reduction in elimination *a* above	(46,000)
Adjusted net income of subsidiary	$44,000
Minority share: 5% × $44,000	$ 2,200

3 The first consolidation elimination cancels Sage Company's retained earnings *at the beginning of the year.* This step is essential for the preparation of all three consolidating financial statements.

4 The parent company's use of the equity method of accounting results in the following equalities:

Parent company net income = consolidated net income
Parent company retained earnings = consolidated retained earnings

5 Purchase accounting theory requires the exclusion from consolidated retained earnings of a purchased subsidiary's retained earnings at date of a business combination. Post Corporation's use of the equity method of accounting meets this requirement. Post Corporation's retained earnings—which are equal to consolidated retained earnings—include Post's $41,800 share of the subsidiary's adjusted net income for the year ended April 30, Year 7—the first year of the parent-subsidiary relationship.

6 One of the effects of the first consolidation elimination is to reduce the difference between the fair values of the subsidiary's net assets at the business combination date and their carrying values at that date. The reduction's effect is as follows:

Difference at date of business combination (Apr. 30, Year 6)	$286,000
Reduction in consolidation elimination *a* ($43,500 + $2,500)	46,000
Difference at Apr. 30, Year 7	$240,000

The joint effect of Post Corporation's use of the equity method of accounting and the annual consolidation eliminations will be to extinguish the remaining $240,000 difference through Post's Investment in Subsidiary account. This will be illustrated further in Chapter 7.

7 The minority interest in subsidiary at April 30, Year 7, may be verified as follows:

Sage Company's total stockholders' equity, Apr. 30, Year 7	$1,019,000
Unamortized difference computed in no. 6, page 217	240,000
Sage Company's adjusted stockholders' equity, Apr. 30, Year 7	$1,259,000
Minority interest therein: 5% × $1,259,000	$ 62,950

Closing entries As indicated in a previous section of this chapter, legal considerations necessitate the following condensed closing entry for Post Corporation at April 30, Year 7:

Net Sales	5,600,000	
Intercompany Investment Income	41,800	
Intercompany Revenue	11,000	
Costs and Expenses		5,191,000
Retained Earnings of Subsidiary [95% × ($44,000 −		
$40,000)]		3,800
Retained Earnings ($461,800 − $3,800)		458,000

To close revenue and expense accounts; to transfer net income legally available for dividends to retained earnings; and to segregate 95% share of adjusted net income of subsidiary not distributed as dividend by subsidiary.

Illustration of cost method of accounting

~~Cost Method: Partially Owned Purchased Subsidiary~~ If Post Corporation used the cost method, rather than the equity method, of accounting for Sage Company's operating results for the year ended April 30, Year 7, ~~Post would make no entries reflecting Sage's net income for the year.~~ Post ~~would record Sage's dividend declaration as follows on March 24, Year 7.~~

Intercompany Dividend Receivable	38,000	
Intercompany Dividend Revenue		38,000

To record dividend declared by Sage Company, payable Apr. 16, Year 7 to stockholders of record Apr. 1, Year 7 (income tax consequences ignored).

Post Corporation's entries for receipt of the dividend from Sage and for accrual of the management fee from Sage would be the same under the cost method as under the equity method of accounting illustrated previously in this chapter.

Consolidating financial statements Condensed consolidating financial statements and the related consolidation eliminations for Post Corporation and subsidiary for the year ended April 30, Year 7, appear below and on pages 220–221.

The following points should be noted:

1 The consolidated amounts in the cost-method consolidating financial statements working papers are identical to the consolidated amounts in the equity method working papers (page 215). This outcome results from the differing consolidation eliminations used in the two methods.

2 Three cost-method consolidation eliminations (*a, b,* and *c*) are required to accomplish what a single equity method consolidation elimination (*a,* page 216) does. The reason is that the parent's accounting records are used in the equity method to reflect the parent's share of the subsidiary's adjusted net income or net loss.

3 The first cost-method consolidation elimination deals with the intercompany investment and subsidiary equity accounts *at the date of the business combination.* Thus, the elimination is identical to the one on page 179 of Chapter 5. This accounting is necessary because the parent's Investment in Subsidiary account is maintained at the *cost of the original investment* in the cost method.

4 Although the parent company's dividend from the subsidiary is *intercompany revenue,* it cannot be handled as is other intercompany revenue in the consolidating income statement. The offset in the subsidiary's records is an *equity account,* not an *intercompany expense.*

POST CORPORATION AND SUBSIDIARY
Consolidation Eliminations
April 30, Year 7

(a) Capital Stock—Sage	400,000	
Paid-in Capital in Excess of Par—Sage	235,000	
Retained Earnings—Sage	334,000	
Inventories—Sage	26,000	
Property, Plant, and Equipment—Sage	190,000	
Leasehold—Sage	30,000	
Goodwill—Sage	40,000	
Investment in Subsidiary—Post		1,192,250
Minority Interest in Subsidiary		62,750

To eliminate intercompany investment and equity accounts of subsidiary at date of business combination; to allocate excess of cost over carrying values of identifiable assets acquired, with remainder to goodwill; and to establish minority interest in subsidiary at date of business combination.

(b) Cost of Goods Sold—Sage 43,500
    Selling, General, and Administrative Expenses—Sage . . 2,500
        Inventories—Sage 26,000
        Property, Plant, and Equipment—Sage 14,000
        Leasehold—Sage 5,000
        Goodwill—Sage 1,000

To provide for Year 7 depreciation and amortization on differences between combination date fair values and carrying values of Sage's assets, as follows:

	To cost of goods sold	To selling, general, and administrative expenses
Inventories sold	$26,000	$ –0–
Building depreciation . . .	2,000	2,000
Machinery and equipment depreciation	10,000	–0–
Leasehold amortization . .	5,000	–0–
Goodwill amortization . . .	500	500
Totals	$43,500	$2,500

(Income tax effects are ignored.)

(c) Intercompany Dividend Revenue—Post 38,000
    Minority Interest in Subsidiary 2,000
        Dividends—Sage 40,000

To eliminate intercompany dividends and minority share thereof (5% × $40,000 = $2,000).

(d) Minority Interest in Net Income of Subsidiary 2,200
    Minority Interest in Subsidiary 2,200

To establish minority interest in subsidiary's adjusted net income for Year 7, as follows:

Net income reported by subsidiary	$90,000
Net reduction in elimination **b** above	(46,000)
Adjusted net income of subsidiary	$44,000
Minority share: 5% × $44,000	$ 2,200

POST CORPORATION AND SUBSIDIARY
Consolidating Financial Statements
Year Ended April 30, Year 7

	Post Corporation	Sage Company	Consolidation Eliminations Increase (Decrease)	Consolidated
Income Statement				
Revenue				
Net sales	$5,600,000	$1,100,000		$6,700,000
Intercompany dividend revenue	38,000	-0-	(c) $ (38,000)	-0-
Intercompany revenue (expenses)	11,000	(11,000)		-0-
	$5,649,000	$1,089,000	$ (38,000)	$6,700,000
Costs and expenses				
Cost of goods sold	$3,925,000	$ 700,000	(b) $ 43,500	$4,668,500
Selling, general, and administrative				
expenses	556,000	129,000	(b) 2,500	687,500
Interest and income taxes expense	710,000	170,000		880,000
Minority interest in net income of				
subsidiary	-0-	-0-	(d) 2,200	2,200
	$5,191,000	$ 999,000	$ 48,200	$6,238,200
Net income	$ 458,000	$ 90,000	$ (86,200)	$ 461,800
Statement of Retained Earnings				
Retained earnings, May 1, Year 6	$1,050,000	$ 334,000	(a) $(334,000)	$1,050,000
Net income	458,000	90,000	(86,200)	461,800
	$1,508,000	$ 424,000	$(420,200)	$1,511,800
Dividends	158,550	40,000	(c) (40,000)	158,550
Retained earnings, April 30, Year 7	$1,349,450	$ 384,000	$(380,200)	$1,353,250
Balance Sheet				
Assets				
Intercompany receivables	$ 11,000	$ (11,000)		$ -0-
Inventories	850,000	450,000	(a) $ 26,000 (b) (26,000)	1,300,000
Other current assets	639,000	371,000		1,010,000
Investment in subsidiary	1,192,250	—	(a) (1,192,250)	-0-
Property, plant, and equipment	3,600,000	1,150,000	(a) 190,000 (b) (14,000)	4,926,000
Leasehold	-0-	-0-	(a) 30,000 (b) (5,000)	25,000
Goodwill	95,000	-0-	(a) 40,000 (b) (1,000)	134,000
	$6,387,250	$1,960,000	$(952,250)	$7,395,000
Liabilities & Stockholders' Equity				
Liabilities	$2,420,550	$ 941,000		$3,361,550
Minority interest in subsidiary	-0-	-0-	(a) $ 62,750 (c) (2,000) (d) 2,200	62,950
Common stock, $1 par value	1,057,000	-0-		1,057,000
Capital stock, $10 par value	-0-	400,000	(a) (400,000)	-0-
Paid-in capital in excess of par	1,560,250	235,000	(a) (235,000)	1,560,250
Retained earnings	1,349,450	384,000	(380,200)	1,353,250
	$6,387,250	$1,960,000	$(952,250)	$7,395,000

5 The parent's cost method net income and retained earnings are not the same as the consolidated amounts. Thus, the consolidated amounts at April 30, Year 7, should be proved as follows, to assure their accuracy:

Consolidated net income:

Net income of Post Corporation	$458,000
Post Corporation's share of Sage Company's adjusted net income not distributed as dividends [95% × ($44,000 − $40,000)]	3,800
Consolidated net income	$461,800

Consolidated retained earnings:

Retained earnings of Post Corporation	$1,349,450
Post Corporation's share of adjusted net increase in Sage Company's retained earnings [95% × ($50,000 − $46,000)]	3,800
Consolidated retained earnings	$1,353,250

Concluding comments on equity method and cost method

In today's accounting environment, the equity method of accounting for a subsidiary's operations is preferable to the cost method. First, the equity method emphasizes *economic substance* of the parent-subsidiary relationship, while the cost method emphasizes *legal form.* More and more, modern accounting stresses substance over form.

Second, the equity method permits the use of *parent company accounting entries* to reflect many items that must be included in *consolidation eliminations* in the cost method. Formal accounting entries provide a better record than do working paper entries.

Third, the equity method facilitates issuance of separate financial statements for the parent company, if required by Securities and Exchange Commission regulations or other considerations. Current accounting standards[3] require the equity method of accounting for unconsolidated subsidiaries in separate parent company financial statements.

Fourth, except when intercompany profits (discussed in Chapter 7) exist in assets to be consolidated, the parent company's net income and retained earnings are identical in the equity method to the related consolidated amounts. Thus, the equity method provides a self-checking technique.

Fifth, as demonstrated in this chapter, the cost method is not appropriate for accounting for a pooled subsidiary's operations.

For these reasons, the equity method of accounting for a subsidiary's operations will be emphasized in the remainder of this text.

[3] *APB Opinion No. 18,* "The Equity Method of Accounting for Investments in Common Stock," AICPA (New York: 1971), pp. 353–354.

REVIEW QUESTIONS

1 How should a parent and subsidiary account for intercompany transactions and balances to assure their correct elimination for consolidated financial statements? Explain.

2 What are five common intercompany transactions between a parent and its subsidiary?

3 Princeton Corporation rents a sales office to its wholly owned subsidiary under an operating lease requiring rent of $500 per month. What are the income tax effects of the elimination of Princeton's $6,000 rent revenue and the subsidiary's $6,000 rent expense for a consolidated income statement? Explain.

4 "Consolidated financial statement balances will be the same, regardless of whether a parent company uses the equity method or the cost method to account for a subsidiary's operations." Why is this statement true?

5 Both Parnell Corporation and Plankton Company have wholly owned subsidiaries. Parnell Corporation's general ledger has an Intercompany Dividend Revenue account, while an Intercompany Investment Income account appears in Plankton Company's ledger. Do both companies use the same method of accounting for their subsidiaries' operating results? Explain.

6 When there are no intercompany profits or losses in consolidated assets, the equity method of accounting produces parent company net income which equals consolidated net income. The equity method also results in parent company retained earnings of the same amount as consolidated retained earnings. Why, then, are consolidated financial statements considered superior to parent company financial statements when the parent uses the equity method? Explain.

7 Describe the special features of closing entries for a parent company which accounts for its subsidiary's operating results by the equity method.

8 Plumstead Corporation's 92%-owned subsidiary declared a dividend of $3 per share on its 50,000 outstanding shares of common stock. How would Plumstead record this dividend in the general journal under
a The equity method of accounting?
b The cost method of accounting?

9 Discuss some of the advantages which result from the use of the equity method, rather than the cost method, of accounting for a subsidiary's operating results.

10 Strake Company, a 90%-owned subsidiary of Peale Corporation, reported net income of $50,000 for the first fiscal year following the business combination. However, the consolidation elimination for the minority interest in the subsidiary's net income was in the amount of $3,500 rather than $5,000. Can this difference be justified? Explain.

11 Is an intercompany note receivable which has been discounted at a bank eliminated for a consolidated balance sheet? Explain.

12 Is a Retained Earnings of Subsidiary account required for a parent company using the cost method of accounting for the subsidiary's operations? Explain.

EXERCISES

Ex. 6-1 The condensed balance sheets of Pate Corporation and Shale Company as of December 31, Year 4, are as follows:

	Pate Corporation	Shale Company
Assets	$600,000	$400,000
Liabilities	$150,000	$100,000
Capital stock	300,000	250,000
Retained earnings	150,000	50,000
Total liabilities & stockholders' equity	$600,000	$400,000

Select the best answer for each of the following multiple-choice questions.

1 If Pate Corporation acquired a 90% interest in Shale Company on December 31, Year 4, for $290,000 and the cost method of accounting for the investment was used, the amount of the debit to Investment in Subsidiary would have been **a** $360,000.   **b** $300,000.   **c** $290,000.   **d** $270,000.

2 If Pate Corporation acquired an 80% interest in Shale Company on December 31, Year 4, for $210,000 and the equity method of accounting for the investment was used, the amount of the debit to Investment in Subsidiary would have been **a** $320,000.   **b** $240,000.   **c** $210,000.   **d** $200,000.

3 If Pate Corporation acquired a 90% interest in Shale Company on December 31, Year 4, for $270,000 and during Year 5 Shale Company had net income of $22,000 and paid a cash dividend of $7,000, applying the cost method would give a debit balance in the Investment in Subsidiary account at the end of Year 5 of **a** $285,000.   **b** $283,500.   **c** $276,300.   **d** $270,000.

4 If Pate Corporation acquired a 90% interest in Shale Company on December 31, Year 4, for $270,000 and during Year 5 Shale Company had net income of $30,000 and paid a cash dividend of $15,000, applying the equity method would give a debit balance in the Investment in Subsidiary account at the end of Year 5 of **a** $285,000.   **b** $283,500.   **c** $276,300.   **d** $270,000.

Ex. 6-2 On March 1, Year 2, Prawn Corporation loaned $10,000 to its subsidiary, Stone Company, on a 90-day, 8% promissory note. On March 31, Year 2, Prawn Corporation discounted the Stone note at the bank at a 10% discount rate. Prepare the general journal entry to record the discounting of the note.

Ex. 6-3 Phillips Corporation uses the equity method of accounting for the operating results of its 97%-owned pooled subsidiary, Stake Company. For Year 6, Phillips had net sales of $2,000,000 and total costs and expenses of $1,700,000. Stake Company reported net income of $150,000 and paid dividends aggregating $70,000. Prepare Phillips Corporation's journal entry to record its share of Stake Company's operating results for Year 6.

Ex. 6-4 On March 31, Year 1, Peeler Corporation acquired for cash 90% of the outstanding capital stock of Spiegel Company. The $100,000 excess of fair value over the carrying values of Spiegel's net assets was allocable to goodwill having an estimated useful life at March 31, Year 1, of 25 years. For the year ended March 31, Year 2, Spiegel Company reported a net loss of $30,000 and paid no dividends. What amount should Peeler Corporation record in its Intercompany

Investment Income account under the equity method of accounting for the year ended March 31, Year 2? (Supporting computations should be in good form.)

Ex. 6-5 Following are all details of three ledger accounts of a parent company which uses the equity method of accounting for its subsidiary's operating results.

Intercompany Dividends Receivable

Aug. 16, Year 8	36,000	Aug. 27, Year 8	36,000

Investment in Subsidiary

Sept. 1, Year 7	630,000	Aug. 16, Year 8	36,000
Aug. 31, Year 8	72,000	Aug. 31, Year 8	5,000

Intercompany Investment Income

Aug. 31, Year 8	5,000	Aug. 31, Year 8	72,000

What is the most logical explanation for each of the transactions recorded in the above ledger accounts?

Ex. 6-6 Perch Corporation erroneously used the cost method of accounting for the operating results of its 94%-owned pooled subsidiary, Spears Company, with which Perch combined on May 31, Year 3. Details of Spears Company's Retained Earnings account for the three years since that date follow.

Div. *Net. Inc.*

Retained Earnings

May 26, Year 4 Dividends	30,000	May 31, Year 3 Balance	470,000
May 31, Year 5 Net loss	20,000	May 31, Year 4 Net income	60,000
May 24, Year 6 Dividends	30,000	May 31, Year 6 Net income	80,000

80,000 (140,00) = 60,000

Prepare an adjusting journal entry for Perch Corporation at May 31, Year 6, to convert its accounting for its subsidiary's operating results to the equity method. The entry should include the account or accounts necessary for Perch Corporation's income statement for the year ended May 31, Year 6.

SHORT CASES FOR ANALYSIS AND DECISION

Case 6-1 You have recently been hired for the position of controller of Plait Corporation, a manufacturer which has begun a program of expansion through business combinations. On February 1, Year 4, two weeks prior to your controllership appointment, Plait Corporation completed the acquisition of 85% of the outstanding common stock of Strait Company for $255,000 cash. You are presently engaged in a discussion with Plait Corporation's chief accountant concerning the appropriate accounting method for Plait's interest in Strait Company's operating results. The chief accountant strongly supports the cost method of accounting, offering the following arguments:

1 The cost method recognizes that Plait Corporation and Strait Company are separate legal entities.

2 The existence of a minority interest in Strait Company requires emphasis on the legal separateness of the two companies.

3 A parent company recognizes revenue under the cost method only when the subsidiary declares dividends. Such dividend revenue is consistent with the accounting theory of revenue realization. The Intercompany Investment Income account recorded in the equity method of accounting does not fit the definition of realized revenue.

4 Use of the equity method of accounting might result in Plait Corporation declaring dividends to its shareholders out of "paper" retained earnings which in reality belong to Strait Company.

5 The cost method is consistent with other aspects of historical cost accounting, since working paper consolidation eliminations, rather than entries in ledger accounts, are used to recognize amortization of differences between fair values and carrying values of Strait Company's net assets.

Instructions Write a rebuttal to each of the chief accountant's arguments.

Case 6-2 As independent auditor of a new client, Aqua Water Company, you are reviewing the consolidating financial statements working papers prepared by Aqua Water Company's chief accountant. Aqua Water Company distributes water to home-owners in a suburb of a large city. Aqua Water Company purchases the water from Aqua Well Company, a subsidiary. Aqua Water organized Aqua Well five years ago and purchased all its capital stock for cash on that date.

During the course of your audit, you have learned the following:

(1) Both Aqua Water Company and Aqua Well Company are public utilities subject to the jurisdiction of a state regulatory agency.

(2) Aqua Well charges Aqua Water for the transmission of water from wells to consumers. The transmission charge, at the customary utility rate, was approved by the state regulatory agency.

(3) Aqua Well charges Aqua Water separately for the volume of water delivered to Aqua Water's customers.

(4) Your audit working papers show the following audited amounts for the separate companies' financial statements:

	Aqua Water Company	Aqua Well Company
Total revenue	$3,500,000	$ 300,000
Net income	300,000	50,000
Total assets	5,700,000	1,000,000
Stockholders' equity	2,500,000	600,000

The consolidating financial statements working papers prepared by Aqua Water Company's chief accountant appear in order, except that Aqua Well's Transmission Revenue account of $60,000 is not offset against Aqua Water's Transmission Expense account of the same amount. The chief accountant explains that, since the transmission charge by Aqua Well is at the customary utility rate approved by the state regulatory agency, he does not consider the charge to be *intercompany* revenue and expense. Furthermore, he points out, his consolidating financial statements working papers do offset Aqua Well Company's Water Sales account of $200,000 against Aqua Water Company's Water Purchases account of the same amount.

Do you concur with the chief accountant's position in this issue? Explain fully.

PROBLEMS

6-3 Pumice Corporation owns 90% of the outstanding common stock of Solar Company, acquired in a pooling business combination January 31, Year 1. For the year ended January 31, Year 2, Pumice Corporation's condensed unconsolidated income statement was as follows:

Revenue:	
Net sales	*$500,000*
Intercompany investment income	*27,000*
Intercompany revenue	*23,000*
Total revenue	*$550,000*
Costs and expenses	*510,000*
Net income	*$ 40,000*

During the year ended January 31, Year 2, Solar Company declared and paid dividends aggregating $10,000.

Instructions Prepare in good form a condensed closing entry for Pumice Corporation at January 31, Year 2.

6-4 Pristine Corporation has begun making working capital loans to its wholly owned subsidiary, Saline Company, on 9% promissory notes. The following 120-day loans were made prior to June 30, Year 3, the close of the fiscal year:

May 1, Year 3	*$15,000*
May 31, Year 3	*20,000*

On June 6, Year 3, Pristine discounted the May 1 note at the bank, at a 12% discount rate.

Instructions Prepare in good form general journal entries to record the note transactions and related June 30, Year 3, adjustments:
a In the accounts of Pristine Corporation.
b In the accounts of Saline Company.

6-5 Pontus Corporation completed a business combination with Sicily Company on April 30, Year 7. Immediately thereafter, Pontus began making cash advances on open account to Sicily, at a 10% annual interest rate. In addition, Sicily agreed to pay a monthly management fee to Pontus of 2% of monthly net sales. Payment was to be made no later than the tenth day of the month following Sicily's accrual of the fee.

During your examination of the financial statements of Pontus Corporation and Sicily Company at July 31, Year 7, you discover that each company has set up only one account—entitled Intercompany Account—to record all intercompany transactions. Details of the two accounts at July 31, Year 7, are given on page 228.

Your audit working papers show audited net sales of $330,000 for Sicily Company for the three months ended July 31, Year 7. You agree to the companies' use of a 360-day year for computing interest.

Instructions Prepare in good form adjusting journal entries for Pontus Corporation and Sicily Company at July 31, Year 7. Establish appropriate separate intercompany accounts in your journal entries.

Pontus Corporation Ledger
Intercompany Account—Sicily Company

Date		Ref.	Debit	Credit	Balance
May 2	Cash advance	CD	4,500		4,500 dr
May 27	Cash advance	CD	9,000		13,500 dr
June 11	Management fee	CR		2,000	11,500 dr
June 12	Repayment of May 2 advance	CR		4,550	6,950 dr
June 21	Cash advance	CD	10,000		16,950 dr
July 11	Management fee	CR		2,200	14,750 dr
July 27	Repayment of May 27 advance	CR		9,150	5,600 dr
July 31	Cash advance	CD	5,000		10,600 dr

Sicily Company Ledger
Intercompany Account—Pontus Corporation

Date		Ref.	Debit	Credit	Balance
May 3	Cash advance	CR		4,500	4,500 cr
May 28	Cash advance	CR		9,000	13,500 cr
June 10	Management fee: 2% × $100,000	CD	2,000		11,500 cr
June 11	Repayment of May 2 advance	CD	4,550		6,950 cr
June 22	Cash advance	CR		10,000	16,950 cr
July 10	Management fee: 2% × $110,000	CD	2,200		14,750 cr
July 26	Repayment of May 27 advance	CD	9,150		5,600 cr

6-6 Platen Corporation consummated a pooling business combination with Slater Company on December 31, Year 6. 48,000 of Slater's 50,000 shares of outstanding common stock were exchanged in the combination.

Slater Company reported net income of $0.80 per share for Year 7 and declared dividends of $0.35 per share on December 13, Year 7, payable January 6, Year 8, to stockholders of record December 23, Year 7. There were no other intercompany transactions during Year 7.

Instructions Prepare general journal entries in good form to record:
a Slater Company's dividend declaration in its accounts.
b Slater Company's operating results for Year 7 in Platen's accounts under the equity method of accounting.

6-7 Postern Corporation purchased 82% of Southern Company's outstanding common stock for $328,000 cash on March 31, Year 8. Costs of the business combination may be ignored. On that date, Southern's stockholders' equity accounts were as follows:

Capital stock, $2 par value	$ 50,000
Paid-in capital in excess of par	75,000
Retained earnings	135,000
Total stockholders' equity	$260,000

All of Southern Company's identifiable net assets were fairly valued at their March 31, Year 8, carrying values except for the following:

	Carrying value	Fair value
Land	$100,000	$120,000
Building (10-year remaining useful life)	200,000	250,000
Patent (8-year remaining useful life)	60,000	80,000

Southern Company uses the straight-line method for depreciation and amortization.

During the year ended March 31, Year 9, Southern Company reported net income of $1.20 per share and paid no dividends. There were no intercompany transactions between Postern Corporation and Southern Company.

Instructions

a Prepare in good form Postern Corporation's general journal entries to record Southern Company's operating results for the year ended March 31, Year 9.

b Prepare in good form the working paper consolidation eliminations for Postern Corporation and subsidiary at March 31, Year 9.

6-8 On January 1, Year 3, Premier Corporation exchanged its capital stock for 100% of Scientific Company's capital stock on a 1 for 4 basis. Premier stock was selling on the market for $7 per share at the time and the investment was recorded on this basis. The Premier stock exchanged was treasury stock that had been purchased for $4.50 per share three years prior to the business combination. The combination qualified for pooling-of-interests accounting. Costs of the combination may be ignored.

There was no market price available for Scientific Company stock at the date of the business combination. The stockholders' equity per share of Scientific stock was $1.60. Premier's board of directors justified the exchange ratio for the Scientific stock on the grounds that the values of Scientific's plant assets were understated.

The balance sheets of the two companies at December 31, Year 3, were as follows:

PREMIER CORPORATION AND SCIENTIFIC COMPANY

Balance Sheets

December 31, Year 3

	Premier Corporation	Scientific Company
Assets		
Cash	$ 50,000	$ (1,800)
Notes receivable	42,000	
Notes receivable discounted	(15,000)	
Accrued interest receivable	1,450	
Accounts receivable	68,000	68,800
Advances to Scientific Company	25,000	
Inventories	177,000	22,500
Investment in Scientific Company	70,000	
Property, plant, and equipment	290,000	240,000
Accumulated depreciation	(40,000)	(60,000)
Other assets	42,000	3,000
Total assets	$710,450	$272,500

Liabilities & Stockholders' Equity

Notes payable	$ 45,000	$ 25,000
Accrued interest payable	300	1,750
Accounts payable	85,400	36,800
Advances from Premier Corporation		25,000
Other accrued liabilities	13,000	9,075
6% bonds payable, due Apr. 1, Year 13		100,000
Capital stock, $5 par value	300,000	
Capital stock, $1 par value		40,000
Paid-in capital in excess of par	150,000	
Retained earnings	116,750	34,875
Total liabilities & stockholders' equity	$710,450	$272,500

The following information is available also:
(1) Condensed income statement data for the two companies for the year ended December 31, Year 3—were as follows:

	Premier Corporation	Scientific Company
Net sales	$600,000	$200,000
Costs and expenses	550,000	189,125
Net income	$ 50,000	$ 10,875

(2) Premier Corporation wired $13,000 to Scientific Company's bank on January 2, Year 4, to cover the cash overdraft and to provide cash for working capital. The $13,000 was considered an additional advance to Scientific.
(3) Scientific's notes payable include a $10,000, 5% demand note payable to the president of Premier Corporation, who is not an officer of Scientific Company. The note is dated July 1, Year 2, and interest is payable on July 1 and January 1. The remaining Scientific Company notes payable are non-interest-bearing and are payable to Premier Corporation, which discounted them at the bank.

Instructions
a Prepare adjusting journal entries, in good form, for Premier Corporation at December 31, Year 3.
b Prepare consolidating balance sheet working papers at December 31, Year 3, and related consolidation eliminations in good form. Balances for Premier Corporation should reflect the adjusting journal entries in *a*.
Ignore income taxes in your solution.

6-9 Peck Corporation, a wholesaler, purchased 80% of the issued and outstanding stock of Sayles Company, a retailer, on December 31, Year 2, for $120,000. At that date Sayles Company had one class of common stock outstanding at a stated value of $100,000 and retained earnings of $30,000. Peck Corporation had a $50,000 deficit in retained earnings.

Peck Corporation purchased the Sayles Company stock from Sayles's major stockholder primarily to acquire control of signboard leases owned by Sayles Company. The leases will expire on December 31, Year 7, and Peck Corporation executives estimated that the leases, which cannot be renewed, were worth at least $20,000 more than their carrying value when the Sayles Company stock was purchased.

The financial statements for both companies for the year ended December 31, Year 6, are as follows:

PECK CORPORATION AND SUBSIDIARY
Financial Statements
Year Ended December 31, Year 6

	Peck Corporation	Sayles Company
Income Statement		
Net sales	$420,000	$300,000
Costs and expenses:		
Cost of goods sold	$315,000	$240,000
Expenses	65,000	35,000
	$380,000	$275,000
Net income	$ 40,000	$ 25,000
Statement of Retained Earnings		
Retained earnings, Jan. 1, Year 6	$ 15,000	$ 59,000
Net income	40,000	25,000
	$ 55,000	$ 84,000
Dividends	–0–	9,000
Retained earnings, Dec. 31, Year 6	$ 55,000	$ 75,000
Balance Sheet		
Assets		
Current assets	$172,000	$199,100
Investment in subsidiary	120,000	
Land	25,000	10,500
Building and equipment	200,000	40,000
Accumulated depreciation.	(102,000)	(7,000)
Signboard leases		42,000
Accumulated amortization.		(33,600)
	$415,000	$251,000
Liabilities & Stockholders' Equity		
Dividends payable.	$ –0–	$ 9,000
Other current liabilities.	60,000	67,000
Capital stock	300,000	100,000
Retained earnings.	55,000	75,000
	$415,000	$251,000

Sayles Company declared a 9% cash dividend on December 20, Year 6, payable January 16, Year 7, to stockholders of record December 31, Year 6. Peck Corporation carries its investment at cost and had not recorded this dividend on December 31, Year 6. Neither company paid a dividend during Year 6.

Instructions

a Prepare adjusting journal entries, in good form, for Peck Corporation at December 31, Year 6, to convert its accounting for Sayles Company's operating results to the equity method.

b Prepare consolidating financial statements working papers at December 31, Year 6, and related consolidation eliminations in good form. Balances for Peck Corporation should reflect the adjusting journal entries in *a*.

Ignore income taxes in your solution.

7

Consolidated financial statements: intercompany profits and losses

Many transactions between a parent and its subsidiary may involve an *actual* element of profit or loss. Among these transactions are intercompany sales of merchandise (inventory), intercompany sales of property and equipment, and intercompany sales of intangible assets. In addition, a parent or subsidiary company's purchase of its affiliate's bonds *in the open market* may result in an *imputed* intercompany profit or loss. In this chapter we shall discuss the consolidation eliminations for intercompany transactions of the types described above. We shall purposely illustrate intercompany transactions involving *profits,* because such transactions seldom involve losses.

Importance of eliminating intercompany profits and losses

At the outset, we must stress the importance of eliminating intercompany profits and losses for consolidated income statements. Failure to eliminate these amounts would result in consolidated income statements reflecting not only results of transactions with those *outside* the consolidated entity, but also the results of non-arm's-length activities *within* the affiliated group. The parent company's management would have free rein to manipulate reported results of operations if the accountant did not eliminate intercompany profits and losses for consolidated income statements.

INTERCOMPANY SALES OF MERCHANDISE (INVENTORY)

Intercompany sales of merchandise are a natural outgrowth of a **vertical** business combination, which involves a corporation and one or more of its customers or suppliers. **Downstream** intercompany sales of merchandise are those from a parent company to its subsidiaries. **Upstream** intercompany sales are those from subsidiaries to the parent company. **Lateral** intercompany sales are between two subsidiaries of the same parent.

The intercompany sales of merchandise between a parent and its subsidiary are similar to the **intracompany** shipments by a home office to a branch, described in Chapter 3.

Intercompany sales of merchandise at cost

Intercompany sales of merchandise may be made at a price equal to the selling company's cost. If so, the consolidation elimination is the same whether all the goods were sold by the purchasing affiliate or whether some of the goods remained in the purchaser's inventory at the date of the consolidated financial statements. For example, assume that Palm Corporation (the parent) during the year ended December 31, Year 12, sold merchandise costing $150,000 to Starr Company (the subsidiary) at a selling price equal to the cost of the merchandise. Assume further that Starr Company's December 31, Year 12, inventory included $25,000 cost of merchandise obtained from Palm Corporation, and that Starr still owed Palm $15,000 for merchandise purchases as of December 31, Year 12. (Starr Company also purchased merchandise from other suppliers during Year 12.)

The two companies would make the combined general journal entries illustrated on page 235 to reflect the above, assuming that both companies used the perpetual inventory system.

Consolidating financial statements working papers for Palm Corporation and subsidiary for the year ended December 31, Year 12, would include the data on page 236 with regard to intercompany sales of merchandise only.

Note that Starr Company's cost of goods sold for Year 12 and inventories at December 31, Year 12, are not affected by consolidation eliminations. From a consolidated entity viewpoint, Starr's cost of goods sold and inventories are both stated at **cost;** no element of intercompany profit is involved. In effect, Starr Company served as a **conduit** to outside customers for Palm Corporation's merchandise.

Intercompany profit in ending inventory

More typical than the intercompany sales of merchandise at cost described in the preceding section are intercompany sales involving a gross profit. The gross profit margin may be equal to, greater than, or less than

Explanations	Palm Corporation	Starr Company

(1) Palm sales of merchandise to Starr	Intercompany Accounts Receivable 150,000
	    Intercompany Sales 150,000
	
	Intercompany Cost of Goods Sold 150,000
	    Inventories 150,000
		Inventories 150,000
		    Intercompany Accounts Payable .. 150,000

(2) Starr payments to Palm for merchandise	Cash 135,000
	    Intercompany Accounts Receivable 135,000
		Intercompany Accounts Payable 135,000
		    Cash 135,000

(3) Starr sales of merchandise purchased from Palm (Starr sales prices assumed)		Accounts Receivable 160,000
		    Sales 160,000
		Cost of Goods Sold 125,000
		    Inventories 125,000

	Palm Corporation	Starr Company	Consolidation eliminations Increase (decrease)	Consolidated
Income Statement				
Revenue				
Intercompany revenue (expenses)	$ -0-	$ -0-*	$ -0-	$ -0-
Balance Sheet				
Assets				
Intercompany receivables (payables) . .	$15,000	$(15,000)	$ -0-	$ -0-

*Palm Corporation's $150,000 intercompany sales and intercompany cost of goods sold are offset in Palm's separate income statement.

the margin on sales to outsiders. The intercompany gross profit is **realized** through the purchasing affiliate's sales to outsiders. Consequently, any goods purchased from an affiliated company which remain unsold at the date of a consolidated balance sheet result in the **overstatement,** from a **consolidated** point of view, of the purchaser's ending inventory. The overstatement is equal to the amount of intercompany gross profit contained in the ending inventory. This overstatement is disposed of through an appropriate consolidation elimination.

Suppose, for example, that Sage Company (the partially owned subsidiary) during the year ended April 30, Year 8, began selling merchandise to Post Corporation (the parent) at a gross profit margin of 20%. Sales by Sage to Post for the year totaled $120,000, of which $40,000 remained unsold by Post at April 30, Year 8. At that date, Post owed $30,000 to Sage for merchandise. Both companies used the perpetual inventory system.

The transactions described in the preceding paragraph would be recorded in summary form by the two companies as illustrated on page 237.

The intercompany profit in Sage Company's sales to Post Corporation may be analyzed as follows:

	Selling price	Cost	Gross profit
Beginning inventory	$ -0-	$ -0-	$ -0-
Sales	120,000	96,000	24,000
Total	$120,000	$96,000	$24,000
Ending inventory	40,000	32,000	8,000
Cost of goods sold	$ 80,000	$64,000	$16,000

Explanations	Post Corporation	Sage Company

(1) Sage sales of merchandise to Post	Inventories 120,000
	  Intercompany Ac-
	  counts Payable . . 120,000
		Intercompany Accounts
		  Receivable 120,000
		    Intercompany
		      Sales 120,000
		Intercompany Cost of
		  Goods Sold 96,000
		    Inventories 96,000

(2) Post payments to Sage for merchandise	Intercompany Accounts
	  Payable 90,000
	    Cash 90,000
		Cash 90,000
		  Intercompany Ac-
		  counts Receivable 90,000

(3) Post sales of merchandise purchased from Sage (Post sales prices assumed)	Accounts Receivable . . . 100,000
	  Sales 100,000
	Cost of Goods Sold 80,000
	  Inventories 80,000	

This analysis demonstrates that the intercompany gross profit on sales by Sage Company to Post Corporation totaled $24,000, and that $16,000 of this intercompany profit was realized through Post Corporation's sales to outside customers. The remaining $8,000 of intercompany profit remains *unrealized* in Post Corporation's inventory at April 30, Year 8.

The following working paper consolidation elimination would be required for Sage Company's intercompany sales of merchandise to Post Corporation for the year ended April 30, Year 8:

Intercompany Sales—Sage	120,000	
Intercompany Cost of Goods Sold—Sage		96,000
Cost of Goods Sold—Post		16,000
Inventories—Post		8,000

To eliminate intercompany sales, cost of goods sold, and unrealized profit in inventories. (Income tax effects are ignored.)

The consequences of the above consolidation elimination are threefold. First, it eliminates Sage Company's sales to Post Corporation and the related cost of goods sold. This avoids the overstatement of the consolidated amounts for sales and cost of goods sold, which should represent merchandise transactions with customers *outside* of the consolidated entity. Second, the consolidation elimination removes the intercompany profit portion of Post Corporation's cost of goods sold, thus restating it to the cost of the *consolidated* entity. Finally, the above elimination reduces the consolidated inventories to the cost incurred by the consolidated entity.

Entering the above consolidation elimination in the consolidating financial statements working paper would result in the balances shown on page 239 (amounts for total outsider sales and cost of goods sold assumed).

Note that the $120,000 elimination of intercompany sales, less the $112,000 total ($16,000 + $96,000) of the cost of goods sold eliminations, equals $8,000—the amount of the intercompany profit eliminated from inventories. This $8,000 unrealized intercompany profit is attributable to Sage Company—the seller of the merchandise—and must be taken into account in the determination of the minority interest in Sage Company's net income for the year ended April 30, Year 8. The $8,000 also enters into the computation of Sage Company's retained earnings at April 30, Year 8. These matters are illustrated in the next section of this chapter.

	Post Corporation	Sage Company	Consolidation eliminations Increase (decrease)	Consolidated
Income Statement				
Revenue				
Sales	$5,800,000	$1,200,000		$7,000,000
Intercompany sales . .	–0–	120,000	$(120,000)	–0–
Costs and expenses				
Cost of goods sold . .	$4,100,000	$ 760,000	$ (16,000)	$4,844,000
Intercompany cost of				
goods sold	–0–	96,000	(96,000)	–0–
Balance Sheet				
Assets				
Intercompany receiv-				
ables (payables) . .	$ (30,000)	$ 30,000		$ –0–
Inventories	900,000	475,000	$ (8,000)	1,367,000

Intercompany profit in beginning and ending inventories

The consolidation elimination for intercompany sales of merchandise is complicated by intercompany profits in the *beginning* inventory of the purchaser. It is generally assumed that, on a first-in, first-out basis, the intercompany profit in the purchaser's *beginning* inventory is realized through sales to outsiders during the ensuing year. Only intercompany profit in *ending* inventory remains unrealized at the end of the year.

Continuing the illustration from the preceding section, assume that Sage Company's intercompany sales of merchandise to Post Corporation during the year ended April 30, Year 9, are analyzed as follows:

	Selling price	Cost	Gross profit
Beginning inventory	$ 40,000	$ 32,000	$ 8,000
Sales	150,000	120,000	30,000
Total	$190,000	$152,000	$38,000
Ending inventory	60,000	48,000	12,000
Cost of goods sold	$130,000	$104,000	$26,000

Sage Company's intercompany sales and intercompany cost of goods sold for the year ended April 30, Year 8, had been closed to Sage's

Retained Earnings account. As a consequence, Sage's April 30, Year 8, retained earnings was overstated by $7,600—95% of the amount of the unrealized intercompany profit in Post Corporation's April 30, Year 8, inventory. (The $400 remainder of the $8,000 unrealized profit at April 30, Year 8, is attributable to the minority interest in Sage Company.) The following working paper consolidation elimination at April 30, Year 9, reflects these facts:

Retained Earnings—Sage (95% × $8,000)	7,600	
Minority Interest in Subsidiary (5% × $8,000)	400	
Intercompany Sales—Sage	150,000	
Intercompany Cost of Goods Sold—Sage		120,000
Cost of Goods Sold—Post		26,000
Inventories—Post		12,000
To eliminate intercompany sales, cost of goods sold, and profit		
in inventories. (Income tax effects are ignored.)		

Intercompany profit in inventory and minority interest

Accountants have given considerable thought to the problem of intercompany profits in transactions with a partially owned subsidiary. There is general agreement that all the intercompany profit in a partially owned subsidiary's inventory should be eliminated for consolidated financial statements. This holds true whether the sales to the subsidiary are downstream from the parent or are made by a wholly owned subsidiary of the same parent.

There has been no such agreement on the treatment of intercompany profit in the parent's or a subsidiary's inventory from upstream or lateral sales by a partially owned subsidiary. Two alternative approaches have been advanced.

1 The first approach is elimination of intercompany profit only to the extent of the parent's ownership interest in the selling subsidiary's stock. This approach builds upon the "parent company" concept of consolidated financial statements (see Chapter 5, pages 185–186), in which the minority interest is considered to be a *liability* of the consolidated entity. If the minority shareholders are considered *outside creditors,* intercompany profit in the parent's inventory has been *realized* to the extent of the minority shareholders' ownership interest in the selling subsidiary's stock.

2 The second approach is elimination of all the intercompany profit. The "entity" concept of consolidated financial statements (see Chapter 5, page 186), in which the minority interest is considered to be a *part of consolidated stockholders' equity,* underlies this approach. If minority shareholders are *part owners* of consolidated assets, their share of intercompany profits in inventories has not been realized.

The AICPA sanctioned the second of the preceding approaches, in the following passage from *Accounting Research Bulletin No. 51:*

The amount of intercompany profit or loss to be eliminated . . . is not affected by the existence of a minority interest. The complete elimination of the inter-company profit or loss is consistent with the underlying assumption that the consolidated statements represent the financial position and operating results of a single business enterprise. The elimination of the intercompany profit or loss may be allocated proportionately between the majority and minority interests.[1]

Consequently, intercompany profits or losses in inventories resulting from sales by a partially owned subsidiary must be considered in the determination of minority interest in net income of the subsidiary, and in the computation of retained earnings of the subsidiary. The subsidiary's reported net income must be *increased* by the *realized* intercompany profit in the parent's *beginning* inventory, and *decreased* by the *unrealized* inter-company profit in the parent's *ending* inventory. Failure to do so would attribute the *entire* intercompany profit effects to the *consolidated* net income.

Elimination of net profit versus elimination of gross profit

Some accounting theorists have discussed the propriety of eliminating intercompany *net* profit, rather than *gross* profit, in inventories of the consolidated entity. There is little theoretical support for such a proposal. First, elimination of intercompany *net* profit would in effect capitalize selling, general, and administrative expenses in consolidated inventories. Selling expenses are *always* period costs, and only in unusual circum-stances are some general and administrative expenses capitalized in inventories. Second, determination of *net* profit for a particular inventory item or line requires many assumptions as to allocations of common costs. The resultant profit figure may be more a product of conjecture than an objectively determined amount.

INTERCOMPANY SALES OF PROPERTY AND EQUIPMENT AND INTANGIBLE ASSETS

Intercompany sales of property and equipment and intangible assets differ from intercompany sales of merchandise in two significant respects. First, intercompany sales of property or intangibles between affiliated companies are rare transactions. In contrast, intercompany sales of merchandise recur frequently throughout each fiscal year, once a pro-gram of such sales has been established. Second, the relatively long lives of property and intangible assets require the passage of many accounting periods before intercompany profits or losses on sales of these assets are realized in transactions with outsiders. Conversely, intercompany

---

[1]*ARB No. 51,* "Consolidated Financial Statements," AICPA (New York: 1959), p. 45.

profits in consolidated inventories at the end of one accounting period are usually realized in sales to outsiders during the ensuing period.

These differences have their counterparts in the consolidation eliminations for intercompany profits or losses on sales of property or intangible assets described in the following sections.

Intercompany profit on sale of land

Suppose that, during the year ended April 30, Year 8, Post Corporation (the parent) sold to Sage Company (the subsidiary) for $175,000 a parcel of land which had cost Post $125,000. Sage Company acquired the land for a new building site. The two companies would account for the transaction as follows (ignoring income tax effects to Post Corporation):

Post Corporation			**Sage Company**		
Cash	175,000		Land for Building		
Land		125,000	Site	175,000	
Intercompany			Cash		175,000
Gain on			To record pur-		
Sale of			chase of		
Land		50,000	land from		
To record sale of			Post		
land to Sage			Corporation.		
Company.					

In consolidated financial statements for the year ended April 30, Year 8, the land must be presented at its historical cost to the consolidated entity. Also, the $50,000 intercompany gain must be eliminated, since it has not been realized in a transaction with an outsider. Accordingly, the following working paper consolidation elimination is required at April 30, Year 8:

Intercompany Gain on Sale of Land—Post	50,000	
Land for Building Site—Sage		50,000
To eliminate unrealized intercompany profit on sale of land.		
(Income tax effects are ignored.)		

The consolidation elimination above would appear as follows in consolidating financial statements working papers for the year ended April 30, Year 8:

	Post Corporation	Sage Company	Consolidation eliminations Increase (decrease)	Consolidated
Income Statement				
Revenue				
Intercompany gain on				
sale of land	$ 50,000	$ –0–	$ (50,000)	$ –0–
Balance Sheet				
Assets				
Land for building site	$ –0–	$ 175,000	$ (50,000)	$ 125,000

Since land is not a depreciable asset, in subsequent years no entries affecting the land would be made by Sage Company unless the land were resold to an outsider (or back to Post Corporation). Of course, Sage Company would transfer the $175,000 to the Land account from Land for Building Site once the building was completed and occupied.

Nevertheless, in ensuing years, as long as Sage Company owns the land, its $175,000 cost to Sage is overstated $50,000 for consolidated financial statement purposes. Since the $50,000 gain on the sale of the land was closed to Post Corporation's Retained Earnings account at April 30, Year 8, the following working paper consolidation elimination is required for Year 9 and subsequent years:

```
Retained Earnings—Post . . . . . . . . . . . . . . . . . . . . . . . .   50,000
        Land for Building Site (or Land)—Sage . . . . . . . . . .             50,000
To eliminate unrealized intercompany profit in land. (Income tax
effects are ignored.)
```

Suppose that, instead of constructing a building on the land, Sage Company sold the land to an outsider for $200,000 during the year ended April 30, Year 10. Sage Company would make the following entry to record the sale:

```
Cash  . . . . . . . . . . . . . . . . . . . . . . . . . . . . . . . . . .   200,000
        Land for Building Site . . . . . . . . . . . . . . . . . . .             175,000
        Gain on Sale of Land . . . . . . . . . . . . . . . . . . . .              25,000
To record sale of land to outsider. (Income tax effects are
ignored.)
```

The consolidated income statement for the year ended April 30, Year 10, must reflect the fact that, for **consolidated** purposes, a **$75,000** gain was realized on Sage's sale of the land. This $75,000 gain consists of the $25,000 gain recorded by Sage Company, and the $50,000 inter-company gain on Post Corporation's sale of the land to Sage Company. The following working paper consolidation elimination at April 30, Year 10, is required:

Retained Earnings—Post	50,000	
Gain on Sale of Land—Sage		50,000
To attribute $50,000 unrealized profit on Post Corporation's sale		
of land to Sage Company to Sage Company's gain on sale of		
the land to an outsider. (Income tax effects are ignored.)		

Intercompany profit on sale of depreciable asset

Annual depreciation provisions cause a significant difference in the consolidation elimination for intercompany profit on the sale of a depreciable asset, compared to the eliminations described in the preceding section. Since the intercompany profit must be eliminated from the valuation of the depreciable asset for a consolidated balance sheet, the appropriate profit element must be eliminated from the related depreciation expense in the consolidated income statement. This technique will be illustrated in the following pages.

Intercompany Profit at Date of Sale of Depreciable Asset The consolidation elimination at date of sale for intercompany profit on the sale of a **depreciable asset** is identical to the comparable elimination for **land.** As of the date of sale, no depreciation has been recognized by the purchaser.

To illustrate, assume that on April 30, Year 8, Sage Company (the partially owned subsidiary) sold to Post Corporation (the parent) a machine which Post required for a new product line. Details of the sale and of the machine follow:

Selling price of machine to Post Corporation	$60,000
Cost to Sage Company when acquired Apr. 30, Year 5	50,000
Estimated residual value:	
To Sage Company as of Apr. 30, Year 5	$ 4,000
To Post Corporation as of Apr. 30, Year 8	4,000
Estimated useful life:	
To Sage Company as of Apr. 30, Year 5	10 years
To Post Corporation as of Apr. 30, Year 8	5 years
Annual depreciation expense:	
To Sage Company—10% × $46,000	$ 4,600
To Post Corporation—20% × $56,000	11,200

Both companies use the straight-line method of depreciation for machinery.

The two companies would account for the sale at April 30, Year 8, as follows (ignoring income tax consequences to Sage Company):

Post Corporation		Sage Company	
Machinery	60,000	Cash	60,000
Cash	60,000	Accumulated Depreciation	13,800
To record purchase of		Machinery	50,000
machinery from Sage		Intercompany Gain	
Company.		on Sale of Machin-	
		ery	23,800
		To record sale of ma-	
		chinery to Post Corpo-	
		ration.	

The following working paper consolidation elimination would be required for consolidated financial statements at April 30, Year 8 (date of intercompany sale of the machinery):

Intercompany Gain on Sale of Machinery—Sage	23,800	
Machinery—Post		23,800
To eliminate unrealized intercompany profit on sale of machinery. (Income tax effects are ignored.)		

The consolidation elimination above would result in the machinery being reflected in the consolidated balance sheet at its undepreciated cost to Sage Company—the seller—as follows:

Cost of machinery to Post Corporation	$60,000
Amount of consolidation elimination, above	23,800
Difference—equal to cost ($50,000), less accumulated depreciation ($13,800) of machinery to Sage Company	$36,200

Elimination of the $23,800 intercompany gain on the sale of machinery would be taken into account in the determination of the minority interest in Sage Company's net income for Year 8. The $23,800 elimination would also enter into the computation of Sage Company's retained earnings, from a consolidated viewpoint, at April 30, Year 8.

Intercompany Profit Subsequent to Date of Sale of Depreciable Asset An appropriate intercompany profit element must be eliminated from depreciation expense for a plant asset sold by one affiliate to another at a profit. The following working paper consolidation elimination for Post Corporation and subsidiary at April 30, Year 9 (one year after the intercompany sale of machinery), illustrates this point:

Retained Earnings—Sage (95% × $23,800)	22,610	
Minority Interest in Subsidiary (5% × $23,800).	1,190	
Accumulated Depreciation—Post	4,760	
Machinery—Post		23,800
Depreciation Expense—Post		4,760
To eliminate intercompany profit in machinery and related depreciation. (Income tax effects are ignored.) Profit element in depreciation computed as ⅕ × $23,800 = $4,760, based on five-year estimated useful life of machinery.		

Since Sage Company's gain on sale of the machinery was closed to Sage's Retained Earnings account, the preceding consolidation elimination corrects the resultant overstatement of Sage's beginning-of-year retained earnings from the viewpoint of the consolidated entity. In addition, the minority interest's share of the overstatement is accounted for.

The intercompany profit eliminated from Post Corporation's depreciation expense may be verified as follows:

Post Corporation's annual depreciation expense [⅕ × ($60,000 − $4,000)]	$11,200
Depreciation expense for a five-year useful life, based on Sage Company's undepreciated cost at date of intercompany sale [⅕ × ($36,200 − $4,000)]	6,440
Difference—equal to intercompany profit element in Post Corporation's annual depreciation expense	$ 4,760

Intercompany Profit in Depreciation and Minority Interest From the point of view of the consolidated entity, the intercompany profit element of annual depreciation expense represents a *realization* of a portion of the intercompany profit on the sale of the machinery. Depreciation, in this view, is in effect an *indirect sale* of a portion of the machinery to Post Corporation's customers. The selling prices of Post's products which are produced by the machine are established in amounts adequate to cover all costs of producing the products, including depreciation expense.

Thus, the $4,760 credit to Post Corporation's depreciation expense in the April 30, Year 9, consolidation elimination illustrated on page 246 in effect *increases* Sage Company's reported net income for consolidated purposes. This increase must be considered in the computation of the minority interest in Sage Company's net income for the year ended April 30, Year 9, and of the subsidiary's retained earnings at that date.

Intercompany Profit in Later Years Consolidation eliminations for later years in the useful life of a machine sold at an intercompany profit must reflect the fact that the intercompany profit element in annual depreciation expense in effect represents a *realization* of the intercompany profit. For example, the working paper consolidation elimination for Post Corporation and subsidiary at April 30, Year 10 (two years following the intercompany sale of machinery), would be as follows:

Retained Earnings—Sage [95% × ($23,800 − $4,760)]	18,088	
Minority Interest in Subsidiary [5% × ($23,800 − $4,760)] . . .	952	
Accumulated Depreciation—Post (2 × $4,760)	9,520	
Machinery—Post		23,800
Depreciation Expense—Post		4,760
To eliminate intercompany profit in machinery and related depreciation. (Income tax effects are ignored.)		

The credit amounts of the preceding consolidation elimination for Year 10 are the same as those for Year 9. The credit amounts will remain unchanged for all consolidation eliminations during the remaining useful life of the machinery. The $19,040 total of the debits to Sage Company's Retained Earnings account and to the minority interest in subsidiary represents the *unrealized* portion of the intercompany profit at the beginning of Year 10. Each succeeding year, the unrealized portion of the intercompany profit decreases, as indicated by the following summary of the consolidation elimination *debits* for those years:

	Year ended April 30		
	Year 11	**Year 12**	**Year 13**
Retained earnings—Sage	$13,566	$ 9,044	$ 4,522
Minority interest in subsidiary	714	476	238
Accumulated depreciation—Post	14,280	19,040	23,800

At the end of Year 13, the entire $23,800 of intercompany profit on the machinery has been realized through Post Corporation's annual depreciation expense charges. Thereafter, no consolidation eliminations are required for the machine until it is sold.

Intercompany profit on sale of intangible asset

The consolidation eliminations for intercompany profits on sales of intangible assets are similar to those for intercompany profits in depreciable assets. The unrealized intercompany profit of the selling affiliate is realized through the annual amortization expense charges of the purchasing affiliate.

PURCHASES OF AFFILIATE'S BONDS

The intercompany profits or losses on sales of merchandise, property and equipment, and intangible assets are *actual* gains or losses resulting from transactions between two affiliated corporations. Intercompany gains and losses may also be *imputed* when one affiliate purchases in the open market bonds issued by another affiliate. The gain or loss on such a transaction is *imputed,* because the transaction is not consummated between the two affiliates. No intercompany gain or loss would result from the *direct purchase* of one affiliate's bonds by another affiliate. The cost of the investment to the purchaser would be *exactly offset* by the carrying value of the debt to the issuer.

Illustration of purchase of affiliate's bonds

Assume that on May 1, Year 7, Sage Company (the subsidiary) issued to the public $500,000 principal amount of 6% debentures due May 1, Year 12. The debentures were issued at a price to yield an 8% return to investors. Interest was payable each May 1, Year 8 through Year 12. Debenture issue costs will be ignored in this example.

The net proceeds of the debenture issue to Sage Company were $460,081, computed as follows:[2]

Present value of $500,000 in five years @ 8%, with interest paid annually ($500,000 × .6806)	$340,300
Present value of $30,000 each year for five years @ 8% ($30,000 × 3.9927)	119,781
Proceeds of debenture issue	$460,081

---

[2] *Intermediate Accounting* of this series and Chapter 13 of this text contain comprehensive discussions of computations of debt issuance proceeds.

During the year ended April 30, Year 8, Sage Company would make the following journal entries for the debentures:

```
Year 7
May 1    Cash  . . . . . . . . . . . . . . . . . . . . . . . . .    460,081
             Discount on Debentures Payable  . . . . . . . . . . .     39,919
                  Debentures Payable  . . . . . . . . . . . . . .                500,000
             Issuance of 6% debentures due May 1, Year 12,
             at a discount.
Year 8
Apr. 30  Interest Expense  . . . . . . . . . . . . . . . . . . .     36,806
             Interest Payable . . . . . . . . . . . . . . . . . .                 30,000
             Discount on Debentures Payable  . . . . . . . .                  6,806
         Accrual of annual interest on 6% debentures.
         Interest computed as 8% × $460,081 = $36,806.
```

At April 30, Year 8, the balance of Sage Company's Discount on Debentures Payable account was $33,113.

Assume that on April 30, Year 8, Post Corporation (the parent) had idle cash available for investment. With a market yield rate of 10% on that date, Sage Company's 6% debentures due May 1, Year 12, could be purchased at a substantial discount. Consequently, Post Corporation purchased in the open market on April 30, Year 8, $375,000 principal amount of the debentures for $327,448 plus $22,500 accrued interest for one year. The $327,448 purchase price is computed as follows:

```
Present value of $375,000 in four years @ 10%, with interest paid
    annually ($375,000 × .6830)  . . . . . . . . . . . . . . . . . . . . . . . . .    $256,125
Present value of $22,500 each year for four years @ 10% ($22,500 ×
    3.1699)  . . . . . . . . . . . . . . . . . . . . . . . . . . . . . . . . . . .      71,323
Cost of $375,000 principal amount of debentures . . . . . . . . . . . . . .    $327,448
```

Post Corporation would make the following journal entry at April 30, Year 8, to record the purchase of Sage Company's debentures:

```
Investment in Subsidiary's Debentures . . . . . . . . . . . . . . .    327,448
Intercompany Interest Receivable . . . . . . . . . . . . . . . . .     22,500
    Cash  . . . . . . . . . . . . . . . . . . . . . . . . . . . . .                 349,948
Purchase of $375,000 principal amount of Sage Company's 6%
debentures due May 1, Year 12, and accrued interest.
```

From the standpoint of the consolidated entity, Post Corporation's purchase of Sage Company's debentures is equivalent to the reacquisition of the debentures for the treasury at an *imputed* gain of $22,717. Computation of the $22,717 gain is as follows:

Carrying value of Sage Company's debentures at Apr. 30, Year 8
($500,000 − $33,113) $466,887
Post Corporation's purchased share—$375,000/$500,000 × $466,887 . $350,165
Cost of Post Corporation's investment 327,448
Imputed gain on reacquisition of debentures . . . . $ 22,717

The $22,717 imputed gain **would not** be recorded in the accounting records of either the parent or the subsidiary. Instead, it would be reflected **only** in the following working paper consolidation elimination for Post Corporation and subsidiary at April 30, Year 8:

Debentures Payable—Sage 375,000
    Discount on Debentures Payable—Sage
      ($375,000/$500,000 × $33,113) 24,835
    Investment in Subsidiary's Debentures—Post 327,448
    Gain on Reacquisition of Debentures—Sage 22,717
To eliminate subsidiary's debentures purchased by parent, and
to recognize imputed gain on reacquisition of the debentures.
(Income tax effects are ignored.)

Disposition of Gain on Reacquisition The consolidation elimination illustrated above attributes the imputed gain on Post Corporation's purchase of its subsidiary's debentures to Sage Company—the subsidiary. This treatment of the gain follows from the assumption that the parent company's open-market purchase of the subsidiary's debentures was in effect the acquisition of the debentures for the consolidated entity's treasury. The parent company acted as *agent* for the subsidiary in the open-market transaction; hence the imputed gain is allocable to the subsidiary. Under this consolidated approach, the accounting for the imputed gain on the reacquisition of the subsidiary's debentures is the same as if the *subsidiary itself* had reacquired the debentures.

The entire imputed gain of $22,717 is reported in the consolidated income statement of Post Corporation and subsidiary for the year ended April 30, Year 8. This treatment is consistent with the provisions of **APB Opinion No. 26** (as amended by **APB Opinion No. 30,** "Reporting the Results of Operations"), which reads as follows:

A difference between the reacquisition price and the net carrying amount of the extinguished debt should be recognized currently in income of the period of extinguishment as losses or gains and identified as a separate item. The criteria in APB Opinion No. 30 should be used to determine whether the losses or gains are ordinary or extraordinary items. Gains and losses should not be amortized to future periods.[3]

Minority Interest in Gain on Reacquisition of Debentures As discussed in the preceding section, the imputed gain on Post Corporation's reacquisition of its subsidiary's debentures is attributed to the subsidiary. It follows that the gain should be considered in the computation of the minority interest in the subsidiary's net income for the year ended April 30, Year 8. Also, the imputed gain is included in the computation of the subsidiary's retained earnings at April 30, Year 8, for consolidated purposes.

Accounting for imputed gain in subsequent years

In the four years following Post Corporation's purchase of Sage Company's debentures, the gain *imputed* at the date of purchase is in effect *realized* by the consolidated entity through the differences in the two affiliates' amortization of discount. (It is essential that the affiliate which purchased the debentures undertake an amortization program consistent with that of the affiliate which issued the debentures.) To illustrate this concept, the accounting for the debenture interest by the two companies for the year ended April 30, Year 9, is presented on page 252.

The $4,732 difference between Post Corporation's $32,745 interest revenue and 75% of Sage Company's $37,351 interest expense— $28,013—represents to the consolidated entity a *realization* of a portion of the $22,717 *imputed* gain on the reacquisition of the subsidiary's debentures. The entire $22,717 would be realized as follows during the remaining term of the debentures:

Year ended April 30	Post Corporation interest revenue	75% of Sage Company's interest expense	Difference—representing realization of imputed gain
Year 9	$ 32,745	$ 28,013	$ 4,732
Year 10	33,769	28,454	5,315
Year 11	34,896	28,930	5,966
Year 12	36,142	29,438	6,704
	$137,552	$114,835	$22,717

---

[3] *APB Opinion No. 26*, "Early Extinguishment of Debt," AICPA (New York: 1973), pp. 501–502.

	Post Corporation		**Sage Company**		
Year 8					
May 1	Cash 22,500		Interest Payable 30,000		
	Intercompany		Cash		30,000
	Interest		Payment of accrued interest		
	Receivable	22,500	on 6% debentures.		
	Receipt of				
	accrued in-				
	terest pur-				
	chased on				
	Sage Com-				
	pany's 6%				
	debentures.				
Year 9					
Apr. 30	Intercompany		Interest Expense 37,351		
	Interest		Intercompany Interest		
	Receivable . . . 22,500		Payable		22,500
	Investment		Interest Payable . . .		7,500
	in Subsidiary's		Discount on Deben-		
	Debentures . . . 10,245		tures Payable		7,351
	Intercompany		Accrual of annual interest		
	Interest		on 6% debentures. Interest		
	Revenue	32,745	computed as 8% × $466,887		
	Accrual of		= $37,351.		
	annual interest				
	on Sage Com-				
	pany's 6% debentures.				
	Interest com-				
	puted as 10% ×				
	$327,448 = $32,745.				

Working Paper Consolidation Elimination at April 30, Year 9 The consolidation elimination for the debentures and interest at April 30, Year 9, would be as shown on page 253.

The consolidation elimination on page 253 effectively reduces consolidated income before minority interest by $4,732. As indicated previously, the $4,732 is the difference between the eliminated interest revenue of the parent—$32,745—and 75% of the subsidiary's $37,351 interest expense—$28,013. Failure to eliminate intercompany interest in this manner would result in a $4,732 overstatement of pre-minority interest consolidated income, because the *entire* $22,717 imputed gain on the reacquisition of the subsidiary's debentures was recognized in the consolidated income statement for the year of reacquisition.

Intercompany Interest Revenue—Post	32,745	
Debentures Payable—Sage	375,000	
Discount on Debentures Payable—Sage ($375,000/		
$500,000 × $25,762)		19,322
Investment in Subsidiary's Debentures—Post		337,693
Interest Expense—Sage		28,013
Retained Earnings—Sage (95% × $22,717)		21,581
Minority Interest in Subsidiary (5% × $22,717)		1,136

To eliminate subsidiary's debentures owned by parent, and related interest revenue and expense; and to increase parent's share of subsidiary's beginning retained earnings by amount of unamortized imputed gain on the reacquisition of the debentures. (Income tax effects are ignored.)

The $4,732 reduction of consolidated income before minority interest is attributable to the subsidiary, since the original imputed gain to which the $4,732 relates was allocated to the subsidiary. Consequently, the $4,732 must be considered in the computation of minority interest in net income of the subsidiary for the year ended April 30, Year 9. The $4,732 also enters into the computation of the subsidiary's retained earnings at April 30, Year 9, for consolidated purposes.

The amounts associated with Sage Company's debentures would be reflected in the consolidating financial statements working papers for the year ended April 30, Year 9, as illustrated on page 254.

Working Paper Consolidation Elimination at April 30, Year 10 The consolidation elimination for Post Corporation and subsidiary at April 30, Year 10, would be as follows:

Intercompany Interest Revenue—Post	33,769	
Debentures Payable—Sage	375,000	
Discount on Debentures Payable—Sage ($375,000/		
$500,000 × $17,823)		13,368
Investment in Subsidiary's Debentures—Post		348,962
Interest Expense—Sage		28,454
Retained Earnings—Sage (95% × $17,985)		17,086
Minority Interest in Subsidiary (5% × $17,985)		899

To eliminate subsidiary's debentures owned by parent, and related interest revenue and expense; and to increase subsidiary's beginning retained earnings by amount of unamortized imputed gain on the reacquisition of the debentures. (Income tax effects are ignored.)

	Post Corporation	Sage Company	Consolidation eliminations Increase (decrease)	Consolidated
Income Statement				
Revenue				
Intercompany interest				
revenue	$ 32,745	$ –0–	$ (32,745)	$ –0–
Costs and expenses				
Interest expense . . .	$ –0–	$ 37,351	$ (28,013)	$ 9,338
Statement of Retained Earnings				
Retained earnings,				
May 1, Year 8	$ x,xxx,xxx	$ xxx,xxx	$ 21,581	$ x,xxx,xxx
Balance Sheet				
Assets				
Investment in subsidiary's debentures	$ 337,693	$ –0–	$ (337,693)	$ –0–
Liabilities & Stockholders' Equity				
Debentures payable .	$ –0–	$ 500,000	$ (375,000)	$ 125,000
Discount on debentures payable	–0–	(25,762)	(19,322)	(6,440)
Minority interest in subsidiary	–0–	–0–	1,136	xxx,xxx

Comparable consolidation eliminations would be appropriate for Years 11 and 12. After Sage Company paid the debentures in full at their May 1, Year 12, maturity date, no further consolidation eliminations for debentures would be required.

Reissuance of intercompany debentures

The orderly amortization of an imputed gain on the reacquisition of an affiliate's debentures is disrupted if the acquiring affiliate reissues the debentures before they mature. A *transaction* gain or loss on such a reissuance is not *realized* by the consolidated entity. Logic requires that a consolidation elimination must be prepared to treat the transaction gain or loss as premium or discount on the reissued debt, as appropriate. These complex issues are rarely encountered, however; hence they will not be illustrated.

COMPREHENSIVE ILLUSTRATION OF CONSOLIDATING FINANCIAL STATEMENTS WORKING PAPERS

In this chapter and in Chapter 6, we have explained and illustrated a number of aspects of consolidating financial statements working papers. The comprehensive illustration which follows incorporates most of these aspects. The illustration is for Post Corporation and its partially owned subsidiary, Sage Company, for the year ended April 30, Year 9.

The ledger accounts for Post Corporation's Investment in Subsidiary, Retained Earnings, and Retained Earnings of Subsidiary, and for Sage Company's Retained Earnings, are presented below and on page 256. Review of these accounts should aid in understanding the illustrative consolidating financial statements working papers on pages 257–261.

POST CORPORATION
Investment in Subsidiary

Date	Explanation	Debit	Credit	Balance
4/30/6	Cost of business combination	1,192,250		1,192,250 dr.
3/24/7	Dividends (95% × $40,000)		38,000	1,154,250 dr.
4/30/7	Earnings (95% × $90,000)	85,500		1,239,750 dr.
4/30/7	Amortization (95% × $46,000)		43,700	1,196,050 dr.
3/22/8	Dividends (95% × $50,000)		47,500	1,148,550 dr.
4/30/8	Earnings (95% × $105,000)	99,750		1,248,300 dr.
4/30/8	Amortization (95% × $20,000)		19,000	1,229,300 dr.
3/25/9	Dividends (95% × $60,000)		57,000	1,172,300 dr.
4/30/9	Earnings (95% × $115,000)	109,250		1,281,550 dr.
4/30/9	Amortization (95% × $20,000)		19,000	1,262,550 dr.

Retained Earnings

Date	Explanation	Debit	Credit	Balance
4/30/6	Balance			1,050,000 cr.
4/30/7	Dividends	158,550		891,450 cr.
4/30/7	Net income ($461,800 − $3,800)		458,000	1,349,450 cr.
4/30/8	Dividends	158,550		1,190,900 cr.
4/30/8	Net income ($352,600 − $33,250)		319,350	1,510,250 cr.
4/30/9	Dividends	158,550		1,351,700 cr.
4/30/9	Net income ($460,200 − $33,250)		426,950	1,778,650 cr.

Retained Earnings of Subsidiary

Date	Explanation	Debit	Credit	Balance
4/30/7	Undistributed income (95% × $4,000)		3,800	3,800 cr.
4/30/8	Undistributed income (95% × $35,000)		33,250	37,050 cr.
4/30/9	Undistributed income (95% × $35,000)		33,250	70,300 cr.

SAGE COMPANY
Retained Earnings

Date	Explanation	Debit	Credit	Balance
4/30/6	Balance		334,000	334,000 cr.
3/24/7	Dividends	40,000		294,000 cr.
4/30/7	Net income		90,000	384,000 cr.
3/22/8	Dividends	50,000		334,000 cr.
4/30/8	Net income		105,000	439,000 cr.
3/25/9	Dividends	60,000		379,000 cr.
4/30/9	Net income		115,000	494,000 cr.

Equity Method: partially owned purchased subsidiary

POST CORPORATION AND SUBSIDIARY
Consolidating Financial Statements
Year Ended April 30, Year 9

	Post Corporation	Sage Company	Consolidation eliminations Increase (decrease)	Consolidated
Income Statement				
Revenue				
Net sales	$ 5,900,000	$ 1,400,000		$ 7,300,000
Intercompany sales	–0–	150,000	$(b) (150,000)	–0–
Intercompany interest revenue . . .	32,745	–0–	(e) (32,745)	–0–
Intercompany investment income .	90,250	–0–	(a) (90,250)	–0–
Intercompany revenue (expenses) .	14,000	(14,000)		–0–
	$ 6,036,995	$1,536,000	$ (272,995)	$ 7,300,000
Costs and expenses			$ (a) 17,500	
			(b) (26,000)	
Cost of goods sold	$ 4,300,000	$ 950,000	(d) (4,760)	$5,236,740
Intercompany cost of goods sold .	–0–	120,000	(b) (120,000)	–0–
Selling, general, and				
administrative expenses	670,352	141,149	(a) 2,500	814,001
Interest expense	51,518	37,351	(e) (28,013)	60,856
Income taxes expense	554,925	172,500		727,425
Minority interest in net income of				
subsidiary	–0–	–0–	(f) 4,551	4,551
	$ 5,576,795	$1,421,000	$ (154,222)	$ 6,843,573
Net income	$ 460,200	$ 115,000	$ (118,773)	$ 456,427
Statement of Retained Earnings			$ (a) (439,000)	
			(b) (7,600)	
Retained earnings, May 1, Year 8 . .	$ 1,547,300	$ 439,000	(c) (50,000)	$ 1,488,671
			(d) (22,610)	
			(e) 21,581	
Net income	460,200	115,000	(118,773)	456,427
	$ 2,007,500	$ 554,000	$ (616,402)	$ 1,945,098
Dividends	158,550	60,000	(a) (60,000)	158,550
Retained earnings, Apr. 30, Year 9 .	$ 1,848,950	$ 494,000	$ (556,402)	$ 1,786,548

POST CORPORATION AND SUBSIDIARY
Consolidating Financial Statements (Concluded)
Year Ended April 30, Year 9

	Post Corporation	Sage Company	Consolidation eliminations Increase (decrease)		Consolidated
Balance Sheet					
Assets					
Intercompany receivables (payables).............	$ (3,500)	$ 3,500			$ –0–
Inventories	950,000	500,000	$(b)	(12,000)	1,438,000
Other current assets	750,000	429,000			1,179,000
Investment in subsidiary......	1,262,550	–0–	(a)	(1,262,550)	–0–
Investment in subsidiary's debentures............	337,693	–0–	(e)	(337,693)	–0–
Property, plant, and equipment, net	3,700,000	1,300,000	(a) (d)	148,000 (19,040)	5,128,960
Land for building site	–0–	175,000	(c)	(50,000)	125,000
Leasehold	–0–	–0–	(a)	15,000	15,000
Goodwill	95,000	–0–	(a)	37,000	132,000
	$7,091,743	$2,407,500	$	(1,481,283)	$8,017,960
Liabilities & Stockholders' Equity					
Debentures payable	$ –0–	$ 500,000	$(e)	(375,000)	$ 125,000
Discount on debentures payable.	–0–	(25,762)	(e)	(19,322)	(6,440)
Other liabilities	2,625,543	804,262			3,429,805
Minority interest in subsidiary ..	–0–	–0–	(a) (b) (d) (e) (f)	61,700 (400) (1,190) 1,136 4,551	65,797
Common stock, $1 par value....	1,057,000	–0–			1,057,000
Capital stock, $10 par value ...	–0–	400,000	(a)	(400,000)	–0–
Paid-in capital in excess of par .	1,560,250	235,000	(a)	(235,000)	1,560,250
Retained earnings	1,848,950	494,000		(556,402)	1,786,548
	$7,091,743	$2,407,500	$	(1,481,283)	$8,017,960

POST CORPORATION AND SUBSIDIARY
Consolidation Eliminations
April 30, Year 9

(a) Capital Stock—Sage	400,000	
Paid-in Capital in Excess of Par—Sage	235,000	
Retained Earnings—Sage	439,000	
Intercompany Investment Income—Post	90,250	
Property, Plant, and Equipment—Sage ($190,000 —		
$42,000)	148,000	
Leasehold—Sage ($30,000 — $15,000)	15,000	
Goodwill—Sage ($40,000 — $3,000)	37,000	
Cost of Goods Sold—Sage	17,500	
Selling, General, and Administrative Expenses—Sage . . .	2,500	
Investment in Subsidiary—Post		1,262,550
Dividends—Sage		60,000
Minority Interest in Subsidiary		61,700

To carry out the following:

(1) Eliminate intercompany investment and equity accounts of subsidiary at beginning of year, and subsidiary dividend.

(2) Provide for Year 9 depreciation and amortization on differences between combination date fair values and carrying values of Sage's assets, as follows:

	To cost of goods sold	To selling, general, and administrative expenses
Building depreciation	$ 2,000	$2,000
Machinery and equipment depreciation	10,000	–0–
Leasehold amortization . . .	5,000	–0–
Goodwill amortization	500	500
	$17,500	$2,500

(3) Allocate remaining unamortized differences between combination date fair values and carrying values to appropriate assets.

(4) Establish minority interest in subsidiary at beginning of year ($64,700), less minority share of dividends declared by subsidiary during year (5% × $60,000 = $3,000). (Income tax effects are ignored.)

(b) Minority Interest in Subsidiary   400
    Retained Earnings—Sage   7,600
    Intercompany Sales—Sage 150,000
        Intercompany Cost of Goods Sold—Sage   120,000
        Cost of Goods Sold—Post   26,000
        Inventories—Post   12,000
    To eliminate intercompany sales, cost of goods sold, and
    profits in inventories. (Income tax effects are ignored.)

(c) Retained Earnings—Post   50,000
        Land for Building Site—Sage   50,000
    To eliminate intercompany profit in land. (Income tax
    effects are ignored.)

(d) Minority Interest in Subsidiary   1,190
    Retained Earnings—Sage   22,610
    Accumulated Depreciation: Machinery—Post   4,760
        Machinery—Post   23,800
        Depreciation Expense—Post   4,760
    To eliminate intercompany profit in machinery and in
    related depreciation. (Income tax effects are ignored.)

(e) Intercompany Interest Revenue—Post   32,745
    Debentures Payable—Sage 375,000
        Discount on Debentures Payable—Sage   19,322
        Investment in Subsidiary's Debentures—Post . . .   337,693
        Interest Expense—Sage   28,013
        Minority Interest in Subsidiary   1,136
        Retained Earnings—Sage   21,581
    To eliminate subsidiary's debentures owned by parent,
    and related interest revenue and expense; and to in-
    crease parent's share of subsidiary's beginning retained
    earnings by amount of unamortized imputed gain on the
    reacquisition of the debentures. (Income tax effects are
    ignored.)

(f) Minority Interest in Net Income of Subsidiary   4,551
        Minority Interest in Subsidiary   4,551
    To establish minority interest in subsidiary's adjusted net
    income for Year 9, as follows:

Net income reported by subsidiary	$115,000
Adjustments due to consolidation elimi-	
nations:	
(a)	(20,000)
(b) ($150,000 − $146,000)	(4,000)
(d)	4,760
(e) ($32,745 − $28,013)	(4,732)
Adjusted net income of subsidiary	$91,028
Minority share—5% × $91,028 = $4,551 . .	$ 4,551

Following are important features of the consolidating financial statements working papers for Post Corporation and subsidiary at April 30, Year 9:

1 Intercompany investment income of Post Corporation for Year 9 is computed as follows:

95% × $115,000 (Sage Company's reported net income for Year 9) . .	$109,250
Less: 95% × $20,000 (Year 9 amortization of differences between fair	
values and carrying values of Sage Company's net assets at date of	
business combination)	19,000
Intercompany investment income of Post Corporation for Year 9	$ 90,250

2 Post Corporation's intercompany revenue of $14,000 is the management fee from Sage Company, computed as 1% of Sage's $1,400,000 net sales for Year 9.

3 The income tax effects of Post Corporation's use of the equity method of accounting for its subsidiary's operating results are not reflected in Post's income tax expense for Year 9. Income tax consequences associated with the equity method of accounting are considered in Chapter 8.

4 Post Corporation's retained earnings balances in the consolidating statement of retained earnings are the totals of Post's two accounts for retained earnings, as follows:

	Balance, May 1, Year 8	Balance, Apr. 30, Year 9
Post Corporation:		
Retained earnings	$1,510,250	$1,778,650
Retained earnings of subsidiary	37,050	70,300
Total	$1,547,300	$1,848,950

5 The net intercompany payable of Post Corporation at April 30, Year 9, consists of the following amounts:

Account payable to Sage Company for merchandise purchases		$40,000
Less: Interest receivable from Sage Company	$22,500	
Management fee receivable from Sage Company . . .	14,000	36,500
Net intercompany payable		$ 3,500

6 Consolidation elimination (*a*) continues the amortization of differences between fair values and carrying values of the subsidiary's net assets at date of the business combination of Post Corporation and Sage Company (see Chapter 6, page 217).

7 The $64,700 minority interest at beginning of year, as set forth in the explanation for consolidation elimination (*a*), is computed as follows:

Stockholders' equity of Sage Company at May 1, Year 8:		
Capital stock		$ 400,000
Paid-in capital in excess of par.		235,000
Retained earnings		439,000
Subtotal		$1,074,000
Unamortized differences between fair values and carrying values of Sage Company's net assets as of May 1, Year 8 (see page 213):		
Land		$ 60,000
Building ($80,000 − $8,000).		72,000
Machinery and equipment ($50,000 − $20,000).		30,000
Leasehold ($30,000 − $10,000)		20,000
Goodwill ($40,000 − $2,000)		38,000
Subtotal		$ 220,000
Total adjusted net assets of Sage Company, May 1, Year 8		$1,294,000
Minority interest therein: 5% × $1,294,000 = $64,700		$ 64,700

8 Consolidation eliminations (*b*), (*c*), (*d*), and (*e*) are identical to the eliminations illustrated in this chapter at pages 240, 243, 246, and 252 to 253, respectively. For posting to the consolidating financial statements working papers, consolidation elimination (*d*) was condensed. The credit to Depreciation Expense in elimination (*d*) is posted to Cost of Goods Sold in the consolidating income statement.

9 The $19,322 *decrease* in Discount on Debentures Payable in the consolidating balance sheet is actually an *increase* for purposes of computing the $(1,481,283) total of the consolidation eliminations column for liabilities and stockholders' equity.

10 Because of the elimination of intercompany profits, consolidated net income is not equal to the parent company's equity method net income. Consolidated net income may be verified as follows:

Post Corporation's net income		$460,200
Less: Post Corporation's share of adjustments to subsidiary's		
reported net income for intercompany profits:		
Consolidation elimination (b)	$(4,000)	
Consolidation elimination (d)	4,760	
Consolidation elimination (e)	(4,732)	
Total	$(3,972)	
Post Corporation's share—95% × $(3,972)		(3,773)
Consolidated net income		$456,427

11 Similarly, consolidated retained earnings does not equal parent company retained earnings. Consolidated retained earnings is verified as follows:

Post Corporation retained earnings		$1,848,950
Adjustments:		
Post Corporation's share of adjustments to subsidiary's reported		
net income (see 10, above)		(3,773)
Intercompany profit in Post Corporation's retained earnings—		
consolidation elimination (c)		(50,000)
Post Corporation's share of adjustments to subsidiary's beginning		
retained earnings for intercompany profits:		
Consolidation elimination (b)	$(7,600)	
Consolidation elimination (d)	(22,610)	
Consolidation elimination (e)	21,581	(8,629)
Consolidated retained earnings		$1,786,548

12 The consolidated balances in the consolidating financial statements working papers represent the financial position and operating results of Post Corporation and subsidiary resulting from the consolidated entity's transactions with **outsiders.** All intercompany transactions, profits, and balances have been eliminated in arriving at the consolidated amounts.

Concluding comments

The most common features of consolidating financial statements working papers have been discussed in this chapter and in Chapters 5 and 6. Chapter 8 includes the less frequent aspects of consolidations, as well as the more complex problems of consolidating financial statements working papers.

REVIEW QUESTIONS

1 How are consolidated financial statements affected if intercompany profits resulting from transactions between parent and subsidiaries are not eliminated? Explain.

2 What consolidated financial statement categories are affected by intercompany sales of merchandise at a profit? Explain.

3 Some accountants advocate the elimination of intercompany profit in the parent's ending inventory only to the extent of the parent's ownership interest in the selling subsidiary's stock. What argument can be advanced in opposition to this treatment of intercompany profit?

4 How do intercompany sales of property and equipment and intangible assets differ from intercompany sales of merchandise?

5 Is intercompany profit on the sale of land ever *realized?* Explain.

6 Sayles Company, a 90% owned subsidiary of Partin Corporation, sold to Partin for $10,000 a machine with an undepreciated cost of $8,000, no salvage value, and an estimated remaining useful life of four years. Explain how the intercompany profit element of Partin Corporation's annual depreciation expense for the machine is accounted for in consolidating financial statements working papers.

7 "No intercompany gain or loss should be recognized when a parent purchases in the open market outstanding bonds of its subsidiary, because the transaction is not an *intercompany* transaction." Do you agree? Explain.

8 What accounting problems result from the reissuance by a subsidiary of parent company bonds acquired in the open market by the subsidiary? Explain.

9 Intercompany profits or losses in inventories, plant assets, or bonds result in consolidated net income which differs from the parent company's equity-method net income. Why is this true? Explain.

10 How is the intercompany profit in a subsidiary's *beginning* inventory resulting from the parent's sales to the subsidiary accounted for in a consolidation elimination? Explain.

EXERCISES

Ex. 7-1 Select the best answer for each of the following multiple choice questions.
1 Paul Company owns 75% of the outstanding common stock of Saul Company. During Year 3, Paul's profits on its transactions with Saul amounted to $50,000. The elimination for intercompany profit is:
a Not necessary
b $50,000

    c $37,500

    d Allocated between Paul Company and the minority shareholders of Saul Company

    e None of the above

2 On April 1, Year 5, Prynn Corporation sold equipment costing $1,000,000 with accumulated depreciation of $250,000 to its wholly owned subsidiary, Swynn Company, for $900,000. Prynn was depreciating the equipment on the straight-line method over 20 years with no salvage value, which Swynn continued. In the "Swynn Company" column of consolidating financial statements working papers at March 31, Year 6, the cost and accumulated depreciation, respectively, are:

    a $1,000,000 and $300,000

    b $900,000 and $50,000

    c $900,000 and $60,000

    d $750,000 and $50,000

3 In the preparation of consolidated financial statements, the intercompany profit on inventory acquired by a parent from its subsidiary should:

    a Not be eliminated

    b Be eliminated in full

    c Be eliminated to the extent of the parent's controlling interest in the subsidiary

    d Be eliminated to the extent of the minority interest in the subsidiary

Ex. 7-2 Pilar Corporation supplies all the inventory of its wholly owned subsidiary, Soule Company. Both Pilar and Soule use perpetual inventory accounting. Pilar bills merchandise to Soule at a price 20% in excess of Pilar's cost. For the fiscal year ended November 30, Year 8, Pilar Corporation's sales to Soule aggregated $120,000 at billed prices. At billed prices, Soule's December 1, Year 7, inventory was $18,000 and its November 30, Year 8, inventory was $24,000. Prepare an analysis of intercompany sales, cost of sales, and profit in inventory for the year ended November 30, Year 8. Your analysis should show selling price, cost, and gross profit for each item.

Ex. 7-3 On October 1, Year 4, Pease Corporation purchased new equipment for $14,500 from its 90%-owned subsidiary, Steap Company. The equipment cost Steap $9,000 and had an estimated useful life of 10 years as of October 1, Year 4. Pease uses the sum-of-the-years'-digits depreciation method. Prepare a working paper consolidation elimination for Pease Corporation and subsidiary at September 30, Year 6.

Ex. 7-4 Searles Company, the wholly owned subsidiary of Parcell Corporation, issued 8%, five-year bonds May 1, Year 1, at their principal amount of $100,000. Interest is payable annually. On April 30, Year 2, Parcell Corporation purchased in the open market 40% of Searles Company's outstanding bonds at a 10% yield, plus accrued interest. Compute the amount of cash paid by Parcell Corporation and the imputed consolidated gain on the reacquisition of the bonds. Round all computations to the nearest dollar.

Ex. 7-5 Pastel Corporation acquired 90% of the outstanding common stock of Sortie Company on August 1, Year 2. During the year ended July 31, Year 3, Pastel made merchandise sales to Sortie in the amount of $100,000; the merchandise was priced at 25% above Pastel's cost. Sortie had 20% of this merchandise in inventory at July 31, Year 3. Prepare a working paper consolidation elimination for Pastel Corporation and subsidiary at July 31, Year 3.

Ex. 7-6 On January 2, Year 1, Stage Company, an 80%-owned subsidiary of Paige Corporation, sold to its parent for $10,000 cash a machine with undepreciated cost of $8,000, a five-year remaining useful life, and no salvage value. Both Paige Corporation and Stage Company use straight-line depreciation for all machinery. Compute the missing amounts in the working paper consolidation eliminations below. Use the identifying numbers for the missing amounts in your solution.

	December 31, Year 2	December 31, Year 4
Minority Interest in Subsidiary	(1)	(4)
Retained Earnings—Stage	(2)	(5)
Accumulated Depreciation, Machinery—Paige	(3)	(6)
Machinery—Paige	2,000	2,000
Depreciation Expense—Paige	400	400

To eliminate intercompany profit in machinery and in related depreciation. (Income tax effects are ignored.)

SHORT CASES FOR ANALYSIS AND DECISION

Case 7-1 The existence of intercompany profits in consolidated inventories as a result of sales by a partially owned subsidiary to its parent has given rise to the following three viewpoints as to how such profits should be treated for consolidated financial statements:

1 Only the parent company's share of intercompany profits in inventory should be eliminated.

2 The entire amount of intercompany profits in inventories should be eliminated against the equities of the controlling and minority groups in proportion to their interests.

3 The entire amount of intercompany profits in inventories should be eliminated against consolidated retained earnings.

Instructions Give arguments to support each treatment.

Case 7-2 Poynter Corporation has begun selling idle equipment from a discontinued product line to a wholly owned subsidiary, Stacey Company. The idle equipment had been transferred from the Equipment account to an Idle Equipment account and had been written down to net realizable value based on quotations from used machinery dealers. Depreciation expense on the idle equipment was terminated when the product line was discontinued.

During Year 3, Poynter Corporation's sales of idle equipment to Stacey Company totaled $50,000; they were accounted for by Poynter and Stacey in the following aggregate journal entries:

Poynter Corporation

Cash	50,000	
Sales of Idle Equipment		50,000

To record sales of idle equipment to Stacey Company.

Cost of Idle Equipment Sold	40,000	
Idle Equipment		40,000

To write off net realizable value of idle equipment sold to Stacey Company.

Stacey Company

Equipment	50,000	
Cash		50,000

To record purchases of used equipment from Poynter Corporation. . .

Depreciation: Equipment	5,000	
Accumulated Depreciation: Equipment		5,000

To provide, in accordance with regular policy, depreciation for one-half
year in year of acquisition of equipment, based on estimated useful
life of five years and no salvage value.

At December 31, Year 3, the controller of Poynter Corporation prepared the
following working paper consolidation elimination:

Retained Earnings—Poynter	10,000	
Equipment—Stacey.		10,000

To eliminate intercompany profit in machinery and equipment.

Instructions Evaluate the accounting entries given above.

Case 7-3 Pleasure Crafts, Inc., sells sailboats for cash or on two-year installment contracts
with no down payment and a 12% nominal rate of interest. For example, the
installment contract for a $6,000 cash-price boat would be in the aggregate
amount of $7,440, computed as follows:

Cash selling price	$6,000
Interest on $6,000 @ 12% for two years	1,440
Total contract balance	$7,440

Under the above contract, 24 monthly installments would be $310 each,
beginning one month after the date of the contract. The resultant effective
annual rate of interest would be 21.6% (1.8026% per month), computed as
follows:

$$\$6,000 = \$310 \, P_{\overline{24}|i}$$
$$19.3548 = P_{\overline{24}|i}$$
$$i = 1.8026\%$$

Pleasure Crafts, Inc., sells all its installment contracts for boat sales to its
wholly owned sales finance subsidiary, Sailboat Financing, Inc. Sailboat Financing pays Pleasure Crafts the cash sales price of the boat. Pleasure Crafts uses
the **nominal rate** of interest (12% compounded monthly) in computing the sales
price for a boat financed on an installment contract. For the contract illustrated
above, the computed sales price would be as follows:

$$S = \$310 \, P_{\overline{24}|\frac{1}{2}\%}$$
$$S = \$310 \times 22.5629$$
$$S = \$6,994$$

Pleasure Crafts, Inc., would record the preceding sales of the boat and the
contract as follows:

Contract Receivable	7,440	
Unearned Interest Revenue		446
Sales		6,994

To record sale of boat on contract for 24 monthly installments of $310 each, discounted at 12% compounded monthly.

Cost of Goods Sold	4,200	
Inventories		4,200

To reduce inventories for cost of boat sold.

Cash	6,000	
Unearned Interest Revenue	446	
Interest Expense	994	
Contract Receivable		7,440

To record sale of contract to Sailboat Financing, Inc.

Sailboat Financing, Inc., would record the purchase of the contract by the following entry:

Contract Receivable	7,440	
Unearned Interest Revenue		1,440
Cash		6,000

To record purchase of contract for 24 monthly installments of $310 each from Pleasure Crafts, Inc.

In consolidating financial statements working papers for Pleasure Crafts, Inc., and subsidiary, the $994 Interest Expense account of Pleasure Crafts would be eliminated against the $1,440 Unearned Interest Revenue account of Sailboat Financing, Inc.

Executives of Pleasure Crafts, Inc., defend the use of the 12% nominal interest rate for determining the $6,994 sale price of a boat sold on an installment contract for two reasons. First, the sales price of a financed boat should be higher than the cash sales price because of the costs incurred in setting up the contract (credit investigation of purchaser, etc.) and selling it to the subsidiary. Second, Sailboat Financing, Inc., can resell contracts to an unrelated financial institution for an amount somewhat in excess of the $6,994 contract sales price.

Instructions Do you concur with the accounting techniques described above? Explain.

PROBLEMS

7-4 Phyll Company sells merchandise to its 90%-owned subsidiary, Stream Company, at a markup of 25% on cost. Stream Company sells merchandise to Phyll Company at a markup of 33⅓% on cost. Merchandise transactions between the two companies for the year ended June 30, Year 2, were as follows:

	Phyll sales to Stream	Stream sales to Phyll
July 1, Year 1, inventory of purchaser	$ 48,000	$ 30,000
Sales during year	600,000	800,000
	$648,000	$830,000
June 30, Year 2, inventory of purchaser.	60,000	40,000
Cost of goods sold during year	$588,000	$790,000

Instructions Prepare in good form working paper consolidation eliminations at June 30, Year 2, for Phyll Company and subsidiary. Ignore income taxes.

7-5 Porter Corporation owns 90% of the outstanding capital stock of Sanders Company. On March 1, Year 4, Sanders sold to Porter for $100,000 cash a warehouse carried in Sanders's Leasehold Improvements account at that date at unamortized cost of $80,000. Porter is amortizing the warehouse on the straight-line basis over the remaining life of the lease, which expires February 28, Year 14.

On March 1, Year 5, Porter Corporation purchased in the open market for $48,262 cash (a 10% yield) one-half of Sanders Company's $100,000 principal amount 8% bonds due February 28, Year 7. The bonds had been issued at their principal amount March 1, Year 2, with interest payable annually each February 28.

Instructions Prepare in good form working paper consolidation eliminations at February 28, Year 6, for Porter Corporation and subsidiary. Ignore income taxes.

7-6 On July 1, Year 8, Palmdale Corporation and its wholly owned subsidiary San Marino Company entered into the following transactions:
(1) Palmdale sold to San Marino for $16,000 cash a machine having undepreciated cost to Palmdale at date of sale in the amount of $12,000. San Marino estimated a remaining useful life of eight years and no salvage value for the machine. San Marino Company uses straight-line depreciation for all plant and equipment.
(2) Palmdale purchased in the open market for $361,578 (a 12% yield) four-fifths of San Marino's outstanding 8% debentures due June 30, Year 11. On San Marino's accounting records at July 1, Year 8, were the following balances:

8% debentures payable, due June 30, Year 11	$500,000
Discount on 8% debentures	24,881

The 8% debentures (interest payable each June 30) had been issued by San Marino July 1, Year 6, to yield 10%. Interest expense recorded by San Marino through Year 8 was as follows:

Year ended June 30, Year 7	$46,208
Year ended June 30, Year 8	46,829

Instructions Prepare in good form working paper consolidation eliminations at June 30, Year 9, for Palmdale Corporation and subsidiary. Ignore income taxes.

7-7 Preble Corporation acquired 80% of Solo Company's 1,250 shares of $100 par value common stock outstanding on July 1, Year 6, for $158,600. The excess of the implied fair value of Solo's net assets over their carrying values at July 1, Year 6, was attributable as follows:

To inventories $3,000

To equipment (five-year remaining useful life at July 1, Year 6) 4,000

To goodwill (five-year remaining useful life at July 1, Year 6) . . . . Remainder
of excess

In addition, on July 1, Year 6, Preble Corporation purchased in the open market at their face amount $40,000 of Solo Company's 6% bonds payable. Interest is payable by Solo each July 1 and January 1.

Financial statements for Preble Corporation and Solo Company for the period ended December 31, Year 6, appear at the bottom of this page and on page 271. The following information is also available:

(1) Intercompany sales data for the six months ended December 31, Year 6, were as follows:

	Preble Corporation	Solo Company
Intercompany payables at end of year	$13,000	$ 5,500
Intercompany purchases in inventory at end of year	25,000	18,000

(2) On October 1, Year 6, Preble Corporation sold to Solo Company for $12,000 equipment having undepreciated cost to Preble at that date in the amount of $14,000. Solo Company established a five-year useful life, no residual value, and straight-line depreciation for the equipment.

PREBLE CORPORATION AND SOLO COMPANY
Financial Statements
Period Ended December 31, Year 6

	Preble Corporation (Year ended 12-31-6)	Solo Company (Six months ended 12-31-6)
Income Statement		
Revenue		
Net Sales	$ 902,000	$400,000
Intercompany sales	60,000	105,000
Intercompany interest revenue (expense)	1,200	(1,200)
Intercompany investment income	12,940	–0–
Intercompany (loss) on sale of equipment	(2,000)	–0–
	$ 974,140	$503,800
Costs and expenses		
Cost of goods sold	$ 720,000	$300,000
Intercompany cost of goods sold	50,000	84,000
Operating expenses	124,140	99,800
	$ 894,140	$483,800
Net income	$ 80,000	$ 20,000

Statement of Retained Earnings

Retained earnings at beginning of period	$ 220,000	$ 50,000
Net income	80,000	20,000
	$ 300,000	$ 70,000
Dividends	36,000	9,000
Retained earnings, Dec. 31, Year 6	$ 264,000	$ 61,000

Balance Sheet

Assets

Intercompany receivables (payables)	$	100	$ (100)
Inventories, at fifo-cost		300,000	75,000
Investment in subsidiary		164,340	-0-
Investment in subsidiary's bonds		40,000	-0-
Plant and equipment		794,000	280,600
Accumulated depreciation		(260,000)	(30,000)
Other assets		610,900	73,400
		$1,649,340	$398,900

Liabilities & Stockholders' Equity

Dividends payable	$ -0-	$ 1,600
Bonds payable	600,000	85,000
Other liabilities	376,340	114,300
Capital stock	360,000	125,000
Paid-in capital in excess of par	49,000	12,000
Retained earnings	264,000	61,000
	$1,649,340	$398,900

(3) Dividends were declared by Solo Company as follows:

Sept. 30, Year 6	$1,000
Dec. 31, Year 6	8,000
Total dividends declared	$9,000

Instructions Prepare consolidating financial statements working papers and related consolidation eliminations for Preble Corporation and subsidiary for the year ended December 31, Year 6. Ignore income taxes.

7-8 On January 2, Year 1, Pence Corporation issued 5,000 shares of its $10 par value capital stock in exchange for all 3,000 shares of Swain Company $20 par value common stock outstanding on that date. Out-of-pocket costs of the combination were negligible. The business combination qualified for pooling-of-interests accounting, and Pence Corporation adopted the equity method of accounting for Swain Company's operating results.

Condensed financial statements of the two companies for the year ended December 31, Year 1, are on pages 272 and 273.

The following additional information is available:

(1) On December 31, Year 1, Swain Company owed Pence Corporation $16,000 on open account and $8,000 on 6% demand notes dated July 1, Year 1

(interest payable at maturity). Pence Corporation discounted $3,000 of the notes received from Swain Company with the First State Bank on July 1, Year 1, without notifying Swain of this action.

(2) During Year 1, Pence Corporation sold to Swain Company for $40,000 merchandise which cost $30,000. Swain Company's December 31, Year 1, inventory included $10,000 of this merchandise priced at Swain's cost.

PENCE CORPORATION AND SWAIN COMPANY
Financial Statements
Year Ended December 31, Year 1

	Pence Corporation	Swain Company
Income Statement		
Revenue		
Net sales	$500,000	$298,000
Intercompany sales	40,000	6,000
Intercompany interest revenue (expense)	150	(240)
Intercompany investment income	10,200	–0–
Intercompany gain on sale of equipment	–0–	2,000
	$550,350	$305,760
Costs and expenses		
Cost of goods sold	$400,000	$225,000
Intercompany cost of goods sold	30,000	4,800
Operating expenses	88,450	65,760
	$518,450	$295,560
Net income	$ 31,900	$ 10,200
Statement of Retained Earnings		
Retained earnings, Jan. 1, Year 1	$ 67,000	$ 22,100
Net income	31,900	10,200
	$ 98,900	$ 32,300
Dividends	–0–	4,500
Retained earnings, Dec. 31, Year 1	$ 98,900	$ 27,800
Balance Sheet		
Assets		
Intercompany receivables (payables)	$ 21,150	$(22,740)
Inventories	81,200	49,600
Investment in subsidiary	112,300	–0–
Plant and equipment	83,200	43,500
Accumulated depreciation	(12,800)	(9,300)
Other assets	71,150	56,200
	$356,200	$117,260

Liabilities & Stockholders' Equity

Liabilities	$ 56,700	$ 9,460
Capital stock, $10 par value	120,000	–0–
Capital stock, $20 par value	–0–	60,000
Paid-in capital in excess of par	58,500	20,000
Retained earnings	98,900	27,800
Retained earnings of subsidiary	22,100	–0–
	$356,200	$117,260

(3) On July 1, Year 1, Swain Company sold equipment with undepreciated cost of $15,000 to Pence Corporation for $17,000. Pence Corporation recorded depreciation on the equipment in the amount of $850 for Year 1. The remaining useful life of the equipment at the date of sale was 10 years.

(4) Swain Company shipped merchandise to Pence Corporation on December 31, Year 1, and recorded an account receivable of $6,000 for the sale. Swain Company's cost for the merchandise was $4,800. Because the merchandise was in transit, Pence Corporation did not record the transaction. The terms of the sale were F.O.B. shipping point.

(5) Swain Company declared a dividend of $1.50 per share on December 31, Year 1, payable on January 10, Year 2. Pence Corporation made no entry for the dividend declaration.

Instructions

a Prepare in good form any necessary adjusting journal entry or entries for Pence Corporation and Swain Company at December 31, Year 1.

b Prepare consolidating financial statements working papers and related consolidation eliminations for Pence Corporation and subsidiary for the year ended December 31, Year 1. Ignore income taxes.

7-9 The condensed financial statements on pages 274 and 275 were prepared following completion of the December 31, Year 4, audit of Placentia Corporation and its subsidiaries, Sawyer Company and Stallman Company. The subsidiary investments are accounted for by the equity method.

The following additional information is available:

(1) Sawyer Company was formed by Placentia Corporation on January 2, Year 4. To secure additional capital, 25% of the capital stock was sold at par value in the securities market. Placentia purchased the remaining capital stock at par value for cash.

(2) On July 1, Year 4, Placentia acquired from stockholders 4,000 shares of Stallman Company capital stock for $175,000. A condensed balance sheet for Stallman Company at July 1, Year 4, follows:

STALLMAN COMPANY

Balance Sheet

July 1, Year 4

Assets

Current assets	$165,000
Property and equipment, net	60,000
	$225,000

Liabilities & Stockholders' Equity

Current liabilities	$ 45,000
Capital stock, $20 par value	100,000
Retained earnings	80,000
	$225,000

The fair values of Stallman Company's identifiable net assets at July 1, Year 4, were the same as their carrying values at that date. Placentia Corporation's board of directors determined that Stallman Company's goodwill had an estimated life of five years.

PLACENTIA CORPORATION, SAWYER COMPANY, AND STALLMAN COMPANY

Financial Statements

Period Ended December 31, Year 4

	Placentia Corporation	Sawyer Company	Stallman Company
	(Year ended 12-31-4)		(Six months ended 12-31-4)
Income Statement			
Revenue			
Net sales	$ 920,000	$245,000	$310,000
Intercompany sales	40,000	30,000	60,000
Dividend revenue	6,800	–0–	–0–
Gain on sales of property and equipment	9,000	–0–	–0–
Intercompany revenue (expenses)	12,000	(6,000)	(6,000)
Intercompany investment (loss)— Sawyer	(45,000)	–0–	–0–
Intercompany investment income— Stallman	105,700	–0–	–0–
	$1,048,500	$269,000	$364,000
Costs and expenses			
Cost of goods sold	$ 788,000	$273,000	$168,000
Intercompany cost of goods sold . .	32,000	27,000	42,000
Operating expenses	70,100	29,000	18,000
	$ 890,100	$329,000	$228,000
Net income (loss)	$ 158,400	$ (60,000)	$136,000
Statement of Retained Earnings			
Retained earnings at beginning of period	$ 611,000	$ –0–	$ 80,000
Net income (loss)	158,400	(60,000)	136,000
	$ 769,400	$ (60,000)	$216,000
Dividends	48,000	–0–	14,000
Retained earnings (deficit), Dec. 31, Year 4	$ 721,400	$ (60,000)	$202,000

Balance Sheet

Assets

Intercompany receivables (payables)	$ 12,000	$ (6,000)	$ (6,000)
Inventories	242,900	70,000	78,000
Investment in Sawyer Company . . .	105,000	-0-	-0-
Investment in Stallman Company . .	269,500	-0-	-0-
Other investments	185,000	-0-	-0-
Property and equipment, net	279,000	51,000	78,000
Other assets	174,000	52,000	170,000
	$1,267,400	$167,000	$320,000

Liabilities & Stockholders' Equity

Accounts payable	$ 46,000	$ 27,000	$ 18,000
Capital stock, $20 par value	500,000	200,000	100,000
Retained earnings (deficit)	721,400	(60,000)	202,000
	$1,267,400	$167,000	$320,000

(3) The following intercompany sales of certain products were made during Year 4:

	Sales	Included in pur- chaser's Dec. 31, Year 4, inventory
Placentia to Stallman	$ 40,000	$15,000
Sawyer to Stallman	30,000	10,000
Stallman to Placentia	60,000	21,900
Total	$130,000	$46,900

(4) On January 2, Year 4, Placentia Corporation sold a punch press to Sawyer Company. The machine was purchased on January 2, Year 2, and was being depreciated by the straight-line method over a ten-year life. Sawyer Company computed depreciation by the same method based on the remaining useful life. Details of the sale were as follows:

Cost of punch press	$25,000
Accumulated depreciation	5,000
Undepreciated cost	$20,000
Sales price	24,000
Gain on sale	$ 4,000

(5) Cash dividends were paid on the following dates in Year 4:

	Placentia Corporation	Stallman Company
June 30	$22,000	$ 6,000
Dec. 31	26,000	14,000
Total	$48,000	$20,000

(6) Placentia Corporation billed each subsidiary $6,000 at year-end for management fees in Year 4. The invoices were paid in January, Year 5.

Instructions Prepare consolidating financial statements working papers and related consolidation eliminations for Placentia Corporation and subsidiaries for the year ended December 31, Year 4. Ignore income taxes.

7-10 On June 30, Year 2, Pearce Corporation purchased all the outstanding common stock of Scales Company for $3,605,000 cash and Pearce's common stock valued at $4,100,000. Costs of the combination were negligible. At the date of the business combination, the carrying values and fair values of Scales Company's assets and liabilities were as follows:

	Carrying value	Fair value
Cash	$ 160,000	$ 160,000
Accounts receivable, net	910,000	910,000
Inventories	860,000	1,025,186
Building	9,000,000	7,250,000
Furniture, fixtures, and machinery	3,000,000	2,550,000
Accumulated depreciation	(5,450,000)	-0-
Intangible assets, net	150,000	220,000
	$8,630,000	
Notes payable	$ 500,000	500,000
Accounts payable	580,000	580,000
5% mortgage note payable	4,000,000	3,710,186
Common stock	2,900,000	-0-
Retained earnings	650,000	-0-
	$8,630,000	

Condensed financial statements of the two companies at December 31, Year 2, appear on pages 277 and 278.

By the year-end, December 31, Year 2, the net balance of Scales Company's accounts receivable at June 30, Year 2, had been collected; the inventory on hand at June 30, Year 2, had been charged to cost of goods sold; the $500,000 note had been paid; and the accounts payable at June 30, Year 2, had been paid.

As of June 30, Year 2, Scales Company's building and furniture, fixtures, and machinery had estimated remaining useful lives of ten years and eight years, respectively. All intangible assets had an estimated remaining life of 20 years. All depreciation and amortization is computed using the straight-line method.

As of June 30, Year 2, the 5% mortgage note payable had eight equal annual payments remaining, with the next payment due June 30, Year 3. The fair value of the note was based on a 7% rate.

Prior to June 30, Year 2, there were no intercompany transactions between Pearce Corporation and Scales Company; however, during the last six months of Year 2 the following intercompany transactions occurred:
(1) Pearce sold $400,000 of merchandise to Scales. The cost of the merchandise to Pearce was $360,000. Of this merchandise, $75,000 remained on hand at December 31, Year 2.
(2) On December 31, Year 2, Scales purchased in the open market $300,000 of Pearce's 7½% bonds payable for $303,845, including $22,500 interest receivable. Pearce had issued $1,000,000 of these five-year, 7½% bonds on January 1, Year 1, for $980,053 (a yield of 8%).

(3) Many of the management functions of the two companies have been combined since the business combination. Pearce Corporation charges Scales
Company a $30,000 per month management fee.
(4) At December 31, Year 2, Scales owed Pearce two months' management fees
and $18,000 for merchandise purchases.

PEARCE CORPORATION AND SCALES COMPANY
Financial Statements
Period Ended December 31, Year 2

	Pearce Corporation (Year ended 12-31-2)	Scales Company (Six months ended 12-31-2)
Income statement		
Revenue		
Net sales	$25,600,000	$6,000,000
Intercompany sales	400,000	-0-
Intercompany revenue (expenses).	180,000	(180,000)
Intercompany investment income	82,082	-0-
	$26,262,082	$5,820,000
Costs and expenses		
Cost of goods sold	$17,640,000	$3,950,000
Intercompany cost of goods sold	360,000	-0-
Depreciation expense	3,701,000	600,000
Amortization expense	-0-	3,750
Selling, general, and administrative expenses . .	3,130,000	956,000
Interest expense	662,000	100,000
	$25,493,000	$5,609,750
Net income	$ 769,082	$ 210,250
Statement of Retained Earnings		
Retained earnings at beginning of period	$ 2,167,500	$ 650,000
Net income	769,082	210,250
Retained earnings, Dec. 31, Year 2	$ 2,936,582	$ 860,250
Balance Sheet		
Assets		
Intercompany receivables (payables)	$ 55,500	$ (55,500)
Inventories	2,031,000	1,009,500
Other current assets	2,326,457	1,031,652
Investment in subsidiary	7,787,082	-0-
Investment in Pearce Corporation 7½% bonds . .	-0-	276,223
Buildings	17,000,000	9,000,000
Furniture, fixtures, and machinery	4,200,000	3,000,000
Accumulated depreciation	(8,000,000)	(6,050,000)
Intangible assets	-0-	146,250
	$25,400,039	$8,358,125

Liabilities & Stockholders' Equity

Current liabilities	$ 2,017,323	$ 597,875
Mortgage notes payable	6,786,500	4,000,000
7½% bonds payable	1,000,000	-0-
Discount on 7½% bonds	(12,866)	-0-
8¼% bonds payable	3,900,000	-0-
Common stock	8,772,500	2,900,000
Retained earnings	2,936,582	860,250
	$25,400,039	$8,358,125

Instructions Prepare consolidating financial statements working papers and related consolidation eliminations for Pearce Corporation and subsidiary for the year ended December 31, Year 2. Round all computations to the nearest dollar. Ignore income taxes.

8

Consolidated financial statements: special problems

In this chapter we shall consider a number of special problems which may arise in the preparation of consolidated financial statements. These problems are as follows:

   Installment acquisition of parent company's controlling interest in a subsidiary
   Changes in parent company's ownership interest in a subsidiary
   Subsidiary with preferred stock
   Stock dividends distributed by a subsidiary
   Treasury stock transactions of a subsidiary
   Parent company stock owned by a subsidiary
   Accounting for income taxes for a consolidated entity

Installment acquisition of parent company's controlling interest in a subsidiary

A parent company may obtain control of a subsidiary company in a series of stock acquisitions, rather than in a single transaction constituting a business combination. The reasons for such an *installment acquisition* program may include unfavorable money market or stock market conditions, as well as nonfinancial considerations.

In accounting for installment acquisitions of stock in the eventual subsidiary, the accountant is faced with a difficult question: At what point in the installment acquisition sequence should fair values be determined

for the subsidiary's net assets, in accordance with the purchase accounting theory for business combinations?[1]

A practical answer to the preceding question is: Fair values for the
subsidiary's net assets should be ascertained at the date when the parent
company attains a controlling interest in the subsidiary. At that date, the
business combination is completed, and purchase accounting should be
applied.

This answer is not completely satisfactory, however, because current
accounting standards[2] require use of the equity method of accounting
for investments in common stock sufficient to enable the investor to
significantly influence the operating and financial policies of the investee
company. A 20% common stock investment is presumed, in the absence
of contrary evidence, to be the minimum ownership interest for exercising
significant operating and financial influence over the investee company.
Furthermore, **APB Opinion No. 18** requires retroactive application of the
equity method of accounting when an investor's ownership interest
reaches the 20% cutoff point. The following example of an installment
acquisition of the parent company's controlling interest in the subsidiary
illustrates these points.

Illustration of Installment Acquisition of Parent Company's Controlling Interest
Prinz Corporation acquired shares of Scarp Company's 10,000 shares
of outstanding $5 par value common stock as follows:

Date	Number of shares of Scarp Company common stock acquired	Medium of payment by Prinz Corporation	Carrying value of Scarp Company's net assets
Mar. 1, Year 2. . .	1,000	$ 10,000 cash	$80,000
Mar. 1, Year 3. . .	2,000	22,000 cash	85,000
Mar. 1, Year 4. . .	6,500	28,000 cash 50,000 8%, 5- year note	90,000
Totals	9,500	$110,000	

The above analysis indicates that Prinz Corporation made investments
at a cost of $10, $11, and $12 per share in Scarp Company's common
stock at dates when the net assets (or book value) per share of Scarp's

[1] As indicated in Chapter 4, pooling-of-interests accounting is appropriate only for business
combinations involving the exchange of 90% or more of the combining company's voting
common stock.

[2] *APB Opinion No. 18*, "The Equity Method of Accounting for Investments in Common Stock,"
AICPA (New York: 1971), pp. 355–356.

common stock was $8, $8.50, and $9, respectively. The wisdom of ascertaining fair values for Scarp Company's net assets at March 1, Year 4—the date Prinz Corporation attained a controlling interest in Scarp—should be readily apparent.

Assume that, in addition to the Capital Stock account with a balance of $50,000 and a Paid-in Capital in Excess of Par account of $10,000, Scarp Company had a Retained Earnings account with the following entries:

SCARP COMPANY
Retained Earnings

Date	Explanations	Debit	Credit	Balance
Mar. 1, Year 2	Balance			20,000 cr.
Feb. 10, Year 3	Dividends: $1 per share	10,000		10,000 cr.
Feb. 28, Year 3	Net income		15,000	25,000 cr.
Feb. 17, Year 4	Dividends: $1 per share	10,000		15,000 cr.
Feb. 28, Year 4	Net income		15,000	30,000 cr.

Parent Company's Entries for Installment Acquisition Prinz Corporation would make the following entries (in addition to conventional end-of-period adjusting and closing entries) to record its investment in Scarp Company's common stock. (All Scarp Company dividends are assumed to have been paid in cash on the declaration date.)

```
Year 2
Mar. 1   Investment in Scarp Company. . . . . . . . . . . . .   10,000
             Cash  . . . . . . . . . . . . . . . . . . . . . . .            10,000
         To record purchase of 1,000 shares of Scarp Com-
         pany's 10,000 outstanding shares of common stock.


Year 3
Feb. 10  Cash  . . . . . . . . . . . . . . . . . . . . . . . . .    1,000
             Dividend Revenue . . . . . . . . . . . . . . . .             1,000
         To record receipt of $1 per share cash dividend on
         1,000 shares of Scarp Company common stock.


Mar. 1   Investment in Scarp Company. . . . . . . . . . . . .   22,000
             Cash  . . . . . . . . . . . . . . . . . . . . . . .            22,000
         To record purchase of 2,000 shares of Scarp Com-
         pany's 10,000 outstanding shares of common stock.
```

Mar. 1	Investment in Scarp Company.	450	
	Retained Earnings of Investee		450

To convert accounting for investment in Scarp Company to equity method from cost method, and retroactively reflect 10% share of operating results of Scarp Company for year ended Feb. 28, Year 3, as follows:

Scarp Company net income, Year 3	$15,000	
Less: Amortization of goodwill implied by Mar. 1, Year 2, cost of 1,000 shares of Scarp common: ($10,000 ÷ 10%) − $80,000 = $20,000 implied goodwill; $20,000 ÷ 40 years = amortization of goodwill for Year 3	500	
Scarp Company adjusted net income, Year 3	$14,500	
Prinz Corporation's share (10% × $14,500)	$ 1,450	
Less: Dividend revenue recorded by Prinz Corporation during Year 3	1,000	
Prior period adjustment to Prinz Corporation's Retained Earnings of Investee account	$ 450	

(Income tax effects are ignored.)

Year 4			
Feb. 17	Cash	3,000	
	Investment in Scarp Company.		3,000

To record receipt of $1 per share cash dividend on 3,000 shares of Scarp Company common stock.

Feb. 28	Investment in Scarp Company. . . . . ·. .	4,500	
	Investment Income		4,500

To record share of Scarp Company's reported net income for year ended Feb. 28, Year 4 (30% × $15,000 = $4,500). (Income tax effects are ignored.)

Feb. 28	Investment Income	191	
	Investment in Scarp Company.		191

To record amortization of implied goodwill for Year 4 as follows:

Acquisition of Mar. 1, Year 2: ($\frac{1}{40}$ × $20,000)		$500
Acquisition of Mar. 1, Year 3: ($22,000 ÷ 20%) − ($85,000 ÷ $19,500) = $5,500 implied goodwill; $\frac{1}{40}$ × $25,000		138
Total		$638
Prinz Corporation's share: 30% × $638		$191

Mar. 1 Investment in Scarp Company	78,000	
Cash		28,000
Notes Payable		50,000

To record purchase of 6,500 shares of Scarp Company's 10,000 shares of outstanding common stock for cash and an 8%, five-year note.

Prinz Corporation's purchase of 6,500 shares of Scarp Company's outstanding common stock on March 1, Year 4, is in essence a business combination which should be accounted for as a purchase. Accordingly, Prinz Corporation should apply the principles of purchase accounting described in Chapters 4 and 5, including the valuation of Scarp Company's identifiable tangible and intangible net assets at their fair values at March 1, Year 4. Any excess of the $120,000 ($78,000 ÷ 65% = $120,000) implied fair value of 100% of Scarp Company's net assets at March 1, Year 4, over the fair values of Scarp's identifiable net assets should be assigned to goodwill and amortized over a period not in excess of 40 years.

Criticism of Preceding Approach The preceding illustration of accounting for the installment acquisition of an eventual subsidiary's common stock can be criticized for its handling of goodwill. On three separate dates spanning two calendar years, goodwill was recognized in Prinz Corporation's three purchases of outstanding common stock of Scarp Company. Furthermore, the three goodwill amounts are amortized over three different 40-year (or shorter) terms.

It might be argued that the fair values of Scarp Company's identifiable net assets should be determined at each of Prinz Corporation's three stock purchase dates. However, such a theoretically precise application of accounting standards for long-term investments in corporate securities appears unwarranted in terms of cost benefit analysis. Until Prinz Corporation attained a controlling interest in Scarp Company, the amortization elements of Prinz's investment income would presumably not be material. Furthermore, it is questionable whether implicit fair values of 100% of an investee company's net assets can be computed logically unless the parent company has acquired a substantial percentage of the investee company's outstanding common stock. Thus, the goodwill approach illustrated in the preceding section of this chapter appears to be practical and consistent with the following passage from *APB Opinion No. 18:*

> The carrying amount of an investment in common stock of an investee that qualifies for the equity method of accounting . . . may differ from the underlying equity in net assets of the investee. . . . if the investor is unable to relate the difference to specific accounts of the investee, the difference should be considered to be goodwill and amortized over a period not to exceed forty years, . . .[3]

Consolidating Financial Statements Working Papers for Prinz Corporation and Subsidiary Consolidating financial statements working papers for Prinz Corporation and subsidiary at March 1, Year 4, and for subsequent periods would be prepared in accordance with the procedures outlined in Chapters 5, 6, and 7. Prinz Corporation's retroactive application of the equity method of accounting for its investment in Scarp Company's common stock results in a Retained Earnings of Subsidiary (Investee) account as follows at March 1, Year 4:

PRINZ CORPORATION
Retained Earnings of Subsidiary (Investee)

Date	Explanations	Debit	Credit	Balance
Mar. 1, Year 3	Retroactive application of equity method		450	450 cr.
Feb. 28, Year 4	Share of Scarp Company adjusted net income not distributed as a dividend [($4,500 − $191) − $3,000]		1,309	1,759 cr.

The $3,000 portion of Scarp Company's Year 4 adjusted net income, which represents Scarp's cash dividends to Prinz, would be closed to Prinz's Retained Earnings account, since it is available for dividend declaration to Prinz's shareholders. Thus, Prinz's share of the increases in Scarp Company's retained earnings from March 1, Year 2, until the March 1, Year 4, business combination would be included in Prinz Corporation's two retained earnings accounts, and in consolidated retained earnings. For fiscal years subsequent to March 1, Year 4, Prinz Corporation would reflect in its accounts 95% of the operating results of Scarp Company.

[3] *Ibid.,* p. 360.

Changes in parent company's ownership interest in a subsidiary

Subsequent to the date of a business combination, a parent company may acquire stockholdings of the subsidiary's minority shareholders; or the parent may sell some of its subsidiary stockholdings to outsiders. Also, the subsidiary itself may issue additional shares of stock to the public. We shall consider the accounting treatment for each of these situations in the following sections.

Parent Company Acquisition of Minority Interest Purchase accounting should be applied to the parent company's acquisition of all or part of the subsidiary's minority interest, even though the original business combination was accounted for as a pooling of interests.[4] Any other approach would be inconsistent with pooling-of-interests accounting theory.

To illustrate, assume that on March 1, Year 5, Prinz Corporation acquired for $7,000 the remaining 500 shares of Scarp Corporation's outstanding common stock owned by minority shareholders. If the minority interest in the consolidated balance sheet of Prinz Corporation and subsidiary amounted to $6,000 at February 28, Year 5, an implicit additional $1,000 of goodwill must be amortized by Prinz Corporation over a maximum of 40 years, beginning March 1, Year 5. Prinz would accrue under the equity method of accounting 100% of Scarp Company's operating results for periods subsequent to March 1, Year 5.

If Prinz Corporation paid *less* than the carrying value of the minority interest purchased, the appropriate accounting treatment of the difference is not clear. Presumably, the excess of minority interest carrying value over Prinz's cost should be allocated pro rata to the carrying values of Scarp Company's noncurrent assets other than long-term investments in corporate securities. This approach would be consistent with the theory of purchase accounting set forth in Chapter 4 (pages 129–131). However, assuming that the difference between carrying value and cost is immaterial, it may be treated as an offset to previously recognized goodwill and amortized over the remaining useful life of that goodwill.

Parent Company Sale of a Portion of Its Subsidiary Stockholdings A parent company with a substantial ownership interest in a subsidiary may sell a portion of that interest for several reasons. Perhaps the parent company is experiencing a severe shortage of cash, or the earnings of the subsidiary have been unsatisfactory. The parent company may recognize that a subsidiary may be effectively controlled with just over 50% ownership of its voting common stock, and that an 80% or 90% ownership interest in a subsidiary may tie up resources unnecessarily. Some corporations which have engaged extensively in business combinations during recent

[4]*APB Opinion No. 16,* "Business Combinations," AICPA (New York: 1970), p. 294.

years have sold a portion of a newly acquired subsidiary's stock in order to generate cash for additional business combinations.

Sale of *all* of an ownership interest in a subsidiary involves accounting for and presentation of the disposal of a segment of a business. That topic is considered in Chapter 9.

Accounting for a parent company's sale of a part of its investment in a subsidiary is similar to the accounting for disposal of any noncurrent asset. The carrying value of the subsidiary stock sold is removed from the parent company's Investment in Subsidiary account, and the difference between that carrying value and the cash or fair value of other consideration received is treated as a gain or loss on disposal of the stock. Under current accounting standards, the gain or loss is not considered to be an *extraordinary item* for consolidated income statement presentation.[5]

Unless the original business combination with the subsidiary resulted from an installment acquisition of the subsidiary's stock, there is no significant change in the working paper consolidation eliminations after the parent's sale of part of its ownership interest in the subsidiary. The minority interest in the subsidiary's net income and net assets increases, however. The parent company's equity method entries for the subsidiary's operations are changed only for the decrease in the percentage of the parent's ownership interest in the subsidiary.

When control was acquired by installment purchases of the subsidiary's stock, *specific identification* should be used to account for the carrying value of the subsidiary shares sold. There must be an accompanying adjustment in the parent's application of the equity method of accounting for the subsidiary's operating results. For example, implicit goodwill may no longer be accounted for in consolidating financial statements working papers if the block of subsidiary stock to which it applies was sold by the parent company.

Subsidiary Issuance of Additional Shares to the Public   Instead of obtaining funds by selling a portion of its ownership interest in a subsidiary, the parent company may instruct the subsidiary to issue additional shares of stock to the public. The cash so obtained would be available to the consolidated group. Unless the parent company acquires shares on a pro rata basis in the stock issuance, as in a stock rights offering, the parent's percentage ownership interest in the subsidiary will change. In addition, unless the subsidiary issues additional shares to the public at a price per share equal to the per-share carrying value of the subsidiary's outstanding stock, there will be an implicit gain or loss to the parent company. These two points are illustrated in the following section.

---

[5]*APB Opinion No. 30,* "Reporting the Results of Operations," AICPA (New York: 1973), p. 566.

Illustration of Subsidiary Issuance of Additional Stock to the Public On January 2, Year 1, Paulson Corporation acquired 80% of the outstanding common stock of Spaulding Company for $240,000. Out-of-pocket costs of the business combination were negligible and are not considered in this illustration. Spaulding Company's stockholders' equity accounts at January 2, Year 1, were as follows:

Common stock, $5 par value	$ 50,000
Paid-in capital in excess of par	75,000
Retained earnings	100,000
Total stockholders' equity	$225,000

The fair values of Spaulding Company's identifiable net assets at January 2, Year 1, were equal to their carrying values. Thus, the $75,000 excess of the implied fair value of 100% of Spaulding's net assets ($300,000, computed as $240,000 ÷ 80%) over the $225,000 fair value of Spaulding's identifiable net assets was attributable to goodwill, which will be amortized over an estimated useful life of 40 years.

For the year ended December 31, Year 1, Spaulding Company reported net income of $20,000 and paid cash dividends of $10,000 (or $1 per share). On December 31, Year 1, Spaulding issued 2,000 shares of common stock in a public offering at $33 per share, net of costs of issuing the stock. Thus, after the closing process, Spaulding Company's stockholders' equity at December 31, Year 1, amounted to $301,000 ($225,000 + $10,000 + $66,000 = $301,000), and consisted of the following account balances:

Common stock, $5 par value	$ 60,000
Paid-in capital in excess of par	131,000
Retained earnings	110,000
Total stockholders' equity	$301,000

Paulson Corporation's Investment in Subsidiary account under the equity method of accounting appears on page 288.

The December 31, Year 1, entry of $2,917 in Paulson Corporation's Investment in Subsidiary account is offset by a credit to a nonoperating gain account. The $2,917 is Paulson Corporation's share of the increase in Spaulding Company's net assets resulting from Spaulding's issuance of stock to the public at $33 per share. The $33 per share issuance price

PAULSON CORPORATION
Investment in Subsidiary

Date	Explanations	Debit	Credit	Balance
Year 1				
Jan. 2	Purchase of 8,000 shares	240,000		240,000 dr.
Dec. 31	Dividend: 80% × $10,000		8,000	232,000 dr.
Dec. 31	Share of reported net income: 80% × $20,000	16,000		248,000 dr.
Dec. 31	Amortization of goodwill: 80% × ($75,000 ÷ 40)		1,500	246,500 dr.
Dec. 31	Gain on subsidiary's issuance of stock to public		2,917	249,417 dr.

exceeds the $30.81 carrying value ($246,500 ÷ 8,000 shares = $30.81) per share of Paulson Corporation's investment in Spaulding Company prior to Spaulding's stock issuance. The $2,917 amount is computed as follows:

	Total	Paulson Corporation's share	Minority interest
Carrying value of Spaulding Company's net assets after stock issuance to public . . .	$374,125*	(66⅔%) $249,417	(33⅓%) $124,708
Carrying value of Spaulding Company's net assets before stock issuance to public . . .	308,125	(80%) 246,500	(20%) 61,625
Difference	$ 66,000	$ 2,917	$ 63,083

* Spaulding Company's total stockholders' equity at Dec. 31, Year 1 . . . . $301,000
 Spaulding Company's unamortized goodwill at Dec. 31, Year 1 (³⁹⁄₄₀ × $75,000) . . 73,125
 Total $374,125

The analysis above reflects the effect of the decrease of Paulson Corporation's percentage interest to 66⅔% of Spaulding Company's outstanding common stock after the public stock issuance from 80% before the issuance. Nevertheless, the issuance price of $33 per share exceeded the $30.81 carrying value per share of Paulson's original investment in Spaulding—hence the $2,917 nonoperating gain to Paulson.

The following working paper consolidation eliminations would be appropriate for Paulson Corporation and subsidiary at December 31, Year

1, assuming that there were no other intercompany transactions, balances, or profits for Year 1:

(a) Common Stock—Spaulding 60,000
    Paid-in Capital in Excess of Par—Spaulding 131,000
    Retained Earnings—Spaulding 100,000
    Amortization Expense—Spaulding ($\frac{1}{40}$ × $75,000) . 1,875
    Goodwill—Spaulding ($75,000 − $1,875) 73,125
    Intercompany Investment Income—Paulson
        ($16,000 − $1,500) 14,500
            Investment in Subsidiary—Paulson 249,417
            Dividends—Spaulding 10,000
            Minority Interest in Subsidiary ($60,000 −
                $2,000 + $63,083) 121,083
    To eliminate intercompany investment and related
    equity accounts of subsidiary (retained earnings of
    subsidiary is at beginning of year); to eliminate sub-
    sidiary's dividends declared; to record amortization
    of goodwill for Year 1 and related unamortized bal-
    ance of the goodwill at Dec. 31, Year 1; and to pro-
    vide for minority interest in subsidiary at beginning
    of year ($300,000 × 20% = $60,000), less dividends
    to minority shareholders ($10,000 × 20% = $2,000),
    plus minority interest's share of proceeds of public
    stock issuance ($66,000 − $2,917 = $63,083).

(b) Minority Interest in Net Income of Subsidiary 3,625
        Minority Interest in Subsidiary 3,625
    To provide for minority interest in subsidiary's Year
    1 net income, as follows:
      Net income for Year 1, as
        reported $20,000
      Less: Goodwill amortization,
        per consolidation elimination (a) . . . 1,875
      Adjusted net income for Year 1 . . . . $18,125
      Minority share thereof
        (20% × $18,125) . . . . $ 3,625

The **nonoperating gain** treatment accorded to the $2,917 increase in Paulson Corporation's interest in Spaulding Company is not universally accepted. As one authority has written:

> . . . the SEC has adopted the position that the issue of shares by a subsidiary company to the public at an amount per share in excess of book value does

not give rise to a gain to the parent interest in the consolidated income statement. In such circumstances, the SEC has generally required the gain to be credited direct to paid-in capital in consolidated financial statements. However, many accountants hold the view that consolidated paid-in capital should arise solely from transactions with stockholders of the parent company, and accordingly that subsidiary capital changes which affect the parent's share of stockholders' equity of the subsidiary should generally result in recognition of gain or loss or adjustment of goodwill on consolidation.[6]

Subsidiary with preferred stock

Some acquired companies in a business combination have outstanding preferred stock. If a parent company acquires all of a subsidiary's preferred stock together with all or a majority of its voting common stock, the consolidating financial statements working papers and related consolidation eliminations are similar to those illustrated in Chapters 5, 6, and 7. If less than 100% of the subsidiary's preferred stock is acquired by the parent company, the preferences associated with the preferred stock must be considered in determining the minority interest in the net income and net assets of the subsidiary. The interest of minority preferred stockholders is not *residual,* as is the interest of minority common stockholders.

Illustration of Minority Interest in Subsidiary with Preferred Stock Suppose, for example, that on July 1, Year 4, Praeger Corporation paid.$200,000 for 60% of Simmons Company's 10,000 shares of outstanding $1 par value, 6% cumulative preferred stock and 80% of Simmons's 50,000 shares of outstanding $2 par value common stock. The preferred stock has a liquidation preference of $1.10 per share and is callable at $1.20 per share plus any cumulative preferred dividends in arrears. In addition to the two capital stock issues, Simmons Company had the following stockholders' equity accounts at July 1, Year 4:

Paid-in capital in excess of par	*$30,000*
Retained earnings	*50,000*

There were no cumulative preferred dividends in arrears at July 1, Year 4. The fair values of Simmons Company's identifiable net assets at July 1, Year 4, were equal to their carrying values at that date.

The presence of preferred stock raises two questions:

1 What part, if any, does the preferred stock play in the determination of the implied fair value of Simmons Company's net assets at July 1, Year 4?

[6]*Consolidated Financial Statements,* Accountants International Study Group (Plaistow, England: 1973), p. 13.

2 Which per-share amount—$1 par value, $1.10 liquidation preference, or $1.20 call price—should enter into the determination of the minority interest in Simmons Company's net assets at July 1, Year 4?

In the opinion of the authors, the following are logical answers to the two questions:

1 The preferred stock does not enter into the determination of the implied fair value of Simmons Company's net assets at July 1, Year 4. Typically, preferred stockholders have no voting rights; hence, in a business combination, preferred stock may in substance be considered **debt** rather than **owners' equity.** Thus, the amount paid by the acquiring company for the subsidiary's **common stock** should be the measure of the implied value of the subsidiary's net assets.

2 The call price should be used in determining the minority interest of the preferred shareholders in Simmons Company's net assets at July 1, Year 4. The call price is usually the maximum claim on net assets imposed by the preferred stock contract. Furthermore, the call price is the amount which Simmons Company would pay, on a going-concern basis, to liquidate the preferred stock. Use of the preferred stock's liquidation value per share in determining the minority shareholders' interest in the subsidiary's net assets would stress a **quitting-concern** approach, rather than a going-concern assumption. Finally, the par value of the preferred stock has no real significance as a measure of **value** for the preferred.

In accordance with the preceding discussion, Praeger Corporation would make the following journal entry to record the business combination with Simmons Company at July 1, Year 4. (Out-of-pocket costs of the combination are ignored.)

Investment in Simmons Company Preferred Stock (6,000		
shares × $1.20)	7,200	
Investment in Simmons Company Common Stock ($200,000 −		
$7,200)	192,800	
Cash		200,000
To record business combination with Simmons Company		
under the purchase method of accounting.		

The working paper consolidation elimination for Praeger Corporation and subsidiary at July 1, Year 4, since the fair values of Simmons Company's identifiable net assets were equal to their carrying values at that date, would be as shown on page 292.

The following aspects of the preceding working paper consolidation elimination should be emphasized:

1 Simmons Company's goodwill is measured by the difference between the implied fair value of 100% of Simmons's common stock over the fair value of the subsidiary's net assets applicable to common stock. The subsidiary's preferred stock does not enter into the computation of the goodwill.

Preferred Stock—Simmons	10,000
Common Stock—Simmons	100,000
Paid-in Capital in Excess of Par—Simmons	30,000
Retained Earnings—Simmons	50,000
Goodwill—Simmons [($192,800 ÷ 80%) − ($190,000 −	
$12,000) call value of preferred stock]	63,000
Investment in Simmons Company Preferred Stock—	
Praeger	7,200
Investment in Simmons Company Common Stock—	
Praeger	192,800
Minority Interest in Subsidiary—Preferred (4,000	
shares × $1.20)	4,800
Minority Interest in Subsidiary—Common ($241,000 ×	
20%)	48,200

To eliminate intercompany investment and related equity accounts of subsidiary at date of business combination; to record excess of implied value of 100% of common stock ($241,000) over fair value of subsidiary's identifiable net assets applicable to common stock ($178,000) as goodwill; and to provide for minority interest in subsidiary's preferred stock and in net assets applicable to common stock at date of business combination.

2 The minority interest in the subsidiary's preferred stock is measured by the $1.20 call price per share multiplied by the 4,000 shares of preferred stock owned by minority shareholders.

3 The minority interest in the subsidiary's common stock is computed as 20% of the implied fair value of 100% of Simmons Company's common stock ($241,000).

Preferred Stock Considerations Subsequent to Date of Business Combination Regardless of whether Simmons Company's preferred dividend is paid or omitted in years subsequent to July 1, Year 4, the preferred dividend affects the computation of the minority interest of common shareholders in the net income of Simmons Company. For example, assume that Simmons Company reported net income of $50,000 for the year ended June 30, Year 5, and declared and paid the preferred dividend and a common dividend of $0.50 per share on June 30, Year 5. Praeger Corporation would record these elements of Simmons's operating results as follows at June 30, Year 5, under the equity method of accounting:

Cash 20,360		
Investment in Simmons Company Common Stock		20,000
Intercompany Dividend Revenue		360

To record receipt of dividends declared and paid by Simmons
Company as follows:

Preferred stock: 6,000 shares × $0.06	$ 360	
Common stock: 40,000 shares × $0.50	20,000	
Total cash received	$20,360	

Investment in Simmons Company Common Stock 39,520		
Intercompany Investment Income		39,520

To record share of Simmons Company's reported net income
applicable to common stock, as follows:

Simmons Company's reported net income	$50,000	
Less: Preferred dividend—10,000 shares × $0.06 . . .	600	
Net income attributable to common stock	$49,400	
Parent company's share—80% × $49,400	$39,520	

Intercompany Investment Income 1,260		
Investment in Simmons Company Common Stock		1,260

To provide for parent company's share of Year 5 amortization of
Simmons Company's goodwill at date of business combination, as
follows:

Simmons's goodwill at date of business combination	$63,000	
Amortization thereof: $\frac{1}{40}$ × $63,000	$ 1,575	
Parent company's share thereof: 80% × $1,575 . . .	$ 1,260	

Investment in Simmons Company Preferred Stock 360		
Intercompany Investment Income		360

To accrue cumulative preferred dividend "passed" by subsidiary's
board of directors: 60% × $600 = $360.

If there were no other intercompany transactions, balances, or profits,
the June 30, Year 5, working paper consolidation eliminations for Praeger
Corporation and subsidiary would be as shown on page 294.

In the review of the preceding journal entries of Praeger Corporation
and working paper consolidation eliminations for Praeger Corporation
and subsidiary, the following should be noted:

(a) Preferred Stock—Simmons   10,000
    Common Stock—Simmons   100,000
    Paid-in Capital in Excess of Par—Simmons   30,000
    Retained Earnings—Simmons   50,000
    Intercompany Dividend Revenue—Praeger   360
    Intercompany Investment Income—Praeger   38,260
    Amortization Expense—Simmons ($\frac{1}{40} \times$ $63,000)   1,575
    Goodwill—Simmons ($63,000 − $1,575)   61,425
        Investment in Simmons Company Preferred Stock—
            Praeger   7,200
        Investment in Simmons Company Common Stock—
            Praeger   211,060
        Minority Interest in Subsidiary—Preferred ($4,800 −
            $240)   4,560
        Minority Interest in Subsidiary—Common
            [$48,200 − (20% × $25,000)]   43,200
        Dividends—Simmons ($600 + $25,000)   25,600
    To eliminate intercompany investment and related equity
    accounts of subsidiary at beginning of year; to eliminate
    subsidiary's dividends declared; to record amortization of
    subsidiary's goodwill for Year 5 and related unamortized
    balance of the goodwill at June 30, Year 5; and to provide
    for minority interest in subsidiary's preferred stock and
    common stock at beginning of year, less dividends to
    minority shareholders.

(b) Minority Interest in Net Income of Subsidiary   9,805
        Minority Interest in Subsidiary—Preferred   240
        Minority Interest in Subsidiary—Common [20% ×
            ($50,000 − $1,575 − $600)]   9,565
    To provide for minority interest in adjusted net income of
    subsidiary for Year 5.

1 Praeger Corporation's accounting for its investment in the subsidiary's preferred stock is essentially the cost method. This method is appropriate as long as the subsidiary declares and pays the cumulative preferred dividend annually. If the subsidiary had "passed" the preferred dividend of $600 for the year ended June 30, Year 5, Praeger Corporation would have used the equity method of accounting for the "passed" preferred dividend, as follows:

The working paper consolidation eliminations in the year of a "passed" cumulative preferred dividend would essentially be the same as those illustrated above, except that the minority interest in the subsidiary's preferred stock would be $240 (40% × $600) greater for the effect of the "passed" dividend.

(Of course, no common dividend could be declared if the cumulative preferred dividend were "passed.")

2 The net result of the preceding journal entries and working paper consolidation eliminations is that the subsidiary's adjusted net income of $48,425 (computed as $50,000 reported net income less $1,575 goodwill amortization) is allocated as follows:

	Total	Consolidated net income	Minority interest
To preferred shareholders: 10,000 shares × $0.06	$ 600	$ 360	$ 240
To common shareholders: in ratio of 80% and 20%	47,825*	38,260	9,565
Total adjusted net income of subsidiary . .	$48,425	$38,620	$9,805

* $50,000 − $1,575 − $600 = $47,825

Other Types of Preferred Stock   Treatment similar to that illustrated in the preceding section is appropriate for the minority interest in a subsidiary having other types of outstanding preferred stock. If the preferred stock were **noncumulative,** there would be no parent company accrual of "passed" dividends. If the preferred stock were **participating** (which is seldom the case), the subsidiary's retained earnings would be allocated to the minority interests in preferred stock and common stock according to the terms of the participation clause.

Stock dividends distributed by a subsidiary

If a parent company uses the equity method of accounting for the operating results of a subsidiary, the subsidiary's declaration and issuance of a stock dividend has no effect on the parent's Investment in Subsidiary account. As emphasized in **Intermediate Accounting** of this series, receipt of a stock dividend does not represent revenue to the investor.

After the declaration of a stock dividend not exceeding 20 to 25%, the subsidiary's retained earnings will have been reduced by an amount equal to the fair value of the stock issued as the dividend. This reduction and the offsetting increase in the subsidiary's paid-in capital accounts must be incorporated in the working paper consolidation eliminations subsequent to the issuance of the stock dividend. The amount of consolidated retained earnings thus is not affected by a subsidiary's stock dividend. As emphasized by the AICPA:

> . . . the retained earnings in the consolidated financial statements should reflect the accumulated earnings of the consolidated group not distributed to the shareholders of, or capitalized by, the parent company.[7]

[7] ARB No. 51, "Consolidated Financial Statements," AICPA (New York: 1959), p. 46.

Treasury stock transactions of a subsidiary

Treasury stock held by a subsidiary at the date of a business combination is logically treated as **retired** stock in the preparation of consolidated financial statements. A working paper consolidation elimination should be prepared to account for the "retirement" of the treasury stock by the **par** or **stated value method.** For example, assume that Palance Corporation acquired all the **outstanding** capital stock of Sizemore Company on March 1, Year 6, for $147,000. Sizemore's stockholders' equity on that date was as follows:

Capital stock, $1 par value	$ 50,000
Paid-in capital in excess of par	25,000
Retained earnings	50,000
Total paid-in capital and retained earnings	$125,000
Less: 1,000 shares of treasury stock, at cost	2,000
Stockholders' equity	$123,000

The first working paper consolldation elimination for Palance Corporation and subsidiary at March 1, Year 6, would be as follows:

Capital Stock—Sizemore	1,000	
Paid-in Capital in Excess of Par—Sizemore	500	
Retained Earnings—Sizemore	500	
Treasury Stock—Sizemore		2,000
To account for subsidiary's treasury stock as though it had been retired.		

The preceding consolidation elimination allocates the original per-share capital contributed by stockholders in excess of par ($25,000 ÷ 50,000 shares = $0.50 per share) to the Paid-in Capital in Excess of Par account of the subsidiary. The remainder of the cost of the treasury stock is allocated to the subsidiary's retained earnings.

If, subsequent to the date of a business combination, a subsidiary acquires for the treasury some or all of the shares owned by minority shareholders, a working paper consolidation elimination similar to the preceding one is appropriate. In addition, a gain or loss to the parent company must be recognized in a manner similar to that illustrated in a preceding section of this chapter for subsidiary issuances of stock to the public.

Parent company stock owned by a subsidiary

In the early history of business combinations resulting in parent-subsidiary relationships, complex indirect or reciprocal shareholdings were frequently encountered. *Indirect shareholdings* are those involving such relationships as one subsidiary and the parent company jointly owning a controlling interest in another subsidiary, or a subsidiary company being itself the parent company of its own subsidiary. *Reciprocal shareholdings* involve subsidiary ownership of shares of the parent company's voting common stock.

Business combinations in recent years have generally been far less complex than those described above. There has usually been a single parent company and one or more subsidiaries in recent business combinations, and indirect shareholdings have been the exception rather than the rule. Consequently, the accountant faced with the problem of preparing consolidating financial statements working papers for parent-subsidiary relationships involving indirect shareholdings needs only to follow carefully the stock ownership percentages and apply the equity method of accounting for the various subsidiaries' operating results accordingly.

The traditional approach by accountants to problems of reciprocal shareholdings involved complex mathematical allocations of the individual affiliated companies' net income or net loss to consolidated net income and to minority interest. These allocations typically involved matrices or simultaneous equations.

Accountants have come to question the traditional approach to reciprocal shareholdings. The principal criticism is that strict application of mathematical allocations for reciprocal shareholdings violates the *going-concern* aspect of consolidated financial statements in favor of a *liquidation* approach. A related criticism is the emphasis of the traditional approach upon *legal form* of the reciprocal shareholdings, rather than upon *economic substance.* When a subsidiary acquires voting common stock of the parent, it has been argued, the shares owned by the subsidiary are substantively *treasury stock* to the consolidated entity. The treasury stock treatment for reciprocal shareholdings was sanctioned by the American Accounting Association and by the AICPA as follows:

> Shares of the controlling company's capital stock owned by a subsidiary before the date of acquisition of control should be treated in consolidation as treasury stock. Any subsequent acquisition or sale by a subsidiary should likewise be treated in the consolidated statements as though it had been the act of the controlling company.[8]
>
> Shares of the parent held by a subsidiary should not be treated as outstanding stock in the consolidated balance sheet.[9]

[8] *Accounting and Reporting Standards for Corporate Financial Statements,* "Consolidated Financial Statements," AAA (Madison: 1957), p. 44.
[9] *ARB No. 51,* p. 45.

The authors concur with the view that a subsidiary's shareholdings of parent company voting common stock are in essence treasury stock to the consolidated entity. This position is analogous to that set forth in Chapter 7 for intercompany bondholdings. There, the point was made that a subsidiary acquiring parent company bonds in the open market is acting on behalf of the parent in the reacquisition of the bonds for the consolidated entity's treasury.

Illustration of Parent Company Stock Owned by a Subsidiary On May 1, Year 7, Springer Company acquired in the open market for $50,000 cash 5,000 shares, or 5%, of the outstanding $1 par value common stock of its parent company, Prospect Corporation. During the year ended April 30, Year 8, Prospect Corporation declared and paid a cash dividend of $1.20 per share.

Springer Company should make the following journal entries for its investment in Prospect Corporation:

Investment in Prospect Corporation	50,000	
Cash		50,000
To record purchase of 5,000 shares of parent company's outstanding common stock at $10 per share.		
Cash	6,000	
Intercompany Dividend Revenue		6,000
To record dividend of $1.20 per share on 5,000 shares of parent company common stock owned.		

Working paper consolidation eliminations for Prospect Corporation and subsidiary at April 30, Year 8, would include the following:

Treasury Stock—Prospect	50,000	
Investment in Prospect Corporation—Springer		50,000
To transfer subsidiary's investment in parent company's common stock to treasury stock category.		
Intercompany Dividend Revenue—Springer	6,000	
Dividends—Prospect		6,000
To eliminate parent company dividends received by subsidiary.		

The effect of the second of the two preceding working paper consolidation eliminations is to remove the parent company dividends applicable to the consolidated treasury stock. The outcome is that, in the consolidated statement of retained earnings, dividends are in the amount of $114,000 ($120,000 − $6,000 = $114,000), representing the $1.20 per share dividend on 95,000 shares of parent company common stock which are *outstanding* from the viewpoint of the consolidated entity. Thus, the principle that treasury stock does not receive dividends is not violated.

Accounting for income taxes for a consolidated entity

The final special problem in consolidated statements to be discussed in this chapter involves accounting for income taxes. This subject has received considerable attention from accountants in recent years, primarily because of the growing emphasis in financial statements upon income tax allocation and disclosure. Accounting for income taxes in consolidated financial statements may be subdivided into two sections: (1) income taxes attributable to undistributed earnings of subsidiaries and (2) income taxes paid on intercompany profits.

Income Taxes Attributable to Undistributed Earnings of Subsidiaries Current accounting standards for income taxes associated with the undistributed earnings of subsidiaries are contained in *APB Opinion No. 23,* "Accounting for Income Taxes—Special Areas." The principal provisions are as follows:

> The Board concludes that including undistributed earnings of a subsidiary in the pretax accounting income of a parent company, either through consolidation or accounting for the investment by the equity method, may result in a timing difference, in a difference that may not reverse until indefinite future periods, or in a combination of both types of differences, depending on the intent and actions of the parent company.
> *Timing difference.* The Board believes it should be presumed that all undistributed earnings of a subsidiary will be transferred to the parent company. Accordingly, the undistributed earnings of a subsidiary included in consolidated income (or in income of the parent company) should be accounted for as a timing difference, except to the extent that some or all of the undistributed earnings meet the criteria in [the paragraph entitled "Indefinite reversal criteria"].
>
> . . . .
>
> *Indefinite reversal criteria.* The presumption that all undistributed earnings will be transferred to the parent company may be overcome, and no income taxes should be accrued by the parent company, if sufficient evidence shows that the subsidiary has invested or will invest the undistributed earnings indefinitely or that the earnings will be remitted in a tax-free liquidation.[10]

Thus, in the usual case, income tax allocation accounting is appropriate for undistributed earnings of a subsidiary. Measurement problems involved in computing the appropriate income taxes are no excuse for ignoring the required allocation, according to *APB Opinion No. 23:*

[10]*APB Opinion No. 23,* "Accounting for Income Taxes—Special Areas," AICPA (New York: 1972), pp. 446–447.

Income taxes of the parent company applicable to a timing difference in undistributed earnings of a subsidiary are necessarily based on estimates and assumptions. For example, the tax effect may be determined by assuming that unremitted earnings were distributed in the current period and that the parent company received the benefit of all available tax-planning alternatives and available tax credits and deductions. The income tax expense of the parent company should also include taxes that would have been withheld if the undistributed earnings had been remitted as dividends.[11]

Illustration of Income Tax Allocation for Undistributed Earnings of Subsidiaries
Pinkley Corporation owns 75% of the outstanding capital stock of Sea-bright Company, which it acquired for cash April 1, Year 2. Goodwill resulting from the business combination was $40,000; Seabright's identifiable net assets were fairly valued at their carrying values. For the year ended March 31, Year 3, Pinkley Corporation had pre-tax accounting income, exclusive of intercompany investment income under the equity method of accounting, of $100,000. Seabright Company's pre-tax accounting income was $50,000, and dividends paid by Seabright during Year 3 totaled $10,000. The combined federal and state income tax rate for both companies is 60%. Both federal and state income tax laws provide for a dividend received deduction rate of 85%. Neither Pinkley nor Seabright had any other timing differences; neither had any income subject to capital gains or preference income tax rates; and there were no intercompany profits resulting from transactions between Pinkley Corporation and Seabright Company.

Seabright's income tax accrual entry at March 31, Year 3, would be as follows:

Income Taxes Expense	30,000	
Income Taxes Payable		30,000
To provide for income taxes for Year 3, as follows: 60% ×		
$50,000 = $30,000.		

At March 31, Year 3, Pinkley Corporation would make the following entries for income taxes payable, the subsidiary's operating results, and deferred income taxes:

Income Taxes Expense	60,000	
Income Taxes Payable		60,000
To provide for income taxes for Year 3 on income exclu-		
sive of intercompany investment income, as follows: 60% ×		
$100,000 = $60,000.		

[11] *Ibid.*, p. 446.

Cash	7,500	
Investment in Subsidiary		7,500

To record dividend received from subsidiary: 75% × $10,000 = $7,500.

Investment in Subsidiary	15,000	
Intercompany Investment Income		15,000

To accrue share of subsidiary's reported net income for Year 3, as follows: 75% × $20,000 = $15,000.

Intercompany Investment Income	750	
Investment in Subsidiary		750

To record share of amortization of subsidiary's goodwill for Year 3: 75% × ($40,000 ÷ 40) = $750.

Income Taxes Expense	1,350	
Income Taxes Payable		675
Deferred Income Tax Liability		675

To provide for income taxes on intercompany investment income from subsidiary, as follows:

Reported net income of subsidiary	$20,000
Less: Goodwill amortization	1,000
Adjusted net income of subsidiary	$19,000
Add: Goodwill amortization, not deductible for in-	
come taxes	1,000
Income of subsidiary subject to taxes	$20,000
Parent company's share (75% × $20,000)	$15,000
Less: Dividend received deduction (85% × $15,000)	12,750
Amount subject to taxes	$ 2,250
Income taxes expense (60% × $2,250)	$ 1,350
Taxes currently payable based on dividend received	
[60% × (15% × $7,500)]	$ 675
Taxes deferred until earnings remitted by subsidiary	675
Income taxes expense	$ 1,350

Income Taxes Paid on Intercompany Profits Current federal income tax laws and regulations permit an affiliated group of corporations to file a consolidated income tax return rather than separate returns. Intercompany profits and losses are eliminated in a consolidated income tax return just as they are in consolidated financial statements. An "affiliated group" for federal income tax purposes is defined as follows:

... the term "affiliated group" means one or more chains of includible corporations connected through stock ownership with a common parent corporation which is an includible corporation if—

(1) Stock possessing at least 80 percent of the voting power of all classes of stock and at least 80 percent of each class of the nonvoting stock of each of the includible corporations (except the common parent corporation) is owned directly by one or more of the other includible corporations; and

(2) The common parent corporation owns directly stock possessing at least 80 percent of the voting power of all classes of stock and at least 80 percent of each class of the nonvoting stock of at least one of the other includible corporations

As used in this subsection, the term "stock" does not include nonvoting stock which is limited and preferred as to dividends.[12]

If a parent company and its subsidiaries do not qualify for the "affiliated group" status, or if they otherwise elect to file separate income tax returns, the following accounting standard governs the treatment of income taxes attributable to intercompany profits:

If income taxes have been paid on intercompany profits remaining within the group, such taxes should be deferred.[13]

The deferral of income taxes provided or paid on intercompany profits can best be illustrated by returning to the intercompany profits examples in Chapter 7.

Income Taxes Attributable to Intercompany Profits in Inventories For intercompany profits in inventories at the end of the first year of an affiliated group's operations, income tax allocation would accompany the working paper consolidation elimination on page 238 by means of the following additional elimination, assuming a combined federal and state income tax rate of 60%:

Prepaid Income Taxes—Sage	*4,800*
Income Taxes Expense—Sage	*4,800*

To defer income taxes provided on separate income tax returns of subsidiary applicable to intercompany profits in parent company's inventories at Apr. 30, Year 8, computed as 60% × $8,000 = $4,800.

The $4,800 reduction in the income tax expense of Sage Company (the partially owned subsidiary) would enter into the computation of the minority interest in the net income of the subsidiary.

With regard to intercompany profits in beginning and ending inventories (illustrated in the working paper consolidation elimination on page 240), the following additional eliminations would be appropriate:

---

[12]U.S., *Internal Revenue Code of 1954*, sec. 1504(a).
[13]*ARB No. 51*, p. 46.

Prepaid Income Taxes—Sage	7,200	
Income Taxes Expense—Sage		7,200

To defer income taxes provided on separate income tax returns of subsidiary applicable to intercompany profits in parent company's inventories at Apr. 30, Year 9: 60% × $12,000 = $7,200.

Income Taxes Expense—Sage	4,800	
Prepaid Income Taxes—Sage		4,800

To provide for income taxes attributable to intercompany profits in parent company's inventories at Apr. 30, Year 8: 60% × $8,000 = $4,800.

The latter working paper consolidation elimination reflects the tax effects of the *realization* by the consolidated group, on a first-in, first-out basis, of the intercompany profits in the parent company's *beginning* inventories.

Income Taxes Attributable to Intercompany Profits in Land Under currently prevailing accounting standards, gains and losses from sales of property, plant, and equipment are not reported as extraordinary items.[14] Thus, intraperiod income tax allocation is not appropriate for such gains and losses. Accordingly, for the intercompany profit on sale of land illustrated in Chapter 7, the following working paper consolidation elimination would accompany the one illustrated on page 242, assuming a relevant combined federal and state "capital gains" income tax rate of 35%:

Prepaid Income Taxes—Post	17,500	
Income Taxes Expense—Post		17,500

To defer income taxes provided on separate income tax returns of parent company applicable to intercompany profit in subsidiary's land at Apr. 30, Year 8: 35% × $50,000 = $17,500.

In years subsequent to Year 8, so long as the subsidiary owned the land, the following working paper consolidation elimination would be appropriate:

Prepaid Income Taxes—Post	17,500	
Retained Earnings—Post		17,500

To defer income taxes attributable to intercompany profit in subsidiary's land.

[14] *APB Opinion No. 30,* pp. 566 and 568.

In a year in which the subsidiary resold the land to an outsider, the appropriate working paper consolidation elimination would be a debit to Income Taxes Expense—Post and a credit to Retained Earnings—Post, in the amount of $17,500.

Income Taxes Attributable to Intercompany Profit in a Depreciable Asset As pointed out in Chapter 7, the intercompany profit in the sale of a depreciable asset is realized through the periodic depreciation of the asset. Therefore, the related deferred income taxes "turn around" as depreciation expense is taken on the asset with intercompany profit in its carrying value.

To illustrate, refer to the example in Chapter 7, pages 244–245. Assuming a combined federal and state income tax rate of 60%, the tax deferral consolidation elimination at April 30, Year 8 (date of the intercompany sale of machinery), would be as follows:

Prepaid Income Taxes—Sage	14,280	
Income Taxes Expense—Sage		14,280

To defer income taxes provided on separate income tax returns of subsidiary applicable to intercompany profit in parent's machinery at Apr. 30, Year 8: 60% × $23,800 = $14,280.

The $14,280 increase in the subsidiary's reported net income would be included in the computation of the minority interest in the subsidiary's net income for Year 8.

For the year ended April 30, Year 9, the consolidation elimination for income taxes attributable to the intercompany profit would be as follows:

Income Taxes Expense—Sage	2,856	
Prepaid Income Taxes—Sage ($14,280 − $2,856)	11,424	
Retained Earnings—Sage		14,280

To provide for income tax expense on intercompany profit realized through parent company's depreciation: 60% × $4,760 = $2,856; and to defer income taxes attributable to remainder of unrealized profit.

Comparable working paper consolidation eliminations would be necessary at April 30, Years 10, 11, and 12.

Income Taxes Attributable to Intercompany Gain on Reacquisition of Debt As pointed out in Chapter 7, the gain or loss on one affiliate's open-market purchase of another affiliate's bonds or debentures is *imputed,* rather than real. Nonetheless, income taxes attributable to the gain or loss should be provided for in a working paper consolidation elimination. The appropriate elimination to accompany the one illustrated on page 250 of Chapter 7 would be as follows, assuming a 60% combined income tax rate:

Income Taxes Expense—Sage	13,630	
Deferred Income Tax Liability—Sage		13,630

To provide for income taxes attributable to subsidiary's imputed gain on parent company's reacquisition of its debentures: 60% × $22,717 = $13,630.

The additional expense of the subsidiary recorded in the preceding elimination would enter into the computation of the minority interest in net income of the subsidiary.

In years **subsequent** to the date of the reacquisition of the debentures, the **actual** income tax expense of both the parent company and the subsidiary would reflect the effects of the intercompany interest revenue and expense. The income tax effects of the difference between intercompany interest revenue and expense would represent the turnaround of the $13,630 deferred income tax liability in the preceding working paper consolidation elimination.

Concluding comments

In this chapter we have discussed a number of special problems which might arise in the preparation of consolidated financial statements. We have purposely not discussed earnings per share computations for a consolidated entity, for in most circumstances the standards for earnings per share set forth in **Intermediate Accounting** of this series apply to consolidated net income per share of parent company common stock and common stock equivalents outstanding. The problems that arise in earnings per share computations when a subsidiary has securities which are common stock equivalents or are otherwise dilutive are highly technical and too specialized to warrant inclusion in our discussion of basic concepts.

REVIEW QUESTIONS

1 How is the equity method of accounting applied when a parent company attains control of a subsidiary in a series of stock acquisitions? Explain.

2 At what stage in the installment purchase of an eventual subsidiary's voting common stock should the parent company ascertain the fair values of the subsidiary's identifiable net assets? Explain.

3 *APB Opinion No. 16* requires use of the purchase method of accounting for parent company acquisitions of minority interest in a subsidiary, even though the original business combination was accounted for as a pooling of interests. Discuss the reasoning supporting this requirement.

4 If a parent company purchases the minority interest in a subsidiary at less than its carrying value, what accounting treatment is appropriate for the difference? Explain.

5 Why does a parent company realize a gain or a loss when a subsidiary issues voting common stock to the public at a price per share greater or less than the carrying value per share of the parent company's investment in the subsidiary's stock? Explain.

6 Should a subsidiary's outstanding preferred stock enter into the determination of implied fair value of the subsidiary's net assets at the date of a business combination? Discuss.

7 Explain how the minority interest in a subsidiary is affected by the parent company's ownership of 70% of the subsidiary's outstanding voting common stock and 60% of the subsidiary's outstanding 7%, cumulative, fully participating preferred stock.

8 Describe how the parent company's accounts are affected when a subsidiary purchases for its treasury all or part of its outstanding voting common stock owned by minority shareholders.

9 "The treasury stock treatment for shares of parent company voting common stock owned by a subsidiary overstates consolidated net income and understates the minority interest in net income of the subsidiary." Do you agree? Explain.

10 Shares of its own stock held by a corporation in its treasury are not entitled to dividends. However, a subsidiary receives dividends on shares of its parent company's outstanding voting common stock owned by the subsidiary. For consolidated financial statements, these parent company shares are considered equivalent to treasury stock of the consolidated entity. Is there an inconsistency in this treatment? Explain.

11 Discuss the following quotation:

> (The "indefinite reversal criteria" provisions of *APB Opinion No. 23*) allow the decision to remit cash from a subsidiary to a parent to affect the income of the parent. This occurs because the full tax expense associated with the earnings of the subsidiary has not been recorded.

12 A parent company and its subsidiary file separate income tax returns. How do the consolidated deferred income taxes associated with the intercompany profit on the parent company's sale of a depreciable asset to its subsidiary "turn around"? Explain.

EXERCISES

Ex. 8-1 Select the best answer for each of the following multiple choice questions.

1 Prigg Company purchased the outstanding capital stock of Selmon Company as follows:

10%, Jan. 2, Year 3
25%, June 1, Year 3
25%, Aug. 1, Year 3
40%, Sept. 30, Year 3
The fiscal year of each of the companies ends on September 30. Selmon's stock was acquired by Prigg at its carrying value. Consolidated net income for the year ended September 30, Year 3, would include the following earnings of the subsidiary:

a 10% of earnings, January–May, Year 3
b 35% of earnings, June–July, Year 3
c 60% of earnings, August–September, Year 3
d 60% of earnings, January–September, Year 3
e None of the above

2 Palter Corporation had 300,000 shares of voting common stock outstanding. It owned 75% of the oustanding capital stock of Swain Company. Swain owned 20,000 shares of Palter's voting common stock. In the consolidated balance sheet, Palter Corporation's outstanding voting common stock may be shown as:

a 280,000 shares
b 300,000 shares less 20,000 shares of treasury stock
c 300,000 shares
d 300,000 shares, footnoted to indicate that Swain Company holds 20,000 shares
e None of the above

3 Poule Corporation and its subsidiary Stoss Company filed separate income tax returns. Poule's income taxes included $70,000 attributable to profits on sales of merchandise to Stoss Company. In the preparation of consolidated financial statements:

a The entire intercompany profit should be eliminated; taxes need not be adjusted
b Taxes of $70,000 should be deferred
c The intercompany profit should be reduced by $70,000 before elimination, and taxes of $70,000 should be deferred
d Income taxes should be recomputed, and a revised return should be filed
e None of the above should take place

4 Pismo Corporation issued voting common stock in exchange for 90% of the outstanding capital stock of Salinas Company. The combination was accounted for by the pooling-of-interests method. If Pismo later issued voting common stock, which had a par value of $1,000 and a fair value of $100,000, for the remaining 10% of the Salinas capital stock, which had a stated value of $5,000, Pismo Corporation's consolidated assets would increase:

a $100,000
b $5,000
c $1,000
d $0
e None of the above

Ex. 8-2 On August 1, Year 6, Pater Corporation purchased 1,000 of the 10,000 out-standing shares of Sibling Company's $1 par value capital stock for $5,000. Sibling's identifiable net assets had a fair value and carrying value of $40,000 at that date. Sibling Company reported net income of $3,000 and declared and paid dividends of the same amount for the year ended July 31, Year 7. On August 1, Year 7, Pater Corporation purchased 4,500 more shares of Sibling Company's outstanding capital stock for $22,500. Sibling's fair values and carrying values for its identifiable net assets were still $40,000 at that date. Sibling Company reported net income of $7,500 and paid no dividends for the year ended July 31, Year 8.

Prepare journal entries in Pater Corporation's accounts for the above facts for the two years ended July 31, Year 8. Omit income tax effects. Journal entry explanations are not required.

Ex. 8-3 On August 1, Year 4, Pylon Corporation acquired 95% of the outstanding capital stock of Sprocket Company in a business combination accounted for as a pooling of interests. Among the intercompany transactions between Pylon and Sprocket subsequent to August 1, Year 4, were the following:

(1) On May 31, Year 5, Sprocket Company declared a 10% stock dividend on its 10,000 outstanding shares of $10 par value capital stock having a market value of $18 per share. The 1,000 shares of the stock dividend were issued June 18, Year 5.

(2) On November 28, Year 5, Sprocket Company purchased in the open market, for $15,000 cash, 1,000 of the 100,000 outstanding shares of Pylon Corporation's $1 par value voting common stock. Pylon Corporation does not presently declare dividends.

Prepare working paper consolidation eliminations at July 31, Year 5, in good form, for Pylon Corporation and subsidiary. Disregard income taxes.

Ex. 8-4 Intercompany profit in the Year 3 merchandise transactions between Philo Corporation and its 80%-owned subsidiary, Silas Company, may be analyzed as follows:

	Selling price	Cost	Gross profit
Beginning inventory	$ 60,000	$ 50,000	$ 10,000
Sales	720,000	600,000	120,000
Total	$780,000	$650,000	$130,000
Ending inventory.	90,000	75,000	15,000
Cost of goods sold	$690,000	$575,000	$115,000

Each of the two companies, which are subject to a combined federal and state income tax rate of 60%, files separate income tax returns.

Prepare working paper consolidation eliminations at December 31, Year 3, for the deferred income taxes attributable to Philo Corporation's intercompany merchandise transactions with its subsidiary.

Ex. 8-5 Petrov Corporation's purchases of Slavik Company's 10,000 shares of outstanding $1 par value capital stock were as follows:

Date	No. of shares acquired	Cash paid	Carrying value of Slavik's net assets
Jan. 2, Year 6	1,500	$ 16,500	$ 90,000
May 1, Year 6	1,000	12,000	95,000
Aug. 1, Year 6	7,500	93,750	101,000
Totals	10,000	$122,250	

At December 31, Year 6, the carrying value of Slavik's net assets was $116,000. Slavik Company paid no dividends during Year 6 and had no change in its paid-in capital during that year; hence the changes in the carrying value of Slavik's net assets during Year 6 were due solely to profitable operations.

Compute in good form Petrov Corporation's intercompany investment income for Year 6, under the equity method of accounting, attributable to its investment in Slavik Company. Ignore income taxes.

Ex. 8-6 The stockholders' equity section of Stoup Company's August 31, Year 2, balance sheet was as follows:

8% cumulative preferred stock, $1 par value, dividends in arrears two years, authorized, issued, and outstanding 100,000 shares, callable at $1.10 per share plus dividends in arrears	$ 100,000
Common stock, $2 par value, authorized, issued, and outstanding 100,000 shares	200,000
Paid-in capital in excess of par—common	150,000
Retained earnings	750,000
Total stockholders' equity	$1,200,000

On August 31, Year 2, Perch Corporation acquired 50,000 shares of Stoup Company's outstanding preferred stock and 75,000 shares of Stoup Company's outstanding common stock for a total cost—including out-of-pocket costs—of $1,030,500. The fair values of Stoup's identifiable net assets were equal to their carrying values at August 31, Year 2.

Answer the following questions. Supporting computations should be in good form.

a What amount of the $1,030,500 purchase price is assignable to Stoup Company's preferred stock?

b What is the minority interest of preferred shareholders in Stoup Company's net assets at August 31, Year 2?

c What is Stoup Company's goodwill purchased by Perch Corporation August 31, Year 2?

d What is the minority interest of common shareholders in Stoup Company's net assets at August 31, Year 2?

Ex. 8-7 Select the best answer for each of the following multiple choice questions.

1 With respect to the difference between taxable income and pre-tax accounting income, the tax effect of the undistributed earnings of a subsidiary included in consolidated income should normally be:

a Accounted for as a timing difference

b Accounted for as a permanent difference

c Ignored because it must be based on estimates and assumptions

d Ignored because it cannot be presumed that all undistributed earnings of a subsidiary will be transferred to the parent company

2 Under the equity method, the effect on the investor of dividends received from the investee is usually:

a A reduction of deferred income taxes and a reduction of investment

b A reduction of deferred income taxes and no effect on investment

c No effect on deferred income taxes and a reduction of investment

d No effect on deferred income taxes and no effect on investment

3 Spicer Company, a subsidiary of Placer Corporation, did not distribute its Year 5 earnings in Year 5. Placer should recognize income taxes on its share of the earnings in its Year 5 financial statements only if:

    a Spicer Company is a domestic corporation

    b The earnings will be remitted in a tax-free transaction within the foreseeable future

    c The earnings will be remitted in a taxable transaction on or before March 15, Year 6

    d Remittance of the earnings in a taxable transaction will not be postponed indefinitely

  4 Accounting for the tax effect of a difference between taxable income and pre-tax accounting income with respect to undistributed earnings of a subsidiary is similar to a situation involving:

    a Profits on assets within the consolidated group which are eliminated in consolidated financial statements

    b Profits on intercompany transactions which are taxed when reported in separate tax returns

    c Rents and royalties which are taxed when collected and deferred in financial statements until earned

    d Profits on installment sales which are recognized in financial statements at the date of sale and reported in tax returns when the installment receivables are collected

SHORT CASES FOR ANALYSIS AND DECISION

Case 8-1 On March 1, Year 1, Primary Corporation, a manufacturer, organized a wholly owned subsidiary finance company, Secondary Company, to purchase Primary's installment contracts for sales of Primary's durable goods products. Primary purchased all 10,000 shares of Secondary's $5 par value capital stock on March 1, Year 1.

    By February 28, Year 4, Secondary Company had accumulated a retained earnings balance of $120,000, which was also reflected in Primary Corporation's Retained Earnings of Subsidiary account, under the equity method of accounting. As of the close of business February 28, Year 4, under a directive from the state regulatory body for finance companies, Secondary Company declared and issued a 100% stock dividend. In connection with the dividend, Secondary transferred $50,000 from its Retained Earnings account to its Capital Stock account.

    The bank which provides Secondary Company's line of credit has requested separate financial statements for both Primary Corporation and Secondary Company, as well as consolidated financial statements, for the year ended February 28, Year 4. The controller of Primary Corporation is concerned about the inconsistency resulting from the fact that Primary Corporation's Retained Earnings of Subsidiary account has a balance of $120,000 at February 28, Year 4, while Secondary Company's Retained Earnings account is $70,000 at that date. The controller asks your opinion of the propriety of transferring $50,000 from Primary Corporation's Retained Earnings of Subsidiary account to its Paid-in Capital in Excess of Par account.

    Instructions What is your opinion of the controller's proposal? Explain.

Case 8-2 Spillane Company, a wholly owned subsidiary of Piltdown Corporation, is in need of additional long-term financing. Under instructions from Piltdown Corporation, Spillane Company offers 5,000 shares of its previously unissued $2 par value capital stock to shareholders of Piltdown Corporation at a price of $10 per share. The offer is fully subscribed by Piltdown's shareholders, and the stock is issued for $50,000 cash on June 30, Year 6.

    After the stock issuance, Piltdown Corporation owns 45,000 shares, or 90%, of the 50,000 shares of Spillane Company capital stock outstanding; and shareholders of Piltdown Corporation own 5,000 shares, or 10%, of Spillane's out-standing stock. By comparing Piltdown Corporation's 90% interest in Spillane Company's net assets after the stock issuance to the parent company's 100% interest in the subsidiary's net assets before the stock issuance, Piltdown's chief accountant computed a $4,000 nonoperating gain for entry into Piltdown's accounts. The controller of Piltdown objected to the chief accountant's entry. He pointed out that the 5,000 shares of Spillane Company stock were issued to Piltdown's shareholders, not to **outsiders,** and that it is a basic principle of accounting that a corporation cannot profit from stock issuances to its share-holders.

Instructions   Evaluate the objections of Piltdown Corporation's controller.

Case 8-3   Pilgrim Corporation needed working capital early in Year 7. Therefore, on January 31, Year 7, Pilgrim sold in the open market 1,000 shares of its 10,000-share investment in Saltine Company's $1 par value capital stock for $15,000. Pilgrim had purchased the 10,000 shares of Saltine Company's stock for $12,000 on February 1, Year 5—the date Saltine Corporation was organized with an author-ized capital stock of 10,000 shares.

Just prior to the stock sale, Pilgrim Corporation's Investment in Subsidiary account, which was maintained by the equity method of accounting, had a balance of $110,000. Pilgrim Corporation's controller asks your advice on how to present the following in consolidated financial statements for the year ended January 31, Year 7:

(1) The $4,000 gain [computed as $15,000 − ($110,000 × 1,000/10,000)] on Pilgrim Corporation's sale of 1,000 shares of Saltine Company's capital stock.
(2) The offset for the $11,000 minority interest (computed as 1,000/10,000 × $110,000) in the net assets of Saltine Company at January 31, Year 7.

Instructions   What is your advice to the controller of Pilgrim Corporation? Support the position you take.

PROBLEMS

8-4   Condensed balance sheets of Plantation Corporation and its subsidiary, Salvador Company, on the dates indicated, appear on page 312.

Plantation Corporation purchased 60,000 shares of Salvador Company's outstanding capital stock January 2, Year 3, at a cost of $1,470,000; and 30,000 shares on September 30, Year 3, at a cost of $888,000. Plantation's desire to attain control over Salvador was due to the valuable patents owned by Salvador.

Salvador Company amortizes the cost of patents on a straight-line basis. Any amount allocated to patents as a result of the business combination is to be amortized over the five-year remaining useful life of the patents as of January 2, Year 3.

Salvador Company paid a cash dividend of $300,000 on December 31, Year 3. Plantation Corporation has not recorded the declaration or the receipt of the dividend.

Instructions   Prepare journal entries, in good form, for Plantation Corporation at December 31, Year 3, to account for its investment in Salvador Company by the equity method of accounting. Ignore income taxes.

8-5   Phosphate Corporation owns 99% of the outstanding capital stock of Stargell Company, acquired July 1, Year 5, in a pooling of interests, and 90% of the outstanding capital stock of Spartan Company, acquired July 1, Year 5, in a purchase which reflected Spartan Company goodwill of $58,000. All identifiable

	Plantation Corporation	Salvador Company		
	Dec. 31, Year 3	Jan. 2, Year 3	Sept. 30, Year 3	Dec. 31, Year 3
Assets				
Cash	$ 400,000	$ 550,000	$ 650,000	$ 425,000
Fees and royalties				
receivable	–0–	250,000	450,000	500,000
Investment in Salvador				
Company	2,358,000	–0–	–0–	–0–
Patents.	–0–	1,000,000	850,000	800,000
Other assets	4,242,000	–0–	–0–	200,000
	$7,000,000	$1,800,000	$1,950,000	$1,925,000
Liabilities & Stockholders' Equity				
Liabilities	$ 400,000	$ 200,000	$ 150,000	$ 275,000
Capital stock, $10 par value	5,000,000	1,000,000	1,000,000	1,000,000
Retained earnings	1,600,000	600,000	800,000	650,000
	$7,000,000	$1,800,000	$1,950,000	$1,925,000

net assets of Spartan Company were fairly valued at their carrying values at July 1, Year 5.

Condensed financial statements of Phosphate Corporation, Stargell Company, and Spartan Company at June 30, Year 6, prior to income tax provisions and equity method accruals in the accounts of Phosphate Corporation, appear on page 313. Intercompany profits in inventories resulting from Phosphate Corporation's sales to its subsidiaries during the year ended June 30, Year 6, are as follows:

In Stargell Company's inventories—$6,000

In Spartan Company's inventories—$7,500

Instructions Prepare in good form Phosphate Corporation's June 30, Year 6, journal entries for income taxes and equity method accruals. Phosphate's combined federal and state income tax rate is 60%. All three companies declared dividends on June 30, Year 6.

8-6 Condensed individual and consolidated financial statements of Peerless Corporation and its wholly owned subsidiary, Supreme Company, for the year ended May 31, Year 4, appear on page 314. Other information about the affiliated companies includes the following:
(1) All of Supreme Company's identifiable net assets were fairly valued at their carrying values at May 31, Year 2—the date of the Peerless-Supreme business combination. Thus, the $50,000 excess of Peerless Corporation's investment in Supreme Company over the carrying value of Supreme's identifiable net assets was attributable to goodwill with an estimated useful life of 40 years.
(2) Peerless Corporation sells merchandise to Supreme Company at Peerless's regular markup.
(3) Supreme Company owns 1,000 shares of Peerless Corporation's outstanding capital stock.

PHOSPHATE CORPORATION AND SUBSIDIARIES
Financial Statements
Year Ended June 30, Year 6

	Phosphate Corporation	Stargell Company	Spartan Company
Income Statement			
Revenue			
Net sales	$1,000,000	$ 550,000	$ 220,000
Intercompany sales	100,000	–0–	–0–
	$1,100,000	$ 550,000	$ 220,000
Costs and expenses			
Cost of goods sold	$ 700,000	$ 357,500	$ 143,000
Intercompany cost of goods sold	70,000	–0–	–0–
Selling, general, and administrative			
expenses	130,000	92,500	27,000
Interest expense	50,000	–0–	–0–
Income taxes expense	–0–	60,000	30,000
	$ 950,000	$ 510,000	$ 200,000
Net income	$ 150,000	$ 40,000	$ 20,000
Statement of Retained Earnings			
Retained earnings, July 1, Year 5	$ 400,000	$ 300,000	$ 150,000
Net income	150,000	40,000	20,000
	$ 550,000	$ 340,000	$ 170,000
Dividends	50,000	20,000	10,000
Retained earnings, June 30, Year 6	$ 500,000	$ 320,000	$ 160,000
Balance Sheet			
Assets			
Inventories	$1,000,000	$ 800,000	$ 700,000
Investment in Stargell Company	990,000	–0–	–0–
Investment in Spartan Company	574,200	–0–	–0–
Other assets	1,501,300	1,260,000	790,000
	$4,065,500	$2,060,000	$1,490,000
Liabilities & Stockholders' Equity			
Liabilities	$1,965,500	$1,040,000	$ 900,000
Capital stock, $1 par value	1,000,000	500,000	300,000
Paid-in capital in excess of par	600,000	200,000	130,000
Retained earnings	500,000	320,000	160,000
	$4,065,500	$2,060,000	$1,490,000

PEERLESS CORPORATION AND SUBSIDIARY
Individual and Consolidated Financial Statements
Year Ended May 31, Year 4

	Peerless Corporation	Supreme Company	Consolidated
Income Statement			
Revenue			
Net sales	$10,000,000	$4,600,000	$12,900,000
Other revenue	270,000	20,000	38,250
	$10,270,000	$4,620,000	$12,938,250
Costs and expenses			
Cost of goods sold	$ 6,700,000	$3,082,000	$ 8,085,300
Other operating expenses	2,920,000	1,288,000	4,209,250
	$ 9,620,000	$4,370,000	$12,294,550
Net income	$ 650,000	$ 250,000	$ 643,700
Statement of Retained Earnings			
Retained earnings, June 1, Year 3	$ 2,420,000	$ 825,000	$ 2,406,800
Net income	650,000	250,000	643,700
	$ 3,070,000	$1,075,000	$ 3,050,500
Dividends	300,000	175,000	297,000
Retained earnings, May 31, Year 4	$ 2,770,000	$ 900,000	$ 2,753,500
Balance Sheet			
Assets			
Intercompany receivables (payables) . .	$ 520,000	$ (520,000)	$ –0–
Marketable securities	400,000	150,000	530,000
Inventories	1,100,000	610,000	1,693,500
Investment in subsidiary	1,097,500	–0–	–0–
Other assets	2,800,000	1,370,000	4,170,000
Goodwill	–0–	–0–	47,500
	$ 5,917,500	$1,610,000	$ 6,441,000
Liabilities & Stockholders' Equity			
Liabilities	$ 2,075,000	$ 560,000	$ 2,635,000
Capital stock, $10 par value	1,000,000	150,000	1,000,000
Retained earnings	2,770,000	900,000	2,753,500
Retained earnings of subsidiary	122,500	–0–	122,500
Treasury stock	(50,000)	–0–	(70,000)
	$ 5,917,500	$1,610,000	$ 6,441,000

Instructions Reconstruct the working paper consolidation eliminations for Peerless Corporation and subsidiary at May 31, Year 4. Omit explanations. Ignore income taxes.

8-7 Condensed financial statements of Petrie Corporation and its two subsidiaries for the year ended December 31, Year 8, appear on page 316. Additional information available includes the following:

(1) Petrie Corporation's Investment in Standish Company Stock account appears as follows:

Investment in Standish Company Stock

Date	Explanations	Debit	Credit	Balance
Year 8				
Jan. 2	*Cost of 5,000 shares*	*71,400*		*71,400 dr.*
June 30	*20% of dividend declared*		*9,000*	*62,400 dr.*
June 30	*20% of net income for Jan. 2–June 30*	*12,000*		*74,400 dr.*
July 1	*Cost of 15,000 shares*	*223,200*		*297,600 dr.*
Dec. 31	*80% of dividend declared*		*24,000*	*273,600 dr.*
Dec. 31	*80% of net income for July 1–Dec. 31*	*32,000*		*305,600 dr.*

(2) The accountant for Petrie Corporation made no equity method entries for Petrie's investments in Sprouse Company preferred and common stock. Petrie Corporation acquired 250 shares of Sprouse's fully participating non-cumulative preferred stock for $7,000 and 14,000 shares of Sprouse's common stock for $196,000 on January 2, Year 8.
(3) Sprouse Company's December 31, Year 8, inventory included $22,400 of merchandise acquired from Petrie Corporation for which no payment had been made.
(4) Petrie Corporation acquired in the open market twenty-five $1,000 principal amount 6% bonds of Standish Company for $20,800 on December 31, Year 8. The bonds have a December 31 interest payment date, and a maturity date of December 31, Year 10.
(5) Standish Company owed Petrie Corporation $17,000 at December 31, Year 8, for a non-interest-bearing cash advance.

Instructions
a Prepare adjusting journal entry or entries for Petrie Corporation, in good form, to account for investments in Sprouse Company preferred and common stock by the equity method. Disregard income taxes.
b Prepare consolidating financial statements working papers and related consolidation eliminations, in good form, for Petrie Corporation and subsidiaries at December 31, Year 8. Ignore income taxes.

8-8 Purcell Corporation purchased for $151,000 cash 100% of the common stock and 20% of the preferred stock of Shilling Company on June 30, Year 1. At that date, Shilling's retained earnings balance was $41,000. The fair values of Shilling's identifiable assets and liabilities and preferred stock did not differ materially from their carrying values at June 30, Year 1.

Transactions between Purcell Corporation and Shilling Company during the year ended December 31, Year 2, follow.
(1) On January 2, Year 2, Purcell sold land with an $11,000 carrying value to Shilling for $15,000. Shilling made a $3,000 down payment and signed an 8% mortgage note payable in 12 equal quarterly payments of $1,135, including interest, beginning March 1, Year 2.
(2) Shilling produced equipment for Purcell under two separate contracts. The first contract, which was for office equipment, was begun and completed during Year 2 at a cost to Shilling of $17,500. Purcell paid $22,000 cash for

PETRIE CORPORATION AND SUBSIDIARIES
Financial Statements
Year Ended December 31, Year 8

	Petrie Corporation	Standish Company	Sprouse Company
Income Statement			
Revenue			
Net sales	$1,120,000	$900,000	$700,000
Intercompany sales	140,000	–0–	–0–
Intercompany investment income	44,000	–0–	–0–
	$1,304,000	$900,000	$700,000
Costs and expenses			
Cost of goods sold	$ 800,000	$650,000	$550,000
Intercompany cost of goods sold	100,000	–0–	–0–
Other operating expenses	300,000	150,000	130,000
	$1,200,000	$800,000	$680,000
Net income	$ 104,000	$100,000	$ 20,000
Statement of Retained Earnings			
Retained earnings, Jan. 1, Year 8	$ 126,200	$107,000	$100,000
Net income	104,000	100,000	20,000
	$ 230,200	$207,000	$120,000
Dividends	22,000	75,000	–0–
Retained earnings, Dec. 31, Year 8	$ 208,200	$132,000	$120,000
Balance Sheet			
Assets			
Intercompany receivables (payables) . .	$ 63,400	$ (41,000)	$ (22,400)
Inventories	290,000	90,000	115,000
Investment in Standish Company stock	305,600	–0–	–0–
Investment in Standish Company bonds	20,800	–0–	–0–
Investment in Sprouse Company			
preferred	7,000	–0–	–0–
Investment in Sprouse Company			
common	196,000	–0–	–0–
Other assets	836,400	555,000	510,000
	$1,719,200	$604,000	$602,600
Liabilities & Stockholders' Equity			
Dividends payable	$ 22,000	$ 6,000	$ –0–
Bonds payable	285,000	150,000	125,000
Discount on bonds payable	(8,000)	(12,000)	–0–
Other liabilities	212,000	78,000	107,600
Preferred stock, $20 par value	400,000	–0–	50,000
Common stock, $10 par value	600,000	250,000	200,000
Retained earnings	208,200	132,000	120,000
	$1,719,200	$604,000	$602,600

the equipment on April 17, Year 2. The second contract was begun on February 15, Year 2, but will not be completed until May of Year 3. Shilling has incurred $45,000 costs under the second contract as of December 31, Year 2, and anticipates additional costs of $30,000 to complete the $95,000 contract. Shilling accounts for all contracts under the percentage-of-completion method of accounting. Purcell has made no entry in its accounts for the uncompleted contract as of December 31, Year 2. Purcell depreciates all its equipment over a 10-year estimated useful life with no salvage value. Purcell takes a half year's depreciation in the year of purchase.

(3) On December 1, Year 2, Shilling declared a 5% cash dividend on its preferred stock, payable January 15, Year 3, to stockholders of record December 14, Year 2.

(4) Purcell sells merchandise to Shilling at an average markup of 12% of cost. During the year, Purcell billed Shilling $238,000 for merchandise shipped, of which Shilling paid $211,000 by December 31, Year 2. Shilling has $11,200 of this merchandise on hand at December 31, Year 2.

The individual financial statements of Purcell Corporation and Shilling Company for Year 2 appear below and on page 318.

Instructions

a Reconstruct the Intercompany Receivables (Payables) accounts of the affiliates as of December 31, Year 2.

b Prepare in good form any necessary adjusting journal entry or entries as of December 31, Year 2, based on your analysis in *a* above.

c Prepare consolidating financial statements working papers and related consolidation eliminations for Purcell Corporation and subsidiary for Year 2. Round all computations to the nearest dollar. Ignore income tax considerations.

PURCELL CORPORATION AND SUBSIDIARY
Financial Statements
Year Ended December 31, Year 2

	Purcell Corporation	Shilling Company
Income Statement		
Revenue		
Net sales	$1,562,000	$ -0-
Intercompany sales.	238,000	-0-
Earned revenue on contracts.	-0-	1,210,000
Intercompany earned revenue on contracts	-0-	79,000
Interest revenue	19,149	-0-
Intercompany investment income	45,000	-0-
Intercompany dividend revenue	500	-0-
Intercompany gain on sale of land	4,000	-0-
Intercompany interest revenue (expense)	851	(851)
	$1,869,500	$1,288,149

PURCELL CORPORATION AND SUBSIDIARY
Financial Statements (Concluded)
Year Ended December 31, Year 2

	Purcell Corporation	Shilling Company
Costs and expenses		
Cost of goods sold	$ 942,500	$ –0–
Intercompany cost of goods sold	212,500	–0–
Cost of earned revenue on contracts	–0–	789,500
Intercompany cost of earned revenue on contracts . .	–0–	62,500
Selling, general, and administrative expenses	497,000	360,000
Interest expense	49,000	31,149
	$1,701,000	$1,243,149
Net income	$ 168,500	$ 45,000
Statement of Retained Earnings		
Retained earnings, Jan. 1, Year 2	$ 139,311	$ 49,500
Net income	168,500	45,000
	$ 307,811	$ 94,500
Dividends	–0–	2,500
Retained earnings, Dec. 31, Year 2	$ 307,811	$ 92,000
Balance Sheet		
Assets		
Intercompany receivables (payables)	$ 35,811	$ 21,189
Costs and estimated earnings in excess of billings on uncompleted contracts	–0–	30,100
Inventories	217,000	117,500
Investment in subsidiary	204,500	–0–
Land	34,000	42,000
Other property and equipment, net	717,000	408,000
Other assets	153,000	84,211
	$1,361,311	$ 703,000
Liabilities & Stockholders' Equity		
Dividends payable	$ –0–	$ 2,000
Mortgages payable	592,000	389,000
Other liabilities	203,000	70,000
5% noncumulative nonparticipating preferred stock . .	–0–	50,000
Common stock	250,000	100,000
Retained earnings	307,811	92,000
Retained earnings of subsidiary	8,500	–0–
	$1,361,311	$ 703,000

8-9 Purl Corporation acquired 10% of the 100,000 outstanding shares of $2.50 par value common stock of Sine Company on December 31, Year 6, for $38,000. An additional 70,000 shares were acquired for $331,800 on June 30, Year 8 (at which time there was no material difference between the fair values and carrying values of Sine Company's identifiable net assets).

The financial statements of Purl Corporation and subsidiary for the year ended December 31, Year 8, appear below and on page 320. The following information is also available:

(1) An analysis of Purl Corporation's Investment in Sine Company Stock account:

Date	Description	Amount
Dec. 31, Year 6	Investment	$ 38,000
June 30, Year 8	Investment	331,800
Dec. 15, Year 8	Dividend: 80% × $11,000	(8,800)
Dec. 31, Year 8	80% of $56,000 net income for Year 8	44,800
Dec. 31, Year 8	Balance	$405,800

(2) An analysis of the companies' Retained Earnings accounts:

	Purl Corporation	Sine Company
Balance, Dec. 31, Year 6	$540,000	$101,000
Net income for Year 7	55,000	40,000
Cash dividends in Year 7	–0–	(5,000)
Balance, Dec. 31, Year 7	$595,000	$136,000
Net income, first half of Year 8	31,000	23,000
Net income, second half of Year 8	40,800	33,000
Cash dividends declared, Dec. 15, Year 8	(20,000)	(11,000)
Balance, Dec. 31, Year 8	$646,800	$181,000

PURL CORPORATION AND SUBSIDIARY
Financial Statements
Year Ended December 31, Year 8

	Purl Corporation	Sine Company
Income Statement		
Revenue		
Net sales	$840,000	$360,000
Intercompany sales	80,600	65,000
Intercompany gain on sale of equipment	9,500	–0–
Intercompany interest revenue	2,702	–0–
Intercompany investment income	44,800	–0–
	$977,602	$425,000

Costs and expenses

Cost of goods sold	$546,000	$252,000
Intercompany cost of goods sold	56,420	48,750
Interest expense	32,000	11,382
Other operating expenses.	271,382	56,868
	$905,802	$369,000
Net income	$ 71,800	$ 56,000

Statement of Retained Earnings

Retained earnings, Jan. 1, Year 8	$595,000	$136,000
Net income	71,800	56,000
	$666,800	$192,000
Dividends	20,000	11,000
Retained earnings, Dec. 31, Year 8	$646,800	$181,000

Balance Sheet

Assets

Intercompany receivables (payables)	$ 35,800	$(35,800)
Inventories	180,000	96,000
Investment in Sine Company stock	405,800	–0–
Investment in Sine Company bonds	27,917	–0–
Plant and equipment	781,500	510,000
Accumulated depreciation	(87,000)	(85,000)
Other assets	333,783	146,500
	$1,677,800	$631,700

Liabilities & Stockholders' Equity

Dividends payable	$ 20,000	$ 2,200
Bonds payable.	400,000	150,000
Discount on bonds payable.	–0–	(5,347)
Other liabilities	97,000	24,847
Capital stock.	500,000	250,000
Paid-in capital in excess of par	14,000	29,000
Retained earnings	646,800	181,000
	$1,677,800	$631,700

(3) Data on intercompany sales for Year 8:

	Purl Corporation	Sine Company
Year-end inventory of intercompany merchandise purchases, at		
first-in, first-out cost	$26,000	$22,000
Intercompany payables at year-end	12,000	7,000

(4) Purl Corporation acquired $30,000 principal amount of Sine Company's 6% bonds in the open market January 2, Year 8, for $27,015—a 10% yield. Sine Company had issued the bonds on January 2, Year 6, to yield 8% and has been paying the interest each December 31.

(5) On September 1, Year 8, Purl Corporation sold equipment with a cost of $40,000 and accumulated depreciation of $9,300 to Sine Company for $40,200. Sine Company recorded the equipment at a cost of $49,500, with accumulated depreciation of $9,300. At September 1, Year 8, the equipment had an estimated useful life of 10 years and no residual value.

(6) Sine Company owed Purl Corporation $32,000 at December 31, Year 8, for non-interest-bearing cash advances.

Instructions

a Draft in good form any necessary adjusting journal entries indicated by the above information. Disregard income taxes.

b Prepare consolidating financial statements working papers and related consolidation eliminations for Purl Corporation and subsidiary at December 31, Year 8. Disregard income taxes. Any amortization required by **APB Opinion No. 17,** "Intangible Assets," should be over a 40-year useful life.

8-10 On January 2, Year 6, Penn Corporation purchased a controlling interest of 75% in the outstanding capital stock of Stice Company for $96,000. Financial statements for the two companies for the year ended December 31, Year 6, appear on pages 322 and 323.

The following information is also available:

(1) Stice Company's stockholders' equity accounts at January 2, Year 6, were as follows:

Capital stock, $5 par value	$ 20,000
Paid-in capital in excess of par	10,000
Retained earnings	112,000
Total stockholders' equity	$142,000

(2) Both companies lease their land and buildings used in operations.

(3) Stice Company's marketable securities consist of 1,500 shares of Penn Corporation capital stock purchased on June 15, Year 6, in the open market for $18,000.

(4) On December 10, Year 6, Penn Corporation declared a cash dividend of $0.50 per share payable January 10, Year 7, to stockholders of record December 20, Year 6. Stice Company paid a cash dividend of $1 per share on June 30, Year 6, and distributed a 10% stock dividend on September 30, Year 6. The stock's ex-dividend fair value was $15 per share on September 30, Year 6.

(5) Stice Company sold machinery with a carrying value of $4,000, no residual value, and a remaining useful life of five years to Penn Corporation for $4,800 on December 31, Year 6.

(6) Stice Company's machinery and equipment had a composite estimated remaining useful life of five years at January 2, Year 6.

(7) Data on intercompany sales of merchandise follow:

	In purchaser's inventory, Dec. 31, Year 6	Amount payable by purchaser, Dec. 31, Year 6
Penn Corporation to Stice Company	$24,300	$24,000
Stice Company to Penn Corporation	18,000	8,000

PENN CORPORATION AND STICE COMPANY
Financial Statements
Year Ended December 31, Year 6

	Penn Corporation	Stice Company
Income Statement		
Revenue		
Net sales	$772,000	$426,000
Intercompany sales	78,000	104,000
Intercompany dividend revenue	–0–	750
Intercompany gain on sale of machinery	–0–	800
Intercompany investment income	30,600	–0–
Other revenue	9,000	2,900
	$889,600	$534,450
Costs and expenses		
Cost of goods sold	$445,000	$301,200
Intercompany cost of goods sold	65,000	72,800
Depreciation expense	65,600	11,200
Selling, general, and administrative expenses	149,900	52,375
Income taxes expense	80,100	58,125
	$805,600	$495,700
Net income	$ 84,000	$ 38,750
Statement of Retained Earnings		
Retained earnings, Jan. 1, Year 6	$378,000	$112,000
Net income	84,000	38,750
	$462,000	$150,750
Dividends	7,500	10,000
Retained earnings, Dec. 31, Year 6	$454,500	$140,750
Balance Sheet		
Assets		
Marketable securities	$ –0–	$ 18,000
Intercompany receivables (payables)	15,250	(15,250)
Inventories	275,000	135,000
Other current assets	309,100	106,000
Investment in subsidiary	123,600	–0–
Machinery and equipment	518,000	279,000
Accumulated depreciation	(298,200)	(196,700)
	$942,750	$326,050

Liabilities & Stockholders' Equity

Dividends payable	$ 6,750	$ -0-
Income taxes payable	80,100	58,125
Other current liabilities	215,400	91,175
Capital stock, $10 par value	150,000	-0-
Capital stock, $5 par value	-0-	22,000
Paid-in capital in excess of par	36,000	14,000
Retained earnings	454,500	140,750
	$942,750	$326,050

(8) Both companies are subject to a combined federal and state income tax rate of 60%. Penn Corporation is entitled to a dividend received deduction of 85%. Each company will file separate income tax returns for Year 6. Except for Penn Corporation's Intercompany Investment Income account, there are no timing differences for either company.

Instructions

a Prepare December 31, Year 6, adjusting journal entry or entries, in good form, to provide for income tax allocation in accounts of Penn Corporation due to Penn's use of the equity method of accounting for the subsidiary's operating results.

b Prepare consolidating financial statements working papers and related consolidation eliminations, including those for income tax allocation, for Penn Corporation and subsidiary at December 31, Year 6.

24 pages

9

Segment reporting; interim statements; forecasts

In this chapter we shall deal with three issues which have received much attention from accounting authorities in recent years. Segment reporting, interim financial statements, and financial forecasts have been the subject of pronouncements by the AICPA, the FASB, and the SEC. In addition, the Cost Accounting Standards Board and other professional organizations have issued statements on one or more of these topics.

SEGMENT REPORTING

The AICPA has defined a **segment of a business** as follows:

> For purposes of this Opinion, the term **segment of a business** refers to a component of an entity whose activities represent a separate major line of business or class of customer. A segment may be in the form of a subsidiary, a division, or a department, and in some cases a joint venture or other non-subsidiary investee, provided that its assets, results of operations, and activities can be clearly distinguished, physically and operationally and for financial reporting purposes, from the other assets, results of operations, and activities of the entity.[1]

The expression **line of business** is often used interchangeably with **segment of a business.**

[1] *APB Opinion No. 30,* "Reporting the Results of Operations," AICPA (New York: 1973), pp. 560–561.

In 1974, the FASB held a public hearing on the subject of financial reporting for segments of a business enterprise. As a basis for identifying matters for discussion at the public hearing, the Board distributed a *Discussion Memorandum,* which analyzed, but did not take a stand on, the various issues involved in segment reporting. In accordance with the Board's operating procedures, an Exposure Draft of a Proposed Statement of Financial Accounting Standards was expected to result from the Board's deliberations following the public hearing.

Much of this section draws upon the above-described *FASB Discussion Memorandum,* entitled "An Analysis of Issues Related to Financial Reporting for Segments of a Business Enterprise." Following a historical survey of the background of segment reporting, we shall identify and investigate some principal issues of segment reporting dealt with in the *Discussion Memorandum.*

Background of segment reporting

The FASB traces a chronological history of segment reporting from the start of hearings, in September of 1964, before the U.S. Senate Judiciary Committee's Subcommittee on Antitrust and Monopoly. The Subcommittee was considering economic concentration in American industry, especially in the so-called *conglomerate,* or *diversified,* business organizations.

Out of these hearings came a great deal of discussion among academicians, Congressmen, SEC officials, financial analysts and executives, and AICPA representatives regarding the propriety of financial reporting for segments of an entity. The concept of segment reporting was controversial in that it was opposed to the philosophy that *consolidated financial statements,* rather than separate financial statements, fairly present the financial position and operating results of a single economic entity, regardless of the legal or product-line structure of the entity.

The AICPA In September 1967, the Accounting Principles Board of the AICPA issued *Statement No. 2,* "Disclosure of Supplemental Financial Information by Diversified Companies." In this statement, which did not have the effect of an APB Opinion, the Board recognized that there were few practical problems in determining *sales* or *revenue* for segments of a diversified company. The Board acknowledged, however, that reporting *profitability* for a segment might entail estimates, assumptions, and arbitrary allocations, with the result that investors might be misled. Consequently, the Board recommended thorough research on the problems associated with segment reporting and urged diversified companies in the interim to voluntarily disclose supplemental financial information as to industry segments.

In June 1973, the AICPA's Accounting Principles Board issued *Opinion No. 30,* "Reporting the Results of Operations." Included in the provisions of **Opinion No. 30** were guidelines for reporting in the income statement the effects of disposal of a segment of a business.

The NAA In April 1968, the National Association of Accountants, an organization emphasizing managerial accounting concepts, issued a Research Study in Managerial Reporting entitled **External Reporting for Segments of a Business,** by Morton Backer and Walter B. McFarland. The authors concluded from their research that investors and creditors need information on operating results of major segments of diversified companies; that management can best define the reporting segments; and that segment contribution margin (revenue less separable costs of the segment) is the most reliable measure of segment profitability for a diversified company having substantial joint revenue and joint costs.[2]

In June 1972, the Committee on Management Accounting Practices of the NAA issued **Statement No. 3,** "Financial Reporting by Diversified Companies." The Committee recommended that all diversified companies include financial information for segments of the business in their annual reports to shareholders. Management should define the segments and should report for each segment the sales or revenue, costs and expenses specific to the segment, costs and expenses allocated to the segment, and income or loss before income taxes and extraordinary items.[3]

The FEI In June 1968, the research foundation of the Financial Executives Institute, an organization devoted to financial accounting concepts, published **Financial Reporting by Diversified Companies,** by R. K. Mautz. The principal conclusions of the author were that managements of diversified companies should identify material segments and report the segments' revenue and contribution to income. Material segments were defined as those producing 15% or more of a diversified company's gross revenue. Each segment's contribution to income could be determined either before or after the allocation of common costs.[4] Subsequently, in May 1971, the Financial Executives Institute issued a policy statement recommending disclosure in annual reports to shareholders of financial information on separable and measurable lines of business. The Institute sanctioned disclosure of line-of-business information as a supplement to the basic financial statements, rather than as a formal part of the statements.[5]

The SEC In August 1969, the SEC adopted requirements for segment disclosures for companies issuing securities interstate to the public, and

[2] Morton Backer and Walter B. McFarland, *External Reporting for Segments of a Business,* NAA (New York: 1968), pp. 99–100.
[3] "Financial Reporting by Diversified Companies," *Management Accounting,* September 1972, pp. 53, 59.
[4] R. K. Mautz, *Financial Reporting by Diversified Companies,* Financial Executives Research Foundation (New York: 1968), pp. 157–158.
[5] *Financial Executives Institute Bulletin No. 213,* May 1971.

for companies registering their securities for trading on a national exchange. In October 1970, comparable segment reporting techniques were mandated by the SEC for companies required to file annual reports with the Commission. The SEC's position was that companies subject to its jurisdiction having revenue of $50 million or less should report revenue and income before income taxes and extraordinary items for segments accounting for 15% or more of either of these measures. For companies with revenue exceeding $50 million, the percentage cutoff was 10%. Definitions of segments were left to the discretion of managements of companies reporting to the SEC.

The CASB The Cost Accounting Standards Board is a federal agency created by Congress in 1970 to establish cost accounting standards to be used by defense contractors in negotiated contracts and subcontracts exceeding certain amounts. In December 1972, the CASB issued **Cost Accounting Standard 403,** "Allocation of Home Office Expenses to Segments." Defining a **home office** as an office responsible for directing or managing two or more, but not necessarily all, segments of an organization,[6] this standard provided guidelines for allocation of residual home office expenses to all segments. Included in **Cost Accounting Standard 403** was the controversial provision that home office state and local taxes based on income should be allocated to segments based upon sales, property, or payroll ratios of each segment, rather than upon income or loss of each segment.

The FTC In March 1974, the Federal Trade Commission approved Form LB, an annual line-of-business report. In August 1974, the FTC mailed Form LB to 345 of the largest United States manufacturing companies. The form required detailed financial information on 219 designated separate manufacturing segments for fiscal years ended between July 1, 1973, and June 30, 1974. For each line of business which produced revenue of $10 million or more, total revenue, income, assets, and expenses such as media advertising and research and development were to be reported on Form LB. Strenuous opposition to the FTC's reporting requirements was expressed by companies required to report. Officials of the FTC countered with assertions that the Commission required the information to carry out its goal of assuring healthy competition in the United States economy. Nevertheless, continued opposition to the FTC's reporting requirements led to the filing of a suit against the FTC by several large companies. The suit charged that the FTC line-of-business reporting requirements would cause irreparable injury to the companies.

Summary of Segment Reporting History Thus, prior to the issuance of a Financial Accounting Standards Board **Statement** on segment reporting,

[6] *Cost Accounting Standard 403,* sec. 403.30(a)(2).

three major professional organizations of accountants and three governmental agencies had issued statements or directives on the subject of financial reporting for segments of a business. There were conflicting approaches and requirements in the various pronouncements, which left segment reporting in an unsatisfactory state prior to action by the FASB.

Voluntary segment reporting

Since reporting of segment operations in annual reports to shareholders was not mandatory as it was for reports to governmental agencies, it is appropriate to note the extent of voluntary segment reporting by large United States industrial companies. A survey of the annual reports of 100 large companies by **Business Week** disclosed the following:

	1973	1972	1971	1970
Disclosure of segment operations:				
Sales and earnings by product line	58%	57%	51%	32%
Sales only by product line	22%	21%	19%	24%

SOURCE: "A New Diet of Data Fattens Annual Reports," **Business Week,** Apr. 27, 1974, p. 63.

Thus, the substantial increase in voluntary segment reporting in 1971, subsequent to the SEC's issuance of mandatory segment reporting requirements, did not continue in succeeding years prior to action by the FASB.

Major unresolved issues in segment reporting

The **FASB Discussion Memorandum,** "An Analysis of Issues Related to Financial Reporting for Segments of a Business Enterprise," lists eleven issues, involving 23 separate questions, to be considered in segment reporting. The first issue—Should information about segments of a business enterprise be included in financial statements?—was already virtually settled in view of the voluntary and mandatory reporting of segment operations in effect at the time of the FASB study. Accordingly, we shall consider only the following three issues:

1 What approach should be taken in specifying segments to be reported externally?
2 What segment information related to the results of operations (income statement) should be reported?
3 How should segment information be presented?

Following our consideration of the three issues above, we shall present the stand taken on each issue by the AICPA's Accounting Standards

Division in its *Statement of Position on Financial Reporting for Segments of a Business Enterprise.*

Specification of segments

The *FASB Discussion Memorandum* suggests the following alternative bases for segmentation of a business enterprise:

A. Organizational lines, such as divisions, branches or subsidiaries, or other legal or nonlegal entities.
B. Area of economic activity. For example:
    Industries in which the enterprise operates
    Product lines and types of services rendered
    Markets
    Geographical areas
C. More than one basis of segmentation[7]

Basing segments on the organizational lines of a business has the advantage of ease of identification of segments, since the segments are identical to the organizational structure. Such a basis appears to ignore economic substance of segments in favor of legal or other form. Rarely does each organizational subdivision of a business entity carry on its operations in a single economic activity.

An industry in which a segment operates is usually capable of more precise definition than is a product line of a segment. However, many authorities on segment reporting have commented upon the overlapping and indistinct boundaries between industries and product lines.

Other proponents have gone on record in favor of segmentation according to the *market* for a segment's goods or services—such as commercial, defense contracts, and the like. Another proposed segmentation basis is geographical areas, such as foreign and domestic segments.

The AICPA's Accounting Standards Division supported segmentation by area of economic activity corresponding to broad industry groupings, often referred to as lines of business.[8] The AICPA further recommended:

> The (Financial Accounting Standards) Board should not prescribe detailed rules for identifying segments; rather, it should establish broad guidelines which would be meaningful to users. Such guidelines might relate to different degrees of risk, and extent of vertical integration.
>
> . . . .
>
> While disclosure of data by market or geographical areas may be useful, . . . these areas of economic activity should not form the primary basis for identifying business segments for financial reporting.[9]

[7] *FASB Discussion Memorandum,* "An Analysis of Issues Related to Financial Reporting for Segments of a Business Enterprise" (Stamford, Conn.: 1974), p. 14.
[8] *Statement of Position on Financial Reporting for Segments of a Business Enterprise,* AICPA (New York: 1974), p. 5.
[9] *Ibid.*

Segment operating results to be reported

The FASB offered the following alternatives for presenting a segment's operating results for a fiscal period:

A. Segment sales should be reported.
B. Some measure of segment income should be reported (e.g., net income or some intermediate level of income).
C. A complete or condensed segment income statement should be presented.[10]

Segment Sales As indicated on page 328, 80 of 100 large industrial companies reported at least segment sales in their 1973 annual reports. Thus, there appears to be no serious opposition to the position that sales of a segment represent a minimum reporting level. An unresolved issue is whether a segment's *intersegment transfers* ("sales" to another segment) should be included in the reported sales for a segment. Although the FASB indicated there is some support for inclusion of intersegment transfers in a segment's reported sales, the opposition arguments reported by the Board appear to carry more weight:

> Those who argue for exclusion of intersegment transfers from segment sales contend that (1) financial accounting should recognize only those revenues which have been realized through a bargained market transaction; (2) the transfer price is not objectively verifiable because there has been no arm's length transaction; (3) the level of segment activity, including intersegment transfers, may be affected by internal production decisions; and (4) the total reported segment sales, including intersegment transfers, will differ from consolidated figures unless appropriate eliminations are presented.[11]

The AICPA's Accounting Standards Division concurred with the preceding arguments, in the following passage:

> Intersegment transfers should not be included in segment sales. These transfers should be treated as reductions of segment costs. The Division does not believe that intersegment transfers meet the criteria for sales.[12]

Measure of Segment Income Perhaps the most controversial aspect of segment reporting is whether some measure of segment income should be developed. The nature of the controversy over reporting income for segments is discernible in the following questions developed by the FASB:

> Should common costs which are not traceable to individual segments be allocated to the various segments and, if so, on what basis?
>
> Should interest expense be attributed to segments?
>
> Should unusual or infrequently occurring items be attributed to segments?

[10] *FASB Discussion Memorandum,* p. 25.
[11] *Ibid.,* p. 27.
[12] AICPA, *Statement of Position,* pp. 6–7.

Should income from investee companies accounted for by the equity method be attributed to segments?

Should income taxes be allocated to segments and, if so, on what basis?[13]

The two extreme positions on reporting income for segments are (*a*) a *net income* should be reported for each segment, and (*b*) *no income amount* whatsoever should be reported for a segment. Proponents of a net income presentation for segments, while acknowledging that a number of questionable assumptions may underlie the computation of net income, maintain that difficulties of estimation and computation should not preclude the development of a segment net income figure useful to investors and creditors. (The 1973 annual report of Textron Inc., presented in Appendix B, disclosed net income for each "product group.")

The opposition argument is that the arbitrary nature of many allocations of common costs, interest, and taxes to segments make the resultant net income figures misleading rather than informative. Opponents of reporting segment income cite as one allocation problem the difficulty of apportioning income taxes to segments. Income tax apportionment is difficult because of the existence of various tax avoidance alternatives to a diversified entity, the differences between income tax liabilities when a consolidated return is filed as opposed to separate returns, and the existence of net operating loss carrybacks and carryforwards.

Some accountants advocate a compromise position between the two extremes outlined in the preceding paragraphs. These accountants support a *segment contribution approach* for reporting a segment's income. *Segment contribution* is defined as segment sales less *traceable costs—* those costs of the enterprise incurred solely by or for, or directly identified with, a particular segment.[14] The segment contribution approach for reporting segment income was supported by the AICPA's Accounting Standards Division, which also opposed allocation of nontraceable common costs, interest expense, or income taxes to segments. The Accounting Standards group was divided on the questions of attributing to segments unusual or infrequently occurring items and equity-method income from investee companies.[15]

If the FASB does sanction the allocation of nontraceable common costs to segments, it will probably provide for one or more allocation bases. The Cost Accounting Standards Board, in *Cost Accounting Standard 403,* "Allocation of Home Office Expenses to Segments," provided a three-factor formula for the allocation of residual home office expenses to segments. The percentage of residual home office expenses to be allocated to a segment was the arithmetic average of the following three percentages for the same fiscal period:

1 Segment payroll dollars divided by total payroll dollars of all segments

---

[13] *FASB Discussion Memorandum,* p. 26.
[14] *Ibid.,* pp. 29–30.
[15] AICPA, *Statement of Position,* pp. 6–8.

2 Segment operating revenue (including intersegment transfers out, and reduced by intersegment transfers in) divided by total operating revenue of all segments

3 Segment average plant and equipment and inventories, at carrying values, divided by total carrying value of average plant and equipment and inventories of all segments[16]

Illustration of Allocation of Common Costs To illustrate the allocation of nontraceable common costs to segments under the provisions of *Cost Accounting Standard 403,* assume the following data for the home office and two segments of Varied Products Corporation for the year ended April 30, Year 7. There were no intersegment transfers for the year.

	Home office	Pharma-ceutical products	Food products	Total
Net sales	$ –0–	$550,000	$ 450,000	$1,000,000
Traceable costs	$ –0–	$300,000	$ 350,000	$ 650,000
Nontraceable common costs .	200,000	–0–	–0–	200,000
Total costs	$200,000	$300,000	$ 350,000	$ 850,000
Income before income taxes .				$ 150,000
Income taxes expense				90,000
Net income				$ 60,000
Payroll dollars	$ 60,000	$160,000	$ 240,000	$ 460,000
Average plant and equipment and inventories	$ 80,000	$620,000	$1,380,000	$2,080,000

The three-factor formula under *Cost Accounting Standard 403* would be computed as follows for Varied Products Corporation:

	Pharmaceutical products	Food products
Ratio of segment payroll dollars	$\dfrac{\$ 160,000}{\$ 400,000} = 40\%$	$\dfrac{\$ 240,000}{\$ 400,000} = 60\%$
Ratio of segment operating revenue	$\dfrac{\$ 550,000}{\$1,000,000} = 55\%$	$\dfrac{\$ 450,000}{\$1,000,000} = 45\%$
Ratio of average plant and equip-ment and inventories	$\dfrac{\$ 620,000}{\$2,000,000} = 31\%$	$\dfrac{\$1,380,000}{\$2,000,000} = 69\%$
Total	126%	174%
Arithmetic average (divide by 3)	42%	58%

[16] *Cost Accounting Standard 403,* sec. 403.50(c)(1).

The $200,000 nontraceable common costs of the home office of Varied Products Corporation would be allocated to the two segments as follows:

To Pharmaceutical Products segment: 42% × $200,000	$ 84,000
To Food Products segment: 58% × $200,000	116,000
Total nontraceable common costs	$200,000

Pre-tax accounting income (loss) for the two segments of Varied Products Corporation would thus be computed as follows:

	Pharmaceutical products	Food products	Total
Net sales	$550,000	$450,000	$1,000,000
Traceable costs	$300,000	$350,000	$ 650,000
Nontraceable common costs	84,000	116,000	200,000
Total costs	$384,000	$466,000	$ 850,000
Income (loss) before income taxes .	$166,000	$(16,000)	$ 150,000

The authors question the wisdom of applying such an arbitrary formula to the allocation of nontraceable common costs to segments for financial reporting purposes. The CASB allocation formula appears to be one of expediency rather than theoretical soundness. This is borne out in the preceding illustration by the pre-tax loss attributed to the Food Products segment of Varied Products Corporation.

Presentation of segment information

The *FASB Discussion Memorandum* presented four possible alternatives for presenting segment information:

1 Segment information should be incorporated into the basic financial statements, with explanatory disclosures in footnotes.

2 Segment information should be presented in the footnotes to the financial statements of the enterprise.

3 Segment information should be presented in a new basic, separate financial statement (or statements).

4 The method of presentation of segment information in financial statements should be left to the judgment of enterprise management.[17]

Each of these alternatives was considered only briefly in the *Discussion Memorandum.* The AICPA's Accounting Standards Division also de-emphasized the presentation issue:

[17] *FASB Discussion Memorandum,* p. 53.

The Division believes segment information should be viewed as an elaboration or amplification of the financial statements of the enterprise. While segment information should be reported in the basic financial statements, the information itself should not be considered a new basic financial statement.

The method of presentation within the financial statements should be left to the judgment of management.[18]

In the opinion of the authors, the determination of the most theoretically sound method for presenting segment information is a critical issue. The question of segment presentation involves many basic aspects of financial accounting theory, such as the nature of the accounting entity, economic substance versus literal form, and the objectives of financial accounting and financial statements. An approach to segment disclosure which would dilute the traditional consolidated financial statements should be undertaken only after substantial study of the theoretical questions involved.

Reporting the effects of disposal of a segment

To this point, we have discussed issues raised by the Financial Accounting Standards Board in its consideration of financial reporting for segments of a business enterprise. We shall conclude our consideration of segment reporting with the reporting for effects of the disposal of a segment.

In June 1973, the AICPA's Accounting Principles Board issued **APB Opinion No. 30,** "Reporting the Results of Operations." The Board's conclusions included the following with respect to disposal of a segment:

For purposes of this Opinion, the term **discontinued operations** refers to the operations of a segment of a business . . . that has been sold, abandoned, spun off, or otherwise disposed of or, although still operating, is the subject of a formal plan for disposal. . . . The Board concludes that the results of continuing operations should be reported separately from discontinued operations and that any gain or loss from disposal of a segment of a business . . . should be reported in conjunction with the related results of discontinued operations and not as an extraordinary item. Accordingly, operations of a segment that has been or will be discontinued should be reported separately as a component of income before extraordinary items and the cumulative effect of accounting changes (if applicable) in the following manner:

Income from continuing operations before income taxes	$XXXX	
Provision for income taxes	XXX	
Income from continuing operations		$XXXX
Discontinued operations (Note _____):		
Income (loss) from operations of discontinued Division X (less applicable income taxes of $_____)		$XXXX
Loss on disposal of Division X, including provision of $_____ for operating losses during phase-out period (less applicable income taxes of $_____)	XXXX	XXXX
Net income		$XXXX

[18]AICPA, *Statement of Position,* p. 11.

Amounts of income taxes applicable to the results of discontinued operations and the gain or loss from disposal of the segment should be disclosed on the face of the income statement or in related notes. Revenues applicable to the discontinued operations should be separately disclosed in the related notes.[19]

In clarifying the methods for computing the gain or loss on discontinued operations, the Board differentiated between the *measurement date* and the *disposal date* for the discontinuance. The *measurement date* was defined as the date on which management having authority to approve the action commits itself to a formal plan to dispose of a segment of the business. The *disposal date* was defined as the date of closing the sale of the segment, or ceasing operations of an abandoned segment.[20] The period between the measurement date and the disposal date is known as the *phase-out period.* If management expects a *loss* on the disposal of a segment, the estimated loss should be recorded at the *measurement date.* An expected *gain* on disposal of a segment should be recognized when realized—typically on the *disposal date.*[21]

These provisions and other features of *APB Opinion No. 30* are essentially illustrated in the excerpt (including a relevant note) from the 1974 annual report of The Wurlitzer Company, on pages 336 to 337.

INTERIM FINANCIAL STATEMENTS

Generally, financial statements are published for the fiscal year of the accounting entity. However, many companies issue financial statements for interim accounting periods during the course of a fiscal year. For example, a small, closely held company with outstanding bank loans may be required to provide monthly financial statements to the lending bank. However, interim financial statements are usually associated with the quarterly reports issued by publicly owned companies to their shareholders, the SEC, and the stock exchanges which list their stock. The New York Stock Exchange's listing agreement requires listed companies to publish quarterly reports. Companies subject to the periodic reporting requirements of the SEC must file Form 10-Q with the Commission 45 days after the end of each of the first three quarters of their fiscal years.

Problems in interim financial statements

Except for 10-Q quarterly reports filed with the SEC, the form, content, and accounting practices for interim financial statements were left to the discretion of the issuing companies until 1973. In that year, the AICPA's Accounting Principles Board issued *APB Opinion No. 28,* "Interim Financial

[19] *APB Opinion No. 30,* pp. 558–559.
[20] *Ibid.,* pp. 561–562.
[21] *Ibid.,* p. 562.

THE WURLITZER COMPANY AND SUBSIDIARIES

**STATEMENT OF CONSOLIDATED EARNINGS (LOSS) AND
RETAINED EARNINGS**

FOR THE YEARS ENDED MARCH 31, 1974 AND 1973

	Year ended March 31	
	1974	*1973*
Sales and Other Income:		
Net sales	$ 90,069,712	$83,842,546
Carrying charges, discount, and interest earned	3,228,906	2,931,400
Miscellaneous—net	288,743	324,883
Total	93,587,361	87,098,829
Costs and Expenses:		
Cost of products sold	64,750,141	58,437,859
Selling, administrative, and research and development expenses	25,236,225	22,197,678
Interest	3,572,677	2,306,121
Provision for loss on discontinuance of U.S. phonograph operations (Note 1)	11,366,000	
Total	104,925,043	82,941,658
Earnings (Loss) before Income Taxes and Extraordinary Items	(11,337,682)	4,157,171
Provision (Credit) for Federal, State, and Foreign Income Taxes	(3,635,000)	1,966,000
Earnings (Loss) before Extraordinary Items (per share—1974, $(6.23); 1973, $1.77)	(7,702,682)	2,191,171
Extraordinary Items		(313,747)
Net Earnings (Loss) for the Year		
(per share—1974, $(6.23); 1973, $1.52)	(7,702,682)	1,877,424
Retained Earnings—Beginning of year	22,380,086	21,244,011
Total	14,677,404	23,121,435
Less—Cash dividends declared (per share—$.60)	742,183	741,349
Retained Earnings—End of year	$ 13,935,221	$22,380,086

The accompanying Notes to Financial Statements are an integral part of this statement.

THE WURLITZER COMPANY AND SUBSIDIARIES

NOTES TO FINANCIAL STATEMENTS
FOR THE YEAR ENDED MARCH 31, 1974

1. DISCONTINUANCE OF U.S. PHONOGRAPH OPERATIONS

In March 1974, the Board of Directors decided to terminate the Company's business of manufacturing and selling coin-operated phonographs in the United States. The provision for loss on discontinuance of these operations is based upon presently available information, not definitely ascertainable until the discontinuance is completed, and is summarized as follows:

Estimated losses on disposition of inventories and collection of receivables	$ 6,080,000
Estimated losses on disposition of tooling, machinery, etc.	813,000
Operating, administrative, and other costs estimated to be incurred in the phase-out period	4,473,000
Total	$11,366,000

The principal assets of the U.S. phonograph business are included in the balance sheet at March 31, 1974 at their estimated net realizable values as follows:

Trade receivables—net	$ 7,719,000
Inventories	2,990,000
Properties and equipment—net	271,000
Total	$10,980,000

Sales of United States manufactured coin-operated phonographs and auxiliary equipment in 1974 and 1973 were $9,391,000 and $11,806,000, respectively.

Reporting." Prior to the issuance of *Opinion No. 28,* there were unresolved problems regarding interim statements. These problems included the following:

1 Interim financial statements were not audited by independent CPAs. As a result, issuing companies employed a wider variety of accounting practices and estimating techniques for interim statements than they would apply in the annual financial statements examined by independent auditors. The companies' implicit view was that any misstatements in interim financial statements would be taken care of by auditors' adjustments for the annual statements.

2 Seasonal fluctuations in revenue and irregular incurrence of costs and expenses during the course of a business entity's fiscal year limited the comparability of operating results for interim periods of the fiscal year. Furthermore, time constraints in the issuance of interim statements limited the available time for accumulating accurate end-of-period data on inventories, payables, and related expenses.

3 Accountants held divergent views on the theoretical issues underlying interim financial statements. These differing views were described as follows:

> Some view each interim period as a basic accounting period and conclude that the results of operations for each interim period should be determined in essentially the same manner as if the interim period were an annual accounting period. Under this view deferrals, accruals, and estimations at the end of each interim period are determined by following essentially the same principles and judgments that apply to annual periods.

> Others view each interim period primarily as being an integral part of the annual period. Under this view deferrals, accruals, and estimations at the end of each interim period are affected by judgments made at the interim date as to results of operations for the balance of the annual period. Thus, an expense item that might be considered as falling wholly within an annual accounting period (no fiscal year-end accrual or deferral) could be allocated among interim periods based on estimated time, sales volume, productive activity, or some other basis.[22]

Misleading interim financial statements

The problems discussed in the preceding section led to a number of notorious examples of published interim income statements with substantial quarterly earnings, and fiscal year financial statements showing a substantial net loss. One such example was Mattel, Inc., a manufacturer of toys and leisure-time products whose stock was traded on the New York Stock Exchange. In 1974, the SEC filed in court a complaint that Mattel, Inc., had issued false and misleading interim earnings reports for the first three quarters of its 1973 fiscal year. The reports showed first quarter net income of $3.9 million; second quarter net income of $6.1 million; and third quarter net income of $6.4 million—for a three-quarters net income of $16.4 million. According to the SEC, Mattel ultimately reported a net loss of $32 million for its 1973 fiscal year. The SEC charged Mattel with failing to make adequate interim adjustments for doubtful accounts, sales returns, excess and obsolete inventories, and amortization of tool costs. Further, Mattel was accused of failing to disclose that it had deferred significant amounts of expenses from the first three quarters of 1973 to the fourth quarter of that year.

APB Opinion No. 28

In 1973, the AICPA's Accounting Principles Board issued *APB Opinion No. 28,* "Interim Financial Reporting." The stated objectives for the *Opinion* were to provide guidance on accounting and disclosure issues peculiar to interim reporting and to set forth minimum disclosure requirements for interim financial reports of publicly traded companies.[23] Part I of the *Opinion* dealt with standards for determining interim financial information and Part II covered disclosure of summarized interim financial data by publicly traded companies.

[22]*APB Opinion No. 28,* "Interim Financial Reporting," AICPA (New York: 1973), p. 521.
[23]*Ibid.,* p. 522.

In Part I of **APB Opinion No. 28,** the Board established guidelines for the following components of interim financial statements: revenue, costs associated with revenue, all other costs and expenses, and income tax provisions. These guidelines are discussed in the following sections.

Revenue According to **APB Opinion No. 28,** revenue from products sold or services rendered should be recognized as earned during an interim period on the same basis as followed for the full year. Further, businesses having significant seasonal variations in revenue should disclose the seasonal nature of their activities.[24]

Costs Associated with Revenue Costs and expenses associated directly with or allocated to products sold or services rendered include raw materials costs, direct labor costs, and manufacturing overhead. **APB Opinion No. 28** required the same accounting for these costs and expenses in interim financial statements as in fiscal-year financial statements.[25] The **Opinion,** however, provided the following exceptions with respect to determination of cost of goods sold for interim financial statements:[26]

1 Companies which use the gross profit method at interim dates to estimate cost of goods sold should disclose this fact in interim financial statements. In addition, any material adjustments reconciling estimated interim inventories with annual physical inventories should be disclosed.

2 Companies which use the lifo inventory method and which **temporarily** deplete base lifo inventories during an interim reporting period should include in cost of goods sold for the interim period the estimated cost of replacing the depleted lifo base.

3 Lower-of-cost-or-market write-downs of inventories should be provided for interim periods as for complete fiscal years, unless the interim date market declines in inventory are considered **temporary,** and not applicable at the end of the fiscal year. If an inventory market write-down in one interim period is offset by an inventory market price **increase** in a subsequent interim period, a gain is recognized in the subsequent period to the extent of the loss provided in the preceding period.

For example, assume that Reynolds Company, which uses lower-of-cost-or-market fifo accounting for its single merchandised inventory item, had 10,000 units of merchandise with fifo cost of $50,000, or $5 per unit, on hand at the beginning of Year 3. Assume further for simplicity that Reynolds Company made no merchandise purchases during Year 3. Quarterly sales, and end-of-quarter replacement costs for inventory, were as follows during Year 3:

Quarter	Quarterly sales (units)	End-of-quarter inventory replacement cost (per unit)
1	2,000	$6
2	1,500	4
3	1,000	7
4	1,200	3

[24] *Ibid.*, pp. 523, 527.
[25] *Ibid.*, p. 524.
[26] *Ibid.*, pp. 524–525.

If the market decline in the second quarter was not considered to be *temporary,* Reynolds Company's cost of goods sold for the four quarters of Year 3 would be as follows:

| | | Cost of goods sold | |
| | | For quarter | Cumulative |
Quarter	Computation for quarter		
1	2,000 × $5	$10,000	$10,000
2	(1,500 × $5) + (6,500 × $1)	14,000	24,000
3	1,000 × $4	4,000	22,500*
4	(1,200 × $5) + (4,300 × $2)	14,600	37,100

* The $28,000 cumulative total ($24,000 + $4,000) is reduced by $5,500, the recovery of the market value of the ending inventory to the extent of the previous quarter's write-down (5,500 units × $1).

The $37,100 cumulative costs of goods sold for Reynolds Company for Year 3 may be verified as follows:

5,700 units sold during Year 3, at $5 fifo cost per unit.	$28,500
Write-down of Year 3 ending inventory to replacement cost (4,300 units × $2)	8,600
Cost of goods sold for Year 3	$37,100

4 Companies using standard costs for inventory and cost of goods sold accounting should generally report standard cost variances for interim periods as they do for fiscal years. Planned materials price variances and volume or capacity variances should be deferred at the end of interim periods if the variances are expected to be absorbed by the end of the fiscal year.

All Other Costs and Expenses The following guidelines for all costs and expenses other than those associated with revenue are set forth in *APB Opinion No. 28:*

Costs and expenses other than product costs should be charged to income in interim periods as incurred, or be allocated among interim periods based on an estimate of time expired, benefit received or activity associated with the periods. Procedures adopted for assigning specific cost and expense items to an interim period should be consistent with the bases followed by the company in reporting results of operations at annual reporting dates. However, when a specific cost or expense item charged to expense for annual reporting purposes benefits more than one interim period, the cost or expense item may be allocated to those interim periods.

Some costs and expenses incurred in an interim period, however, cannot be readily identified with the activities or benefits of other interim periods and should be charged to the interim period in which incurred. Disclosure should be made as to the nature and amount of such costs unless items of a comparable nature are included in both the current interim period and in the corresponding interim period of the preceding year.

Arbitrary assignment of the amount of such costs to an interim period should not be made.

Gains and losses that arise in any interim period similar to those that would not be deferred at year end should not be deferred to later interim periods within the same fiscal year.

. . . .

The amounts of certain costs and expenses are frequently subjected to year-end adjustments even though they can be reasonably approximated at interim dates. To the extent possible such adjustments should be estimated and the estimated costs and expenses assigned to interim periods so that the interim periods bear a reasonable portion of the anticipated annual amount. Examples of such items include inventory shrinkage, allowance for uncollectible accounts, allowance for quantity discounts, and discretionary year-end bonuses.[27]

APB Opinion No. 28 includes a substantial number of specific applications of the preceding guidelines.

Income Tax Provisions The techniques for computing income tax provisions in interim financial statements were described as follows in *APB Opinion No. 28:*

At the end of each interim period the company should make its best estimate of the effective tax rate expected to be applicable for the full fiscal year. The rate so determined should be used in providing for income taxes on a current year-to-date basis. The effective tax rate should reflect anticipated investment tax credits, foreign tax rates, percentage depletion, capital gains rates, and other available tax planning alternatives. However, in arriving at this effective tax rate no effect should be included for the tax related to significant unusual or extraordinary items that will be separately reported or reported net of their related tax effect in reports for the interim period or for the fiscal year.[28]

To illustrate, assume that at the end of the first quarter of Year 7, Carter Company's actual first quarter and forecast fiscal year operating results were as follows:

	First quarter (actual)	Fiscal year (estimated)
Revenue	$400,000	$1,800,000
Costs and expenses other than income taxes	300,000	1,500,000
Income before income taxes.	$100,000	$ 300,000

Assume further that there were no *timing differences* between Carter Company's pre-tax accounting income and taxable income, but that the company had the following estimated *permanent differences* between pre-tax accounting income and federal and state taxable income for the fiscal year:

[27] *Ibid.*, pp. 525–526, 527.
[28] *Ibid.*, pp. 527–528.

Dividend exclusion	$17,000
Goodwill amortization	5,000

If Carter Company's **nominal** combined federal and state income tax rates total 60%, the company would estimate its **effective** combined total income tax rate for Year 7 as follows:

Estimated income before income taxes	$300,000
Add: Nondeductible goodwill amortization	5,000
Deduct: Dividend exclusion	(17,000)
Estimated taxable income	$288,000
Estimated combined federal and state income taxes ($288,000 × 60%	
= $172,800)	$172,800
Estimated effective combined federal and state income tax rate for	
Year 7 ($172,800 ÷ $300,000 = 57.6%)	57.6%

Carter Company's journal entry for income taxes for the first quarter of Year 7 would be as follows:

Income Taxes Expense	57,600	
Income Taxes Payable		57,600
To provide for estimated federal and state income taxes for the		
first quarter of Year 7 as follows: 57.6% × $100,000 = $57,600.		

For the second quarter of Year 7, Carter Company would again estimate an effective combined federal and state income tax rate based on more current projections for permanent differences between pre-tax accounting income and taxable income for the entire year. However, the new effective rate **would not** be retroactively applied to restate the first quarter's tax expense.

Disclosure of Interim Financial Data As a minimum, **APB Opinion No. 28** provided that the following data should be included in publicly traded companies' interim financial reports to shareholders. The data are to be reported for the just-completed quarter and the year to date, or twelve months to date of the quarter's end.

   a. Sales or gross revenues, provision for income taxes, extraordinary items (including related income tax effects), cumulative effect of a change in accounting principles or practices, and net income.

b. Primary and fully diluted earnings per share data for each period presented, . . .

c. Seasonal revenue, costs or expenses.

d. Significant changes in estimates or provisions for income taxes.

e. Disposal of a segment of a business and extraordinary, unusual or
infrequently occurring items.

f. Contingent items.

g. Changes in accounting principles or estimates.

h. Significant changes in financial position.[29]

Conclusions on interim statements

APB Opinion 28 represented a substantial effort to upgrade the quality of
interim financial statements. However, as long as independent CPAs do
not attest to the fairness of interim statements, it is questionable whether
misleading interim statements can be eliminated from financial reporting.
Conceivably, the SEC may require that the 10-Q reports of companies
subject to the Commission's jurisdiction are to be subject to some type
of review by independent auditors, if not a complete audit. Alternatively,
the public accounting profession may follow the lead of one international
CPA firm, which has offered to *review* its clients' interim financial statements. The product of the review would be a letter from the CPA firm
to the client describing the scope of the review, and stating, if appropriate, that the firm had no recommended adjustments for the interim
statements.

FINANCIAL FORECASTS

In February 1973, the SEC issued *Securities Act Release No. 5362* entitled
"Statement by the Commission on the Disclosure of Projections of Future
Economic Performance." The *Release* grew out of a series of public
hearings by the Commission on the propriety of the inclusion of projected
sales and earnings in companies' filings with the Commission.

The principal conclusions of the SEC in *Release No. 5362* were as
follows:

1 Disclosure of forecast data should not be *required* in filings with the SEC unless
a company subject to the reporting requirements of the Commission reports
projected sales and earnings outside of filings of the Commission to financial
media or financial analysts. In such cases, the subject companies would be
required to report the forecast data, with comparative actual results, in their
annual reports to the SEC.

2 Companies subject to the SEC's jurisdiction which meet certain standards of
earnings history and forecasting experience would be *permitted* to include
forecast data in filings with the Commission if they so choose. Filed forecasts
should meet standards with respect to disclosure of underlying assumptions,
setting forth of reasonably definite amounts for sales and earnings, and reasonable time periods. Companies which filed forecast information with the SEC

[29]*Ibid.*, p. 532.

would be required to update the data periodically and whenever the forecasts were significantly changed by the issuers. A company which had filed forecasts with the SEC could later discontinue the practice if it disclosed its decision and the underlying reasons.

3 For the time being, no statement of attestation of the forecasts by CPAs or other third parties would be permitted. The SEC would establish standards for the preparation and dissemination of financial forecasts by managements, financial analysts, and others, and would establish rules to limit the liability of forecast issuers under the Securities Acts.[30]

Prior to the action of the SEC described above, accountants, financial executives, and financial analysts had sporadically debated the propriety of including forecasts of future periods' operating results in annual reports to shareholders. Since the SEC's *Release No. 5362* was permissive rather than mandatory regarding forecast disclosure, its issuance triggered a series of pro and con arguments on the propriety of published forecasts.

Arguments in support of published forecasts

Proponents of the publishing of business financial forecasts advance the following arguments in support of their position:

1 Publication of financial forecasts would make them available to *all* interested parties, rather than to selected financial analysts.

2 The availability of a company's published forecasts would make the company more competitive in the search for scarce debt and equity capital.

3 Disclosure of assumptions underlying published forecasts would alert users to the uncertainties and risks inherent in forecasting.

4 Forecasts are already used for managerial purposes by most progressive companies. Thus, publication of forecasts would not add unduly to the costs of financial communications of those companies.

5 Mathematical models and computers have substantially enhanced the reliability of forecasting techniques.

Arguments in opposition to published forecasts

Following are the principal objections to published forecasts expressed by opponents:

1 Unsophisticated users of published forecasts might consider them to be commitments rather than estimates. These users would not comprehend the uncertainties and risks in the forecasting process.

2 Companies which did not attain forecast results might lose the confidence of current and prospective shareholders and creditors.

3 The forecasts used for managerial purposes are designed more for motivation and control than for achievability.

4 Potential legal liability in published forecasts might lead to ultraconservative forecasting or manipulation of actual operating results by managements.

---

[30] U.S. Securities and Exchange Commission, *Securities Act Release No. 5362* (Feb. 2, 1973).

5 Economic disruptions such as inflation, energy and commodity shortages, increasing labor costs, and high interest rates make forecasts for periods longer than one or two months extremely unreliable.

Despite the persuasiveness of the arguments in support of forecasting, the opponents' counterarguments have considerable merit, especially the last one. There has been some speculation that interest in voluntary published financial forecasts is waning, not to be revived unless further action is taken by the SEC.

Standards for financial forecasts

As indicated earlier, the SEC has undertaken to establish standards for financial forecasts in filings with the Commission. In addition, the Accounting Standards Division of the AICPA has begun consideration of guidelines for the presentation and disclosure of forecast information in annual reports to shareholders. In 1974 the AICPA's Management Services Division circulated for comment an Exposure Draft entitled *Standards for Systems for the Preparation of Financial Forecasts.* Following are the standards set forth in that Exposure Draft:

1 A financial forecasting system should provide a means for management to determine what it considers to be the single most probable forecasted result.

2 The accounting principles used in the preparation of a financial forecast should be those which are expected to be used when the events and transactions envisioned in the forecast will be recorded in financial statements.

3 Financial forecasts should be prepared with appropriate care by qualified personnel.

4 A financial forecasting system should provide for seeking out the best information available at the time.

5 The information used in preparing a financial forecast should reflect the plans of the enterprise.

6 The assumptions utilized in preparing a financial forecast should be reasonable and appropriate and be suitably supported.

7 The financial forecasting system should provide the means to determine the relative effect of variations in the major underlying assumptions.

8 A financial forecasting system should provide adequate documentation of both the forecast and the forecasting process.

9 A financial forecasting system should include the regular comparison of the forecast with attained results.

10 The preparation of a financial forecast should include adequate review and approval by management at the appropriate levels.[31]

The Management Advisory Services Division proposed the above standards for enterprises which prepare financial forecasts on a recurring basis, and which typically update their forecasts. In amplification of the standards, the Division established the following definitions:

---

[31] Exposure Draft: *Standards for Systems for the Preparation of Financial Forecasts,* AICPA (New York: 1974), pp. 14–15.

Financial Forecast. A financial forecast is a statement for an enterprise showing the most probable financial position, financial results of operations and cash flow for one or more future periods.

"Most Probable." "Most probable" means that the assumptions have been evaluated and that the forecast is based on management's judgment of the most likely set of conditions and the most likely course of action planned by the enterprise. The most probable result will usually be prepared as a single forecasted result, although, under certain circumstances, the most probable result may be expressed as a probabilistic statement or a range.

Financial Forecasting System. A financial forecasting system consists of a set of related procedures, methods and practices used to prepare financial forecasts, to monitor attained results relative to the forecast and to prepare revisions or otherwise update the forecast. The system may or may not employ mechanized data processing techniques.[32]

Importance of assumptions in forecasting

A frequently heard statement is that a financial forecast is only as good as the assumptions which underlie it. The AICPA's Management Advisory Services Division recognized the importance of assumptions in a lengthy discussion of the sixth financial forecasting standard on page 345. Among the points made in the Division's discussion were the following:

1 Assumptions with large impact should receive more attention and support than those with less impact. Generally, assumptions pertaining to sales volume and revenue have the greatest single impact on a company. Significant assumptions should be made explicit to focus attention on them and to facilitate review by management.

2 Assumptions should be supported by evidence. While it is not possible to absolutely prove that any given assumption will be true, much evidence consisting of data and logical argument or theory can usually be developed to support an assumption.

3 Care should be exercised to avoid unrealistic assumptions in situations where assumptions may involve a certain degree of arbitrariness. For example, it may be difficult to predict the precise rate of future cost inflation but it is generally more realistic to estimate such a rate than to assume no inflation.

4 The conditions assumed in arriving at the sales or revenue forecast should be consistent with those assumed in forecasting the cost of operations. Care should be exercised to ensure that likely costs and revenue have been considered, that sufficient capacity and resources will be available to produce the expected revenue, that capital expenditures have been recognized as appropriate, that provision has been made for applicable taxes and that appropriate financing has been considered.[33]

One interesting proposal with respect to financial forecast assumptions recommends a three-category grouping for the assumptions—technical assumptions, planning assumptions, and standard assumptions. *Technical assumptions* relate to the mathematical model underlying a forecast. *Planning assumptions* are those dealing with marketing and production plans as well as with sporadic matters such as the outcome of litigation.

[32] *Ibid.,* pp. 5, 6, 7.
[33] *Ibid.,* pp. 23–26.

Standard assumptions are those which are basic to a going concern; for example, the business will continue to operate without disruptions such as strikes.[34]

Illustration of a financial forecast

Introductory and managerial accounting textbooks generally contain illustrations of the techniques of assembling financial budgets or forecasts. Consequently, the illustration below is limited to a forecast statement of income and the related underlying assumptions. The illustration is related to the one previously presented on page 333, which involves the allocation of nontraceable common costs to segments of a business.

VARIED PRODUCTS CORPORATION
Forecast Income Statement
Year Ending April 30, Year 8

	Pharmaceutical products	Food products	Total
Net sales	$600,000	$475,000	$1,075,000
Traceable costs	$400,000	$375,000	$ 775,000
Nontraceable common costs	94,500	130,500	225,000
Total costs	$494,500	$505,500	$1,000,000
Income (loss) before income taxes .	$105,500	$(30,500)	$ 75,000
Income taxes expense			45,000
Net income			$ 30,000

The accompanying assumptions are an integral part of this forecast.

Assumptions for the year ending April 30, Year 8

1 The Corporation's mathematical model for financial forecasts is described in the Corporation's annual report to shareholders for the year ended April 30, Year 7.

2 The Corporation anticipates no disruption of sources of supply or of scheduled production by strikes, lockouts, or natural catastrophes. No major changes are expected in the board of directors or the officers of the company.

3 The Corporation's combined federal and state income tax rate is expected to total 60% in Year 8, the same as in Year 7.

4 The Corporation's borrowing rate on its bank line of credit is anticipated to be 12%, which is 2% greater than the expected prime bank lending rate for Year 8.

5 The rate of inflation during Year 8 is expected to be 9%. This rate is incorporated

---

[34] Pieter Elger, John J. Clark, and Richard E. Speagle, "The Role of Assumptions in Financial Forecasts," *The Journal of Accountancy* (July 1974), p. 64.

in an anticipated across-the-board wage rate increase for the Corporation's employees who benefit from the escalator clause in the union contract with the
Corporation.

6 The Pharmaceutical Products segment's share of the market is expected to remain
the same as it was in Year 7. The Food Products segment's market share is
expected to decline 5% from its level of Year 7.

Conclusion

A great amount of effort is currently being expended by accountants in
research and in setting standards for the three topics discussed in this
chapter—segment reporting, interim financial statements, and financial
forecasts. We can anticipate a number of releases on these topics in the
future from the FASB, the AICPA, and the SEC. The standards, principles,
and guidelines described in this chapter inevitably will be changed in the
coming years. One unresolved question which must be dealt with is the
extent, if any, of independent certified public accountants' attestation or
review of published segment reports, interim financial statements, and
financial forecasts. Until the extent of the CPA's participation in these
matters is resolved, the credibility of segment reports, interim statements,
and forecasts will be subject to challenge.

REVIEW QUESTIONS

1 What is a **segment of a business?**

2 Is the concept of segment reporting consistent with the theory of consolidated
financial statements? Explain.

3 What stand was taken by the AICPA's Accounting Principles Board with
respect to segment reporting? Discuss.

4 Outline the segment reporting requirements of the SEC.

5 In view of the fact that companies subject to the line-of-business reporting
requirements of the FTC were already disclosing segment operations in their
reports to the SEC, how do you account for the strenuous opposition to the
FTC's requirements? Discuss.

6 Identify three alternative bases for segmentation of a business enterprise.

7 What arguments have been advanced in opposition to inclusion of **intersegment transfers** in a segment's reported sales?

8 Why is the question of whether some measure of segment income should
be reported so controversial? Explain.

9 What advantages are claimed for a **segment contribution approach** for reporting a segment's income?

10 Describe the formula for the allocation of residual home office expenses set forth in **Cost Accounting Standard 403,** "Allocation of Home Office Expenses to Segments."

11 Differentiate between the **measurement date** and the **disposal date** for the discontinuance of a segment of a business.

12 Discuss the provisions of **APB Opinion No. 28** dealing with the accounting for costs associated with revenue in interim financial statements.

13 Tarleton Company's interim financial statements for the first quarter of Year 5 included cost of goods sold of $10,000. For the second quarter of Year 5, Tarleton's interim statements presented cost of goods sold for the quarter of $11,000, and for the first six months of Year 5 of $19,000. What is the probable explanation for the fact that Tarleton's cost of goods sold reported for the first half of Year 5 does not equal the total of reported cost of goods sold amounts for the first two quarters of Year 5?

14 Explain the technique included in **APB Opinion No. 28** for the computation of income tax provisions in interim financial statements.

15 Does the SEC require disclosure of a company's forecast data in that company's filings with the Commission? Explain.

16 List three arguments advanced by proponents of published financial forecasts for business enterprises.

17 Discuss the role of assumptions in the publication of financial forecasts.

EXERCISES

Ex. 9-1 Select the best answer for each of the following multiple choice questions.

1 Measuring the net income of an enterprise segment:
  a Avoids arbitrary cost allocations.
  b Involves consideration of more than the controllable and traceable items.
  c Is identical to measuring its activity (traceable items only).
  d Is identical to measuring the performance of its manager.

2 "Segment contribution" is:
  a Synonymous with "segment net income."
  b Segment sales less segment variable costs.
  c Segment sales less segment traceable costs.
  d None of the above.

3 A loss on the disposal of a segment of a business should be reported as:
  a A component of income before extraordinary items.
  b An extraordinary item.
  c A prior period adjustment.
  d None of the above.

4 Companies which temporarily deplete their base lifo inventories during an interim period should include in interim statement cost of goods sold:
  a The average cost of the goods sold during the interim period.
  b The fifo cost of the goods sold during the interim period.
  c The estimated cost of the goods sold during the period.
  d None of the above.

5 Minimum requirements for disclosure of interim financial data by publicly traded companies do **not** include:

   a Contingent items.
   b Earnings per share.
   c Significant accounting policies.
   d Seasonal costs or expenses.

6 According to the AICPA's Management Services Division, the accounting standards used in the preparation of a financial forecast should be:

   a Those expected to be used when the transactions envisioned in the forecast will be recorded in financial statements.
   b Those listed in the forecasting company's "Summary of Significant Accounting Policies" footnote in its most recent published financial statements.
   c Those sanctioned by the FASB for financial forecasts.
   d None of the above.

7 Technical assumptions underlying a financial forecast are:

   a Those dealing with marketing and production plans.
   b Those basic to a going concern.
   c Those related to the mathematical model for the forecast.
   d None of the above.

Ex. 9-2 Fulton Company's accounting records for the year ended May 31, Year 2, included the following data for its three segments:

	Segment 1	Segment 2	Segment 3
Net sales to outsiders	$500,000	$400,000	$300,000
Intersegment transfers out	40,000	50,000	60,000
Traceable costs:			
Intersegment transfers in	70,000	60,000	20,000
Other	300,000	200,000	200,000

Nontraceable common costs of Fulton Company totaled $120,000 for the year ended May 31, Year 2.

Compute the income of each of Fulton Company's three segments for the year ended May 31, Year 2, in accordance with the method recommended by the AICPA's Accounting Standards Division.

Ex. 9-3 The nontraceable common costs of Wallace Company's home office for Year 8 totaled $150,000. Other financial data for Wallace Company's home office and two segments follow:

	Home office	Segment A	Segment B
Net sales	$-0-	$600,000	$400,000
Payroll dollars	50,000	200,000	150,000
Average plant and equipment and inventories . .	80,000	400,000	320,000

Allocate the nontraceable common costs of Wallace Company to its two segments in accordance with the provisions of **Cost Accounting Standard 403.** Round all percentage computations to the nearest tenth.

Ex. 9-4 Thoreson Company's accounting records for the year ended August 31, Year 4, include the following data with respect to its Modern Products Division. Sale of that division to Diversified Enterprises, Inc., for $300,000 was authorized by Thoreson's board of directors on August 31, Year 4. Closing date of the sale was expected to be February 28, Year 5.

THORESON COMPANY
Modern Products Division

Net sales, year ended Aug. 31, Year 4	$200,000
Costs and expenses, year ended Aug. 31, Year 4	150,000
Estimated operating losses, six months ending Feb. 28, Year 5	30,000
Estimated carrying value of net assets at Feb. 28, Year 5	330,000

Thoreson Company's combined federal and state income tax rate is 60%.

Prepare a partial income statement for Thoreson Company for the year ended August 31, Year 4, to present the above data.

Ex. 9-5 Ralston Company sells a single product, which it purchases from three different vendors. On May 1, Year 8, Ralston's inventory of the product consisted of 1,000 units priced at fifo cost of $7,500. Ralston's inventory transactions for the year ended April 30, Year 9, were as follows:

Quarter	Units purchased	Cost per unit purchased	Units sold	End-of-quarter replacement cost (per unit)
1	5,000	$8.00	4,500	$8.50
2	6,000	8.50	7,000	9.00
3	8,000	9.00	6,500	8.50*
4	6,000	8.50	5,500	9.50

*Decline not considered to be temporary.

Compute Ralston Company's cost of goods for each of the four quarters of the year ended April 30, Year 9. Show details of your computations.

Ex. 9-6 Stallings Petroleum Company's actual pre-tax operating results for the first two quarters of its fiscal year ending April 30, Year 4, and its related estimates for the entire fiscal year, were as follows:

	Year ended April 30, Year 4		
	First quarter (actual)	Second quarter (actual)	Full year (estimated)
Revenue	$600,000	$700,000	$2,700,000
Costs and expenses other than income taxes .	400,000	450,000	2,000,000
Income before income taxes	$200,000	$250,000	$ 700,000

Stallings Petroleum Company's financial executives anticipated no timing differences between pre-tax accounting income and taxable income for the year ending April 30, Year 4. However, these executives estimated the following permanent differences between pre-tax accounting income and taxable income for the first and second quarters:

	Estimate of permanent differences for year ending April 30, Year 4	
	Made for first quarter	Made for second quarter
Dividend exclusion	$ 15,000	$ 20,000
Excess of statutory depletion over cost depletion	150,000	140,000
Goodwill amortization	50,000	50,000

Stallings Petroleum Company's combined federal and state income tax rate is expected to be 60% for the year ending April 30, Year 4.

Prepare general journal entries for Stallings Petroleum Company's estimated income tax expense for the first quarter and second quarter of the year ending April 30, Year 4. Round all effective tax rate percentages to the nearest tenth.

Ex. 9-7 Selected assumptions underlying Halvorson Company's financial forecast for the year ending November 30, Year 9, follow:

1 Markups on merchandise will continue to be 25% of gross purchase cost.
2 Merchandise purchases will continue to be made on account with terms of 1/10, net 60. Purchase discounts will always be taken and will be recorded as usual in the Purchase Discounts account.
3 Payments of each month's purchases will be made as follows:
   60% in month of purchase
   40% during first 10 days of first month following purchase
4 Merchandise inventories at the end of each month will be maintained at 30% of the following month's cost of goods sold.
5 Merchandise sales on account will continue to bear terms of 2/10, net 30. Cash sales will not be subject to discount.
6 Collections of each month's sales on account will be made as follows:
   50% in month of sale
   45% in month following month of sale
7 5% of each month's sales on account will be uncollectible.
8 70% of collections on account in the month of sale will be subject to discount; 10% of the collections in the succeeding month will be subject to discount.
9 Forecast sales for the first four months of the year ending November 30, Year 9, are as follows:

	Sales on account—gross	Cash sales
Year 8:		
December	$1,900,000	$400,000
Year 9:		
January	1,500,000	250,000
February	1,700,000	350,000
March	1,600,000	300,000

Select the best answer for each of the following multiple choice questions for Halvorson Company:

1 Forecast gross purchases for January, Year 9, are:
 a $1,400,000.
 b $1,470,000.
 c $1,472,000.
 d $1,248,000.
 e None of the above.

2 Forecast inventory at the end of December, Year 8, is:
 a $420,000.
 b $441,600.
 c $552,000.
 d $393,750.
 e None of the above.

3 Forecast payments to suppliers during February, Year 9, are:
 a $1,551,200.
 b $1,535,688.
 c $1,528,560.
 d $1,509,552.
 e None of the above.

4 Forecast sales discounts to be taken by customers making remittances during February, Year 9, are:
 a $5,250.
 b $15,925.
 c $30,500.
 d $11,900.
 e None of the above.

5 Forecast total collections from customers during February, Year 9, are:
 a $1,875,000.
 b $1,861,750.
 c $1,511,750.
 d $1,188,100.
 e None of the above.

SHORT CASES FOR ANALYSIS AND DECISION

Case 9-1 **Part a** The quarterly income statements issued by publicly traded companies to their stockholders are usually prepared on the same basis as annual statements, the statement for each quarter reflecting the transactions of that quarter.

Instructions
1 Why do problems arise in using such quarterly statements to predict the income (before extraordinary items) for the year? Explain.
2 Discuss the ways in which quarterly income can be affected by the behavior of the costs recorded in a Repairs and Maintenance of Factory Machinery account.
3 Do such quarterly statements give management opportunities to manipulate the results of operations for a quarter? If so, explain or give an example.

Part b The controller of Ogden Company wants to issue to stockholders quarterly income statements that will be predictive of expected annual results. He proposes to allocate all fixed costs for the year among quarters in proportion to the number of units expected to be sold in each quarter, stating that the annual income can then be predicted through use of the following equation:

$$\frac{\text{Annual}}{\text{income}} = \frac{\text{quarterly}}{\text{income}} \times \frac{100\%}{\begin{array}{c}\text{\% of unit sales}\\\text{applicable to quarter}\end{array}}$$

Ogden has forecast the following activity for the year (in thousands of dollars):

	Units	Average per unit	Total (000 omitted)
Sales revenue:			
First quarter.	500,000	$2.00	$1,000
Second quarter	100,000	1.50	150
Third quarter	200,000	2.00	400
Fourth quarter	200,000	2.00	400
	1,000,000		$1,950
Costs to be incurred:			
Variable:			
Manufacturing		$0.70	$ 700
Selling and administrative		0.25	250
		$0.95	$ 950
Fixed:			
Manufacturing			$ 380
Selling and administrative			220
			$ 600
Income before income taxes			$ 400

Instructions (ignore income taxes)
1 Assuming that Ogden's activities do not vary from expectations, will the controller's plan achieve his objective? If not, how can it be modified to do so? Explain and give illustrative computations.
2 How should the effect of variations of actual activity from expected activity be treated in Ogden's quarterly income statements?
3 What assumption has the controller made in regard to inventories? Discuss.
4 Does the proposal of Ogden's controller comply with the requirement of *APB Opinion No. 28,* "Interim Financial Reporting"? Explain.

Case 9-2 You are the independent CPA for two audit clients, Arlington Company and Beaverton Company. Both companies maintain their accounts on a calendar-year basis, and both have a combined federal and state income tax rate of 60%. The controllers of both companies have requested your advice on the accounting for federal and state income taxes in their interim income statements for the first quarter of Year 7. You are provided with the following data for each company:

	Arlington Company	Beaverton Company
Actual pre-tax accounting income (loss) for first quarter of Year 7	$(200,000)	$(150,000)
Expected pre-tax accounting income (loss) for Year 7	(600,000)	400,000
Actual federal and state income taxes paid:		
Year 4	100,000	50,000
Year 5	150,000	75,000
Year 6	200,000	100,000
Expected timing differences and permanent differences for Year 7	None	None

Instructions State the advice you would give to the controllers of Arlington Company and Beaverton Company for their accounting for income taxes in the companies' interim financial statements for the first quarter of Year 7.

Case 9-3 The most recently published consolidated income statement of Broad Company appears as follows:

BROAD COMPANY
Consolidated Income Statement
For the Year Ended March 31, Year 8

Net sales	$38,041,200
Other revenue	407,400
	$38,448,600
Cost of goods sold	$27,173,300
Selling and administrative expenses	8,687,500
Interest expense	296,900
Income taxes	1,005,200
	$37,162,900
Net income	$ 1,285,700

Walter Wyatt, a representative of a firm of security analysts, visited the headquarters of Broad Company for the purpose of obtaining more information about the company's operations.

In the annual report, Broad's president stated that Broad was engaged in the pharmaceutical, food processing, toy manufacturing, and metalworking industries. Wyatt complained that the published consolidated income statement was of limited utility in his analysis of the operations. He said Broad should have disclosed separately the income earned by each of its segments.

Instructions
a Discuss the accounting problems involved in measuring net income for each segment within a company.
b With reference to Broad Company's consolidated income statement, identify the specific items where difficulty might be encountered in measuring income for each of its segments, and explain the nature of the difficulty.

PROBLEMS

9-4 Earhart Company has an excellent financial forecasting system. For the year ending July 31, Year 6, Earhart Company forecast pre-tax accounting income of $800,000. The company did not anticipate any timing differences between pre-tax accounting income and taxable income. However, the following permanent differences between accounting and taxable income for Year 6 were forecast:

Dividend exclusion	$150,000
Goodwill amortization	20,000
Officers' life insurance premium expense	15,000

In addition, Earhart Company anticipated investment tax credits of $50,000 for Year 6. The company's combined federal and state income tax rates totaled 60%, and federal and state laws coincided with respect to taxable income determination.

During the year ended July 31, Year 6, Earhart Company realized pre-tax accounting income as follows:

Quarter ended:

Oct. 31, Year 5	$180,000
Jan. 31, Year 6	230,000
Apr. 30, Year 6	195,000
July 31, Year 6	215,000

During Year 6, Earhart Company did not alter its forecast of pre-tax accounting income for the year. However, effective January 31, Year 6, the company revised its permanent difference estimate for the Year 6 dividend exclusion to $180,000 from $150,000, and its investment tax credit estimate for the year to $80,000 from $50,000. The actual amounts for the permanent differences and investment credit computed by the company as of July 31, Year 6, were as follows:

Dividend exclusion	$175,000
Goodwill amortization	20,000
Officers' life insurance premium expense	16,000
Investment tax credit	90,000

Instructions
a Compute the effective combined federal and state income tax rates which Earhart Company should use for its quarterly interim financial statements for the year ended July 31, Year 6. Round all percentage computations to the nearest tenth.
b Prepare Earhart Company's general journal entries for income taxes at October 31, Year 5, and January 31, April 30, and July 31, Year 6.

9-5 The general ledger of Walpole Company included the following amounts for the year ended December 31, Year 6:

Cost of goods sold	$ 8,000,000
Estimated loss on disposal of Wellington Division, to be consummated in	
first quarter of Year 7	50,000
Income taxes expense ($540,000 × 60%)	324,000
Interest expense	100,000
Judgment paid in lawsuit of **Justin Company v. Walpole Company,** initiated	
in Year 4	80,000
Loss from bankruptcy of customer	150,000
Loss from operations of Wellington Division, discontinued effective	
Dec. 31, Year 6	120,000
Net sales	10,000,000
Selling, general, and administrative expenses	800,000
Uninsured loss from earthquake at Wonmouth Division	160,000

Walpole Company's combined federal and state income tax rate is 60%. The company had no timing or permanent differences between pre-tax accounting income and taxable income, and no investment tax credits for Year 6. The company's retained earnings balance at January 1, Year 6, was $800,000; it declared and paid dividends of $50,000 during Year 6.

Instructions Prepare an income statement and a statement of retained earnings for Walpole Company for the year ended December 31, Year 6, in accordance with the provisions of **APB Opinion No. 30,** "Reporting the Results of Operations." Ignore earnings per share or dividends per share disclosures.

9-6 Dalton Company, a manufacturer of molded plastic containers, determined in October, Year 8, that it needed cash to continue operations. The company began negotiating for a one-month bank loan of $100,000 which would be discounted at 6% per annum on November 1. In considering the loan, the bank requested a forecast income statement and a cash forecast for the month of November. The following information is available:
(1) Sales were forecast at 120,000 units per month in October, Year 8, December, Year 8, and January, Year 9, and at 90,000 units in November, Year 8.
    The selling price is $2 per unit. Sales are billed on the fifteenth and last day of each month on terms of 2/10, net 30. Past experience indicates that sales are even throughout the month and 50% of the customers pay the billed amount within the discount period. The remainder pay at the end of 30 days, except for uncollectible accounts, which average $\frac{1}{2}$% of gross sales. On its income statement the company deducts from sales the estimated amounts for cash discounts on sales and losses on uncollectible accounts.
(2) The inventory of finished goods on October 1 was 24,000 units. The finished goods inventory at the end of each month is to be maintained at 20% of sales anticipated for the following month. There is no work in process.
(3) The inventory of raw materials on October 1 was 22,800 pounds. At the end of each month the raw materials inventory is to be maintained at not less than 40% of production requirements for the following month. Materials are purchased as needed in minimum quantities of 25,000 pounds per shipment. Raw material purchases of each month are paid in the next succeeding month on terms of net 30 days.
(4) All salaries and wages are paid on the fifteenth and last day of each month for the period ending on the date of payment.
(5) All manufacturing overhead and selling and administrative expenses are paid on the tenth of the month following the month in which incurred. Selling expenses are forecast at 10% of gross sales. Administrative expenses, which

include depreciation of $500 per month on office furniture and fixtures, total $33,000 per month.

(6) The standard cost of a molded plastic container, based on "normal" production of 100,000 units per month, is as follows:

Materials—½ pound	$0.50
Labor	.40
Variable overhead	.20
Fixed overhead	.10
Total	$1.20

Fixed overhead includes depreciation on factory equipment of $4,000 per month. Over- or underabsorbed overhead is included in cost of goods sold.

(7) The cash balance on November 1 is expected to be $10,000.

Instructions Prepare the following for Dalton Company, assuming that the bank loan is granted. (Do not consider income taxes.)

a Working papers computing inventory forecasts by months for:
  (1) Finished goods production in units for October, November, and December.
  (2) Raw material purchases in pounds for October and November.
b A forecast income statement for the month of November.
c A cash forecast for the month of November showing the opening balance, receipts (itemized by dates of collection), disbursements, and balance at end of month.

9-7 Shoppers' Mart, Inc., operates a chain of three food stores, each of which is considered a segment, in a state which recently enacted legislation permitting municipalities within the state to levy an income tax on corporations operating within their respective municipalities. The legislation established a uniform tax rate which the municipalities may levy, and regulations which provided that the tax is to be computed on income derived within the taxing municipality after a reasonable and consistent allocation of general overhead expenses. General overhead expenses, which have not been allocated to individual stores previously, include warehouse, home office, advertising, and delivery expenses.

Each of the municipalities in which Shoppers' Mart, Inc., operates a store has levied the corporate income tax as provided by state legislation, and management is considering two plans for allocating general overhead expenses to the stores. The Year 9 operating results for each store, before general overhead expense and taxes, were as follows:

	Store			
	Evans	Fargo	Grant	Total
Net sales	$416,000	$353,600	$270,400	$1,040,000
Cost of goods sold	215,700	183,300	140,200	539,200
Gross profit on sales	$200,300	$170,300	$130,200	$ 500,800
Less local operating expenses:				
Fixed	$ 60,800	$ 48,750	$ 50,200	$ 159,750
Variable	54,700	64,220	27,448	146,368
Total	$115,500	$112,970	$ 77,648	$ 306,118
Income before general overhead and income taxes	$ 84,800	$ 57,330	$ 52,552	$ 194,682

General overhead expenses in Year 9 were as follows:

Warehousing and delivery expenses:

Warehouse depreciation	$20,000	
Warehouse operations	30,000	
Delivery expense	40,000	$ 90,000

Home office expenses:

Advertising	$18,000	
Home office salaries	37,000	
Other home office expenses	28,000	83,000
Total general overhead expenses		$173,000

Additional information includes the following:

(1) One-fifth of the warehouse space is used to house the home office, and depreciation on this space is included in other home office expenses. Warehouse operating expenses vary with the quantity of merchandise sold.

(2) Delivery expense varies with distance and the number of deliveries. The distances from the warehouse to each store and the number of deliveries made in Year 9 were as follows:

Store	*Miles*	*Number of deliveries*
Evans	120	140
Fargo	200	64
Grant	100	104

(3) All advertising is arranged by the home office and is distributed in the areas in which stores are located.

(4) As each store was opened, the fixed portion of home office salaries increased $7,000 and other home office expenses increased $2,500. Basic fixed home office salaries amount to $10,000 and basic fixed other home office expenses amount to $12,000. The remainder of home office salaries and the remainder of other home office expenses vary with sales.

Instructions

a For each of the following plans for allocating general overhead expenses, compute the income of each store that would be subject to the municipal levy on corporation income:

Plan 1 Allocate all general overhead expenses on the basis of sales volume.

Plan 2 First, allocate home office salaries and other home office expenses evenly to warehouse operations and each store. Second, allocate the resulting warehouse operations expenses, warehouse depreciation, and advertising to each store on the basis of sales volume. Third, allocate delivery expense to each store on the basis of delivery miles times number of deliveries.

b Management has decided to expand one of the three stores to increase annual sales by $50,000. The expansion will increase local fixed operating expenses by $7,500 per year and require ten additional deliveries from the warehouse. Determine which store management should select for expansion to maximize profits.

9-8 In June, Year 11, after ten years with a large CPA firm, Arnold Walsh, CPA, opened an office as a sole practitioner.

In Year 13, Baxter Young, CPA, joined Walsh as a senior accountant. The partnership of Walsh and Young was organized July 1, Year 18, and a fiscal year ending June 30 was adopted and approved by the Internal Revenue Service.

Continued growth of the firm has required additional personnel. The current complement, including approved salaries for the fiscal year ending June 30, Year 24, is as follows:

	Annual salary
Partners:	
Arnold Walsh, CPA	$24,000
Baxter Young, CPA	18,000
Professional staff:	
Manager:	
Carol Zale, CPA	17,500
Senior accountant:	
David Ashe, CPA	12,500
Assistants:	
Earl Bowles	10,500
Frances Carter	10,500
Secretaries:	
Georgia Davis	7,800
Helen Evans	6,864
Janice Falcon	6,864

A severe illness kept Walsh away from the firm for more than four months in Year 22. The firm suffered during this period, mainly because other personnel lacked knowledge about the practice.

After Walsh's illness, a plan was developed for delegation of administrative authority and responsibility and for standardization of procedures.

The goals of the plan included (1) income objectives, (2) standardized billing procedures (with flexibility for adjustments by the partners), and (3) assignment schedules to eliminate overtime and to allow for nonchargeable time such as vacations and illness. The firm plans a 52-week year with five-day, 40-hour weeks.

The partners have set an annual income target (after partners' salaries) of at least $55,000. The forecast for Fiscal Year 24 is 700 hours of chargeable time at $45 per hour for Walsh and 1,100 hours at $40 per hour for Young. Walsh and Young are to devote all other available time, except as specified below, to administration. The billing rates for all other employees including secretaries are to be set at a level to recover their salaries plus the following overhead items: fringe benefits of $15,230, other operating expenses of $49,380, and a contribution of $20,500 to target income.

The partners agree that salary levels are fair bases for allocating overhead in setting billing rates, with the exception that salary costs of the secretaries' nonchargeable time are to be added to overhead to arrive at total overhead to be allocated. Thus the billing rate for each secretary will be based upon the salary costs of her chargeable time plus her share of the total overhead. No portion of total overhead is to be allocated to partners' salaries.

The following information is available for nonchargeable time:

(1) Because of his recent illness, Walsh expects to be away an additional week.

Young expects no loss of time from illness. All other employees are to be allowed one illness day per month (12 days each).
(2) Allowable vacations are as follows:

1 month	Walsh
	Young
3 weeks	Zale
	Davis
2 weeks	All other employees

(3) The firm observes seven holidays annually. If the holiday falls on a weekend, the office is closed the preceding Friday or following Monday.
(4) Bowles and Carter should each be allotted three days to sit for the November, Year 23, CPA examination.
(5) Hours are forecast for other miscellaneous activities of the personnel as follows:

	Walsh	Young	Zale	Ashe	Bowles	Carter	Davis	Evans	Falcon
Firm projects		100	40	40	40		200		
Professional development . .	80	80	56	40	40	50	24	16	24
Professional meetings	184	120	40	40	16	16	24	8	8
Firm meetings	48	48	48	24	24	24	48	8	8
Community activities	80	40	40	24	16	16	12		
Office time other than firm administration				84	72		1,000	716	808
Total other miscellaneous .	392	388	308	240	136	106	1,308	748	848

(6) Unassigned time is forecast for Ashe, Bowles, and Carter as 8, 38, and 78 hours, respectively.

Instructions
a Prepare a time allocation forecast for Walsh, Young, and each employee, ending with forecast chargeable time for the year ending June 30, Year 24.
b Independent of your solution to part *a* and assuming the following data as to forecast chargeable hours, prepare a working paper computing billing rates by employee for the year ending June 30, Year 24. The working paper should show the proper allocation of appropriate expenses and target income contribution to salaries applicable to chargeable time in accordance with the objective established by the partners. (Round allocation calculations to one decimal place. Round billing rate calculations to the nearest dollar.)

Forecast chargeable hours

Zale	1,600
Ashe	1,650
Bowles	1,550
Carter	1,450
Davis	500
Evans	1,150
Falcon	1,200

c Independent of your solutions to parts *a* and *b* and assuming the following data as to forecast chargeable hours and billing rates, prepare a condensed statement of forecast income for the year ending June 30, Year 24.

	Forecast chargeable hours	Forecast hourly billing rate
Walsh	700	$45
Young	1,100	40
Zale	1,600	32
Ashe	1,650	25
Bowles	1,550	15
Carter	1,450	17
Davis	500	5
Evans	1,150	7
Falcon	1,200	7

10

Financial reporting by multinational companies

A *multinational company* is a business enterprise which carries on operations in more than one nation, through a network of branches, divisions, and subsidiaries. These companies attempt to obtain raw materials and debt or equity capital in countries where such resources are plentiful. Multinational companies manufacture their products in nations where wages and other operating costs are lowest, and they sell their products in countries which provide the most profitable markets.

The worldwide scope of the operations of multinational companies has resulted in enormous growth for many of them. This growth was evidenced by a 1971 United Nations study, which developed operating data for the 25 largest multinational companies as shown on page 364.

As indicated in this chart, the majority of the largest multinational companies are headquartered in the United States. One source has estimated the total number of multinational companies in the United States at 200. The magnitude of these companies' operations was pointed up in a survey which demonstrated that the sales volume of General Motors Corporation in 1969 was exceeded by the gross national products of only 22 countries.[1]

In this chapter, we shall discuss the three principal accounting and reporting issues of multinational companies—variations in international accounting standards, accounting for transactions involving foreign currencies, and combined or consolidated financial statements for a United States company and its foreign branches or subsidiaries.

[1] U.S. Senate, Committee on Finance, *The Multinational Corporation and the World Economy* (Washington: 1973), p. 8.

THE 25 LARGEST MULTINATIONAL CORPORATIONS

Company	Total 1971 sales (billions of dollars)	Foreign sales as percentage of total	Foreign earnings as percentage of total	Number of countries where subsidiaries are located
General Motors (United States)	$28.3	19%	19%	21
Exxon (United States)	18.7	50	52	25
Ford (United States)	16.4	26	24	30
Royal Dutch Shell (Netherlands–United Kingdom)	12.7	79	—	43
General Electric (United States)	9.4	16	20	32
IBM (United States)	8.3	39	50	80
Mobil Oil (United States)	8.2	45	51	62
Chrysler (United States)	8.0	24	—	26
Texaco (United States)	7.5	40	25	30
Unilever (Netherlands–United Kingdom)	7.5	80	—	31
ITT (United States)	7.3	42	35	40
Gulf Oil (United States)	5.9	45	21	61
British Petroleum (United Kingdom)	5.2	88	—	52
Philips Gloeilampenfabrieken (Netherlands)	5.2	—	—	29
Standard Oil of California (United States)	5.1	45	43	26
Volkswagenwerk (Federal Republic of Germany)	5.0	69	—	12
U.S. Steel (United States)	4.9	54	62	—
Nippon Steel (Japan)	4.1	31	—	5
Standard Oil (Ind.) (United States)	4.1	—	—	24
du Pont (United States)	3.8	18	—	20
Siemens (Federal Republic of Germany)	3.8	39	—	52
Imperial Chemical (United Kingdom)	3.7	35	—	46
Hitachi (Japan)	3.6	39	—	—
Goodyear Tire & Rubber (United States)	3.6	30	30	22
Nestlé (Switzerland)	3.5	98	—	15

SOURCE: *Multinational Corporations in World Development*, United Nations Department of Economic and Social Affairs, New York, 1973, reproduced in *Financial Executive*, December 1973, p. 32.

VARIATIONS IN INTERNATIONAL ACCOUNTING STANDARDS

The wide variety of accounting standards and practices among the nations of the world presents a substantial problem to the multinational company. The international public accounting firm of Arthur Andersen & Co. commented upon this problem as follows:

> No internationally recognized standards of accounting exist today. In the case of certain basic concepts, there is some consensus in practice among several of the more industrialized countries of the world, and this consensus is likely to be more pronounced in the case of larger multinational companies, especially those that are audited by accounting firms associated with an international practice. Yet even among the world's principal industrial countries, significant variations in accounting standards can be found. Since accounting problems have been approached from various perspectives, differing, and often conflicting, solutions have been developed.
>
> The principal problems that impede the development of internationally recognized accounting standards and that must be overcome before such standards can be established include:
>
> Failure of accountants and users to consider or agree on the objectives of financial statements.
>
> Differences in the extent to which the accounting profession has developed in various countries.
>
> Influence of tax laws on financial reporting.
>
> Provisions of company laws.
>
> Requirements of governmental and other regulatory bodies.
>
> Failure to consider differences among countries in basic economic factors affecting financial reporting.
>
> Inconsistencies in practices recommended by the accounting professions in different countries.[2]

The extent of just one aspect of the problem—the influence of tax laws on financial reporting—was surveyed by Price Waterhouse International, a major worldwide CPA firm. Price Waterhouse International found that accounting practices in nine surveyed countries adhered strictly to tax requirements in a majority of matters. Accounting practices in 11 countries adhered strictly to tax requirements in a minority of matters; while in four countries (including the United States) strict adherence of accounting practices to tax requirements was not permitted.[3]

Actions to narrow differences in international accounting standards

Two major steps taken in the quest for greater uniformity in international accounting standards were the establishment in 1966 of the Accountants International Study Group and the organization in 1973 of the International Accounting Standards Committee. The Accountants International

---

[2] *Accounting Standards for Business Enterprises throughout the World* (Arthur Andersen & Co., 1974), pp. 2–3.

[3] *Accounting Principles and Reporting Practices: A Survey in 38 Countries* (Price Waterhouse International, 1973), sec. 233.

Study Group, formed jointly by the AICPA and the Institutes of Chartered Accountants of Canada, England and Wales, Scotland, and Ireland, has issued a number of reports which survey accounting thought and practices of the Study Group's member countries. These reports have covered areas such as materiality, consolidated financial statements, and reporting by diversified companies.

The International Accounting Standards Committee was comprised at the time of its organization of representatives from the professional accounting societies of Australia, Canada, France, Germany, Japan, Mexico, Netherlands, United Kingdom, and United States. Subsequently, associate membership status was given to accounting profession representatives of Belgium, Fiji, Greece, India, Israel, New Zealand, Pakistan, Rhodesia, South Africa, Trinidad and Tobago, and Zambia. The Committee's stated goals were to formulate and solicit general acceptance of basic international standards in accounting, financial reporting, and auditing. The first three pronouncements of the Committee dealt with disclosure of accounting policies, valuation of inventories, and consolidation of subsidiaries. These pronouncements set forth standards comparable in most respects to those used in the United States.

The work of the International Accounting Standards Committee, which is headquartered in London, should in time exercise a great deal of influence on accounting standards for multinational companies.

ACCOUNTING FOR TRANSACTIONS INVOLVING FOREIGN CURRENCIES

In most countries of the world, a foreign country's currency is treated as though it were a *commodity,* or a *money market instrument.* In the United States, for example, foreign currencies are bought and sold by the international banking departments of commercial banks. These foreign currency transactions are entered into on behalf of the bank's multinational company customers, and for the bank's own account.

The buying and selling of foreign currencies as though they were commodities result in variations in the *exchange rate* between the currencies of two countries. For example, a daily newspaper at the end of 1974 quoted the exchange rates for foreign banknotes shown on page 367.

The quoted rates are *spot rates* applicable to current exchanges of money. *Forward market rates* apply to foreign currency transactions which are to be consummated at a future date. The *agio,* or *spread,* between the buying rates and the selling rates represents the gross profit to a trader in foreign currency. If, for example, a United States multinational company required £10,000 (10,000 British pounds), it would have had to pay the foreign currency trader $23,700 (£10,000 × $2.37 selling rate) in the market illustrated on page 367.

Prices for foreign banknotes, as quoted on the last business day (in dollars):

	Buying	Selling
Argentina (Peso)	$ .04	$ .0520
Australia (Dollar)	1.20	1.30
Austria (Schilling)	.054	.059
Belgium (Franc)	.024	.028
Brazil (Cruzeiro)	.1150	.13
Britain (Pound)	2.31	2.37
Canada (Dollar)	.99	1.02
China-Taiwan (Dollar)	.024	.029
Colombia (Peso)	.031	.04
Denmark (Krone)	.16	.18
Egypt (Pound)	1.35	1.65
Finland (Markka)	.2625	.2725
France (Franc)	.20	.22
Greece (Drachma)	.027	.035
Hong Kong (Dollar)	.19	.2050
India (Rupee)	.0975	.1075
Italy (Lira)	.00135	.00155
Japan (Yen)	.0032	.0035
Malaysia (Dollar)	.39	.46
Mexico (Peso)	.078	.082
Netherlands (Guilder)	.38	.40
New Zealand (Dollar)	1.00	1.15
Norway (Krone)	.17	.19
Pakistan (Rupee)	Z	Z
Philippines (Peso)	.1350	.1475
Portugal (Escudo)	.035	.04
Singapore (Dollar)	.39	.46
South Korea (Won)	.0018	.0025
Spain (Peseta)	.016	.018
Sweden (Krona)	.22	.24
Switzerland (Franc)	.35	.37
Turkey (Lira)	.06	.0725
Uruguay (Peso)	.0003	.0005
Venezuela (Bolivar)	.2275	.2340
West Germany (Mark)	.39	.42

Supplied by one major New York bank.
Z-not available.

Factors influencing fluctuations in exchange rates include the individual nation's balance of payments surpluses or deficits, differing global rates of inflation, money market variations, such as interest rates, in individual countries, and capital investment levels.

Accounting standards

The AICPA, during the period in which it exercised the responsibility for establishing accounting standards, did not publish standards for the accounting problems associated with transactions involving foreign currencies. It remained for the Financial Accounting Standards Board, in its *Discussion Memorandum* entitled "An Analysis of Issues Related to Accounting for Foreign Currency Translation," to recognize the theoretical and practical accounting problems in foreign currency transactions. Three of these problems were described as follows:

1 What is the nature of the exchange adjustment that may result from the foreign currency risk on a purchase or sale denominated in a foreign currency?

2 What is the nature of the exchange adjustment that may result from the foreign currency risk on a loan receivable or loan payable denominated in a foreign currency?

3 When should exchange adjustments be recorded?[4]

To understand the issues in the problems outlined above, we shall briefly describe the nature of business transactions involving foreign currencies.

Transactions involving foreign currencies

A multinational company headquartered in the United States engages in innumerable sales, purchases, and loans with independent entities in foreign countries, as well as with its branches, divisions, or subsidiaries in other countries. If the transactions with independent foreign entities are consummated in terms of the United States dollar, no accounting problems arise for the United States multinational company. The sale, purchase, or loan transaction is recorded in dollars in the accounts of the United States company; the independent foreign entity must obtain the dollars necessary to complete the transaction through the *foreign exchange* department of its bank.

Often, however, the transactions outlined above are negotiated and settled in terms of the foreign entity's *local currency.* In such circumstances, the United States company must account for the transaction valued in foreign currency in terms of United States dollars. This accounting, described as *foreign currency translation,* is accomplished by applying the *exchange rate* between the foreign currency and the United States dollar.

To illustrate, assume that on April 18, Year 6, Worldwide Enterprises, Inc., purchased merchandise from a Federal Republic of Germany supplier at a cost of 100,000 deutsche marks (symbol DM). The April 18, Year 6, selling exchange rate was DM1 = $0.40. Because Worldwide Enter-

---

[4]*FASB Discussion Memorandum,* "An Analysis of Issues Related to Accounting for Foreign Currency Translation" (Stamford, Conn.: FASB, 1974), p. xi.

prises, Inc., was a customer of good credit standing, the German supplier made the sale on 30-day open account.

Assuming that Worldwide Enterprises, Inc., uses a perpetual inventory system, the company would record the April 18, Year 6, purchase as follows:

Inventory	40,000	
Accounts Payable		40,000
Purchase from German supplier for DM 100,000, translated at		
selling exchange rate of DM1 = $0.40.		

The use of the selling exchange rate as in the above transaction was recommended by the AICPA in response to the issue "What is the current exchange rate?" raised by the FASB in its *Discussion Memorandum* on foreign currency translation.[5]

Exchange adjustments

During the period that the account payable to the German supplier remains unpaid, Worldwide Enterprises, Inc., is subject to the risk that the exchange rate for deutsche marks may have changed substantially when payment of the liability is made May 18, Year 6. Worldwide Enterprises, Inc., could have *hedged* the risk by buying deutsche marks in the forward market on April 18 for delivery May 18. The forward market rate would generally be less than the spot rate, reflecting the currency dealer's assumption of the risk of exchange rate fluctuation. For example, on April 18 the forward market rate might have been DM1 = $0.405. The AICPA has suggested that the difference between the spot rate and the forward market rate is of a financing nature and should be charged to expense when the forward exchange contract is purchased.[6]

Purchase of Forward Exchange Contract The following journal entry illustrates Worldwide Enterprises' April 18, Year 6, purchase of a 30-day forward exchange contract at DM1 = $0.405.

Investment in Forward Exchange Contract	40,000	
Interest Expense	500	
Contract Payable		40,500
Purchase of DM 100,000 forward exchange contract for 30 days,		
at forward market rate of DM1 = $0.405.		

[5] *Statement of Position on Accounting for Foreign Currency Translation* AICPA, (New York: 1974), p. 8.
[6] *Ibid.*

On May 18, Year 6, when the forward exchange contract matured and the account payable to the German supplier was paid, the following entries would be appropriate for Worldwide Enterprises, Inc.:

Contract Payable	*40,500*	
Investment in Deutsche Marks	*40,000*	
Investment in Forward Exchange Contract		*40,000*
Cash		*40,500*
Payment of DM 100,000 forward exchange contract, and receipt of deutsche marks.		
Accounts Payable	*40,000*	
Investment in Deutsche Marks		*40,000*
Payment of April 18, Year 6, purchase from German supplier.		

If financial statements were prepared prior to the payment of the forward exchange contract, the unexpired portion of the $500 charge to Interest Expense would be deferred by an adjusting entry.

Exchange Gain or Loss If Worldwide Enterprises, Inc., did not purchase a forward exchange contract, it would obtain 100,000 deutsche marks on May 18, Year 6, to pay the liability to the German supplier. If the May 18 selling exchange rate was DM1 = $0.39, Worldwide Enterprises, Inc., would expend only $39,000 for a bank draft for DM 100,000 to pay the German supplier. The first issue identified by the FASB (see page 368) concerned the nature of the $1,000 difference (called an *exchange adjustment*) between the $40,000 liability established by Worldwide Enterprises, Inc., on April 18, Year 6, and the $39,000 expended by the company on May 18, Year 6, to settle the debt. Following are two approaches to resolving this issue.

The One-transaction Perspective One school of accounting theorists holds that the $1,000 difference described above should be applied to reduce the cost of the inventory acquired. Under this approach, Worldwide Enterprises, Inc., would make the following entry on May 18, Year 6 (assuming that one-fourth of the goods purchased April 18 remained unsold on May 18):

Accounts Payable	*40,000*	
Cost of Goods Sold		*750*
Inventory		*250*
Cash		*39,000*
Payment for DM 100,000 draft to settle liability to German supplier, and allocation of resultant exchange adjustment to cost of goods sold and to inventory.		

In effect, supporters of the *one-transaction perspective* for foreign trade activities consider the original amount recorded for a foreign merchandise purchase as an *estimate,* subject to adjustment when the *exact cash outlay* required for the purchase is known. Essentially, the one-transaction proponents emphasize the *cash payment* aspects of the transaction, rather than the *bargained price* aspects as of the date of the foreign trade transaction.

The Two-transaction Perspective A contrasting view is that a foreign trade action is essentially *two separate transactions.* One transaction is the purchase of the merchandise; the second is the purchase of the foreign currency required to settle the liability for the merchandise purchased. Supporters of the *two-transaction perspective* for foreign trade transactions, including the AICPA,[7] argue that an importer's assumption of the exchange adjustment risk, rather than hedging the risk, is a financial-type decision, not a merchandising decision.

Under the two-transaction perspective, Worldwide Enterprises, Inc., would make the following entry at May 18, Year 6:

Accounts Payable	40,000	
Exchange Gains and Losses		1,000
Cash		39,000
Payment for DM 100,000 draft to settle liability to German supplier, and recognition of favorable exchange adjustment as a gain.		

The authors join the AICPA in support of the two-transaction perspective for foreign trade activities and for loans receivable and payable denominated in a foreign currency (see the second FASB issue set forth on page 368). In the authors' view, the separability of the merchandising and financing aspects of a foreign trade action is an undeniable fact. In delaying payment of a foreign trade purchase transaction, an importer has made a decision to assume the risk of fluctuations in the exchange rate for the foreign currency required to pay for the purchase. This risk assumption is measured by the exchange gain or loss recorded at the time of payment of the purchase. To offset the exchange gain or loss against the cost of the merchandise would be a violation of the widely accepted accounting prohibition against setoffs.

Timing of recording of exchange adjustments

The preceding example under the two-transaction perspective included recognition of the exchange gain when Worldwide Enterprises, Inc., paid

[7] *Ibid.,* p. 2.

the liability to the German supplier. If, however, the company had pre-pared financial statements as of April 30, Year 6, and the exchange rate at that date differed from the rate at the date of the purchase from the German supplier, should an exchange adjustment be recorded at April 30? This question is the essence of the third FASB issue listed on page 368.

Opponents of recording exchange adjustments prior to settlement of the related receivable or payable assert that an exchange gain or loss is not *realized* until the settlement date. In the view of the authors, this assertion emphasizes *cash basis* accounting. Under accrual accounting, many losses, and some gains, are recorded in the accounts prior to their actual realization in a cash transaction. Therefore, the authors con-cur with the position of the AICPA in the issue of the timing of the recording of exchange adjustments:

> In general, . . . exchange adjustments should be recorded when exchange rate changes occur in order to record exchange gains or losses in the period of the event—the exchange rate change—rather than at the date the account balance is settled.[8]

To illustrate, assume that on April 30, Year 6, the selling exchange rate for deutsche marks was DM1 = $0.396, and Worldwide Enterprises, Inc., planned to prepare financial statements as of that date. The company would make the following journal entry with respect to the account payable to the German supplier:

Accounts Payable	400	
Exchange Gains and Losses		400
To record exchange adjustment applicable to April 18, Year 6,		
purchase from German supplier, as follows:		
Liability recorded at April 18, Year 6	$40,000	
Liability translated at exchange rate DM1 = $0.396		
(DM 100,000 × $0.396 = $39,600)	39,600	
Exchange gain	$ 400	

In these circumstances, the May 18, Year 6, journal entry for Worldwide Enterprises, Inc.'s, payment of the liability to the German supplier would be as follows:

Accounts Payable	39,600	
Exchange Gains and Losses		600
Cash		39,000
Payment for DM 100,000 draft to settle liability to German sup-		
plier, and recognition of favorable exchange adjustment as a		
gain.		

[8] *Ibid.,* p. 3.

Income statement presentation and disclosure of exchange adjustments

There appears to be general agreement that the effects of material exchange adjustments should be disclosed in the income statement. This disclosure was required by the FASB in its first *Statement of Financial Accounting Standards,*[9] and has been supported by the AICPA.[10] An "Other Revenue and Expenses" section of the income statement is an appropriate classification for exchange adjustments.

At one time, substantial exchange adjustments resulting from a foreign government's major *revaluation* or *devaluation* of its currency in relation to gold or to other countries' currencies were accounted for as extraordinary gains or losses. This accounting treatment was prohibited by *APB Opinion No. 30,* as follows:

> Certain gains and losses should not be reported as extraordinary items because they are usual in nature or may be expected to recur as a consequence of customary and continuing business activities. Examples include:
> . . . .
> (b) Gains or losses from exchange or translation of foreign currencies, including those relating to major devaluations and revaluations.[11]

COMBINED OR CONSOLIDATED FINANCIAL STATEMENTS FOR FOREIGN SUBSIDIARIES OR BRANCHES

When a United States multinational company prepares consolidated or combined financial statements which include the assets, liabilities, and operations of foreign subsidiaries or branches, the United States company must *translate* the financial statements of the foreign entities to United States dollars. Similar treatment must be given to the assets and income statement amounts associated with foreign subsidiaries which are not consolidated, and with other foreign investees for which the United States company uses the equity method of accounting.[12]

If the exchange rate for the foreign currency of the country in which a foreign subsidiary or branch operated remained constant instead of fluctuating, translation of the investee's financial statements to United States dollars would be simple. *All* financial statement amounts would be translated to United States dollars at the constant exchange rates.

We have already noted, however, that exchange rates fluctuate frequently. Thus, the accountant charged with translating amounts in a foreign investee's financial statements to United States dollars faces a

[9] *Statement of Financial Accounting Standards No. 1,* "Disclosure of Foreign Currency Translation Information" (Stamford, Conn.: FASB, 1973), p. 5 (quoted on pages 379–380).
[10] *Statement of Position on Accounting for Foreign Currency Translation,* p. 12.
[11] *APB Opinion No. 30,* "Reporting the Results of Operations" (New York: AICPA, 1973), p. 566.
[12] The wide range of United States multinational companies' consolidation practices for foreign subsidiaries was discussed in Chapter 5 (p. 165).

problem similar to that involving inventory valuation during a period of price fluctuations. Which exchange rate or rates should be used to translate the foreign investee's financial statements? Several answers have been proposed for this question,[13] just as several valuation methods have been adopted for inventories. However, the several methods for foreign currency translation may be grouped into three basic classes: *current/noncurrent, monetary/nonmonetary,* and *current rate.* (A fourth method, the *temporal* method, is essentially the same as the monetary/nonmonetary method.) The three classes differ principally in translation techniques for balance sheet accounts.

Current/noncurrent method

In the *current/noncurrent method* of translation, current assets and current liabilities are translated at the exchange rate in effect at the balance sheet date of the foreign investee (the *current rate*). All other assets and liabilities, and the elements of owners' equity, are translated at the *historical rates* in effect at the time the assets, liabilities, and equities were first recorded in the accounts. In the income statement, depreciation and amortization are translated at historical rates applicable to the related assets, while all other expenses and revenue items are translated at an *average* exchange rate for the accounting period.

The current/noncurrent method of translating foreign investees' financial statements was sanctioned by the AICPA for many years following World War II. This method supposedly best reflected the *liquidity* aspects of the foreign investee's financial position. However, the current/noncurrent method has few adherents among today's accountants. The principal theoretical objection to the current/noncurrent method is that, with respect to inventories, it represents a departure from historical cost. Inventories are translated at the *current rate,* rather than at *historical rates,* when the current/noncurrent method of translating foreign currency accounts is followed.

Monetary/nonmonetary method

The *monetary/nonmonetary method* of translating foreign currencies focuses upon the *characteristics* of assets and liabilities of the foreign investee, rather than upon their *balance sheet classifications.* This method is founded upon the same monetary/nonmonetary aspects of assets and liabilities that are employed in general price-level accounting.[14] *Monetary assets and liabilities*—those representing claims or obligations expressed in a fixed monetary amount—are translated at the current exchange rate.

[13]*Nine* distinct methods of foreign currency translation are illustrated in the Financial Accounting Standards Board's *Financial Statement Model on Accounting for Foreign Currency Translation* (Stamford, Conn.: FASB, 1974).
[14]*Intermediate Accounting* of this series includes expanded coverage of general price-level accounting.

All other assets, liabilities, and owners' equity accounts are translated at appropriate historical rates. In the income statement, average exchange rates are applied to all revenue and expenses except depreciation, amortization, and cost of goods sold, which are translated at appropriate historical rates.

The AICPA supports the monetary/nonmonetary method, because it retains the historical cost concept in the foreign investee's financial statements.[15] Since the foreign investee's financial statements are combined or consolidated with those of the United States multinational company, consistent accounting standards are applied in the combined or consolidated financial statements.

Current rate method

Critics of the monetary/nonmonetary method point out that this method emphasizes the *parent company* aspects of a foreign investee's financial position and operating results. By reflecting the foreign investee's changes in resources and obligations, and operating results, as though they were made in the parent company's *reporting currency,* the monetary/nonmonetary method misstates the *actual* financial position and operating relationships of the foreign investee.

The critics of the monetary/nonmonetary method of foreign currency translation have proposed the *current rate method.* Under the current rate method, *all* balance sheet accounts other than owners' equity accounts are translated at the current exchange rate. Owners' equity accounts are translated at historical rates.

To emphasize the *local currency* aspects of the foreign investee's operations, *all* revenue and expense may be translated at the current rate. Otherwise, an average exchange rate is used for all revenue and expenses. The current rate method has not been generally accepted in the United States in the past, and the FASB rejected the method in a Proposed Statement of Financial Accounting Standards on foreign currency translation issued December 31, 1974.

Illustration of monetary/nonmonetary method

We shall illustrate the monetary/nonmonetary method of translating a foreign investee's financial statements, since this method is supported by the AICPA. To simplify the illustration, we shall model it upon the home office–branch illustration in Chapter 3, with inventories billed to the branch in excess of cost. We shall further assume that both home office and branch use the perpetual inventory system, and that the branch is located in France.

---

[15] *Statement of Position on Accounting for Foreign Currency Translation,* p. 4. In a proposed Statement of Financial Accounting Standards issued December 31, 1974, the FASB sanctioned the monetary/nonmonetary method, although the Board used the term *temporal method,* in harmony with the AICPA's *Accounting Research Study No. 12.*

The Year 1 transactions illustrated in Chapter 3 are repeated below. Following each transaction is the exchange rate for French francs (symbol F) at the date of the transaction.

Transactions for Year 1
(1) Cash of $1,000 sent to branch (F1 = $0.20)
(2) Merchandise with a cost of $60,000 shipped to branch at a billed price of $90,000 (F1 = $0.20)
(3) Equipment purchased by branch for F 2,500, to be carried in home office records (F1 = $0.20)
(4) Sales by branch on credit, F 500,000 (F1 = $0.16). Cost of goods sold F 337,500
(5) Collections of accounts receivable by branch, F 248,000 (F1 = $0.25)
(6) Payment of operating expenses by branch, F 80,000 (F1 = $0.25)
(7) Cash remitted to home office, F 156,250 (F1 = $0.24)
(8) Operating expenses incurred by home office charged to branch, $3,000 (F1 = $0.24)
The exchange rate at the end of Year 1 was F1 = $0.23.

The preceding transactions would be recorded by the home office and by the branch with the journal entries on page 377.

In the home office accounts, the Investment in Branch X account would appear (*in dollars* before the accounts are closed), as follows:

Investment in Branch X

Explanation of transactions	Debit	Credit	Balance
Cash sent to branch	$ 1,000		$ 1,000 dr
Merchandise shipped to branch	90,000		91,000 dr
Equipment purchased by branch, recorded			
in home office accounts		$ 500	90,500 dr
Cash received from branch		37,500	53,000 dr
Operating expenses billed to branch	3,000		56,000 dr

In the branch records, the home office account would appear *in francs* before the branch accounting records are closed as follows:

Home Office

Explanation of transactions	Debit	Credit	Balance
Cash received from home office		F 5,000	F 5,000 cr
Merchandise received from home office		450,000	455,000 cr
Equipment purchased by branch	F 2,500		452,500 cr
Cash sent to home office	156,250		296,250 cr
Operating expenses billed by home office		12,500	308,750 cr

Home Office Records ($)			Branch Records (F)		
(1) Investment in			Cash	5,000	
Branch X	1,000		Home Office . .		5,000
Cash		1,000			
(2) Investment in					
Branch X	90,000		Inventory	450,000	
Shipments to			Home Office . .		450,000
Branch X .		90,000			
Cost of Goods					
Shipped to					
Branch X . . .	60,000				
Inventory . . .		60,000			
(3) Equipment:			Home Office . . .	2,500	
Branch X	500		Cash		2,500
Investment in					
Branch X .		500			
(4) None			Accounts		
			Receivable . . .	500,000	
			Sales		500,000
			Cost of Goods		
			Sold	337,500	
			Inventory . . .		337,500
(5) None			Cash	248,000	
			Accounts		
			Receivable		248,000
(6) None			Operating		
			Expenses	80,000	
			Cash		80,000
(7) Cash	37,500		Home Office . . .	156,250	
Investment in			Cash		156,250
Branch X . .		37,500			
(8) Investment in			Operating		
Branch X	3,000		Expenses	12,500	
Operating			Home Office .		12,500
Expenses .		3,000			

The branch trial balance *(in francs)* would be as follows at the end of Year 1:

	Debit	Credit
Cash	F 14,250	
Accounts receivable	252,000	
Inventory	112,500	
Home office		F308,750
Sales		500,000
Cost of goods sold	337,500	
Operating expenses	92,500	
Totals	F808,750	F808,750

Translation of Branch Trial Balance Translation of the branch trial balance by the monetary/nonmonetary method is illustrated below.

	Balance, francs dr (cr)	×	Exchange rate	=	Balance, dollars dr (cr)
Cash	F 14,250		$ 0.23(1)		$ 3,278
Accounts receivable	252,000		0.23(1)		57,960
Inventory	112,500		0.20(2)		22,500
Home office	(308,750)		(3)		(56,000)
Sales	(500,000)		0.215(4)		(107,500)
Cost of goods sold	337,500		0.20(2)		67,500
Operating expenses	92,500		0.215(4)		19,887
Subtotal	F -0-				$ 7,625
Exchange gain	-0-				(7,625)
Total	F -0-				$ -0-

(1) *Current rate (at end of Year 1)*
(2) *Historical rate (when goods were shipped to branch by home office)*
(3) *Translated at balance of Investment in Branch X account in home office records*
(4) *Average of beginning (F1 = $0.20) and ending (F1 = $0.23) exchange rates for Year 1*

In the review of the translation of the branch trial balance by the monetary/nonmonetary method, the following should be noted:

1 Monetary assets are translated at the current rate; the single nonmonetary asset—inventory—is translated at the appropriate historical rate.

2 To quickly achieve the same result as a translation of the Home Office account transactions at appropriate historical rates, the balance of the home office's Investment in Branch X account *(in dollars)* is substituted for the branch's

Home Office account **(in francs).** All equity accounts—regardless of legal form of the investee—are translated at historical rates in the monetary/nonmonetary method.

3 A simple average of beginning-of-year and end-of-year exchange rates is used to translate revenue and expense accounts other than cost of goods sold, which is translated at the appropriate historical rates. In practice, a quarterly, monthly, or even daily average might be computed, either unweighted or weighted.

4 A balancing figure labeled as an "exchange gain" is used to reconcile the total debits and total credits of the branch's translated trial balance. This exchange gain is accounted for in the same manner as the one illustrated earlier in this chapter (page 373).

After the branch trial balance has been translated from francs to dollars, combined financial statements for home office and branch may be prepared as previously illustrated in Chapter 3.

Translation of accounts of foreign subsidiaries

In the translation of a foreign subsidiary's financial statements from the local currency to United States dollars prior to consolidation with the United States parent, techniques comparable to those used for translation of branches are appropriate. Under the monetary/nonmonetary method of translation, monetary assets and liabilities of the foreign subsidiary other than intercompany items are translated at the current exchange rate; nonmonetary assets and liabilities and stockholders' equity accounts are translated at appropriate historical rates. The foreign subsidiary's nonintercompany revenue and expenses other than depreciation, amortization, and cost of goods sold are translated at average exchange rates. The latter three expenses are translated at appropriate historical rates.

All intercompany receivables, payables, revenue, and expenses in the foreign subsidiary's accounts are translated at the United States dollar amounts in the comparable United States parent company accounts. This technique represents a "shortcut" translation of the subsidiary's accounts at appropriate exchange rates.

If the foreign subsidiary is not consolidated with the United States parent company, the same translation techniques described above are necessary before the parent company accounts for the foreign subsidiary's operations under the equity method of accounting described in Chapter 6.

Footnote disclosures of foreign currency matters

In **Statement of Financial Accounting Standards No. 1,** "Disclosure of Foreign Currency Translation Information," the FASB provided the following guidelines, which remain in effect until modified by the FASB:

> The FASB has concluded that certain disclosures shall be made in financial statements that include amounts denominated in a foreign currency which

have been translated into the currency of the reporting entity. The amounts may result from transactions, the consolidations of subsidiaries, and the equity method of accounting for investees. The following information shall be disclosed:

a) A statement of translation policies including identification of: (1) the balance sheet accounts that are translated at the current rate and those translated at the historical rate, (2) the rates used to translate income statement accounts (e.g., historical rates for specified accounts and a weighted average rate for all other accounts), (3) the time of recognition of gain or loss on forward exchange contracts, and (4) the method of accounting for exchange adjustments (and if any portion of the exchange adjustment is deferred, the method of disposition of the deferred amount in future years).

b) The aggregate amount of exchange adjustments originating in the period, the amount thereof included in the determination of income and the amount thereof deferred.

c) The aggregate amount of exchange adjustments included in the determination of income for the period, regardless of when the adjustments originated.

d) The aggregate amount of deferred exchange adjustments, regardless of when the adjustments originated, included in the balance sheet (e.g., such as in a deferral or in a "reserve" account) and how this amount is classified.

e) The amount by which total long-term receivables and total long-term payables translated at historical rates would each increase or decrease at the balance sheet date if translated at current rates.

f) The amount of gain or loss which has not been recognized on unperformed forward exchange contracts at the balance sheet date.[16]

The following excerpts from the "accounting policies" notes of recent annual reports of Mobil Oil Corporation and Rockwell International, respectively, illustrate applications of the preceding guidelines:

Mobil Oil Corporation

Foreign Currency Translation

Foreign currency items are expressed in U.S. dollars as follows: (a) nonmonetary items, such as inventories, properties, plants, and equipment, and long-term investments, at exchange rates prevailing when acquired; (b) monetary assets and liabilities, including long-term receivables and long-term debt, at current rates of exchange; (c) reserves, except for depreciation, depletion, and amortization, at exchange rates prevailing when provided; (d) revenues, costs, and expenses, at average rates during the period, except depreciation, depletion, and amortization, which are calculated on the U.S. dollar cost of properties.

When currencies change in value in relation to the dollar, the translation of foreign currency monetary assets and liabilities, including uncompleted forward exchange contracts, may result in a net charge. The charge that is applicable to long-term borrowings, or the net charge, whichever is lesser, is considered to be a part of the cost of these long-term borrowings. As such, it is deferred and amortized over the remaining life of the borrowings. Generally, other gains and losses arising from foreign currency translations are included in revenues, costs, and expenses.

[16] *Statement of Financial Accounting Standards No. 1*, "Disclosure of Foreign Currency Translation Information" (Stamford, Conn.: FASB, 1973), pp. 5–6.

Rockwell International

Foreign Currency Translation

Accounts of foreign subsidiaries and affiliates are translated into United States dollars as follows: Current assets, current liabilities and, beginning in fiscal 1973, long-term debt at year-end exchange rates; property and other non-current assets and liabilities at rates prevailing at dates of transactions; revenues and costs and expenses at average rates during the year except that depreciation and amortization charges are translated at exchange rates prevailing when the related assets were acquired. Beginning in 1973, net gains and losses relating to the translation of foreign currency long-term debt obligations are amortized by the interest method over the remaining life of the debt. Other translation gains are deferred to the extent they exceed previously recorded losses and other translation losses are included currently in consolidated net income.

Concluding comments on foreign currency translation

The example of the monetary/nonmonetary method of foreign currency translation illustrated in this chapter was deliberately simplified to exclude a number of complex unsettled issues which remain to be resolved by the Financial Accounting Standards Board. Among these issues are the following:

1 Should different translation principles be applied for imported inventories, in contrast to inventories acquired locally by a foreign investee?

2 Should different translation principles be applied for imported plant assets, in contrast to plant assets acquired locally by a foreign investee?

3 Are deferred income taxes **monetary** or **nonmonetary** assets or liabilities for purposes of foreign currency translation?

4 How should the income tax allocation problems associated with foreign currency translation be resolved?

The incorporation of logical answers to these questions into a cohesive body of accounting theory poses a substantial challenge to the Financial Accounting Standards Board.

REVIEW QUESTIONS

1 What is a **multinational company?**

2 Identify four of the principal problems that impede the development of internationally recognized accounting standards.

3 Distinguish between the Accountants International Study Group and the International Accounting Standards Committee.

4 Define the following terms associated with foreign currencies:
   a Exchange rate
   b Forward market rate
   c Selling rate
   d Spot rate

5 Today's newspaper listed quoted prices for the Japanese yen (symbol ¥) as follows:
    Buying rate: ¥1 = $0.0032
    Selling rate: ¥1 = $0.0035
How many United States dollars would a United States importer have had to exchange for ¥50,000 at the above prices to settle an account payable in that amount to a Japanese supplier? Explain.

6 On March 27, Year 3, a United States multinational company purchased merchandise on 30-day credit terms from a Philippines exporter at an invoice cost of ₱80,000. (₱ is the symbol for the Philippines peso.) What United States dollar amount would the United States company credit to the Accounts Payable account if the March 27, Year 3, exchange rates for Philippines pesos were as follows:
    Buying rate: ₱1 = $0.1350
    Selling rate: ₱1 = $0.1475

7 How does a United States multinational company *hedge* against the risk of fluctuations in exchange rates for foreign currencies? Explain.

8 Explain the *one-transaction perspective* regarding the nature of an exchange adjustment.

9 What arguments are advanced in support of the *two-transaction perspective* for exchange adjustments? Explain.

10 Should exchange gains or losses be recorded in the accounts prior to collection of a receivable or payment of a liability in foreign currency? Explain.

11 How are substantial exchange adjustments resulting from revaluations or devaluations of a foreign currency presented in financial statements? Explain.

12 Differentiate between the *current/noncurrent* and the *current rate* methods of translating foreign currencies.

13 Present arguments supporting the *monetary/nonmonetary* method of translating foreign currencies.

14 What exchange rate is used to translate the Intercompany Accounts Payable account of a foreign subsidiary of a United States parent company which uses the *monetary/nonmonetary* method of translation? Explain.

EXERCISES

Ex. 10-1 Select the best answer for each of the following multiple choice questions.

    1 In the translation of the financial statements of a foreign branch to United States dollars under the monetary/nonmonetary method, the average exchange rate for the current year should be applied to:
    a Sales
    b Notes payable
    c Home office account
    d Accumulated depreciation

    2 Parent Company acquired 80% of the outstanding stock of Subsidiary Company, which is in a foreign country. In the monetary/nonmonetary method of translating Subsidiary Company's financial statements for consolidated state-

ments, the paid-in capital of Subsidiary Company should be translated at the:
a Exchange rate in effect when Subsidiary Company was organized
b Current exchange rate
c Average exchange rate for the period Subsidiary Company's stock has been owned by Parent Company
d Exchange rate in effect on the date of Parent Company's acquisition of the stock of Subsidiary Company

3 Under the monetary/nonmonetary method of translation, the item or items in a foreign subsidiary's financial statements that should *not* be translated to United States dollars in terms of the current exchange rate would be:
a Sales
b Intercompany accounts payable
c Long-term debt
d Long-term receivables
e Both *a* and *b*
f Both *b* and *c*

4 In the translation of the trial balance of a foreign branch, increases in the translated value of foreign net current assets resulting from an upward fluctuation in the exchange rate should be:
a Credited to a gain account in the income statement
b Charged to a loss account in the income statement
c Offset against prior provisions for unrealized losses, the excess of the increase being credited to a "suspense" account
d Credited to the Retained Earnings account in order to state net income fairly

Ex. 10-2 International Trading Company, a United States multinational company, issued a purchase order to a Netherlands supplier for merchandise at a price of 60,000 guilders (symbol f.). The merchandise was received on 30-day open account on May 1, Year 5; the spot exchange rates for Netherlands guilders on that date were as follows:
Buying rate: f.1 = $0.38
Selling rate: f.1 = $0.40
International Trading Company purchased a draft for 60,000 guilders on May 31, Year 5, for remittance to the Netherlands supplier. On that date, the exchange rates for guilders were as follows:
Buying rate: f.1 = $0.39
Selling rate: f.1 = $0.41
Prepare journal entries for International Trading Company to reflect the above transactions, under the perpetual inventory system.

Ex. 10-3 On August 6, Year 7, Foreign Traders, Inc., a United States company which uses the perpetual inventory system, purchased from a Belgian supplier on 30-day open account goods costing 80,000 francs. On that date, various exchange rates for Belgian francs (symbol BF) were as follows:
Spot rates:
Buying: BF1 = $0.025
Selling: BF1 = $0.029
Forward market rate: BF1 = $0.031
Also on August 6, Year 7, Foreign Traders, Inc., purchased a 30-day forward exchange contract for BF 80,000.
Prepare journal entries to record the August 6, Year 7, transactions described above, as well as the related transactions on September 5, Year 7.

Ex. 10-4 On January 2, Year 6, Marks Company established a branch in a foreign country. In connection with your preparation of combined financial statements for the home office and branch of Marks Company at December 31, Year 6, you note the following accounts in the trial balance of the branch. In addition, you learn

that all transfers of funds from the home office of Marks Company to the foreign branch are executed at the selling spot rate.
1 Sales
2 Home Office
3 Accounts Receivable, Trade
4 Office Equipment (purchased in the United States and paid for in United States dollars)
5 Factory Building
6 Inventory, Dec. 31, Year 6
7 Mortgage Payable on Factory Building (due Dec. 31, Year 16)
8 Inventory, Jan. 2, Year 6 (shipped from home office)
9 Notes Payable to Bank (due Jan. 31, Year 7)
10 Accumulated Depreciation: Factory Building

Following the AICPA recommendations in **Statement of Position on Accounting for Foreign Currency Translation,** indicate at which of the following exchange rates each of the above accounts would be translated into United States dollars:
(1) The selling spot rate at the date of payment, acquisition, or entry in the accounts
(2) The selling spot rate at December 31, Year 6
(3) An average of selling spot rates for Year 6
(4) None of the above (If you select this answer, indicate what rate you would use.)

Ex. 10-5 Intercontinental Corporation, a United States multinational company with subsidiaries in foreign countries, prepares consolidated financial statements which include all subsidiaries. The accounting records and financial statements of the foreign subsidiaries are maintained in the respective local currencies of the countries in which they operate.
a Explain the monetary/nonmonetary basis of translating the subsidiaries' financial statements to United States dollars with respect to each of the following items:
(1) Accounts receivable, trade
(2) Sales
(3) Building
(4) Accrued payroll
(5) Depreciation, building
(6) Intercompany accounts payable to Intercontinental Corporation
b Explain the nature of any difference between the debits and credits of a foreign subsidiary's trial balance after it has been translated to United States dollars.

Ex. 10-6 On June 30, Year 6, Wayland Company, a United States corporation, sold merchandise costing $75,000 to a Portuguese customer, receiving in exchange a 60-day, 12% note for 2,500,000 escudos (symbol Esc). The buying rate for escudos on June 30, Year 6, was Esc 1 = $0.04. On August 29, Year 6, Wayland Company received from the Portuguese customer a draft for Esc 2,550,000, which Wayland Company converted on that date to United States dollars at the buying rate for escudos of Esc 1 = $0.05.

Prepare journal entries for Wayland Company to record the June 30, Year 6, sale (under the perpetual inventory system), and the August 29, Year 6, conversion of the Portuguese customer's Esc 2,550,000 draft to United States dollars.

SHORT CASES FOR ANALYSIS AND DECISION

Case 10-1 Haden Company, a United States multinational company, has a subsidiary in Austria. On April 1, Year 3, Haden Company purchased for $50,000 a draft for

500,000 Austrian schillings (symbol S) and remitted it to the Austrian subsidiary as a long-term, non-interest-bearing advance. The advance was to be repaid ultimately in United States dollars.

You were engaged as independent auditor for the examination of the March 31, Year 4, consolidated financial statements of Haden Company and subsidiaries (including the Austrian subsidiary). On March 31, Year 4, the selling spot rate for schillings was S1 = $0.05. Haden Company's controller translated the Advance from Parent Company account in the Austrian subsidiary's balance sheet from S500,000 to $25,000 (S500,000 × $0.05 = $25,000). Since the $25,000 translated balance of the subsidiary's Advance from Parent Company account did not offset the $50,000 balance of Haden Company's Advance to Austrian Subsidiary account as of March 31, Year 4, Haden's controller prepared the following working paper consolidation elimination for Haden Company and subsidiaries at March 31, Year 4:

Exchange Loss—Austrian Subsidiary	25,000	
Advance to Austrian Subsidiary—Haden		25,000

To record exchange loss resulting from decline in exchange rate for schillings to S1 = $0.05 on March 31, Year 4, from S1 = $0.10 on April 1, Year 3.

Instructions Evaluate the accounting treatment described above.

Case 10-2 Michigan Company, a United States multinational company, has a branch in Hong Kong. The Hong Kong branch purchases locally all its merchandise acquired for resale. The branch sells to Hong Kong customers exclusively, and measures its cost of goods sold by the fifo method.

For many years, the exchange rate between the United States dollar and the Hong Kong dollar (symbol HK$) has remained stable. However, there were substantial fluctuations in the exchange rate during Year 6, as evidenced by the following selling spot rates for Hong Kong dollars on the dates of the Hong Kong branch's purchases of merchandise:

Year 6	Exchange rate
Jan. 2	HK$1 = $0.20
Apr. 1	HK$1 = $0.16
July 1	HK$1 = $0.24
Oct. 1	HK$1 = $0.22
Dec. 31	HK$1 = $0.26

Instructions Discuss the propriety of translating the Year 6 cost of goods sold of Michigan Company's Hong Kong branch to United States dollars at the following alternative exchange rates:
a Historical fifo rates
b Average rate
c Current rate (as of December 31, Year 6)

Case 10-3 The chief accountant of Overseas Company, a United States multinational company, completed the translation of the financial statements of a foreign subsidiary for its first year of operations as follows:

	Local currency	Exchange rate	U.S. dollars	Rate used
Income and retained earnings statement				
Sales	LC10,000,000	$.230	$2,300,000	A
Costs and expenses				
Cost of goods sold:				
Purchases	LC 6,100,000	.215	$1,311,500	A
Less: Ending inventory	1,800,000	.209	376,200	H
	LC 4,300,000		$ 935,300	
Salaries and wages	2,200,000	.205	451,000	A
Depreciation expense . .	2,500,000	.250	625,000	H
Income taxes expense . .	450,000	.200	90,000	A
	LC 9,450,000		$2,101,300	
Income after taxes	LC 550,000		$ 198,700	
Exchange loss (Exhibit A)	-0-		(361,750)	
Net income (loss)	LC 550,000		$ (163,050)	
Dividends	400,000	.200	(80,000)	T
Retained earnings at end of year	LC 150,000		$ (243,050)	
Balance sheet				
Net assets at risk (monetary items)				
Cash	LC 2,800,000	.145	$ 406,000	C
Accounts receivable . . .	2,000,000	.145	290,000	C
Bank loan payable in local currency.	(2,000,000)	.145	(290,000)	C
Income taxes payable . .	(450,000)	.145	(65,250)	C
	LC 2,350,000		$ 340,750	
Net assets not at risk (nonmonetary items)				
Inventory	LC 1,800,000	.209	$ 376,200	H
Plant assets	7,500,000	.250	1,875,000	H
Accumulated depreciation	(2,500,000)	.250	(625,000)	H
Long-term debt payable in U.S. dollars.	(1,000,000)	.210	(210,000)	H
	LC 5,800,000		$1,416,200	
Net assets.	LC 8,150,000		$1,756,950	
Stockholders' equity				
Capital stock (no change during year) . .	LC 8,000,000	.250	$2,000,000	H
Retained earnings	150,000		(243,050)	
	LC 8,150,000		$1,756,950	

A Average rate for the year
C Current rate at end of the year
H Historical rate (rate at date of purchase of subsidiary's capital stock—.250; rate at date of acquisition of plant assets—.250; rate prevailing during accumulation of inventory)
T Transaction rate (rate in effect when dividend paid)

The chief accountant then prepared the analysis of the exchange loss for the year, as shown below.

Exhibit A

Analysis of Exchange Loss Resulting from the Translation Process

	Net monetary assets at risk (local currency)	Exchange loss or (gain) (U.S. dollars)
Net assets at risk (*monetary items*) at beginning of year, and exchange loss (*measured by change in rate from .250 to .145*) during year	LC 8,000,000*	$ 840,000
Additions to net assets at risk during year:		
a Net addition from operations, and exchange loss (*details below*)	1,250,000	266,250

	LC	Exchange rate†	Exchange loss or (gain)
Sales	LC 10,000,000	$.085	$850,000
Purchases	(6,100,000)	.070	(427,000)
Salaries and wages	(2,200,000)	.060	(132,000)
Income taxes	(450,000)	.055	(24,750)
	LC 1,250,000		$266,250

	Net monetary assets at risk (local currency)	Exchange loss or (gain) (U.S. dollars)
b Additional cash resulting from **dollar** financing, and exchange loss (*measured by change in rate from .210 to .145*)	1,000,000	65,000
Reduction in net assets at risk during year (*details below*) . . .	(7,900,000)	(809,500)

	LC	Exchange rate‡	Exchange loss or (gain)
Purchase of plant assets	LC(7,500,000)	$.105	$(787,500)
Payment of dividends	(400,000)	.055	(22,000)
	LC(7,900,000)		$(809,500)

	Net monetary assets at risk (local currency)	Exchange loss or (gain) (U.S. dollars)
Transaction not affecting net assets at risk: Local currency bank loan obtained (*increased cash and increased liability offset*)	–0–	–0–
Net assets at risk (*monetary items*) at end of year, and total exchange loss for year	LC 2,350,000	$ 361,750

* *Cash paid by parent company for subsidiary's capital stock*
† *Difference between average rate used to translate income statement item and current rate of .145*
‡ *Difference between historical or transaction rate and current rate of .145*

Instructions Appraise the chief accountant's translation methods and the analysis of the exchange loss. (Adapted from case prepared by Joseph E. Conner of Price Waterhouse & Co. and published in *Financial Executives Handbook*, pp. 1110–1111.)

PROBLEMS

10-4 Transocean Corporation, a United States multinational company with an April 30 fiscal year, had the following transactions, among others, during March and April, Year 8:

Date	Explanation of transactions	Spot Buying	Spot Selling	Forward market
Year 8				
Mar. 6	Purchased goods from Brazilian supplier on 30-day open account, cost 100,000 cruzeiros (symbol Cr$). Purchased 30-day forward exchange contract for Cr$100,000.	$0.12	$0.13	$0.135
18	Purchased goods from Danish supplier on 30-day open account, cost 75,000 kronen (symbol DKr).	0.16	0.18	0.184
25	Sold goods to Swiss customer on 30-day open account for 50,000 francs (symbol Sfr.). Cost of goods $15,000.	0.36	0.38	0.382
Apr. 4	Purchased goods from Spanish supplier on 30-day open account for 150,000 pesetas (symbol Ptas.).	0.015	0.02	0.025
5	Liquidated Cr$100,000 forward exchange contract, and paid Brazilian supplier for Mar. 6 purchase.	0.11	0.12	0.126
17	Purchased draft for DKr75,000 for payment to Danish supplier for Mar. 18 purchase.	0.17	0.19	0.195
24	Received draft for Sfr.50,000 from Swiss customer for sale of Mar. 25. Exchange draft for U.S. dollar credit to bank checking account.	0.37	0.39	0.393
30	Obtained exchange rate quotation for Spanish pesetas.	0.02	0.025	0.03

Instructions

a Prepare journal entries for Transocean Corporation to record the above transactions in United States dollars, under the perpetual inventory system.

b Prepare the necessary adjusting journal entry or entries for Transocean Corporation at April 30, Year 8.

10-5 On August 1, Year 8, Orient Trading Company, a United States multinational company, established a sales branch in Singapore. The transactions of Orient's home office with the Singapore branch, and the branch's own transactions, during August, Year 8, are set forth below. Following each transaction is the appropriate spot exchange rate for Singapore dollars (symbol S$).

Transactions for August, Year 8

(1) Cash of $50,000 sent to branch (S$1 = $0.45)
(2) Merchandise with a cost of $75,000 shipped to branch at a billed price of $100,000 (S$1 = $0.45)
(3) Rent of leased premises for August paid by branch, S$1,000 (S$1 = $0.45)
(4) Store and office equipment purchased by branch for S$5,000, to be carried in home office records (S$1 = $0.45)
(5) Sales by branch on credit, S$25,000 (S$1 = $0.46). Cost of goods sold S$15,000
(6) Collections of accounts receivable by branch, S$20,000 (S$1 = $0.455)
(7) Payment of operating expenses by branch, S$5,000 (S$1 = $0.47)
(8) Cash remitted to home office by branch, S$10,000 (S$1 = $0.44)
(9) Operating expenses incurred by home office charged to branch, $2,000 (S$1 = $0.445)
(10) Uncollectible account receivable written off by branch, S$1,000 (S$1 = $0.44)

Instructions Prepare journal entries for the home office of Orient Trading Company in United States dollars, and for the Singapore branch in Singapore dollars, to record the above transactions. Both segments use the perpetual inventory system. Round all amounts to the nearest dollar. Omit journal entry explanations.

10-6 Hastings Company, a United States multinational company, acquired Compañia Producción on January 2, Year 3, by the purchase at carrying value of all outstanding capital stock. Compañia Producción is located in Argentina, whose monetary unit is the peso (symbol $A). Compañia Producción's accounting records were continued without change; a trial balance, in pesos, of the balance sheet on January 2, Year 3, follows:

COMPAÑIA PRODUCCIÓN
Trial Balance (pesos)
January 2, Year 3

	Debit	Credit
Cash	$A 3,000	
Accounts receivable	5,000	
Inventory	32,000	
Machinery and equipment	204,000	
Accumulated depreciation		$A 42,000
Accounts payable		81,400
Capital stock		50,000
Retained earnings		70,600
	$A244,000	$A244,000

Compañia Producción's trial balance, in pesos, at December 31, Year 4, follows:

COMPAÑIA PRODUCCIÓN
Trial Balance (pesos)
December 31, Year 4

	Debit	Credit
Cash	$A 25,000	
Accounts receivable	20,000	
Allowance for doubtful accounts		$A 500
Due from Hastings Company	33,000	
Inventory, Dec. 31, Year 4	110,000	
Machinery and equipment	210,000	
Accumulated depreciation		79,900
Notes payable		60,000
Accounts payable		22,000
Income taxes payable		40,000
Capital stock		50,000
Retained earnings		100,600
Sales—local		170,000
Sales—foreign		200,000
Cost of goods sold	207,600	
Depreciation expense	22,400	
Selling and administrative expenses	60,000	
Income taxes expense	40,000	
Gain on sale of assets		5,000
	$A728,000	$A728,000

The following additional information is available:
(1) All of Compañia Producción's foreign sales are made to Hastings Company, and are accumulated in the account Sales—Foreign. The balance in the Due from Hastings Company account is the total of unpaid invoices. All foreign sales are billed in United States dollars. The reciprocal accounts in Hastings Company's records show total Year 4 purchases as $471,000 and the total of unpaid invoices as $70,500.
(2) Depreciation is computed by the straight-line method over a 10-year service life for all depreciable assets, with no residual value. Machinery costing $A20,000 was purchased on December 31, Year 3, and no depreciation was recorded for this machinery in Year 3, There have been no other depreciable assets acquired since January 2, Year 3, and no assets are fully depreciated.
(3) Certain assets that were in the Machinery and Equipment account at January 2, Year 3, were sold on December 31, Year 4. For Year 4 a full year's depreciation was recorded before the assets were removed from the accounts. Information regarding the sale follows:

Cost of assets	$A14,000
Accumulated depreciation	4,900
Undepreciated cost	$A 9,100
Proceeds of sale	14,100
Gain on sale	$A 5,000

(4) No entries have been made in the Retained Earnings account of the subsidiary since its acquisition other than the net income for Year 3. The Retained Earnings account at December 31, Year 3, was translated to $212,000.
(5) The prevailing exchange rates follow:

Dollars per peso

Jan. 2, Year 3	$2.00
Year 3 average	2.10
Dec. 31, Year 3	2.20
Year 4 average	2.30
Dec. 31, Year 4	2.40

(6) The December 31, Year 4, inventory translates to $258,500. Cost of goods sold for Year 4 translates to $481,632.

Instructions Prepare a working paper to translate the December 31, Year 4, trial balance of Compañia Producción from pesos to dollars, under the monetary/nonmonetary method. The working paper should show the trial balance in pesos, the exchange rate, and the trial balance in dollars. Supporting computations should be in good form.

10-7 Continental Trading Company, a United States multinational company, established a branch in Bolivia in Year 2 to purchase local products for resale by the home office and to sell company products locally.

You were engaged to examine the company's combined financial statements for the year ended December 31, Year 9. You engaged a licensed professional accountant in Bolivia to examine the branch accounts. He reported that the branch accounts were fairly stated in pesos (symbol $b), except that a Bolivian franchise fee and any possible adjustments required by home office accounting procedures were not recorded. Trial balances for both the branch and the home office as of December 31, Year 9, appear on page 392.

Your examination disclosed the following information:
(1) The Bolivian peso was devalued July 1, Year 9, from $b1 = $0.25 to $b1 = $0.20. The former exchange rate had been in effect since Year 1.
(2) Included in the balance of the home office's Branch Account was a $4,000 billing for merchandise shipped to the branch December 29, Year 9. The branch did not receive the shipment during Year 9. Home office sales to the branch are marked up 33⅓% on cost and shipped FOB home office. Branch sales to home office are made at branch cost. There were no seasonal fluctuations in branch sales to outsiders during the year.
(3) The branch had a beginning and ending inventory valued at fifo cost of $b80,000 (exclusive of the amount in (2), above), of which one-half at each date had been acquired from the home office. The home office had a December 31, Year 9, inventory valued at fifo cost of $520,000.
(4) The Branch Account balance is the unamortized portion of a $15,000 fee paid in January, Year 8, to a United States firm for marketing research for the branch. Currency restrictions prevented the branch from paying the fee, which was paid by the home office. The home office agreed to accept merchandise from the branch over a five-year period, during which the fee is to be amortized.
(5) The government of Bolivia imposes a franchise fee of 10 pesos per 100 pesos of net income before franchise fee of the branch, in exchange for certain exclusive trading rights granted to the branch. The fee is payable each May 1 for the preceding calendar year's trading rights; it had not been recorded by the branch at December 31, Year 9.

CONTINENTAL TRADING COMPANY
Home Office and Branch
Trial Balances
December 31, Year 9

	Branch (pesos) dr (cr)	Home office (dollars) dr (cr)
Cash	$b 110,000	$ 90,000
Accounts receivable, trade	150,000	160,000
Inventory, Jan. 1, Year 9	80,000	510,000
Prepaid expenses	-0-	18,000
Investment in branch	-0-	10,000
Branch account.	-0-	12,000
Property and equipment	1,000,000	750,000
Accumulated depreciation	(650,000)	(350,000)
Current liabilities	(220,000)	(240,000)
Long-term debt	(230,000)	(200,000)
Home office	(30,000)	-0-
Capital stock	-0-	(300,000)
Retained earnings, Jan. 1, Year 9	-0-	(145,000)
Sales	(1,680,000)	(4,035,000)
Intracompany sales	-0-	(160,000)
Purchases	1,180,000	3,010,000
Intracompany purchases	-0-	140,000
Depreciation expense	100,000	50,000
Other operating expenses	190,000	680,000
	$b -0-	$ -0-

Instructions Prepare a working paper to combine the income statement and balance sheet of Continental Trading Company's home office and Bolivian branch, with all amounts stated in United States dollars under the monetary/nonmonetary method of translation. Formal combined financial statements are not required. Do not prepare formal adjusting journal entries or working paper combination eliminations; instead, explain the adjustments and eliminations, including supporting computations, at the bottom of the working paper. Disregard income taxes.

The following columnar headings are suggested for your working paper:
Branch trial balance (in pesos):
    Unadjusted—dr (cr)
    Adjustments—dr (cr)
    Adjusted—dr (cr)
Exchange rate
Branch trial balance (in dollars)—dr (cr)
Home office trial balance (in dollars):
    Unadjusted—dr (cr)
    Adjustments—dr (cr)
    Adjusted—dr (cr)
Combination eliminations—increase (decrease)
Combined income statement—dr (cr)
Combined balance sheet—dr (cr)

10-8 Individual financial statements of Polestar Company, a United States multinational company, and its two subsidiaries for the year ended December 31, Year 6, appear on page 394. ($ is the symbol for the Mexican peso as well as for the United States dollar.)

Additional data regarding the companies follow:

(1) On December 31, Year 5, Polestar Company acquired 900 of the 1,000 issued and outstanding shares of capital stock of United States Subsidiary for $9,000, and all 1,000 shares of the issued and outstanding capital stock of Mexico Subsidiary for $12,000. The tangible and identifiable intangible net assets of both investee companies were fairly valued at their carrying values on December 31, Year 5. Polestar Company planned to use the equity method of accounting for its investments in both subsidiaries.

(2) Both of Polestar Company's subsidiaries depreciate plant assets on the straight-line basis over 10-year service lives, with no residual values. None of the subsidiaries' plant assets were fully depreciated at December 31, Year 5, or at December 31, Year 6. There were no additions to or retirements of Mexico Subsidiary's plant assets during Year 6.

(3) On December 31, Year 6, Polestar Company shipped merchandise billed at $4,000 to United States Subsidiary.

(4) On December 18, Year 6, United States Subsidiary declared a dividend of $1 per share, payable January 16, Year 7, to stockholders of record January 10, Year 7.

(5) Exchange rates for the Mexican peso were as follows:

Dec. 31, Year 5, through Mar. 31, Year 6 . . . . $U.S. 0.12

Apr. 1, Year 6, through Dec. 31, Year 6 . . . . $U.S. 0.08

Instructions

a Prepare a working paper to translate Mexico Subsidiary's financial statements from Mexican pesos to United States dollars, under the monetary/nonmonetary method of translation. Use **weighted** average of exchange rates where appropriate. Translate the Mexican Subsidiary's inventory at $U.S. 7,885, and its cost of goods sold at $U.S. 31,500.

b Prepare necessary adjusting journal entries for Polestar Company and for the United States Subsidiary at December 31, Year 6.

c Prepare consolidating financial statements working papers, and related consolidation eliminations, for Polestar Company and subsidiaries at December 31, Year 6. Your working papers should reflect the translated balances in **a** and the adjustments in **b.** Disregard income taxes in your solution.

POLESTAR COMPANY AND SUBSIDIARIES
Financial Statements
Year Ended December 31, Year 6

	Polestar Company (dollars)	United States Subsidiary (dollars)	Mexico Subsidiary (pesos)
Income statement			
Revenue			
Sales	$400,000	$21,000	$381,000
Intercompany sales—United States			
Subsidiary	10,000	–0–	–0–
	$410,000	$21,000	$381,000
Costs and expenses			
Cost of goods sold	$300,000	$15,000	$300,000
Intercompany cost of goods sold	7,500	–0–	–0–
Depreciation expense	3,000	550	17,500
Selling expenses	34,500	2,400	16,500
General and administrative expenses	35,000	1,650	18,000
Income taxes expense	15,000	400	15,000
	$395,000	$20,000	$367,000
Net income	$ 15,000	$ 1,000	$ 14,000
Statement of retained earnings			
Retained earnings, Jan. 1, Year 6	$ 25,000	$ 2,000	$ 7,000
Net income	15,000	1,000	14,000
	$ 40,000	$ 3,000	$ 21,000
Dividends	–0–	1,000	–0–
Retained earnings, Dec. 31, Year 6	$ 40,000	$ 2,000	$ 21,000
Balance sheet			
Assets			
Cash	$ 10,000	$ 1,500	$ 10,000
Accounts receivable	30,000	8,000	35,000
Intercompany receivables (payables)	4,000	(900)	–0–
Inventory	20,000	–0–	83,000
Investment in United States Subsidiary	9,000	–0–	–0–
Investment in Mexico Subsidiary	12,000	–0–	–0–
Property, plant, and equipment	45,000	5,500	175,000
Accumulated depreciation	(15,000)	(2,000)	(75,000)
	$115,000	$12,100	$228,000
Liabilities & stockholders' equity			
Accounts payable	$ 25,000	$ –0–	$ 7,000
Dividends payable	–0–	100	–0–
Long-term debt	–0–	–0–	100,000
Capital stock, 1,000 shares	50,000	10,000	100,000
Retained earnings	40,000	2,000	21,000
	$115,000	$12,100	$228,000

11

Bankruptcy and corporate reorganization

Business failures are a common occurrence in the United States economy. According to the national credit rating company, Dun & Bradstreet, Inc., there were nearly 10,000 business failures in 1972—a number representing 0.4% of the approximately 2.5 million concerns in business that year.[1] Another measure of the extent of business failures is found in the report that approximately 176,000 businesses and persons entered bankruptcy proceedings in the first 11 months of 1974.[2] As might be expected, mismanagement is the most commonly cited cause of business failures.

The situation which precedes the typical business failure is inability to pay liabilities as they become due. Unsecured creditors often resort to lawsuits to satisfy their unpaid claims against a company. Secured creditors may force foreclosure proceedings for real property or may repossess personal property covered by a secured transaction. The Internal Revenue Service may seize the properties of a business enterprise which has failed to pay payroll taxes withheld from employees.

A business may be unable to pay its liabilities as they become due even though the fair values of its assets exceed its liabilities. For example, a company may experience a severe cash shortage in times of "double-digit" price inflation because of the lag between the purchase or produc-

---

[1] U.S. Department of Commerce, *Pocket Data Book: U.S.A. 1973* (Washington: U.S. Government Printing Office, 1973), p. 242.
[2] *Los Angeles Times,* January 9, 1975.

tion of goods at inflated costs and the recovery of the inflated costs through increased selling prices.

More typical of the failing business than the conditions described in the preceding paragraph is the state of *insolvency,* which is defined in the United States Bankruptcy Act as follows:

> A person shall be deemed insolvent within the provisions of this Act whenever the aggregate of his property, exclusive of any property which he may have conveyed, transferred, concealed, removed, or permitted to be concealed or removed, with intent to defraud, hinder, or delay his creditors, shall not at a fair valuation be sufficient in amount to pay his debts.[3]

The terms *insolvent* and *bankrupt* are often used as interchangeable adjectives. Such usage is technically incorrect; *insolvent* refers to a person's or company's financial condition, while *bankrupt* refers to a legal state. In this chapter we shall discuss various legal and accounting issues associated with bankruptcy, as well as with arrangements with creditors and corporate reorganizations.

BANKRUPTCY

Article 1, Section 8 of the Constitution of the United States gives Congress the power to establish uniform laws on the subject of bankruptcies throughout the United States. For the first eighty-nine years under the Constitution, the United States had a national bankruptcy law for only a total of sixteen years—1800 to 1803, 1841 to 1843, and 1867 to 1878. During the periods in which national bankruptcy laws were not in effect, state laws on insolvency prevailed. In 1898 the present Bankruptcy Act was first enacted; it has been amended frequently and extensively since that time. Enactment of the Bankruptcy Act in effect caused state laws on insolvency to be relatively dormant.

Composition of the Bankruptcy Act

The Bankruptcy Act presently contains fourteen effective chapters. The first seven chapters of the Act cover ordinary bankruptcy. Chapter 8 of the Act, entitled "Provisions for the Relief of Debtors," now has only one effective section: Section 77, titled "Reorganization of Railroads Engaged in Interstate Commerce." Chapter 9 of the Act deals with the composition of indebtedness of certain taxing agencies or instrumentalities. Chapters 10 and 11 of the Act, which will be covered in the final sections of this chapter, deal with corporate reorganizations and arrangements, respectively. The three remaining chapters of the Bankruptcy Act are as follows: Chapter 12, "Real Property Arrangements by Persons Other than Corporations"; Chapter 13, "Wage Earners' Plans"; and Chapter 14, "Maritime

[3]U.S. *Bankruptcy Act,* sec. 1(19).

Commission Liens." Chapters 8, 9, 12, 13, and 14 of the Act are very specialized and will not be covered in this discussion.

Section 2075 of Title 28, Chapter 131 of the U.S. Code provides that the United States Supreme Court may prescribe by general rules the various legal practices and procedures under the Bankruptcy Act. Thus, the Bankruptcy Rules constitute important interpretations of provisions of the Bankruptcy Act.

Ordinary bankruptcy

The legal process known as *ordinary bankruptcy* involves the liquidation of the assets of a bankrupt individual or business enterprise and the distribution of the cash proceeds to the bankrupt's creditors. Creditors having security interests collateralized by specific assets of the debtor are entitled to obtain satisfaction of their claims from the assets pledged as collateral. The Bankruptcy Act provides for priority treatment for certain other unsecured creditors; their claims are satisfied in full, if possible, from proceeds of realization of the debtor's noncollateralized assets. Unsecured creditors without priority receive *dividends,* in proportion to the amounts of their claims, from the remaining proceeds of liquidation of the debtor's assets.

Voluntary Petition Sections 4a and 59a of the Bankruptcy Act provide that any "person," except a municipal, railroad, insurance, or banking corporation, or a savings and loan association, may file a petition in a federal district court to be adjudged a *voluntary bankrupt.* The official form for a voluntary bankruptcy petition must be accompanied by supporting schedules of the petitioner's debts and property. The debts are classified as follows: (1) creditors having priority; (2) creditors holding security; and (3) creditors having unsecured claims without priority. The debtor's property is reported as follows: real property; personal property; property not otherwise scheduled; and property claimed as exempt. Valuations of property are at *market* or *current fair values.* Also accompanying the voluntary bankruptcy petition is a *statement of affairs* (not to be confused with the *accounting* statement of affairs illustrated in a subsequent section of this chapter), which contains a series of questions to be answered by the debtor concerning all aspects of his financial condition and operations.

Creditors Having Priority Section 64 of the Bankruptcy Act provides that the following debts are to have priority over other unsecured debts, and are to be paid in full out of bankrupt estates before any dividends are paid to other unsecured creditors:

1 Costs and expenses of administering the bankrupt estate
2 Unpaid wages and commissions not in excess of $600 per claimant, earned

by employees within three months before the date of filing of the voluntary petition

3 Costs incurred by creditors in successfully opposing the discharge of a bankrupt, or in providing evidence, leading to conviction, of crime committed by the bankrupt during the bankruptcy proceeding

4 Taxes owed to the United States or to any state or subdivision thereof, unless the taxes are released by a discharge in bankruptcy

5 Debts, other than for taxes, having priority under United States law (for example, amounts owed to agencies of the United States), and rent owed to a lessor entitled to priority under applicable state law

Property Claimed as Exempt Certain property of a bankruptcy petitioner is not includable in the bankruptcy estate. Section 6 of the Bankruptcy Act excludes from coverage of the Act the various allowances provided in the laws of the United States or of the state of the bankrupt's residence. Typical of these allowances are residential property exemptions provided by homestead laws and exemptions for life insurance policies payable on death to the spouse or a relative of the bankrupt.

Involuntary Petition If a debtor other than the types excluded in the Bankruptcy Act owes unpaid amounts to twelve or more unsecured creditors who are not employees, relatives, stockholders, or other "insiders," three or more of the creditors having unsecured claims aggregating $500 or more may file in a federal district court a creditor's petition for bankruptcy, also known as an *involuntary petition.* If less than twelve creditors are involved, one or more creditors having unsecured claims of $500 or more in the aggregate may file the petition. Excluded from the involuntary bankruptcy petition process are wage earners earning $1,500 or less per year, farmers, savings and loan associations, and municipal, railroad, insurance, or banking corporations. The petitioning creditors must claim that the debtor owes debts aggregating $1,000 or more, and that the debtor committed an *act of bankruptcy* within four months preceding the filing of the petition.[4]

Acts of Bankruptcy Sections 3a and 60 of the Bankruptcy Act identify six *acts of bankruptcy* by a debtor, as follows:

1 Concealing, removing, or permitting to be concealed or removed, any part of the debtor's assets, in order to hinder, delay, or defraud creditors; or fraudulently making or allowing a transfer of property

2 Transferring assets to a creditor while the debtor is insolvent, with the objective of enabling the creditor to obtain a greater percentage of the unpaid claim than some other creditor of the same classification (Such a transfer of assets is called a *preference.*)

3 Permitting a creditor to obtain a lien upon any part of the debtor's property while the debtor is insolvent, and not having discharged the lien on a timely basis

[4] *Ibid.,* secs. 3b, 4b, 59b, 59e.

4 Making a general assignment of assets to a trustee; the assets to be converted by the trustee into cash for the benefit of creditors

5 Permitting or initiating, while the debtor is insolvent or unable to pay debts as they mature, the appointment of a receiver or trustee to take charge of the debtor's property

6 Admitting in writing an inability to pay debts and a willingness to be adjudged a bankrupt

Role of court in ordinary bankruptcy

The federal district court in which a voluntary or involuntary petition for bankruptcy is filed oversees all aspects of the bankruptcy proceedings.

The officer of the court in charge of the bankruptcy proceedings is the *referee.* Referees are appointed for a six-year term by the judges of bankruptcy courts. Jurisdiction and duties of referees are set forth in Sections 38 and 39 of the Bankruptcy Act.

Adjudication One of the first acts of the referee is to either dismiss or *adjudicate* the voluntary or involuntary bankruptcy petition. *Adjudication* is defined as the determination, whether by decree or by operation of law, that a person or a business enterprise is a bankrupt.[5] The filing of a voluntary petition in bankruptcy is in effect adjudication;[6] in an involuntary petition, adjudication is made by the referee after a hearing at which the debtor may attempt to refute the creditor's charges that the debtor committed an act of bankruptcy.[7] Any suits which are pending against a debtor for whom a voluntary or involuntary bankruptcy petition is filed are *stayed* until adjudication or dismissal of the petition; after adjudication, such suits are further stayed until the question of the bankrupt's *discharge* is determined by the court.[8]

Receiver Before or after adjudication, a *receiver* may be appointed by the bankruptcy court to preserve the assets of a bankrupt's estate and protect the interest of creditors therein. The receiver, like the referee, is an officer of the bankruptcy court. A receiver, as instructed by the court, may take possession of, but not title to, the property of a bankrupt, conduct the business of the bankrupt, or represent the bankrupt estate in any legal proceeding.[9]

Accounting duties of the receiver include taking an inventory of the bankrupt's property (unless an inventory was filed with the bankruptcy petition), maintaining records of cash and properties received and disposed of, and reporting on the financial condition and administration of

---

[5] *Ibid.,* sec. 1(2).
[6] *Ibid.,* sec. 18f.
[7] *Ibid.,* secs. 3c, 3d, 18d.
[8] *Ibid.,* sec. 11.
[9] *Ibid.,* secs. 2a(3), 2a(5), 11c; Rule 201.

the bankrupt's estate at periodic intervals and at the end of the receivership.[10]

Appraisal of Bankrupt's Estate The bankruptcy court is required under Section 70f of the Bankruptcy Act to obtain an appraisal of all the real and personal property included in a bankrupt's estate. The purpose of the appraisal is to facilitate sale of the bankrupt's property and use of the sales proceeds for dividends to unsecured, nonpriority creditors. Estate property cannot be sold for less than 75% of appraised value without court approval.

Role of Bankrupt's Creditors Within a period of 10 to 30 days after an adjudication, the bankruptcy court must call a meeting of the bankrupt's creditors. At this first meeting of creditors, the presiding referee may allow or disallow creditors' claims which have been submitted. Also at the first meeting, the "outsider" creditors appoint a trustee or three trustees to manage the bankrupt's estate. A majority vote in number and amount of claims of all unsecured and nonpriority creditors present is required for actions by creditors. Creditors must submit their claims within six months after the date of the first meeting of creditors in order for the claims to be allowed against the bankrupt's estate. Creditors must receive from the court at least 30 days notice of the last day set for filing objections to a bankrupt's discharge.[11]

Role of Trustee The trustee elected by the creditors or appointed by the court assumes custody of and title to the bankrupt's nonexempt property, either directly or from a receiver if one had been previously appointed by the bankruptcy court. The principal duties of the trustee are to continue operating the bankrupt's business if directed by the court, liquidate the property of the bankrupt's estate, and pay dividends to unsecured, nonpriority creditors within 10 days after they are declared by the referee.[12] The trustee is responsible for keeping accounting records similar to those described for receivers on page 399.[13]

Dividends to Creditors Dividends are declared by the referee and paid by the trustee to unsecured, nonpriority creditors. Section 65 of the Bankruptcy Act sets out procedures for and timing of dividend declarations.

Discharge of Bankrupt Once the bankrupt's property has been liquidated, all secured and priority creditor claims have been paid, and all possible dividends have been paid to unsecured, nonpriority creditors, the bank-

[10]*Ibid.,* Rule 218.
[11]*Ibid.,* secs. 44a, 55b, 56a, 56b, 57n, 58b.
[12]*Ibid.,* secs. 2a(5), 47a(1), 70a.
[13]*Ibid.,* Rule 218.

rupt may receive a *discharge,* defined as the release of the bankrupt from all unliquidated debts except the following:[14]

1 Taxes which became legally due and owing by the bankrupt to the United States or to any state or subdivision thereof within three years preceding the bankruptcy, including taxes attributable to improper return preparation by the bankrupt

2 Liabilities arising from the bankrupt's obtaining money or property under false pretenses or representations, or willful conversion of the property of others

3 Debts not properly scheduled by the bankrupt in support of the bankruptcy petition, with the creditor accordingly uninformed of the bankruptcy proceedings

4 Debts arising from embezzlement or other fraudulent acts by the bankrupt when acting in a fiduciary capacity

5 Wages and commissions entitled to priority (see pages 397–398) but remaining unpaid

6 Liabilities for amounts furnished to the bankrupt by an employee of the bankrupt, to secure performance of terms of the employment contract

7 Amounts due for alimony or child support

8 Liabilities for willful and malicious injuries to the person or property of others [other than the conversion described in (*2*), above][15]

A bankrupt will not be discharged if any crimes, misstatements, or other malicious acts were committed by the bankrupt in connection with the court proceedings. In addition, a bankrupt will not be discharged if the current bankruptcy petition was filed within 6 years of a previous bankruptcy discharge to the same bankrupt.[16]

Role of the accountant in ordinary bankruptcy

The accountant's role in ordinary bankruptcy proceedings is concerned with proper reporting of the financial condition of the debtor company, and adequate accounting and reporting for the receiver or trustee for the bankrupt's estate.

Financial condition of debtor company: the statement of affairs

A company which enters ordinary bankruptcy proceedings is a *quitting concern,* not a *going concern.* Consequently, the balance sheet, which reports the financial position of a going concern, is inappropriate for a business enterprise in bankruptcy.

The financial statement designed by accountants for a concern entering bankruptcy is the *statement of affairs* (not to be confused with the legal bankruptcy form with the same title described on page 397). The purpose of the statement of affairs is to present the assets and liabilities of the company from a *liquidation* viewpoint, since liquidation is the outcome

[14] *Ibid.,* sec. 1(15).
[15] *Ibid.,* sec. 17a.
[16] *Ibid.,* sec. 14c.

of ordinary bankruptcy. Accordingly, assets in the statement of affairs are valued at *current fair values;* carrying values of assets are presented only on a memorandum basis. In addition, assets and liabilities in the statement of affairs are classified according to the rankings and priorities set forth in the Bankruptcy Act; the current/noncurrent classification used in a balance sheet for a going concern is not appropriate.

Illustration of Statement of Affairs The balance sheet of Sanders Company at June 30, Year 4, the date the company filed a voluntary bankruptcy petition, appears on page 403.

Other information available from notes to financial statements and from estimates of current fair values of assets follows:

1 Notes receivable with a face amount plus accrued interest aggregating $15,800, and an estimated realizable value of $13,300, collateralize the notes payable to Pacific National Bank.

2 Finished goods are estimated to be salable at a markup of 33⅓% over cost, with disposal costs estimated at 20% of selling prices. Estimated cost to complete goods in process is $15,400, of which $3,700 would be cost of raw materials and factory supplies used. Estimated selling prices of goods in process when completed total $40,000, with disposal costs estimated at 20% of selling prices. Estimated realizable values for raw materials and factory supplies not required to complete goods in process are $8,000 and $1,000, respectively. All short-term prepayments are expected to be used up in the course of liquidation.

3 Land and buildings, which have an aggregate appraised value of $95,000, collateralize the first mortgage bonds payable. Machinery with undepreciated cost of $18,200 and estimated realizable value of $10,000 collateralizes notes payable to suppliers with a balance, including accrued interest, of $12,000. Estimated realizable value of the remaining machinery is $9,000, net of disposal costs of $1,000. Estimated realizable value of tooling, after its use in completing the goods in process inventory, is $3,000.

4 Accrued salaries and wages are debts having priority under Section 64 of the Bankruptcy Act.

The statement of affairs for Sanders Company at June 30, Year 4, appears on pages 404–405.

The following points should be stressed in the review of the June 30, Year 4, statement of affairs for Sanders Company:

1 The "carrying value" columns in the statement of affairs serve as a tie-in to the balance sheet of Sanders Company at June 30, Year 4, as well as a basis for determination of expected losses or gains on liquidation of Sanders Company's assets.

2 Assets are assigned to one of three categories: pledged with fully secured creditors, pledged with partially secured creditors, and free. This categorization of assets facilitates the computation of estimated amounts available for unsecured creditors—those with priority and those without priority.

3 Liabilities are ranked into the categories reported by a debtor in the schedules supporting a bankruptcy petition (see page 397): priority, fully secured, partially secured, and unsecured.

4 A *contra,* or *offset* technique is used where the legal right of set off exists. For example, amounts due to fully secured creditors are deducted from the

SANDERS COMPANY
Balance Sheet
June 30, Year 4
Assets

Current assets:

Cash		$ 2,700
Notes receivable and accrued interest, less allowance for doubtful notes, $6,000		13,300
Accounts receivable, less allowance for doubtful accounts, $23,240		16,110
Inventories; at fifo cost:		
Finished goods		12,000
Goods in process		35,100
Raw materials		19,600
Factory supplies		6,450
Short-term prepayments		950
Total current assets		$106,210
Property, plant, and equipment:		
Land	$20,000	
Buildings, less accumulated depreciation, $33,750	41,250	
Machinery, less accumulated depreciation, $32,100	48,800	
Tooling, less accumulated amortization, $2,300	14,700	
Total property, plant, and equipment		124,750
Total assets		$230,960

Liabilities & Stockholders' Equity

Current liabilities:

Notes payable:		
Pacific National Bank, plus accrued interest		$15,300
Suppliers, plus accrued interest		51,250
Accounts payable		52,000
Accrued salaries and wages		8,850
Property taxes payable		2,900
Accrued interest on bonds		1,800
Payroll taxes withheld and accrued		1,750
Total current liabilities		$133,850
First mortgage bonds payable		90,000
Total liabilities		$223,850
Stockholders' equity:		
Capital stock, $100 par value, 750 shares authorized and issued	$75,000	
Deficit	(67,890)	7,110
Total liabilities & stockholders' equity		$230,960

SANDERS COMPANY
Statement of Affairs
June 30, Year 4

Carrying value	Assets	Current fair value	Estimated amount available	Loss or (gain) on realization
	Assets pledged with fully secured creditors:			
$ 20,000	Land	$95,000		$(33,750)
41,250	Building			
	Less: Fully secured claims (contra)	91,800	$ 3,200	
	Assets pledged with partially secured creditors:			
13,300	Notes and interest receivable (deducted contra)	$13,300		
18,200	Machinery (deducted contra)	$10,000		8,200
	Free assets:			
2,700	Cash	$ 2,700	2,700	
–0–	Notes and interest receivable	–0–	–0–	
16,110	Accounts receivable	16,110	16,110	
	Inventories:			
12,000	Finished goods	12,800	12,800	(800)
35,100	Goods in process	20,300*	20,300*	14,800
19,600	Raw materials	8,000	8,000	11,600
6,450	Factory supplies	1,000	1,000	5,450
950	Short-term prepayments . . .	–0–	–0–	950
30,600	Machinery	9,000	9,000	21,600
14,700	Tooling	3,000	3,000	11,700
	Total estimated amount available		$76,100	$39,750
	Liabilities with priority (contra)		13,500	
	Estimated amount available for unsecured creditors		$62,610	
	Estimated deficiency to unsecured creditors . .		32,640	
$230,960			$95,250	

*Estimated selling price $40,000
Less: Estimated "out-of-pocket" completion costs
($15,400–$3,700) . . . . (11,700)
Estimated disposal costs (20% × $40,000) . . (8,000)
Net realizable value $20,300

Carrying value	Liabilities & stockholders' equity		Amount unsecured
	Liabilities with priority:		
$ 8,850	Accrued salaries and wages	$ 8,850	
2,900	Property taxes payable	2,900	
1,750	Payroll taxes withheld and accrued	1,750	
	Total (deducted contra)	$13,500	
	Fully secured creditors:		
90,000	First mortgage bonds payable	$90,000	
1,800	Accrued interest on bonds	1,800	
	Total (deducted contra)	$91,800	
	Partially secured creditors:		
15,300	Notes and interest payable to Pacific National Bank .	$15,300	
	Less: Net realizable value of notes pledged as collateral (contra)	13,300	$ 2,000
12,000	Notes and accrued interest payable to suppliers . . .	$12,000	
	Less: Estimated realizable value of machinery pledged as collateral (contra)	10,000	2,000
	Unsecured creditors:		
39,250	Notes payable to suppliers		39,250
52,000	Accounts payable		52,000
7,110	Stockholders' equity		
$230,960			$95,250

estimated current fair value of the assets serving as collateral; and liabilities with priority are deducted from estimated amounts available to unsecured creditors from the proceeds of asset liquidation.

5 An "estimated settlement per dollar of unsecured liabilities" may be computed by dividing the estimated amount available for unsecured creditors by the total unsecured liabilities, thus:

$$\frac{\$62,610}{\$95,250} = 65.73 \text{ cents on the dollar}$$

The above computation enables the bankruptcy referee to estimate the aggregate dividends which will be available to unsecured, nonpriority creditors in a bankruptcy proceeding.

Some accountants recommend the preparation of a **statement of estimated deficiency to unsecured creditors** as an adjunct to the statement of affairs. This supplementary statement appears unnecessary, however, since the information it contains is included entirely in the "Estimated amount available" column of the statement of affairs. If the balance sheet prepared on the same date as a statement of affairs includes adequate provisions for doubtful accounts and for estimated liabilities, the statement of affairs will be adequate for a comprehensive analysis of the financial condition of the "quitting concern."

Accounting and reporting for receiver or trustee

As pointed out previously in this chapter, Bankruptcy Rule 218 requires a receiver or trustee to keep records of cash and properties received and disposed of for the bankrupt's estate, and to report on the financial condition and administration of the bankrupt's estate at periodic intervals and at the end of the receivership or trusteeship. Traditionally, records and reports proposed by accountants for receivers and trustees have been extremely detailed and elaborate. However, the provisions of Rule 218 are very general; consequently, simple records and reports should be adequate under the Rule. The authors therefore recommend the following with respect to the accountant's performance under Rule 218:

1 Maintenance of the accounting records of the debtor should be continued during the period that a receiver or trustee carried on the operations of the debtor's business.

2 An **accountability** technique should be used once the trustee begins liquidation of the bankrupt's assets. In the accountability method of accounting the assets and liabilities for which the trustee is responsible are recorded in the accounts of the trustee at their statement of affairs valuations, with an offset to a memorandum-type balancing account with a title such as Estate Deficit. Appropriate cash receipts and cash disbursements entries would be made for the trustee's liquidation of assets and payment of liabilities; no "gain" or "loss" account is necessary, since the business in liquidation does not require a statement of operations. Differences between cash amounts realized and carrying values of the related assets or liabilities may be charged or credited directly to the Estate Deficit account.

3 The periodic and final reports of the trustee to the bankruptcy court will be a statement of cash receipts and disbursements, a statement of realization and liquidation, and, for interim reports, supporting schedules of assets not yet realized and liabilities not yet liquidated.

Illustration of Accountability Technique Assume that Arline Wells, the trustee in the bankruptcy proceedings for Sanders Company (see pages 402–406), took custody of and title to the property of Sanders Company as of June 30, Year 4. The accountant for the trustee would make the following entry on June 30, Year 4:

Cash	2,700	
Notes and Interest Receivable	13,300	
Accounts Receivable	16,110	
Finished Goods Inventory	12,800	
Goods in Process Inventory	20,300	
Raw Materials Inventory	8,000	
Factory Supplies	1,000	
Land and Building	95,000	
Machinery	19,000	
Tooling	3,000	
Estate Deficit	32,640	
Notes and Interest Payable		66,550
Accounts Payable		52,000
Accrued Salaries and Wages		8,850
Property Taxes Payable		2,900
Payroll Taxes Withheld and Accrued		1,750
Accrued Interest on Bonds		1,800
First Mortgage Bonds Payable		90,000

To record current fair values of assets and liabilities of Sanders Company, in voluntary bankruptcy proceedings this date.

As the trustee liquidated the Sanders Company assets, the accounting entry would be a debit to Cash, a credit to the appropriate asset account, and a debit or credit to the Estate Deficit account for a loss or gain on liquidation, respectively. Cost of administering the estate would also be charged to the Estate Deficit account.

Statement of Realization and Liquidation The traditional statement of realization and liquidation was a complex and not very readable accounting presentation. A form of realization and liquidation statement which should be more useful to the bankruptcy court than the traditional statement is set forth on page 408. This financial statement is based on the assumed activities of the trustee for the bankrupt estate of Sanders Company during the month of July, Year 4, including operating the business long enough to complete the goods in process.

Sanders Company, in Bankruptcy
Arline Wells, Trustee
Statement of Realization and Liquidation
Month Ended July 31, Year 4

Estate deficit, June 30, Year 4 . . . . $32,640

Assets realized:

	Current fair value, June 30, Year 4	Realization proceeds	Loss or (gain)	
Accounts receivable .	$14,620	$12,807	$ 1,813	
Finished goods inventory	12,800	11,772	1,028	
Goods in process inventory	14,820	15,075	(255)	
	$42,240	$39,654		2,586

Liabilities with priority liquidated at carrying values:

Accrued salaries and wages	$ 8,850	
Property taxes payable	2,900	
Payroll taxes withheld and accrued	1,750	
Total	$13,500	

Estate administration expenses paid 1,867

Estate deficit, July 31, Year 4 . . . . $37,093

An accompanying statement of cash receipts and disbursements for the month ended July 31, Year 4, would show the sources of the $39,654 total realization proceeds, and the dates, check numbers, payees, and amounts of the $13,500 disbursed for liabilities with priority and the $1,867 paid for estate administration expenses.

Concluding comment on ordinary bankruptcy

Ordinary bankruptcy, covered by Chapters 1 through 7 of the Bankruptcy Act, involves liquidation of the bankrupt's estate. In many cases, an insolvent business may be salvaged and put on a sound financial footing if it can defer payment of its debts. Chapter 11 of the Bankruptcy Act, dealing with *arrangements,* enables a business to continue operations under court protection from creditor lawsuits, while it formulates a plan to pay its debts. Arrangements are discussed in the following section.

ARRANGEMENTS

An *arrangement* is defined in Chapter 11 of the Bankruptcy Act as any plan of a debtor for the settlement, satisfaction, or extension of the time of payment of his unsecured debts, upon any terms.[17] An arrangement includes provisions modifying or altering the rights of unsecured creditors generally or some class of them, upon any terms or for any consideration.[18]

Petition for arrangement

Although any debtor eligible for ordinary bankruptcy (see page 397) is also eligible to file a petition for an arrangement under Chapter 11 of the Bankruptcy Act, generally only debtors with no large amounts of debt payable to the public file petitions for arrangements. The petition for an arrangement must state that the debtor is insolvent or unable to pay his debts as they mature. The petition must also set forth provisions of the debtor's proposed arrangement, or must state that the debtor intends to propose an arrangement.

A petition for a corporation debtor includes an exhibit of key components of the corporation's financial position, as well as the supporting schedules and statement of affairs required for an ordinary bankruptcy petition.[19] The court in which the petition is filed has exclusive jurisdiction over the debtor and its property, wherever located, until provisions of the arrangement have been performed.[20] The filing of the petition operates as a stay of the commencement or continuation of any court or other proceedings or the enforcement of any judgments against the debtor or the enforcement of any liens against the property of the debtor.[21]

Appointment of receiver or control by debtor

Section 332 of the Bankruptcy Act provides that the court may, upon the application of any party in interest such as a stockholder or creditor of the debtor company, appoint a receiver of the property of the debtor. The receiver has the power, subject to court control, to operate the business and manage the property of the debtor for as long as the court authorizes. The receiver must file reports with the court as directed. If a receiver is not appointed, the debtor continues in possession and ownership of its property, and continues to operate the business.[22]

Role of creditors

The court must hold a first meeting of creditors not less than 25 nor more than 40 days after the debtor files the petition for an arrangement. The

[17] *Ibid.*, sec. 306(1).
[18] *Ibid.*, sec. 356.
[19] *Ibid.*, secs. 321, 323, 324.
[20] *Ibid.*, secs. 311, 357(7).
[21] *Ibid.*, Rule 11-44(a).
[22] *Ibid.*, secs. 342, 343.

notice of the first meeting is generally accompanied by a copy of the debtor's proposed arrangement and a summary of the debtor's assets, including any appraisals, and liabilities. At the first meeting, the judge or referee of the court receives proof of creditors' claims and may allow or disallow them. The creditors' written acceptances of the proposed arrangement are also received by the court at the first meeting of creditors.[23]

Confirmation of arrangement

If, at the first meeting of creditors, all or a majority of creditors affected by the arrangement have accepted the arrangement in writing, the court confirms the arrangement once the debtor has deposited with a fiduciary funds adequate to pay liabilities with priority, any amounts to be distributed to creditors as part of the arrangement and amounts adequate to cover the costs of the bankruptcy proceedings.[24] Once the arrangement is confirmed, it is binding upon the debtor, upon all creditors whether or not they have accepted it in writing, and upon any person issuing securities or acquiring property under the arrangement. The effect of the confirmation of the arrangement is to discharge the debtor from all unsecured liabilities except as provided for in the arrangement, other than debts not dischargeable in bankruptcy (see page 401).[25]

Although Chapter 11 of the Bankruptcy Act does not require stockholder acceptance of an arrangement in order for the court to confirm it, some state laws or corporate bylaws of the debtor may require such approval. The board of directors of the debtor corporation should submit the plan of arrangement to stockholders for their approval if the plan requires a change in the capital stock structure of the debtor corporation.

Accounting for an arrangement

The accountant for a debtor involved in a Chapter 11 arrangement proceeding must account for all provisions of the arrangement as confirmed by the court.

To illustrate the accounting for an arrangement, assume that Sanders Corporation (see pages 402–406) filed a petition for an *arrangement,* rather than for *ordinary bankruptcy,* on June 30, Year 4. The proposed arrangement, which was approved by stockholders and all unsecured creditors and confirmed by the court, included the following:

1 Deposit of $25,000 with escrow agent, as soon as cash becomes available, to cover liabilities with priority and costs of bankruptcy proceedings.
2 Amend articles of incorporation to provide for 10,000 shares of authorized capital stock of $1 par value per share. The new capital stock to be exchanged

[23] *Ibid.,* secs. 334, 335(1), 336(2), 336(4).
[24] *Ibid.,* secs. 337(2), 361, 362.
[25] *Ibid.,* secs. 367(1), 371.

on a share-for-share basis for the 750 shares of old $100 par value capital stock already issued to shareholders.

3 Extend due date of unsecured notes payable to suppliers aggregating $15,250 for four years, until May 31, Year 9.

4 Exchange 1,600 shares of new $1 par value capital stock (at fair value of $15 per share) for unsecured notes payable to suppliers totaling $24,000.

5 Pay vendors 70 cents per dollar of accounts payable owed.

Illustrative Journal Entries for Arrangement The following journal entries, numbered to correspond with the provisions of the arrangement outlined above, were recorded by Sanders Company in connection with the confirmed arrangement, as cash became available from operations:

(1) *Cash with Escrow Agent*	25,000	
Cash		25,000
Deposit with escrow agent under terms of		
Chapter 11 bankruptcy		
arrangement.		
Accrued Salaries and Wages	8,850	
Property Taxes Payable	2,900	
Payroll Taxes Withheld and Accrued	1,750	
Cash with Escrow Agent		13,500
Escrow agent's payment of liabilities		
with priority as of June 30,		
Year 4.		
Costs of Bankruptcy Proceedings	11,000	
Cash with Escrow Agent		11,000
Escrow agent's payment of costs of		
bankruptcy proceedings.		
(2) *Capital Stock, $100 par value*	75,000	
Capital Stock, $1 par value		750
Paid-in Capital Excess of Par		74,250
Issuance of 750 shares of $1 par value		
capital stock in exchange for 750 shares		
of $100 par value capital stock.		
(3) *Notes Payable to Suppliers, due May 31,*		
Year 5	15,250	
Notes Payable to Suppliers,		
due May 31, Year 9		15,250
Extension of due dates of notes		
payable to suppliers.		

(4) Notes Payable to Suppliers	24,000	
Capital Stock, $1 par value		1,600
Paid-in Capital in Excess		
of Par		22,400
Exchange of 1,600 shares of $1 par		
value capital stock for $24,000		
principal amount of notes payable,		
at agreed-upon current fair value		
of $15 per share.		
(5) Accounts Payable	52,000	
Cash		36,400
Gain from Discharge of		
Indebtedness in Bankruptcy		15,600
Payment of $0.70 per dollar of		
accounts payable to vendors.		

After the arrangement had been carried out, the following journal entry would be appropriate for eliminating the $67,890 accumulated deficit of Sanders Company at June 30, Year 4 (assuming approval of stockholders):

Paid-in Capital in Excess of Par.	63,290	
Gain from Discharge of Indebtedness		
in Bankruptcy	15,600	
Costs of Bankruptcy Proceedings.		11,000
Retained Earnings		67,890
To eliminate deficit at June 30, Year 4,		
and close bankruptcy gain and costs to		
additional paid-in capital.		

The effect of the preceding entries is to show a "clean slate" for Sanders Company as a result of the Chapter 11 bankruptcy arrangement and the write-off of the accumulated deficit existing at the date of the petition for arrangement. The extension of due dates of some debts, conversion of other debts into equity securities, and liquidation of accounts payable at less than their face amount, should enable Sanders Company to resume operations as a going concern. For a reasonable number of years subsequent to the arrangement, Sanders Company should "date" the retained earnings in its balance sheets to disclose that the earnings arose after the arrangement with unsecured creditors.

Footnote disclosure of arrangements

Because of the unusual and pervasive effects of arrangements under Chapter 11 of the Bankruptcy Act, full disclosure in notes to financial statements is essential for the period in which the arrangement was carried out. The following note, from the 1973 annual report of Astrodata, Inc., is an example of such disclosure.

> On December 2, 1970, the Company filed proceedings for an arrangement under Chapter XI of the Bankruptcy Act and was operated under the direction of a Receiver until August 17, 1972. On that date, the court entered an order confirming a Plan of Arrangement between the Company and certain of its creditors and returned control to the Company of its assets, business, and operations, which theretofore had been administered by the Receiver. The court's order became final on or about August 28, 1972.
>
> In accordance with the Plan of Arrangement, the following significant events transpired, the effects of which have been included in the accompanying financial statements [all common stock shares are after the reverse stock split referred to in item (a)]:
>
> (a) On August 3, 1972, the Company's stockholders approved a reverse split of common stock on a one-for-ten basis (fractional shares were redeemed) with no change in the number of authorized shares of common stock without par value of 10,000,000 shares, a Qualified Stock Option Plan for the issuance of up to 300,000 shares of common stock, and the aforementioned Plan of Arrangement.
>
> (b) On or about August 28, 1972:
>
> 1. The 50,000 shares of convertible preferred stock with a par value of $100 per share and their claim to unpaid dividends since the date of issue in the amount of $553,000 were converted to 103,472 shares of common stock.
>
> 2. The Company issued 3,190,394 shares of common stock, warrants for the purchase of 200,000 shares of common stock at $.31 per share, and a $500,000 subordinated note payable due in increasing annual installments from 1974 through 1977 bearing interest at the rate of 1% over prime rate to an investor group for aggregate consideration of $1,500,000.
>
> 3. The Receiver's Certificates of Indebtedness payable to Security Pacific National Bank in the amount of $4,618,000 and accrued interest in the amount of $584,000 were converted to 331,109 shares of common stock and secured notes valued at $307,000. One of the notes stated at $232,000 was noninterest bearing except that early retirement provided for a discount. Accordingly, for purposes of recording the issuance, the principal was reduced by $43,000 to state the note at its present value computed in accordance with the terms of the agreement. All of the notes were paid in full prior to March 31, 1973.
>
> (c) As finally determined by the court on January 31, 1973, the unsecured liabilities at December 2, 1970 were satisfied by the issuance of 206,943 shares of the Company's common stock and $5,000 cash for claims of $100 and less. The total of the recorded liabilities settled in this fashion was $4,581,000. (d) From the proceeds of the stock issuance mentioned in item (b.2), $450,000 was set aside for the payment of unsecured claims of $100 and less [item (c)], certain priority claims, and the expenses of administration under Chapter XI proceedings. After payment of the unsecured claims and the certain priority claims, $187,000 remains toward payment of the maximum expenses of administration. In addition, the court, in approving the Plan of Arrangement, has established as part of the maximum consideration to be used in payment of the administrative expenses, a subordinated note payable in the amount of $100,000 payable in three annual installments plus interest at 1% over prime, and 100,000 shares of the Company's common stock. The expenses of administration have been accrued at the maximum and charged to income over

the period of the bankruptcy proceeding. The consideration is held by the Receiver pending resolution by the court of the distribution of the above to satisfy such administrative claimants. To the extent that the expenses of administration as determined by the court result in issuance of subordinated notes of less than $100,000 or cash payments of less than $187,000, stockholders' equity will be increased. In the event that the full 100,000 shares are not used, they will be issued to the investment group [see item (c) above] for no additional consideration. (e) On March 30, 1973, a majority in interest of the Company's stockholders approved the offset of the cumulative deficit at August 31, 1972 of $25,494,000 against the capital stock account, which offset has been given effect to in the accompanying financial statements.

Retroactive effect has been given to the reverse stock split in the accompanying financial statements.

CORPORATE REORGANIZATION

Chapter 10 of the Bankruptcy Act provides for the court-supervised reorganization of a corporation which is insolvent or unable to pay its debts as they mature. For all but very small corporations, the reorganization is carried out by a court-appointed trustee. Chapter 10 reorganizations are used primarily by large corporations with extensive debt owed to the public. In recent years, a number of widely publicized corporate reorganizations have involved corporations which were victims of "management fraud."

Petition for reorganization

The Bankruptcy Act provides that any one of the following may file a petition for a corporate reorganization:

1 A corporation which is insolvent or unable to pay its debts when they mature
2 Three or more creditors of a corporation, as described in (1), with claims aggregating $5,000 or more
3 A trustee under an indenture for securities of a corporation as described in (1)[26]

The petition must show the reasons why reorganization is required, and why an arrangement under Chapter 11 of the Bankruptcy Act is inadequate for relief.[27] In addition, a petition filed by creditors or by an indenture trustee must state one of the following:

1 That the corporation was adjudged a bankrupt in a pending proceedings in bankruptcy; or
2 That a receiver or trustee has been appointed for or has taken charge of all or the greater portion of the property of the corporation in a pending equity proceeding; or
3 That an indenture trustee or a mortgagee under a mortgage is, by reason of a default, in possession of all or the greater portion of the property of the corporation; or

[26] *Ibid.*, secs. 126, 130(1).
[27] *Ibid.*, sec. 130(7).

4 That a proceeding to foreclose a mortgage or to enforce a lien against all or the greater portion of the property of the corporation is pending; or

5 That the corporation has committed an act of bankruptcy within four months prior to the filing of the petition.[28]

The bankruptcy court judge approves a petition unless dissatisfied as to the petition's compliance with provisions of Chapter 10 of the Bankruptcy Act. If a petition is filed by creditors or by an indenture trustee, the debtor corporation is subpoenaed by the court. The corporation is authorized to contest the allegations of a creditor's or indenture trustee's petition. The judge's approval of a petition operates as a stay of any pending ordinary bankruptcy, mortgage foreclosure, equity receivership, or lien enforcement proceeding against the debtor corporation.[29]

Appointment of trustee

After approval of a petition involving a corporation with debts aggregating $250,000 or more, the bankruptcy court judge appoints one or more trustees for the corporation. Among the powers and duties of the trustee are the following:

1 Prepare and file in court a list of creditors of each class and their claims and a list of stockholders of each class

2 Investigate the acts, conduct, property, liabilities, and business operations of the corporation, consider the desirability of continuing operations, and formulate a plan for such continuance for submission to the judge

3 Report to the judge any facts ascertained as to fraud against or mismanagement of the corporation[30]

Plan of reorganization

The plan of reorganization submitted by the trustee to the bankruptcy court judge is given to the debtor corporation, its creditors, stockholders, and trustees, the Secretary of the Treasury, and the Securities and Exchange Commission. The plan must include provisions altering or modifying the interests and rights of the creditors and stockholders of the corporation, as well as a number of additional provisions.[31] The judge must submit plans involving corporations with more than $3 million of indebtedness to the SEC for review and advisory comment; submission of other plans to the SEC for comment is optional with the judge.[32] Before a plan of reorganization is confirmed by the bankruptcy court, the plan must be deemed *feasible* as well as *fair* and *equitable* to the various creditor and stockholder groups. To be feasible, the plan should afford reasonable

---

[28] *Ibid.*, sec. 131.
[29] *Ibid.*, secs. 133, 136, 141, 142, 143, 144, 148.
[30] *Ibid.*, secs. 156, 164, 167, 169.
[31] *Ibid.*, secs. 171, 216.
[32] *Ibid.*, sec. 172.

prospect of financial integrity and success for the reorganized corporation.

Once a plan of reorganization is approved by the judge of the bankruptcy court, the trustee submits the plan, the judge's opinion thereon,
and the report of the SEC to all creditors and stockholders affected by
the plan. In order for the plan to be confirmed by the judge, two-thirds
of all affected creditors and a majority of the shareholders of a solvent
corporation must approve the plan.[33] Confirmation of the plan of reorganization by the judge serves to make the plan binding upon the
corporation, upon *all* creditors and stockholders of the corporation, and
upon any other corporation issuing securities or acquiring property under
the plan.[34]

Accounting for a corporate reorganization

The accounting problems associated with a corporate reorganization are
similar to those involved in arrangements, as illustrated on pages
410–412. Journal entries are made to reflect write-downs of assets;
reductions of par or stated value of capital stock (with recognition of
resultant paid-in capital in excess of par or stated value); extensions of
due dates of notes payable; exchanges of debt securities for equity
securities; and write-off of a deficit. The journal entries for a Chapter 10
corporate reorganization thus resemble the entries to record a *quasi-
reorganization,* as illustrated in *Intermediate Accounting* of this series. In
essence, the only difference for accounting purposes between a Chapter
10 corporate reorganization and a quasi-reorganization is the authority
for the entries. Chapter 10 corporate reorganization journal entries result
from a directive of the bankruptcy court, while journal entries for a
quasi-reorganization are authorized by action of stockholders.

It is important for the accountant to be thoroughly familiar with the
plan of a corporate reorganization, in order to properly account for its
implementation. The accountant must be careful to avoid charging post-
reorganization operations with losses which arose before the reorganization.

Footnote disclosure of corporate reorganizations

The elaborate and often complex issues involved in a corporate reorganization must be disclosed in a note to the financial statements for the
period in which the plan of reorganization was carried out. The following
illustrative footnote appeared in the 1973 annual report of Anta Corporation, successor to two corporations which were victims of a massive
management fraud.

[33] *Ibid.,* secs. 175, 179.
[34] *Ibid.,* sec. 224(1).

Anta Corporation was formed (effective July 1, 1972) by the reorganization under Chapter X of the Federal Bankruptcy Act of Four Seasons Nursing Centers of America, Inc., and Four Seasons Equity Corporation and their subsidiaries (the reorganized companies). A Court-appointed Board of Directors assumed responsibility for the operations of the Company September 15, 1972.

The Plan of Reorganization provided for the issuance of common stock of the Company at the rate of one share of $1 par value stock for each $7 of unsecured indebtedness (over $200) of the reorganized companies, and for distribution to persons who suffered losses as a result of acquiring for value any stock, warrant or other security of the reorganized companies before July 22, 1970 and who filed a claim for such losses with the Trustee, on a pro rata basis (based on the dollar amount of loss) of one-half the number of shares of common stock issued to unsecured creditors. All previously issued common stock, warrants and options have been canceled under the Terms of the Plan. Creditors who had approved claims against the reorganized companies for work performed or material delivered (Class B-2) were paid in cash in full under the terms of the Plan of Reorganization.

At July 1, 1972 the Company, after reflecting the Plan of Reorganization, owned 26 operating nursing centers, 2 operating child care centers, 22 nonoperating nursing or child care center sites and 33 tracts of undeveloped land.

The Company's consolidated financial statements include the accounts of Anta Corporation and its subsidiaries after giving effect to the Plan of Reorganization as of July 1, 1972. As a result of the Plan of Reorganization, the following adjustments to the historical financial records, on a combined basis, of the predecessor companies were made effective July 1, 1972:

1 Retention by the Trustee of $1,979,614 to pay the estimated cost of the reorganization and $2,531,680 to pay Class B-2 creditors.
2 Retention by the Trustee of title to nonoperating nursing centers located in Canton and Dayton, Ohio (net book value $1,178,000) which were subsequently sold for the benefit of a certain creditor.
3 Recognition of adjustments totaling $8,876,645 to reduce the carrying value of property and equipment and land held for development or sale to the Trustee's estimate of the fair market value.
4 Elimination of the combined stockholders' equity of the reorganized companies.
5 Recognition of stockholders' equity in the Company through issuance of common stock (8,000,000 shares of $1 par value authorized): 3,132,858 shares were issued in settlement of unsecured liabilities totaling $21,933,112 and 1,566,429 shares were issued in settlement of claims of creditor stockholders. Included in issued shares are 88,540 shares which will be issued upon the adjudication of certain pending litigation.

Reorganization compared to an arrangement

Some of the significant differences between a corporate reorganization under Chapter 10 of the Bankruptcy Act and an arrangement under Chapter 11 of the Act are as follows:

1 Only a corporation can reorganize; an arrangement can be carried out by the various classes of debtors eligible for ordinary bankruptcy.
2 Reorganization involves all classes of a corporation's creditors and shareholders; an arrangement involves only unsecured creditors.
3 A trustee is appointed for all but the smallest corporations undergoing re-

organization; in many cases the debtor continues to operate a business involved in arrangement proceedings.

4 Two-thirds of a corporation's creditors must approve a reorganization; a majority of unsecured creditors may approve an arrangement.

5 The Securities and Exchange Commission reviews and advises the bankruptcy court on plans for reorganization. The SEC has no such role in arrangements, although the SEC is authorized to apply to the court to dismiss a Chapter 11 arrangement proceeding and require the petitioning corporation to reorganize under the more stringent provisions of Chapter 10 of the Bankruptcy Act.[35]

Concluding comments

In this chapter we have highlighted the principal aspects of bankruptcy and corporate reorganization, without becoming involved in extensive details of this highly complex area of accounting. An accountant is apt to be exposed to bankruptcy proceedings at some time during his or her professional career; thus a knowledge of the basic legal issues in bankruptcy and corporate reorganization is essential to an understanding of the accounting issues involved. The accountant who serves a company receiver or trustee in bankruptcy proceedings should consult the Bankruptcy Act and legal counsel for guidance in the various accounting matters involved.

REVIEW QUESTIONS

1 Define *insolvency* as that term is used in the United States Bankruptcy Act.

2 What are *Bankruptcy Rules?*

3 Identify the various classes of creditors whose claims are dealt with in ordinary bankruptcy.

4 What are dividends in a bankruptcy proceeding?

5 Differentiate between a *voluntary* and *involuntary* bankruptcy petition.

6 May *any* corporation file a voluntary bankruptcy petition? Explain.

7 What is a *statement of affairs* under the Bankruptcy Act?

8 List the debts having priority over other unsecured debts under the provisions of the Bankruptcy Act.

9 Who may file an *involuntary petition* in ordinary bankruptcy?

10 Identify four *acts of bankruptcy.*

11 Differentiate between the following officers of a bankruptcy court: *referee; receiver; trustee.*

---

[35] *Ibid.,* sec. 328.

12 What are the effects of a *discharge* in bankruptcy proceedings? Explain.

13 What use is made of the accounting financial statement known as a *statement of affairs?* Explain.

14 Describe the *accountability* method of accounting used by a trustee in bankruptcy.

15 What is an *arrangement* under the Bankruptcy Act?

16 Describe the role of stockholders of a bankrupt company involved in Chapter 11 arrangement proceedings.

17 What is a *corporate reorganization* under the Bankruptcy Act?

18 Describe three differences between arrangements and corporate reorganizations under the Bankruptcy Act.

EXERCISES

Ex. 11-1 John Clark owns all of the stock of Clark Corporation. Recently the corporation has been unprofitable. A supplier who in the past sold to Clark Corporation on credit now demands cash on delivery because he believes the corporation is becoming insolvent. Determine whether each of the following legal conclusions is true or false according to general principles of bankruptcy law.
  a Clark Corporation is insolvent in the equity sense if it is unable to meet its debts as they mature.
  b Clark Corporation is insolvent in the bankruptcy sense if its assets valued on the basis of a voluntary sale are less than its liabilities.
  c Clark Corporation cannot be considered insolvent so long as John Clark has adequate personal funds which he can invest in the corporation.
  d Proof of insolvency is itself an act of bankruptcy.
  e If an involuntary petition in bankruptcy should be filed against John Clark charging him with concealing his personal assets with intent to defraud his creditors, proof by John Clark that he was personally solvent at the time the petition was filed would be a complete defense to the action.

Ex. 11-2 Determine whether each of the following legal conclusions is true or false according to the general principles of bankruptcy law:
  a Bankruptcy proceedings may be instituted against any person or corporation, including:
    (1) A married woman
    (2) A municipal corporation
    (3) A banking corporation
    (4) A savings and loan association
    (5) A partnership
  b Classes of claims which have priority under the provisions of the Bankruptcy Act include:
    (6) Expenses of administering the bankrupt estate
    (7) Wages earned within two years before the date of bankruptcy
    (8) Debts of less than $100
    (9) Taxes owed to the United States
    (10) Claims of creditors which have been outstanding for more than two years
  c In order for a person to be adjudged a bankrupt under the Bankruptcy Act:
    (11) He must owe debts totaling more than $10,000
    (12) There must be at least three creditors

(13) A petition in bankruptcy must be filed by a majority of creditors
(14) The creditors must agree to the commencement of bankruptcy proceedings
(15) A petition in bankruptcy must be filed
d Acts of bankruptcy include a debtor:
(16) Making a fraudulent conveyance of property
(17) Intentionally making a preference to one or more creditors
(18) Permitting a creditor to obtain a lien upon any part of his property while he is insolvent
(19) Orally admitting his willingness to be adjudged a bankrupt
(20) Permitting the appointment of a receiver to take charge of his property

Ex. 11-3 The statement of affairs for Andrews Corporation shows that approximately $0.77 on the dollar probably will be paid to unsecured creditors. The corporation owes Jamison Company $23,000 on a note, which includes accrued interest of $940. Inventory with an estimated current fair value of $19,200 was pledged as collateral on the note payable. Compute the amount that Jamison Company can reasonably expect to receive from Andrews Corporation, assuming that actual payments to unsecured creditors consist of 77% of total acknowledged claims.

Ex. 11-4 Compute the amount that will probably be paid to each class of creditors, using the following data taken from the statement of affairs for Ralph Williams, Inc.:

Assets pledged with fully secured creditors (estimated current fair value, $75,000)	$ 90,000
Assets pledged with partially secured creditors (estimated current fair value, $52,000)	74,000
Free assets (estimated current fair value, $40,000)	70,000
Liabilities with priority	7,000
Fully secured creditors	30,000
Partially secured creditors	60,000
Unsecured creditors	112,000

Ex. 11-5 The following information for Hill Publishing Company was gathered by an attorney-accountant retained by a committee of the company's creditors:
a Furniture and fixtures: Carrying value, $70,000; estimated current fair value, $60,500; pledged on a note payable of $42,000 on which unpaid interest of $800 has accrued.
b Book manuscript owned: Carrying value, $15,000; estimated current fair value, $7,200; pledged on a note payable of $9,000; no interest has accrued on the note.
c Books in process of production: Accumulated cost (direct materials, direct labor, and factory overhead), $37,500; estimated cash realizable value upon completion, $60,000; additional out-of-pocket costs of $14,200 will be required to complete the books in process.
  Prepare the headings for the asset side of a statement of affairs and illustrate how each of the three items described above should be shown in the statement.

Ex. 11-6 From the traditional statement of realization and liquidation shown on page 421, prepare a more concise statement of realization and liquidation similar to the one illustrated on page 408:

CONNER COMPANY, IN BANKRUPTCY
Frank Johnson, Trustee
Statement of Realization and Liquidation
For Month of January, Year 2

Assets to be realized:		Liabilities to be liquidated:	
Accounts receivable	$ 7,500	Accounts payable	$30,000
Inventory	12,500	Notes payable	5,000
Equipment	10,000	Interest payable	150
	$30,000		$35,150

Supplementary charges:		Liabilities assumed:	
Administration expenses	2,950	Interest payable	50
Interest expense	50	Assets realized:	
Liabilities liquidated:		Accounts receivable	6,500
Accounts payable	6,000	Inventory	14,500
Liabilities not liquidated:		Assets not realized:	
Accounts payable	24,000	Equipment	10,000
Notes payable	5,000	Net loss	2,000
Interest payable	200		
Total	$68,200	Total	$68,200

Ex. 11-7 In auditing the financial statements of Newley Company as of December 31, Year 10, you find the following items had been charged or credited to the Retained Earnings account during the six months immediately following a Chapter 10 reorganization, which was finalized and made effective July 1, Year 10:

a Debit of $25,000 arising from an income tax assessment applicable to Year 9.

b Credit of $48,000 resulting from gain on sale of equipment which was no longer used in the business. This equipment had been written down by a $50,000 increase in the accumulated depreciation at July 1, Year 10.

c Debit of $15,000 resulting from the loss on plant assets destroyed in a fire on November 2, Year 10.

d Debit of $32,000 representing cash dividends declared on common and preferred stock.

e Credit of $60,400, the net income for the six-month period ending December 31, Year 10.

For each of these items, state whether you believe it to be correctly charged or credited to the Retained Earnings account. Give a brief reason for your conclusion.

SHORT CASES FOR ANALYSIS AND DECISION

Case 11-1 The following news item appeared in *The Wall Street Journal* late in 1974:

M. H. Fishman, 20 Subsidiaries to File Today for Bankruptcy Act Protection

NEW YORK—M. H. Fishman Co. said it and 20 of its subsidiaries will file petitions under Chapter 11 of the Bankruptcy Act tomorrow in the U.S. District Court in the Southern District of New York.

Fishman operates 55 discount and variety stores in the Eastern U.S., under the names Masons, Fishman and Centers Stores.

Under Chapter 11 a company files for court protection from its creditors while it tries to work out a plan for paying its debts.

The company will list consolidated liabilities totaling $18.5 million and assets totaling $22.1 million.

In an affidavit accompanying the petitions, M. L. Polk, chief executive, attributed the company's financial problems to what he called substantial sales difficulties in the last quarter of the year and the operation of a number of unprofitable stores.

Further details weren't available.

For the nine months ended Sept. 28 the company reported net income of $205,000, or 17 cents a share, up from $199,000, or 16 cents a share, for the like 1973 period. Sales were $48.2 million, up from $45 million for the year-earlier period.

The company's stock wasn't traded yesterday. It closed at $1.25 in the previous session on the American Stock Exchange.

Instructions

a Since a parent company and its subsidiaries are separate legal entities, what are the possible reasons for M. H. Fishman Co. and its subsidiaries filing a joint bankruptcy petition under Chapter 11 of the Bankruptcy Act?

b Explain why a corporation whose assets exceed its liabilities and whose sales and net income increased over the year-earlier period would find it necessary to file a bankruptcy petition under Chapter 11 of the Bankruptcy Act.

Case 11-2 Zeta Corporation is insolvent. It has 20 unsecured creditors and 3 creditors who have liens on its assets. Zeta, while insolvent, paid $20,000 to Jones, one of its unsecured creditors, in partial payment of goods sold and delivered by Jones to Zeta six months earlier. Adams, one of the secured creditors, loaned Zeta funds ten months ago and, two months ago, when he knew Zeta was insolvent, obtained from Zeta a security interest in the company's accounts receivable which he duly perfected under applicable state law. Collins, another of the secured creditors, sold Zeta some machinery six months ago and obtained a security interest therein which he has neglected to perfect. Barton, the remaining secured creditor, holds a mortgage on Zeta's plant which he obtained two years ago and which is duly filed and recorded under applicable state law.

Instructions

a Has Zeta committed an act of bankruptcy? Explain.

b Assuming Zeta has committed an act of bankruptcy, how many of its creditors must join in an involuntary petition in bankruptcy? How much in provable claims must such petitioning creditors have? Explain.

c Assume an involuntary petition has been filed against Zeta and Zeta has been adjudicated bankrupt, all other facts recited above remaining the same. Discuss the rights of Adams, Collins and Barton in relation to Zeta's trustee in bankruptcy.

d Assuming Jones received a preference, might the trustee be able to recover the $20,000 from Jones? Explain.

Case 11-3 During your examination of the financial statements of Athens Corporation, you note that as of September 30, Year 5:

(1) Current liabilities exceed current assets

(2) Total assets substantially exceed total liabilities

(3) Cash position is poor and current payables are considerably past due

(4) Trade and secured creditors are pressing for payment and several lawsuits have been commenced against Athens Corporation

Further investigation reveals the following:

On August 31, Year 5, Athens Corporation made a $1,000 payment to Davis on a $20,000 mortgage indebtedness over one year in arrears. The fair value of the mortgaged property on August 31, Year 5, was $35,000.

On September 20, Year 5, a trade creditor, Mann, obtained a judgment against Athens Corporation, which under applicable law constitutes a lien on Athens Corporation's real property.

On September 22, Year 5, Athens Corporation paid a substantial amount to Stanich, a supplier, on an account over one year old.

On September 27, Year 5, Athens Corporation executed and delivered a financing statement to Barajas, a vendor, from whom Athens Corporation had purchased some new machinery six months earlier. Barajas duly filed and perfected the financing statement.

Instructions

a As of September 30, Year 5, did any of the above transactions legally constitute acts of bankruptcy? Explain.

b As of September 30, Year 5, could the creditors of Athens Corporation file an involuntary petition in bankruptcy against Athens if a sufficient number of them having a sufficient amount of claims decide to do so? Explain.

c Independent of your answers to parts *a* and *b,* assume the same facts set out above except that Athens Corporation's total liabilities exceed total assets and that on October 2, Year 5, Athens Corporation filed a voluntary petition in bankruptcy, and a trustee has been appointed.

(1) What are the rights, if any, of the trustee against each of the creditors involved in the four transactions stated in the problem? Explain.

(2) What are the general requirements for creditors to be entitled to vote on and participate in a bankruptcy proceeding? Explain for each of the four creditors involved whether he meets these requirements, and why.

Case 11-4 The Short Corporation, a retail furniture dealer, has been operating at a loss for several years, and it has no new sources of capital. A creditor's committee wishes to determine the loss to the creditors should the company be placed in bankruptcy. You have been asked to review the accounting records of the company.

Instructions

a List the sections and column headings of the statement you would prepare for the guidance of the creditors' committee. Include a brief description of the items which you would include in each section of the statement.

b List the information you would require in order to prepare the statement.

Case 11-5 The following letter was received by Clayton Grimstad, a professor of accounting at a large university, who is frequently consulted on accounting and reporting matters by businessmen and certified public accountants:

Two years ago our client was a wholly owned subsidiary and went through a reorganization, along with its parent corporation, under Chapter 11 of the Bankruptcy Act. Shortly after the reorganization one of the former stockholders acquired all of the stock of the subsidiary and is now operating the business. In the financial statements of his business, he showed in the stockholders' equity section the amount of the additional paid-in capital arising from the reorganization under Chapter 11, and he described it as such. In other words, he called it "Additional paid-in capital arising from reorganization under Chapter 11." The client is now financially sound and is disturbed by the reference to Chapter 11 in his balance sheets. This reference has raised questions in the minds of suppliers and customers. Our question is: How long does our client have to continue labeling this stockholders' equity item as "Additional paid-in capital arising from the reorganization under Chapter 11?"

Instructions Prepare a short memorandum answering the question raised in the letter to Professor Grimstad.

PROBLEMS

11-6 The following information is available at October 10, Year 5, for the Sunset Trading Company, which is having considerable difficulty paying its bills as they fall due:

	Carrying value
Cash	$ 4,000
Accounts receivable, net of appropriate allowance	46,000
Inventory: Net realizable value, $18,000; pledged on	
$20,000 of notes payable	39,000
Plant assets: Current fair value, $67,400; pledged on	
mortgage payable	134,000
Accumulated depreciation	27,000
Supplies: Current fair value, $1,500	2,000
Wages payable, all earned during latest month	5,800
Property taxes payable	1,200
Accounts payable	60,000
Notes payable, $20,000 unsecured	40,000
Mortgage payable, including interest of $400	50,400
Capital stock, $5 par value	100,000
Deficit	59,400

Instructions

a Prepare a statement of affairs using the form illustrated on pages 404–405.
b Prepare a schedule showing the estimated percentage of claims each group of creditors should reasonably expect to receive if the Sunset Trading Company is forced into bankruptcy.

11-7 Woodbury Corporation found itself in financial difficulty because of low sales and poor cost controls. Its stockholders and principal creditors had asked for an estimate of the financial results of the liquidation of the assets, the payment of liabilities, and the dissolution of the corporation. The independent accountant for Woodbury Corporation subsequently prepared the statement of affairs which appears on pages 426–427.

On January 2, Year 4, Woodbury Corporation filed a voluntary petition for bankruptcy under the Bankruptcy Act. Michael Moore was appointed as trustee by the bankruptcy court to take custody of the assets, authorize the payment of creditors, and implement an orderly dissolution of the company. In January of Year 4, the trustee completed the following transactions:

Jan. 2 Recorded the assets and liabilities of Woodbury Corporation in a separate set of accounting records. The assets were recorded at current fair value and all liabilities were recorded at the estimated amounts payable to the various groups of creditors.

Jan. 7 Sold the land and buildings at an auction for $52,000 cash and paid $42,550 to the mortgagee. The payment included interest of $50 which accrued in January.

Jan. 10 Made cash payments as follows:

Wages payable	$1,500
Payroll taxes withheld and accrued	800
Completion of inventory	400
Liquidation expenses	600

Jan. 31 Cash receipts for the period from January 7 to January 31 were:

Collection on accounts receivable at carrying value, including	
$10,000 assigned accounts	$17,500
Sale of inventory	18,000
Sale of Public Service Company bonds	1,200

Jan. 31 Additional cash payments were:

Liquidation expenses	$ 1,250
Note payable to bank (from proceeds on collection of assigned	
accounts receivable)	10,000
Dividend of $0.50 on the dollar to unsecured creditors	30,500

Instructions

a Record the transactions listed above in journal entry form in the records of the trustee.

b Prepare a statement of realization and liquidation for the month of January, Year 4. Use the form illustrated on page 408.

c Prepare a trial balance for the trustee at January 31, Year 4.

11-8 Newton Becker, Inc., advises you that it is facing bankruptcy proceedings. As the company's independent CPA, you are aware of its financial condition.

The unaudited balance sheet of Newton Becker, Inc., at July 10, Year 10, and additional information are presented below:

Assets

Cash	$ 12,000
Marketable securities, at cost	20,000
Accounts receivable, less allowance for doubtful accounts	90,000
Inventory, finished goods	60,000
Inventory, raw materials.	40,000
Short-term prepayments	5,000
Land	13,000
Buildings, less accumulated depreciation	90,000
Machinery, less accumulated depreciation	120,000
Goodwill	20,000
Total assets	$470,000

Liabilities & Stockholders' Equity

Notes payable	$135,000
Accounts payable	94,200
Accrued wages	15,000
Mortgages payable	130,000
Capital stock	100,000
Retained earnings (deficit)	(4,200)
Total liabilities & stockholders' equity	$470,000

Additional information

(1) Cash includes a $500 travel advance which has been spent.

(2) Accounts receivable of $40,000 have been pledged in support of notes payable to banks in the amount of $30,000. Credit balances of $5,000 are

WOODBURY CORPORATION

Statement of Affairs

December 31, Year 3

Carrying value	Assets	Current fair value	Estimated amount available	Loss or (gain) on realization
	Assets pledged with fully secured creditors:			
$ 4,000	Land	$20,000		$(16,000)
25,000	Buildings	30,000		(5,000)
	Total	$50,000		
	Less: Fully secured claims			
	(contra)	42,500	$ 7,500	
	Assets pledged with partially secured creditors:			
	Accounts receivable			
10,000	(deducted contra)	$10,000		
	Free assets:			
700	Cash	$ 700	700	
10,450	Accounts receivable	10,450	10,450	
40,000	Inventory $19,350			
	Less: Cost to			
	complete 400	18,950	18,950	21,050
9,100	Factory supplies	–0–	–0–	9,100
5,750	Public Service Company			
	bonds	900	900	4,850
38,000	Machinery and equipment . . .	18,000	18,000	20,000
	Total estimated amount			
	available		$56,500	$34,000
	Liabilities with priority (contra)		5,500	
	Estimated amount available for unsecured			
	creditors		$51,000	
	Estimated deficiency to unsecured creditors . . .		10,000	
$143,000			$61,000	

netted in the accounts receivable total. All accounts are expected to be collected except those for which an allowance has been established.

(3) Marketable securities consist of government bonds costing $10,000 and 500 shares of Owens Company stock. The market value of the bonds is $10,000; the market value of the stock is $18 per share. The bonds have accrued interest due of $200. The marketable securities are collateral for a $20,000 note payable to bank.

Carrying value	Liabilities & stockholders' equity	Amount unsecured
	Liabilities with priority:	
$ 1,500	Wages payable	$ 1,500
800	Payroll taxes withheld and accrued	800
	Estimated liquidation expenses	3,200
	Total (deducted contra)	$ 5,500
	Fully secured creditors:	
42,000	Mortgage payable	$42,000
500	Mortgage interest payable.	500
	Total (deducted contra)	$42,500
	Partially secured creditors:	
25,000	Notes payable—bank	$25,000
	Less: Assigned accounts receivable	10,000	$15,000
	Unsecured creditors:	
20,000	Notes payable—suppliers	20,000
26,000	Accounts payable	26,000
27,200	Stockholders' equity	
$143,000		$61,000

(4) Estimated realizable value of finished goods is $50,000 and of raw materials is $30,000. For additional out-of-pocket costs of $10,000 the raw materials would realize $59,900 as finished goods.
(5) Short-term prepayments will be exhausted during the liquidation period.
(6) The appraised value of plant and equipment is as follows: Land, $25,000; buildings, $110,000; machinery, $65,000.
(7) Accounts payable include $15,000 withheld payroll taxes and $6,000 due

to creditors who had been reassured by the president of Newton Becker, Inc., that they would be paid. There are unrecorded employer's payroll taxes in the amount of $500.

(8) Wages payable are not subject to any limitations under bankruptcy laws.

(9) Mortgages payable consist of $100,000 on land and buildings, and a $30,000 installment contract on machinery. Total unrecorded accrued interest for these liabilities amounts to $2,400.

(10) Probable judgment on a pending damage suit is estimated at $50,000.

(11) Expenses in connection with the liquidation are estimated at $10,000.

(12) You have not submitted an invoice for $5,000 for the April 30, Year 10, annual audit of Newton Becker, Inc., and you estimate a $1,000 fee for liquidation work.

Instructions

a Prepare a statement of affairs for Newton Becker, Inc., at July 10, Year 10.

b Prepare a working paper which explains the amount of the estimated deficiency to unsecured creditors of Newton Becker, Inc.

11-9 On June 30, Year 6, Dell Mortimer was appointed receiver of Sears Mfg. Company. The company's general ledger trial balance on that date is presented on page 429.

Additional information

(1) Notes receivable of $25,000 were pledged to collateralize the $18,000 note payable to City Bank. Interest of $500 was accrued on the pledged notes and $600 was accrued on the $18,000 note payable to the bank. All of the pledged notes were collectible. Of the remaining notes receivable a $1,000 noninterest-bearing note was uncollectible.

(2) Accounts receivable include $7,000 from Ames Mfg. Co. which is currently being liquidated. Creditors expect to realize $0.40 on the dollar. The allowance for doubtful accounts is adequate to cover any other uncollectible accounts. A total of $3,200 of the remaining collectible accounts receivable was pledged as collateral for the notes payable to Municipal Trust Co. of $6,000 with accrued interest of $180 at June 30, Year 6.

(3) The subscriptions receivable from stockholders for no-par capital stock are due July 31, Year 6, and are considered fully collectible.

(4) Inventory is valued at cost and is expected to realize 25% of cost on a forced liquidation sale after the write-off of $10,000 of obsolete stock.

(5) Land and buildings, which are appraised at 110% of their carrying value, are mortgaged as collateral for the bonds. Interest of $1,820 was accrued on the bonds to June 30, Year 6. The company expects to realize 20% of the cost of its machinery and equipment, and 50% of the cost of its furniture and fixtures after incurring refinishing costs of $800.

(6) Estimated expenses of liquidation are $4,500. Depreciation, prepayments, and accruals have been adjusted to June 30, Year 6.

(7) The company has net operating loss carryovers for income tax purposes of $22,000 for Year 4, and $28,000 for Year 5. Assume the tax rate in effect for those years was 50%.

Instructions

a Prepare a statement of affairs classifying assets according to their availability for secured and unsecured creditors and classifying liabilities according to their legal priority and secured status. The column headings at the bottom of page 429 are suggested for the statement:

SEARS MFG. COMPANY
General Ledger Trial Balance
June 30, Year 6

Cash	$ 14,135	
Notes receivable	29,000	
Accrued interest on notes receivable	615	
Accounts receivable	19,500	
Stock subscriptions receivable	5,000	
Allowance for doubtful accounts		$ 800
Inventory	48,000	
Land	10,000	
Building	50,000	
Accumulated depreciation, building		15,000
Machinery and equipment	33,000	
Accumulated depreciation, machinery and equipment		19,000
Furniture and fixtures	21,000	
Accumulated depreciation, furniture and fixtures		9,500
Goodwill	8,000	
Organization costs	1,600	
Note payable to City Bank		18,000
Notes payable to Municipal Trust Co.		6,000
Notes payable to vendors		24,000
Accrued interest on notes payable		1,280
Accounts payable		80,520
Wages payable		1,400
Payroll taxes payable		430
Mortgage bonds payable		32,000
Accrued interest payable on mortgage bonds		1,820
Capital stock		65,000
Capital stock subscribed		5,000
Retained earnings	39,900	
Totals	$279,750	$279,750

For assets:	Carrying value	Assets	Current fair value	Estimated amount available	Loss or (gain) on realization
For liabilities and stockholders' equity:	Carrying value	Liabilities & stockholders' equity		Amount unsecured	

b Compute the estimated settlement per dollar of unsecured liabilities.

11-10 Pratt Corporation had $105,000 of dividends in arrears on its preferred stock at March 31, Year 20. While retained earnings were adequate to permit the payment of accumulated dividends, the company's management did not wish to weaken its working capital position. They also realized that a portion of the plant assets were no longer used or useful in their operation. Therefore, they proposed the following reorganization, which was approved by stockholders, to be effective as of April 1, Year 20:

(1) The preferred stock was to be exchanged for $300,000 of 5% debentures. Dividends in arrears were to be settled by the issuance of $120,000 of $10 par value, 5%, noncumulative preferred stock.

(2) Common stock was to be assigned a value of $50 per share.

(3) Goodwill was to be written off; property, plant, and equipment were to be written down, based on appraisal and estimates of useful value, by a total of $103,200 consisting of $85,400 increase in Accumulated Depreciation and $17,800 decrease in certain assets; other current assets were to be written down by $10,460 to reduce receivables and inventories to net realizable values.

The condensed balance sheet at March 31, Year 20, is presented below:

PRATT CORPORATION
Balance Sheet
March 31, Year 20

Assets

Cash		$ 30,000
Other current assets		252,890
Property, plant, and equipment	$1,458,250	
Less: Accumulated depreciation	512,000	946,250
Goodwill		50,000
Total assets		$1,279,140

Liabilities & Stockholders' Equity

Current liabilities	$ 132,170
7% cumulative preferred stock, $100 par value ($105,000 dividends in arrears)	300,000
Common stock, no-par value, 9,000 shares outstanding	648,430
Paid-in capital in excess of par: preferred	22,470
Retained earnings	176,070
Total liabilities & stockholders' equity	$1,279,140

Instructions

a Prepare journal entries to give effect to the reorganization as of April 1, Year 20. Give complete explanations with each entry and comment on any possible options in recording the reorganization.

b Prepare a balance sheet at April 30, Year 20, assuming that net income for April was $15,000. The operations resulted in $11,970 increase in cash, $18,700 increase in other current assets, $7,050 increase in current liabilities, and $8,620 increase in Accumulated Depreciation.

11-11 Morocco Corporation is considering dissolution because one of the three stockholders, Turk, cannot get along with the other two, Kane and Levy. At the end of Year 7, Kane and Levy agree to reorganize the corporation into a partnership. The information relative to the reorganization plan follows:

(1) The balance sheet of Morocco Corporation at December 31, Year 7, is shown on page 431.

MOROCCO CORPORATION
Balance Sheet
December 31, Year 7

Assets

Current assets:

Cash		$105,000
Accounts receivable, less allowance of $22,000		135,000
Inventory		225,000
Short-term prepayments		4,500
Total current assets		$469,500
Building, stated at appraisal value determined at December 31,		
Year 7	$125,000	
Less: Accumulated depreciation	27,500	97,500
Investment in land		20,000
Other assets		10,000
Total assets		$597,000

Liabilities & Stockholders' Equity

Current liabilities:

Note payable to Turk, a stockholder		$ 30,000
Accounts payable		110,000
Accrued liabilities		32,000
Total current liabilities		$172,000

Stockholders' equity:

Preferred stock—par value, $100 (entitled to $110 in liquidation); authorized, 1,000 shares; in treasury, 400 shares; outstanding, 600 shares	$100,000	
Common stock, no-par; authorized, 200,000 shares; issued and outstanding, 100,000 shares; stated at value of $1 per share	100,000	
Paid-in capital in excess of stated value	150,000	
Total paid-in capital	$350,000	
Appraisal capital arising from appraisal of building at December 31, Year 7	50,000	
Retained earnings	72,250	
Subtotal	$472,250	
Less: Treasury stock, 400 shares of preferred (at cost)	47,250	425,000
Total liabilities & stockholders' equity		$597,000

(2) The capital stock records of Morocco Corporation at December 31, Year 7, indicate that there are three stockholders who have retained their respective interests since corporate organization five years ago as follows:

Stockholder	Total invested	Preferred		Common	
		Shares	Amount	Shares	Amount
Kane	$115,000	300	$30,000	35,000	·$ 85,000
Levy	105,000	100	10,000	40,000	95,000
Turk	90,000	200	20,000	25,000	70,000
Total	$310,000	600	$60,000	100,000	$250,000

(3) In accordance with a reorganization agreement, the corporation will acquire Turk's stock and thereafter the corporation will be dissolved by an appropriate disposition of its net assets.

(4) In order to finance the acquisition of Turk's stock interest, the building was appraised as a basis for an $80,000 mortgage loan arranged by the corporation with an insurance company. The appraisal was made at December 31, Year 7, and was recorded in the accounting records as follows:

	Appraisal	Cost	Appraisal capital
Building	$125,000	$70,000	$55,000
Accumulated depreciation . .	27,500	22,500	5,000
Total	$ 97,500	$47,500	$50,000

(5) Turk's stock is to be acquired by the cash payment of $110 per share for the preferred stock and $3 per share for the common stock. The stock acquired from Turk is to be canceled.

(6) After acquisition of Turk's stock, disposition of the net assets of the corporation in complete liquidation and dissolution is to be made as follows:

a The note payable to Turk is to be paid in cash.

b The investment in land is to be transferred to Levy at its fair value of $36,000.

c The remaining assets are to be acquired and the liabilities (including the $80,000 mortgage) are to be assumed by a partnership organized by Kane and Levy. Kane is to withdraw cash from the partnership as necessary to equalize his capital account with that of Levy.

Instructions Prepare a working paper giving effect to the reorganization of the Morocco Corporation into a partnership as of December 31, Year 7, in accordance with the agreement among the three stockholders. Use the following columnar headings in the working paper:

Accounts	Morocco Corporation balance sheet Dec. 31, Year 7	Transactions to carry out reorganization	Kane and Levy balance sheet Dec. 31, Year 7

12

Installment sales and consignments

INSTALLMENT SALES

Although the concept of the installment sale was first developed in the field of real estate and for high-priced durable goods such as automobiles, it has spread through nearly every sector of the economy. Almost all single-family residences are sold on the installment plan, with monthly payments extending as long as 25 to 30 years. Installment sales also are very widely used by dealers in home furnishings and appliances and in farm equipment. For these products the installment payments are usually due monthly for periods of from 6 to 36 months.[1]

For many types of business, the technique of installment sales has been a key factor in achieving large-scale operation. The automobile industry, for example, could hardly have developed to anything like its present size without the use of installment sales. The huge volume of output achieved by the auto industry has in turn made possible economies in tooling, production, and distribution which could not have been achieved on a small scale of operation. Credit losses are often increased when a business adopts an installment sales plan but this disadvantage is generally more than offset by the expanded sales volume.

To the accountant, installment sales pose some puzzling problems. The most basic of these issues is the matching of costs and revenue.

[1] In the middle of 1973, the installment debt of consumers in the United States was $167 billion, including $48.5 billion owed on installment purchases of automobiles. In contrast, the total installment debt of consumers 25 years earlier was only $9 billion.

Should the gross profit from an installment sale be treated as revenue in the period the sale occurs, or should it be spread over the life of the installment contract? What should be done with costs which occur in periods subsequent to the sale? How should defaults and repossessions be handled?

Regardless of the accounting issues raised by installment sales, we can assume that installment contracts will continue to be a major element in the economy. The accountant, therefore, must examine the issues and develop the most effective techniques possible for measuring, controlling, and reporting installment sales. As we progress through this chapter, it will be apparent that installment sales are one of the many thorny problems confronting the accounting profession as it searches for a consistent set of universally useful accounting standards.

Special characteristics of installment sales

An installment sale is a sale of real or personal property or services which provides for a series of payments over a period of months or years. A down payment is usually but not always required. Since the seller must wait a considerable period of time to collect the full sales price, it is customary to provide for interest on the unpaid balance, and to add service and carrying charges to the listed selling price.

The risk to the seller of noncollection is greatly increased by use of the installment plan. The customers generally are in weaker financial condition than those who buy on open account; furthermore, the credit rating of the customer and his ability to pay may change significantly during the period covered by an installment contract. To protect himself against this greater risk of noncollection, the seller of real or personal property usually selects a form of contract called a *secured transaction* which enables him to repossess the property if the buyer fails to make all the agreed payments.

The seller's right to protect his *security interest* (uncollected balance of sales contract) and to repossess the property varies by type of industry, the form of the contractual arrangement, and the statutes relating to repossessions. For the service-type business, repossession is obviously not available as a safeguard against the failure to collect. In reality, for many types of personal property as well, the seller's right to repossess the goods may be more of a threat than a real assurance against loss. The merchandise may have been damaged or may have depreciated to a point that it is worth less than the balance due on the installment contract. A basic rule in attempting to minimize losses from nonpayment of installment contracts is to require a sufficient down payment to cover the loss of value when property moves out of the "new merchandise" category. A corollary rule is that the payment schedule should not be outstripped by the projected decline in value of the article sold. For example, if a customer buying an automobile on the installment plan finds after a year or so that his car is currently worth less than the balance still owed on the contract, his motivation to continue the payments may be considerably reduced.

Often competitive pressures within an industry will not permit a business to adhere to these standards. Furthermore, repossession may be a difficult and expensive process, especially if the customer is non-cooperative or has disappeared. Reconditioning and repair may be necessary to make the goods salable, and the resale of such goods may be difficult. For these reasons, uncollectible accounts expense is likely to be significantly higher on installment sales than on regular credit sales.

A related problem is the increased collection expense when payments are spread over an extended period. Accounting expenses also are multiplied by the use of installment sales, and large amounts of working capital are tied up in receivables. In recognition of these problems, many businessmen have concluded that the handling of installment receivables is a separate business and they therefore sell their installment contracts receivable to finance companies which specialize in credit and collection activities.

Methods for recognition of profits on installment sales

The determination of net income on installment sales is complicated by the fact that the amounts of revenue and related costs and expenses are seldom known in the period when the sale is made. Substantial expenses (as for collection, accounting, repairs, and repossession) are likely to be incurred in subsequent periods. In some businesses, *the risk of noncollection may even be so great as to raise doubts as to the recognition of any revenue or profit at the point of sale.*

The first objective in developing accounting policies for installment sales should be a reasonable matching of costs and revenue. In recognition of the diverse business conditions under which installment sales are made, however, accountants have used three approaches to the problem.

Recognition of Gross Profit at Time of Sale To recognize the entire gross profit at the time of making an installment sale is to say in effect that installment sales should be treated like regular sales on credit. The goods have been delivered to the customer and an enforceable receivable of definite amount has been acquired. The excess of the receivable contract over the cost of goods delivered is *realized* gross profit in the traditional meaning of the term. The accounting entry consists of a debit to Installment Contracts Receivable and a credit to Installment Sales. If perpetual inventories are maintained, a companion entry is needed to transfer the cost of the goods from the Inventory account to the Cost of Installment Sales account. No recognition is given to the seller's retention of title to the goods, since the normal expectation is completion of the contract through collection of the receivable. Implicit in this recognition of gross profit at the time of sale is the assumption that all expenses relating to the sale will be recognized in the same period so that the determination of net income will be a valid process of matching realized revenue with the expired costs.

The expenses associated with the sale include collection and uncollectible accounts expenses. Recognition of these expenses in the period of sale requires an estimate of the customer's performance over the entire life of the installment contract. Such an estimate may be considerably more difficult to make than the normal provision made for uncollectible accounts from regular sales, which generally involve credit extension for 30 to 60 days. However, with careful analyses of experience in the industry and in the particular business, reasonably satisfactory estimates can be made in most situations. The accounting entry would consist of debits to expense accounts and credits to asset valuation accounts such as Allowance for Uncollectible Accounts and Allowance for Collection Costs. The allowance accounts would be debited in later periods as uncollectible installment contracts became known and as collection costs are incurred.

Cost Recovery Method   In some cases accounts receivable may be collectible over a long period of time. In addition, the terms of sale may not be definite and the financial position of customers may be extremely unpredictable, thus making it virtually impossible to find a reasonable basis for estimating the degree of collectibility of the receivables. In such cases, either the installment method or the cost recovery method of accounting may be used for installment sales. Under the *cost recovery method,* no profit is recognized until all costs of the item sold have been fully recovered. After all costs have been recovered, additional collections on the installment receivables would be recognized as revenue and only current collection expenses would be charged to such revenue. The cost recovery method of accounting is rarely used; therefore it will not be illustrated in this chapter.

Recognition of Gross Profit in Installments   The third approach to the measurement of income from installment sales is to recognize gross profit in installments over the life of the contract on the basis of cash collections. Emphasis is shifted from the acquisition of a receivable to the collection of that receivable as the basis for realization of profit; in other words, *a modified cash basis of accounting is substituted for the accrual basis.* This modified cash basis of accounting is known as the *installment method.*

The installment method of accounting

Under the installment method of accounting, each cash collection on the contract is regarded as including both a return of cost and a realization of gross profit in the ratio in which these two elements were included in the sales price.

For example, assume that a farm equipment dealer sells for $10,000 a machine which cost him $7,000. The $3,000 excess of the sales price over cost is regarded as *deferred gross profit.* Since cost and gross profit constituted 70% and 30%, respectively, of the sales price, this 70:30 ratio is used to divide each collection under the contract between the recovery of cost and realization of gross profit. If $1,000 is received as a down payment, then $300 of the deferred gross profit has become realized and is taken into income of the current period. At the end of each accounting period, the Deferred Gross Profit account will equal 30% of the installment receivable remaining uncollected. The account Realized Gross Profit on Installment Sales will show for each period an amount equal to 30% of the collections during that period. In this example the question of interest and carrying charges is purposely omitted; it is considered later in the chapter.

The method described is acceptable under income tax regulations. In fact, the opportunity to postpone the recognition of taxable income has been responsible for the popularity of the installment method of accounting for income tax purposes. Although the tax advantages are readily apparent, the theoretical support for the installment method of accounting is much less impressive.

More than 20 years ago the Committee on Concepts and Standards Underlying Corporate Financial Statements of the American Accounting Association stated:

> There is no sound accounting reason for the use of the installment method for financial statement purposes in the case of closed transactions in which collection is dependent upon lapse of time and the probabilities of realization are properly evaluated. In the opinion of the Committee, such income has accrued and should be recognized in the financial statements, . . .[2]

In 1962, authors of *Accounting Research Study No. 3* stated that revenue should be recognized in the accounting period in which the major economic activity necessary to the production and disposition of goods is performed. The authors of *ARS No. 3* rejected the use of the installment method of accounting in published financial statements:

> Collectibility of receivables is not necessarily less predictable because collections are scheduled in installments. The postponement of recognition of revenues until they can be measured by actual cash receipt is not in accordance with the concept of an accrual accounting. Any uncertainty as to collectibility should be expressed by a separately calculated and separately disclosed estimate of uncollectibles rather than by a postponement of the recognition of revenue.[3]

[2] *Accounting and Reporting Standards for Corporate Financial Statements and Preceding Statements and Supplements,* "Supplementary Statement No. 4," dated Aug. 1, 1952, American Accounting Association (Sarasota: 1957), p. 33.

[3] Robert T. Sprouse and Maurice Moonitz, *Accounting Research Study No. 3,* "A Tentative Set of Broad Accounting Principles for Business Enterprises," AICPA (New York: 1962), p. 149.

The Accounting Principles Board practically removed the installment method of accounting from the body of generally accepted accounting principles when it reaffirmed the general concept that income is realized when a sale is made, unless the circumstances are such that the collection of the sale price is not reasonably assured. The Board stated:

> . . . .Revenues should ordinarily be accounted for at the time a transaction is completed, with appropriate provision for uncollectible accounts. Accordingly, . . . in the absence of the circumstances referred to above, the installment method of recognizing revenue is not acceptable.[4]

The circumstances in which the use of the installment method was permitted by the Accounting Principles Board were: (1) Collection of installment receivables is not reasonably assured; (2) receivables are collectible over an extended period of time; and (3) there is no reasonable basis for estimating the degree of collectibility. In such circumstances either the installment method or the cost recovery method of accounting may be used.

Because the installment method may still be used for financial reporting purposes in some cases and because *it is widely used for income tax purposes,* we shall illustrate its use in the following pages, first for a single sale of real estate and then for sales of merchandise by a dealer.

Single sale of real estate on the installment plan

The holder of real estate which has appreciated greatly in value is often willing to sell only on the installment plan so that he can spread the profit (gain) over several years for income tax purposes. Federal tax regulations presently permit the use of the installment method for the sale of real estate if the payment received during the year of the sale does not exceed 30% of the sales price.

Let us assume that on November 1, Year 1, Tom Long sold for $110,000 a parcel of land acquired some years ago for $40,000. Commission and other expenses pertaining to the sale were $10,000. Since Long was not in the real estate business, he treated these expenses as a deduction in determining the gross profit on the sale rather than charging them to specific expense accounts. The net amount receivable from the sale was therefore $100,000, of which 40% represented the return of the investment in land and 60% represented deferred gain (profit). All collections from the buyer, including the down payment, were regarded as consisting of 40% cost recovery and 60% realization of gain. Long maintained his accounting records on a calendar-year basis.

The sales agreement signed by Long called for a down payment of $20,000 and a secured note, with payments every six months in the amount of $7,500 plus interest at the annual rate of 8% on the unpaid balance. One-half of the down payment was applied in the escrow state-

---

[4]*APB Opinion No. 10,* "Omnibus Opinion—1966," AICPA (New York: 1966), p. 149.

ment to pay commissions and other expenses of sale. The entries below show the sale of the land on November 1 of Year 1, the interest accrual at the end of Year 1, the collections on the note during Year 2, and the realization of a portion of the deferred gain in Years 1 and 2. Since this transaction was an isolated sale by a nondealer, there was no need to use an Installment Sales account; the deferred gain on sale of land was recorded at the time of sale.

General Journal

Year 1

Nov. 1   Cash 10,000
Notes Receivable..................... 90,000
     Land   40,000
     Deferred Gain on Sale of Land   60,000
Sold land on installment plan, receiving note calling for payments of $7,500 every six months plus 8% annual interest on the unpaid balance. Broker's commissions and other expenses of $10,000 were deducted in computing the gain.

Dec. 31   Deferred Gain on Sale of Land 6,000
     Realized Gain on Sale of Land   6,000
Realized gain computed at 60% of cash collected on the contract during Year 1.

31   Accrued Interest Receivable 1,200
     Interest Revenue   1,200
To accrue interest for two months at 8% on note receivable of $90,000.

Year 2

May 1   Cash 11,100
     Accrued Interest Receivable   1,200
     Interest Revenue   2,400
     Notes Receivable.................   7,500
Collected semiannual installment on note receivable plus interest for six months at 8% on $90,000.

Nov. 1   Cash 10,800
     Interest Revenue   3,300
     Notes Receivable.................   7,500
Collected semiannual installment on note receivable plus interest for six months at 8% on unpaid balance of $82,500.

Dec. 31	Deferred Gain on Sale of Land	9,000	
	Realized Gain on Sale of Land		9,000
	Realized gain computed at 60% of amount collected		
	on principal of note during Year 2 ($15,000 ×		
	0.60 = $9,000).		
31	Accrued Interest Receivable	1,000	
	Interest Revenue		1,000
	To accrue interest for two months at 8% on $75,000		
	unpaid balance of note receivable.		

Entries for the remaining life of the note would follow the same pattern illustrated for Year 1 and Year 2, assuming that the buyer makes all payments as required by the note.

This example brings out the contrast between the timing of profits on ordinary sales and on sales accounted for by the installment method. If the land sold by Tom Long had been recorded as an ordinary sale, a profit of $60,000 would have been reported in the year of sale. Use of the installment method resulted in the recognition of only $6,000 profit in the year of sale, followed by a profit of $9,000 ($15,000 × 60%) in each of the next six years. If a sale on the installment plan results in a loss, the entire loss should be recognized in the year of the sale.

Sales of merchandise on the installment plan by a dealer

In the preceding example we dealt with a single sale of real property on the installment plan by a nondealer. Now we shall consider a large volume of installment sales of merchandise by a retailer.

A first requirement is to keep separate all sales made on the installment plan as distinguished from ordinary sales. The records of installment receivables are usually maintained by contract rather than by customer; if several articles are sold on the installment plan to one customer, it is convenient to account for each contract separately. However, it is not necessary to compute the rate of gross profit on each individual installment sale or to apply a different rate to collections on each individual contract. The average rate of gross profit on all installment sales during a given year is computed and applied to all collections received (net of interest and carrying charges) on installment receivables originating in that year.

Data for Illustration To illustrate the procedures of accounting for merchandise sales on the installment plan, assume that the Harned Company sells merchandise on the installment plan as well as on regular terms (cash or 30-day open accounts). The company uses a perpetual inventory system. On an installment sale the customer's account is debited for the full amount of the sale price, including interest and carrying charges, and is credited for the amount of the down payment. The installment contract receivable thus provides a complete record of the transaction. Uncollectible accounts expense is recognized at the time the accounts are known to be uncollectible. Assume that at the beginning of Year 5, the company's ledger included the following accounts:

Installment contracts receivable—Year 3	$20,000 debit
Installment contracts receivable—Year 4	85,000 debit
Deferred interest and carrying charges on installment sales	17,500 credit
Deferred gross profit—Year 3 installment sales	4,500 credit
Deferred gross profit—Year 4 installment sales	19,460 credit

The gross profit rate on installment sales (excluding interest and carrying charges) was 25% in Year 3 and 28% in Year 4.

During Year 5, the following transactions relating to installment sales were completed by the Harned Company:

(1)   Sales and cost of sales:

Installment sales (not including $30,000 deferred interest and carrying charges)	$200,000
Cost of installment sales	138,000
Deferred gross profit—Year 5 installment sales	62,000
Rate of gross profit on installment sales	31%

(2)   Cash collections on installment contracts during Year 5 are summarized below:

	Sales price	Interest and carrying charges	Total cash collected
Installment contracts receivable—			
Year 5	$ 80,000	$10,000	$ 90,000
Installment contracts receivable—			
Year 4	44,500	12,500	57,000
Installment contracts receivable—			
Year 3	17,000	1,850	18,850
Total	$141,500	$24,350	$165,850

(3) Customers who purchased merchandise in Year 3 were unable to pay the balance of their contracts, $1,150. The contracts consisted of $1,000 sales price and $150 in interest and carrying charges, and included $250 of deferred gross profit ($1,000 × 25%). The fair (net realizable) value of the merchandise repossessed was $650.

(4) Deferred gross profit realized in Year 5 is determined as follows:

Relating to Year 5 sales, $80,000 × 31%	$24,800
Relating to Year 4 sales, $44,500 × 28%	12,460
Relating to Year 3 sales, $17,000 × 25%	4,250

Recording Transactions   The journal entries to record the transactions relating to installment sales for Year 5 are given below:

Installment Contracts Receivable—Year 5	230,000	
Installment Sales		200,000
Deferred Interest and Carrying Charges on Installment		
Sales		30,000
To record installment sales during Year 5.		
Cost of Installment Sales	138,000	
Inventory		138,000
To transfer cost of installment sales out of inventory.		
Cash	165,850	
Installment Contracts Receivable—Year 5		90,000
Installment Contracts Receivable—Year 4		57,000
Installment Contracts Receivable—Year 3		18,850
To record collections on installment accounts during Year 5.		
Inventory	650	
Deferred Gross Profit—Year 3 Installment Sales	250	
Deferred Interest and Carrying Charges on Installment Sales	150	
Uncollectible Accounts Expense	100	
Installment Contracts Receivable—Year 3		1,150
To record default on installment contracts originating in Year 3 and repossession of merchandise.		

Adjusting Entries   The adjusting entries at December 31, Year 5, are as follows:

Installment Sales 200,000
    Cost of Installment Sales   138,000
    Deferred Gross Profit—Year 5 Installment Sales   62,000
To set up deferred gross profit on Year 5 installment sales.

Deferred Gross Profit—Year 5 Installment Sales 24,800
Deferred Gross Profit—Year 4 Installment Sales 12,460
Deferred Gross Profit—Year 3 Installment Sales 4,250
    Realized Gross Profit on Installment Sales   41,510
To record realized gross profit as computed below:
    Year 5: $80,000 × 31% $24,800
    Year 4: $44,500 × 28%   12,460
    Year 3: $17,000 × 25%   4,250
    Total $41,510

Deferred Interest and Carrying Charges on Installment Sales   24,350
    Revenue from Interest and Carrying Charges   24,350
To record interest and carrying charges earned during Year 5,
consisting of following:
    On Year 5 accounts $10,000
    On Year 4 accounts   12,500
    On Year 3 accounts   1,850
    Total $24,350

The Realized Gross Profit on Installment Sales and the Revenue from Interest and Carrying Charges accounts would be closed to the Income Summary account at the end of Year 5. The accounts relating to installment sales appear in the ledger at the end of Year 5 as follows:

Installment contracts receivable—Year 4 . . . . $ 28,000 debit
Installment contracts receivable—Year 5 . . . . 140,000 debit
Deferred interest and carrying charges on installment sales . . . 23,000 credit
Deferred gross profit—Year 4 installment sales . . . . 7,000 credit
Deferred gross profit—Year 5 installment sales . . . . 37,200 credit

These amounts may be rearranged in slightly different form to test the accuracy of the deferred gross profit on installment contracts at the end of Year 5:

	Contracts receivable	Deferred interest and carrying charges	Net contracts receivable	Gross profit, %	Deferred gross profit
Year 4 accounts .	$ 28,000	$ 3,000	$ 25,000	28	$ 7,000
Year 5 accounts .	140,000	20,000	120,000	31	37,200
Totals	$168,000	$23,000	$145,000		$44,200

Instead of segregating the collections applicable to the sales price and to the interest and carrying charges, it would be possible to determine the gross profit rate by including the interest and carrrying charges in the selling price in arriving at the gross profit rate. The resulting *larger* gross profit rate would then be applied to the total amount collected each period in determining the realized gross profit. Applying this approach to the Harned Company example above, the gross profit rate for Year 5 would be determined as follows:

Sales, including interest and carrying charges of $30,000 . . . . $230,000
Gross profit on installment sales, $230,000 − $138,000 cost of install-
ment sales 92,000
Gross profit rate on installment sales, $92,000 ÷ $230,000 . . . . 40%

The 40% gross profit rate thus determined would be applied to the total collections each year to compute the realized gross profit. Using this approach, the realized gross profit on Year 5 sales would have been $36,000 ($90,000 × 40% = $36,000).[5]

The use of the installment method of accounting requires installment contracts and collections to be segregated by year of origin. In addition, the gross profit rate must be computed separately for each year. However, a single controlling account for installment contracts may be used if the accounting records are computerized or if the accounts are analyzed at the end of each year to ascertain uncollected balances by year of origin.

The entry to record the default on installment contracts originating in Year 3 and the repossession of merchandise by the Harned Company is explained below.

Defaults and repossessions

If a customer defaults on an installment contract for services and no further collection can be made, we have an example of default with-

---

[5] This procedure must be used for income tax purposes by dealers in personal property who compute taxable income on the installment basis [Sec. 453 (a) of Internal Revenue Code].

out the possibility of repossession. A similar situation exists for certain types of merchandise which have no significant resale value. The accounting entry required in such cases is to write off the uncollectible installment contract receivable, cancel the deferred gross profit related to the receivable, and debit Uncollectible Accounts Expense for the difference. In other words, the uncollectible accounts expense is equal to the *unrecovered cost* contained in the installment contract receivable.

For many lines of business, however, a default by a customer leads to repossession of merchandise. The uncollectible accounts expense is reduced by the value of the property repossessed and it is possible, though not likely, for the repossession to result in a gain.

The principal difficulty in accounting for defaults followed by repossession is in estimating the fair value of the merchandise at the time of repossession. In setting a fair value, the objective is to choose an amount that will allow for any necessary reconditioning costs and provide a normal gross profit on resale. As reconditioning costs are incurred, they should be added to the Inventory account, provided this does not become unreasonable in relation to the expected selling price. In other words, the carrying value of the repossessed merchandise should not exceed its *net realizable value.*

The entry on page 442 to record the default and repossession by the Harned Company accomplished the following: (1) It eliminated the defaulted installment receivable of $1,150; (2) it canceled the deferred gross profit of $250 (or $1,000 × 25%) and the deferred interest and carrying charges of $150 applicable to the defaulted contracts receivable; (3) it recognized an asset equal to the $650 fair value of the repossessed merchandise; and (4) it recognized an uncollectible accounts expense of $100, the difference between the unrecovered cost in the defaulted receivables ($750) and the value of the repossessed merchandise ($650). When the installment method of accounting is used, no loss or expense can be recognized with respect to the deferred gross profit and interest and carrying charges contained in the defaulted installment contracts because their amounts had not previously been recognized as realized revenue.

Other accounting issues relating to installment sales

Special accounting issues arise in connection with (1) acceptance of used property as a trade-in, (2) computation of interest on installment contracts receivable, (3) the use of the installment method of accounting solely for income tax purposes, and (4) retail land sales. These issues are briefly discussed in the following sections.

Trade-ins The automobile business is a familiar example of the use of trade-ins; that is, the acceptance by the dealer of a used automobile as partial payment for a new car. An accounting problem is raised only if the dealer grants an **overallowance** on the used car taken in trade. An overallowance is the excess of the trade-in allowance over the inventory value of the used merchandise in terms of the dealer's ability to resell it at a price covering his costs and a normal profit. A rough approximation of inventory value or "fair value" of the used automobile to the dealer may be the currently quoted wholesale price for used cars of the particular make and model.

An overallowance on trade-ins is significant to the accountant because it actually represents a reduction in the stated sales price of the new merchandise. **The stated sales price must be reduced by the amount of the overallowance** to arrive at a valid amount for the net sales price. This net sales price as compared with cost indicates the rate of gross profit.

As an illustration, assume that an article with a cost of $2,400 is sold for $3,300. Used merchandise is accepted as a trade-in at a "value" of $1,100, but the dealer expects to spend $50 in reconditioning the used merchandise before reselling it for only $1,000. Assume that the customary gross profit rate on used merchandise of this type is 15%, which will cover the selling costs, various overhead costs, and also provide a reasonable net profit on the resale of the used merchandise. The fair value of the trade-in and the amount of the overallowance may be computed as follows:

Trade-in allowance given to customer			$1,100
Deduct fair value of trade-in:			
Estimated sales value of article traded in		$1,000	
Less: Reconditioning cost expected to be incurred	$ 50		
Gross profit margin ($1,000 × 15%)	150	200	
Fair value of article traded in			800
Overallowance given on trade-in			$ 300

Assuming that a perpetual inventory system is used, the journal entry to record the sale and the merchandise traded in follows:

Inventory (trade-ins)	800	
Installment Contracts Receivable ($3,300 − $1,100)	2,200	
Cost of Installment Sales	2,400	
Installment Sales ($3,300 − $300)		3,000
Inventory		2,400
To record sale of merchandise for $3,000 consisting of gross sales price of $3,300 minus an overallowance of $300 given on the trade-in.		

Cost of the new article was $2,400; therefore the deferred gross profit on the installment sale of $3,000 amounts to $600. The gross profit rate is 20% ($600 ÷ $3,000). This rate will be applied in determining the realization of deferred gross profit on the basis of collections. The fair value of the merchandise accepted as a trade-in, $800, is viewed as a collection for this purpose.

Interest on Installment Contracts Receivable Installment contracts usually provide for interest and other so-called "carrying charges" to be paid concurrently with each installment payment. Such *deferred payment charges,* regardless of the label placed on them, represent a cost of borrowing to the buyer and logically may be referred to as interest. Only that portion of the payment which is applied to reduce the principal of the contract is considered in measuring the realized gross profit under the installment method of accounting.

The arrangement for adding interest to installment contracts may follow one of the following plans:

1 Equal periodic payments, with a portion of each payment representing interest on the uncollected balance of the principal and the remainder of the payment representing a reduction in the principal.

2 Interest computed on each individual installment from the beginning date of the contract to the date each installment is received.

3 Interest computed each month on the balance of the principal outstanding during the month.

4 Interest computed throughout the entire contract period on the original amount of the sale minus any down payment.

The first plan is probably the most widely used. Contracts with customers usually state how payments are to be allocated between principal and interest. Regardless of the plan used by dealers for adding interest to installment contracts, interest revenue for financial reporting purposes should be computed periodically by applying the *effective interest rate* to the unpaid balance of the installment contracts receivable.

Installment Method for Income Tax Purposes Only The popularity of the installment method for income tax purposes is readily explained by its capacity for postponing the recognition of taxable income and the payment of income taxes. For example, assume that the Woods Company uses the accrual method of accounting for financial reporting purposes as required by generally accepted accounting standards. The income before income taxes for Year 10 is $200,000, as indicated by the following condensed partial income statement:

WOODS COMPANY
Partial Income Statement (accrual basis)
For Year 10

Sales	$800,000
Cost of goods sold	500,000
Gross profit on sales	$300,000
Operating expenses	100,000
Income before income taxes	$200,000

Assume that the deferred gross profit on installment sales was $55,000 at the beginning of Year 10 and $105,000 at the end of Year 10. To take advantage of the installment method of accounting for income tax purposes, the taxable income for Year 10 would be determined as follows:

Income before income taxes for Year 10 (accrual basis of accounting)		$200,000
Less: Deferred gross profit on installment sales at end of Year 10	$105,000	
Add: Deferred gross profit on installment sales at the beginning of Year 10	55,000	50,000
Taxable income for Year 10 using installment method		$150,000

Income taxes for Year 10 would be recorded as follows, assuming that the income tax rate is 45% of taxable income:

Income Tax Expense	90,000	
Current Income Tax Liability		67,500
Deferred Income Tax Liability		22,500
To record income taxes for Year 10, determined as follows:		
Income tax expense: $200,000 × 45% = $90,000.		
Current income tax liability: $150,000 × 45% = $67,500.		
Deferred income tax liability: $50,000 × 45% = $22,500.		

For a thorough discussion of the problem of income tax allocation, the reader should refer to the *Intermediate Accounting* text of this series.

Accounting for Retail Land Sales In 1973, the AICPA published a booklet, "Accounting for Retail Land Sales," which was prepared by the Committee on Land Development Companies and approved by the Accounting Principles Board. The committee called for the use of the accrual method of accounting for land development projects in which collections on contracts are reasonably assured and *all* of the following conditions are present:

1 The properties clearly will be useful for residential or recreational purposes at the end of the normal payment period.

2 The project's improvements have progressed beyond preliminary stages, and there is evidence that the project will be completed according to plan.

3 The receivable is not subject to subordination to new loans on the property (except for home construction purposes).

4 Collection experience for the project indicates that collectibility of receivable balances is reasonably predictable and that 90% of the contracts in force six months *after sales are recorded* will be collected in full.[6]

Unless all four of these conditions for the use of the accrual method of accounting are met for the entire project, the installment method of accounting should be used for all recorded sales of land. If all four conditions are subsequently satisfied, a change to the accrual method of accounting should be adopted for the entire project and the effect accounted for as a change in accounting estimate.[7]

The *AICPA Industry Accounting Guide* suggested that the procedures to be applied under the installment method of accounting for retail land sales should include the following:[8]

1 The entire contract price applicable to the installment sale, without reduction for cancellations or discounts, should be reported as revenue in the income statement of the year the sale is recorded.

2 Cost of sales (including provision for future improvement costs) and nondeferable operating expenses (except to the extent deferred in 3 below) should be charged to income of the current period.

3 Gross profit less selling costs directly associated with the project should be deferred and recognized in income as payments of principal are received on the sales contract receivable.

4 Interest at the stated contract rate should be recorded as revenue when received and the unamortized deferred profit *should be deducted from related contracts receivable* in the balance sheet.

5 Disclosure should be made of the portion of sales and receivables applicable to the installment method.

Financial statement presentation

The presentation of accounts relating to installment sales in periodic financial statements raises some interesting theoretical issues, regardless of whether the accrual or installment method of accounting is used.

[6] *An AICPA Industry Accounting Guide,* "Accounting for Retail Land Sales," AICPA (New York: 1973), pp. 7–8.

[7] *Ibid.,* pp. 8–9.

[8] *Ibid.,* pp. 15–16.

Income Statement A partial income statement for Year 5 for the Harned Company, which uses the installment method of accounting, is presented below. This statement is based on the installment sales information illustrated on pages 440 to 444, plus additional assumed data for regular sales.

HARNED COMPANY
Partial Income Statement
For Year Ended December 31, Year 5

	Installment sales	Regular sales	Combined
Sales	$200,000	$300,000	$500,000
Cost of goods sold	138,000	222,000	360,000
Gross profit on sales	$ 62,000	$ 78,000	$140,000
Less: Deferred gross profit on Year 5 installment sales	37,200		37,200
Realized gross profit on Year 5 sales . . .	$ 24,800	$ 78,000	$102,800
Add: Realized gross profit on prior years' installment sales (see page 443)			16,710
Total realized gross profit on sales			$119,510

If the accrual method of accounting were used for all sales, a gross profit of $140,000 would be reported in Year 5. The three-column form illustrated above, while useful for internal purposes, generally would not be used in reporting the results of operations to outsiders. In a single-step income statement, revenue from interest and carrying charges on installment contracts is frequently added to sales in arriving at total revenue; in a classified income statement such revenue is generally reported as Other Income.

Balance Sheet Installment contracts receivable, net of deferred interest and carrying charges, are classified as current assets although the collection period often extends more than a year beyond the balance sheet date. This rule is equally applicable whether the accrual or installment method of accounting is used. The definition of current assets specifically includes installment accounts and notes receivable if they conform generally to normal trade practices and terms within the industry. This classification is implicit in the concept that current assets include all resources expected to be realized in cash or sold or consumed during the normal operating cycle of the business.

A recent balance sheet for General Motors Acceptance Corporation included the following notes and accounts receivable:

Notes and accounts receivable (including installments maturing after one year, $4,212,023,193; less unearned income,
  $678,406,977; and reserves for losses, $121,693,670) $11,766,336,782

The listing of installment receivables in the current asset section may be made most informative by showing separately the amounts maturing each year or by disclosing this information in notes accompanying the financial statements.

The classification of deferred gross profit on installment sales in the balance sheet **when the installment method of accounting is used for financial reporting purposes** has long troubled accountants. A common practice for many years was to classify it as a deferred credit at the end of the liability section. Critics of this treatment pointed out that no obligation to an outsider existed and that the liability classification was improper.

The existence of a deferred gross profit account is based on the argument that the profit element of an installment sale has not yet been realized. Acceptance of this view suggests that the related installment receivable will be overstated unless the deferred gross profit account is shown as a deduction from installment contracts receivable. This classification as an asset valuation account seems theoretically preferable and was recommended in the **AICPA Industry Accounting Guide,** "Accounting for Retail Land Sales."[9]

Efforts to find an acceptable compromise to these conflicting views have brought forth the suggestion that deferred gross profit be subdivided into three parts: (1) an allowance for collection costs and uncollectible accounts which would be deducted from installment receivables; (2) a liability representing future income taxes on the profit not yet realized; and (3) a residual income element. The residual income element would be classified by some accountants as a separate item in the stockholders' equity section and by others in an undefined "no-man's land" between liabilities and stockholders' equity. Such a detailed classification of deferred gross profit in the balance sheet is rarely, if ever, encountered in actual practice.

The lack of agreement on the proper classification of deferred gross profit in the balance sheet is evidence of the inherent contradiction between the installment method of accounting and the basic assumptions of accrual accounting. Since the chief reason for the use of the installment method is the income tax advantage it affords, the most satisfactory solution in most cases is to recognize profits on installment sales on the accrual basis for financial reporting purposes and to defer recognition of profits for income tax purposes until the installment contracts are collected.

[9]*Ibid.,* p. 16.

CONSIGNMENTS

The meaning of consignments

The term *consignment* means a transfer of goods from the owner to another person who acts as the sales agent of the owner. Title to the goods remains with the owner, who is called a *consignor;* the sales agent who has possession of the goods is called a *consignee* or a *commission merchant.*

From a legal viewpoint a consignment represents a *bailment.*[10] The relationship between the consignor and consignee is that of principal and agent, and the law of agency controls the determination of the obligations and rights of the two parties to the consignment contract.

The consignee is responsible to the consignor for the goods placed in his custody until they are sold or returned. Since the consignee does not acquire title to the goods, he does not include them in his inventory and records no account payable or other liability. His only obligation is to give reasonable care to the consigned goods and to account for them to the consignor. When the goods are sold by the consignee, the resulting account receivable is the property of the consignor. At this point the consignor recognizes the passage of title to the goods to the purchaser and also recognizes any profit or loss on the sale.

The shipment of goods on consignment may be referred to by the consignor as a *consignment out,* and by the consignee as a *consignment in.*

Distinguishing between a consignment and a sale

Although both a sale and a consignment involve the shipment of goods, a clear distinction between the two is necessary for the proper measurement of income. Since the title does not pass when goods are shipped on consignment, the consignor continues to carry the consigned goods as part of his inventory. No profit can be recognized at the time of the consignment shipment because there is no change in ownership of goods. If the consignee's business should fail, the consignor would not be in the position of a creditor hoping to recover a part of his claim; instead he would have the right to take possession of the consigned goods to which he has legal title.

Why should a producer or wholesaler of goods prefer to consign goods rather than to make outright sales? One possible reason, especially with new products, is that he may be able to persuade dealers to stock the items on consignment whereas they would not be willing to purchase the goods outright. Secondly, the consignor avoids the risk inherent in selling goods on credit to dealers of questionable financial strength.

[10]A *bailment* is a contract for the delivery or transfer of possession of money or personal property for a particular purpose such as for safekeeping, repairs, or sale.

From the viewpoint of a consignee, the acquisition of a stock of goods on consignment rather than by purchase has the obvious advantage of requiring less capital investment in his business. He also avoids the risk of loss if he is unable to sell all the goods, and he avoids the risks of style obsolescence and physical deterioration of inventory.

Rights and duties of the consignee

When goods are shipped on consignment, a written contract is needed to provide specific rules on such points as credit terms to be granted to customers by the consignee, expenses of the consignee to be reimbursed by the consignor, commissions allowable to the consignee, frequency of reporting and payment by the consignee, and handling and care of the consigned goods. In addition to the explicit contractual arrangements, the general rights and duties of the consignee may be summarized as follows:

Rights of Consignee	*Duties of Consignee*
1 To receive **compensation** for goods sold for the account of consignor.	*1* To give **care and protection** reasonable in relation to the nature of the consigned goods.
2 To receive **reimbursement** for expenses (such as freight and insurance) incurred in connection with the consignment.	*2* To keep the consigned goods **separate from his own inventory** or be able to identify the consigned goods. Similarly, the consignee must **identify** and **segregate the consignment receivables** from his own receivables.
3 To sell consigned goods on **credit** if the consignor has not forbidden him to do so.	*3* To use care **in extending credit** on the sale of consigned goods and to be diligent in **setting prices** on consigned goods and in collecting receivables.
4 To make the usual **warranties** as to the quality of the consigned goods and to bind the consignor to honor such warranties.	*4* To **render complete reports** of sales of consigned goods and to make appropriate and timely payments to the consignor.

In granting credit, as in caring for the consigned goods, the consignee is obliged to act prudently and to protect the interests of the consignor. Since the receivables from the sale of consigned goods are the property of the consignor, he bears any credit losses, providing the consignee has exercised due care in granting credit and making collections. However, by special agreement, the consignee may guarantee the collection of receivables; under this type of consignment contract, he is said to be a *del credere agent.*

The consignee must also follow any special instructions by the consignor as to care of the goods. If the consignee acts prudently in providing appropriate care and protection, he is not liable for any damage to the goods which may occur. Although he is not usually obligated to maintain a separate bank account for cash from consignment sales, a strict legal view of the relationship between consignor and consignee requires separate identification of all property belonging to the consignor.

The account sales

The report rendered by the consignee is called an **account sales;** it shows the goods received, goods sold, expenses incurred, advances made, and amounts owed or remitted. Payments may be scheduled as agreed portions of the shipment are sold or may not be required until the consigned goods either have been sold or returned to the consignor.

Assume that Lane Company ships on consignment to Ralph & Co. 10 television sets to be sold at $400 each. The consignee is to be reimbursed for transportation costs of $135 and is to receive a commission of 20% of the authorized selling price. After selling all the consigned goods, Ralph & Co. sends the consignor an account sales similar to the one shown below, accompanied by a check for the amount due.

Ralph & Co.
Rockport, Missouri

ACCOUNT SALES

August 31 ____, 19____

Sales for account and risk of:

Lane Company

Pittsburgh, Pennsylvania

Sales: 10 TV sets @ $400		$4,000
Charges:		
Transportation in	$135	
Commission (20% of $4,000)	800	935
Balance (check enclosed)		$3,065
Consigned TV sets on hand		none

Accounting methods for consignee

The receipt of the consignment shipment of 10 television sets by Ralph & Co. could be recorded in any of several ways. The objective is to create a memorandum record of the consigned goods; no purchase has been made and no account payable exists. The receipt of the consignment could be recorded by a memorandum notation in the general journal, or by an entry in a separate ledger of consignment shipments, or by a memorandum entry in a general ledger account entitled Consignment In—Lane Company. In this illustration, the latter method is used and the ledger account would appear as follows:

Consignment In—Lane Company	
Received 10 TV sets to be sold for $400 each at a 20% commission.	

The entries by Ralph & Co. to record the incurring of transportation charges on the shipment and subsequently the sale of the goods would be as follows:

Consignment In—Lane Company	135	
Cash		135
Charges for transportation in.		
Cash	4,000	
Consignment In—Lane Company		4,000
Sold 10 TV sets at $400 each.		

The entry to record the 20% commission earned by the consignee consists of a debit to the Consignment In account and a credit to a separate revenue account, as follows:

Consignment In—Lane Company	800	
Commissions Revenue—Consignment Sales		800
Commission of 20% earned on sets sold.		

The payment by the consignee of the full amount owed will be recorded by a debit to the Consignment In account and will result in closing that account. The entry is:

Consignment In—Lane Company	3,065	
Cash		3,065
Payment in full to consignor.		

After the posting of this entry, the ledger account for the consignment will appear as follows in the consignee's records:

Consignment In—Lane Company

Received 10 TV sets to be		Sales—10 sets @ $400 each	4,000
sold for $400 each at a			
20% commission.			
Transportation	135		
Commissions earned	800		
Payment to consignor	3,065		
	4,000		4,000

Several variations from the basic pattern of entries illustrated might be mentioned. If the policy of Ralph & Co. is to charge inbound freight on both consignment shipments and purchases of merchandise to a Freight In account, the portion applicable to the Lane Company consignment should later be reclassified by debiting Consignment In—Lane Company and crediting Freight In. If an advance is made by the consignee to the consignor, it is recorded as a debit to the Consignment In account, and the final payment is reduced by the amount of the advance. If goods are received on consignment from several consignors, a controlling account entitled Consignments In may be established in the general ledger, and a supporting account for each consignment set up in a subsidiary consignments ledger.

If the consignee, Ralph & Co., does not wish to determine profits from consignment sales separately from regular sales, the sale of the consigned goods may be credited to the regular Sales account. Concurrently, an entry should be made debiting Cost of Goods Sold (or Purchases) and crediting the Consignment In account for the amount payable to the consignor for each unit sold (sales price minus agreed commission). Costs chargeable to the consignor would be recorded by debiting the Consignment In account and crediting Cash or expense accounts if the costs were previously recorded in expense accounts. No entry would be made for commissions earned since the profit element would be represented by the difference between the amount credited to Sales and the amount debited to Cost of Goods Sold (or Purchases). The Consignment In account would be closed by debiting it with the payment made to the consignor in settlement for the consigned goods. This method is usually less desirable, since information on the profits earned on consignment sales as compared with other sales is usually needed by the consignee as a basis for sound business decisions.

At the end of the accounting period when financial statements are prepared, some Consignment In accounts in the subsidiary consignment ledger may have debit balances and others credit balances. A debit balance will exist in a Consignment In account if the total of expenses, commissions, and advances to the consignor is larger than the proceeds of sales of that particular lot of consigned goods. A credit balance will exist if the proceeds of sales are in excess of the expenses, commissions, and advances to the consignor. The total of the Consignment In accounts with debit balances should be shown as an asset on the balance sheet; the total of the Consignment In accounts with credit balances should be classified as a liability. Any commissions earned but not recorded should be entered in the accounts before financial statements are prepared. The balance of the Consignments In controlling account represents the difference between the Consignment In accounts with debit balances and those with credit balances. This net figure should not be presented in the balance sheet, because it would violate the accounting policy against offsetting asset and liability accounts.

Accounting methods for consignor

When the consignor ships merchandise to consignees, it is essential that he have a record of the location of this portion of his inventory. Therefore, he may establish in the general ledger a Consignment Out account for every consignee (or every shipment on consignment). If consignment shipments are numerous, the consignor may prefer to use a controlling account for subsidiary consignment accounts. If the inventory records are computerized, special coding may be used to identify inventories in the hands of consignees. The Consignment Out accounts should not be intermingled with accounts receivable, because they represent a special category of inventory rather than receivables.

Should gross profits on consignments be determined separately?

First, let us distinguish between a separate determination of *net income* on consignment sales and a separate determination of *gross profits* on consignment sales. Another possibility to consider is merely a separate determination of consignment revenue apart from other sales revenue.

Naturally, it would be useful to have very detailed information on the relative profitability of selling through consignees as compared with selling through other channels of distribution. However, our inclination to develop such information must be influenced by several practical considerations. First, the determination of a separate net income from consignment sales is seldom feasible because this would require allocations of many operating expenses on a rather arbitrary basis. The work required would be extensive and the resulting data would be no better than the arbitrary decisions underlying such expense allocations. In general, therefore, the determination of **net income** from consignment sales cannot be justified.

The determination of gross profits from consignment sales as distinguished from gross profits on other sales is much simpler, since it is based on the identification of **direct costs** associated with the consignments. However, the compilation of these direct costs can be an expensive process, especially if the gross profit is computed by individual consignments or consignees. Management should weigh the cost of this extra work against the need for information on consignment gross profits. In general, a separate determination of gross profits on consignments becomes more desirable if consignment transactions are substantial in relation to other sales.

A separation of consignment sales from other sales is usually a minimum step to develop information needed by management if consignment sales are an important part of total sales volume. On the other hand, no separation of consignment sales from other sales may be justified if only an occasional sale is made on a consignment basis.

Illustration of accounting methods for consignor

The choice of accounting methods by the consignor depends upon whether (1) consignment gross profits are to be determined separately from gross profits on regular sales or (2) sales on consignment are to be merged with regular sales without any effort to measure gross profits separately for the two types of transactions.

The entries required under these alternative methods of accounting for consignment shipments will now be illustrated, first under the assumption that gross profits on consignment sales are to be determined separately and secondly on the assumption that consignment sales are to be merged with regular sales without a separate determination of gross profits. The assumed transactions for these illustrations have already been described from the consignee's viewpoint but are now restated to include the cost data available to the consignor. In all remaining illustrations, we shall assume that the consignor uses a perpetual inventory system.

Lane Company shipped on consignment to Ralph & Co. 10 television sets which cost $250 each. Authorized selling price was $400 each. The cost of packing the merchandise for shipment was $30; all costs incurred in the packing department are charged to the Packing Expense account. Transportation charges of $135 by an independent truck line to deliver the shipment to Ralph & Co. were paid by the consignee. All 10 sets were sold by the consignee for $400 each. After deducting the agreed commission of 20% and the transportation charges of $135, Ralph & Co. sent Lane Company a check for $3,065 and the account sales illustrated on page 454.

The entries for the consignor, assuming that gross profits on consignment sales are determined separately and gross profits on consignment sales are not determined separately, are summarized as on pages 460–461.

If the consigned goods are sold on credit by the consignee, he may send the consignor an account sales but no check. In this case the debit will be to Account Receivable rather than to the Cash account. When sales are reported by the consignee and profits are not determined separately, the account credited is not Consignment Sales but Sales, since there is no intent to separate regular sales from consignment sales. Similarly, commissions paid to consignees are merged with other commissions expense, and freight applicable to the consignment shipment is combined with other freight expense.

Accounting for partial sale of consigned goods

In the preceding examples, we have assumed that the consignor received an account sales showing that the entire consignment had been sold by the consignee. The account sales was accompanied by remittance in full, and the consignor's accounting entries were designed to record the profit from the completed consignment.

Let us now change our conditions by assuming that only four of the ten TV sets consigned by Lane Company to Ralph & Co. had been sold by the end of the accounting period. In order to prepare financial statements, the consignor must determine the amount of profit realized on the four units sold and also determine the inventory value of the six unsold units. The account sales received by Lane Company at the end of the current period includes the following information:

Account Sales		
Sales: 4 TV sets at $400		$1,600
Charges: Transportation in	$135	
Commission ($1,600 × 20%)	320	455
Balance payable to consignor		$1,145
Check enclosed	$500	
Balance due to consignor	645	$1,145
Consigned merchandise on hand		6 TV sets

The entries for the consignor to account for this uncompleted consignment are presented on pages 462 and 463.

Accounting for Complete Consignment

Explanations	Profits determined separately	Profits not determined separately

(1) Shipment of goods costing $2,500 on consignment; consigned goods are transferred to a separate inventory account. Consignor uses a perpetual inventory system.	Consignment Out—
	Ralph & Co. 2,500
	  Inventory 2,500
		Consignment Out—
		Ralph & Co. 2,500
		  Inventory 2,500

(2) Packing expense of $30 is allocated to consigned goods; this expense was previously recorded in the Packing Expense account.	Consignment Out— Ralph & Co. . . . . 30 Packing Expense . . 30	No entry required; total packing expense is reported among operating expenses.

(3) Consignment sales of $4,000 reported by consignee and payment of $3,065 received. Charges by consignee: freight, $135; commissions, $800.	Cash 3,065
	Consignment Out—
	Ralph & Co. 135
	Commissions Expense—
	Consignment Sales 800
	  Consignment Sales 4,000
		Cash 3,065
		Freight Expense 135
		Commissions Expense . . 800
		  Sales 4,000

(4) To record the cost of consignment sales, $2,665 ($2,500 + $30 + $135).

Cost of Consignment Sales............	2,665	
Consignment Out—Ralph & Co.		2,665
Cost of Goods Sold	2,500	
Consignment Out—Ralph & Co.		2,500

(5) Summary of Consignment Out account.

Consignment Out—Ralph & Co.

2,500	2,665
30	
135	
2,665	2,665

Consignment Out—Ralph & Co.

2,500	2,500

(6) Presentation in income statement.

Consignment sales		$4,000
Less: Cost of consignment sales	$2,665	
Commissions expense	800	
		3,465
Gross profit on consignment sales		$ 535

Included in total sales.........	$4,000
Included in cost of all goods sold..........	2,500
Included in total packing expense	30
Included in total freight expense	135
Included in total commissions expense	800

Accounting for Partial Sale of Consigned Goods

Explanations	Profits determined separately	Profits not determined separately

(1) Shipment of goods costing $2,500 on consignment; consigned goods are transferred to a separate inventory account. Consignor uses a perpetual inventory system.	Consignment Out—Ralph & Co. 2,500
	     Inventory 2,500
		Consignment Out—Ralph & Co. 2,500
		     Inventory 2,500

(2) Packing expense of $30 is allocated to consigned goods; this expense was previously recorded in the Packing Expense account.	Consignment Out—Ralph & Co. ...... 30 Packing Expense ... 30	No entry required; total packing expense is reported among operating expenses.

(3) Consignment sales of $1,600 reported by consignee and payment of $500 received. Charges by consignee: freight, $135; commissions, $320.	Cash 500
	 Accounts Receivable ... 645
	 Consignment Out—Ralph & Co. ... 135
	 Commissions Expense—Consignment Sales ... 320
	     Consignment Sales 1,600
		Cash 500
		 Accounts Receivable ... 645
		 Freight Expense 135
		 Commissions Expense ... 320
		     Sales 1,600

(4) To record cost of consignment sales:

4 × ($250 + $3 + $13.50) = $1,066

4 × $250 = $1,000

| Cost of Consignment Sales .... | 1,066 | |
| Consignment Out— Ralph & Co. ..... | | 1,066 |

| Cost of Goods Sold ..... | 1,000 | |
| Consignment Out— Ralph & Co. ... | | 1,000 |

(5) To defer direct costs relating to unsold goods in hands of consignee when profits are not separately determined:

Packing costs, 6 × $3	$18
Freight costs, 6 × $13.50 ..	81
Total	$99

No entry required.

Consignment Out—Ralph & Co.	99	
Packing Expense ..		18
Freight Expense ..		81

(6) Summary of Consignment Out account.

Consignment Out—Ralph & Co.

2,500		1,066	
30			
135	Balance	1,599	
2,665		2,665	
1,599			

Consignment Out—Ralph & Co.

2,500		1,000	
99	Balance	1,599	
2,599		2,599	
1,599			

(7) Presentation in balance sheet.

Current assets:

Inventory on consignment $1,599

Current assets:

Inventory on consignment $1,599

In the preceding illustration of a partial consignment sale, we have employed the familiar accounting principle of carrying forward as part of inventory valuation a pro rata portion of those costs incurred to place the goods in a location and condition necessary for their sale. The selling commission allowed to the consignee on the units sold is an operating expense of the current period.

Return of unsold goods by consignee

We have stressed that the costs of packing and shipping goods to a consignee, whether paid directly by the consignor or by the consignee, are properly included in inventory. However, if the consignee for any reason returns goods to the consignor, the packing and freight costs incurred on the original outbound shipment should be written off as expense of the current period. The "place utility" originally created by these costs was lost when the goods were returned. Any charges borne by the consignor on the return shipment should also be treated as expense, along with any repair expenditures necessary to place the goods in salable condition.

Finally, a clear distinction should be made between freight costs on consignment shipments and outbound freight on regular sales. The latter is a current expense because the revenue from sale of the goods is recognized in the current period. The transportation cost of shipping goods to a consignee creates an increment in value of the goods, which are still the property of the consignor. This increment, along with the cost of acquiring or producing the goods, is to be offset against revenue in the period in which the consigned goods are sold.

Advances from consignees

Although cash advances from a consignee are sometimes credited to the Consignment Out account, a better practice is to credit a liability account, Advances from Consignees. The Consignment Out account will then continue to show the inventory value of goods on consignment rather than being shown net of a liability to the consignee.

Nature of the Consignment Out account

When the student of accounting encounters for the first time a ledger account such as Consignment Out, he may gain a clear understanding of its function more quickly by considering where it belongs in the basic five types of accounts: assets, liabilities, owners' equity, revenue, and expenses. Classification of the Consignment Out account within this structure will depend upon the methods employed by a particular company in accounting for consignments.

Whether or not a company uses a system of determining profits on consignment sales separately from regular sales, the Consignment Out account belongs in the asset category. The account is debited with the cost of goods shipped to a consignee; when the consignee reports sale of all or a portion of the goods, the cost is transferred from Consignment Out to Cost of Consignment Sales. To be even more specific, Consignment Out is a current asset, one of the inventory group to be listed on the balance sheet as Inventory on Consignment, or perhaps merged with other inventories if the amount is not material. As stated earlier, the costs of packing and transporting consigned goods constitute an element of inventory cost, and these costs should be charged to the Consignment Out account.

Another concept of the Consignment Out account *not* illustrated in this chapter but used by some companies will now be summarized briefly. The Consignment Out account may be debited with the cost of goods shipped to the consignee and credited with the sales proceeds remitted by the consignee. This will normally result in a credit balance in Consignment Out when the entire shipment has been sold. This credit balance represents the profit earned by the consignor. The account is closed by debiting Consignment Out and crediting an account such as Profit on Consignment Sales. No separate account is used for Consignment Sales, and the income statement does not show the amount of sales made through consignees. Under this system the Consignment Out account does not fit into any of the five basic classes of accounts. It is a mixture of asset elements and revenue and must be closed or reduced to its asset element (cost of unsold consigned goods) before financial statements are prepared.

The methods we have illustrated in accounting for consignments are widely used, but many variations from these methods are possible. Our real concern lies in recognizing the theoretical issues which arise in accounting for consignments.

REVIEW QUESTIONS

1 What do you consider to be the most important characteristics that distinguish an installment sale from an ordinary sale on 30-day credit?

2 In a discussion of the theoretical support for the installment method, one student made the following statement: "If a business is going to sell personal property over a period as long as 36 months, no one can predict how difficult or costly collections may be. To recognize the gross profit as earned at the time of sale would violate well-established accounting principles such as conservatism and the 'completed-transaction' concept." What opposing arguments can you offer?

3 What position did the Accounting Principles Board take in *Opinion No. 10* on the use of the installment method of accounting for financial reporting purposes?

4 On December 1, Jones agreed to sell for $150,000 a tract of land acquired by him several years ago at a cost of $60,000. The buyer offered to pay $50,000 down and the balance in 20 semiannual installments plus 6% interest on the unpaid balance. Jones agreed to these terms except that he insisted that the down payment be only $44,000 and the semiannual payments increased accordingly. The buyer quickly agreed and the deal was completed. Why did Jones insist on reducing the down payment? Assume that Jones (who is not a dealer in real estate) computes his net income on a calendar-year basis and chooses to use the installment method of accounting. How much profit did he realize in the year of sale on this transaction?

5 The following journal entry appears in the records of a real estate sales company using the installment method of accounting:

Inventory	1,750	
Deferred Gross Profit on Installment Sales—Year 10	1,505	
Uncollectible Accounts Expense	1,045	
Installment Contracts Receivable		4,300

What was the rate of gross profit on the original sale? What was the probable source of the $1,750 debit to the Inventory account?

6 How should the *fair value* of merchandise traded in be determined? What accounting treatment would you recommend for any *overallowance* granted to customers on merchandise accepted as a trade-in?

7 According to the AICPA, what conditions must be present before the accrual method of accounting can be used to account for the sale of land on the installment plan?

8 Discuss briefly the balance sheet classification of deferred gross profit on the installment sales of real estate, touching on both current practice and theoretical considerations in your answer.

9 How does a *consignment* of goods differ from a *sale*?

10 Magruder Corporation sells goods outright for cash and on 30-day credit; it also makes sales through consignees. Explain how the two methods of marketing differ with respect to the time when income is recognized. What relationship, if any, exists between the recognition of profit and the receipt of payment by Magruder Corporation?

11 Give reasons why the use of consignments may be advantageous from the viewpoint of both the consignor and the consignee.

12 On December 31, Lowe Company received a report from one of its consignees that 40 motors out of a consignment of 100 had been sold. No check was enclosed but the report indicated that payment would be made later. Lowe Company keeps its records on a calendar-year basis and maintains perpetual inventory records. It determines profits on consignment sales separately from profits on regular sales. What accounting action, if any, should be taken by Lowe Company at December 31 with respect to the consignee's report?

13 A Denver manufacturer of outboard motors accumulates production costs on job cost sheets. On March 20, Lot No. K-37, consisting of 100 identical motors, was completed at a cost of $14,000. Of the motors 25 were immediately shipped on consignment to a dealer in Florida and another 25 were sent to a consignee in California. The remaining 50 motors were still in the manufacturer's stockroom at March 31, the end of the fiscal year. Neither of the consignees submitted an account sales for March. Explain the quantity and valuation of motors in the manufacturer's balance sheet at March 31.

14 Identify each of the following accounts by indicating whether it belongs in the ledger of the consignor or the consignee; whether it normally has a debit or credit balance; and how the account would be classified in the financial statements.

a Cost of Consignment Sales
b Consignment Out
c Consignment Sales
d Consignment In

15 What difference, if any, do you see between outbound freight expense on regular sales and outbound freight expense on consignment shipments?

16 Ken-Most Company makes a number of shipments on consignment, although most of its output is sold outright on 30-day credit. Consignment shipments are recorded on sales invoices which are posted as debits to Accounts Receivable and credits to Sales. The Ken-Most Company has never before been audited by independent public accountants, but at the suggestion of the company's bank you are retained to make an audit for the current year.

Would you as an independent auditor take exception to the company's method of accounting for consignments? Explain. What adjustments, if any, would be needed at year-end?

EXERCISES

Ex. 12-1 On September 30, Year 1, the El Dorado Corporation sold for $50,000 (net of selling expenses) a tract of land which had a cost of $30,000. The company received a down payment of $8,000, the balance to be received at the rate of $3,000 every three months starting December 31, Year 1. In addition, the buyer agreed to pay interest at the rate of 2% per quarter on the unpaid balance. Because collection of the installment was highly uncertain, the El Dorado Corporation elected to report the gain on the installment basis, both for financial reporting and for income tax purposes.

Prepare journal entries (**a**) to record the sale of the land, (**b**) to record the receipt of the first installment on December 31, and (**c**) to recognize at December 31 the portion of gain realized in Year 1 under the installment method of accounting.

Ex. 12-2 Early in Year 1, Strawser Company sold a parcel of land which had a carrying value of $40,000 for a net selling price of $100,000. The buyer paid $10,000 down and agreed to pay the balance plus interest in three equal annual installments starting on December 31, Year 1. Assuming that collections are made as agreed, prepare a schedule showing the profit that Strawser Company would recognize each year using (**a**) the accrual method of accounting, (**b**) the installment method of accounting, and (**c**) the cost recovery method of accounting.

Ex. 12-3 Gross profits were 35, 33, and 30% of sales price for Year 1, Year 2, and Year 3, respectively. The following account balances are available at the end of Year 3:

Sales	Installment contracts receivable	Deferred gross profit (before adjustment)
Year 1	$ 4,000	$ 4,820
Year 2	41,000	40,500
Year 3	130,000	80,100

The installment contracts receivable and the gross profit rates include both interest and carrying charges. Prepare a compound journal entry at the end of Year 3 to recognize the realized gross profit on installment sales.

Ex. 12-4 Merchandise was sold for $1,600 in Year 5 at a gross profit of 25% on cost. In Year 6 no collections were made on this contract and the merchandise was repossessed. The fair value of the merchandise was $680; however, the accountant recorded the repossession as follows:

Uncollectible Accounts Expense	1,000	
Installment Contract Receivable—Year 5		1,000

To write off balance of defaulted installment contract.

Prepare a journal entry to correct the accounts, assuming that the accounts are still open for Year 6 and that an allowance for uncollectible installment contracts receivable is not used. Ignore interest and carrying charges.

Ex. 12-5 Motors Corporation sold a new automobile for a list price of $6,600. Cash of $300 was received on the sale together with an old-model automobile accepted at a trade-in value of $1,500. The balance of $4,800 was due in 24 monthly installments. Cost of the new automobile sold was $5,100. The company anticipated reconditioning cost on the trade-in of $200 and a sales price of $1,300. Used automobiles are normally sold at a gross profit of 25% of selling price.

Prepare journal entries to record (**a**) the sale of the new automobile, (**b**) reconditioning costs of $200 on the automobile acquired as a trade-in, and (**c**) the sale of the used automobile for cash at a "sacrifice" price of $1,250. Ignore interest and carrying charges.

Ex. 12-6 Sellers, Inc., sells merchandise on three-year installment sales contracts. At February 28, Year 5, the end of its first fiscal year, the results of operations prior to provision for income taxes are summarized below:

Sales	$1,000,000
Cost of goods sold	700,000
Operating expenses	80,000

The balance at February 28, Year 5, in the Installment Contracts Receivable account was $600,000. No allowance for possible uncollectible contracts receivable is required.

Prepare a journal entry to record federal and state income taxes at February 28, Year 5, assuming Sellers, Inc., accounts for sales on the accrual basis for financial reporting purposes and on the installment basis for income tax purposes. Assume a combined income tax rate of 55%.

Ex. 12-7 The Consignment Out account in the records of Bulk Sales Company for Year 1 appears on page 469.

Consignment Out—Retailer's Oasis

Shipped 20 units	3,200	Sales price 12 units	
Freight out paid by consignor	260	(per account sales)	3,500
Charges by consignee:			
Unpacking	100		
Commissions on sale of 12			
units	350		

The company charged the Consignment Out account for all costs relating to the consignment and credited the account for the full sales price of units sold.

a Prepare a journal entry in the records of the consignor to correct the Consignments Out account at the end of Year 1, assuming that consignment profits are separately determined. (Show computations clearly.)

b Give the entries that would appear in the records of the consignee, assuming that consignment profits are separately determined. The consignee sold the units for cash and made remittance in full at the end of Year 1.

Ex. 12-8 Howard A. David consigns radios to retailers, debiting Accounts Receivable for the retail sales value of the radios consigned and crediting Sales. All costs relating to consigned radios are charged to expense of the current period. Net remittances from consignees are credited to Accounts Receivable.

In December, 500 radios costing $60 per unit and retailing for $100 per unit were sent to the Sunset Shop. Freight costs of $1,100 were charged to Freight Expense by the consignor. On December 31, the Sunset Shop remitted $35,550 to Howard A. David in full settlement to date; Accounts Receivable was credited for this amount. The consignee deducted a commission of $10 on each radio sold and $450 for delivering the radios sold.

a Compute the number of radios sold by the Sunset Shop.

b Give a single correcting entry required in the records of the consignor at December 31, assuming that the accounts are still open, that perpetual inventories are maintained, and that profits on consignments are to be separately determined. Prepare a schedule allocating costs between radios sold and radios on hand in support of the correcting entry.

Ex. 12-9 Information relating to regular and consignment sales of Olive Growers, Inc., for Year 1 is shown below:

	Regular sales	Consignment sales	Total
Sales	$120,000	$30,000	$150,000
Cost of goods sold	84,000	26,000	110,000
Operating expenses	?	1,760	16,910

Income tax expense is 40% of income before income taxes.

You ascertain that an inventory of $6,500 is in the hands of consignees and is included in cost of consignment goods sold. Operating expenses of $15,150 (more than half of which are fixed) are to be allocated to regular and consignment sales on the basis of sales volume. The $1,760 of operating expenses relating to consignment sales includes a commission of 5% and $260 of costs incurred by consignees relating to the entire shipment costing $26,000.

Prepare a three-column income statement showing the net income on regular sales, consignment sales, and total sales. Advise management whether the company should continue to sell on a consignment basis.

SHORT CASES FOR ANALYSIS AND DECISION

Case 12-1 The Meadow Company sells furniture on the installment plan. For its federal income tax returns, it reports its profit from sales on the installment basis. For its financial reports, it considers the entire profit to be earned in the year of sale.

Instructions
a Discuss the relative merits of the two methods of reporting income.
b Explain the installment basis as used for income tax purposes.
c Discuss the effects of the concurrent use of these two bases by the Meadow Company on the significance of its reported annual income. What recommendation would you make to the company to produce an income statement in accordance with generally accepted accounting principles?

Case 12-2 The Rock Music Parlor, which maintains its accounts on a calendar-year basis, sold a stereo set to Edie on October 1, Year 1. Cost of the set was $800 and the sales price was $1,200. A down payment of $300 was received along with a contract calling for the payment of $50 on the first of each month for the next 18 months. No interest or carrying charge was added to the contract.

Edie paid the monthly installments promptly on November 1 and December 1, Year 1. She also made seven payments in Year 2 but then defaulted on the contract. Rock Music Parlor repossessed the set on November 1, Year 2.

Instructions
a State three different amounts which **might** be reported as realized income from this transaction for Year 1, and indicate the circumstances under which each of the three amounts might be acceptable.
b Without regard to income tax advantages or disadvantages, which of the three amounts do you believe has the strongest support from a theoretical standpoint? Which has the weakest support? Explain.
c If the stereo set repossessed on November 1, Year 2, has a wholesale value of $200 and a retail value of $300, prepare a journal entry to record the repossession under the installment method of accounting. Explain fully the reasoning applicable to your entry.

Case 12-3 The firm of Wolfe and Hill, certified public accountants, is attempting to develop the management advisory services area of its practice. One of the firm's tax clients, Powrie Corporation, affords an opportunity for work along this line. Powrie Corporation, a manufacturer of machinery, has in the past sold its products through wholesalers and also directly to some large retail outlets.

During a telephone conversation on tax matters between the president of Powrie Corporation and Lawrence Wolfe, the president posed the following question: "We are considering making sales of our products on a consignment basis as well as through our present outlets; would it be feasible to establish accounting methods that would show separately the net income we earned on the consignment transactions? I don't have time to discuss it now, but write me a memo and let me have your reactions."

Instructions Write the memo requested, making any assumptions you deem necessary, and summarizing the issues involved and the alternatives available.

Case 12-4 Beef King, Inc., sells franchises to independent operators. The contract with the franchisee includes the following provisions:
(1) The franchisee is charged an initial fee of $25,000. Of this amount $5,000 is payable when the agreement is signed and a $4,000 non-interest-bearing note is payable at the end of each of the five subsequent years.
(2) All the initial franchise fee collected by the franchisor is to be refunded and

the remaining obligation canceled if, for any reason, the franchisee fails to open his franchise.

(3) In return for the initial franchise fee, the franchisor agrees to (1) assist the franchisee in selecting the location for his business, (2) negotiate the lease for the land, (3) obtain financing and assist with building design, (4) supervise construction, (5) establish accounting and tax records, and (6) provide expert advice over a five-year period relating to such matters as employee and management training, quality control, and promotion.

(4) In addition to the initial franchise fee, the franchisee is required to pay to Beef King, Inc., a monthly fee of 2% of sales for menu planning, recipe innovations, and the privilege of purchasing ingredients from Beef King, Inc., at or below prevailing market prices.

Management of Beef King, Inc., estimates that the value of the services rendered to the franchisee at the time the contract is signed amounts to at least $5,000. All franchisees to date have opened their locations at the scheduled time and none has defaulted on any of the notes receivable.

The credit ratings of all franchisees would entitle them to borrow at the current interest rate of 10%. The present value of an ordinary annuity of five annual receipts of $4,000 each discounted at 10% is $15,163. (See Table 4 in Appendix A.)

Instructions

a Discuss the alternatives that Beef King, Inc., might use to account for the initial franchise fee, evaluate each by applying generally accepted accounting principles to this situation, and give illustrative entries for each alternative. Assume that a Discount on Notes Receivable account is used.

b Given the nature of Beef King's agreement with its franchisees, when should revenue be recognized? Discuss the question of revenue recognition for both the initial franchise fee and the additional monthly fee of 2% of sales and give illustrative entries for both types of revenue.

c Assume that Beef King, Inc., sells some franchises for $35,000 which includes a charge of $10,000 for the rental of equipment for its useful life of ten years, that $15,000 of the fee is payable immediately and the balance on non-interest-bearing notes at $4,000 per year, that no portion of the $10,000 rental payment is refundable in case the franchisee goes out of business, and that title to the equipment remains with the franchisor. What would be the preferable method of accounting for the rental portion of the initial franchise fee? Explain.

PROBLEMS

12-5 The Provo Corporation accounts for its retail sales of land on the installment basis because the collection of contracts is not reasonably assured. The balances in the accounts for installment contracts receivable at the beginning and end of Year 10 were:

	January 1, Year 10	December 31, Year 10
Installment contracts receivable—Year 8 (sales and cost of sales for Year 8 were $600,000 and $480,000)	$ 41,000	$ 1,000
Installment contracts receivable—Year 9 (sales and cost of sales for Year 9 were $675,000 and $526,500)	324,500	92,500
Installment contracts receivable—Year 10 (sales and cost of sales for Year 10 were $900,000 and $675,000)		500,000

An allowance for uncollectible contracts is not used. Interest and carrying charges are included in the sales price and are included in the computation of the yearly gross profit rates.

Upon default in payment by customers in Year 10, the company repossessed land which had a fair value of $2,000; in recording the repossession, the company debited Inventory and credited Installment Contracts Receivable—Year 9 for $2,000. The sale of the land had been made in Year 9 for $5,000 and $2,200 had been collected prior to the default. The $1,000 receivable at December 31, Year 10, from sales made in Year 8 is considered uncollectible.

Instructions

a Prepare a general journal entry to record realized gross profits at the end of Year 10.

b Prepare a general journal entry to write off the uncollectible contracts originating in Year 8.

c Prepare any correcting entries required as a result of the incorrect treatment of the repossessions in Year 10.

12-6 Bargain Fair, Inc., started business in Year 1. It sells merchandise on the installment plan and on regular 30-day open accounts. Activities for Year 1 are summarized below:

Regular sales	$350,000
Installment sales, including $90,000 deferred interest and carrying charges .	690,000
Cost of regular sales	203,000
Cost of installmont salos	360,000
Operating expenses	125,000
Collections on regular sales	310,000
Collections on installment sales, including $30,000 interest and carrying	
charges	250,000

The company uses a perpetual inventory system and does not include interest and carrying charges in computing the gross profit on installment sales. Income taxes are levied at 45% of taxable income. Accrued interest and carrying charges at the end of the year may be ignored.

Instructions

a Prepare journal entries to record all transactions and adjustments for Year 1, using only the information given in the problem. Assume that the accrual method of accounting is used for financial reporting purposes and the installment method is used for income tax purposes. Closing entries are not required.

b Prepare journal entries to record all transactions for Year 1 (including the setting up of deferred gross profit and adjusting entries), using only the information given in the problem. Assume that the installment method of accounting is used both for financial reporting and income tax purposes. Closing entries are not required.

12-7 Riviera Corporation sold a parcel of undeveloped land on December 31, Year 1, for "a consideration of $318,610," net after commissions and all other expenses of sale. The land had a carrying value of $180,000. The consideration received consisted of the following:

Cash down payment on Dec. 31, Year 1	$ 51,310
Three notes of $100,000 each with payments starting Dec. 31, Year 2, includ-	
ing interest at an annual rate of 6% (present value of an ordinary annuity of	
three rents of $1 at 6% = $2.6730)	267,300
Total	$318,610

You conclude that 10% is a more reasonable rate of interest and that the present fair value of the three notes of $100,000 each should be computed as follows:

Annual payments due on three notes $100,000

Present value of ordinary annuity of three rents of $1 discounted at 10% . . . ×2.4869

Present fair value of notes $248,690

The notes are recorded by the Riviera Corporation at present fair value on a 10%-yield basis without using a Discount on Notes Receivable account. The gain realized each year on this transaction should be recorded net of a 30% income tax rate applicable to long-term capital gains.

Instructions

a Assuming that the installment method is used to account for this transaction, both for accounting and income tax purposes, prepare journal entries to record all transactions through Year 4. Round all computations to nearest dollar.

b Assuming that the installment method is used to report the gain for income tax purposes and that the accrual basis is used for accounting purposes, prepare journal entries to record all transactions through Year 4.

12-8 On January 2, Year 5, Wilshire Company entered into a contract with a manufacturing company to purchase room-size air conditioners and to sell the units on an installment plan with collections over 30 months, with no separately identified interest or carrying charge.

For income tax purposes, Wilshire Company elected to report income from its sales of air conditioners on the installment basis.

Purchases and sales of new units were as follows:

	Units purchased		Units sold	
	Quantity	Price (each)	Quantity	Price (each)
Year 5	1,200	$100	1,000	$150
Year 6	1,800	90	2,000	140
Year 7	800	105	700	143

Collections on installment contracts receivable were as follows:

	Collections received		
	Year 5	Year 6	Year 7
Year 5 sales	$30,000	$60,000	$ 60,000
Year 6 sales		70,000	115,000
Year 7 sales			21,000

In Year 7, 40 units from the Year 6 sales were repossessed and sold for $72.50 each on the installment plan. At the time of repossession, $1,200 had been collected from the original purchasers and the units had a fair value of $2,520.

General and administrative expenses for Year 7 were $50,000. No charge has been made against current income for the applicable insurance expense from a three-year policy expiring June 30, Year 8, costing $2,400, and for an advance payment of $10,000 on a new contract to purchase air conditioners beginning January 2, Year 8.

Instructions Assuming that the weighted-average method is used for determining the inventory cost, including repossessed merchandise, prepare schedules computing the following:

a (1) The cost of goods sold on the installment plan for each year

(2) The average unit cost of goods sold on the installment plan for each year

b The gross profit percentages for each year

c The gain or loss on repossessions in Year 7

d The taxable income from installment sales for Year 7

12-9 The Electronic Appliance Company began business on January 1, Year 1. All sales of new merchandise are made on installment contracts. Because of the risks of noncollection, the company recognizes income from the sale of new merchandise under the installment method and employs the periodic inventory system. The following information was extracted from the company's accounts at December 31 for the years indicated:

	Year 2	Year 1
Installment contracts receivable:		
Year 1 contracts	$ 17,300	$ 40,000
Year 2 contracts	56,000	
Cash sales of trade-ins	20,500	
Installment sales	310,000	221,000
Purchases	176,700	170,180
Inventory, new merchandise—Jan. 1	42,000	
Operating expenses	59,006	53,718
Loss on defaulted contracts (uncollectible accounts expense) . .	10,400	

Your audit as of December 31, Year 2, disclosed the following:

(1) The inventories of new and repossessed merchandise on hand at December 31, Year 2, were $36,432 and $4,100, respectively.

(2) When a customer defaults on a contract the repossessed merchandise is recorded at its approximate wholesale market value in a separate inventory account. Differences between the unpaid balance on the contract and the wholesale market value are charged to the Loss on Defaulted Contracts account. Repossessed merchandise is sold on the installment contract basis.

(3) The wholesale value of repossessed merchandise is determined as follows:

a Merchandise repossessed during year of sale is valued at 40% of original sales price.

b Merchandise repossessed subsequent to the year of sale is valued at 20% of original sales price.

(4) There were no defaulted contracts during Year 1. An analysis of contracts defaulted and written off during Year 2 follows:

	Original sale price	Unpaid contract balance
Year 1 contracts	$19,500	$10,500
Year 2 contracts	11,000	8,200

(5) On January 1, Year 2, the company began granting allowances on merchandise traded in as part payment on new sales. During Year 2 the company granted trade-in allowances of $22,600. The wholesale value of traded-in

merchandise was $15,800. All merchandise traded in during the year was sold for cash.

(6) The company uses the installment method of reporting income on merchandise sold on the installment basis for both accounting and income tax purposes. Assume that the income tax rate is 48%.

Instructions

a Prepare a schedule of deferred gross profit at December 31, Year 2 and Year 1, from installment sales. Include a supporting schedule calculating the gross profit percentage on installment sales for each year.

b Compute the adjustment (if any) that you would recommend be made in the Loss on Defaulted Contracts account.

c Prepare an income statement (showing cash sales, installment sales, and total sales) for the year ended December 31, Year 2. A total of 10,000 shares of capital stock is outstanding. The following supporting schedules should be in good form:

(1) Unrealized gross profit on Year 2 installment sales
(2) Realized gross profit on Year 1 installment sales
(3) Realized gross profit on sales of traded-in merchandise

12-10 Allen's Machine Works derives a major part of its revenue from sales made through numerous consignees throughout the New England area and Canada. The company determines profits on consignment sales by using separate sales, cost of goods sold, and expense accounts. Under the perpetual inventory system designed by Allen's accountants, all costs relating to consigned goods are initially recorded in the Inventory on Consignment account. During the last quarter of Year 1, the following transactions were completed with Joe Golemme, a new consignee in Boston:

Oct. 2   *Consigned 25 lathes costing $12,000 and paid $350 shipping costs.*

Dec. 28   *Sent a mechanic to Boston to install safety devices on 10 lathes which have not been sold by Joe Golemme. The costs of this alteration were: parts from inventory, $60; cash expenditure, $40.*

Dec. 31   *Received an account sales from Joe Golemme as follows:*

Sales: 20 lathes @ $800		$16,000
Charges: Commission (15% of $16,000)	$2,400	
Advertising	75	
Delivery and installation costs on 20 lathes sold	140	2,615
Balance (check no. 1269 enclosed)		$13,385

Instructions

a Prepare a schedule showing the allocation of costs to lathes sold and to the consignment inventory at the end of Year 1.

b Prepare journal entries for the consignor to record the transactions with the consignee, including an entry to recognize the cost of consignment sales at December 31, Year 1.

12-11 Mary Lee sells pianos for Visalia Company on a consignment basis. Her ledger shows the following account summarizing consignment activities for the month of November:

Consignment In—Visalia Company

Memo: Received 10 pianos		Sale of 6 pianos	4,848
Paid freight and insurance	120		
Delivery to customers of 6 pianos	80		
Commissions earned	723		
Storage fees on 4 unsold pianos			
(as agreed)	24		
Remittance	2,130		

The cost of the pianos to Visalia Company was $480 each. The accounting policies of Visalia Company provide for a separate determination of profits on consigned goods as distinguished from profits on direct sales. The company maintains perpetual inventory records and also maintains a separate Consignment Out account for each consignee. All costs applicable to a consignment of pianos are charged to the Consignment Out account. When sales are reported by a consignee, the gross sales price is credited to Consignment Sales. The Consignment Out account is then relieved of the cost of the units sold by transferring this amount to a Cost of Consignment Sales account.

Instructions
a Give all entries required in the accounts of the consignor, Visalia Company, during November.
b Construct the Consignment Out ledger account applicable to the transactions with Mary Lee showing all entries during November.
c How should the month-end balances in the Consignment Out and Consignment In accounts appear on the financial statements of the consignor and the consignee at November 30?

12-12 The Pasadena Corporation sells a limited number of its products through agents on a consignment basis. In the spring of Year 1, the company arranged to sell outboard motors through a consignee, the Mar Supply Co. The motors were to be sold by the consignee at a fixed price of $300 each, and the consignee allowed a 15% commission on gross sales price. The consignee agreed to guarantee the accounts receivable and to remit all collections less the commission on accounts collected. The consignee was also allowed to deduct certain agreed reimbursable costs; these costs were chargeable to the consignor as incurred. Both companies maintain perpetual inventory records.

Transactions relating to the consignment during the first six months of Year 1 were as follows:

Consignor's transactions:

Apr. 10	Sent 30 motors to Mar Supply Co., cost of each motor $180.
	Total packing costs paid for shipment $120.
June 30	Received account sales from Mar Supply Co. and check for $4,255.

Consignee's transactions:

Apr. 15	Received 30 motors and paid freight charges, $150.
May 1–June 23	Sold 20 motors and collected $5,200.
June 2	Paid $15 for minor repairs on two motors sold.
June 30	Sent account sales to Pasadena Corporation with a check for $4,255 enclosed.

Instructions

a Prepare all entries in the accounts of the Pasadena Corporation and in the accounts of the Mar Supply Co., assuming that both companies wish to report profits on consignment sales separately. Closing entries are not required.

b Prepare all entries in the accounts of the Pasadena Corporation and in the accounts of the Mar Supply Co., assuming that consignment sales are combined with regular sales. Closing entries are not required.

c Would the balance of the Consignment In account maintained by Mar Supply Co. be of the same amount at June 30 under the differing assumptions in *a* and *b* above? What is the balance of that account and how should it be shown in the financial statements of Mar Supply Co. at June 30?

12-13 You are examining the December 31, Year 7, financial statements of the Nelson Sales Company, a new client. The company was established on January 1, Year 6, and is a distributor of air-conditioning units. The company's income statements for Year 6 and Year 7 were presented to you as follows:

NELSON SALES COMPANY

Income Statement

For Years Ended December 31, Year 7 and Year 6

	Year 7	Year 6
Sales	$1,287,500	$1,075,000
Cost of goods sold	669,500	559,000
Gross profit on sales	$ 618,000	$ 516,000
Selling and administrative expenses	403,500	330,000
Income before income taxes	$ 214,500	$ 186,000
Income taxes, at 50%	107,250	93,000
Net income	$ 107,250	$ 93,000

Your examination disclosed the following:

(1) Some sales were made on open account; other sales were made through dealers to whom units were shipped on a consignment basis. Both sales methods were in effect in Year 6 and Year 7. In both years, however, the company treated all shipments as outright sales.

(2) The sales price and cost of the units were the same in Year 6 and Year 7. Each unit had a cost of $130 and was uniformly invoiced at $250 to open-account customers and to consignees.

(3) During Year 7 the amount of cash received from consignees in payment for units sold by them was $706,500. Consignees paid for the units as soon as they were sold. Confirmations received from consignees showed that they had a total of 23 unsold units on hand at December 31, Year 7. Consignees were unable to confirm the unsold units on hand at December 31, Year 6.

(4) The cost of goods sold for Year 7 was determined by the client as follows:

	Units		
Inventory on hand in warehouses, Dec. 31, Year 6	1,510		
Purchases	4,454		
Available for sale	5,964		
Inventory on hand in warehouses, Dec. 31, Year 7	814		
Shipments to: Open-account customers	3,008		
Consignee customers	2,142	5,150 @ $130 = $669,500	

Instructions

a Compute the total amount of the Nelson Sales Company's inventory at December 31, Year 7, and December 31, Year 6.

b Prepare the auditor's working-paper entries to correct the financial statements for the year ended December 31, Year 6.

c Prepare the formal adjusting journal entries to correct the accounts at December 31, Year 7. Record corrections to Year 6 net income in a Prior Period Adjustment (or Retained Earnings) account. (The accounts have not been closed. Do not prepare closing entries.)

13

Present value: concepts and applications

The concept of the time value of money is familiar to students of accounting. Cash of $100 in hand today is worth more than cash of $100 to be received at some future date, because money can be invested to earn a fee called *interest.* Assuming a stable general price level, we should be willing to accept a smaller sum today in settlement of a receivable than we would a year from now. This rather self-evident fact has a wide application in the analysis of alternative choices for management decision making and in the measurement of assets and liabilities for financial reporting.

When interest on the *principal* (sum of money invested or owed) *is not computed* on the already accumulated interest, the computation is said to be at *simple interest.* For example, the simple interest I on $10,000 at 10% for five years may be computed by using the basic interest formula $I = prt$ (interest = principal × annual rate of interest × number of years interest accrues) as follows:

$$I = prt$$
$$I = \$10,000 \times 0.10 \times 5$$
$$I = \underline{\underline{\$5,000}}$$

When interest *is computed* on the sum of money invested or owed as well as on the already accumulated interest, the computation is said to be at *compound interest.* For example, the compound interest on $10,000 at 10% for five years (interest compounded annually) may be determined as follows:

Year	Principal	×	Rate	×	Time	=	Compound interest, I	Accumulated amount
1	$10,000	×	0.10	×	1	=	$1,000	$11,000
2	11,000	×	0.10	×	1	=	1,100	12,100
3	12,100	×	0.10	×	1	=	1,210	13,310
4	13,310	×	0.10	×	1	=	1,331	14,641
5	14,641	×	0.10	×	1	=	1,464	16,105

Compound interest on $10,000 at 10% for
five years $6,105

Note that in the computation of compound interest the accumulated amount (which includes the interest accrued to date) at the end of each year becomes the principal sum for purposes of computing the interest for the following year. Interest may be compounded annually, quarterly, or at more frequent intervals. In recent years many banks and savings and loan associations have compounded interest on savings accounts on a daily basis.

Amount of $1 formula

The accumulated amount (or simply *amount*) of any number of dollars invested at compound interest can be computed period by period by a series of multiplications as illustrated above for the $10,000 invested for five years at 10% interest compounded annually. If n is used to represent the number of periods that interest is to be compounded, such a series of multiplications to compute the accumulated amount of a principal sum can be stated in formula form as follows:

Accumulated amount $a = p\,(1 + rt)^n$

$a = \$10,000\,[1 + (0.10 \times 1)]^5$

$a = \$10,000\,(1.10)^5$

$a = \$16,105$

The total compound interest which accrued during the five-year period may be calculated as follows:

> **Compound interest accrued** I = **accumulated amount** a **less principal** p
>
> I = \$16,105 − \$10,000
>
> I = \$6,105

To simplify our subsequent discussion, let us substitute the term i for rt in the formula for the accumulated amount. The term i thus becomes the *rate of interest per time period,* and we have the *amount of \$1 formula* as follows:

$$a_{\overline{n}|i} = p(1 + i)^n$$

If we assume p to be \$10,000, the accumulated amount at 10% for five periods is:

$$\$10,000 \times a_{\overline{5}|10\%} = \$10,000 (1.10)^5 = \$16,105$$

The symbol $a_{\overline{n}|i}$ is the amount to which \$1 will accumulate at i rate of interest per period for n periods. This symbol should be read as "small a angle n at i." If the annual interest of 10% is compounded quarterly for five years, the rate of interest per time period (one-fourth of a year) is 2½%, and the number of interest periods (n) in the five-year period is 20 (5 years $\times$ 4 quarters per year). Thus the amount of \$1 formula at 10% interest compounded quarterly for five years would be:

$$a_{\overline{n}|i} = p (1 + i)^n$$
$$a_{\overline{20}|2\frac{1}{2}\%} = \$1 (1 + 0.025)^{20}$$

Obviously, it would be a laborious task to multiply 1.025 by 1.025 twenty times without an electronic calculator programmed to perform such computations. To reduce the computational work, tables are available which give the value of $a_{\overline{n}|i}$. Use of these tables involves reference to a line showing the desired number of periods and a column showing the desired rate of interest per period. For example, Table 1 in Appendix A shows that $a_{\overline{5}|10\%}$ is equal to 1.610510, which means that \$1 would accumulate to \$1.61 in five years at 10% compounded annually, or that \$10,000 would accumulate to $16,105. Table 1 also shows that $a_{\overline{20}|2\frac{1}{2}\%}$ is equal to 1.638616, which means that $10,000 would accumulate to $16,386.16 in five years at 10% compounded every three months, or that $0.50 would accumulate to approximately $0.82 ($0.50 × 1.638616). Compound interest tables are generally prepared for $1. This provides a convenient means of finding the accumulated amount of any number of dollars by multiplying the amount of $1 by the number of dollars involved in any given situation.

Summary The amount of $1 formula, $a_{\overline{n}|i}$, is used to compute the future value a of a given sum p which earns compound interest i at a fixed interest rate per period for a specific number of periods n.

Example 1: Amount accumulated when interest rate changes Albert Abrams deposited $1,000 in a trust fund which will earn 8% interest compounded quarterly for four years, and 10% interest compounded semiannually for the next six years. How much will Abrams have in the trust fund at the end of 10 years? Using Table 1 in Appendix A, we have the following amount at the end of four years:

$$\$1,000 \times a_{\overline{16}|2\%} = \$1,000 (1 + 0.02)^{16}$$
$$\$1,000 \times a_{\overline{16}|2\%} = \$1,000 (1.372786), \text{ or } \$1,373$$

And for the next six years, we have:

$$\$1,373 \times a_{\overline{12}|5\%} = \$1,373 (1 + 0.05)^{12}$$
$$\$1,373 \times a_{\overline{12}|5\%} = \$1,373 (1.795856), \text{ or } \underline{\$2,466}$$

In this case the interest rate per period changed at the end of four years from 2% per period to 5% per period. Therefore, it was first necessary to compute the amount in the trust fund at the end of four years ($1,373) and then to accumulate compound interest on the $1,373 for six additional years at 10% interest compounded semiannually, thus accumulating a fund of $2,466 in 10 years.

Present value of $1 formula

Many valuation and measurement problems in the areas of financial accounting and management decision making require the computation of the discounted present value of a fixed sum of money scheduled to be paid or received at a fixed future date. Discounted present value is closely related to the concept of accumulated amount discussed in the previous section, and it may be computed by a series of sequential divisions. Each division discounts the future fixed sum of money for one period at the stated compound interest rate per period. For example, assume that Beran Company received on January 1, Year 1, a non-interest-bearing note for $16,105 due on December 31, Year 5. If the current fair rate of interest is 10% compounded annually, what is the present value of this note today? The present discounted value of the note p and the compound discount D can be computed as follows:

Year	Value of note at end of year ÷	Discount at 10% per year =	Value of note at beginning of year, p	Compound discount, D
5	$16,105 ÷	1.10 =	$14,641	$1,464
4	14,641 ÷	1.10 =	13,310	1,331
3	13,310 ÷	1.10 =	12,100	1,210
2	12,100 ÷	1.10 =	11,000	1,100
1	11,000 ÷	1.10 =	10,000	1,000
Compound discount on $16,105 at 10% interest for five years				$6,105

A careful comparison of this schedule with the schedule on page 480 for the computation of the accumulated amount of $10,000 at 10% interest for five years shows that in computing the discounted present value of a future sum, we are reversing the procedure previously used for computing the future sum (accumulated amount) of a principal sum invested at compound interest. In other words, $10,000 is multiplied by 1.10 to obtain the accumulated amount at the end of the first year, or $11,000; and if $11,000 is the accumulated amount a year hence, we would discount this future value to a present value (or principal sum) by dividing it by 1.10 to obtain the beginning-of-year present value of $10,000. We can restate this relationship between accumulated amount a and the present value p of a principal sum to develop the **present value of $1 formula**, $p_{\overline{n}|i}$, as follows:

Since $a = p\,(1 + i)^n$

Then $p = \dfrac{a}{(1 + i)^n}$ **or** $p_{\overline{n}|i} = \dfrac{1}{(1 + i)^n}$ **or** $(1 + i)^{-n}$

Previously we determined the value of $(1 + 0.10)^5$ as 1.6105; therefore, the present value p of a $16,105 non-interest-bearing note discounted for five years at a 10% annual rate of interest may be determined as follows:

$$\$16,105 \times p_{\overline{5}|10\%} = \frac{\$16,105}{1.6105} = \underline{\underline{\$10,000}}$$

The computation above suggests the following rule: The present value of a future sum a at i rate of interest for n periods can be computed by dividing the future sum a by the amount of $1 at i rate of interest for n periods. Alternatively, we can use the formula $p = a/(1 + i)^n$ to compute p for $1 by dividing 1 by $(1 + i)^n$. We can thus solve present value problems by the process of multiplication rather than by division. Discounted present values of $1 at selected interest rates are given in Table 2 of Appendix A. For example, the present value of $1 for five periods at 10% interest in Table 2 is 0.620921, which was derived by dividing 1 by 1.610510 (the amount of $1 for five periods at 10% in Table 1).

At this point it may be helpful to summarize the preceding discussion of the accumulated amount and present value with the following diagram:

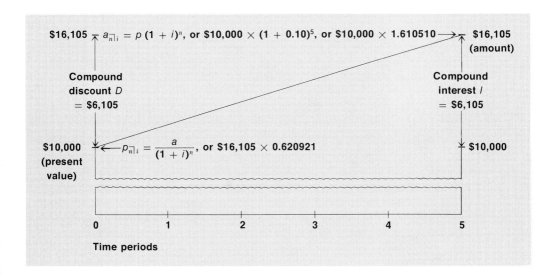

$\$16,105$ ↗ $a_{\overline{n}|i} = p (1 + i)^n$, or $\$10,000 \times (1 + 0.10)^5$, or $\$10,000 \times 1.610510$ → $\$16,105$ (amount)

Compound discount D = $\$6,105$

Compound interest I = $\$6,105$

$\$10,000$ (present value) ← $p_{\overline{n}|i} = \dfrac{a}{(1 + i)^n}$, or $\$16,105 \times 0.620921$ $\$10,000$

0   1   2   3   4   5

Time periods

Summary The present value of $1 formula, $p_{\overline{n}|i}$, is used to compute the discounted present value p of a given sum a due at some future date, discounted at a fixed compound interest rate per period i for a specific number of periods n.

Example 2: Present value when interest rate changes Alice Cooper wants to deposit a lump sum at the beginning of Year 1 in a savings account so that she will have $100,000 at the end of Year 4. How much must she deposit at the beginning of Year 1 if the interest rate is 8% compounded annually for Years 1 and 2 and 8% compounded quarterly for Years 3 and 4? Using Table 2 in Appendix A, we have the following present value at the beginning of Year 3 of the $100,000 required at the end of Year 4:

$$\$100,000 \times p_{\overline{8}|2\%} = \$100,000 \ (0.853490), \text{ or } \$85,349$$

And at the beginning of Year 1, we have:

$$\$85,349 \times p_{\overline{2}|8\%} = \$85,349 \ (0.857339), \text{ or } \underline{\$73,173}$$

Thus, Alice Cooper must deposit $73,173 at the beginning of Year 1 in order to have $100,000 at the end of Year 4.

Because the interest rate per period changed at the beginning of Year 3, it was necessary to prepare the solution in two separate steps. Even though the rate of interest remained unchanged at 8% per year, the interest rate *per period* changed from 8% to 2% because interest was compounded annually for the first two years (Years 1 and 2) and quarterly for the next two years (Years 3 and 4).

Annuities—a series of equal receipts or payments

Many business situations involve regular periodic deposits, receipts, withdrawals, or payments (called *rents*), with interest compounded at a stated rate at the time that each periodic rent is paid or received. These situations are called *annuities* when (1) the time intervals (periods) between rents are equal (for example, one month, three months, or a year); (2) the interest rate per time period remains constant; and (3) the interest is compounded regularly at the end of each time period. When rents are paid or received at the end of each period and the total amount on deposit is determined at the time the final rent is made, the annuity is an *ordinary annuity*. When rents are paid or received at the beginning of each period and the total amount on deposit is determined one period after the final rent is made, the annuity is an *annuity due*. When the amount on deposit continues to accumulate interest after the last rent (or, in the computation of the present value of an annuity, when withdrawals are postponed for a number of periods), we have a *deferred annuity*.

Amount of ordinary annuity of $1 formula

The amount of an ordinary annuity consists of the sum of the equal periodic rents and compound interest on the rents immediately after the final rent. The amount A to which an ordinary annuity of n rents of R dollars each will accumulate in n periods at i rate of interest per period is illustrated below:

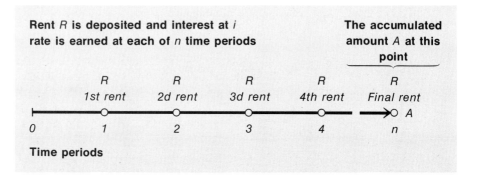

Before we continue with the discussion of annuities, it might be helpful to explain how the formula for the amount of an ordinary annuity is developed. From the table on page 480, we can see that $1 deposited at 10% compounded annually for a five-year period would accumulate to $1.6105, with compound interest I of $0.6105. This compound interest accumulated as a series of five periodic rents of $0.10 in interest plus the compound interest on these rents. It follows that the amount of an ordinary annuity of five rents of $0.10 at 10% compound interest equals $0.6105. The amount of an ordinary annuity of five annual rents of $0.10 at 10% can be converted to an amount of an ordinary annuity of five rents of $1 at 10% as follows: $0.6105 ÷ $0.10 = $6.105. Because division by $0.10 is the same as dividing by the interest rate of 0.10, the following *amount of ordinary annuity of $1 formula* may be developed:

$$\text{Amount of ordinary annuity of 5 rents of \$1 at 10\%} = \frac{(\$1 + \$0.10)^5 - \$1}{0.10}$$

Therefore, the formula for the amount of an ordinary annuity of n rents of $1 at i interest rate per period is:

$$A_{\overline{n}|i} = \frac{(1 + i)^n - 1}{i}, \quad \text{or} \quad I_{\overline{n}|i}$$

For example, the amount of an ordinary annuity of 25 rents of $1 at 2% is given in Table 3 of Appendix A as $32.0303, which can also be computed from Table 1 by subtracting $1 from $1.640606 (the amount of $1 for 25 periods at 2%) and dividing the resultant compound interest of $0.640606 by the interest rate as follows:

$$A_{\overline{25}|2\%} = \frac{\$1.640606 - \$1}{0.02} = \$32.0303$$

Tables showing the amount of an ordinary annuity for rents of $1 each may be used to compute the accumulated amount of an ordinary annuity for rents of any dollar amount by the process of multiplication. For example, since the amount of an annuity of 25 rents of $1 at 2% is $32.0303, the amount of an ordinary annuity of 25 rents of $200 would be $6,406.06 (32.0303 × $200).

Summary The amount of an ordinary annuity of $1 formula $A_{\overline{n}|i}$, is used to compute the future value A of n equal periodic rents of R dollars which earn compound interest i at a fixed rate per period. The amount of an ordinary annuity of n rents of $1 at i interest is obtained by dividing the compound interest I that would accumulate on $1 in n periods at i interest rate by that interest rate.

Example 3: Amount of ordinary annuity known; periodic rents not known Damon Corporation plans to accumulate $500,000 in a pension fund by making ten equal annual deposits. The fund will earn interest at 8% compounded annually. How much should be deposited at the end of each year to accumulate $500,000 immediately after the final (tenth) deposit? The answer may be determined as follows:

$$\$500,000 = R(A_{\overline{10}|8\%})$$

$$\$500,000 = R\,(14.486562) \text{ (from Table 3 in Appendix A)}$$

$$\$500,000 = R\,(14.486562)$$

$$R = \frac{\$500,000}{14.486562}$$

$$R = \$34,515$$

Stated concisely, the periodic rent may be computed by dividing the dollar amount to be accumulated by the amount of an ordinary annuity of $1 at the given interest rate for the number of periods equal to the number of rents (deposits).

Amount of an Annuity Due We have previously defined the amount of an annuity due as the total amount on deposit one period after the final rent, as illustrated below:

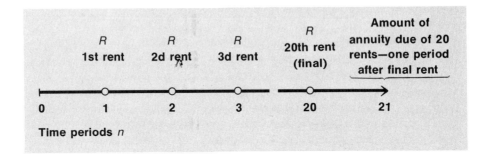

This diagram suggests that there are two ways of computing the amount of an annuity due of 20 rents of $1 at 4% interest per period as follows:

1 Take the amount of an ordinary annuity of 20 rents of $1 at 4% from Table 3 in Appendix A and accrue interest at, say, 4% for one additional period: $29.778079 \times 1.04 = 30.969202$

2 Take the amount of an ordinary annuity of 21 rents of $1 at 4% from Table 3 in Appendix A and subtract 1, the rent not made at this date: $31.969202 - 1 = 30.969202$

Example 4: Application of amount of an annuity due formula James Edwards wants to make four equal annual deposits in a savings fund starting January 1, Year 1, and ending January 1, Year 4, so that he will have $5,000 on deposit at December 31, Year 4. How much should Edwards deposit if the fund will earn interest at 10% compounded annually? The solution calls for the division of $5,000 by the amount of an annuity due of four $1 rents (or the amount of an ordinary annuity of five rents, taken from Table 3 in Appendix A less $1) as follows: $5,000 \div (6.1051 - 1) = 979.41. The accumulation of the $5,000 fund through December 31, Year 4, is summarized below:

Accumulation of Annuity Due of Four Rents of $979.41 at 10%

Year	Rent at January 1	Balance at January 1 (after rent)	Interest earned at 10%	Balance of fund at December 31
1	$979.41	$ 979.41	$ 97.94	$1,077.35
2	979.41	2,056.76	205.68	2,262.44
3	979.41	3,241.85	324.19	3,566.04
4	979.41	4,545.45	454.55	5,000.00

Amount of Deferred Annuity When the accumulated amount of an ordinary annuity remains on deposit for a number of periods beyond the final rent, the arrangement is known as a **deferred annuity.** If you refer to the diagram on page 488 you will see that the amount of an annuity due of 20 rents is also the amount of an ordinary annuity deferred for only one period. When the amount of an ordinary annuity continues to earn interest for one additional period, we have an annuity due situation; when the amount of an ordinary annuity continues to earn interest for more than one additional period, we have a deferred annuity situation.

The amount of a deferred annuity may be computed by multiplying the amount of the ordinary annuity by the amount of $1 for the period of deferral to accrue compound interest. Alternatively, we can take the amount of an ordinary annuity for all periods (including the period of deferral) and subtract from this the amount of the ordinary annuity for the deferral period when rents **were not made** but interest continued to accumulate.

Example 5: Amount of deferred annuity Find the amount of an ordinary annuity of 20 rents of $1 at 4% deferred for five periods as diagrammed below:

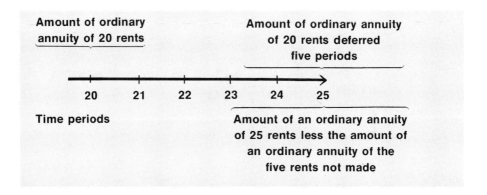

The amount of this deferred annuity (rounded to two decimal places) may be computed using Appendix A by either of the two methods below:

(1) $A_{\overline{20}|4\%} \times (1 + 0.04)^5 = \$29.78\ (1.2167) = \underline{\$36.23}$

(2) $A_{\overline{25}|4\%} - A_{\overline{5}|4\%} = \$41.65 - \$5.42 = \underline{\$36.23}$

Present value of ordinary annuity of $1 formula

Perhaps the most frequent application of compound interest in financial reporting and decision making involves the **present value of annuity formula.**

For example, financing leases which are equivalent to a purchase of an asset, past service costs under newly adopted pension plans, proceeds on issuance of bonds, installment contracts, and mortgage notes all require the computation of the present value of an annuity.

The present value of an ordinary annuity is the value, at a point in time one period before the first rent, of the equal periodic rents discounted at compound interest. The present value of an ordinary annuity may be computed as the sum of the present values of the individual rents, but the use of the present value of an ordinary annuity table considerably shortens the computations. We have seen that the amount of an ordinary annuity of n rents at i interest is computed by dividing the compound interest I for n periods at i rate of interest by the interest rate per period i. Similarly, the present value of an ordinary annuity P of n rents at i rate of interest can be computed by dividing the compound discount D for n periods at i rate of interest by the interest rate per period, as illustrated below:

$$P_{\overline{n}|i} = \frac{1 - \dfrac{1}{(1 + i)^n}}{i}, \quad \text{or} \quad \frac{D_{\overline{n}|i}}{i}$$

If we wish to compute the present value of an ordinary annuity of five rents of $1 at 10% and we know that $(1 + i)^n$ for five periods at 10% is 0.6209, applying the formula above, we have

$$P_{\overline{5}|10\%} = \frac{1 - 0.6209}{0.10} = \$3.791$$

In Table 4 of Appendix A, the present value of an ordinary annuity of five rents of $1 at 10% is given as 3.790787, or 3.791 if rounded, thus confirming our computation above.

Summary The *present value of an ordinary annuity of $1 formula*, $P_{\overline{n}|i}$, is used to compute the sum P that would settle a debt one period before the first rent of n equal rents of R dollars discounted at compound interest i at a fixed rate per period. Stated differently, $P_{\overline{n}|i}$ is used to compute the dollar worth one period before the first rent of a series of equal future cash inflows discounted at a fixed interest rate per period. The present value of an ordinary annuity of n rents of $1 at i interest is obtained by dividing the compound discount D on $1 for n periods at i interest rate by that interest rate.

Example 6: Proceeds on issuance of bonds at a discount Farmer Company issued $1 million face amount of 7%, 10-year bonds on March 1, Year 1. The bonds pay interest semiannually on March 1 and September 1 and were issued to yield 8% compounded semiannually. What amount was received by the Farmer Company on the issuance of the bonds?

Since the coupon rate of interest on the bonds is less than the market rate of interest, the bonds were sold at a discount equal in amount to the present value of the semiannual interest *deficiency* (interest which will not be received by bondholders) of $5,000 [$1,000,000 × (0.040 − 0.035)] for 20 semiannual periods discounted at the 4% *market rate* of interest per period. Therefore, the proceeds on the issuance of the bonds would be determined as follows:

Face amount of bonds	$1,000,000
Less: Present value of ordinary annuity of 20 rents of $5,000 discounted at 4% per period: $5,000 × 13.590326	67,952
Proceeds on issuance of bonds	$ 932,048

It would also be possible to compute the proceeds on the bonds by computing the sum of (1) the present value of the $1 million maturity value discounted at the 4% semiannual rate of interest for 20 periods, plus (2) the present value of an ordinary annuity of 20 rents of $35,000 also discounted at 4% per period, as illustrated below:

Present value of $1 million discounted at 4% for 20 six-month periods: $1,000,000 × 0.456387	$456,387
Add: Present value of ordinary annuity of 20 rents of $35,000 discounted at 4%: $35,000 × 13.590326	475,661
Proceeds on issuance of bonds	$932,048

Example 7: Proceeds on issuance of bonds at a premium Assume the same facts as in Example 6, except that the Farmer Company issued the 7%, 10-year bonds to yield 6% compounded semiannually. What amount would be received from the issuance of the bonds?

Since the coupon rate of interest on the bonds is greater than the market rate of interest, the bonds will be sold at a premium equal in amount to the present value of the *extra* semiannual interest to be paid to bondholders, or $5,000 [$1,000,000 × (0.035 − 0.030)] for 20 periods discounted at the 3% market rate of interest per period. Therefore, the proceeds on the issuance of the bonds would be determined as follows:

Face amount of bonds	$1,000,000
Add: Present value of ordinary annuity of 20 rents of $5,000 discounted at 3% per period: $5,000 × 14.877475	74,387
Proceeds on issuance of bonds	$1,074,387

Or by the following alternative computation:

Present value of $1 million discounted at 3% for 20 six-month periods: $1,000,000 × 0.553676	$ 553,676
Add: Present value of ordinary annuity of 20 rents of $35,000 discounted at 3%: $35,000 × 14.877475	520,712
Proceeds on issuance of bonds	$1,074,388*

*$1 discrepancy due to rounding of present values

Present Value of Annuity Due You may recall that the present value of an ordinary annuity falls one period before the first rent. In contrast, the present value of an annuity due falls *on the date* the first rent is deposited or withdrawn, as illustrated below:

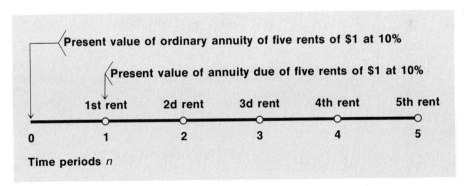

The present value of an annuity due of *n* rents of $1 is needed, for example, to compute the periodic rental payments on an equipment contract or a lease when the first payment is due at the beginning of the period. The diagram above suggests that the present value at time period 1 of an annuity due of five rents at 10% can be computed (1) by adding interest for one period to the present value of an ordinary annuity of five rents or (2) by obtaining the present value of an ordinary annuity of four rents and then adding $1, representing the "extra" rent on this date (time period 1). These calculations are presented on page 493 using Table 4 in Appendix A:

(1) *Present value of ordinary annuity of five rents of $1 at 10% plus interest on such present value for one period: $3.7908 + ($3.7908 × 10%)* $4.1699

(2) *Present value of ordinary annuity of four rents of $1 at 10% plus $1, the fifth rent on this date: $3.1699 + $1* $4.1699

Example 8: Use of present value of annuity due to determine periodic rents
On January 1, Year 1, the George Company acquired a machine for $20,849.50. The company agreed to make five equal annual payments starting immediately and ending on January 1, Year 5. Compute the annual payments, assuming that the agreed rate of interest on the unpaid balance is 10% per year.

Periodic payments = $20,849.50 ÷ 4.1699 (see above) = $5,000

The payment schedule for this contract is shown below:

Payment Schedule for Liability of $20,849.50 at 10% Interest

January 1, year	Liability at beginning of year	Payment at beginning of year	Balance accruing interest	Interest at 10%	Liability at end of year
1	$20,849.50	$5,000.00	$15,849.50	$1,584.95	$17,434.45
2	17,434.45	5,000.00	12,434.45	1,243.45	13,677.90
3	13,677.90	5,000.00	8,677.90	867.79	9,545.69
4	9,545.69	5,000.00	4,545.69	454.31*	5,000.00
5	5,000.00	5,000.00			

*Adjusted for slight discrepancy because the present value of annuity due of five rents of $1 at 10% was rounded to 4.1699.

Present Value of Deferred Annuity When periodic rents on a contract are postponed for more than one period and the present value of such an annuity at some date prior to the first rent is to be computed, two approaches may be followed: The first is to discount the present value of the ordinary annuity portion of the contract at compound interest for the periods the annuity is deferred. The alternative is to determine the present value of an ordinary annuity equal to the number of periods involved in the contract and subtract from such value the present value of the "missing" ordinary annuity for rents equal in number to the number of periods the actual annuity is deferred. To illustrate, assume that we wish to know the sum at time period 0 which would settle a debt of five payments of $1,000 each, payments starting at time period 4 and interest compounded at 10% per time period. First it would be helpful to diagram this situation as follows:

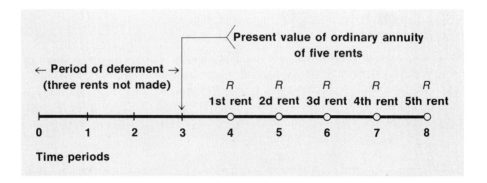

Using Tables 2 and 4 in Appendix A, we compute the present value of the ordinary annuity of five rents of $1 deferred for three periods as follows:

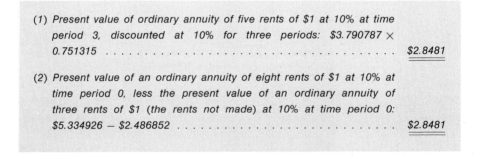

(1) *Present value of ordinary annuity of five rents of $1 at 10% at time period 3, discounted at 10% for three periods: $3.790787 ×0.751315* *$2.8481*

(2) *Present value of an ordinary annuity of eight rents of $1 at 10% at time period 0, less the present value of an ordinary annuity of three rents of $1 (the rents not made) at 10% at time period 0: $5.334926 − $2.486852* *$2.8481*

Many complex situations involving compound interest may be encountered in the business world. An understanding of the concepts discussed in the preceding pages should enable the student to analyze and solve problems requiring the application of compound interest principles and to evaluate the possibilities of expanding the use of direct valuation techniques in financial reporting and management decision making.

Compound interest methods of depreciation

For many years the *annuity* and *sinking fund* methods of depreciation have received attention from accounting theorists because they focus on the critical issues of cost recovery and rate of return on the investment in depreciable assets. A depreciable asset represents a bundle of services to be received periodically over the useful life of the asset. The cost of such an asset may be logically viewed as the present value of the approximately equal periodic rents (services) discounted at a rate of interest commensurate with the risk factors surrounding the investment in the asset.

Annuity Method The annuity method of depreciation would be appropriate when the periodic cost (depreciation) of using a long-lived asset is considered to be equal to the total of the expired cost of the asset and the interest on the unrecovered investment in the asset. Depreciation Expense is debited and Accumulated Depreciation and Interest Revenue are credited periodically, as explained in the example below.

Assume that a computer with a useful life of five years and estimated net residual value of $67,388 at the end of five years is acquired for $800,000. If the fair rate of interest for this type of investment is 10% compounded annually, annual depreciation would be computed, using Table 2 and Table 4 in Appendix A, as follows:

$$\text{Depreciation} = \frac{\text{cost of asset less present value of net residual value}}{\text{present value of ordinary annuity of five rents at 10\%}}$$

$$\text{Depreciation} = \frac{\$800,000 - (\$67,388 \times 0.620921^*)}{3.790787},$$

$$\text{or} \quad \frac{\$800,000 - \$41,843}{3.790787}$$

$$\text{Depreciation} = \underline{\underline{\$200,000}}$$

*Present value of $1 for five periods at 10%

A schedule summarizing the results of the annuity method of depreciation and the journal entries to record depreciation for the first two years are presented on page 496.

The schedule below shows that: (1) Depreciation computed by the annuity method is debited for $200,000 each year; (2) interest revenue is credited each year with 10% of the unrecovered investment (carrying value of the computer); (3) the difference between annual depreciation expense and interest revenue is credited to Accumulated Depreciation; and (4) the carrying value of the computer at the end of Year 5 is $67,388, the estimated net residual value at the end of its useful life. The total depreciation expense over the useful life of the computer exceeds its depreciable cost by $267,388 ($1,000,000 − $732,612), an amount equal to the interest revenue recorded during the useful life of the computer. The *net* charge to revenue over the five-year period is equal to the

Annuity Method of Depreciation

Year	Depreciation expense	Interest revenue (10% of carrying value)	Credit to Accumulated Depreciation account	Balance in Accumulated Depreciation account	Carrying value of computer
0					$800,000
1	$ 200,000	$ 80,000	$120,000	$120,000	680,000
2	200,000	68,000	132,000	252,000	548,000
3	200,000	54,800	145,200	397,200	402,800
4	200,000	40,280	159,720	556,920	243,080
5	200,000	24,308	175,692	732,612	67,388
	$1,000,000	$267,388	$732,612		

Journal entries:	Year 1	Year 2
Depreciation Expense	200,000	200,000
Interest Revenue	80,000	68,000
Accumulated Depreciation	120,000	132,000
To record depreciation using the		
annuity method.		

depreciable *cost* of the computer and *increases* each year. The annuity method of depreciation thus tends to produce a more constant rate of return on investment than, say, the straight-line method of depreciation. Consequently, the use of the annuity method of depreciation for assets acquired under financing leases has been advocated by some accountants in recent years.

Sinking Fund Method   The sinking fund method of depreciation might be used when a fund is to be accumulated to replace an asset at the end of its estimated useful life. Under the sinking fund method, the amount of annual depreciation is equal to the increase in the asset replacement fund. The increase in the fund would consist of the equal periodic deposits (rents) plus the interest revenue at the assumed rate on the fund balance.

We shall illustrate the sinking fund method of depreciation using the same example as we used to illustrate the annuity method, that is, a computer purchased for $800,000 with an estimated useful life of five years and a net residual value of $67,388 at the end of five years. If we again assume a 10% annual compound rate of interest, the annual deposits to the sinking fund may be determined, using Table 3 in Appendix A, as follows:

$$\text{Sinking fund deposits} = \frac{\text{cost of asset less net residual value}}{\text{amount of ordinary annuity of 5 rents at 10\%}}$$

$$\text{Sinking fund deposits} = \frac{\$800,000 - \$67,388}{6.1051}$$

$$\text{Sinking fund deposits} = \underline{\underline{\$120,000}}$$

A schedule summarizing the results of the sinking fund method of depreciation and the journal entries for the first two years follow:

Sinking Fund Method of Depreciation

	Sinking fund				Depreciation and carrying value		
Year	Annual deposit	Interest revenue (10% of fund balance)	Total fund increase	Fund balance	Depreciation expense	Balance in Accumulated Depreciation account	Carrying value of computer
0							$800,000
1	$120,000	$ -0-	$120,000	$120,000	$120,000	$120,000	680,000
2	120,000	12,000	132,000	252,000	132,000	252,000	548,000
3	120,000	25,200	145,200	397,200	145,200	397,200	402,800
4	120,000	39,720	159,720	556,920	159,720	556,920	243,080
5	120,000	55,692	175,692	732,612	175,692	732,612	67,388
	$600,000	$132,612	$732,612		$732,612		

Journal entries:		Year 1		Year 2
Sinking Fund		120,000		132,000
Depreciation Expense		120,000		132,000
Cash			120,000	120,000
Interest Revenue			-0-	12,000
Accumulated Depreciation			120,000	132,000
To record depreciation using the sinking fund method.				

The schedule above shows that: (1) Depreciation computed by the sinking fund method is debited each year for *increasing* amounts equal to the total increase in the sinking fund; (2) interest revenue is credited each year with earnings at 10% on the fund balance; (3) the net charges to revenue (depreciation less interest earned) each year remain constant at $120,000; and (4) the carrying value of the computer at the end of Year 5 is $67,388, the estimated net residual value at this date.

The sinking fund method of depreciation may be used without accumulating a sinking fund. However, depreciation would still be recorded equal to the hypothetical fund increases as illustrated above. The sinking fund method of depreciation is actually used by a few public utility companies.

Refunding a bond issue

When a company has a bond issue outstanding and the market rate of interest is less than the contractual rate on the bonds outstanding, it may be profitable for the company to **refund** the bonds outstanding, that is, call the old bonds and issue new bonds paying a lower interest rate. The decision to refund requires careful analysis when (1) the carrying value of bonds to be refunded differs from the face amount of the bonds; (2) a call premium is to be paid on the retirement of the bonds outstanding; and (3) issuance costs will be incurred on the new bonds.

To illustrate the type of analysis required for a bond refunding decision, assume the following for the Piper Company on December 31, Year 10:

10% bonds now outstanding; due Dec. 31, Year 20, callable currently at 105, interest payable at June 30 and Dec. 31	$10,000,000
Unamortized bond discount and issuance costs on bonds now outstanding	300,000
New 8% bonds to be issued at 100, due Dec. 31, Year 20, callable at any time at 103, interest payable at June 30 and Dec. 31	10,000,000
Estimated out-of-pocket costs of issuing new bonds	250,000
Effective combined federal and state income tax rate	50%

Since the life of the new 8% bonds is the same as the remaining life of the old 10% bonds and $10 million will have to be paid to bondholders at the end of Year 20 in either case, the decision whether or not to refund rests on a comparison between the net after-tax cost of refunding and the present value of 20 rents representing the semiannual after-tax interest saving. Assuming straight-line amortization for income tax purposes, the analysis of the bond refunding may be made as follows:

After-tax cost of refunding:		
Call premium on old bonds, $500,000, and costs of issuing new bonds, $250,000, to be paid in cash.		$750,000
Less: Tax saving from loss on call of old bonds, 50% × $800,000 (call premium, $500,000, and unamortized bond discount and issuance costs on old bonds, $300,000)		400,000
Net after-tax cost of refunding		$350,000
Net after-tax cash outlay for semiannual interest expense:		
On old 10% bonds:		
Semiannual after-tax interest paid in cash		
($10,000,000 × 10% × ½) × 50%	$250,000	

(continued)

Less: Tax saving from amortization of bond discount		
and issuance costs ($300,000 × $\frac{1}{20}$) × 50%	*7,500*	
Net after-tax cash outlay		*$242,500*
On new 8% bonds:		
Semiannual after-tax interest paid in cash		
($10,000,000 × 8% × $\frac{1}{2}$) × 50%	*$200,000*	
Less: Tax savings from amortization of bond issuance		
costs ($250,000 × $\frac{1}{20}$) × 50%	*6,250*	
Net after-tax cash outlay		*193,750*
Net semiannual after-tax interest saving if refunding is carried		
out		*$ 48,750*

If we assume that the after-tax cost of capital is 4% (50% of 8% interest rate on new bonds compounded semiannually), the refunding would be advantageous, as summarized below:

Present value at Dec. 31, Year 10, of ordinary annuity of 20 rents of	
$48,750 at 2%: $48,750 × 16.351433 from Table 4 of Appendix A	*$797,132*
Less: Net after-tax cost of refunding at Dec. 31, Year 10 (see page 498)	*350,000*
Net present value at Dec. 31, Year 10, of advantage from refunding . .	*$447,132*

In our example the new 8% bonds had a life of 10 years, a period exactly equal to the remaining life of the old 10% bonds. If the new 8% bonds had a life of, say, 25 years, a question would arise whether there is any interest saving during the 15 years beyond the life of the old 10% bonds. If we assumed that the Piper Company could borrow at 8% when the 10% bonds mature in 10 years, the same analysis would apply, since the company would be in approximately the same position at the end of Year 20 whether the bonds are refunded or not.

Direct valuation by discounting future cash flows

Economists have generally taken the position that the fair value of an asset at any point in time is equal to the present value of the future net cash inflows (or cost savings) expected to be generated from the investment (or use) of the asset. The value would be computed by discounting the expected cash inflows (or cost savings) at the current fair rate of interest. Liabilities would be similarly valued by discounting the scheduled future payments at the current fair rate of interest. This technique for the measurement of assets and liabilities is known as *direct valuation.*

Direct valuation techniques are widely used in evaluating alternative choices for decision making, particularly in situations where the future cash inflows or outflows are reasonably predictable. To be able to effectively accumulate and analyze relevant data for decision makers, management accountants should understand the benefits and shortcomings of direct valuation. On the other hand, financial accountants must be aware of the limitations of historical cost valuations and should search for effective means of narrowing the gap which has always existed between *objectivity* and *relevance* of accounting information.

Direct valuation techniques have not been widely used in the area of financial reporting, except in the measurement of long-term receivables and payables and in the valuation of assets acquired through financing leases.[1] Future cash flows are highly unpredictable and are virtually impossible to identify with specific assets in most situations. Furthermore, the *timing* of net future cash flows is uncertain and the selection of the current fair rate of interest for discounting purposes is often a matter of personal opinion. Nevertheless, the concept of direct valuation is a useful frame of reference in accounting theory, particularly in evaluating *indirect valuation* techniques (such as *liquidation* or *exit value,* *replacement value,* and *specific-price index replacement value* described in the *Intermediate Accounting* text of this series) in the preparation of current value financial statements.

Can greater use be made of direct valuation in financial reporting?

The direct valuation concept may be used in situations involving the computation of the present value of a single future sum or a series of equal future receipts, as illustrated in the earlier sections of this chapter. In recent years, some accountants have applied the discounted cash flows concept to the measurement of a business entity's total wealth at a particular point in time, as well as to the measurement of changes in its wealth. In 1973, the Study Group on the Objectives of Financial Statements stated that creditors and investors are generally concerned with the ability of business enterprises to generate future cash flows. One of the objectives of financial statements identified by the Study Group was the following:

> An objective of financial statements is to provide information useful to investors and creditors for predicting, comparing, and evaluating potential cash flows to them in terms of amount, timing, and related uncertainty.[2]

In a paper prepared for consideration by the Study Group, Joshua Ronen found that the preparation of discounted cash flow financial

---

[1] See *APB Opinion No. 21,* "Interest on Receivables and Payables," AICPA (New York: 1971) and *APB Opinion No. 31,* "Disclosure of Lease Commitments by Lessees," AICPA (New York: 1973).

[2] *Objectives of Financial Statements, vol. 1,* AICPA (New York: 1973), p. 20.

statements was entirely feasible.[3] Ronen used three-year forecasted financial statements for an actual company as the basis for his study. With encouragement from the Study Group on the Objectives of Financial Statements, belief by the Securities and Exchange Commission that financial forecasts would be useful to investors (see Chapter 9), and the growing emphasis placed by creditors and investors on the liquidity of corporations, accountants will probably continue to give considerable attention to direct valuation techniques in the years ahead.

Use of direct valuation in current value accounting

Under generally accepted accounting standards, financial statements are prepared using objectively verifiable historical costs. Furthermore, accountants generally assume that the dollar is a stable unit of value and that changes in value of specific assets and liabilities are not relevant in the preparation of financial statements for a going concern. These assumptions have been adopted because continuity of operations rather than termination of activities (liquidation) of the reporting entity is the normal expectation by management and by users of financial statements. An increasing number of accountants and users of financial statements have questioned the assumption that the dollar is a stable unit of value and that current values can be ignored in the preparation of financial statements. Furthermore, the focus in financial reporting in recent years has been shifting from cost-oriented financial statements which report on management's stewardship to a policy of providing financial data which are useful to creditors and investors in making economic decisions.

Issues relating to the restatement of historical-cost financial statements for the changes in the general price level and proposals to incorporate current fair values in the accounting model are included in the *Intermediate Accounting* text of this series. At this point we are primarily interested in pointing out that the concepts of direct valuation described earlier in this chapter promise to play an important role in efforts to expand the use of current value data in financial reports to stockholders.

The Study Group on the Objectives of Financial Statements also called for the disclosure of current values of assets to assist users of financial statements in predicting, comparing, and evaluating the earning power of the reporting company:

> An objective is to provide a statement of financial position useful for predicting, comparing, and evaluating enterprise earning power. This statement should provide information concerning enterprise transactions and other events that are part of incomplete earnings cycles. Current values should also be reported when they differ significantly from historical costs. Assets and liabilities should be grouped or segregated by the relative uncertainty of the amount and timing of prospective realization or liquidation.

[3] *Objectives of Financial Statements, vol. 2, Selected Papers,* Joshua Ronen, "A Test of the Feasibility of Preparing Discounted Cash Flow Accounting Statements," AICPA (New York: 1974), pp. 202–212.

. . . Various current value measurements could be used as indicators of the prospective benefits of assets and sacrifices for liabilities, and of the current sacrifice or benefit aspects of holding them. Each of the current value measurements represents a discounting of expected cash flows, either implicitly by the market (for exit values and current replacement cost) or explicitly by the preparer (for discounted cash flows). The discount rate used by the market or the preparer reflects a subjective assessment of the degree of risk involved. Thus, because he has his own risk preference, disclosure of the current values would be of most help to the user if the amounts of the expected cash flows and the discount rates are disclosed separately. It is, of course, impossible to provide both those components for values determined by the market, but they can be made available when discounted cash flows are reported.

Historical cost is probably, for the present, the only reliable measure of the sacrifice incurred in obtaining assets and the only measure of the benefit realized by incurring liabilities. Value measures probably provide the best current indication of the outcome of incomplete cycles. The choice among these value measures will vary depending on circumstances.[4]

Proposed current value reporting model

In a comprehensive research study on current value accounting prepared for the Financial Executives Institute, Morton Backer listed the following generally recognized financial reporting models:

1 Historical Cost System

2 Price-Level Adjusted Historical Cost System

3 Replacement Cost System

4 Market Value System

5 Current Cash Equivalent System

6 Multi-Measurement System[5]

Backer raised the question whether "current cash equivalent" should be computed for individual assets, groups of assets, or the business entity as a whole. He observed that it has not been sufficiently demonstrated that the current cash equivalent system would enhance the decision processes of users of financial statements, and that current cash equivalent values may not be sufficiently reliable for use in financial reports issued to the public.[6] He also questioned whether the financial community would accept any financial reporting model which did not conform to the basic criteria of objectivity, relevance, verifiability, and realization. As a possible interim solution, Backer proposed the multimeasurement value reporting model illustrated on page 503.[7]

[4] *Objectives of Financial Statements, vol. 1,* pp. 35–36.

[5] Morton Backer (assisted by Richard Simpson), *Current Value Accounting,* Financial Executives Research Foundation (New York: 1973), p. 29.

[6] *Ibid.,* p. 35.

[7] *Ibid.,* p. 38.

PROPOSED VALUE REPORTING MODEL

	Formal Reporting (Balance Sheet and Income Statement)					Informal Reporting (Management Provided Supplemental Information)
	Severable Assets			Nonseverable Assets		
	Objectively Determinable		Not Objectively Determinable	Objectively Determinable	Not Objectively Determinable	
	Relatively Certain Realization	Relatively Uncertain Realization				
Inventories		CRC				
Land in use					OC	EMV
Buildings in use				CRC		
Machinery and equipment				ACRC		
Marketable securities	MV					
Real estate not in use			OC			EMV
Natural resources					OC	EMV
Film libraries			OC			EMV
Unconsolidated nonmarketable securities (affiliated companies)					AOC	EMV
Measurable intangibles					OC	EMV

Key: MV = Market value; CRC = Current replacement cost; ACRC = Current replacement cost adjusted for changes in technology; OC = Original cost less depreciation or amortization; AOC = Original cost adjusted for proportionate share of profits or losses; EMV = Management's estimate of market value.

SOURCE: Morton Backer, *Current Value Accounting*, Financial Executives Research Foundation (New York: 1973), p. 38.

Personal financial statements

Late in the 1960s the accounting profession sanctioned the use of esti-mated current values in the preparation of *personal financial statements* for an individual, a husband and a wife, or a larger family group. Recog-nizing that considerable disparity frequently exists between cost and estimated current values of personal assets, the Committee on Personal Financial Statements of the AICPA recommended a two-column pre-sentation, the first showing financial data on the cost basis and the second showing estimated current values.[8] A set of personal financial statements adapted from the report of the Committee on Personal Finan-cial Statements is illustrated in the Appendix below and on pages 505 to 507.

The Committee believed that it was not acceptable to present personal financial statements on the estimated current value basis without inclu-sion of the related cost data. It also recommended that a personal balance sheet be titled "Statement of Assets and Liabilities" because this would be more readily understood by users of personal financial statements and that the owner's equity section be labeled "Excess of Assets over Liabili-ties."[9]

APPENDIX: PERSONAL FINANCIAL STATEMENTS

MR. AND MRS. RICHARD NELSON
Statement of Assets and Liabilities
December 31, Year 10

Assets	Column A Cost basis	Column B Estimated value basis
Cash	$ 11,079	$ 11,079
Marketable securities (Note 2)	29,578	42,227
Cash value of life insurance	4,647	4,647
Net assets of ABC Proprietorship (Notes 1 and 3)	47,970	65,280
Interest in net assets of XYZ, Inc. (Note 4)	3,000	4,730
Residence, pledged on mortgage note (Note 6)	42,000	67,000
Automobiles	3,000	3,000
Jewelry (Note 6)	6,300	8,400
Paintings (Note 5)	10,000	20,000
Household furnishings	2,000	2,000
Vested interest in QM, Inc., Pension Trust	–0–	17,810
Investment in real estate (Note 6)	30,678	41,000
Contingent asset (Notes 8 and 9)	–0–	–0–
Total assets	$190,252	$287,173

[8] *Audits of Personal Financial Statements*, AICPA (New York: 1968), pp. 2–3.
[9] *Ibid.*, p. 3.

Liabilities

Accounts payable and accrued expenses	$ 3,290	$ 3,290
8% note payable, unsecured, due Jan. 15, Year 13	15,000	15,000
7% mortgage, maturing in Year 17, secured by residence (annual amortization and interest payments, $2,880)	19,790	19,790
Accrued income taxes payable, net of prepayments	2,400	2,400
Accrued income taxes on unrealized asset appreciation (Note 7)	–0–	24,230
Total liabilities	$ 40,480	$ 64,710
Excess of assets over liabilities	$149,772	$222,463

The Notes to the financial statements are an integral part of this statement.

SOURCE: *Audits of Personal Financial Statements; AICPA* (New York: 1968), modified by the authors.

MR. AND MRS. RICHARD NELSON
Statement of Changes in Net Assets
Year Ended December 31, Year 10

	Column A	Column B
	Cost basis	Estimated value basis
Net assets, Jan. 1, Year 10	$146,046	$215,998
Add: Revenue and other increases in net assets:		
Dividends on stock	$ 1,565	$ 1,565
Interest earned	845	845
Salaries and bonuses from XYZ, Inc.	4,040	4,040
Drawings from ABC Proprietorship	16,000	16,000
Gain on sale of securities	3,989	1,743
Increase in value since January 1, Year 10:		
Marketable securities	–0–	2,936
Net assets of ABC Proprietorship (net of drawings)	3,618	4,300
Interest in net assets of XYZ, Inc.	–0–	613
Vested interest in QM, Inc., Pension Trust	–0–	547
Residence	–0–	1,120
Total increases in net assets	$ 30,057	$ 33,709
Deduct: Expenses and other decreases in net assets:		
Interest expense	$ 1,870	$ 1,870
Decrease in value of automobiles	1,125	1,125
Income taxes	4,000	4,000
Real estate taxes	1,873	1,873
Personal expenditures	17,463	17,463
Provision for income taxes on unrealized asset appreciation	–0–	913
Total decreases in net assets	$ 26,331	$ 27,244
Net assets, Dec. 31, Year 10	$149,772	$222,463

The Notes to the financial statements are an integral part of this statement.

Notes to the Financial Statements

Note 1—Net Assets of ABC Proprietorship:

A summary statement of the net assets of the proprietorship at December 31, Year 10, follows:

Current assets	$37,694	
Land, building, and equipment (net)	25,570	
Other assets	2,110	$65,374
Current liabilities	$ 5,790	
Deferred items	3,094	
Long-term debt	8,520	17,404
Net assets		$47,970

Income before provision for income taxes for the year ended December 31, Year 10, amounted to $19,618. Drawings by Mr. Nelson during the year were $16,000.

A certified public accounting firm has examined the financial statements of the proprietorship at December 31, Year 10, and has expressed an unqualified opinion on them.

Note 2—Marketable Securities:

The amounts shown as market value at December 31, Year 10, were arrived at as follows:

Stocks—Quoted closing or latest bid prices

Bonds, U.S.—Quoted latest bid prices

Bonds, other—Quoted latest bid prices

Marketable securities consist of the following:

Stocks:	Shares	Cost	Market value
American Industries, Inc.	100	$ 1,647	$ 4,003
Colleen Fabrics Corp.	1,000	9,696	15,322
Do-All Manufacturing, Ltd.	50	913	401
Thomas Lighting Company	75	1,097	4,243
Maureen Fashions, Inc.	225	7,674	8,949
United Products	500	2,312	1,676
U.S. Equipment Rentals	100	239	920
Total stocks		$23,578	$35,514
Bonds:			
United Products, 9% due July 1, Year 27.		$ 2,000	$ 2,713
U.S. Government, 7% due Mar. 15, Year 19		4,000	4,000
Total bonds		$ 6,000	$6,713
Total marketable securities		$29,578	$42,227

Note 3—ABC Proprietorship:

Estimated value is based on an offer to purchase the net assets of the business, dated September 17, Year 10. Mr. Nelson has refused the offer.

Note 4—Interest in Net Assets of XYZ, Inc.:

Estimated value of the 25% interest in the net assets of the corporation is based on audited financial statements at September 30, Year 10. Management of XYZ, Inc., has reported that no material financial changes have occurred since that date.

Note 5—Paintings:

Estimated value is based upon a firm offer to purchase the paintings by Modern Galleries on December 10, Year 10.

Note 6—Appraisals:

Estimated value is based upon independent appraisals obtained from individuals and/or firms for the following assets:

Residence	$67,000	(1)
Jewelry	8,400	(2)
Real estate	41,000	(3)

(1) Recent purchases of homes within the same area approximate the appraised valuation. The assessed real estate value (100% valuation) was determined in Year 9 to be $61,000.

(2) Mrs. Nelson's jewelry has been insured in the amount of $8,400.

(3) The assessed real estate value (100% valuation) was determined in Year 8 to be $38,000.

Note 7—Accrued Income Taxes on Unrealized Appreciation:

Unrealized appreciation in value of assets would, if realized, require payment of taxes at capital gains rates. Therefore, the accrual has been made on that basis.

Note 8—Stock Option:

Mr. Nelson has been granted an option to purchase 300 shares, or any part thereof, of QM, Inc., common stock at a price of $9 per share. The option expires on August 31, Year 13. The market price of QM, Inc., common stock is approximately $10 per share.

Note 9—Interest in Property Subject to Life Estate:

Mrs. Nelson is the beneficiary of the estate of William Dudley, her father, remaining at the time of the death of her mother. Contingencies within the bequest preclude the actuarial determination of a present value of Mrs. Nelson's interest in the estate.

REVIEW QUESTIONS

1 Differentiate between *simple* and *compound* interest.

2 Explain the meaning of the symbols i and n in the formula $(1 + i)^n$. If interest at 12% is compounded monthly, what is the formula for computing the amount to which $500 would accumulate in three years?

3 Compute the present value of $296 discounted for ten periods at 4% per period if the amount of $1 at 4% for ten periods is $1.48.

4 From the basic compound interest formula $(1 + i)^n$, give the formula for:
  a The present value of $1 for n periods discounted at i rate of interest per period
  b The amount of an ordinary annuity of n rents at i rate of interest per period

    c The present value of an ordinary annuity of *n* rents at *i* rate of interest per period

5 Given the amount of an ordinary annuity for *n* periods at *i* rate of interest, how would you determine:

    a The amount on deposit immediately after making the tenth deposit of $1,000 each?

    b The dollar amount of each of ten equal deposits if $5,000 is to be accumulated at a point in time one period after the tenth deposit?

6 Describe how the "present value of $1 at 5%" formula can be used to compute:

    a The sum that must be deposited at December 31, Year 1, so that 20 equal annual withdrawals of $200 can be made starting on December 31, Year 2

    b The dollar amount of 20 equal annual rents that can be withdrawn starting on December 31, Year 1, if $10,000 is deposited on that date

7 Define each of the following:

    a Amount of an annuity due

    b Present value of an annuity due

    c Amount of a deferred annuity

    d Present value of a deferred annuity

    e Annuity method of depreciation

    f Sinking fund method of depreciation

8 Sarah Chatfield owes Vickie Kubota $8,710, which will be paid in six equal installments of $2,000 starting in one year. Using Table 4 in Appendix A, determine the approximate annual rate of interest that Sarah Chatfield will be paying on this loan.

9 What is the meaning of **direct valuation?** Describe some uses of direct valuation techniques in the preparation of financial statements or in other financial accounting situations.

10 The Study Group on the Objectives of Financial Statements called for disclosure of information for predicting, comparing, and evaluating potential cash flows to investors and creditors in terms of amount, timing, and related uncertainty. Do you consider such information useful to investors and creditors? Why?

11 What position was taken by the Study Group on the Objectives of Financial Statements with respect to the disclosure by publicly owned companies of current values of assets in their financial statements?

12 Describe a **multi-measurement** current value reporting model. How can such a model be used in the preparation of **personal financial statements?**

EXERCISES

Ex. 13-1 The Stanaway Company has a choice of paying for an insurance policy as follows:

One-year premium	$1,050
Three-year premium	2,783
Five-year premium	4,743

Assuming that premiums are payable in advance and that the current fair rate of interest is 8%, which of the three alternatives is most advantageous? Use tables in Appendix A in your analysis.

Ex. 13-2 Assuming that the amount of $1 at 3% for 31 periods is $2.50 and that interest at 6% is compounded semiannually, compute answers for the following to the nearest dollar:

a Amount of $1,000 for 16 years
b Compound interest on $10,000 for 15 years
c Present value of $5,000 discounted for 15½ years
d Amount of an annuity due of 31 rents of $1,000
e Present value of an ordinary annuity of 31 rents of $1,000
f Amount of an ordinary annuity of 31 rents of $1,000 deposited semiannually, 16 years after the final deposit

Ex. 13-3 On January 1, Year 1, Pepe Gonzales acquired $100,000 face amount of 10% bonds with a remaining life of 12 years. The current market rate of interest is 9%, compounded semiannually. Assuming that interest on the bonds is payable semiannually, compute the cost to the nearest dollar of the bonds to Pepe Gonzales. Use the appropriate table or tables in Appendix A.

Ex. 13-4 Bob Hamilton plans to make five equal deposits beginning January 1, Year 1, in order to be able to withdraw $10,000 each year at eight annual intervals beginning January 1, Year 6. If the money on deposit will earn interest at 5% compounded annually, what equal deposits should be made? The following rounded values for $1 are available from compound interest tables:

$$A_{\overline{5}|5\%} = \$\ 5.526 \qquad P_{\ \overline{5}|5\%} = \$4.329$$
$$A_{\overline{12}|5\%} = \$15.917 \qquad P_{\ \overline{8}|5\%} = \$6.463$$
$$A_{\overline{13}|5\%} = \$17.713 \qquad P_{\overline{12}|5\%} = \$8.863$$

Ex. 13-5 Rose Mary Marquez has agreed to sell a property for $110,000. She received $30,000 cash at the date of sale and 20 non-interest-bearing notes of equal amount. The notes are due serially, one each six months starting six months from the date of sale. It was agreed that the notes will include interest in their face amount at 10% compounded semiannually.

Compute to the nearest dollar the face amount of each note. Show your computations in good form. Use Appendix A in completing your solution.

Ex. 13-6 The Krueger Company issued 10-year, 7% bonds on January 1, Year 5. On December 31, Year 5, the accountant for the Krueger Company made the following entry to record the effective interest expense for the last half of Year 5:

Bond Interest Expense	37,373	
Discount on Bonds Payable		2,373
Cash		35,000

Semiannual bond interest expense for the last
half of Year 5:

Bond interest paid		$35,000
Add: Discount at June 30, Year 5	$65,670	
Less: Discount at Dec. 31, Year 5	63,297	2,373
Bond interest expense		$37,373

On the basis of the information presented above, prepare the journal entry that must have been made by Krueger Company to record the issuance of bonds at January 1, Year 5. Round all computations to the nearest dollar.

Ex. 13-7 The following are symbols relating to compound interest formulas:

$P_{\overline{n}|i}$ = the present value of an ordinary annuity of n payments of $1 each at interest rate i per period.

$p_{\overline{n}|i}$ = the present value of $1 for n periods at interest rate i per period.

$A_{\overline{n}|i}$ = the future value of an ordinary annuity of n payments of $1 each at interest rate i per period.

$a_{\overline{n}|i}$ = the future value of $1 for n periods at interest rate i per period.

R = periodic cash payment (or receipt).

1 If Jeffrey wishes to earn interest at an annual rate of 8% compounded quarterly on an investment that promises to pay the lump sum of $1,000 at the end of six years, the formula that could be used to compute the amount that should be paid now is:

a $1,000 $(A_{\overline{24}|2\%})$

b $1,000 $(a_{\overline{24}|2\%})$

c $1,000 $(P_{\overline{24}|2\%})$

d $1,000 $(p_{\overline{24}|2\%})$

e None of the above

2 If Lori wishes to earn interest at the annual rate of 8% compounded semi-annually on an investment contract that promises to pay $1,000 at the end of 20 years along with semiannual interest payments of $50, the formula that could be used to compute the amount that Lori should invest now is:

a $1,000 $(p_{\overline{20}|8\%})$ + $50 $(P_{\overline{20}|8\%})$

b $1,000 $(p_{\overline{40}|4\%})$ + $50 $(P_{\overline{40}|4\%})$

c $1,000 $(p_{\overline{20}|10\%})$ + $50 $(P_{\overline{20}|10\%})$

d $1,000 $(p_{\overline{40}|5\%})$ + $50 $(P_{\overline{40}|5\%})$

e None of the above

3 On May 1, Year 1, Lisa wishes to know the amount of the equal payments that must be made semiannually beginning on November 1, Year 1, to have a fund of $10,000 at the end of 20 years. If Lisa is certain that the fund will earn interest at the annual rate of 6% compounded semiannually, a formula that could be used to compute the periodic payment is:

a $10,000 = R $(A_{\overline{40}|3\%})$

b $10,000 = R $(A_{\overline{20}|6\%})$

c $10,000 = R $(P_{\overline{40}|3\%})$

d $10,000 = R $(P_{\overline{20}|6\%})$

e None of the above

4 On May 1, Year 1 a new car was purchased on a four-year installment contract which required payments of $100 now and $100 on the first day of each month with the last payment due on April 1, Year 5. If the annual interest rate is 12% compounded monthly, the formula that could be used to compute the cash price for the car is:

a $1,200 $(P_{\overline{4}|12\%})$

b $100 $(P_{\overline{47}|1\%})$ + $100

c $100 $(P_{\overline{48}|1\%})$

d $100 $(p_{\overline{47}|1\%})$ + $100

e None of the above

SHORT CASES FOR ANALYSIS AND DECISION

Case 13-1 The following letter was written by George Gustafson to L. C. Dull, an insurance company executive:

Dear Mr. Dull:

I recently purchased a home on which your company holds a first mortgage, with a balance of $21,290, issued 21 years ago and bearing interest at 6% compounded monthly. My payments for the remaining four years of the loan period are $500 per month. The next payment is due one month from today.

With the current high cost of mortgage money (12% compounded monthly), you may find it profitable to allow me to pay off this mortgage loan at, say, $20,000 so that you can reinvest the money in other mortgage loans yielding a much higher current return. Would you consider my offer?

This loan is of course quite attractive for me but if I can pay it off for $20,000, I would be happy to do so. I sincerely hope that as rational businessmen we can complete a transaction which would be profitable for both of us. Please let me hear from you at your earliest convenience.

Sincerely,

George Gustafson

Dull's reply to Gustafson's letter follows:

Dear Mr. Gustafson:

Thank you for your inquiry concerning the early payoff of the mortgage which we hold on your property. As you undoubtedly are aware, under FHA regulations you can now pay this mortgage in full without penalty.

Your proposal that we consider discounting your present balance in order to reacquire these low-yielding funds for reinvestment at higher rates is a very logical one. From our standpoint, however, there are other factors to be considered. When we originally purchased the mortgage on the property you now own, it was at a yield that was very satisfactory to us in relation to the long-term liabilities we were attempting to cover. This is still true. Secondly, since we are under no compulsion to sell this asset at a loss, there is little incentive to do it as the net effect on our mortgage portfolio would be imperceptible.

We hope this reply, while not being the one you perhaps wanted, satisfies your question.

Sincerely,

L. C. Dull
Assistant Mortgage Secretary

Instructions   Evaluate Gustafson's offer to pay off the mortgage and Dull's response, with appropriate computations (using Appendix A) to support your conclusions.

Case 13-2 Ivan Vodka has just accepted a position with a state agency. The state has a retirement pension plan which calls for joint contributions by the employee and employer; however, the retirement fund earns a very low rate of return. Vodka, who is 10 years from the retirement age of sixty-five, expects to contribute $3,000 per year to the plan and after 10 years of contributions to be eligible to receive approximately $5,000 per year for life.

Vodka is uncertain whether he should accept the plan. Since the retirement plan is optional, he is considering the alternative of investing annually an amount equal to his contribution under the plan, with the idea that the higher rate of earnings on such an investment might well more than offset the loss of his employer's contribution. Vodka is firmly convinced that he can invest $3,000 per year to earn a return of 8% annually for the next 10 years and also after his retirement. After his retirement, Vodka would plan to exhaust his investment fund by withdrawing (starting one year after his retirement) an equal amount each year from his investment for a period of 15 years, which is his life expectancy at age sixty-five.

Instructions Assuming that Vodka can carry out his investment plan and that he will realize earnings on his investment at the expected rate, prepare a schedule (using Appendix A) to show whether he is likely to be better or worse off if he accepts his employer's pension plan. How would you advise Vodka with respect to this decision?

Case 13-3 The Rapid-Growth Corporation recently acquired equipment for $2 million. The company made a down payment of $200,000, with the balance payable at the rate of $300,000 per year at the end of each of the next six years, plus 10% interest on the unpaid balance. The estimated useful life of the equipment is eight years and the residual value at the end of eight years is estimated at $250,000.

The president of the company informs you that he would like to take the maximum amount of depreciation for income tax purposes. However, because the company's volume of business is expected to grow at an annual compound rate of 15% and because of the high interest expense in the early years, he would prefer to take the lowest possible amount of depreciation for financial reporting purposes in the early years and correspondingly larger amounts in later years. He also mentions to you that a president of a public utility company told him at a cocktail party to "pick one of those compound interest methods of depreciation; they will do the job for you."

Instructions What advice would you give to the president, assuming that an accumulation of a sinking fund for the replacement of the equipment is not contemplated? (**Hint:** The depreciation for the first year, using the sinking fund method of depreciation at 10%, is $153,027).

Case 13-4 Professor Smedley received the following note from a former student who was a partner of a medium-sized CPA firm:

"We would like to have your opinion as to the proper balance sheet treatment of the potential liability arising under the following circumstances:

"One of our clients purchased a parcel of real estate, the consideration being $10,000 per year for the joint lives of the sellers, who are married. It would seem to us that since each annual payment is contingent upon the sellers living another year, only the actual payments should be capitalized as paid and the remaining liability disclosed in a footnote.

"Please let us know if you concur. If you do not agree, we would appreciate knowing how you would determine the liability and whether or not any portion of the annual payments should be treated as interest expense. We propose to pay you a fee of $100 for your advice on this matter."

Instructions Prepare a response to the question raised by the CPA which, in your opinion, would be in conformity with generally accepted accounting standards.

PROBLEMS

13-5 Using appropriate tables in Appendix A, prepare solutions for each of the following independent situations. (Round all amounts to the nearest dollar.)
 a Compute the semiannual deposit necessary to accumulate a fund of $46,071 at the end of four years, if the fund earns interest at the rate of 8% compounded semiannually. Prepare a schedule showing the fund accumulation for the four-year period.
 b If $39,927 is invested in a savings account at the beginning of Year 3, to earn 8% annually, what equal amounts may be withdrawn at the end of each year for five years? Compute the amount of the equal withdrawals and prepare a schedule showing that the savings account will be exhausted at the end of five years.

c If $46,993 is invested now to earn an annual return of 10%, what equal amounts can be withdrawn at the end of the third year and for each of the next four years? Compute the amount of the periodic withdrawals and prepare a schedule showing that the sum invested will be exhausted at the end of seven years.

13-6 On April 1, Year 9, Lease Financing Company acquired rental equipment at a cost of $20,849 cash, with an estimated salvage value equal to the cost of disposal at the end of its useful life. On the same date, Lease Financing Company entered into a lease for the equipment with Gilles Corporation. The lease is for a five-year period, with rent payable in advance the first day of each year in an amount sufficient to return Lease Financing Company's unrecovered investment, together with interest at 10% on the unrecovered investment. Rental payments are to be equal. The present value of an annuity due of five rents of $1 at 10% is 4.169865.

Instructions
a Compute the annual rental payment to be made by Gilles Corporation to Lease Financing Company and prepare a schedule showing the recovery of the investment over the life of the lease. Assume that the lease is not considered equivalent to a sale and purchase of property.
b Prepare journal entries in the accounts of Lease Financing Company to record the lease transactions for the year ended March 31, Year 10.

13-7 The County of Tulare has decided to build a toll bridge across a river between two towns. The construction contract was awarded to the Pinto Company with a bid of $2 million to complete the bridge by the end of the current year. The Pinto Company agrees to accept the county's 20-year, 4% tax-free bonds (with interest payable annually) in payment for the bridge when construction is completed. The county plans to provide for a schedule of toll rates that will produce revenue sufficient to cover interest, operating costs, and an annual deposit in a sinking fund to retire the bonds at maturity.

Engineers estimate that the ratio of automobiles to trucks will be 10 to 1, and that tolls of 25 cents for automobiles and 50 cents for trucks can be established. The cost of collecting tolls and maintaining the bridge is estimated to be $30,000 per year.

Instructions Determine the number of automobile and truck tolls that must be collected annually in order to meet annual sinking fund, interest, and operating costs. Assume that the sinking fund will earn 4% compounded annually. (Use Appendix A to obtain the appropriate value for $1.)

13-8 *a* Sandman Company has made annual payments of $10,000 into a fund at the close of each year for the past four years. The fund balance immediately after the fourth payment totaled $45,061. Sandman Company's controller asks you to determine how many more $10,000 annual payments will be required to bring the fund to $100,000, assuming that the fund continues to earn interest at 8% compounded annually.

Instructions Compute the number of full payments required and the amount of the final payment (to the nearest dollar) if a full $10,000 is not required. (Use Appendix A.)

b Sandman Company also wishes to provide for the retirement of an obligation of $500,000 due on March 1, Year 8. The company plans to deposit $40,000 in a special fund each March 1 for eight years, starting March 1, Year 1. The company wishes to deposit on March 1, Year 0, an amount which, with accumulated interest at 7% compounded annually, will bring the fund up to $500,000 at the maturity of the obligation on March 1, Year 8.

Instructions Compute (to the nearest dollar) the amount to be deposited on March 1, Year 0. (Use Appendix A.)

13-9 On January 2, Year 1, Purvis Corporation purchased a printing press for $500,000. Installation and freight costs on the printing press were $45,093. The printing press had an estimated service life of 15 years and an estimated net residual value at the end of that time of $100,000. The current rate of return on this type of investment is 8%.

Instructions
a Prepare a depreciation schedule for the printing press for the first two years of service life under the annuity method of depreciation, and the journal entries to record depreciation for the first two years of service life. Use Appendix A and carry all computations to the nearest dollar.
b Prepare a depreciation schedule for the printing press for the first two years of service life under the sinking fund method of depreciation, and the journal entries to record depreciation for the first two years of service life. Use Appendix A and carry all computations to the nearest dollar.

13-10 At December 31, Year 10, the Boyce Corporation has outstanding $20 million of 20-year, 9% bonds that were issued on January 1, Year 1. Unamortized bond discount and issuance costs of $100,000 remain in the accounts. The bonds were callable at 103 in Years 11 through 15, and at reduced call prices thereafter.

Wally Boyce, the president of the company, is considering the possibility of refunding the 9% bonds by issuing, at their face amount, $20 million of 8%, 10-year bonds. Issuance costs that would be incurred in connection with the new issue of 8% bonds are estimated at $400,000. Interest on both the 9% bond and the 8% bonds is payable semiannually at June 30 and December 31.

Instructions Prepare a schedule analyzing the proposed refunding and advise Boyce whether or not the refunding of the old 9% bonds would be profitable. Your analysis should be similar to the schedule on pages 498–499. Assume that the company is subject to an average income tax rate of 50% and that the after-tax cost of capital is 4% compounded semiannually. (Use Appendix A.)

13-11 For many years you have prepared George Mora's income tax return on a cash basis and have provided him with tax-planning advice. He has recently inherited $100,000 which will be paid to him about January 1, Year 7, when the estate is settled. He is considering the following investments for the $100,000:

(1) Lease of a downtown parking lot which is the site of a proposed office building whose construction will begin in January, Year 17. Mora would be required to make an advance payment of $90,000 for the lease and to make monthly rental payments of $1,000. In addition he would spend $10,000 for the erection of a shelter which would be completed by the beginning of the lease period, January 1, Year 7. The shelter would be depreciated by the straight-line method. Parking revenue is estimated to be $44,000 yearly and annual cash expenses, in addition to the rent, would amount to $8,500.

(2) Purchase of an interest in a producing oil well on January 1, Year 7, for $100,000. Mora's share of the well's yearly income would be $20,000 less cash expenses of $8,250. The estimated value of his share of the well at the end of 10 years is $65,000. The percentage depletion rate applicable to oil wells is 22%.

The net cash flow after income taxes derived from these alternative investments would be invested at the end of each year in tax-exempt securities offering a 4% return paid in one annual payment at December 31. This annual payment would, in turn, be reinvested in the same kind of tax-exempt securities. Tables for compounding interest at the rate of 4% to be used in arriving at the solution to this problem are given on page 515.

Periods	Amount of $1	Amount of an ordinary annuity of $1
1	$1.040	$1.000
2	1.082	2.040
3	1.125	3.122
4	1.170	4.246
5	1.217	5.416
6	1.265	6.633
7	1.316	7.898
8	1.369	9.214
9	1.423	10.583
10	1.480	12.006

Taxable income derived from the investment of the $100,000 would be subject to a tax rate of 60%. Long-term capital gains would be taxed at a rate of 30%.

Instructions Prepare schedules computing for a 10-year period the total cash flow after income taxes for each alternative investment, the parking lot and the oil well, including the cash flow derived from the reinvestment of available funds in the described tax-exempt securities. Total cash flow is the amount of cash accumulated over the 10-year period. In the computation of the gain or loss on the sale of the oil well, the total amount of percentage depletion allowed for income tax purposes reduces the basis (unrecovered cost) of the oil well.

13-12 Whittier Enterprises designs and manufactures toys. Past experience indicates that the product life cycle of a toy is three years. Promotional advertising produces large sales in the early years, but there is a substantial sales decline in the final year of a toy's life.

Consumer demand for new toys placed on the market tends to fall into three classes. About 30% of the new toys sell well above expectations, 60% sell as anticipated and 10% have poor consumer acceptance.

A new toy has been developed. The following sales projections were made by carefully evaluating consumer demand for the new toy:

Consumer demand for new toy	Chance of occurring	Estimated sales in		
		Year 1	Year 2	Year 3
Above average	30%	$1,200,000	$2,5000,000	$600,000
Average	60%	700,000	1,700,000	400,000
Below average	10%	200,000	900,000	150,000

Variable costs are estimated at 30% of the selling price. Special machinery must be purchased at a cost of $860,000 and will be installed in an unused portion of the factory which Whittier Enterprises has unsuccessfully been trying to rent to someone for several years at $50,000 per year and has no prospects for future utilization. Fixed expenses (excluding depreciation) of a cash flow nature are estimated at $50,000 per year on the new toy. The new machinery will be depreciated by the sum-of-the-years' digits method with an estimated residual value of $110,000 and will be sold at the beginning of the fourth year. Advertising and promotional expenses will be incurred uniformly and will total $100,000 the first year, $150,000 the second year, and $50,000 the third year. These expenses will be deducted as incurred for income tax purposes.

Whittier Enterprises believes that state and federal income taxes will total 60% of income in the foreseeable future and may be assumed to be paid uniformly over the year income is earned.

Instructions

a Prepare a schedule computing the probable sales of this new toy in each of the three years, taking into account the probability of above average, average, and below average sales occurring.

b Assume that the probable sales computed in a are $900,000 in the first year, $1,800,000 in the second year, and $410,000 in the third year. Prepare a schedule computing the probable net income for the new toy in each of the three years of its life.

c Prepare a schedule of net cash flows from sales of the new toy for each of the years involved and from the disposition of the machinery purchased. Use the sales data given in part b.

d Assuming a minimum desired rate of return of 10%, prepare a schedule of the present value of the net cash flows calculated in c. The following data are to be used in arriving at your answer.

Year	Present value of $1 due at the end of each year discounted at 10%	Present value of $1 earned uniformly throughout the year discounted at 10%
1	$0.91	$0.95
2	0.83	0.86
3	0.75	0.78

13-13 Lee Wong, M.D., and John Zorb, M.D., are applying for a $115,000 loan to purchase additional equipment for their medical practice. The bank has requested a personal statement of assets and liabilities as of June 30, Year 13, from Dr. and Mrs. Wong. Pertinent facts about the Wongs follow. Unless stated otherwise, all facts are presented as of June 30, Year 13.

(1) The Wongs have $8,000 in a checking account and $30,000, including interest through June 30, Year 13, in a savings account.

(2) The Wongs paid $7,500 in Year 11 for a 15% interest in Corona Corporation which has 100,000 shares of stock outstanding. The stock is traded on a midwestern exchange. In recent months the stock has traded in blocks of 100 shares or less at $1.50 per share. Dr. Wong was offered $1.10 per share for all his shares on June 22, Year 13. The offer is still outstanding.

(3) Dr. Wong and Dr. Zorb each own a 50% interest in the South Bay Medical Group, a partnership. The balance sheet of South Bay Medical Group, prepared on a modified cash basis, follows:

Assets

Cash (in non-interest-bearing checking account)	$ 10,400
Treasury bills (maturing July 30, Year 13)	11,000
Drugs and supplies inventory	6,100
Equipment and office furniture (net of $14,000 accumulated depreciation) . .	66,000
Automobiles (net of $1,150 accumulated depreciation)	10,800
Building (purchased June 28, Year 13)	55,000
Total	$159,300

Liabilities & Partners' Capital

6% notes payable (principal and interest payable monthly until Year 20) . . .	$ 39,000
Partners' Capital	120,300
Total	$159,300

At June 30, Year 13, South Bay Medical Group had unrecorded accounts receivable of $12,451 and unrecorded accounts payable of $1,327. Payments on the notes are current. The partnership prepares its tax returns on the accrual basis.

(4) Drs. Wong and Zorb were offered $260,000 for their practice. The offer is still outstanding. Counsel has advised that if the offer is accepted, any difference between the proceeds and the partners' tax bases in the partnership will be taxed as ordinary income.

(5) The Wongs purchased their residence in Year 10 for $85,000. The balance of the 30-year, 6¾% mortgage is $64,498. The current rate charged on similar mortgages is 6¾%. Payments on the mortgage are current. Similar homes in the area have increased in value approximately 30% since Year 10. The assessed real estate value was determined in March of Year 13 to be $108,500 based on fair value.

(6) Mrs. Wong owns an automobile which cost $5,950. Current newspaper advertisements indicate that her car could be sold for $4,800.

(7) Some years ago the Wongs received a painting as a wedding present from Mrs. Wong's aunt, an internationally known artist. At the date of gift, the painting was appraised at $6,000 and this is considered the cost basis for accounting purposes. The income tax basis of the painting to Mrs. Wong is zero. The painting was conservatively appraised in June of Year 13 at $16,000.

(8) The Wongs have maintained cost records on their major household effects. The costs aggregate $27,500. A local business which specializes in auctioning this type of merchandise estimated in July of Year 13 that the household effects have a net realizable value of $12,000. Other household effects are of nominal value.

(9) Dr. Wong has a vested interest of $14,175 in a group-participating pension plan. The present value of the vested benefits is $6,818. Dr. Wong's contributions to the plan (tax basis) have been $5,432.

(10) On July 1, Year 10, Dr. Wong paid $9,000 for 25% of the capital stock of MI, Inc., a closely held business which designs medical instruments. A summary of financial data of MI, Inc., follows:

Balance sheet at June 30, Year 12		Earnings summary for the years ended June 30		Dividends paid	
Assets	$112,800				
Liabilities	$ 46,650	Year 11	$12,050		
Equity	66,150	Year 12	18,100		
	$112,800	Year 13	28,050	$6,200	(June 10)

Similar businesses in the area have been sold recently for 10 times the average of the last three years' earnings.

(11) The Wongs owed $810 on charge accounts and $220 on a national credit card account at June 30, Year 13.

(12) In early July of Year 13, the Wongs estimated their federal income tax for their Year 13 return to be $26,000. Estimated tax payments of $8,000 had

been made as of June 30, Year 13. A tax rate of 40% is assumed for ordinary income and 20% for long-term capital gains. Assume that the gain in the value of the pension trust would be taxed at 40%.

Instructions Prepare a personal statement of assets and liabilities in good form as of June 30, Year 13, for Dr. and Mrs. Wong. Use the Appendix on pages 504–505 as a guide. Supporting calculations should be in good form. Footnotes are not required.

CHAPTER

14

Government entities: funds and programs

The student beginning the study of accounting for government entities must temporarily set aside many of the familiar accounting principles for business entities. Such fundamental concepts of accounting theory for business entities as the nature of the accounting entity, the primacy of the income statement, and the pervasiveness of accrual accounting have little or no relevance in accounting for government entities. Consequently, we shall begin our discussion with those features of government entities which give rise to unique accounting concepts. The second section of the chapter will deal with the various theoretical issues of accounting for government entities. The chapter will conclude with specific examples of accounting for governmental units.

NATURE OF GOVERNMENT ENTITIES

When thinking of government entities of the United States, one tends to focus on the federal government, or on the governments of the 50 states. However, in addition to those major government entities and the governments of the several U.S. territories, there are the following governmental units in the United States:

More than 3,000 counties
Nearly 17,000 townships
More than 18,000 municipalities
Almost 16,000 school districts

Nearly 24,000 special districts (port authorities, airports, public buildings, libraries, and others)[1]

Despite the wide range in size and scope of governance, the government entities listed above have a number of characteristics in common. Among these characteristics are the following:

1 *Organization to serve the citizenry.* A basic tenet of governmental philosophy in the United States is that government entities exist to serve the citizens subject to their jurisdiction. Thus, the citizens as a whole establish government entities through the constitutional and charter process. Business entities, in contrast, are created by only a limited number of individuals.

2 *General absence of the profit motive.* With few exceptions, government entities render services to the citizenry without the objective of profiting from those services. Business enterprises are motivated to a great extent to earn profits.

3 *Taxation as the principal source of revenue.* The citizenry subject to a government's jurisdiction provides resources to the governmental unit principally through taxation. Many of these taxes are paid on a **self-assessment** basis. There is no comparable revenue source for business enterprises.

4 *Impact of the legislative process.* Operations of governmental units are for the most part initiated by various legislative enactments, such as operating budgets, borrowing authorizations, and tax levies. Business enterprises are also affected by federal, state, and local laws and regulations, but not to such a **direct** extent.

5 *Stewardship for resources.* The primary responsibility of governmental entities in financial reporting is to demonstrate adequate stewardship for resources provided by their citizenry. Business enterprises have a comparable responsibility to their owners, but not to the same extent as government entities.

The five preceding characteristics of government entities are major determinants of accounting theory for governmental units. In the next section we shall discuss this theory.

THEORY OF ACCOUNTING FOR GOVERNMENT ENTITIES

In accounting for business entities, **economic substance** of financial transactions is emphasized over their **legal form.** Thus, noncancellable leases which are in substance installment purchases of personal property are accounted for as such in the financial statements of business enterprises. Similarly, minority interest in a consolidated subsidiary, although in form a part of consolidated stockholders' equity, is substantively treated as a liability under the "parent company" concept of consolidated financial statements.

In contrast, accounting for governmental units emphasizes **legal form** over **economic substance.** This emphasis is necessitated by the characteristics of government entities discussed in the preceding section of this chapter—especially the impact of the legislative process and the stewardship for resources. Emphasis on legal form for governmental units

[1] *Audits of State and Local Government Units,* AICPA (New York: 1974), p. 4.

is manifested in several aspects of governmental accounting. Among these are the following:

The governmental accounting entity

The modified accrual basis of accounting

Recording of expenditures rather than expenses

Recording of purchase orders for goods and services

Recording the budget

The governmental accounting entity

Accounting for business enterprises emphasizes the economic entity as an accounting unit. Thus, a partnership is considered to be an accounting entity separate from its partners; and consolidated financial statements are issued for a group of affiliated—but legally separate—corporations which comprise a single economic entity under common control.

There is generally no single accounting entity for a specific governmental unit, such as the Town of Verdant Glen. Instead, the accounting entity for governmental units is the *fund.* A fund is described by the National Committee on Governmental Accounting as follows:

> For governmental accounting purposes, a fund is an independent fiscal and accounting entity composed of a sum of money or other resources which are segregated for the purpose of carrying on specific activities or attaining certain objectives in accordance with special regulations, restrictions or limitations. Unlike a private business enterprise which constitutes a single economic entity with a single group of assets, liabilities, and equity accounts, a governmental unit will normally have within its jurisdiction and sphere of operations several separate entities or funds, each of which has its own designated assets, liabilities and fund equities.[2]

Thus, accounting for a single governmental unit generally involves several different funds. The National Committee on Governmental Accounting has recommended eight types of funds, as follows:

(1) The General Fund to account for all financial transactions not properly accounted for in another fund;

(2) Special Revenue Funds to account for the proceeds of specific revenue sources (other than special assessments) or to finance specified activities as required by law or administrative regulation;

(3) Debt Service Funds to account for the payment of interest and principal on long-term debt other than special assessment and revenue bonds;

(4) Capital Projects Funds to account for the receipt and disbursement of moneys used for the acquisition of capital facilities other than those financed by special assessment and enterprise funds;

(5) Enterprise Funds to account for the financing of services to the general public where all or most of the costs involved are paid in the form of charges by users of such services;

(6) Trust and Agency Funds to account for assets held by a governmental unit as trustee or agent for individuals, private organizations, and other governmental units;

---

[2]*Governmental Accounting, Auditing and Financial Reporting,* National Committee on Governmental Accounting (Ann Arbor: 1968), p. 3.

(7) Intragovernmental Service Funds to account for the financing of special activities and services performed by a designated organization unit within a governmental jurisdiction for other organization units within the same governmental jurisdiction;

(8) Special Assessment Funds to account for special assessments levied to finance public improvements or services deemed to benefit the properties against which the assessments are levied.[3]

In addition, the National Committee on Governmental Accounting recommended that governmental units maintain two *self-balancing groups of accounts*—the general fixed assets and general long-term debt groups.

Every governmental unit has a general fund. Additional funds should be established as required by legislative action and the maintenance of adequate custodianship for resources of the governmental unit. Accounting for each of the eight types of funds and two groups of accounts will be discussed in a subsequent section of this chapter. At this point, we must reemphasize that a governmental unit does not have a single accounting entity to account for *all* its financial resources, obligations, revenues, and expenditures.

The modified accrual basis of accounting

Except for enterprise funds and intragovernmental service funds, which reflect sales of goods and services, governmental accounting does not emphasize the results of the governmental unit's operations for a fiscal year. Financial reporting for governments instead focuses upon the stewardship provided for the governmental unit's assets. One consequence is that a *modified accrual basis* of accounting is appropriate for the general fund, special revenue funds, and debt service funds. The conventional accrual basis of accounting is used for capital projects funds, trust and agency funds, and special assessment funds, in addition to enterprise funds and intragovernmental service funds.

What is the *modified accrual basis* of accounting? The AICPA has described the modified accrual basis as follows:

> Revenues are recorded as received in cash except for (a) revenues susceptible to accrual and (b) revenues of a material amount that have not been received at the normal time of receipt.
>
> . . . .
>
> Expenditures are recorded on the accrual basis, except in the instances discussed below.
>
> Disbursements for inventory items may be considered as expenditures at the time of purchase or at the time the items are used.
>
> Normally expenditures are not divided between years by the recording of prepaid expenses, for example prepaid insurance.
>
> Interest on long-term debt, commonly accounted for in debt service funds, normally should be recorded as an expenditure on its due date. . . .[4]

Few revenues of the general fund, special revenue funds, and debt

---

[3] *Ibid.,* pp. 7–8.
[4] *Audits of State and Local Government Units,* pp. 14, 16.

service funds are susceptible to accrual. For example, there is no basis for the accrual of self-assessed taxes such as income taxes, sales taxes, and taxes on gross business receipts. Similarly, fees for business licenses, marriage licenses, and comparable permits are properly recorded when received in cash, because these fees are not billable in advance of the service or permit granting.

Perhaps the most commonly accrued revenue of a governmental unit is property taxes. These taxes are customarily billed by the governmental unit to the property owner and are usually payable in the fiscal year for which billed.

In summary, cash basis accounting is appropriate for many revenues of the general fund, special revenue funds, and debt service funds.

Recording of expenditures rather than expenses

Because of the lack of emphasis upon operating results, funds other than enterprise funds and intragovernmental service funds account for authorized *expenditures* of the government's resources, rather than accounting for *expenses* of operations. There is no attempt to match *cost expirations* against *earned revenues* in funds other than enterprise funds and intragovernmental service funds. As a result, depreciation is recorded only in enterprise funds and intragovernmental service funds, and occasionally in trust funds. In addition, depreciation may be recorded on a memorandum basis in the general fixed assets group of accounts, which are nothing more than memorandum records themselves.[5] Similarly, there is no uncollectible taxes expense in the general fund or in special revenue funds.

Recording of purchase orders for goods and services

Because of the need for the expenditures of governmental units to be in accordance with authorizations of appropriate legislative bodies, an *encumbrance* accounting technique is used for the general fund, special revenue funds, capital projects funds, and special assessment funds. When a purchase order for goods or services is issued to a supplier by one of the preceding funds, a journal entry similar to the following entry is made in the accounts of the fund:

Encumbrances	18,413	
Reserve for Encumbrances		18,413
To record encumbrance for purchase order no. 1685 issued to		
Wilson Company.		

[5] *Ibid.*, p. 18.

When the supplier's invoice for the ordered goods or services is received by the governmental unit, it is recorded, and the related encumbrance is reversed, as follows:

Expenditures	18,507	
Vouchers Payable		18,507
To record invoice received from Wilson Company under purchase		
order no. 1685.		
Reserve for Encumbrances	18,413	
Encumbrances		18,413
To reverse encumbrance for purchase order no. 1685 issued to		
Wilson Company.		

As indicated by the preceding example, the invoice amount may differ from the governmental unit's purchase order amount, because of such items as shipping charges and sales taxes.

The encumbrances technique is a memorandum method for making certain that total expenditures for a fiscal year do not exceed authorized amounts. Encumbrance entries are not necessary for normal recurring expenditures such as salaries and wages, utilities, and rent. The encumbrance technique used in accounting for government entities has no counterpart in accounting for commercial enterprises.

Recording the budget

Budgets are key elements of legislative control over governmental units. The executive branch of a governmental unit proposes the budgets, the legislative branch reviews, modifies, and enacts the budgets, and finally the executive branch approves the budgets and carries out their provisions.

The two basic classifications of budgets for governmental units are the same as those for commercial enterprises—operating budgets and capital budgets. Operating budgets include the *estimated revenues* and amounts appropriated for *expenditures* for a specific fiscal year of the governmental unit. Operating budgets are appropriate for the general fund and special revenue funds; they are also sometimes used for debt service funds. A trust fund may also have an operating budget, depending upon the terms of the trust indenture. *Capital budgets,* which are used to control the expenditures for long-term construction projects or other property and equipment acquisitions, are appropriate for capital projects funds and special assessment funds. The operating or capital budgets of all these funds are *recorded in their accounts,* to aid in accounting for compliance with legislative authorizations.

As mentioned previously, the operations of enterprise funds and intra-governmental service funds are similar to those of commercial enterprises. Consequently, operating budgets are utilized by these funds as a managerial planning and control device rather than as a legislative control tool. Thus, operating budgets of enterprise funds and intra-governmental service funds are not usually recorded in the accounts of those funds.

Types of Operating Budgets One or more of four types of operating budgets may be used by a governmental unit. A *traditional budget* emphasizes the *object* of each authorized expenditure, by department. For example, under the legislative activity of the general government function, the traditional budget may include authorized expenditures for personal services, supplies, and capital outlays.

A *program budget* stresses measurement of total cost of a specific governmental unit *program,* regardless of how many departments of the governmental unit are involved in the program. Object of expenditure information is of secondary importance in a program budget.

In a *performance budget,* there is an attempt to relate the input of governmental resources to the output of governmental services. For example, the total estimated expenditures of the enforcement section of the taxation department might be compared to the aggregate collections of additional tax assessments budgeted for the fiscal year.

The fourth type of operating budget for a governmental unit is the *planning, programming, budgeting system* (PPBS). This budgeting technique has been described as follows:

> PPBS attempts to apply concepts of program and performance budgeting to the tasks of identifying the fundamental objectives of a government; selections are made from among alternative ways of attaining these objectives, on the basis of the full analysis of respective cost implications and expected benefit results of the alternatives.[6]

Regardless of which types of operating budgets are used by a governmental unit, the final budget adopted by the governmental unit's legislative body will include *estimated revenues* for the fiscal year and the *appropriations* for expenditures authorized for that year. If the budget's estimated revenues exceed appropriations (as required by law for many governmental units), there will be a *budgetary surplus.* If appropriations exceed estimated revenues in the budget, there will be a *budgetary deficit.*

Journal Entries for a General Fund Budget To illustrate the recording of an operating budget in the accounts of a general fund, assume that the Town of Verdant Glen in June of Year 5 adopted the following condensed operating budget for its General Fund for the fiscal year ending June 30, Year 6:

[6]*Ibid.,* pp. 27–28.

Estimated revenues:		
General property taxes		$700,000
Other		100,000
Total estimated revenues		$800,000
Appropriations:		
General government	$420,000	
Other	340,000	
Total appropriations		760,000
Excess of estimated revenues over appropriations (budgetary surplus) .		$ 40,000

The general journal entry to record the above budget on July 1, Year 5, would be as follows:

Estimated Revenues	800,000	
Appropriations		760,000
Fund Balance		40,000
To record operating budget adopted for fiscal year ending June		
30, Year 6.		

Let us analyze each of the accounts of the preceding journal entry.

1 The Estimated Revenues account may be considered a ***pseudo asset*** account, because it reflects revenues expected to be received by the General Fund during the fiscal year. It is not a genuine asset, because it does not fit the accounting definition of an asset as an economic resource of an enterprise that is recognized and measured in conformity with generally accepted accounting principles.[7] Thus, the Estimated Revenues account is in substance a memorandum account, useful for control purposes only, which will be closed prior to the issuance of financial statements for the General Fund at the end of the Town of Verdant Glen's fiscal year on June 30, Year 6.

2 The Appropriations account may be considered a ***pseudo liability*** account, because it reflects the legislative body's commitments to expend General Fund resources as authorized in the operating budget. The Appropriations account is not a genuine liability, because it does not fit the definition of a liability as an economic obligation of an enterprise that is recognized and measured in conformity with generally accepted accounting principles.[8] The Appropriations account, like the Estimated Revenues account, is a memorandum account useful for control purposes only, which will be closed prior to issuance of year-end financial statements for the Town of Verdant Glen General Fund.

3 The Fund Balance account, as its title implies, is an account which balances the asset and liability accounts of a general fund. Although similar to the owners' equity accounts of a commercial enterprise in this balancing feature,

[7] *APB Statement No. 4,* "Basic Concepts and Accounting Principles Underlying Financial Statements of Business Enterprises," AICPA (New York: 1970), p. 49.
[8] *Ibid.,* p. 50.

the Fund Balance account does not purport to show any ownership interest in a general fund's assets.

The general journal entry to record the Town of Verdant Glen General Fund's operating budget for Fiscal Year 6 would be accompanied by detailed entries to subsidiary ledgers for both estimated revenues and appropriations. The Town of Verdant Glen General Fund's budget was purposely condensed; in practice, the general fund's estimated revenues and appropriations would be detailed by source and function, respectively, into one or more of the following widely used subsidiary ledger categories:

Estimated revenues:	Appropriations:
Taxes	General government
Licenses and permits	Public safety
Intergovernmental revenue	Public works
Charges for services	Health and welfare
Fines and forfeits	Culture—recreation
Miscellaneous[9]	Debt service
	Intergovernmental expenditures
	Miscellaneous[10]

In summary, budgets of a governmental unit are recorded in the accounts of the general fund, special revenue funds, debt service funds, capital projects funds, and special assessment funds. A trust fund may also record a budget if required to do so by the trust indenture. The recording of the budget initiates the accounting cycle for each of the funds listed above. Recording the budget also facilitates the preparation of financial statements which compare budgeted and actual amounts of revenues and expenditures.

ILLUSTRATIONS OF ACCOUNTING FOR GOVERNMENT ENTITIES

Having considered several of the theoretical issues in accounting for government entities, we shall now discuss and illustrate the accounting entries for each of the eight types of funds identified previously, as well as for the general fixed assets and general long-term debt groups of accounts.

Accounting for the general fund

As indicated in the first part of this chapter, a *general fund* is used to account for all transactions of a governmental unit not properly accounted for in one of the other seven types of funds. Thus, the general fund as an accounting entity serves the same *residual* purpose as the

[9]*Governmental Accounting, Auditing and Financial Reporting*, pp. 188–190.
[10]*Ibid.*, pp. 192–201.

general journal provides as an accounting record. Although the general fund is residual, it usually accounts for the greatest aggregate dollar amounts of the governmental unit's revenues and expenditures.

In illustrating the accounting for a general fund, we shall expand the example of the Town of Verdant Glen used in the preceding section of this chapter.

Illustration of Accounting for a General Fund Assume that the balance sheet of the Town of Verdant Glen General Fund at June 30, Year 5 (prior to the entry for the Fiscal Year 6 budget illustrated on page 526), was as follows:

TOWN OF VERDANT GLEN GENERAL FUND
Balance Sheet
June 30, Year 5

Assets:

Cash	$160,000
Inventory of supplies	40,000
	$200,000

Liabilities, Reserve, & Fund Balance:

Vouchers payable	$ 80,000
Reserve for inventory of supplies	40,000
Fund balance	80,000
	$200,000

The Reserve for Inventory of Supplies account is analogous to an appropriation of retained earnings in a commercial entity. It represents a segregation of the General Fund's Fund Balance account, so that the $40,000 nonexpendable portion of the General Fund's total assets will not be appropriated accidentally for expenditures in the legislative body's adoption of the next operating budget for the General Fund.

Assume that, in addition to the budget illustrated on page 526, the Town of Verdant Glen General Fund had the following aggregate transactions for the fiscal year ended June 30, Year 6:

1 Property taxes were billed in the amount of $720,000, of which $14,000 was expected to be uncollectible.

2 Property taxes collected in cash totaled $650,000; other revenues collected in cash totaled $102,000.

3 Property taxes in the amount of $13,000 were found to be uncollectible.

4 Purchase orders were issued to vendors and suppliers in the aggregate amount of $360,000.

5 Expenditures for the year totaled $760,000, of which $90,000 applied to additions to inventory of supplies. $350,000 of the total expenditures applied to $355,000 of the purchase orders issued during the year.

6 Cash payments on vouchers payable totaled $770,000.

7 Supplies used during the year cost $80,000.

8 All uncollected property taxes at June 30, Year 6, were determined to be delinquent.

The following general journal entries, numbered to correspond to the transactions outlined above, would be recorded in the general journal of the Town of Verdant Glen General Fund during the year ended June 30, Year 6:

1 *Taxes Receivable—Current* *720,000*

                Estimated Uncollectible Current Taxes *14,000*

                Revenues *706,000*

      To accrue property taxes billed and to provide for estimated uncollectible portion thereof.

As indicated earlier, the modified accrual basis of accounting for a general fund permits the accrual of property taxes, because they are **billed** to the property owners by the Town of Verdant Glen. Since expense accounting is not appropriate for a general fund, the estimated uncollectible property taxes are **offset** against the total taxes billed; the net amount is the **actual** revenue from property taxes for the year.

2 *Cash* *752,000*

                Taxes Receivable—Current *650,000*

                Revenues *102,000*

      To record cash collections of property taxes and other revenues for the year.

Under the modified accrual basis of accounting, revenues not susceptible to accrual are recorded on the cash basis. However, any taxes or other revenues collected in advance of the fiscal year to which they apply would be credited to a liability account in the Town of Verdant Glen General Fund.

3 *Estimated Uncollectible Current Taxes* *13,000*

                Taxes Receivable—Current *13,000*

      To write off receivable for property taxes which are uncollectible.

The above entry represents a shortcut approach. In an actual situation, uncollectible property taxes would first be transferred, together with estimated uncollectible amounts, to the Taxes Receivable—Delinquent account from the Taxes Receivable—Current account. Any amounts collected on these delinquent taxes would include revenues for interest and penalties required by law. If delinquent taxes remained uncollected, they would be transferred, together with estimated uncollectible amounts, to the Tax Liens Receivable account. The governmental unit might satisfy its tax lien by selling the related property.

4 Encumbrances	360,000	
Reserve for Encumbrances		360,000
To record purchase orders issued during the year.		

Encumbrance entries are designed to prevent the overexpending of an appropriated amount in the budget. The general journal entry to the Encumbrances account would be posted in detail to reduce the unexpended balances of each pertinent appropriation in the subsidiary ledger for appropriations. The unexpended balance of each appropriation is thus reduced for the amount committed by the issuance of the applicable purchase orders.

5a Expenditures	670,000	
Inventory of Supplies	90,000	
Vouchers Payable		760,000
To record expenditures for the year.		

The Expenditures account is charged with *all* expenditures—regardless of purpose—except for additions to the inventory of supplies. Debt principal and interest payments, additions to the governmental unit's property and equipment assets, payments for services to be received in the future—all are charged to Expenditures rather than to asset or liability accounts. (Expenditures for debt principal and interest and property and equipment additions are also recorded *on a memorandum basis* in the general long-term debt and general fixed assets groups of accounts, respectively.)

The accounting for General Fund expenditures described above emphasizes once again the importance of the operating budget in the accounting for a general fund. Expenditures are chargeable to amounts appropriated by the legislative body of the governmental unit. The detail items making up the $670,000 total debit to the Expenditures account in the preceding journal entry are posted to the appropriations subsidiary ledger as reductions of unexpended balances of each appropriation.

5b *Reserve for Encumbrances*	*355,000*	
Encumbrances		*355,000*
To reverse encumbrances applicable to vouchered expenditures of $350,000.		

Recording actual expenditures of $350,000 relevant to purchase orders totaling $355,000 makes this amount of the previously recorded encumbrances no longer necessary. Accordingly, $355,000 of encumbrances is reversed; the reversal is posted to the detailed appropriations subsidiary ledger as well as to the general ledger.

6 *Vouchers Payable*	*770,000*	
Cash		*770,000*
To record payment of vouchered liabilities during the year.		
7 *Expenditures*	*80,000*	
Inventory of Supplies		*80,000*
To record cost of supplies used during the year.		
Fund Balance	*10,000*	
Reserve for Inventory of Supplies		*10,000*
To increase inventory of supplies reserve to agree with balance in Inventory of Supplies account at end of year.		

The immediately preceding entry represents a segregation of a portion of the Fund Balance account to prevent its being improperly appropriated to finance a deficit operating budget for the General Fund for Year 7. Only cash and other ***monetary*** assets of a general fund are available for appropriation to finance authorized expenditures of the succeeding fiscal year.

8 *Taxes Receivable—Delinquent*	*57,000*	
Estimated Uncollectible Current Taxes	*1,000*	
Taxes Receivable—Current		*57,000*
Estimated Uncollectible Delinquent Taxes		*1,000*
To transfer delinquent taxes and related estimated uncollectible amounts from the current classification.		

The above entry clears the Taxes Receivable—Current account and the related contra account for uncollectible amounts so that they will be available for accrual of property taxes for the fiscal year ending June 30, Year 7.

After all the preceding general journal entries (including the budget entry on page 526) have been posted, the trial balance for the Town of Verdant Glen General Fund at June 30, Year 6, would be as follows:

TOWN OF VERDANT GLEN GENERAL FUND
Trial Balance
June 30, Year 6

Cash	$ 142,000	
Taxes receivable—delinquent	57,000	
Estimated uncollectible delinquent taxes		$ 1,000
Inventory of supplies	50,000	
Vouchers payable		70,000
Reserve for encumbrances		5,000
Reserve for inventory of supplies		50,000
Fund balance		110,000
Estimated revenues	800,000	
Appropriations		760,000
Revenues		808,000
Expenditures	750,000	
Encumbrances	5,000	
	$1,804,000	$1,804,000

Closing Entries for a General Fund   Before financial statements are prepared for the Town of Verdant Glen General Fund for the year ended June 30, Year 6, the budgetary and actual revenue, expenditure, and encumbrance accounts must be closed. The June 30, Year 6, closing entries for the Town of Verdant Glen General Fund would be as follows:

Revenues	808,000	
Estimated Revenues		800,000
Fund Balance		8,000
To close estimated and actual revenue accounts.		
Appropriations	760,000	
Expenditures		750,000
Encumbrances		5,000
Fund Balance		5,000
To close appropriation, expenditure, and encumbrance accounts.		

The above entries do not close the Reserve for Encumbrances account. Thus, the reserve represents a restriction on the fund balance at June 30, Year 6, because the Town of Verdant Glen General Fund is committed in Fiscal Year 7 to make estimated expenditures of $5,000 attributable to budgetary appropriations carried over from Fiscal Year 6. If the Reserve for Encumbrances account had been closed in the preceding entry, the Fund Balance account would have been overstated $5,000. The Fund Balance account must represent the balance of the General Fund's assets which are available for appropriation for a *deficit* budget in Fiscal Year 7.

On July 1, Year 6—the beginning of Fiscal Year 7—the following general journal entry would be appropriate for the $5,000 balance in the Reserve for Encumbrances account at June 30, Year 6:

Reserve for Encumbrances	*5,000*	
Reserve for Encumbrances—Year 6		*5,000*
To transfer balance in Reserve for Encumbrances account to a separate, earmarked account.		

The entry above clears the Reserve for Encumbrances account for entries applicable to the General Fund's operating budget for Fiscal Year 7. When the invoices applicable to the $5,000 reserve for encumbrances for Year 6 are received during Fiscal Year 7, a separate Expenditures—Year 6 account would be debited for the actual amount of the invoices. One of the closing entries at June 30, Year 7, would close the Expenditures—Year 6 account and the Reserve for Encumbrances—Year 6 account to the Fund Balance account.

Financial Statements for a General Fund We have stated previously that the results of operations (that is, net income or net loss) are not significant for a general fund. Therefore, the following financial statements should be prepared for the Town of Verdant Glen General Fund for the year ended June 30, Year 6.

TOWN OF VERDANT GLEN GENERAL FUND	
Statement of Changes in Fund Balance	
For Year Ended June 30, Year 6	
Fund balance, July 1, Year 5	*$ 80,000*
Add: Excess of revenues over expenditures and encumbrances	*53,000*
Subtotal	*$133,000*
Deduct: Increase in reserve for inventory of supplies	*10,000*
Fund balance, June 30, Year 6	*$123,000*

TOWN OF VERDANT GLEN GENERAL FUND
Statement of Revenues, Expenditures, and Encumbrances
For Year Ended June 30, Year 6

	Budget	Actual	Over (under) budget
Revenues			
Taxes.	$700,000	$706,000	$ 6,000
Other.	100,000	102,000	2,000
Total revenues	$800,000	$808,000	$ 8,000
Expenditures and Encumbrances*			
General government	$420,000	$409,000	$(11,000)
Other.	340,000	346,000	6,000
Total expenditures	$760,000	$755,000	$ (5,000)
Excess of revenues over expenditures			
and encumbrances	$ 40,000	$ 53,000	$ 13,000

*Breakdown of actual amounts between General Government and Other categories is assumed.

TOWN OF VERDANT GLEN GENERAL FUND
Balance Sheet
June 30, Year 6

Assets
Cash $142,000
Property taxes receivable, less allowance of $1,000 for
    uncollectible amounts. 56,000
Inventory of supplies 50,000
                                   $248,000

Liabilities, Reserves, & Fund Balance
Vouchers payable . . . . $ 70,000
Encumbrances outstanding 5,000
Reserve for inventory of supplies. 50,000
Fund balance 123,000
                                   $248,000

The following aspects of the Town of Verdant Glen General Fund financial statements should be emphasized:

1 The statement of revenues, expenditures, and encumbrances compares budgeted to actual amounts. This comparison aids in the appraisal of the stewardship for the General Fund's resources and the compliance with legislative appropriations. (Expenditures in excess of appropriated amounts generally are not permitted unless a supplementary appropriation is made by the legislative body of the governmental unit.)

2 The $8,000 excess of actual revenues over estimated revenues in the statement of revenues, expenditures, and encumbrances coincides with the amount credited to the Fund Balance account in the General Fund's June 30, Year 6, closing entry for estimated and actual revenues. The $5,000 excess of budgeted appropriations over actual expenditures and encumbrances also agrees with the amount credited to the Fund Balance account in the related General Fund closing entry at June 30, Year 6.

3 The excess of *actual* revenues over *actual* expenditures and encumbrances appears in the General Fund's statement of changes in fund balance. The *budgeted* excess of estimated revenues over appropriations does not appear in the fund balance changes statement, although it does appear in the statement of revenues, expenditures, and encumbrances.

4 The assets of the Town of Verdant Glen General Fund include only monetary assets and inventory. Expenditures for prepayments (other than supplies) and property and equipment are not recorded as assets in the General Fund.

5 The $123,000 fund balance at June 30, Year 6, is available, if required, for appropriation for a deficit budget for Fiscal Year 7. As pointed out earlier in this chapter, many government entities are not authorized to enact deficit budgets.

Concluding Comments on Accounting for a General Fund The preceding illustration of accounting for and financial statements of a general fund has obviously been simplified. For example, *interfund* accounts and transactions between the General Fund and other funds of the Town of Verdant Glen were not included in the illustration. "Due from" and "Due to" accounts with other funds of the governmental unit are appropriate for interfund transactions. Accounting for interfund transactions is similar to accounting for intercompany transactions between affiliated commercial entities.

Accounting for special revenue funds

Special revenue funds are very similar to the general fund. They are established to account for the collections and expenditures associated with specialized revenue sources which are earmarked by law or regulation to finance specified governmental operations. Rubbish collection, freeway construction, and rapid transit systems are examples of governmental activities accounted for in special revenue funds.

Account titles, budgetary processes, and financial statements for special revenue funds are similar to those for general funds; hence, they are not illustrated in this section.

On occasion, there may be a question as to whether a particular governmental program should be accounted for in a special revenue fund or in an enterprise fund. The National Committee on Governmental Accounting summarized this issue as follows:

As a general rule, the distinguishing characteristic of a Special Revenue Fund is that most of the revenue involved in the operation comes from tax and non-tax sources not directly related to services rendered rather than from direct charges to users of the services. If a facility or program is financed entirely or predominantly by charges to users, the financial transactions involved should be accounted for in an Enterprise Fund. . . .[11]

Accounting for debt service funds

Payments of principal and interest on all long-term debt of a government entity other than special assessment bonds, revenue bonds, and general obligation bonds serviced by an enterprise fund are accounted for in debt service funds. *Special assessment bonds* are repaid from the proceeds of special assessment levies against specific properties receiving benefits from the special assessment improvements; these bonds accordingly are accounted for in special assessment funds. *Revenue bonds* are payable from the earnings of a governmental enterprise and are accounted for in the appropriate enterprise fund. In some cases, *general obligation bonds,* which are supported by the full faith and credit of the issuing governmental unit, will be repaid from the resources of a governmental enterprise. These general obligation bonds should be carried as liabilities of the appropriate enterprise fund.

We must stress that *the liability for bonds payable from resources of a debt service fund is not recorded in that fund until the debt matures.* Prior to maturity date, the bond liability is recorded on a memorandum basis in the general long-term debt group of accounts.

The three customary types of general obligation long-term debt whose servicing is recorded in debt service funds are the following:

Serial bonds, with principal payable in annual installments over the life of the issue

Term bonds, with principal payable in total at a fixed maturity date from proceeds of an accumulated sinking fund

Notes, maturing more than one year from date of issuance

Journal Entries for a Debt Service Fund A governmental unit's debt service fund operates in a manner very similar to a commercial entity's pension fund. An actuarially determined amount, based on required debt servicing expenditures for the governmental unit's fiscal year, is recorded in the accounts of the debt service fund at the beginning of the fiscal year. In effect, this amount is the operating budget for the debt service fund for the fiscal year.

The budget for a term bond, which requires the accumulation of a sinking fund, is recorded in the accounts of the debt service fund as follows:

[11] *Ibid.,* p. 28.

Required Additions	50,500	
Required Earnings	1,500	
Appropriations		12,200
Fund Balance		39,800

To record budget for required addition and earnings for term bond
sinking fund, and for required expenditures for interest and fiscal
agent's fee.

For a serial bond, which requires annual payments of principal as well
as interest, the debt service fund's budget entry would use the same
Estimated Revenues and Appropriations accounts as the budget entry
for a general fund illustrated on page 526.

We have previously pointed out that the modified accrual basis of
accounting is appropriate for a debt service fund. Thus, any property
taxes specifically earmarked for servicing of a governmental unit's term
or serial general obligation bonds may be accrued in the debt service
fund. The accounting for such a tax accrual is the same as that for the
general fund illustrated in a preceding section of this chapter.

On the due date for any principal and interest payments by the debt
service fund, the Expenditures account is debited and related Bonds
Payable and Interest Payable accounts are credited. (The general long-
term debt group of accounts would simultaneously be relieved of the
corresponding amounts, as explained on page 546.) A debt service fund
does not accrue interest which is not payable at the end of the fiscal
year, because that interest has not been provided for in the debt service
fund's budget for the fiscal year. A debt service fund does not issue
purchase orders or contracts; hence the encumbrance accounting technique is not required.

For a term bond, which requires the accumulation of a sinking fund,
the accounting entries of a debt service fund include the investment of
cash in interest-bearing obligations and the collection of interest on the
investments. Under the modified accrual basis of accounting, interest
accrued on investments at the end of the governmental unit's fiscal year
is recorded in the accounts of the debt service fund.

Financial Statements for a Debt Service Fund The statement of changes in
fund balance for a debt service fund is usually appended to the statement
of revenues and expenditures, since the only change in the fund balance
is the excess of revenues over expenditures. Further, a comparison of
budgeted to actual revenues and expenditures is unnecessary for a debt
service fund, because of the limited sources of revenues and types of
expenditures. Footnote disclosure is appropriate for the actuarially determined required additions to a debt service fund for a term bond. A
balance sheet for a debt service fund might appear as follows:

TOWN OF VERDANT GLEN DEBT SERVICE FUND

Balance Sheet

June 30, Year 6

Assets

Cash	$ 10,000
Cash with fiscal agent	54,000
Investments, at amortized cost plus accrued interest	80,000
Property taxes receivable, less allowance of $2,000 for uncollectible amounts	10,000
	$154,000

Liabilities & Fund Balance

Bonds payable	$ 50,000
Interest payable	4,000
Fund balance.	100,000
	$154,000

The balance sheet above discloses that cash has been deposited with the Town of Verdant Glen's fiscal agent (ordinarily a bank trust department) to pay bonds and interest which have matured at June 30, Year 6. The fiscal agent, however, has not yet completed redemption of the matured bonds and interest coupons.

Accounting for capital projects funds

Capital projects funds of a governmental unit record the receipt and disbursement of cash for the governmental unit's long-lived property and equipment assets, other than those financed by special assessments and government enterprises. The resources for a capital projects fund usually are derived from proceeds of general obligation bonds, but the resources may also come from current tax revenues or from grants or shared revenues of other governmental units.

As stated previously, a capital budget, rather than an operating budget, is the control device appropriate for a capital projects fund. The capital budget should deal with both the authorized expenditures for the project and the bonds or other sources of revenues for the project.

Journal Entries for a Capital Projects Fund Neither an Estimated Revenues account nor an Appropriations account is needed to record the capital budget for a capital projects fund. The capital projects fund is not an authorized taxing agency; it merely receives proceeds of general obligation bond issuances or general fund and special revenue fund tax levies. Furthermore, no annual legislative authorizations are required for the expenditures of a capital projects fund, because the capital budget covers all authorized expenditures of the fund during the life of the project. The Fund Balance account of a capital projects fund may be viewed as serving the same purpose as an Appropriations account of the general fund, special revenue fund, or debt service fund. The opening journal entry for a capital projects fund financed entirely with the proceeds of a general obligation bond issue is as follows:

Cash	1,010,000	
Revenues		1,000,000
Premium on Bonds Payable		10,000
To record receipt of proceeds of general obligation bonds		
issued at 101.		

The proceeds of the bond issue represent *revenue* to the capital projects fund; that fund does not assume the liability for the bonded indebtedness. The liability for the bonds is reflected in the general long-term debt group of accounts until the bonds mature. At maturity date, the bond liability is recorded in the debt service fund and removed from the general long-term debt group of accounts.

Typically, the principal amount of the general obligation bonds represents the total capital budget for the capital projects fund. Accordingly, the $10,000 bond premium in the preceding journal entry would be transferred to the debt service fund, which must pay periodic interest and the bond principal at maturity.

If the bonds had been issued at a discount, the customary accounting treatment would be to offset the discount against the Revenues account of the capital projects fund. Any deficiency in the capital projects fund's resources at the date of completion of the project would usually be financed from the general fund.

For a capital projects fund financed by other than bond proceeds, the opening journal entry would not reflect revenue. For example, if we assume that the general fund was to finance the project from general tax revenues, the capital projects fund's opening journal entry would be as follows:

Due from General Fund	500,000	
Fund Balance		500,000
To record amount due from General Fund for the cost of au-		
thorized capital project.		

In the general fund, a companion entry would debit Expenditures and credit Due to Capital Projects Fund in the amount of $500,000.

Following the opening journal entry, subsequent entries for the capital projects fund would include encumbrance entries for construction contracts and purchase orders issued, and expenditures entries for payments to contractors, architects, and suppliers. These entries would be similar to those illustrated for a general fund. In addition, temporarily idle cash of the capital projects fund might be invested in short-term, interest-bearing securities. Any interest earned on the investments would be transferred from the capital projects fund to the debt service fund or to the general fund, depending on the source of the original financing of the capital projects fund.

Expenditures for construction recorded in the capital projects fund are accompanied by a debit to Construction Work in Progress and a credit to Investment in Fixed Assets from Capital Projects Fund in the general fixed assets group of accounts. The accounting for the general fixed assets group of accounts is illustrated in a subsequent section of this chapter.

At the end of each fiscal year prior to completion of a capital project, the Revenues, Expenditures, and Encumbrances accounts of the capital projects fund are closed to the Fund Balance account. Upon completion of the project, the entire capital projects fund is closed out by a transfer of any unused cash to the debt service fund or the general fund, as appropriate. Any cash deficiency in the capital projects fund would probably be made up by the general fund; this financing would be credited to the Revenues account of the capital projects fund.

Financial Statements for a Capital Projects Fund   Three financial statements are issued for a capital projects fund at the close of each fiscal year prior to completion of the project. The *statement of revenues—estimated and actual* is similar in content to the revenues portion of the general fund statement illustrated on page 534. The statement of changes in fund balance shows the fund balance at the beginning of the fiscal year, increased by the year's *actual* revenues and decreased by the total expenditures and encumbrances for the fiscal year. The statement ends with the fund balance at the end of the fiscal year.

The balance sheet for a capital projects fund shows the fund's assets—cash, short-term investments, and receivables. Liabilities, reserve for encumbrances, and fund balance round out the capital projects fund's balance sheet. To reiterate, the assets constructed with resources of the capital projects fund do not appear in that fund's balance sheet. Constructed plant assets appear in the governmental unit's general fixed assets group of accounts. Furthermore, any general obligation bonds issued to finance the capital projects fund are not a liability of that fund. Prior to the maturity date or dates of the bonds, the liability is carried in the general long-term debt group of accounts. At the date the bonds mature, the related liability is transferred to the debt service fund from the general long-term debt group of accounts.

Accounting for enterprise funds

Enterprise funds account for the operations of commercial-type activities of the governmental unit, such as utilities, airports, seaports, and recreational facilities. These commercial-type enterprises sell services to the public (and in some cases to other activities of the governmental unit) at a profit. Consequently, the accounting for enterprise funds is more like commercial entity accounting than the accounting for any other governmental fund.

For example, full accrual accounting is used for an enterprise fund, with prepaid expenses, depreciation, and doubtful accounts recorded in the fund's accounting records. The enterprise fund's accounts also include the property and equipment assets owned by the enterprise, as well as the liabilities for revenue bonds and any general obligation bonds payable by the enterprise. Encumbrance accounting is not used for enterprise funds, and the operating budget is not recorded in the accounts of an enterprise fund. Retained earnings of an enterprise fund may be charged with cash remittances to the general fund, like dividends paid by a commercial entity.

Financial Statements for an Enterprise Fund The financial statements for an enterprise fund are analogous to those for a commercial entity—a statement of revenue and expenses (income statement), statement of retained earnings, balance sheet, and statement of changes in financial position. However, there are a number of differences between the accounts of an enterprise fund and the accounts of a commercial entity. Among these differences are the following:

1 Enterprise funds are not subject to federal and state income taxes. However, an enterprise fund may be required to make payments in lieu of property or franchise taxes to the general fund.

2 There is no capital stock in an enterprise fund's balance sheet. Instead, Contributions accounts set forth the assets contributed to the enterprise fund by the general fund, by customers of the enterprise fund, or by other members of the public.

3 An enterprise fund has many restricted assets. Cash deposits made by customers of a utility enterprise fund, which are to assure the customers' payment for utility services, are restricted for cash or interest-bearing investments to offset the enterprise fund's liability for the customers' deposits. Cash received from proceeds of revenue bonds issued by the enterprise fund is restricted to payments for construction of plant assets financed by issuance of the bonds. Part of the cash generated by the enterprise fund's operations must be set aside and invested for payment of interest and principal of the revenue bond liabilities of the enterprise fund.

4 A number of retained earnings reserves appear in the accounts of an enterprise fund. These reserves are equal to the cash and investments restricted to payment of revenue bond interest and principal.

The statement of revenue and expenses (income statement) of an enterprise fund may be on a budget-to-actual comparison basis, even though the operating budget is not recorded in the accounts of the fund. In the enterprise fund's balance sheet, the restricted assets of the fund, the liabilities payable from restricted assets, and the retained earnings reserves are all segregated and clearly labeled.

There is a difference among accounting authorities as to the appropriate balance sheet presentation of the governmental unit's general obligation bonds which are to be paid by an enterprise fund. The National Committee on Governmental Accounting has recommended that the liability for such general obligation bonds be recorded in the general long-term debt group of accounts and that a liability account entitled Advance from Municipality—General Obligation Bonds be set up in the enterprise fund to offset the cash received from the issuance of the general obligation bonds.[12] The position of the AICPA is that the actual liability for the general obligation bonds should appear in the balance sheet of the enterprise fund (as stated earlier in this chapter) and that a footnote to the statement of general long-term debt of the governmental unit should describe the contingent liability for payment of the bonds if the enterprise fund fails to do so.[13] The AICPA's position seems the sounder of the two alternatives, from a theoretical point of view, and is supported by the authors.

Accounting for trust and agency funds

Trust and agency funds are used to account for assets held by a governmental unit as a *custodian.* Agency funds are of short duration; they typically account for such items as sales taxes, payroll taxes, and other deductions withheld from salaries of governmental unit employees for transmittal to a federal or state tax collection unit.

Trust funds of a governmental unit are longer-lived than agency funds. An *expendable* trust fund is one whose principal and income may both be expended to achieve the objectives of the trust. A Government Employees' Retirement Trust Fund is an example of an expendable trust fund, for both principal and income of a Retirement Trust Fund are expended for retired government employees' pensions. A *nonexpendable* trust fund is one whose income is expended to carry out the objectives of the trust; the principal remains intact. For example, an *endowment* established by the grantor of a trust may specify that the income from the endowment is to be expended by the governmental unit for student scholarships, but the endowment principal is not to be expended. Nonexpendable trusts actually require two separate trust fund accounting entities—one for principal and one for revenue. Accounting for the two

---

[12] *Ibid.,* p. 57.
[13] *Audits of State and Local Government Units,* p. 79.

separate trust funds requires a careful distinction between transactions affecting the principal—such as changes in the investment portfolio—and transactions affecting income—such as cash dividends and interest on the investment portfolio. The *trust indenture,* which is the legal document establishing the trust, should delineate distinctions between principal and income. If the trust indenture is silent with respect to such distinctions, the trust law of the governmental unit governs separation of principal trust fund and revenue trust fund transactions.

Since the governmental unit serves as a custodian for a trust fund, accounting for a trust fund should comply with the agreement under which the fund was established. Among the terms which might affect the accounting for a trust fund are requirements that the operating budget for the trust fund be recorded in its accounts and that depreciation be recorded for an endowment principal trust fund which includes depreciable assets.

The accrual basis of accounting is appropriate for trust and agency funds. Financial statements required for trust and agency funds are a statement of cash receipts and disbursements, a statement of changes in fund balance, and a balance sheet.

Accounting for intragovernmental service funds

An intragovernmental service fund is established to sell goods and services to other departments of the governmental unit but not to the public at large. This type of fund is created to assure uniformity and economies in the procurement of goods and services for the governmental unit as a whole, such as stationery supplies and the maintenance and repairs of motor vehicles.

An intragovernmental service fund operates like a commercial entity, except that it is not profit-motivated. Its "Billings to Departments" revenue account should be sufficient to cover all its operating costs and expenses, with perhaps a modest profit margin. In this way, the resources of an intragovernmental service fund are "revolving"; the original contribution from the general fund to establish the service fund is expended for supplies, operating equipment, and employees' salaries or wages, and the amounts expended are then recouped through billings to other departments of the governmental unit.

Although an intragovernmental service fund should use an operating budget for managerial planning and control purposes, the budget need not be recorded in the accounts of the fund. The accrual basis of accounting, including the perpetual inventory system and depreciation of property and equipment, is required for an intragovernmental service fund. Encumbrance accounting is not mandatory but may be useful in controlling the purchase orders of the intragovernmental service fund.

The financial statements for an intragovernmental service fund consist of a combined statement of operations and retained earnings and a balance sheet. Since an intragovernmental service fund is not profit-motivated, the term **net income** should not be used in the statement of operations. "Excess of revenue over expenses" or a similar caption is more appropriate. Like an enterprise fund, an intragovernmental service fund has no owners' equity in its balance sheet. A Contribution from General Fund account represents the general fund's "investment" in the intragovernmental service fund.

Accounting for special assessment funds

A special assessment fund accounts for the resources, liabilities, revenues, and expenditures attributable to special tax assessments, payable in installments, which are levied on property owners in the governmental unit's jurisdiction. These tax assessments finance construction projects primarily of benefit to the assessed property owners.

Accounting for a special assessment fund is in many respects a composite of the accounting for a debt service fund and a capital projects fund. The accounts of a special assessment fund include both the proceeds and the servicing of the **special assessment bonds** which are issued to finance the construction project prior to the collection of the assessment installments.

Journal Entries for a Special Assessment Fund Like a capital projects fund, a special assessment fund might have a capital budget. The following general journal entry would record the capital budget:

Special Assessments Receivable—Current	100,000	
Special Assessments Receivable—Deferred	900,000	
Fund Balance		1,000,000
To record levy of special assessments, payable in ten equal		
annual installments, with interest at 8% on unpaid balance.		

The special assessment fund would then record the issuance of special assessment serial bonds, usually equal in amount to the deferred special assessments receivable, with a debit to Cash and a credit to Bonds Payable. Any premium or discount on the bonds would be recorded in the special assessment fund and amortized through interest expense in the customary manner, since the special assessment fund services its own bonds. Accrual accounting is desirable for the special assessment fund. Delinquent assessments receivable, encumbrances, and expenditures are recorded in the same way as illustrated previously for the general fund. At the end of each fiscal year prior to completion of the construction project financed by the special assessments, the Interest

Revenue, Interest Expense, Expenditures, and Encumbrances accounts are closed to the Fund Balance account. Complementary entries would be made to the Construction Work in Progress account in the general fixed assets group of accounts.

At the beginning of each fiscal year following the establishment of the special assessment fund, the current installments of the special assessments receivable are transferred from the Special Assessments Receivable—Deferred account to the Special Assessments Receivable—Current account. Payments of matured serial special assessment bonds are recorded in the accounts of the fund in the usual manner for the liquidation of interest-bearing debt.

Financial Statements for a Special Assessment Fund The financial statements for a special assessment fund are the statement of cash receipts and disbursements, statement of changes in fund balance, and balance sheet. Unlike a capital projects fund, a special assessment fund does not issue a statement of revenues—estimated and actual, since a special assessment fund's revenue consists only of interest on deferred special assessments receivable.

The general fixed assets and general long-term debt account groups

A governmental unit's general fixed assets and general long-term debt groups of accounts are not *funds;* they are memorandum accounts. Their purpose is to provide in one record the governmental unit's property and equipment and long-term liabilities which are not recorded in one of the governmental unit's other funds. We have pointed out earlier that property and equipment assets are recorded, as appropriate, in enterprise, trust, and intragovernmental service funds; and that bond liabilities are recorded, as appropriate, in debt service, enterprise, and special assessment funds.

The AICPA has suggested that the "improvements other than buildings" category of governmental unit–owned assets need not be recorded in the general fixed assets group of accounts, because they are immovable and of value only to the governmental unit.[14] These assets are generally termed "land improvements" in accounting for a commercial entity.

Assets in the general fixed assets group of accounts are recorded at their cost to the government or at their fair value if donated to the governmental unit. The offsetting memorandum account is entitled Investment in General Fixed Assets from Capital Projects Fund, or other sources.

As pointed out earlier, depreciation may be recorded on a memorandum basis in the general fixed assets group of accounts, with a debit to the appropriate Investment in General Fixed Assets account and a

[14] *Ibid.*, p. 17.

credit to an Accumulated Depreciation account. When a property and equipment asset is sold or retired by the governmental unit, the memorandum accounts in the general fixed assets group are relieved of the carrying value of the asset; the sales proceeds are recorded as miscellaneous revenue in the general fund.

General obligation bonds of a governmental unit, both serial and term, which are not recorded in an enterprise fund are recorded as memorandum credits in the general long-term debt group of accounts. The offsetting memorandum debit entry is to an account entitled Amount to be Provided for Payment of (Serial or Term) Bonds. When resources for the ultimate payment of a bond issue have been accumulated in a debt service fund, an Amount Available in Debt Service Fund account is debited and the Amount to be Provided for Payment of Bonds account is credited. When the bonds are paid by the debt service fund, the memorandum accounts are reversed in the general long-term debt account group.

Combined financial statements for governmental units

The annual report for a governmental unit's fiscal year is a complex mass of financial data if separate financial statements are presented in the report for each fund and group of accounts. Consequently, accountants have considered various methods for condensing the financial data within manageable bounds.

It is generally agreed that *consolidated*-type financial statements issued for affiliated commercial enterprises are inappropriate for the funds and account groups of a governmental unit. Despite the presence of "Due from" and "Due to" interfund receivable and payable accounts, the various types of funds and account groups are too heterogeneous and subject to too many legal restrictions to be consolidated into a single reporting entity.

The AICPA has sanctioned the presentation of individual balance sheets of a governmental unit's funds and account groups in adjacent columns of a *combined* balance sheet, with a "memorandum only" total column which aggregates the columnar amounts.[15] The total column *does not* purport to show the financial position of the entire governmental unit.

Checklist for government entity accounting

The discussion in this chapter of accounting for government entities may be conveniently summarized in a checklist such as the one on page 547.

[15] *Ibid.*, pp. 20–21.

Checklist of Accounting for Governmental Entities

	General Fund	Special Revenue Fund	Debt Service Fund	Capital Projects Fund	Enterprise Fund	Trust or Agency Fund	Intragovernmental Service Fund	Special Assessment Fund	General Fixed Assets Group of Accounts	General Long-Term Debt Group of Accounts
Records operating or capital budget	X	X	X	X		X		X		
Uses accrual basis of accounting					X	X	X	X		
Uses modified accrual basis of accounting	X	X	X	X						
Records taxes or assessments receivable	X	X	X					X		
Uses encumbrance technique	X	X		X				X		
Records property and equipment assets					X	X	X		X	
Records depreciation					X	X	X		X	
Records proceeds of bond issuances				X	X			X		
Records liability for bonds issued			X(1)		X			X		X
Records payment of bonds	X	X	X		X			X		
Financial statements issued:									(3)	(3)
Balance sheet	X	X	X	X	X	X	X	X		
Statement of revenues and expenditures	X	X	X(2)							
Statement of operations					X		X			
Statement of cash receipts and disbursements						X		X		
Statement of changes in fund balance	X	X	X(2)	X		X		X		
Statement of changes in retained earnings					X		X			
Statement of changes in financial position					X					

(1) At maturity date of bonds only.
(2) Statement of revenues and expenditures is combined with statement of changes in fund balance.
(3) The two groups of accounts issue *trial balances* rather than *financial statements*.

REVIEW QUESTIONS

1 What characteristics of government entities have a significant influence upon the accounting for governmental units? Explain.

2 What is a *fund* in government entity accounting?

3 What is the support for each of the following aspects of government entity accounting theory?
 a The modified accrual basis of accounting
 b The encumbrance accounting technique
 c Recording the budget in the accounting records

4 Differentiate between a *program budget* and a *performance budget.*

5 The Estimated Revenues account of a governmental unit's general fund is sometimes alluded to as a *pseudo asset.* Why is this true?

6 What does the reference to a general fund as *residual* mean? Explain.

7 *a* What are the basic financial statements for a governmental unit's general fund?
 b What are the major differences between the financial statements of a governmental unit's general fund and the financial statements of a commercial enterprise?

8 What revenues of a general fund are usually accrued? Explain.

9 Distinguish between the Expenditures account of a governmental unit's general fund and the expense accounts of a commercial enterprise.

10 The accounting records for the City of Worthington General Fund include an account titled Reserve for Inventory of Supplies. Explain the purpose of this account.

11 Under what circumstances are general obligation bonds of a governmental unit recorded in the governmental unit's enterprise fund? Explain.

12 Discuss the similarities and differences between a governmental unit's capital projects fund and special assessment fund.

13 The accounting for a governmental unit's enterprise fund is in many respects similar to the accounting for a business entity, yet there are a number of differences between the two types of accounting. Identify at least three of the differences.

14 Accounting for nonexpendable trusts for which a governmental unit acts as custodian requires the establishment of two separate trust funds. Why is this true?

15 Is a consolidated balance sheet appropriate for all funds and account groups of a governmental unit? Explain.

EXERCISES

Ex. 14-1 Select the best answer for each of the following multiple choice questions:

1 When permanent improvements constructed by a governmental unit are to benefit and to be paid for largely by taxpayers in the immediate area, the receipts and expenditures related to the project should be accounted for in:

a A special revenue fund
b A special assessment fund
c An intragovernmental service fund
d The general fixed assets group of accounts

2 Accounting for a governmental unit generally is different from that for a business, but accounting for a business is most like accounting for:

a A special revenue fund
b A special assessment fund
c An enterprise fund
d A capital projects fund

3 When used in government entity accounting, the term *fund* usually refers to:

a A sum of money designated for a special purpose
b A liability to other governmental units
c The equity of a governmental unit in its own assets
d An accounting entity having a set of self-balancing accounts

4 Depreciation on the property and equipment assets of a government entity should be recorded as an expense in the:

a Enterprise fund
b General fund
c Special assessment fund
d Special revenue fund

5 In government entity accounting, the accrual basis is recommended for:

a Only agency, debt service, enterprise, general, and special revenue funds
b Only capital projects, enterprise, intragovernmental service, special assessment, and trust funds
c Only enterprise, general, and intragovernmental service funds
d None of the funds

6 Property and equipment and current assets are not accounted for in the same fund, with the exception of the:

a General fund
b Intragovernmental service fund
c Special assessment fund
d Special revenue fund

7 The balance sheet in the financial report of a governmental unit may be prepared:

a On a consolidated basis after eliminating the effects of interfund transactions
b On a combined basis showing the assets and equities of each fund with a total column labeled "memorandum only" indicating the aggregate balance for each identical account in all the funds
c On a combined basis showing the assets and equities of each fund, but without a total column labeled "memorandum only" indicating the aggregate balance for each identical account in all the funds
d For each fund on a separate page but never presenting all funds together on the same page

8 The budget which relates input of resources to output of services is the:

a Capital budget
b Traditional budget
c Performance budget
d Program budget

9 The activities of a street improvement project which is being financed by requiring each owner of property facing the street to pay a proportionate share of the total cost should be accounted for in the:

  a Capital projects fund
  b General fund
  c Special assessment fund
  d Special revenue fund

Ex. 14-2 On July 1, Year 4, the City of Linden paid $115,000 out of General Fund revenues for a central garage to service its vehicles, with $67,500 being applicable to the building, which has an estimated life of 25 years, $14,500 to land, and $33,000 to machinery and equipment, which has an estimated life of 15 years. A $12,200 cash contribution was received by the garage from the General Fund on the same date. Prepare the journal entry or entries in good form to record the above transactions in the appropriate fund established for the central garage. Identify the fund.

Ex. 14-3 On June 30, Year 1, the Town of Quartile issued $160,000 principal amount of special assessment bonds at 100 to finance in part a street improvement project estimated to cost $215,000. The project is to be paid by a $15,000 contribution from the Town of Quartile General Fund and by a $200,000 special assessment against property owners (payable in five equal annual installments beginning July 1, Year 1). Prepare the journal entry or entries in good form to record the above transactions in the appropriate fund established for the street improvement project. Identify the fund.

Ex. 14-4 On July 1, Year 7, the County of Fairwind issued $400,000 in 30-year, 8% general obligation term bonds of the same date at 100 to finance the construction of a public health center. Prepare the journal entry or entries in good form to record the above transaction in all affected funds or account groups. Identify the funds or account groups.

Ex. 14-5 Select the best answer for each of the following multiple choice questions.

  1 Of the items listed below, those most likely to have parallel accounting procedures, account titles, and financial statements are:
    a Special revenue funds and special assessment funds
    b Intragovernmental service funds and debt service funds
    c The general fixed assets group of accounts and the general long-term debt group of accounts
    d The general fund and special revenue funds

  2 The City of Briggs should use a capital projects fund to account for:
    a Structures and improvements constructed with the proceeds of a special assessment
    b Proceeds of a bond issue to be used to acquire land for city parks
    c Construction in progress on the city-owned electric utility plant, financed by an issue of revenue bonds
    d Assets to be used to retire bonds issued to finance an addition to the city hall

  3 Activities of a central print shop offering printing services at cost to various city departments should be accounted for in:
    a The general fund
    b An intragovernmental service fund
    c A special revenue fund
    d A special assessment fund

  4 Tucker County collects property taxes for the benefit of the state government and the local school districts and periodically remits collections to these units.

These activities should be accounted for in:
a An agency fund
b The general fund
c An intragovernmental service fund
d A special assessment fund

5 In order to provide for the retirement of general obligation bonds, the City of Milburn invests a portion of its receipts from general property taxes in marketable securities. This investment activity should be accounted for in:
a A capital projects fund
b A debt service fund
c A trust fund
d The general fund

6 The transactions of a city police retirement system should be recorded in:
a The general fund
b A special revenue fund
c A trust fund
d An intragovernmental service fund

7 The activities of a municipal golf course which receives three-fourths of its total revenue from a special tax levy should be accounted for in:
a An enterprise fund
b The general fund
c A special assessment fund
d A special revenue fund

8 A performance budget relates a governmental unit's expenditures to:
a Objects of expenditure
b Expenditures of the preceding fiscal year
c Individual months within the fiscal year
d Activities and programs

Ex. 14-6 The city council of Northgate adopted a budget for the general operations of the city government during the fiscal year ending June 30, Year 5. Revenues were estimated at $695,000. Legal authorizations for budgeted expenditures were $650,000. In addition, taxes of $160,000 were levied and billed for the special revenue fund of Northgate, of which 1% was estimated to be uncollectible. Prepare the journal entry or entries to record the above transactions in the appropriate funds. Identify the funds.

Ex. 14-7 On July 25, Year 3, office supplies estimated to cost $2,390 were ordered from a vendor for delivery to the city manager's office of Eaton. Eaton, which operates on the calendar year, maintains a perpetual inventory system for such supplies. The supplies ordered July 25 were received on August 9, Year 3, accompanied by an invoice for $2,500. Prepare the journal entries in good form to record the above transactions in the appropriate fund. Identify the fund.

Ex. 14-8 Wilson Harding, a citizen of Prospect City, donated common stock valued at $22,000 to the city under a trust agreement dated July 1, Year 6. Under the terms of the agreement, the principal amount is to be kept intact; use of revenue from the stock is restricted to financing academic university scholarships for needy students. On December 14, Year 6, dividends of $1,100 were received on the stock donated by Harding. Prepare the journal entries in good form to record the above transactions in the appropriate funds. Identify the funds.

Ex. 14-9 Select the best answer for each of the following multiple choice questions.
1 The operations of a public library receiving the majority of its support from property taxes levied for that purpose should be accounted for in:

a The general fund
b A special revenue fund
c An enterprise fund
d An intragovernmental service fund
e None of the above

2 The liability for general obligation bonds issued for the benefit of a municipal electric company and serviced by its earnings should be recorded in:
a An enterprise fund
b The general fund
c An enterprise fund and the general long-term debt group of accounts
d An enterprise fund and disclosed in a footnote in the statement of general long-term debt
e None of the above

3 The receipts from a special tax levy to retire and pay interest on general obligation bonds issued to finance the construction of a new city hall should be recorded in a:
a Debt service fund
b Capital projects fund
c Revolving interest fund
d Special revenue fund
e None of the above

4 The operations of a governmental unit's swimming pool receiving the majority of its support from charges to users should be accounted for in:
a A special revenue fund
b The general fund
c An intragovernmental service fund
d An enterprise fund
e None of the above

5 The property and equipment assets of a central purchasing and stores department organized to serve all governmental unit departments should be recorded in:
a An enterprise fund and the general fixed assets group of accounts
b An enterprise fund
c The general fixed assets group of accounts
d The general fund
e None of the above

6 The monthly remittance to an insurance company of the lump sum of hospital-surgical insurance premiums collected as payroll deductions from employees should be recorded in:
a The general fund
b An agency fund
c A special revenue fund
d An intragovernmental service fund
e None of the above

7 Several years ago a city provided for the establishment of a sinking fund to retire an issue of general obligation bonds. This year the city made a $50,000 contribution to the sinking fund from general revenues and realized $15,000 in revenue from securities in the sinking fund. The bonds due this year were retired. These transactions require accounting recognition in:
a The general fund
b A debt service fund and the general long-term debt group of accounts
c A debt service fund, the general fund, and the general long-term debt group of accounts

d A capital projects fund, a debt service fund, the general fund, and the general long-term debt group of accounts

e None of the above

8 A transaction in which a governmental unit's electric utility paid $150,000 out of its earnings for new equipment requires accounting recognition in:

a An enterprise fund

b The general fund

c The general fund and the general fixed assets group of accounts

d An enterprise fund and the general fixed assets group of accounts

e None of the above

9 A transaction in which a governmental unit's electric utility issues bonds (to be repaid from its own operations) requires accounting recognition in:

a The general fund

b A debt service fund

c Enterprise and debt service funds

d An enterprise fund, a debt service fund, and the general long-term debt group of accounts

e None of the above

10 A transaction in which a governmental unit issued general obligation serial bonds to finance the construction of a fire station requires accounting recognition in the:

a General fund

b Capital projects and general funds

c Capital projects fund and the general long-term debt group of accounts

d General fund and the general long-term debt group of accounts

e None of the above

SHORT CASES FOR ANALYSIS AND DECISION

Case 14-1 You have been appointed to examine the financial statements of the funds and account groups of Orangegrove City for the fiscal year ended June 30, Year 7. During the course of your examination you learn that on July 1, Year 6, the city issued at face amount $1,000,000 20-year, 8% general obligation serial bonds to finance additional power-generating facilities for the Orangegrove City electric utility. Principal and interest on the bonds are repayable by the Orangegrove City Electric Utility Enterprise Fund. However, for the first five years of the serial maturities of the bonds—July 1, Year 7, through July 1, Year 11—a special tax levy accounted for in the Orangegrove City Special Revenue Fund is to contribute to the payment of 80% of the interest and principal of the general obligation bonds. At the end of the five-year period, it is anticipated that revenue from the electric utility's new power-generating facilities will create cash flow for the Orangegrove City Electric Utility Enterprise Fund sufficient to pay *all* the serial maturities and interest of the general obligation bonds during the period July 1, Year 12, through July 1, Year 26.

You find that the accounts of the Orangegrove City Electric Utility Enterprise Fund include the following amounts relative to the general obligation bonds at June 30, Year 7:

8% *General obligation serial bonds payable ($50,000 due July 1,*	
Year 7)	$1,000,000
Interest payable (interest on the bonds is payable annually each	
July 1)	80,000
Interest expense	80,000

The statement of revenue and expenses for the year ended June 30, Year 7, prepared by the accountant for the Orangegrove City Electric Utility Enterprise Fund shows a net loss of $20,000. You also learn that on July 1, Year 7, the Orangegrove City Special Revenue Fund paid $104,000 (80% × $130,000) and the Orangegrove City Electric Utility Enterprise Fund paid $26,000 (20% × $130,000) to the fiscal agent for the 8% general obligation serial bonds. The $130,000 was the total of the $50,000 principal and $80,000 interest due on the bonds July 1, Year 7.

Instructions Do you concur with the Orangegrove City Electric Utility Enterprise Fund's accounting and reporting treatment for the 8% general obligation serial bonds? Discuss.

Case 14-2 The controller of the City of La Columbia has asked your advice on the accounting for an installment contract payable by the city. The contract covers the costs of installing automatic gates, coin receptacles, and ticket dispensers for the 20 city-owned parking lots in the downtown district. Installation of the self-parking equipment resulted in a decrease in the required number of parking attendants for the city-owned parking lots and a reduction in the city's salaries and related expenditures.

The contract is payable monthly in amounts equal to 40% of the month's total parking revenue for the 20 lots. Since no legal or contractual provisions require the City of La Columbia to establish an enterprise fund for the parking lots, both parking revenue and parking lot maintenance and repairs expenditures are recorded in the City of La Columbia General Fund. The parking-lot sites are carried at cost in the City of La Columbia General Fixed Assets group of accounts.

The City controller outlines to you his plans for accounting for payments on the contract as follows: Monthly payments under the contract are to be charged to the Expenditures account of the General Fund and to the Debt Service section of the Expenditures subsidiary ledger. The payments will also be recorded in the General Fixed Assets group of accounts as additions to the Improvements Other than Buildings account. A footnote to the General Fund balance sheet will disclose the unpaid balance of the installment contract at the end of each fiscal year. The unpaid balance of the contract will not be included in the General Long-term Debt group of accounts, because the contract does not represent a liability for **borrowing of cash,** as do the bond and other long-term debt liabilities of the City of La Columbia.

Instructions What is your advice to the controller of the City of La Columbia? Discuss your position thoroughly.

Case 14-3 Jason and Margaret Means, residents of Littoral City, have donated their historic mansion, "Seabright," in trust to Littoral City to serve as a tourist attraction. For a nominal charge, tourists will be guided through Seabright to observe the paintings, sculptures, antiques, and other art objects collected by Mr. and Mrs. Means, as well as the mansion's unique architectural style.

The trust indenture executed by Mr. and Mrs. Means provides that the admissions charges to Seabright (which was appraised at $5,000,000 as of the date of the trust indenture) are to cover the operating expenditures associated with the tours, as well as maintenance and repairs costs for Seabright. Any excess of admissions revenues over the above costs are to be donated to Littoral University for scholarships to art and architecture students.

Instructions Discuss the fund accounting issues, and related accounting matters such as depreciation, which should be considered by officials of Littoral City with respect to the Means trust.

PROBLEMS

14-4 The following data were taken from the accounting records of the Town of Washburn General Fund after the accounts had been closed for the fiscal year ended June 30, Year 3:

	Balances July 1, Year 2	Fiscal Year 3 Changes		Balances June 30, Year 3
		Debit	Credit	
Assets				
Cash	$180,000	$ 955,000	$ 880,000	$255,000
Taxes receivable	20,000	809,000	781,000	48,000
Estimated uncollectible taxes	(4,000)	6,000	9,000	(7,000)
	$196,000			$296,000
Liabilities, Reserves, & Fund Balance				
Vouchers payable	$ 44,000	880,000	889,000	$ 53,000
Due to Intragovernmental				
Service Fund	2,000	7,000	10,000	5,000
Due to Debt Service Fund	10,000	60,000	100,000	50,000
Reserve for encumbrances	40,000	40,000	47,000	47,000
Fund balance	100,000	20,000	61,000	141,000
	$196,000	$2,777,000	$2,777,000	$296,000

The following additional data are available:
(1) The budget for Fiscal Year 3 provided for estimated revenues of $1,000,000 and appropriations of $965,000.
(2) Expenditures totaling $895,000, in addition to those chargeable against Reserve for Encumbrances, were made.
(3) The actual expenditure chargeable against Reserve for Encumbrances was $37,000.

Instructions Reconstruct in good form the journal entries for the Town of Washburn General Fund indicated by the above data for the year ended June 30, Year 3. Do not attempt to differentiate between current and delinquent taxes receivable, or between reserves for encumbrances for Year 2 and Year 3.

14-5 You were engaged as independent auditor of the City of DeMons as of June 30, Year 2. You found the following accounts, among others, in the General Fund for the Fiscal Year ended June 30, Year 2:

Special Cash

Date		Reference	Debit	Credit	Balance
Year 1					
Aug. 1		CR 58	301,000		301,000 dr.
Sept. 1		CR 60	80,000		381,000 dr.
Dec. 1		CD 41		185,000	196,000 dr.
Year 2					
Feb. 1		CD 45		4,500	191,500 dr.
June 1		CR 64	50,500		242,000 dr.
June 30		CD 65		167,000	75,000 dr.

Construction in Progress—Main Street Sewer

Date		Reference	Debit	Credit	Balance
Year 1					
Dec. 1		CD 41	185,000		185,000 dr.
Year 2					
June 30		CD 65	167,000		352,000 dr.

Bonds Payable

Date		Reference	Debit	Credit	Balance
Year 1					
Aug. 1		CR 58		300,000	300,000 cr.
Year 2					
June 1		CR 64		50,000	350,000 cr.

Premium on Bonds

Date		Reference	Debit	Credit	Balance
Year 1					
Aug. 1		CR 58		1,000	1,000 cr.

Assessment Revenue

Date		Reference	Debit	Credit	Balance
Year 1					
Sept. 1		CR 60		80,000	80,000 cr.

Interest Expense

Date		Reference	Debit	Credit	Balance
Year 2					
Feb. 1		CD 45	4,500		4,500 dr.
June 1		CR 64		500	4,000 dr.

The accounts resulted from the project described below:

The City Council authorized the Main Street Sewer Project and a 5-year, 3% bond issue of $350,000 dated August 1, Year 1, to permit deferral of assessment payments. According to the terms of the authorization, the property owners were to be assessed 80% of the estimated cost of construction; the balance was to be made available by the City of DeMons General Fund on October 1, Year 1. On September 1, Year 1, the first of five equal annual assessment installments was collected from the property owners, and a contract for construction of the sewer was signed. The deferred assessments were to bear interest at 5%% from September 1, Year 1. The project was expected to be completed by October 31, Year 2.

Instructions

a Prepare in good form the journal entries which should have been made in the City of DeMons Special Assessment Fund for the year ended June 30, Year 2. Amortize the bond premium by the straight-line method.

b Prepare the journal entries at June 30, Year 2, for City of DeMons funds, other than the Special Assessment Fund, to record properly therein the results of transactions of the Main Street Sewer Project.

14-6 The following budget was proposed for Year 3 for the Fairdale School District General Fund:

Fund balance, Jan. 1, Year 3	$128,000
Revenues:	
Property taxes	112,000
Investment interest	4,000
Total	$244,000
Expenditures:	
Operating	$120,000
County Treasurer's fees	1,120
Bond interest	50,000
Fund balance, Dec. 31, Year 3	72,880
Total	$244,000

A general obligation bond issue of the School District was proposed in Year 2. The proceeds are to be used for a new school. There are no other outstanding bond issues. Information about the bond issue follows:

Face amount	$1,000,000
Interest rate	5%
Bonds dated	Jan. 1, Year 3
Coupons mature	Jan. 1 and July 1 beginning July 1, Year 3
Bonds mature serially at $100,000 per year starting Jan. 1, Year 5.	

The School District uses a separate bank account for each fund. The General Fund trial balance at December 31, Year 2 follows:

	Debit	Credit
Cash	$ 28,000	
Temporary investments—U. S. Treasury 4% bonds, interest payable		
May 1 and Nov. 1	100,000	
Fund balance		$128,000
	$128,000	$128,000

The county treasurer collects the taxes and charges a standard fee of 1% on all collections. The transactions for Year 3 were as follows:

Jan.   1   The proposed budget was adopted, the general obligation bond issue was authorized, and the property taxes were levied.

Feb. 28   Tax receipts from county treasurer, $49,500, were deposited.

Apr.   1   Bond issue was sold at 101 plus accrued interest. It was directed that the premium be used for payment of interest.
Apr.   2   The School District disbursed $47,000 for new school site.
Apr.   3   A contract for $950,000 for the new school was approved.
May   1   Interest was received on temporary investments.
July   1   Interest was paid on bonds.
Aug. 31   Tax receipts from county treasurer, $59,400, were deposited.
Nov.   1   Payment on new school construction contract, $200,000, was made.
Dec. 31   Operating expenditures during year were $115,000.

Instructions Prepare journal entries in good form to record the foregoing Year 3 transactions in the following funds or groups of accounts. (Closing entries are not required.)
a General Fund
b Capital Projects Fund
c General Fixed Assets group of accounts
d General Long-term Debt group of accounts
Fairdale School District does not use a Debt Service Fund.

14-7 Your examination of the financial statements of the Town of Farmville for the year ended June 30, Year 6 disclosed that the Town's inexperienced accountant was uninformed regarding governmental accounting and recorded all transactions in the General Fund. The following General Fund trial balance was prepared by the accountant:

TOWN OF FARMVILLE GENERAL FUND
Trial Balance
June 30, Year 6

	Debit	Credit
Cash	$ 12,900	
Accounts receivable	1,200	
Taxes receivable—current	8,000	
Vouchers payable		$ 15,000
Appropriations		350,000
Expenditures	344,000	
Estimated revenues	290,000	
Revenues		320,000
Town property	16,100	
Bonds payable	36,000	
Fund balance		23,200
Totals	$708,200	$708,200

Your audit disclosed the following:
(1) The accounts receivable balance was due from the Town's water utility for the sale of scrap iron. Accounts for the water utility operated by the Town are maintained in a separate fund.
(2) The total tax levy for the year was $270,000. The Town's tax collection experience in recent years indicates an average loss of 3% of the net tax levy for uncollectible taxes.
(3) On June 30, Year 6, the Town retired at face value 4% General Obligation Serial Bonds totaling $30,000. The bonds were issued on July 1, Year 4, in

the total amount of $150,000. Interest paid during the year was also recorded in the Bonds Payable account.

(4) On July 1, Year 5, to service various departments the Town Council authorized a supply room with an inventory not to exceed $10,000. During the year supplies totaling $12,300 were purchased and charged to Expenditures. The physical inventory taken at June 30, Year 6, disclosed that supplies totaling $8,400 were used.

(5) Expenditures for Year 6 included $2,600 applicable to purchase orders issued in the prior year. Outstanding purchase orders at June 30, Year 6, not recorded in the accounts amounted to $4,100.

(6) The amount of $8,200, due from the state during Fiscal Year 6 for the town's share of state gasoline taxes, was not recorded in the accounts, since the state was late in remitting the $8,200.

(7) Equipment costing $7,500, which had been purchased by the General Fund, was removed from service and sold for $900 during the year and new equipment costing $17,000 was purchased. These transactions were recorded in the Town Property account. The Town does not record depreciation in the General Fixed Assets group of accounts.

Instructions

a Prepare in good form adjusting and closing entries for the Town of Farmville General Fund at June 30, Year 6.

b Prepare in good form adjusting entries for any other funds or groups of accounts. (The town's accountant had recorded all the above transactions in the General Fund.)

14-8 The City of Gaspar City Hall Capital Projects Fund was established on July 1, Year 2, to account for the construction of a new city hall financed by the sale of bonds. The building was to be constructed on a site owned by the City.

The building construction was financed by the issuance on July 1, Year 2, of $1,000,000 principal amount of 4%, ten-year term bonds.

The only funds in which the transactions pertaining to the new city hall were recorded were the City of Gaspar Capital Projects Fund and General Fund. The Capital Projects Fund's trial balance follows:

CITY OF GASPAR CITY HALL CAPITAL PROJECTS FUND
Trial Balance
June 30, Year 3

	Debit	Credit
Cash	$ 893,000	
Vouchers payable		$ 11,000
Reserve for encumbrances		723,000
Appropriations		1,015,000
Expenditures	140,500	
Encumbrances	715,500	
	$1,749,000	$1,749,000

An analysis of the Reserve for Encumbrances account follows:

	Debit (Credit)
Contract with General Construction Company	$(750,000)
Purchase orders placed for materials and supplies	(55,000)
Receipt of materials and supplies and payment therefor	14,500
Payment of General Construction Company invoice less 10% retention . . .	67,500
	$(723,000)

An analysis of the Appropriations account follows:

	Debit (Credit)
Face amount of bonds sold	$(1,000,000)
Premium on bonds	(15,000)
	$(1,015,000)

An analysis of the Expenditures account follows:

	Debit (Credit)
Progress billing invoice from General Construction Company (with which the City contracted for the construction of the new City Hall for $750,000; other contracts will be let for heating, air conditioning, etc.) showing 10% of the work completed	$ 75,000
Charge from the General Fund for work done in clearing the building site	11,000
Payments to suppliers for building materials and supplies purchased .	14,500
Payment of interest on bonds outstanding	40,000
	$140,500

Instructions

a Prepare a working paper for the City of Gaspar City Hall Capital Projects Fund at June 30, Year 3, showing:
   (1) Preliminary trial balance.
   (2) Adjustments. (Formal adjusting entries are not required; however, explain adjustments at bottom of working paper.)
   (3) Adjusted trial balance.

b Prepare adjusting entries in good form at June 30, Year 3, for the following:
   (1) Debt Service Fund
   (2) General Fixed Assets account group
   (3) General Long-term Debt account group

14-9 The accounting records of the City of Kelton were maintained by an inexperienced accountant during the year ended December 31, Year 5. The following trial balance of the General Fund was available when you began your examination:

CITY OF KELTON GENERAL FUND
Trial Balance
December 31, Year 5

	Debit	Credit
Cash	$ 75,600	
Taxes receivable—current	29,000	
Estimated uncollectible current taxes		$ 9,000
Taxes receivable—delinquent	4,000	
Estimated uncollectible delinquent taxes		5,100
Building addition constructed	25,000	
Special assessment bonds payable		50,000
Serial bonds paid	8,000	
Vouchers payable		13,000
Fund balance		33,500
Estimated revenues	180,000	
Appropriations		174,000
Revenues		177,000
Expenditures	140,000	
	$461,600	$461,600

Your examination disclosed the following:
(1) The estimate of losses of $9,000 for current taxes receivable was found to be a reasonable estimate.
(2) The Building Addition Constructed account balance is the cost of an addition to the municipal building. The addition was constructed during Year 5 and payment was made from the General Fund as authorized.
(3) The Serial Bonds Paid account reports the annual retirement of general obligation bonds issued to finance the construction of the municipal building. Interest payments of $3,800 for this bond issue are included in Expenditures.
(4) A physical count of the current operating supplies at December 31, Year 5, revealed an inventory of $6,500. The decision was made to record the inventory in the accounts; expenditures are to be recorded on the basis of usage rather than purchases.
(5) Operating supplies ordered in Year 4 and chargeable to Year 4 appropriations were received, recorded, and consumed in January Year 5. The outstanding purchase orders for these supplies, which were not recorded in the accounts at December 31, Year 4, amounted to $4,400. The vendors' invoices for these supplies totaled $4,700.
(6) Outstanding purchase orders at December 31, Year 5 for operating supplies totaled $5,300. These purchase orders were not recorded in the accounting records.
(7) The special assessment bonds were issued December 31, Year 5, to finance a street paving project. No contracts have been signed for this project and no expenditures have been made.
(8) The balance in the Revenues account includes credits for $10,000 for a note issued to a bank to obtain cash in anticipation of tax collections to pay current expenses and for $900 for the sale of scrap iron from the city's water utility. The note was still outstanding at year-end. The operations of the water utility are accounted for in a separate fund.

Instructions

a Prepare in good form adjusting and closing entries for the City of Kelton General Fund at December 31, Year 5.

b The foregoing information disclosed by your examination was recorded only in the General Fund, even though other funds or account groups were involved. Prepare in good form adjusting entries for any other funds or account groups involved.

14-10 The City of Harrington has engaged you to examine its financial statements for the year ended December 31, Year 1. The City was incorporated as a municipality and began operations on January 1, Year 1. You find that a budget was approved by the City Council and was recorded, but that all transactions have been recorded on the cash basis in an "Operating Fund." The City's accountant has provided the Operating Fund's trial balance at December 31, Year 1, as follows:

	Debit	Credit
Cash	$238,900	
Bonds payable		$200,000
Premium on bonds payable		3,000
Fund balance		12,100
Estimated revenues	114,100	
Appropriations		102,000
Revenues		108,400
Expenditures	72,500	
	$425,500	$425,500

Additional information is given below:

(1) Your examination of the expenditures subsidiary ledger revealed the following information:

	Budgeted	Actual
Personal services	$ 45,000	$38,500
Supplies	19,000	11,000
Equipment	38,000	23,000
	$102,000	$72,500

(2) Supplies and equipment in the amount of $4,000 and $10,000, respectively, had been received, but the vouchers had not been paid at December 31, Year 1.

(3) At December 31, Year 1, outstanding purchase orders for supplies and equipment not yet received were $1,200 and $3,800, respectively.

(4) The inventory of supplies on December 31, Year 1, was $1,700 by physical count. A city ordinance requires that the expenditures for supplies are to be based on usage, not on purchases.

(5) Your examination of the revenues subsidiary ledger revealed the following information:

	Budgeted	Actual
Property taxes	$102,600	$ 96,000
Licenses	7,400	7,900
Fines	4,100	4,500
	$114,100	$108,400

It was estimated that 5% of the property taxes would not be collected. Accordingly, property taxes were levied in an amount so that collections would yield the budgeted amount of $102,600.

(6) On November 1, Year 1, the City of Harrington issued 8% General Obligation Term Bonds with $200,000 principal amount for a premium of $3,000. Interest is payable each May 1 and November 1 until the maturity date of November 1, Year 15. The City Council ordered that the cash from the bond premium be set aside and restricted for the eventual retirement of the debt principal. The bonds were issued to finance the construction of a city hall, but no contracts had been signed as of December 31, Year 1.

Instructions

a Prepare a working paper for the City of Harrington "Operating Fund" at December 31, Year 1, showing adjustments and distributions to the proper funds or groups of accounts in conformity with generally accepted accounting principles applicable to government entities. Formal adjusting entries are not required; however, explain each adjustment at the bottom of the working paper.

The following column headings are suggested:

Operating Fund Trial Balance
Adjustments
Adjusted Trial Balance
General Fund
Debt Service Fund
Capital Projects Fund
General Fixed Assets Group of Accounts
General Long-term Debt Group of Accounts

b Prepare in good form closing entries for the City of Harrington General Fund at December 31, Year 1.

14-11 The City of Algernon has engaged you to examine the following balance sheet which was prepared by the city's accountant:

CITY OF ALGERNON
Balance Sheet
June 30, Year 6

Assets

Cash	$ 159,000
Investments	250,000
Taxes receivable—current	32,000
Inventory of supplies	9,000
Land	1,000,000
Property and equipment	7,000,000
	$8,450,000

Liabilities, Reserves, & Fund Balance

Vouchers payable	$ 42,000
Term bonds payable	3,000,000
Reserve for inventory of supplies	8,000
Fund balance	5,400,000
	$8,450,000

Your audit disclosed the following information:

(1) An analysis of the Fund Balance account:

Balance, June 30, Year 5		$2,100,000
Add:		
Donated land	$ 800,000	
Federal grant-in-aid	2,200,000	
Creation of endowment fund	250,000	
Excess of actual tax revenue over estimated revenue	24,000	
Excess of appropriations closed out over expenditures and encumbrances	20,000	
Net income from endowment funds	10,000	3,304,000
		$5,404,000
Deduct:		
Excess of Cultural Center operating expenses over revenues		4,000
Balance, June 30, Year 6		$5,400,000

(2) In July, Year 5, land, appraised at a fair market value of $800,000, was donated to the city for a Cultural Center which was opened on April 15, Year 6. Building construction expenditures for the project were financed from a federal grant-in-aid of $2,200,000 and from an authorized 10-year $3,000,000 issue of 6% general obligation bonds sold at face amount on July 1, Year 5. Interest is payable on December 31 and June 30. The fair market value of the land and the cost of the building are included respectively in the Land and Property and Equipment accounts.

(3) The Cultural Center receives no direct state or city subsidy for current operating expenses. A Cultural Center Endowment Trust Fund was established by a gift of marketable securities having a fair market value of $250,000 at date of the gift. The endowment principal is to be kept intact. Income is to be applied to any operating deficit of the center.

(4) Other data:
    a It is anticipated that $7,000 of the Fiscal Year 6 tax levy is uncollectible.
    b The physical inventory of supplies on hand at June 30, Year 6 amounted to $12,500.
    c Unfilled purchase orders for the General Fund at June 30, Year 6 totaled $5,000.
    d On July 1, Year 5, an all-purpose building was purchased for $2,000,000. Of the purchase price, $200,000 was allocated to the land. The purchase had been authorized under the budget for the year ended June 30, Year 6.

Instructions Prepare a working paper for the City of Algernon at June 30, Year 6, showing adjustments and distributions to the proper funds or groups of accounts in conformity with generally accepted accounting principles applicable to government entities. Formal adjusting entries are not required; however, explain each adjustment at the bottom of the working paper. The following column headings are suggested:
    Unadjusted Trial Balance
    Adjustments
    Adjusted Trial Balance
    General Fund
    City Cultural Center Endowment Trust Principal Fund
    City Cultural Center Endowment Trust Revenue Fund
    General Fixed Assets Group of Accounts
    General Long-term Debt Group of Accounts

15

Not-for-profit entities

A *not-for-profit entity* is an organization which is operated for the benefit of society as a whole, rather than for the benefit of an individual proprietor or a group of partners or shareholders. Thus, the concept of *net income* is not meaningful for a not-for-profit entity. Instead, like the intragovernmental service fund described in Chapter 14, a not-for-profit entity strives only to obtain revenue sufficient to cover its expenses.

Not-for-profit entities comprise a significant segment of the United States economy. Colleges and universities, voluntary health and welfare organizations such as United Way, most hospitals, philanthropic foundations such as the Ford Foundation and the Rockefeller Foundation, professional societies such as the AICPA, and civic organizations such as Kiwanis, are familiar examples of not-for-profit entities.

Until recent years, the accounting standards and practices which constitute generally accepted accounting principles were not considered to be entirely applicable to not-for-profit entities. The following quotation, which has appeared in various auditing publications of the AICPA since 1957, outlines this situation:

> . . . the statements . . . of a not-for-profit organization . . . may reflect accounting practices differing in some respects from those followed by enterprises organized for profit. In some cases generally accepted accounting principles applicable to not-for-profit organizations have not been clearly defined. In those areas where the independent auditor believes generally accepted accounting principles have been clearly defined, he may state his opinion as to the conformity of the financial statements either with *generally accepted accounting principles* or (less desirably) with *accounting practices* for not-for-profit organizations in the particular field, and in such circum-

stances he may refer to financial position and results of operations. In those areas where he believes generally accepted accounting principles have not been clearly defined, the provisions covering special reports as discussed under cash basis and modified accrual basis statements are applicable.[1]

In the period 1972 to 1974, the unsettled state of accounting for not-for-profit entities was substantially improved by the AICPA's issuance of three *Industry Audit Guides:* "Hospital Audit Guide" (1972), "Audits of Colleges and Universities" (1973), and "Audits of Voluntary Health and Welfare Organizations" (1974). The status of an *Industry Audit Guide* is set forth in a "Notice to Readers" in each *Guide;* the following language in "Hospital Audit Guide" is typical:

> This audit guide is published for the guidance of members of the Institute in examining and reporting on financial statements of hospitals. It represents the considered opinion of the Committee on Health Care Institutions and as such contains the best thought of the profession as to the best practices in this area of reporting. Members should be aware that they may be called upon to justify departures from the Committee's recommendations.[2]

Thus, the accounting concepts included in an *Industry Audit Guide* have the *substantial authoritative support* required for all accepted accounting standards. The three *Industry Audit Guides* referred to above cover only three types of not-for-profit entities; however, their provisions can be tailored for accounting for other types of not-for-profit entities.

We shall discuss in some detail the hospital, college, and health and welfare *Industry Audit Guides* in subsequent sections of this chapter. Our attention must first be given to the characteristics of not-for-profit entities which have a bearing on their accounting standards and practices.

Characteristics of not-for-profit entities

Not-for-profit entities are in certain respects *hybrid.* These entities have some characteristics comparable to those of governmental entities, and other characteristics similar to those of commercial enterprises.

Characteristics Comparable to Those of Governmental Entities Among the features of not-for-profit entities which resemble characteristics of governmental entities are the following:

1 *Service to society.* Not-for-profit entities render services to society as a whole. The members of this society may range from a limited number of citizens of a community to almost the entire population of a city, state, or nation. Like the services rendered by governmental units, the services of not-for-profit entities are of benefit to the many rather than the few.

2 *No profit motivation.* As previously stated, not-for-profit entities do not operate with the objective of earning a profit. Consequently, not-for-profit entities are usually exempt from federal and state income taxes. Governmental units,

---

[1] *Statement on Auditing Standards No. 1,* "Codification of Auditing Standards and Procedures," AICPA (New York: 1973), p. 136.
[2] "Hospital Audit Guide," AICPA (New York: 1972).

except for enterprise funds, have the same characteristics. (As pointed out in Chapter 14, enterprise funds are sometimes assessed an amount in lieu of taxes by the legislative branch.)

3 *Financing by the citizenry.* Like governmental units, most not-for-profit entities depend on the general population for a substantial portion of their revenue, since charges for their services are not designed to cover all their operating costs. Exceptions are professional societies and the philanthropic foundations established by wealthy individuals or families. Whereas the citizenry's contributions to governmental revenues are mostly *involuntary* taxes, their contributions to not-for-profit entities are *voluntary* donations.

4 *Stewardship for resources.* Since a substantial portion of the resources of a not-for-profit entity are donated, the entity must account for the resources on a stewardship basis similar to that of governmental entities. The stewardship requirement makes *fund accounting* appropriate for not-for-profit entities as well as for governmental entities.

5 *Importance of budget.* The four preceding characteristics of not-for-profit entities cause their *operating budget* to be as important as for governmental entities. Not-for-profit units may employ a *traditional budget,* a *program budget,* a *performance budget,* or a *planning, programming, budgeting system.* These types of operating budgets are described in Chapter 14.

Characteristics Comparable to Those of Commercial Enterprises Among the characteristics of not-for-profit entities which resemble those of commercial enterprises are the following:

1 *Governance by board of directors.* Like a commercial corporation, a not-for-profit corporate entity is governed by elected or appointed directors, trustees, or governors. In contrast, the legislative and executive branches of a governmental unit share the responsibilities of its governance.

2 *Measurement of cost expirations.* Governance by a board of directors means that a not-for-profit entity does not answer to a lawmaking body as does a governmental unit. One consequence is that *cost expirations,* or *expenses,* rather than *expenditures,* are usually reported in the operations statement of a not-for-profit entity. Allocation of expenses (including depreciation) and revenue to the appropriate accounting period is thus a common characteristic of not-for-profit entities and commercial enterprises.

3 *Use of accrual accounting.* Not-for-profit entities employ the same accrual accounting techniques used by commercial enterprises. The modified accrual basis of accounting used by some governmental entity funds is inappropriate for not-for-profit entities.

ACCOUNTING FOR NOT-FOR-PROFIT ENTITIES

The basic accounting unit for a not-for-profit entity is the *fund,* which is defined in Chapter 14 (see page 521). Separate funds are necessary to distinguish between resources which may be used as authorized by the board of directors and resources whose use is restricted by donors. Funds commonly used by not-for-profit entities include the following:

Unrestricted fund (sometimes called *unrestricted current fund* or *current unrestricted fund*)

Restricted fund (sometimes called *restricted current fund* or *current restricted fund*)

Endowment fund

Agency fund (sometimes called *custodian fund*)

Annuity and life income funds

Loan fund

Plant fund (sometimes called *land, building, and equipment fund*)

Unrestricted fund

In many respects, the *unrestricted fund* of a not-for-profit entity is similar to the *general fund* of a governmental unit. The unrestricted fund includes all the resources of a not-for-profit entity which are available for use as authorized by the board of directors and which are not restricted for specific purposes. Thus, like the general fund of a governmental unit, the unrestricted fund of a not-for-profit entity is *residual* in nature.

Designated Fund Balance of Unrestricted Fund The board of directors of a not-for-profit entity may designate a portion of an unrestricted fund's resources for a specific purpose. The earmarked portion should be accounted for as a segregation of the unrestricted fund balance, rather than as a separate restricted fund. For example, if the board of trustees of the Civic Welfare Organization earmarked $5,000 of the unrestricted fund's resources for the purchase of new office equipment, the following journal entry would be made in the Civic Welfare Organization Unrestricted Fund:

Undesignated Fund Balance	5,000	
Designated Fund Balance—Equipment		5,000
Board of trustees' designation of portion of fund balance for purchase of office equipment.		

The Designated Fund Balance—Equipment account is similar to a retained earnings appropriation account of a commercial enterprise and is reported in the Civic Welfare Organization's balance sheet as a portion of the unrestricted fund balance.

Revenue of Unrestricted Fund The revenue of the unrestricted fund of a not-for-profit entity is derived from a number of sources. For example, a hospital derives unrestricted fund revenue from patient services, educational programs, research and other grants, unrestricted gifts, unrestricted income from endowment funds, and miscellaneous sources such as donated goods and services. A university's sources of unrestricted fund revenue include student tuition and fees; governmental appropriation, grants, and contracts; gifts and private grants; unrestricted income from endowment funds; and revenue from auxiliary enterprises such as student residences, food services, and intercollegiate athletics. The principal revenue sources of voluntary health and welfare organizations' unrestricted funds (and all other funds) are cash donations and pledges from the citizenry. Other revenue may include membership dues, interest, dividends, and gains on investments.

Revenue for Services A hospital's patient service revenue and a university's tuition and fee revenue are accrued at full rates, even though part or all of the revenue is to be waived or otherwise adjusted. Suppose, for example, that Community Hospital's patient service revenue for June, Year 3, included the following amounts:

Gross patient service revenue (before recognition of charity allowances and contractual adjustments)	$100,000
Charity allowances for indigent patients	8,000
Amount to be received from Civic Welfare Organization for indigent patients	3,000
Contractual adjustment allowed to Blue Cross	16,000

The journal entries below would be appropriate for the Community Hospital Unrestricted Fund at June 30, Year 3:

Accounts Receivable	100,000	
Patient Service Revenue		100,000
Gross patient service revenue for month of June at full		
rates.		
Accounts Receivable	3,000	
Charity Allowances.	5,000	
Allowances and Uncollectible Accounts		8,000
Gross charity allowances for June ($8,000), less amount re-		
ceivable from Civic Welfare Organization ($3,000).		
Contractual Adjustments	16,000	
Allowances and Uncollectible Accounts		16,000
Contractual adjustments allowed to Blue Cross for June.		

The contractual adjustments recorded in the latter journal entry illustrate a unique feature of a hospital's operations. Many hospital receivables are due from a ***third-party payer,*** rather than from the patient receiving services. Among third-party payers are the U.S. government (Medicare and Medicaid programs), Blue Cross, and private medical insurance carriers. The hospital's contractual agreements with third-party payers usually provide for payments by the third parties at less than full billing rates.

In the statement of revenues and expenses of Community Hospital for June, Year 3, the Charity Allowances and Contractual Adjustments accounts, together with a provision for estimated uncollectible accounts for the month, would be deducted from the Patient Service Revenue account to provide net patient service revenue for the month. The Allowances and Uncollectible Accounts ledger account would be treated as a contra to the Accounts Receivable account in the balance sheet, as in commercial enterprise accounting. The write-off of an account receivable would be accomplished in the customary fashion. For example, the accounts of indigent patients would be written off by Community Hospital by the following entry in the Unrestricted Fund at June 30, Year 3.

Allowances and Uncollectible Accounts	8,000	
Accounts Receivable		8,000
Write off uncollectible balances of indigent patients as follows: .		
J. R. English $1,500		
R. L. Knight 4,000		
S. O. Newman 2,500		
Total $8,000		

Donated Goods and Services In addition to cash contributions, not-for-profit entities receive donations of goods and services from the public. For example, a hospital may receive free drugs, or a "thrift store" may receive donated articles of clothing. The donated goods should be recorded in the Inventory account at their fair value, with a credit to a revenue account in the unrestricted fund.

Donated services should be recorded in the unrestricted fund as salaries expense, with an offset to a revenue account, if the services are rendered to the not-for-profit entity in an employee-employer relationship. The value assigned to the services should be the going salary rate for comparable salaried employees of the entity, less any meals or other living costs absorbed for the donor of the services by the not-for-profit entity.

Pledges A *pledge* is a commitment by a prospective donor to contribute a specific amount of cash to a not-for-profit entity at a future date or in installments. Since the pledge is in writing and signed by the pledgor, it resembles in form the **promissory note** used in commerce.

Accrual accounting requires that unrestricted pledges be recorded as receivables and revenue in the unrestricted fund of a not-for-profit entity, with appropriate provision for estimated uncollectible amounts. Recording of revenue from pledges in this fashion is specifically mandated by the *Industry Audit Guides* "Hospital Audit Guide" and "Audits of Voluntary Health and Welfare Organizations."[3] However, the "Audits of Colleges and Universities" *Industry Audit Guide* makes the recording of pledges *optional* rather than *mandatory,* as indicated in the following passage:

> Pledges of gifts . . . should be disclosed in the notes unless they are reported in the financial statements. The notes to the financial statements should disclose the gross amounts by time periods over which the pledges are to be collected. . . .
>
> If the pledges are reported in the financial statements, they should be accounted for at their estimated net realizable value in the same manner as gifts received. . . .[4]

The reason for the inconsistent treatment of pledges in the three *Industry Audit Guides* is not apparent. The "Audits of Colleges and Universities" *Guide* apparently sanctions use of notes to financial statements to *correct* an error in the application of accounting standards—the omission of receivables and revenue—in the financial statements themselves. The authors believe this to be an improper use of footnotes.

Revenue from Pooled Investments Many of the funds of not-for-profit entities have resources available for investments in securities and other money-market instruments. To provide greater efficiency and flexibility in investment programs, the investment resources of all funds of a single not-for-profit entity may be *pooled* for investment by a single portfolio manager. The pooling technique requires a careful allocation of investment revenue, including gains and losses, to each participating fund of the not-for-profit entity.

To illustrate the pooling of investments, assume that on January 2, Year 5, the four funds of Civic Welfare Organization pooled their individual investments, as follows:

	Value at Jan. 2, Year 5		Original equity, %
	Cost	Market	
Unrestricted Fund	$ 20,000	$ 18,000	15.00
Restricted Fund	15,000	22,000	18.33
Plant Fund	10,000	20,000	16.67
Wilson Endowment Fund	55,000	60,000	50.00
Total	$100,000	$120,000	100.00

[3]*Ibid.,* p. 10; "Audits of Voluntary Health and Welfare Organizations," AICPA (New York: 1974), p. 14.

[4]"Audits of Colleges and Universities," AICPA (New York: 1973), p. 8.

The original equity percentages in the above tabulation are based on *market value,* not on *cost.* The market values of the pooled investments at January 2, Year 5, represent a common "measuring rod" not available in the cost amounts, which represent market values at varied dates of purchase of the investments.

Realized gains and losses, interest revenue, and dividend revenue of the pooled investments during Year 5 would be allocated to the four funds in the ratio of the original equity percentages. For example, if $18,000 realized gains of the investment pool during Year 5 were reinvested, and if interest of $5,000 and dividends of $4,000 were earned by the pool during Year 5, these amounts would be allocated as follows:

	Original equity, %	Realized gains	Interest and dividends
Unrestricted Fund	15.00	$ 2,700	$1,350
Restricted Fund	18.33	3,300	1,650
Plant Fund	16.67	3,000	1,500
Wilson Endowment Fund	50.00	9,000	4,500
Total	100.00	$18,000	$9,000

Each of the funds participating in the investment pool would debit Investments and credit Gains on Sale of Investments for its share of the $18,000. Each appropriate fund would also debit Cash (or Due from Unrestricted Fund) and credit Interest and Dividend Revenue for its share of the $9,000.

If another fund of the Civic Welfare Organization entered the investment pool at December 31, Year 5, the original equity percentages would have to be revised, based on the December 31, Year 5, market values of the investment portfolio. For example, if the Harris Endowment Fund entered the Civic Welfare Organization investment pool at December 31, Year 5, with investments having a cost of $32,000 and a market value of $36,000 at that date, the equity percentages would be revised as illustrated on page 573.

Realized gains and losses, interest revenue, and dividend revenue for periods subsequent to December 31, Year 5, would be allocated in the revised equity percentages. The revised percentages would be maintained until the membership of the investment pool changed again.

Expenses of Unrestricted Fund The expenses of unrestricted funds are similar in many respects to those of a commercial entity—salaries and wages, supplies, maintenance, research, and the like. The question of whether depreciation should be recognized by a not-for-profit entity has

	Value at Dec. 31, Year 5		Revised equity, %
	Cost*	Market†	
Unrestricted Fund	$ 22,700	$ 21,600	12.00
Restricted Fund	18,300	26,400	14.67
Plant Fund	13,000	24,000	13.33
Wilson Endowment Fund	64,000	72,000	40.00
Subtotal	$118,000	$144,000	
Harris Endowment Fund	32,000	36,000	20.00
Total	$150,000	$180,000	100.00

* Cost for four original pool member funds includes $18,000 realized gains of Year 5.
† Market value of original pooled investments totaling $144,000 at December 31, Year 5, allocated to original pool member funds based on original equity percentages on page 571.

not been settled by the AICPA. The "Hospital Audit Guide" and "Audits of Voluntary Health and Welfare Organizations" both specify that depreciation should be recorded as an expense of each accounting period.[5] However, "Audits of Colleges and Universities" takes a position that is contrary:

> Current funds expenditures . . . comprise . . . all expenses incurred, determined in accordance with the generally accepted accrual method of accounting, except for the omission of depreciation. . . .
>
> . . . .
>
> Depreciation expense related to depreciable assets comprising the physical plant is reported neither in the statement of current funds revenues, expenditures, and other changes nor in the statement of changes in unrestricted current funds balance. The reason for this treatment is that these statements present expenditures and transfers of current funds rather than operating expenses in conformity with the reporting objectives of accounting for resources received and used rather than the determination of net income. Depreciation allowances, however, may be reported in the balance sheet and the provision for depreciation reported in the statement of changes in the balance of the investment-in-plant fund subsection of the plant funds group.[6]

In the opinion of the authors, the financial reporting requirements of colleges and universities do not differ sufficiently from those of other not-for-profit entities as to make the recognition of depreciation expense inappropriate.

Assets and Liabilities of Unrestricted Fund The balance sheet of a not-for-profit entity typically presents the assets, liabilities, and fund balance for each fund, one below another. (See the illustrative balance sheet in the Appendix, pages 580–581.) Most assets and liabilities of a not-for-profit entity's unrestricted fund are similar to the *current* assets and liabilities

[5] "Hospital Audit Guide," p. 4; "Audits of Voluntary Health and Welfare Organizations," p. 12.
[6] "Audits of Colleges and Universities," pp. 26, 9–10.

of a commercial enterprise. Cash, investments, receivables, due from other funds, inventories, and prepaid expenses are typical assets of an unrestricted fund.

The "Audits of Colleges and Universities" and "Audits of Voluntary Health and Welfare Organizations" *Guides* segregate plant assets into a separate fund. In contrast, the "Hospital Audit Guide" includes the following quotation:

> Property, plant and equipment and related liabilities should be accounted for as a part of unrestricted funds, since segregation in a separate fund would imply the existence of restrictions on asset use.[7]

In the opinion of the authors, however, segregation of plant assets in a separate fund is logical accounting practice for any not-for-profit entity.

The liabilities of an unrestricted fund include payables, accruals, and deferred revenue comparable to those of a commercial enterprise, as well as Due to Other Funds accounts.

Restricted fund

Not-for-profit entities establish *restricted funds* to account for resources available for current use but expendable only as authorized by the donor or other grantor of the resources. Thus, a *restricted fund* of a not-for-profit entity resembles the *special revenue fund* of a governmental unit, since the resources of both types of funds may be expended only for specified purposes.

The AICPA's "Hospital Audit Guide" includes in the restricted funds category a broad spectrum of restricted resources:

Funds for specific operating purposes
Funds for additions to property, plant, and equipment
Endowment funds[8]

In contrast, "Audits of Colleges and Universities" and "Audits of Voluntary Health and Welfare Organizations" limit the restricted fund category to resources for specific operating purposes.[9] Thus, we once again find contradictory treatment of like items in the three AICPA *Industry Audit Guides.*

The resources of restricted funds are not derived from the operations of the not-for-profit entity. Instead, the resources are obtained from restricted gifts or grants of individuals or governmental units; revenue from restricted fund investments; gains on sales of investments of the restricted fund; and restricted income from endowment funds. These resources are transferred to the unrestricted fund as revenue of that fund at the time the designated expenditure is made.

[7]"Hospital Audit Guide," p. 4.
[8]*Ibid.,* p. 9.
[9]"Audits of Colleges and Universities," p. 16; "Audits of Voluntary Health and Welfare Organizations," p. 2.

To illustrate, assume that on July 1, Year 4, Robert King donated $50,000 to Community Hospital for the purchase of beds for a new wing of the hospital. On August 1, Year 4, Community Hospital expended $51,250 for the beds. These activities would be recorded in the accounts of Community Hospital as follows:

In Robert King Restricted Fund:

Year 4

July 1	Cash	50,000	
	Fund Balance		50,000
	Receipt of gift from Robert King for beds for new wing.		
Aug. 1	Fund Balance	50,000	
	Due to Unrestricted Fund		50,000
	Obligation to Unrestricted Fund for amount expended in accordance with Robert King gift.		

In Unrestricted Fund:

Year 4

Aug. 1	Property, Plant, and Equipment	51,250	
	Cash		51,250
	Purchase of beds for new wing.		
1	Due from Robert King Restricted Fund	50,000	
	Other Operating Revenue		50,000
	Receivable from Robert King Restricted Fund for hospital beds purchased.		

Endowment fund

An *endowment fund* of a not-for-profit entity is comparable to a *nonexpendable trust fund* of a governmental unit, described in Chapter 14. A *pure endowment fund* is one for which the principal must be held indefinitely in revenue-producing investments. Only the income from the pure endowment fund's investments may be expended by the not-for-profit entity. In contrast, the principal of a *term endowment fund* may be expended by the not-for-profit entity after the passage of a period of time or the occurrence of an event stipulated by the donor of the endowment principal. A *quasi-endowment fund* is established by the board of directors of a not-for-profit entity, rather than by an outside donor. At the option of the board, the principal of a quasi-endowment fund may be later expended by the entity which established the fund.

The income of endowment funds is handled in accordance with the instructions of the donor or the board of directors. If there are no restrictions on the use of endowment fund income, it is transferred to the not-for-profit entity's unrestricted fund. Otherwise, the endowment fund income is transferred to an appropriate restricted fund.

Agency fund

An *agency fund* of a not-for-profit entity is identical to its counterpart in a governmental unit. In an agency fund are recorded resources held by a not-for-profit entity as a custodian. The resources are disbursed only as instructed by their owner.

For example, a university may act as custodian of funds of a student organization. The university would disburse the funds as directed by the appropriate officers of the student organization. The net assets of the student organization would appear as a *liability* of the university's agency fund, rather than as *fund balance,* because the university has no equity in the fund.

Annuity and life income funds

Annuity Fund Assets may be contributed to a not-for-profit entity with the stipulation that the entity pay specified amounts periodically to named recipients, for a fixed time period. An *annuity fund* is established by the not-for-profit entity to account for this arrangement. At the end of the designated time period for the periodic payments, the unexpended assets of the annuity fund are transferred to the unrestricted fund, or to a restricted fund or endowment fund specified by the donor.

The following journal entries illustrate the accounting for the Ruth Collins Annuity Fund of Ridgedale College for the fund's first fiscal year ending June 30, Year 2:

Year 1				
July 1	Cash		50,000	
		Annuity Payable		35,000
		Fund Balance		15,000
	Receipt of cash from Andrea Collins for an annuity of			
	$6,000 per year each June 30 to Ruth Collins for her			
	lifetime. Liability is recorded at the actuarially			
	determined present value of the annuity, based on			
	Ruth Collins' life expectancy.			
1	Investments		45,000	
		Cash		45,000
	Purchase of interest in Ridgedale College's invest-			
	ment pool.			

```
Year 2
June 30   Cash ..................................   1,500
          Investments ..........................   2,000
                 Annuity Payable ...............            3,500
          Share of revenue and gains of Ridgedale College in-
          vestment pool.


      30  Annuity Payable .......................   6,000
                 Cash .............................           6,000
          Payment of current year's annuity to Ruth Collins.


      30  Fund Balance ..........................   1,000
                 Annuity Payable ................            1,000
          Actuarial loss based on revised life expectancy actu-
          arial valuation of Ruth Collins' annuity.
```

Note that, in the first entry above, the revenue and gains on the annuity fund's share of the investment pool are credited to the Annuity Payable account. This is necessary because the actuarial valuation of the annuity at date of establishment of the annuity fund set up the annuity liability at its then present value.

Life Income Fund A *life income fund,* like an annuity fund, is used to account for stipulated payments to a named beneficiary (or beneficiaries) during the beneficiary's lifetime. The payments from an annuity fund are made directly from the *principal* of the fund, but in a life income fund only the *income* of the assets is paid to the beneficiary. Thus, payments to a life income fund's beneficiary *vary* from one accounting period to the next. In contrast, payments from an annuity fund are *fixed* in amount.

Loan fund

A *loan fund* may be established by any not-for-profit entity, but loan funds are usually most significant in the accounts of colleges and universities. Student loan funds are usually *revolving;* that is, as old loans are repaid, new loans are made from the receipts. Loans receivable are carried in the loan fund at estimated realizable value; provisions for uncollectible loans are charged directly to the Fund Balance account, not to an expense account. Interest on loans is credited to the Fund Balance account, ordinarily *on the cash basis.*

Plant fund

We have already noted (see page 574) the inconsistent accounting treatment for property and equipment assets of hospitals as compared to colleges and universities and voluntary health and welfare organizations. There are also inconsistencies in the contents of the **plant funds** of the three types of not-for-profit entities, as follows:

1 A **plant replacement and expansion fund** is a subdivision of the **restricted fund** category of a hospital. In the hospital's plant replacement and expansion fund are recorded the cash, investments, and receivables earmarked by donors for expenditure for plant assets.[10]

2 The following excerpt describes the accounting for the plant fund of a voluntary health and welfare organization:

> Land, building and equipment fund (often referred to as plant fund) is often used to accumulate the net investment in fixed assets and to account for the unexpended resources contributed specifically for the purpose of acquiring or replacing land, buildings, or equipment for use in the operations of the organization. Mortgages or other liabilities relating to these assets are also included in this fund. When additions to land, buildings, or equipment used in carrying out the organization's program and supporting services are acquired with unrestricted fund resources, the amount expended for such assets should be transferred from the unrestricted fund to the plant fund and should be accounted for as a direct addition to the plant fund balance. Gains or losses on the sale of fixed assets should be reflected as income items in the plant fund accounts. The proceeds from the sale of fixed assets should be transferred to the unrestricted fund; such transfers should be reflected as direct reductions and additions to the respective fund balances.[11]

3 In contrast to the two preceding types of plant funds, "Audits of Colleges and Universities" provides for the following:

> The plant funds group consists of (1) funds to be used for the acquisition of physical properties for institutional purposes but unexpended at the date of reporting; (2) funds set aside for the renewal and replacement of institutional properties; (3) funds set aside for debt service charges and for the retirement of indebtedness on institutional properties; and (4) funds expended for and thus invested in institutional properties.
>
> Some institutions combine the assets and liabilities of the four subfund groups for reporting purposes; however, separate fund balances should be maintained. Resources restricted by donors or outside agencies for additions to plant should be recorded directly in the particular fund subgroup, generally unexpended plant funds.[12]

Thus, in the three AICPA **Industry Audit Guides** for not-for-profit entities, we find wide variations in the composition and accounting for plant funds. The differences in the plant funds of the three types of not-for-profit entities are not supported by any theoretical differences in their accounting objectives.

[10] "Hospital Audit Guide," pp. 9, 41.
[11] "Audits of Voluntary Health and Welfare Organizations," pp. 2–3.
[12] "Audits of Colleges and Universities," p. 44.

Financial statements for not-for-profit entities

All not-for-profit entities issue a balance sheet incorporating all funds of the entity. The assets, liabilities, and fund balances for each fund are listed in vertical sequence in the single balance sheet. This type of balance sheet presentation emphasizes the unitary nature of the not-for-profit entity, despite its use of separate funds for accountability purposes.

Since a not-for-profit entity does not operate for gain, an income statement is inappropriate. Instead, a statement of revenue and expenses is issued, with the final amount labeled "Excess of revenue over expenses." Changes in fund balances may be summarized in a separate statement or may be annexed to the statement of revenue and expenses.

The AICPA's "Hospital Audit Guide" recommends a statement of changes in financial position for the unrestricted fund.[13] However, "Audits of Voluntary Health and Welfare Organizations" and "Audits of Colleges and Universities" specifically waive a statement of changes, because the information is available in the other financial statements.[14]

Illustrative Financial Statements of a Not-for-Profit Entity Many of the issues discussed in this chapter are illustrated in the financial statements and notes for Civic Welfare Organization, a voluntary health and welfare organization, in the Appendix below and on pages 580–585.

APPENDIX

CIVIC WELFARE ORGANIZATION
Notes to Financial Statements
December 31, Year 2

1 *Summary of significant accounting policies.* The financial statements include the accounts of the Organization and its affiliated chapters. The Organization follows the practice of capitalizing all expenditures for land, buildings, and equipment in excess of $100; the fair value of donated plant assets is similarly capitalized. Depreciation is provided over the estimated useful lives of the assets. Investments are stated at cost. All contributions are considered to be available for unrestricted use unless specifically restricted by the donor. Pledges for contributions are recorded as received and allowances are provided for amounts estimated to be uncollectible. Policies concerning donated material and services are described in Note 6.

2 *Investments.* Market values and unrealized appreciation (depreciation) at December 31, Year 2, and Year 1 are summarized as follows:

[13]"Hospital Audit Guide," p. 38.
[14]"Audits of Voluntary Health and Welfare Organizations," p. 33; "Audits of Colleges and Universities," p. 55.

CIVIC WELFARE ORGANIZATION
Balance Sheets
December 31, Year 2 and Year 1

CURRENT FUNDS
Unrestricted

Assets	Year 2	Year 1
Cash	$2,207,000	$2,530,000
Investments (Note 2):		
For long-term purposes	2,727,000	2,245,000
Other	1,075,000	950,000
Pledges receivable less allowance for uncollectibles of $105,000 and $92,000	475,000	363,000
Inventories of educational materials, at cost	70,000	61,000
Accrued interest, other receivables and prepayments	286,000	186,000
Total	$6,840,000	$6,335,000

Liabilities and Fund Balances	Year 2	Year 1
Accounts payable	$ 148,000	$ 139,000
Research grants payable	596,000	616,000
Contributions designated for future periods	245,000	219,000
Total liabilities and deferred revenue	$ 989,000	$ 974,000
Fund balances:		
Designated by the governing board for:		
Long-term investments	$2,800,000	$2,300,000
Purchases of new equipment	100,000	-0-
Research purposes (Note 3)	1,152,000	1,748,000
Undesignated, available for general activities (Note 4)	1,799,000	1,313,000
Total fund balances	$5,851,000	$5,361,000
Total	$6,840,000	$6,335,000

Restricted

Assets	Year 2	Year 1
Cash	$ 3,000	$ 5,000
Investments (Note 2)	71,000	72,000
Grants receivable	58,000	46,000
Total	$ 132,000	$ 123,000

Liabilities and Fund Balances	Year 2	Year 1
Fund balances:		
Professional education	$ 84,000	$ -0-
Research grants	48,000	123,000
Total	$ 132,000	$ 123,000

LAND, BUILDING, AND EQUIPMENT FUND

Cash	$ 3,000	$ 2,000	Mortgage payable, 8%	$ 32,000	$ 36,000
Investments (Note 2)	177,000	145,000	Fund balances:		
Pledges receivable less allowance for			Expended	$ 484,000	$ 477,000
uncollectibles of $7,500 and $5,000	32,000	25,000	Unexpended—restricted	212,000	172,000
Land, buildings, and equipment, at cost less			Total fund balances	$ 696,000	$ 649,000
accumulated depreciation of $296,000					
and $262,000 (Note 5)	516,000	513,000			
Total	$ 728,000	$ 685,000	Total	$ 728,000	$ 685,000

ENDOWMENT FUNDS

Cash	$ 4,000	$ 10,000	Fund balance	$1,948,000	$2,017,000
Investments (Note 2)	1,944,000	2,007,000			
Total	$1,948,000	$2,017,000	Total	$1,948,000	$2,017,000

(See accompanying notes to financial statements)

Source: Adapted from "Audit of Voluntary Health and Welfare Organizations," AICPA (New York: 1974), pp. 42–50.

CIVIC WELFARE ORGANIZATION
Statement of Support, Revenue, and Expenses
and Changes in Fund Balances
Year Ended December 31, Year 2
with Comparative Totals for Year 1

	Year 2				Total all Funds	
	Current Funds		Land, Building, and Equipment Fund	Endowment Fund	Year 2	Year 1
	Unrestricted	*Restricted*				
Public support and revenue:						
Public support:						
Contributions (net of estimated uncollectible pledges of $195,000 in Year 2 and $150,000 in Year 1)	$3,764,000	$162,000	$ -0-	$ 2,000	$3,928,000	$3,976,000
Contributions to building fund	-0-	-0-	72,000	-0-	72,000	150,000
Special events (net of direct costs of $181,000 in Year 2 and $163,000 in Year 1)	104,000	-0-	-0-	-0-	104,000	92,000
Legacies and bequests	92,000	-0-	-0-	4,000	96,000	129,000
Received from federated and nonfederated campaigns (which incurred related fund-raising expenses of $38,000 in Year 2 and $29,000 in Year 1)	275,000		-0-	-0-	275,000	308,000
Total public support	$4,235,000	$162,000	$72,000	$ 6,000	$4,475,000	$4,655,000
Revenue:						
Membership dues	$ 17,000	$ -0-	$ -0-	$ -0-	$ 17,000	$ 12,000
Investment revenue	98,000	10,000	-0-	-0-	108,000	94,000
Realized gain on investment transactions	200,000	-0-	-0-	25,000	225,000	275,000
Miscellaneous	42,000	-0-	-0-	-0-	42,000	47,000
Total revenue	$ 357,000	$ 10,000	$ -0-	$ 25,000	$ 392,000	$ 428,000
Total support and revenue	$4,592,000	$172,000	$72,000	$ 31,000	$4,867,000	$5,083,000

Expenses:						
Program services:						
Research	$1,257,000	$155,000	$ 2,000	$ -0-	$1,414,000	$1,365,000
Public health education	539,000	-0-	5,000	-0-	544,000	485,000
Professional education and training . .	612,000	-0-	6,000	-0-	618,000	516,000
Community services	568,000	-0-	10,000	-0-	578,000	486,000
Total program services	$2,976,000	$155,000	$ 23,000	$ -0-	$3,154,000	$2,852,000
Supporting services:						
Management and general	$ 567,000	$ -0-	$ 7,000	$ -0-	$ 574,000	$ 638,000
Fund raising	642,000	-0-	12,000	-0-	654,000	546,000
Total supporting services . .	$1,209,000	$ -0-	$ 19,000	$ -0-	$1,228,000	$1,184,000
Total expenses	$4,185,000	$155,000	$ 42,000	$ -0-	$4,382,000	$4,036,000
Excess of public support and revenue over expenses	$ 407,000	$ 17,000	$ 30,000	$ 31,000		
Other changes in fund balances:						
Property and equipment acquisitions from unrestricted funds	(17,000)	-0-	17,000	-0-		
Transfer of realized endowment fund appreciation	100,000	-0-	-0-	(100,000)		
Returned to donor	-0-	(8,000)	-0-	-0-		
Fund balances, beginning of year . .	5,361,000	123,000	649,000	2,017,000		
Fund balances, end of year	$5,851,000	$132,000	$696,000	$1,948,000		

(See accompanying notes to financial statements)

(Thousands of dollars)

	Dec. 31, Year 2		Dec. 31, Year 1	
	Quoted market value	Unrealized appreciation	Quoted market value	Unrealized appreciation (depreciation)
Current unrestricted fund:				
For long-term purposes	$2,735	$ 8	$2,230	$(15)
Other	1,100	25	941	(9)
Current restricted funds	73	2	73	1
Endowment funds	2,125	181	2,183	176
Land, building, and				
equipment fund	184	7	153	8

Interfund transfers include $100,000 for Year 2, which represents the portion of the realized appreciation ($25,000 realized in the current year and $75,000 realized in prior years) in endowment funds that, under the laws of Kansas, were designed by the governing board for unrestricted operations. At December 31, Year 2, $200,000 of realized appreciation was available in endowment funds, which the governing board may, if it deems prudent, also transfer to the unrestricted fund.

3 *Research grants.* The Organization's awards for research grants-in-aid generally cover a period of one to three years, subject to annual renewals at the option of the governing board. At December 31, Year 2, $1,748,000 had been designated by the board for research grants, of which $596,000 had been awarded for research to be carried out within the next year.

4 *Proposed research center.* The Parsons Foundation has contributed $50,000 to the Organization with the stipulations that it be used for the construction of a research center and that construction of the facilities begin within four years. The Organization is considering the construction of a research center, the cost of which would approximate $2,000,000. If the governing board approves the construction of this facility, it is contemplated that its cost would be financed by a special fund drive.

5 *Land, buildings, and equipment and depreciation.* Depreciation of buildings and equipment is provided on a straight-line basis over the estimated useful lives of the assets. At December 31, Year 2 and Year 1, the costs of such assets were as follows:

	Year 2	Year 1
Land	$ 76,000	$ 76,000
Buildings	324,000	324,000
Medical research equipment	336,000	312,000
Office furniture and equipment	43,000	33,000
Automobiles and trucks	33,000	30,000
Total cost	$812,000	$775,000
Less: Accumulated depreciation	296,000	262,000
Net	$516,000	$513,000

6 *Donated materials and services.* Donated materials and equipment are reflected as contributions in the accompanying statements at their estimated values at date of receipt. No amounts have been reflected in the statements for donated services inasmuch as no objective basis is available to measure the value of such services; however, a substantial number of volunteers have donated significant amounts of their time in the Organization's program services and in its fund-raising campaigns

7 *Pension plans.* The Organization has a noncontributory pension and retirement plan covering substantially all its employees. Pension expense for the current year and the prior year was $83,000 and $75,000, respectively, which includes amortization of prior service cost over a 20-year period. The Organization's policy is to fund pension cost accrued. At December 31, Year 2, the actuarially computed value of the vested benefits in the plan exceeded the fund balance of the plan by approximately $50,000.

8 *Leased facilities.* Most of the buildings used by the Organization for ·its community services programs are leased on a year-to-year basis. At December 31, Year 2, fifteen such buildings were being leased for an annual cost of approximately $52,000.

REVIEW QUESTIONS

1 What is a *not-for-profit entity?*

2 List at least four types of not-for-profit entities in the United States economy.

3 What role do the AICPA's *Industry Audit Guides* play in the determination of accounting standards for not-for-profit entities? Explain.

4 What are the three characteristics of not-for-profit entities which resemble those of governmental entities?

5 What characteristics of not-for-profit entities resemble those of commercial enterprises?

6 Define the following terms applicable to not-for-profit entities:
  a Designated Fund Balance
  b Third-party payer
  c Pledge
  d Pooled investments
  e Term endowment fund

7 Differentiate between an *annuity fund* and a *life income fund* of a not-for-profit entity.

8 There are several inconsistencies in the accounting standards for like items set forth in the AICPA's *Industry Audit Guides* for not-for-profit entities. Identify at least three of these inconsistencies.

9 Hospitals and universities often "rebate" or otherwise reduce their basic revenue charges to patients and students, respectively. How are these reductions reflected in the revenue accounting for the two types of not-for-profit entities? Explain.

10 *a* Should a not-for-profit entity record donated goods in its accounts? Explain.

> **b** Should a not-for-profit entity record donated services in its accounts? Explain.

11 Identify the financial statements which are issued by a hospital.

EXERCISES

Ex. 15-1 Select the best answer for each of the following multiple choice questions:

1 Resources of a not-for-profit entity's unrestricted fund which are designated for a specific purpose by the entity's board of directors should be recorded in:

a A quasi-endowment fund
b A restricted fund
c A term endowment fund
d None of the above funds

2 A not-for-profit entity's restricted fund is used to record:

a Gifts which must be invested indefinitely in revenue-producing investments
b Resources available for current use in accordance with authorization of the donor
c Resources held by a not-for-profit entity as a custodian
d None of the above

3 The fund established to record the assets contributed to a not-for-profit entity on the condition that the entity pay a fixed amount periodically to a designated recipient for a fixed time period is:

a Life income fund
b Agency fund
c Annuity fund
d None of the above funds

4 The relevant AICPA *Industry Audit Guide* recommends that a statement of changes in financial position be issued by:

a A hospital
b A college or university
c A voluntary health and welfare organization
d None of the above not-for-profit entities

5 The accrual basis of accounting is not appropriate for a not-for-profit entity's:

a Donated goods
b Pledges
c Revenue for services
d Interest on student loans

Ex. 15-2 For the month of September, Year 6, Repose Hospital's patient service revenue records included the following:

Amount to be received from United Way for indigent patients	$ 6,500
Charity allowances for indigent patients	12,000
Contractual adjustment allowed for Medicare patients	8,500
Gross patient service revenue (before recognition of charity allowances and contractual adjustments)	125,000

Prepare the September 30, Year 6, journal entries to reflect the above in the accounts of Repose Hospital.

Ex. 15-3 On July 1, Year 5, three funds of Covina College pooled their individual investments, as follows:

	Value at July 1, Year 5	
	Cost	Market
Restricted Fund	$ 80,000	$ 90,000
Quasi-Endowment Fund	120,000	126,000
Annuity Fund	150,000	144,000
Total	$350,000	$360,000

During the year ended June 30, Year 6, the Covina College investment pool reinvested realized gains of $10,000 and earned dividends and interest totaling $18,000.

Prepare journal entries at June 30, Year 6, for each of the three Covina College funds to reflect the results of the investment pool's operations during Fiscal Year 6.

Ex. 15-4 In your examination of the financial statements of Civic Health Center, a not-for-profit entity, you find the following journal entries in the Restricted Fund:

Due from Unrestricted Fund	10,000	
Fund Balance		10,000

Board of directors authorization of resources to be expended for clinic equipment.

Clinic Equipment	9,500	
Accounts Payable		9,500

Receipt of invoice for clinic equipment.

Prepare necessary adjusting journal entries at December 31, Year 1, for all affected funds of Civic Health Center.

Ex. 15-5 The "Summary of Significant Accounting Policies" note to the unaudited financial statements drafted by the controller of People's Hospital for the year ended June 30, Year 3, includes the following sentence: "Pledges for contributions are recorded when the cash is received." Another note reads as follows:

Pledges Unrestricted pledges receivable, received, and collected during the year ended June 30, Year 3, were as follows:

Pledges receivable at July 1, Year 2 (10% estimated to be uncollectible) . . .	$ 50,000
New pledges received during year	300,000
Pledges receivable at July 1, Year 2, determined to be uncollectible during year	(15,000)
Pledges collected in cash during year	(275,000)
Pledges receivable at June 30, Year 3 (12% estimated to be uncollectible) .	$ 60,000

All pledges are due six months from the date of the pledge. Pledge revenue is recorded in the Unrestricted Fund.

Assume that you are engaged in the examination of the financial statements of People's Hospital for the year ended June 30, Year 3, and are satisfied with the propriety of the amounts recorded in the hospital's "Pledges" note. Prepare the necessary adjusting journal entry or entries for the Unrestricted Fund of People's Hospital at June 30, Year 3.

SHORT CASES FOR ANALYSIS AND DECISION

Case 15-1 During the June 20, Year 10, meeting of the Board of Directors of Resthaven Nursing Home, a not-for-profit entity, the following transpired:

Chairman. "We shall now hear the report from the controller."

Controller. "Our unrestricted contributions are at an all-time high. I projected an Unrestricted Fund excess of revenue over expenses of $100,000 for the year ended June 30."

Chairman. "That's too high a figure for us to have a successful fund-raising drive next year. I'll entertain a motion that $80,000 of unrestricted contributions be recorded in the Restricted Fund."

Director Walker. "So moved."

Director Hastings. "Second."

Chairman. "All those in favor say 'aye'."

All Directors. "Aye."

Chairman. "The chair directs the controller to prepare the necessary accounting entries for the Unrestricted Fund and the Restricted Fund."

Instructions Do you concur with the action taken by the Board of Directors of Resthaven Nursing Home? Explain.

Case 15-2 The Board of Trustees of Wallington Day Care Center, a not-for-profit entity, has asked you, as independent CPA for the center, to attend the current meeting of the board to participate in the discussion of a proposal to create one or more endowment funds. At the meeting, the board members ask you several questions regarding the required operating and accounting treatment of endowment funds. Among the questions posed by directors were the following:

1 Is only the *income* of an endowment fund expendable for current operations?

2 Under what circumstances, if any, may endowment fund *principal* be expended as decided by the board?

3 Must a separate set of accounts be established for each endowment fund, or may all endowment fund operations be accounted for in the Restricted Fund?

Instructions Draft your reply for each of the directors' questions. Number your replies to correspond with the question numbers.

Case 15-3 The controller of Bishop's Hospital, a not-for-profit entity, proposes to present the Provision for Uncollectible Accounts Receivable account as an *expense* in the statement of revenue and expenses of Bishop's Hospital Unrestricted Fund. As the hospital's independent CPA you oppose this treatment. You point out that the AICPA's "Hospital Audit Guide" requires the provision for uncollectible accounts to be offset against gross patient service revenue in the statement of revenue and expenses of a hospital's unrestricted fund. The controller's rejoinder is that there are so many contradictions among the AICPA's three *Industry Audit Guides* for not-for-profit entities that there should be some latitude for managers of not-for-profit entities to report operating results on the same basis as a commercial entity.

Instructions How would you respond to the statement of the controller of Bishop's Hospital? Support your reply by sound accounting theory for not-for-profit entities.

PROBLEMS

15-4 On July 1, Year 6, the four funds of Municipal Welfare Services, a not-for-profit entity, formed an investment pool. On that date, costs and market values of the four funds' investments were as follows:

	Value at July 1, Year 6	
	Cost	Market
Unrestricted Fund	$ 50,000	$ 60,000
Restricted Fund.....................	20,000	15,000
Plant Fund......................	80,000	90,000
Arnold Life Income Fund	100,000	105,000
Total	$250,000	$270,000

During the six months ended December 31, Year 6, the investment pool reinvested realized gains totaling $15,000 and earned dividends and interest aggregating $25,000. On December 31, Year 6, the Restricted Fund withdrew from the pool and was awarded securities in the amount of its share of the pool's aggregate December 31, Year 6, market value of $300,000. On January 2, Year 7, the Edwards Endowment Fund entered the Municipal Welfare Services investment pool with investments having a cost of $70,000 and a market value of $75,000. During the six months ended June 30, Year 7, the investment pool reinvested realized gains totaling $40,000 and earned dividends and interest aggregating $60,000.

Instructions
a Prepare a working paper for the Municipal Welfare Services investment pool, computing the following:
   (1) Original equity percentages at July 1, Year 6
   (2) Revised equity percentages at January 2, Year 7
b Prepare journal entries to reflect the operations of the Municipal Welfare Services investment pool in the accounts of the participating Unrestricted Fund.

15-5 Among the transactions of the Unrestricted Fund of Convalescent Hospital, a not-for-profit entity, for the month of October, Year 8, were the following:
   (1) Gross patient service revenue of $80,000 was billed to patients. Provision was made for indigent patient charity allowances of $4,000; amounts receivable from Township Welfare Organization for indigent patients of $2,500; contractual adjustments allowed to Medicaid of $6,000; and estimated uncollectible accounts of $8,000.
   (2) Donated services approximating $10,000 at going salary rates were received from volunteer nurses. Meals costing $200 were served to the volunteer nurses at no charge by the Convalescent Hospital cafeteria.
   (3) New pledges, due in three months, totaling $5,000 were received from various donors. Collections on pledges amounted to $3,500, and the provision for uncollectible pledges for October, Year 8, was estimated to be $800.
   (4) Paid the $500 monthly annuity established for Arline E. Walters by a contribution by Ms. Walters to Convalescent Hospital three years ago.
   (5) Received and expended $3,000 from Charles Watson Restricted Fund for new surgical equipment, as authorized by the donor.

Instructions

a Prepare the journal entries for the above October, Year 8, transactions of the Convalescent Hospital Unrestricted Fund. Number each group of entries to correspond to the number of each transactions group.

b Prepare journal entries required for other funds of Convalescent Hospital as indicated by the transactions of the Unrestricted Fund.

15-6 A newly elected board of directors of Forbes Hospital, a not-for-profit entity, decided that effective January 1, Year 98:

a The existing general ledger balances are to be properly adjusted and three separate funds (Unrestricted Fund, James Forbes Endowment Fund, and Plant Replacement Fund) are to be established.

b The fund balance of the James Forbes Endowment Fund and an amount equal to the Accumulated Depreciation account of the Unrestricted Fund are to be fully invested in securities.

c All accounts are to be maintained in accordance with the AICPA's "Hospital Audit Guide."

The board engaged you to determine the proper account balances for each of the funds. The balances in the general ledger at January 1, Year 98, were:

	Debit	Credit
Cash	$ 50,000	
Investment in U.S. Treasury Bills	105,000	
Investment in common stocks	417,000	
Interest receivable	4,000	
Accounts receivable	40,000	
Inventory	25,000	
Land	407,000	
Building	245,000	
Equipment	283,000	
Accumulated depreciation		$ 376,000
Accounts payable		70,000
Bank loan		150,000
James Forbes Endowment Fund		119,500
Surplus		860,500
Totals	$1,576,000	$1,576,000

The following additional information is available:

(1) Under the terms of the will of James Forbes, founder of the hospital, "the principal of the bequest is to be fully invested in trust forevermore in mortgages secured by productive real estate in Webster City and/or in U.S. government securities . . . and the income therefrom is to be used to defray current expenses."

(2) The James Forbes Endowment Fund account balance consists of the following:

Cash received in Year 1 by bequest from James Forbes	$ 81,500
Net gains realized from Year 56 through Year 89 from the sale of real estate acquired in mortgage foreclosures	23,500
Income received from Year 90 through Year 97 from 91-day U.S. Treasury Bill investments	14,500
Balance per general ledger on Jan. 1, Year 98	$119,500

(3) The Land account balance was composed of:

Year 20 appraisal of land at $10,000 and building at $5,000 received by donation at that time. (The building was demolished in Year 40)	$ 15,000
Appraisal increase based on insured value in land title policies issued in Year 57	380,000
Landscaping costs for trees planted	12,000
Balance per general ledger on Jan. 1, Year 98	$407,000

(4) The Building account balance was composed of:

Cost of present hospital building completed in January, Year 57, when the hospital commenced operations	$300,000
Adjustment to record appraised value of building in Year 67	(100,000)
Cost of elevator installed in hospital building in January, Year 83	45,000
Balance per general ledger on Jan. 1, Year 98	$245,000

    The estimated useful lives of the hospital building and the elevator when new were 50 years and 20 years, respectively.

(5) The hospital's equipment was inventoried on January 1, Year 98. The cost of the inventory agreed with the Equipment account balance in the general ledger. The Accumulated Depreciation account at January 1, Year 98, included $158,250 applicable to equipment, and that amount was approved by the board of directors as being accurate. All depreciation is computed on a straight-line basis.

(6) A bank loan was obtained to finance the cost of new operating room equipment purchased in Year 94. Interest on the loan was paid to December 31, Year 97.

Instructions Prepare a working paper to present the adjustments necessary to restate the general ledger account balances properly and to distribute the adjusted balances to establish the required fund accounts. Formal journal entries are not required; however, explain each adjustment (including supporting computations) at the bottom of the working paper. The following column headings are suggested:

    Unadjusted trial balance
    Adjustments
    Adjusted trial balance
    Unrestricted Fund
    James Forbes Endowment Fund
    Plant Replacement Fund

15-7 The accountant for Johnson Vocational School, a not-for-profit entity, resigned on March 1, Year 8, after she prepared the following general ledger trial balance and analysis of cash as of February 28, Year 8:

JOHNSON VOCATIONAL SCHOOL
General Ledger Trial Balance
February 28, Year 8

Debits

Cash for general current operations	$258,000
Cash for restricted current uses	30,900
Stock donated by L. M. Nash	11,000
Bonds donated by O. P. Quinn	150,000
Land	22,000
Building	33,000
General current operating expenses	38,000
Faculty recruitment expenses	4,100
Total	$547,000

Credits

Mortgage payable on plant assets	$ 30,000
Revenue from gifts for general operations	210,000
Revenue from gifts for restricted uses	196,000
Student fees	31,000
Surplus	80,000
Total	$547,000

JOHNSON VOCATIONAL SCHOOL
Analysis of Cash
For the Six Months Ended February 28, Year 8

Cash for general current operations:				
Balance, Sept. 1, Year 7			$ 80,000	
Add: Student fees		$ 31,000		
Gift of H. I. Johnson		210,000	241,000	
Subtotal			$321,000	
Deduct: General current operating expenses	$ 38,000			
Payment on land and building	25,000		63,000	$258,000
Cash for restricted current uses:				
Gift of H. I. Johnson for faculty recruitment			$ 35,000	
Less: Faculty recruitment expenses			4,100	30,900
Checking account balance, Feb. 28, Year 8				$288,900

You were engaged to determine the proper account balances for the school as of August 31, Year 8, the close of the school's first fiscal year. Your examination disclosed the following information:

(1) In September, Year 7, L. M. Nash donated 100 shares of Wilder, Inc., stock with a market value of $110 per share at the date of donation. The terms of the gift provide that the stock and any income thereon are to be retained intact. At any date designated by the board of directors, the assets are to be liquidated and the proceeds used to assist the school's director in acquir-

ing a personal residence. The school will not retain any financial interest in the residence.
(2) O. P. Quinn donated 6% bonds in September, Year 7, with face amount and market value of $150,000 at the date of donation. Annual payments of $3,500 are to be made to the donor during his lifetime. Upon the donor's death the fund is to be used to construct a school cafeteria. The actuarial valuation of the O. P. Quinn annuity at August 31, Year 8, was $122,143.
(3) No transactions have been recorded in the school's accounts since February 28, Year 8. An employee of the school prepared the following analysis of the checking account for the period from March 1 through August 31, Year 8:

Balance, Mar. 1, Year 8				$288,900
Deduct:	General current operating expenses	$14,000		
	Purchase of equipment	47,000	$61,000	
	Less: Student fees		8,000	
	Net expenses		$53,000	
	Payment for director's residence	$11,200		
	Less: Sale of 100 shares of Wilder, Inc.,			
	stock	10,600	600	53,600
	Total			$235,300
Add:	Interest on 6% bonds		$ 9,000	
	Less: Payment to O. P. Quinn		3,500	5,500
Balance, Aug. 31, Year 8				$240,800

Instructions Prepare a working paper presenting the trial balance at February 28, Year 8, adjusting entries, transaction entries from March 1 through August 31, Year 8, and distributions to the proper funds. The following column headings are recommended for your working paper:
Unadjusted trial balance, Feb. 28, Year 8
Adjustments and transactions—Debit
Adjustments and transactions—Credit
Adjusted trial balance, Aug. 31, Year 8
Unrestricted Current Fund
Restricted Current Fund
O. P. Quinn Annuity Fund
Plant Fund—Investment in Plant
Formal journal entries are not required; however, explain each adjustment and transaction (including supporting computations) at the bottom of the working paper. Ignore accrued interest on mortgage payable.

15-8 Fielding College (a not-for-profit entity) has asked your assistance in developing its operating budget for the coming academic year ending June 30, Year 12. You are supplied with the following data for the current year:

(1)

	Lower division (freshman-sophomore)	Upper division (junior-senior)
Average number of students per class	25	20
Average salary of faculty members	$10,000	$10,000
Average number of credit hours carried each year per student	33	30
Enrollment including scholarship students	2,500	1,700
Average faculty teaching load in credit hours per year (10 classes of 3 credit hours)	30	30

For the year ending June 30, Year 12, lower division enrollment is expected to increase by 10%, while the upper division's enrollment is expected to remain stable. Faculty salaries will be increased by a standard 5%, and additional merit increases to be awarded to individual faculty members will be $90,750 for the lower division and $85,000 for the upper division.

(2) The current budget is $210,000 for operation and maintenance of plant and equipment; this includes $90,000 for salaries and wages. Experience of the past three months suggests that the current budget is realistic, but that expected increases for the year ending June 30, Year 12, are 5% in salaries and wages and $9,000 in other expenditures for operation and maintenance of plant and equipment.

(3) The budget for the remaining expenditures for the year ending June 30, Year 12, is as follows:

Administrative and general	$240,000
Library	160,000
Health and recreation	75,000
Athletics	120,000
Insurance and retirement	265,000
Interest	48,000
Capital outlay	300,000

(4) The college expects to award 25 tuition-free scholarships to lower division students and 15 to upper division students. Tuition is $22 per credit hour and no other fees are charged.

(5) Budgeted revenue for the year ending June 30, Year 12, is as follows:

Endowments	$114,000
Net income from auxiliary services	235,000
Athletics	180,000

The college's remaining source of revenue is an annual support campaign held during the spring.

Instructions

a Prepare a working paper computing for the year ending June 30, Year 12, by division (1) the expected enrollment, (2) the total credit hours to be carried, and (3) the number of faculty members needed.

b Prepare a working paper computing the budget for faculty salaries by division for the year ending June 30, Year 12.

c Prepare a working paper computing the tuition revenue budget by division for the year ending June 30, Year 12.

d Assuming that the faculty salaries budget computed in part **b** was $2,400,000 and that the tuition revenue budget computed in part **c** was $3,000,000, prepare a working paper computing the amount which must be raised during the annual support campaign in order to cover the expenditures budget for the year ending June 30, Year 12.

15-9 The administrator of Paulson Hospital (a not-for-profit entity) has presented you with a number of service projections for the hospital's operating budget for the year ending June 30, Year 6. Estimated room requirements for inpatients by type of services are:

Type of patient	Total patients expected	Average number of days in hospital		Percentage of regular patients selecting types of service		
		Regular	Medicare	Private	Semi-private	Ward
Medical	2,100	7	17	10%	60%	30%
Surgical	2,400	10	15	15	75	10

Of the patients served by the hospital, 10% are expected to be Medicare patients, all of whom are expected to select semiprivate rooms. Both the number and proportion of Medicare patients have increased over the past five years. Daily rentals per patient are: $40 for a private room, $35 for a semiprivate room, and $25 for a ward.

Operating room charges are based on man-minutes (number of minutes the operating room is in use multiplied by number of personnel assisting in the operation). The per man-minute charges are $0.13 for inpatients and $0.22 for outpatients. Studies for the current year show that operations on inpatients are divided as follows:

Type of operation	Number of operations	Average number of minutes per operation	Average number of personnel required
A	800	30	4
B	700	45	5
C	300	90	6
D	200	120	8
	2,000		

The same proportion of inpatient operations is expected for the next fiscal year and 180 outpatients are expected to use the operating room. Outpatient operations average 20 minutes and require the assistance of three persons.

The department costs budget for the year ending June 30, Year 6, by departments, is presented on page 596.

General services:

Maintenance of plant	$	50,000
Operation of plant		27,500
Administration		97,500
All other		192,000
Revenue-producing services:		
Operating room		68,440
All other		700,000
Total budgeted costs		$1,135,440

The following information is provided for cost allocation purposes:

	Square feet	Salaries
General services:		
Maintenance of plant	12,000	$ 40,000
Operation of plant	28,000	25,000
Administration	10,000	55,000
All other	36,250	102,500
Revenue-producing services:		
Operating room	17,500	15,000
All other	86,250	302,500
Totals	190,000	$540,000

Basis of allocations:

Maintenance of plant—salaries

Operation of plant—square feet

Administration—salaries

All other—8% to operating room

Instructions Prepare working papers showing the computation of:

a The number of patient days (number of patients multiplied by average stay in hospital) expected by type of patients and service.

b The total number of man-minutes expected for operating room services for inpatients and outpatients. For inpatients show the breakdown of total operating room man-minutes by type of operation.

c Expected gross revenue from routine services.

d Expected gross revenue from operating room services.

e Cost per man-minute for operating room services assuming that the total man-minutes computed in part *b* is 800,000 and that the step-down method of cost allocation is used (that is costs of the general services departments are allocated in sequence first to the general services departments that they serve and then finally to the revenue-producing departments).

16

Accounting for
estates and trusts

Estates and *trusts* are accounting entities; in addition, they are taxable entities under the provisions of federal income tax laws and regulations. The individuals or corporations which manage the assets of estates and trusts are *fiduciaries;* they exercise stewardship for those assets in accordance with the provisions of a will, a trust document, or state laws.

In this chapter we shall first deal with certain legal aspects of estates, including wills, and then discuss and illustrate the accounting for estates. The last section of this chapter will cover the legal aspects of and accounting for trusts.

LEGAL AND ACCOUNTING ASPECTS OF ESTATES

State laws (generally termed *probate codes*) regulate the administration and distribution of estates of decedents, missing persons, and other individuals subject to protection of the court. The many variations among the probate codes of the fifty states led to the drafting of a *Uniform Probate Code* in 1969. This code, developed by the National Conference of Commissioners on Uniform State Laws and approved by the American Bar Association, has been presented to all state legislatures for approval. Although the Uniform Probate Code has not yet been adopted in its entirety by all states, we will use the code to illustrate certain legal issues underlying accounting for estates.

Provisions of Uniform Probate Code governing estates

The Uniform Probate Code identifies an **estate** as all of the property of a decedent, trust, or other person whose affairs are subject to the code.[1] "Person" is defined in the code as an individual, a corporation, an organization, or other legal entity.[2] Thus, the code establishes the accounting entity status of an estate.

In Section 3-101, the Uniform Probate Code provides that the real and personal property of a deceased person be awarded to the persons specified in his will. In the absence of a will—a condition known as **intestacy**—the decedent's property goes to his heirs, as enumerated in the Uniform Probate Code. Thus, as the code points out, the intentions of a **testator** (a person creating a will) control the disposition of his property.[3]

Wills The Uniform Probate Code (Section 2-502) provides that a will shall be in writing, signed by the testator, or in the testator's name by some other person in the testator's presence and by his direction, and also signed by at least two witnesses. The chief exception to these requirements is a **holographic will**—a will having its material provisions and signature in the handwriting of the testator.[4]

Probate of Wills Probate of a will is action by the probate court (also known as **surrogate** or **orphan's** court) to validate the will. Section 3-102 of the Uniform Probate Code provides for two types of probate—**informal** and **formal.** Informal probate is initiated by the application of an interested party filed with a court official known as a **Registrar.**[5] After thorough review of the completeness and propriety of an application for informal probate, the Registrar issues a written statement of informal probate, thus making the will effective.[6]

Formal probate, covered in Article III, Part 4 of the Uniform Probate Code, is litigation to determine whether a decedent left a valid will. Formal probate is initiated by a petition filed by an interested party requesting the probate court to order probate of the will. The petition may also request a finding that the decedent died intestate.[7] During the court hearings, any party to the formal probate proceedings may oppose the will; however, the burden of proof that the will is invalid is on such a contestant of the will.[8] After completion of the hearings, the court enters an order for formal probate of a will found to be valid, or an order that

[1] Uniform Probate Code, Sec. 1-201(11).
[2] *Ibid.,* Sec. 1-201(29).
[3] *Ibid.,* Sec. 2-603.
[4] *Ibid.,* Sec. 2-503.
[5] *Ibid.,* Sec. 1-307.
[6] *Ibid.,* Secs. 3-302, 3-303.
[7] *Ibid.,* Sec. 3-401.
[8] *Ibid.,* Secs. 3-404, 3-407.

the decedent died intestate.[9] Generally, no formal or informal probate proceedings may be undertaken more than three years after the decedent's death.[10]

Appointment of Personal Representative   In both informal and formal probate proceedings, the probate court appoints a *personal representative* of the decedent to administer the decedent's estate. A personal representative named in the decedent's will is called an *executor;* if the decedent died intestate, the court-appointed personal representative is known as an *administrator.* The Uniform Probate Code requires the probate court to issue *letters testamentary* to the personal representative before administration of the estate can begin.[11] Since a personal representative is a fiduciary, he must observe standards of care in administering the estate that a prudent man would observe in dealing with the property of others.[12] The personal representative is entitled to reasonable compensation for his services.[13]

Powers and Duties of Personal Representative   The personal representative of a decedent is empowered to take possession and control of the decedent's property, and to have title to the property in trust for the benefit of creditors and others interested in the estate.[14] The personal representative has many additional powers, which are enumerated in Section 3-715 of the Uniform Probate Code. Among these powers are the right to continue any sole proprietorship business of the decedent for not more than four months following the date of the personal administrator's appointment, and the authority to allocate items of revenue and expenses of the estate to either *estate principal* (corpus) or *estate income,* as provided by will or by law. The allocations to estate principal and estate income comprise the chief accounting problem for an estate and are discussed in a subsequent section of this chapter.

Not later than 30 days after his appointment, the personal representative must inform the decedent's *devisees* or heirs of the appointment.[15] (A *devisee* is any person or trust named in a will to receive real or personal property of the decedent in a transfer known as a *devise.*[16]) Within three months after his appointment, the personal representative must prepare an inventory of property owned by the decedent at date of death, together with a listing of any liens against the property. The property in the inventory must be valued at current fair value at date of death; to this end, the personal representative may retain the services

[9] *Ibid.,* Secs. 3-409, 3-411.
[10] *Ibid.,* Sec. 3-108.
[11] *Ibid.,* Sec. 3-103.
[12] *Ibid.,* Sec. 3-703.
[13] *Ibid.,* Sec. 3-719.
[14] *Ibid.,* Secs. 3-709, 3-711.
[15] *Ibid.,* Sec. 3-705.
[16] *Ibid.,* Secs. 1-201(7), 1-201(8).

of an appraiser. The inventory is filed with the probate court and copies are provided to interested parties who request them. If, after the filing of the original inventory, other unlisted property of the decedent is discovered, the personal representative must file a supplementary inventory.[17]

Exempt Property and Allowances   Like the Bankruptcy Act discussed in Chapter 11, the Uniform Probate Code, in Sections 2-401 through 2-404, provides for certain exemptions from claims against the estate assets, even by devisees. These exemptions are as follows:

1 Homestead allowance   The decedent's surviving spouse, or surviving minor and dependent children, are entitled to an aggregate ***homestead allowance*** of $5,000. This allowance is in addition to any share of the estate passing to the spouse or children by the will.

2 Exempt property   The decedent's surviving spouse or children are entitled to an aggregate $3,500 value of automobiles, household furniture and furnishings, appliances, and personal effects.

3 Family allowance   The surviving spouse and children who were being supported by the decedent are entitled to a reasonable cash allowance, payable in a lump sum not exceeding $6,000 or in installments not exceeding $500 per month for one year, during the administration of the estate. The family allowance has priority over all claims against the estate, but does not have priority over the homestead allowance.

Claims of Creditors against the Estate   Upon his appointment, a personal representative is required by Section 3-801 of the Uniform Probate Code to publish a notice once a week for three successive weeks, in a newspaper of general circulation, requesting creditors of the estate to present their claims to him within four months after the date of the first publication, or be forever barred. If the estate assets not exempt under the Uniform Probate Code are insufficient to pay all claims in full, the personal representative shall pay claims in the following order:

1 Expenses of administering the estate

2 Decedent's funeral expenses and medical and hospital expenses of the decedent's last illness

3 Debts and taxes with preference under federal or state laws

4 All other claims[18]

Four months after publication of the first notice to estate creditors, the personal representative initiates payment of claims in the order outlined above, after first providing for homestead, family, and support allowances.[19]

Distributions to Devisees   The personal representative also has the duty of distributing estate assets to the devisees named in the will. The assets

[17] *Ibid.,* Secs. 3-706, 3-707, 3-708.
[18] *Ibid.,* Sec. 3-805.
[19] *Ibid.,* Sec. 3-807.

are to be distributed in kind to the extent possible, rather than first being converted to cash and then distributing the cash.[20]

If estate assets which are not exempt are insufficient to cover creditors' claims as well as all devises, the devises *abate*—or are reduced—in the sequence provided for in the decedent's will. If the will is silent as to order of abatement, Section 3-902 of the Uniform Probate Code provides the following abatement sequence:

1 Property not disposed of by the will

2 **Residuary devise,** which is a devise of all estate property remaining after general and specific devises are satisfied

3 **General devises,** which are gifts of a sum of money or a number of countable monetary assets, such as 500 shares of Mercury Company common stock

4 **Specific devises,** which are gifts of identified objects, such as named paintings, automobiles, stock certificates, or real property

Devises may be granted to the devisees *in trust,* which requires the establishment of a *testamentary trust,* or one provided for by a will. Trusts are discussed further in a subsequent section of this chapter.

Estate and Inheritance Taxes   The federal estate tax assessed against the net assets of an estate, and inheritance taxes assessed by various states against devisees and heirs of a decedent, often called "death taxes," must be apportioned to the various devisees in the manner outlined in the will. If the will is silent on apportionment, Section 3-916(b) of the Uniform Probate Code applies. This section provides that the estate and inheritance taxes are to be apportioned to the various devisees in the ratio of each devisee's interest to the aggregate interests of all devisees.

Closing Estates   No earlier than six months after the date of his appointment, a personal representative may close an estate by filing a statement with the probate court. The written content of this statement is described in Section 3-1003 of the Uniform Probate Code; the legal statement is usually accompanied by an accounting presentation termed a *charge and discharge statement.*

Provisions of Revised Uniform Principal and Income Act governing estates

We have previously noted that the chief accounting problem for an estate is the allocation of revenue and expenses of the estate to *estate principal* (corpus) or *estate income.* This allocation is important because many wills provide that income from the assets of a testamentary trust may be paid to an *income beneficiary,* while the principal of a trust reverts to a *principal beneficiary* or *remainderman.* A proper accounting for principal and income by the personal representative of a decedent is essential before the estate is closed.

[20] *Ibid.,* Sec. 3-906.

In 1962 the National Conference of Commissioners on Uniform State Laws approved the Revised Uniform Principal and Income Act to provide guidelines for allocation in the absence of instructions in the will or trust agreement. Through 1973, seventeen states had adopted all or part of this act, often with modifications. The provisions of the Revised Uniform Principal and Income Act include the following:

1 *Income* is defined as the return in money or property derived from the use of principal, including rent, interest, cash dividends, and revenue received during administration of a decedent's estate. [Section 3(a).]

2 *Principal* is defined as property set aside by its owner to be held in trust for eventual delivery to a remainderman. Principal includes proceeds of insurance on principal assets, stock and liquidating dividends, and allowances for depreciation. [Section 3(b).] Any accrued rent or other revenue at date of death of the testator is principal. [Section 4(b)(2).]

3 Premium or discount on investments in bonds included in principal is not amortized. All proceeds from sale or redemption of bonds are principal. [Section 7(a).]

4 Income is charged with a reasonable provision for depreciation, computed in accordance with generally accepted accounting standards, on all depreciable assets except property used by a beneficiary as a residence. [Section 13(a)(2).] Income is also charged with expenses of administering and preserving income-producing estate property, such as property taxes, ordinary repairs, and insurance premiums on the interests of the income beneficiary. [Section 13(a)(1).]

5 Principal is charged with expenditures incurred in preparing principal property for sale or rent, cost of investing and reinvesting principal assets, extraordinary repairs to principal assets, and income taxes on receipts or gains allocable to principal. [Section 13(c).]

6 Court costs, attorneys' fees, and other fees for periodic reporting to the probate court, as well as trustees' fees, are apportioned to principal and to income. [Sections 13(a)(3), 13(a)(5), 13(c)(1).]

Illustration of accounting for an estate

Now that we have reviewed certain legal issues involved in estates, we shall illustrate the accounting for estates, including the charge and discharge statement rendered by the personal representative at the closing of the estate. Estate accounting is carried out in accordance with the *accountability* method previously illustrated in Chapter 11. The accounting records of the personal representative reflect only those items for which he is accountable, under the equation Assets = Accountability.

Our illustration is based on the following hypothetical data:

1 Jessica Davis, a single woman who lived alone, died March 18, Year 3, after a brief illness which required her to be hospitalized. Her will, approved for informal probate on March 25, Year 3, contained the following devises:

a $10,000 in cash to each of three household employees: Alice Martin, cook; Angela Wilson, housekeeper; Nolan Ames, gardener and maintenance man. Devisees must waive claims for unpaid wages at date of death.

b 200 shares of Preston Company common stock to Nancy Grimes, a niece.

c Paintings, other art objects, clothing, jewelry, and personal effects to Frances Grimes, a married woman, only sister of Jessica Davis.

d Residence, furniture, and furnishings to Wallace Davis, a single man, only brother of Jessica Davis.

e $5,000 cash to Universal Charities, a not-for-profit organization.
f Residue of estate in trust to Nancy Grimes; income to be paid at the end of each calendar quarter to Miss Grimes until her 21st birthday October 1, Year 8, at which time the principal also reverts to Miss Grimes.

2 Paul Hastings, attorney for Jessica Davis and executor of her estate, published the required newspaper notice to creditors on March 26, April 2, and April 9, Year 3. The following claims were received from creditors within the four-month statutory period:

Description	Amount
Funeral expenses	$ 810
Hospital charges	1,928
Doctor's fees	426
Department store charge account	214
Various residence bills: utilities, telephone, trash disposal	87
Total	$3,465

3 Mr. Hastings prepared final individual federal and state income tax returns for Jessica Davis for the period January 1 to March 18, Year 3. The federal return showed income tax due in the amount of $457; the state return showed no tax due.

4 Mr. Hastings prepared the following inventory of property owned by Jessica Davis at March 18, Year 3:

Description	Current fair value March 18, Year 3
Bank checking account	$ 2,157
Bank savings account (including accrued interest)	30,477
Savings and loan association 2-year certificate of deposit maturing June 30, Year 3 (including accrued interest)	26,475
Accrued salary earned for period March 1 to March 8, Year 3	214
Claim against medical insurance carrier	1,526
Social security benefits receivable	14,820
Proceeds of life insurance policy (payable to estate)	25,000
Common stock:	
200 shares Preston Company	8,000
100 shares Arthur Corporation	6,500
Residence	40,800*
Furniture and furnishings	2,517
Paintings and other art objects	16,522
Clothing, jewelry, personal effects	625
Automobile	2,187
Total	$177,820

*Subject to unpaid trust deed note of $15,500 due $500 monthly on the last day of the month, plus interest at 10% per year on the unpaid balance.

5 Subsequent to preparing the above inventory, Mr. Hastings discovered a certificate for 600 shares of Campbell Company common stock with a market value of $18,000.

6 Mr. Hastings prepared the federal estate tax return for the Estate of Jessica Davis, Deceased. The return showed a tax due in the amount of $18,556. Mr. Hastings also prepared state inheritance tax returns for the devisees showing aggregate taxes due of $5,020.

7 Mr. Hastings administered the estate, charging the estate a fee of $2,500, and closed the estate by filing the required legal statement and an accounting charge and discharge statement prepared by a CPA who was a member of his staff.

The journal entries below and on pages 605–607 would be entered in the accounting records for the Estate of Jessica Davis, Deceased. (Dates for journal entries are assumed.) Comments relating to specific journal entries which require particular emphasis start at the bottom of page 607.

PAUL HASTINGS, EXECUTOR
of the Will of Jessica Davis, Deceased
General Journal

Year 3

Mar. 18	*Principal Cash*	2,157	
	Savings Account	30,477	
	Certificate of Deposit	26,475	
	Accrued Salary Receivable	214	
	Medical Insurance Claim Receivable	1,526	
	Social Security Benefits Receivable	14,820	
	Life Insurance Claim Receivable	25,000	
	Marketable Securities	14,500	
	Residence	40,800	
	Furniture and Furnishings	2,517	
	Paintings and Other Art Objects	16,522	
	Clothing, Jewelry, Personal Effects	625	
	Automobile	2,187	
	Note Payable Secured by Deed of Trust		15,500
	Accrued Interest Payable		
	($15,500 × 10% × 18 days)		78
	Estate Principal Balance		
	($177,820 − $15,578)		162,242
	To record inventory of property owned by decedent Jessica Davis at date of death, net of lien against residence.		
Mar. 25	*Marketable Securities*	18,000	
	Assets Discovered		18,000
	To record supplemental inventory for property discovered subsequent to filing of original inventory.		

Mar. 31 Principal Cash 70,511
       Income Cash 55
              Savings Account 30,477
              Accrued Salary Receivable 214
              Social Security Benefits Receivable 14,820
              Life Insurance Claim Receivable 25,000
              Interest 55
       To record liquidation of various assets in cash,
       including $55 interest received on savings account for
       period Mar. 18–31, Year 3.

Mar. 31 Distributions to Income Beneficiaries 55
            Income Cash 55
       To distribute income cash due to residuary devisee
       Nancy Grimes, as required by will.

Apr. 2 Principal Cash 2,050
      Loss on Disposal of Principal Assets 137
           Automobile 2,187
      To record sale of automobile at a loss.

Apr. 4 Devises Distributed 5,000
           Principal Cash 5,000
      To record distribution of general devise to Universal
      Charities.

Apr. 16 Liabilities Paid 3,922
           Principal Cash 3,922
      To record following liabilities paid:
        Funeral expenses . . . . $ 810
        Hospital charges 1,928
        Doctor's fees 426
        Individual federal income tax 457
        Department store charge account 214
        Various residence bills 87
          Total $3,922

Apr. 19 Principal Cash 1,526
           Medical Insurance Claim Receivable 1,526
      To record collection of medical insurance claim.

Apr. 24	Income Cash	2,500	
	Due to Devisees		1,000
	Dividends		1,500

To record receipt of quarterly cash dividends on
common stock, as follows:

Preston Company:		
200 shares × $5 per share	$1,000	
Arthur Corporation:		
100 shares × $3 per share	300	
Campbell Company:		
600 shares × $2 per share	1,200	
Total	$2,500	

Apr. 25	Due from Devisees	23,576	
	Principal Cash		23,576

To record payment of federal estate tax and state
inheritance taxes on behalf of devisees, as follows:

Federal estate tax	$18,556
State inheritance taxes.	5,020
Total	$23,576

Apr. 26	Principal Cash	6,295	
	Due from Devisees		6,295

To record receipt of cash from specific devisees
for their shares of federal estate tax and state inheritance taxes, as follows:

Frances Grimes: 10.2% × $23,576	$2,405
Wallace Davis: 16.5% × $23,576	3,890
Total	$6,295

Apr. 27	Devises Distributed	30,000	
	Due from Devisees		4,173
	Principal Cash		25,827

To record payment of cash to general devisees, less
amounts due for their shares of federal estate tax and
state inheritance taxes, as follows:

$10,000 devises due to Alice Martin, Angela Wilson,	
Nolan Ames: 3 × $10,000	$30,000
Shares of death taxes:	
(5.9% × $23,576) × 3	4,173
Net cash paid	$25,827

Apr. 30	Note Payable Secured by Deed of Trust	15,500	
	Accrued Interest Payable.	78	
	Devises Distributed	52,886	
	Due to Devisees	1,000	
	Marketable Securities		8,000
	Residence		40,800
	Furniture and Furnishings		2,517
	Paintings and Other Art Objects		16,522
	Clothing, Jewelry, Personal Effects		625
	Income Cash		1,000

To record distribution of following devises:

General devise to Nancy Grimes:

200 shares of Preston Company com-
mon stock . . . . $ 8,000

Specific devise to Frances Grimes:
paintings, other art objects, clothing,
jewelry, personal effects 17,147

Specific devise to Wallace Davis:
Residence, net of deed of trust, with
furniture and furnishings 27,739

Total $52,886

Also, to transfer to devisee Nancy Grimes cash for dividend received on Preston Company common stock.

May 1	Administrative Expenses	2,500	
	Principal Cash		2,500

To record payment of executor's fee.

May 3	Devises Distributed	85,797	
	Distributions to Income Beneficiaries	1,500	
	Principal Cash		21,714
	Income Cash		1,500
	Certificate of Deposit		26,475
	Marketable Securities		24,500
	Due from Devisees		13,108

To record distribution of residuary devise principal
and income to Third National Bank, trustee for Nancy
Grimes, devisee.

Mar. 18 Entry This entry records the executor's inventory of estate assets, including accrued interest and accrued salary as of date of death. Since the decedent was a single woman, there was no homestead allowance, family allowance, or exempt property. The deed of trust note applicable to the residence is recorded as a liability for accountability purposes. Claims of creditors *are not* recorded as liabilities in the estate accounts because the accounting records for an estate are not designed to record all aspects of the estate's financial position. Only the executor's accountability for assets is reflected in the estate accounts.

Mar. 31 Entries A separate cash account, entitled Income Cash, is used to record cash receipts attributable to income. In accordance with provisions of the will, the income attributable to the residuary devise to Nancy Grimes is distributed to the devisee at the end of the calendar quarter.

Apr. 2 Entry No depreciation was recorded on the automobile prior to its sale because it was not a revenue-producing asset for the estate.

Apr. 16 Entry The Liabilities Paid account represents a reduction of the executor's accountability for estate assets. It is not an asset account or an expense account.

Apr. 24 Entry Dividends received on marketable securities required segregation in the accounts because the securities are allocable to separate devises, as follows:

> Preston Company common stock: allocable to general devise to Nancy Grimes
>
> Arthur Corporation and Campbell Company common stock: allocable to residuary devise to Nancy Grimes

Although Nancy Grimes is the recipient of both devises, the residuary devise will ultimately be placed in trust for the devisee.

Apr. 25 Entry The will of Jessica Davis was silent regarding allocation of estate and inheritance taxes. Consequently, in accordance with Section 3-916(b) of the Uniform Probate Code, the federal estate tax and state inheritance taxes are allocated in the ratio of interests of devisees, other than the nontaxable not-for-profit organization, in the estate. The following schedule shows these ratios:

Devisee	Current fair value of estate interest	Ratio to total of all estate interests
Alice Martin	$ 10,000	5.9%
Angela Wilson.	10,000	5.9
Nolan Ames	10,000	5.9
Nancy Grimes (general devise)	8,000	4.7
Frances Grimes.	17,147 (1)	10.2
Wallace Davis	27,739 (2)	16.5
Nancy Grimes (residuary devise)	85,797	50.9
Total	$168,683	100.0%

(1) $16,522 + $625 = $17,147
(2) ($40,800 + $2,517) − ($15,500 + $78) = $27,739

Apr. 26 and Apr. 27 Entries The executor requested the specific devisees to pay in cash their shares of the federal estate tax and state inheritance taxes. The executor withheld the general devisees' death tax shares from the cash due to them.

May 1 Entry The entire fee of the executor was charged to estate principal since his time spent on income assets was nominal. The allocation of fees required by Section 13 of the Revised Uniform Principal and Income Act is more appropriate for a trust than for a short-lived estate.

May 3 Entry No accrual entries are required for interest on the certificate of deposit or any declared but unpaid dividends on the marketable securities. An accrual-basis cutoff for an estate is appropriate only at the time the executor prepares the inventory of estate property in order to facilitate the distinction between estate principal and estate income. If the will provides that accrual accounting must be used, the executor must of course comply.

In the preceding illustration, federal and state *income* taxes on the estate were disregarded. In addition, it was assumed that devisee Wallace Davis immediately occupied the decedent's residence, so that depreciation on the residence was not required as it would be if rent revenue were realized from a lease. A further assumption was that devisee Wallace Davis paid the March 31 and April 30, Year 3, installments on the trust deed note collateralized by the residence.

Trial Balance of Estate Accounts Following is a trial balance of the accounts of the Estate of Jessica Davis, Deceased at May 3, Year 3:

PAUL HASTINGS, EXECUTOR
of the Will of Jessica Davis, Deceased
Trial Balance
May 3, Year 3

Principal		
Estate principal balance		$162,242
Assets discovered		18,000
Loss on disposal of principal assets	$ 137	
Liabilities paid	3,922	
Devises distributed	173,683	
Administrative expenses	2,500	
Totals	$180,242	$180,242
Income		
Interest		$ 55
Dividends		1,500
Distributions to income beneficiaries	$ 1,555	
Totals	$ 1,555	$ 1,555

Charge and Discharge Statement The executor's charge and discharge statement for the Estate of Jessica Davis is presented below and on pages 611–612. The items in the statement were taken from the trial balance of the Estate of Jessica Davis which appears on page 609. Although the executor's activities essentially ended May 3, the Uniform Probate Code precludes closing an estate earlier than six months after the executor's appointment.

PAUL HASTINGS, EXECUTOR

of the Will of Jessica Davis, Deceased

Charge and Discharge Statement

for the period March 18 through September 18, Year 3

First, as to Principal

I charge myself as follows:

Inventory, March 18, Year 3 (Schedule 1)	$162,242	
Assets discovered (Schedule 2)	18,000	$180,242

I credit myself as follows:

Loss on disposal of principal assets (Schedule 3) . . .	$ 137	
Liabilities paid (Schedule 4)	3,922	
Devises distributed (Schedule 5)	173,683	
Administrative expenses (Schedule 6)	2,500	180,242

Balance, September 18, Year 3. . . . . $ –0–

Second, as to Income

I charge myself as follows:

Interest (Schedule 7)	$ 55	
Dividends (Schedule 8)	1,500	$ 1,555

I credit myself as follows:

Distributions of income (Schedule 9)		1,555

Balance, September 18, Year 3. . . . . $ –0–

PAUL HASTINGS, EXECUTOR
of the Will of Jessica Davis, Deceased
Schedules Supporting Charge and Discharge Statement
for the period March 18 through September 18, Year 3

Schedule 1—Inventory, March 18, Year 3

Bank checking account		$ 2,157
Bank savings account (including accrued interest)		30,477
Savings and loan association 2-year certificate of deposit maturing		
June 30, Year 3 (including accrued interest)		26,475
Accrued salary earned for period March 1–8, Year 3		214
Claim against medical insurance carrier		1,526
Social security benefits receivable		14,820
Proceeds of life insurance policy		25,000
Common stock of Preston Company, 200 shares		8,000
Common stock of Arthur Corporation, 100 shares		6,500
Residence	$40,800	
Less: Balance of trust deed note payable; including		
accrued interest of $78	15,578	25,222
Furniture and furnishings		2,517
Paintings and other art objects		16,522
Clothing, jewelry, personal effects		625
Automobile		2,187
Total		$162,242

Schedule 2—Assets discovered

On March 25, Year 3, a certificate for 600 shares of Campbell Company common stock was discovered among the decedent's personal effects. All other securities were located in the decedent's safe deposit box at Third National Bank	$ 18,000

Schedule 3—Loss on disposal of principal assets

Sale of automobile, April 3, Year 3:	
Carrying value	$ 2,187
Cash proceeds	2,050
Loss	$ 137

Schedule 4—Liabilities paid

Watts Mortuary	$ 810
Suburban Hospital	1,928
Charles Carson, M.D.	426
Morningside Department Store	214
Various residence bills: utilities, telephone, trash disposal	87
Final federal income tax	457
Total	$ 3,922

Schedule 5—Devises distributed

General devise to Universal Charities: Cash	$ 5,000
General devise to Alice Martin: Cash	10,000
General devise to Angela Wilson: Cash	10,000
General devise to Nolan Ames: Cash	10,000
General devise to Nancy Grimes: 200 shares of Preston Company common stock	8,000
Specific devise to Frances Grimes: Paintings, other art objects, clothing, jewelry, personal effects	17,147
Specific devise to Wallace Davis: Residence, net of deed of trust note payable, with furniture and furnishings	27,739
Residuary devise to Nancy Grimes: Cash, certificate of deposit, 100 shares of Arthur Corporation common stock, 600 shares of Campbell Company common stock	85,797
Total	$173,683

Schedule 6—Administrative expenses

Fee of executor (charged entirely to principal because income administration activities were nominal)	$ 2,500

Schedule 7—Interest

Bank savings account, March 18–31, Year 3	$ 55

Schedule 8—Dividends

Arthur Corporation common stock	$ 300
Campbell Company common stock	1,200
Total	$ 1,500

Schedule 9—Distributions of income

March 31, Year 3: To residuary devisee Nancy Grimes	$ 55
May 3, Year 3: To Third National Bank, trustee for Nancy Grimes . .	1,500
Total	$ 1,555

The charge and discharge statement shows the executor's *accountability,* not the financial position or cash transactions of the estate. The statement discloses the charges to the executor for estate principal and estate income assets for which he is accountable, and the credits to the executor for the dispositions he made of estate assets.

Closing Entry for Estate Once the executor's closing statement and charge and discharge statement have been accepted by the probate court, the accountant for the estate may prepare an appropriate closing entry. The September 18, Year 3, closing entry for the Estate of Jessica Davis would be as follows:

Estate Principal Balance	162,242
Assets Discovered	18,000
Interest	55
Dividends	1,500

Loss on Disposal of Principal Assets	137
Liabilities Paid	3,922
Devises Distributed	173,683
Administrative Expenses	2,500
Distributions to Income Beneficiaries	1,555

To close estate in accordance with probate court authorization.

Concluding comments on accounting for estates

The example of estate accounting in this chapter was simplified in terms of details and time required for the liquidation of the estate. In practice, many estates—especially those involved in formal probate proceedings—take many months and sometimes years to settle. For many estates, preparation of the federal estate tax return is a complex and time-consuming task. Furthermore, the estate of an *intestate* decedent involves complicated legal issues, such as the rules for intestate succession in Article II, Part 1 of the Uniform Probate Code. The accountant involved in accounting for an estate must be familiar with provisions of the decedent's will and with appropriate state probate laws and principal and income laws, and should maintain close liaison with the attorney for the estate.

LEGAL AND ACCOUNTING ASPECTS OF TRUSTS

A trust created by a will, as illustrated in the preceding sections of this chapter, is termed a *testamentary trust.* A trust created by the act of a living person is known as an *inter vivos,* or *living,* trust. The parties to a trust are (1) the *settlor* (also known as the *donor* or *trustor*)—the individual creating the trust, (2) the *trustee*—the fiduciary individual or corporation who holds legal title to the trust property and carries out provisions of the trust document for a fee, and (3) the *beneficiary*—the party for whose benefit the trust was established. As we have previously noted in this chapter, the income from trust property may be distributed to an income beneficiary, but the principal of a trust ultimately goes to a *principal beneficiary* or *remainderman.*

Provisions of Uniform Probate Code affecting trusts

Article VII of the Uniform Probate Code contains four parts: trust registration, jurisdiction of court concerning trusts, duties and liabilities of trustees, and powers of trustees. The code requires that a trustee of a trust must register the trust with the appropriate state probate court. Registration subjects the trust to the jurisdiction of the court. The court's jurisdiction may include appointing or removing a trustee, reviewing the trustee's fees, and reviewing or settling interim or final accountings of the trustee. The trustee is required by the code to administer the trust expeditiously for the benefit of the beneficiaries, and to use standards of care appropriate for a prudent man in dealing with the property of others. The trustee must keep the trust beneficiaries reasonably informed as to the administration of the trust, and furnish the beneficiaries a statement of the trust accounts annually (or more frequently if necessary) and at the termination of the trust.

Provisions of Revised Uniform Principal and Income Act governing trusts

The provisions for allocations between principal and income included in the Revised Uniform Principal and Income Act (see pages 601–602) are applicable to trusts as well as to estates.

Illustration of accounting for a trust

The accounting entries for a trust usually differ from those of an estate because of the longer life of a trust. Whereas the personal representative for an estate attempts to wind up the administration of the estate as expeditiously as possible, the trustee for a trust must comply with the provisions of the trust document during the stated term of the trust. Accordingly, the trustee's activities include investment of trust property in revenue-producing assets and maintenance of records for both trust principal and trust income.

To illustrate the accounting issues for a trust, we shall return to the testamentary trust created by the will of Jessica Davis (see page 603). The trust was created by the residuary devise to Nancy Grimes, which required the trustee to pay income from the trust to Miss Grimes at the end of each calendar quarter until her 21st birthday October 1, Year 8—at which time the trust principal would revert to Miss Grimes. Thus, Nancy Grimes is both the income beneficiary and the remainderman.

The journal entries on pages 615–616 illustrate the activities of Third National Bank, trustee for Nancy Grimes, during the calendar quarter ended June 30, Year 3. The journal entries for the trust are *cash basis* entries; there is no need to accrue interest or dividends on the trust assets because no financial position or operations statements are normally prepared for the trust.

NANCY GRIMES TRUST
Third National Bank, Trustee
General Journal

Year 3

May 3	Principal Cash	21,714	
	Income Cash	1,500	
	Certificate of Deposit	26,475	
	Marketable Securities	24,500	
	Trust Principal Balance		72,689
	Trust Income Balance		1,500

To record receipt of Principal and Income assets in trust from Paul Hastings, executor of Estate of Jessica Davis.

May 6	Marketable Securities	19,900	
	Accrued Interest Purchased	180	
	Principal Cash		20,080

To record purchase of following securities:

$15,000 principal amount of 12%, 20-year bonds of Warren Company, due March 31, Year 23, purchased at 100	$15,000
Accrued interest purchased	180
$5,000 principal amount of 60-day commercial paper of Modern Finance Company due July 5, Year 3, purchased at 12% discount	4,900
Total cash outlay	$20,080

June 30	Principal Cash	26,475	
	Income Cash	612	
	Certificate of Deposit		26,475
	Interest		612

To record proceeds of matured certificate of deposit and interest since March 18, Year 3, received this date.

June 30	Administrative Expenses	250	
	Expenses Chargeable to Income	250	
	Principal Cash		250
	Income Cash		250

To record payment of trustee fee for period May 3–June 30, Year 3, chargeable equally to principal and to income.

June 30	Marketable Securities	25,000	
	Principal Cash		25,000
	To record purchase of 5-year, 8% U.S. Treasury notes		
	due June 30, Year 8, at principal amount.		
June 30	Distributions to Income Beneficiary	1,862	
	Income Cash		1,862
	To record regular quarterly distribution to income		
	beneficiary Nancy Grimes.		

The May 3, Year 3, opening entry for the trust is the counterpart of the entry for the Estate of Jessica Davis on the same date (see page 607), except that the amount due from the trust beneficiary for federal estate tax and state inheritance tax was offset against the gross amount of the devise, and the $72,689 difference ($85,797 − $13,108 = $72,689) was established as the trust principal balance.

Trial Balance of Trust Accounts The June 30, Year 3, trial balance of the Nancy Grimes trust would be as follows:

NANCY GRIMES TRUST
Third National Bank, Trustee
Trial Balance
June 30, Year 3

Principal		
Principal cash	$ 2,859	
Marketable securities	69,400	
Accrued interest purchased	180	
Trust principal balance		$72,689
Administrative expenses	250	
Total	$72,689	$72,689
Income		
Trust income balance		$ 1,500
Interest		612
Expenses chargeable to income	$ 250	
Distributions to income beneficiary	1,862	
Total	$ 2,112	$ 2,112

Charge and Discharge Statement for Trust A charge and discharge statement for the trustee of the Nancy Grimes trust would resemble the comparable statement for an estate illustrated on pages 610–612. The principal difference would be a schedule for the details of the $72,439 trust principal balance at June 30, Year 3 ($72,689 − $250 = $72,439).

Closing Entry for Trust A closing entry should be made for a trust at the end of each period for which a charge and discharge statement is prepared, in order to clear the nominal trust accounts for the next reporting period. The June 30, Year 3, closing entry for the Nancy Grimes Trust would be as follows:

Trust Principal Balance	250	
Trust Income Balance	1,500	
Interest	612	
Administrative Expenses		250
Expenses Chargeable to Income		250
Distributions to Income Beneficiary		1,862
To close nominal accounts of trust.		

At the time specified in the trust document for transfer of the trust principal to the remainderman, a journal entry would be made to charge the Distributions to Principal Beneficiary account and credit the various trust principal asset accounts. A closing entry for the winding up of the trust would then be required, in the form of the comparable estate journal entry illustrated on page 613.

REVIEW QUESTIONS

1 Is the Uniform Probate Code in effect throughout the United States? Explain.

2 Define the following terms:
  a Estate
  b Intestacy
  c Testator
  d Executor
  e Administrator
  f Letters testamentary
  g Devise
  h Remainderman
  i Inter vivos trust
  j Settlor

3 Compare *informal probate* with *formal probate* of a will.

4 Compare the standards of care required of a *personal representative* with the standards of care required of a *trustee.*

5 Why must there be a sharp distinction between *estate principal* and *estate income* in the administration of an estate?

6 Describe the *exempt property and allowances* provisions of the Uniform Probate Code.

7 What type of *devise* is each of the following? Explain.
  a The beach house at 1411 Ocean Avenue

> *b* $25,000 cash
> *c* $60,000 principal amount of U.S. Treasury Bonds
> *d* 1,000 shares of Rogers Corporation common stock represented by certificate no. G-1472
> *e* All of my remaining property

8 Is *accrual accounting* ever used for an estate or a trust? Explain.

9 Explain the requirements for *depreciation accounting* contained in the Revised Uniform Principal and Income Act.

10 Describe the use of the Assets Discovered account in the accounting for an estate.

11 Compare a personal representative's *charge and discharge statement* with the financial statements issued by a business enterprise.

12 Discuss the similarities and differences in the accounting entries for estates and for trusts.

EXERCISES

Ex. 16-1 Wendy Spiegel is trustee of a testamentary trust established in the will of Sonia Sheldon. The principal of the trust consists of stocks, bonds, and a building subject to a mortgage. The will provides that trust income is to be paid to the surviving husband during his lifetime, that the trust will terminate upon his death, and that the principal is then to be distributed to the Soledad School for Girls. Indicate whether each of the following statements is true or false:
a A cash dividend received on one of the trust securities may not be used without compensating the husband.
b A 5% stock dividend on Z Co. stock should be distributed to the husband.
c The cost of insurance on the office building should be deducted from the income paid to the husband.
d Monthly principal payments to amortize the mortgage are deducted from income.
e Proceeds from fire insurance on the office building would be a part of the trust principal.
f The cost of exercising stock warrants is chargeable to trust income.
g The Soledad School for Girls is the residuary beneficiary of the trust created under Mrs. Sheldon's will.
h If Mr. Sheldon and the Soledad School for Girls agree to terminate the trust and divide the trust principal, the trustee would have to comply with their wishes.

Ex. 16-2 Indicate whether each of the following items would be charged to principal or to income of a testamentary trust, assuming that the Revised Uniform Principal and Income Act is to be followed.
a Depreciation on building
b Legal fees for managing trust assets
c Special assessment tax levied on real estate for street improvements
d Interest on mortgage payable
e Loss on disposal of trust investments
f Extraordinary repairs on property prior to disposal of the property

Ex. 16-3 The accounts on page 619 appear in the trial balance of an estate. Indicate how the balance in each of the accounts should be classified in the charge and discharge statement.

a Executor's fees
b Estate and inheritance taxes
c Fire insurance premium
d Special assessments adding permanent value to real estate
e Monthly allowance to beneficiaries
f Expenses of probating the will of deceased
g Legal fees for defending claims against the estate
h Funeral and terminal-illness expenses

Ex. 16-4 Selected transactions completed by the executor of the estate of Jack Black, who passed away October 15, Year 10, are listed below:

Oct. 20 Inventory of estate assets (at current fair value) was filed with the court as follows:

Cash	$36,700
Real estate	48,000
Capital stock of Leeds Corp.	50,000
9% bonds of Reno Corporation ($40,000 principal amount)	40,000
Accrued interest on Reno Corporation bonds	600
Personal and household effects	23,500

Oct. 29 A certificate for 50 shares of IBM Corporation capital stock valued at $9,000 was found in the coat pocket of an old suit belonging to the deceased.

Nov. 10 A dividend of $520 was received on the capital stock of Leeds Corp. The stock was willed as a specific devise to Junior Black.

Nov. 15 Liabilities of Jack Black in the amount of $30,000 were paid.

Nov. 22 Administrative expenses of $3,240 were paid. All expenses are chargeable to principal.

Nov. 29 The bonds of Reno Corporation were sold at 98, plus accrued interest of $1,050.

Nov. 30 The capital stock of Leeds Corp. and the cash dividend of $520 were transferred to Junior Black.

Prepare journal entries to record the transaction listed above in the accounting records of the executor for the estate of Jack Black.

Ex. 16-5 John Kojima, executor for the estate of William Barnes, who died on September 3, Year 2, prepared the following trial balance at February 10, Year 3:

Principal cash	$ 6,000	
Income cash	300	
Estate principal balance		$ 97,000
Assets discovered		1,800
Gains on disposal of principal assets		1,200
Administrative expenses	3,000	
Liabilities paid	24,500	
Devises distributed	66,500	
Interest		3,400
Distributions to income beneficiaries	2,000	
Expenses chargeable to income	1,100	
Totals	$103,400	$103,400

Prepare a charge and discharge statement.

Ex. 16-6 Pursuant to the will of Ted Groman, the balance of his estate after probate is to be transferred to a testamentary trust. The following trial balance was prepared from the accounts of the estate at June 30, Year 5:

Principal cash	$ 60,000	
Income cash	6,750	
Marketable securities	105,000	
Estate principal balance		$210,000
Assets discovered		13,000
Gains and losses on disposal of principal assets		12,000
Administrative expenses	5,400	
Liabilities paid	16,000	
Devises distributed	48,600	
Income (interest and dividends)		8,500
Expenses chargeable to income	1,750	
Totals	$243,500	$243,500

a Prepare the journal entry to close the accounts of the estate.
b Prepare the journal entry to open a set of accounting records for the trust.

SHORT CASES FOR ANALYSIS AND DECISION

Case 16-1 The estate of James Zupan included the following items at the date of his death at April 16, Year 2:

(1) Skelly Co. 10% bonds due June 16, Year 12; principal amount $100,000, appraised value at April 16, Year 2 (excluding accrued interest), $103,500; interest payable June 16 and December 16 of each year.
(2) Petrol Corporation common stock, 5,000 shares, dividend of $1 declared April 1, payable May 1 to stockholders of record April 14.
(3) Petrol Corporation 8% cumulative preferred stock, 1,000 shares. (Dividends are paid semiannually on January 1 and July 1 and there are no dividends in arrears.)

Instructions
a The executor of the estate asks that you advise him as to which items constitute income and which principal of the estate.
b Suppose that there were dividends in arrears on the Petrol Corporation 8% cumulative preferred stock; would your answer to *(a)* be any different? If so, in what way? Explain.

Case 16-2 Ellwood Lui transferred his manufacturing business and 10,000 shares of MP Company common stock to Fidelity Trust Company to be held in trust for the benefit of his son, Robert, for life, with the remainder to go to Robert's son, Edward. The Fidelity Trust Company insured the business with the Boston Insurance Company by buying two policies. One policy was a standard fire insurance policy covering the buildings and equipment. The other policy was secured for the purpose of covering loss of income during periods when the business was inoperable as a result of fire or other catastrophe. The buildings and equipment were subsequently destroyed by fire and the Boston Insurance Company paid claims under both policies to the Fidelity Trust Company.

Shortly after the 10,000 common shares of MP Company had been transferred to Fidelity Trust Company, MP Company declared a dividend of 10 common shares of Monte Oil Corporation for each 100 shares of MP Company common stock held. The Monte Oil Corporation common stock had been purchased as an investment by MP Company.

During the same year MP Company directors declared that the common stock would be split on a basis of two new shares for each old share. After the distribution of the new shares, Fidelity Trust Company decided to sell 10,000 shares of MP Company common stock.

Instructions How should the Fidelity Trust Company handle the events which have been described above as to distribution between the income beneficiary and the remainderman? State reasons for making the distribution in the manner in which you recommended.

Case 16-3 In analyzing the accounts of Ruben Fairfax, executor of the estate of a decedent who died January 16, Year 7, you review the will and other documents which reveal that (1) the decedent's son had been specifically bequeathed the decedent's only rental property and 6% bonds of the Padre Corporation, $50,000 maturity value, due March 1, Year 21; (2) the decedent's daughter was the beneficiary of a life insurance policy (face amount $100,000) on which the decedent had paid the premiums; and (3) his widow had been left the remainder of the estate in trust, with full powers of appointment.

Your examination reveals the following transactions occurring from the time of the decedent's death to March 1, Year 7:

(1) Jan. 20 $3,105 was collected in connection with the redemption of $3,000 face amount of Camm Corporation 7% bonds due January 15, Year 7.

(2) Jan. 20 $500 was collected from Pittson Corporation as a cash dividend of $1 per share on common stock declared December 1, Year 6, payable January 15, Year 7, to stockholders of record January 2, Year 7.

(3) Jan. 20 $5,040 was paid to Backe and Co., brokers, for the purchase of five Seaboard Co. 8% bonds due June 30, Year 18.

(4) Jan. 21 30 shares of common stock were received from Ragusa Company, constituting receipt of an ordinary 2% stock dividend declared December 14, Year 6, distributable January 20, Year 7, to holders of record January 15, Year 7.

(5) Feb. 1 $200 quarterly interest was paid by the executor on a promissory note due January 31, Year 8.

(6) Feb. 1 Dr. Peter, the decedent's physician, was paid $2,500 for professional services rendered during the deceased's last illness.

(7) Feb. 2 $600 was collected from Zappa Corporation, as a cash dividend of $0.25 per share on common stock declared January 18, Year 7, payable January 30, Year 7, to holders of record January 27, Year 7.

(8) Feb. 3 $575 rental income for February was received and deposited in the bank.

(9) Feb. 10 $890 was paid for real estate taxes covering the period from February 1 to July 31, Year 7.

(10) Mar. 1 $1,802 was paid to the District Director of Internal Revenue as the remaining income tax owed by the decedent on his Year 6 taxable income.

Instructions Indicate whether each transaction should be:
Allocated between principal and income
Allocated between principal and beneficiaries (devisees)
Attributed solely to income
Attributed solely to principal
Attributed solely to beneficiaries (devisees)
Give reasons supporting your conclusions as to how each transaction should be handled.

Case 16-4 Tudor Zeff, a resident of Bend, Oregon, died September 1, Year 7, and by his will established a trust providing that the income, after costs of administration, be paid to his widow Lisa for and during her life.

During the first year of the trust, the trustee received the following:

(1) Dividends:

> Cash dividends declared August 5, Year 7, payable to stock of record
> August 30 . . . . $ 9,200
>
> Cash dividends declared at various times from September 2, Year 7, to
> July 31, Year 8 25,000
>
> Stock dividend declared on December 1, Year 7, and received December 28, Year 7, a total of 75 shares of Rebel Sugar Company common stock. The market value of the stock at date of declaration was $40.

(2) Interest:

> Semiannual interest on municipal bonds paid on December 1, Year 7 . . $ 4,000
>
> Semiannual interest on municipal bonds paid on June 1, Year 8 (bonds
> were purchased by trustee) 5,500
>
> Semiannual interest on corporate bonds paid on February 28 and
> August 31, Year 8 (for the two periods) 21,200

(3) Disposal of marketable securities:

> Marketable securities with an inventory value of $30,000 were sold for $34,750.

The trustee's expenses and fees paid in accordance with the provisions of the trust agreement totaled $2,450.

Instructions

a Prepare an income statement for the year ended August 31, Year 8, to show the amount to which Lisa Zeff is entitled in accordance with the terms of the trust agreement.

b For those items not considered income, explain why they are excluded.

PROBLEMS

16-5 James Anderson passed away on July 5, Year 1. Skip Phelan was named executor of the estate in the will prepared by Anderson's attorney three years ago. On December 31, Year 1, the accountant for the executor prepared the following trial balance:

SKIP PHELAN, EXECUTOR
of the Will of James Anderson, Deceased
Trial Balance
December 31, Year 1

Principal cash	$ 43,100	
Income cash	8,000	
Investments in bonds	168,300	
Investments in stocks	70,000	
Household effects	9,500	
Gains on disposal of principal assets		$ 2,200
Assets discovered		16,800
Liabilities paid	26,200	
Administrative expenses	9,000	
Devises distributed	10,000	
Estate principal balance		317,100
Dividends		4,200
Interest		8,500
Expenses chargeable to income	720	
Distributions to income beneficiaries	3,980	
Total	$348,800	$348,800

Instructions The balance in the Estate Principal Balance account represents the inventory of assets at July 5, Year 1. Prepare a charge and discharge statement for the estate of James Anderson. Supporting schedules are not required for any items except the listing of assets comprising the estate principal balance at December 31, Year 1.

16-6 Connie Suffolk died on March 1, Year 8, leaving a valid will in which she named Dominic Riemma as executor and trustee of her assets pending final distribution to Lee Ablon, a nephew. The will instructed the executor to transfer her personal effects and automobile to the nephew, to pay estate taxes, outstanding liabilities, administrative expenses of the estate, and to transfer the remaining assets to a trust for the benefit of her nephew. Income from the estate and the trust is to be paid to the nephew, who will receive the principal (corpus) upon graduation from medical school.

An inventory of the estate at March 1, Year 8, consisted of the following assets:

Cash	$ 9,440
Certificate of deposit at California Federal Savings and Loan Association,	
includes accrued interest of $1,100	101,100
Personal effects	13,200
Automobile	2,800
Common stocks	42,000

The following transactions were completed by the executor before the trust assets were transferred to the Connie Suffolk Trust on December 10, Year 8:

(1) Discovered a savings account of $6,290 in the name of Connie Suffolk. (Debit Principal Cash.)

(2) Paid administrative expenses for the estate, $5,200. All expenses are chargeable to principal.
(3) Sold common stock with a carrying value of $20,000 for $21,020, net of commissions.
(4) Transferred personal effects and automobile to Lee Ablon.
(5) Received income as follows (there were no expenses chargeable to income):
    Interest, $5,200 (includes accrued interest as of March 1, Year 8)
    Dividends, $1,400
(6) Distributed the income of the estate to Lee Ablon.
(7) Paid liabilities of deceased, $8,050.
(8) Paid estate taxes, $24,000. (Debit Estate Taxes Paid.)

Instructions
a Prepare journal entries to record the transactions and to close the accounting records for the estate. Disregard homestead allowance, exempt property, and family allowance.
b Prepare a charge and discharge statement immediately prior to the transfer of estate assets to the Connie Suffolk Trust. Do not prepare any supporting schedules.
c Prepare a journal entry to establish the accounting records for the testamentary trust.

16-7 Cameron Riley died in Year 1, and under the terms of his will the devisees were listed as follows:

(1) Jane Riley, widow of testator, who was left a general devise of $100,000 payable immediately, and in addition a life interest in 50% of the residuary estate, with the right of appointment.
(2) Sally Riley, his daughter, who was left 25% of the residuary estate. One half of this was left outright and the other half was to remain in trust, with the right of appointment.
(3) Sonora Riley, his daughter, who was left a life interest in 15% of the residuary estate, with the right of appointment.
(4) Jason Riley, his son, who was also left a 10% interest in the residuary estate, to be paid to him outright.

Cameron Riley specified in his will that the executor had the power to defer liquidation of any of the estate assets and to hold such assets in trust until, in his opinion, conditions were favorable, and to make intermediate distributions of principal from the funds so realized to the beneficiaries. The income from the estate (or trust) was to be distributed annually in the proportion of the beneficiaries' interests.

On December 31, Year 3, the following advances were made on account of principal:

Sally Riley	$300,000
Jason Riley	200,000

The general devise to Jane Riley had not been paid as of December 31, Year 3.

The trustee rendered his first accounting to the probate court at December 31, Year 3, on which date all income, after paying all expenses applicable to income, was paid to the beneficiaries.

The probate court's decree on the accounting of December 31, Year 3, specified that (1) in considering the distribution of future income, all intermediate payments of principal should be treated as advances to the beneficiaries; (2) in order to make a fair and equitable division of income, interest at 8% per year should be charged and credited to the beneficiaries subsequent to Year 3.

The income for Year 4 amounted to $900,000 after all expenses applicable to income had been paid. No further distribution of principal had taken place.

Instructions Prepare a journal entry to record the payments to income beneficiaries at December 31, Year 4. Support the journal entry with a statement showing how the amounts payable to the beneficiaries were determined. Disregard homestead allowance, exempt property, and family allowance.

16-8 John Garibaldi died December 31, Year 1, and left his property in trust to his daughter, Sue. Income was to be paid to her as she needed it, and at her death the trust principal was to go to his nephew, Newton Garibaldi. Any income (including accrued interest) not paid to Sue at her death would be paid to her estate. In his will John Garibaldi appointed Jim Price trustee at a fee of $3,100 per year. All expenses of settling the estate were paid and accounted for by the executor before the trustee took over.

Sue Garibaldi died on October 1, Year 5, and left all her property in trust to her cousin, June Lee. Jim Price was also appointed executor and trustee of her estate and he agreed not to charge additional fees for these services. All income subsequent to October 1, Year 5, was to be paid to June Lee as soon as the income was received by the trustee. The estate of Sue Garibaldi consisted solely of Sue's unexpended income from the John Garibaldi Trust. Principal cash of the Sue Garibaldi Trust was immediately invested at 8% interest, payable quarterly.

From October 1, Year 5, to December 31, Year 6, Newton Garibaldi received "advances" from the income of his uncle's trust. On December 31, Year 6, the remainder of the trust was turned over to Newton Garibaldi.

The property received by Jim Price under the will of John Garibaldi on January 1, Year 2, consisted of the following:

(1) 20,000 shares of Armco Corporation common stock with a market price of $25 per share.
(2) $150,000 bonds of Armco Corporation, paying interest on June 30 and December 31 at 9% per year. The bonds had a market value equal to their principal amount.

In the five years ended December 31, Year 6, the trustee received the following dividends on the Armco Corporation common stock: February 1, Year 2, Year 3, and Year 4, $20,000 per year; February 1, Year 5, and Year 6, $30,000 per year. The trustee made the following payments:

Trustee's fees and expenses: $3,100 per year
To beneficiaries:
Sue Garibaldi, beneficiary of John Garibaldi Trust, from December 31, Year 1, to October 1, Year 5:

Year 2	$13,625
Year 3	17,500
Year 4	19,375
Year 5	28,500

Newton Garibaldi, beneficiary of the John Garibaldi Trust, from October 1, Year 5, to December 31, Year 6:

Year 5	$ 8,500
Year 6	23,000

June Lee, beneficiary of the Sue Garibaldi Trust, from October 1, Year 5, to December 31, Year 6:

Year 5 and Year 6, all trust income as determined on cash basis.

The executor of the John Garibaldi Trust kept the remaining cash in a checking account where it earned no interest for the beneficiaries.

Instructions

a Prepare a statement for the John Garibaldi trust from December 31, Year 1, to October 1, Year 5, showing the undistributed income comprising the Sue Garibaldi Trust. Assume that interest on the Armco Corporation bonds was accrued by the trustee from July 1 to October 1, Year 5. Disregard homestead allowance, exempt property, and family allowance.

b Compute the amount to be distributed to Newton Garibaldi at December 31, Year 6.

c Compute the income received by June Lee from the Sue Garibaldi Trust in Year 5 and Year 6.

16-9 Festus Ramsey died in an accident on May 31, Year 1. His will provided that all liabilities and expenses be paid and that his property be distributed as follows:

(1) Personal residence to Martha Ramsey, widow of Festus Ramsey.
(2) U.S. Treasury 6% bonds and Permian Company common stock—to be placed in trust. All income to go to Martha Ramsey during her lifetime, with the right of appointment upon her death.
(3) Sonar Corporation 9% bonds—bequeathed to Emma Ramsey Edwards, daughter of Festus Ramsey.
(4) Cash—a bequest of $10,000 to Martin Ramsey, son of Festus Ramsey.
(5) Residue of estate—to be divided equally between the two children of Festus Ramsey—Emma Ramsey Edwards and Martin Ramsey.

The will further provided that during the administration period Martha Ramsey was to be paid $500 a month out of estate income. Estate and inheritance taxes are to be borne by the residue of the estate. Martin Ramsey was named as executor and trustee.

An inventory of the decedent's property was prepared. The inventory of estate assets follows:

Personal residence	$ 45,000
Jewelry—diamond ring	9,600
Portland National Bank—checking account; balance May 31, Year 1	143,000
$100,000 U.S. Treasury 6% bonds, due Year 20, interest payable March 1 and September 1 (includes accrued interest of $1,500)	101,500
$10,000 Sonar Corporation 9% bonds, due Year 10, interest payable May 31 and November 30	9,900
Permian Company common stock, 800 shares	64,000
Dividends receivable on Permian Company common stock	800
XY Company common stock, 700 shares	70,000

The executor opened an estate checking account to which he transferred the decedent's checking account balance. Other deposits through July 1, Year 2, were as follows:

Interest collected on $100,000 U.S. Treasury 6% bonds:

September 1, Year 1	$ 3,000
March 1, Year 2	3,000

Dividends received on Permian Company common stock:

June 15, Year 1, declared May 7, Year 1, payable to holders of record May 27, Year 1	800
September 15, Year 1	800
December 15, Year 1	1,200
March 15, Year 2	1,500
June 15, Year 2	1,500
Net proceeds of June 19, Year 1, sale of XY Company 700 shares of common stock.	68,810

Payments were made from the estate's checking account through July 1, Year 2, for the following:

Liabilities of decedent paid (including funeral expenses)	$12,000
Additional prior years' federal and state income taxes, plus interest, to May 31, Year 1	1,810
Year 1 income taxes of Festus Ramsey for the period January 1, Year 1, through May 31, Year 1, in excess of amounts paid by the decedent on declarations of estimated tax	9,100
Federal and state fiduciary income taxes, fiscal years ending June 30, Year 1, and June 30, Year 2	2,476
Estate and inheritance taxes	58,000
Monthly payments to Martha Ramsey, 13 payments of $500	6,500
Attorney's and accountant's fees (allocated entirely to principal)	25,000

The executor, Martin Ramsey, waived his fee. However, he desired to receive his father's diamond ring in lieu of the $10,000 cash devise. All parties agreed to this in writing, and the court's approval was secured. All other specific devises were delivered by July 15, Year 1.

Instructions

a Prepare a charge and discharge statement as to principal and income, with supporting schedules, to accompany the attorney's formal court accounting on behalf of the executor of the Estate of Festus Ramsey for the period from May 31, Year 1, through July 1, Year 2. In accordance with the will, the executor accrued the interest and dividends on the estate investments to July 1, Year 2. Disregard homestead allowance, exempt property, and family allowance.

b Prepare a summary showing the allocation of principal and income assets at July 1, Year 2, between the trust for the benefit of Martha Ramsey and the residual estate to be divided between Emma Ramsey Edwards and Martin Ramsey.

16-10 The will of Mean Joe Jackson directed that his executor, Floyd Windal, liquidate the entire estate within two years of the date of death and pay the net proceeds and income to the South Side YMCA. Mean Joe Jackson was a bachelor and died on February 1, Year 10, after a brief illness.

An inventory of the decedent's property was prepared, and the current fair

value of all items was determined. The preliminary inventory, before the computation of any appropriate income accruals on inventory items, follows:

	Current fair value
United California Bank checking account	$ 8,500
$60,000 Sun City bonds, interest rate 6%, payable January 1 and July 1,	
maturity date July 1, Year 14	59,000
2,000 shares Rex Corporation common stock	220,000
Term life insurance: beneficiary, Estate of Mean Joe Jackson	20,000
Residence ($56,500) and furniture ($6,000)	62,500

During Year 10 the following transactions occurred:
(1) The interest on the Sun City bonds was collected. The bonds were sold on
July 1, for $59,000, and the proceeds and interest were paid to the South
Side YMCA.
(2) Rex Corporation paid cash dividends of $1 per share on March 1 and De-
cember 1, and a 10% stock dividend was distributed on July 1. All dividends
were declared 45 days before each payment date and were payable to holders
of record as of 40 days before each payment date. In September, 1,000 shares
were sold at $105 per share, and the proceeds were paid to the South Side
YMCA.
(3) Because of a depressed real estate market, the personal residence was rented
furnished at $300 per month commencing April 1, Year 10. The rent is paid
monthly, in advance. Real estate taxes of $1,200 for the calendar Year 10
were paid. The house and furnishings have estimated lives of 40 years and
8 years, respectively. The part-time gardener was paid 4 months' wages
totaling $500 on April 30 for services performed, and was then released.
(4) The United California Bank checking account was closed and the balance
of $8,500 was transferred to an estate bank account.
(5) The proceeds of the term life insurance were received on March 1 and
deposited in the estate bank account.
(6) The following disbursements were made:
  (a) Funeral expenses and expenses of final illness, $3,500.
  (b) Balance due on Year 9 income taxes of deceased, $700.
  (c) Attorney's and accountant's fees, $12,000, of which $1,000 was allocated
  to income.
(7) On December 31, the balance of the undistributed income, except for $250,
was paid to the beneficiary. The balance of the cash on hand derived from
the principal of the estate was also paid to the beneficiary on December 31.
At December 31, Year 10, the executor resigned and waived all fees.

Instructions Prepare a charge and discharge statement, together with its supporting schedules, for the executor of the Estate of Mean Joe Jackson for the
period February 1–December 31, Year 10. Disregard depreciation.

Compound interest tables

Table 1 Future Amount of $1 at Compound Interest Due in n Periods: $a_{\overline{n}|i} = (1 + i)^n$

n	$\frac{1}{2}\%$	1%	$1\frac{1}{2}\%$	2%	$2\frac{1}{2}\%$	3%
1	1.005000	1.010000	1.015000	1.020000	1.025000	1.030000
2	1.010025	1.020100	1.030225	1.040400	1.050625	1.060900
3	1.015075	1.030301	1.045678	1.061208	1.076891	1.092727
4	1.020151	1.040604	1.061364	1.082432	1.103813	1.125509
5	1.025251	1.051010	1.077284	1.104081	1.131408	1.159274
6	1.030378	1.061520	1.093443	1.126162	1.159693	1.194052
7	1.035529	1.072135	1.109845	1.148686	1.188686	1.229874
8	1.040707	1.082857	1.126493	1.171659	1.218403	1.266770
9	1.045911	1.093685	1.143390	1.195093	1.248863	1.304773
10	1.051140	1.104622	1.160541	1.218994	1.280085	1.343916
11	1.056396	1.115668	1.177949	1.243374	1.312087	1.384234
12	1.061678	1.126825	1.195618	1.268242	1.344889	1.425761
13	1.066986	1.138093	1.213552	1.293607	1.378511	1.468534
14	1.072321	1.149474	1.231756	1.319479	1.412974	1.512590
15	1.077683	1.160969	1.250232	1.345868	1.448298	1.557967
16	1.083071	1.172579	1.268986	1.372786	1.484506	1.604706
17	1.088487	1.184304	1.288020	1.400241	1.521618	1.652848
18	1.093929	1.196147	1.307341	1.428246	1.559659	1.702433
19	1.099399	1.208109	1.326951	1.456811	1.598650	1.753506
20	1.104896	1.220190	1.346855	1.485947	1.638616	1.806111
21	1.110420	1.232392	1.367058	1.515666	1.679582	1.860295
22	1.115972	1.244716	1.387564	1.545980	1.721571	1.916103
23	1.121552	1.257163	1.408377	1.576899	1.764611	1.973587
24	1.127160	1.269735	1.429503	1.608437	1.808726	2.032794
25	1.132796	1.282432	1.450945	1.640606	1.853944	2.093778
26	1.138460	1.295256	1.472710	1.673418	1.900293	2.156591
27	1.144152	1.308209	1.494800	1.706886	1.947800	2.221289
28	1.149873	1.321291	1.517222	1.741024	1.996495	2.287928
29	1.155622	1.334504	1.539981	1.775845	2.046407	2.356566
30	1.161400	1.347849	1.563080	1.811362	2.097568	2.427262
31	1.167207	1.361327	1.586526	1.847589	2.150007	2.500080
32	1.173043	1.374941	1.610324	1.884541	2.203757	2.575083
33	1.178908	1.388690	1.634479	1.922231	2.258851	2.652335
34	1.184803	1.402577	1.658996	1.960676	2.315322	2.731905
35	1.190727	1.416603	1.683881	1.999890	2.373205	2.813862
36	1.196681	1.430769	1.709140	2.039887	2.432535	2.898278
37	1.202664	1.445076	1.734777	2.080685	2.493349	2.985227
38	1.208677	1.459527	1.760798	2.122299	2.555682	3.074783
39	1.214721	1.474123	1.787210	2.164745	2.619574	3.167027
40	1.220794	1.488864	1.814018	2.208040	2.685064	3.262038
41	1.226898	1.503752	1.841229	2.252200	2.752190	3.359899
42	1.233033	1.518790	1.868847	2.297244	2.820995	3.460696
43	1.239198	1.533978	1.896880	2.343189	2.891520	3.564517
44	1.245394	1.549318	1.925333	2.390053	2.963808	3.671452
45	1.251621	1.564811	1.954213	2.437854	3.037903	3.781596
46	1.257879	1.580459	1.983526	2.486611	3.113851	3.895044
47	1.264168	1.596263	2.013279	2.536344	3.191697	4.011895
48	1.270489	1.612226	2.043478	2.587070	3.271490	4.132252
49	1.276842	1.628348	2.074130	2.638812	3.353277	4.256219
50	1.283226	1.644632	2.105242	2.691588	3.437109	4.383906

TABLE 1   **631**

Table 1   Future Amount of $1 (*continued*)

n	3½%	4%	4½%	5%	5½%	6%
1	1.035000	1.040000	1.045000	1.050000	1.055000	1.060000
2	1.071225	1.081600	1.092025	1.102500	1.113025	1.123600
3	1.108718	1.124864	1.141166	1.157625	1.174241	1.191016
4	1.147523	1.169859	1.192519	1.215506	1.238825	1.262477
5	1.187686	1.216653	1.246182	1.276282	1.306960	1.338226
6	1.229255	1.265319	1.302260	1.340096	1.378843	1.418519
7	1.272279	1.315932	1.360862	1.407100	1.454679	1.503630
8	1.316809	1.368569	1.422101	1.477455	1.534687	1.593848
9	1.362897	1.423312	1.486095	1.551328	1.619094	1.689479
10	1.410599	1.480244	1.552969	1.628895	1.708144	1.790848
11	1.459970	1.539454	1.622853	1.710339	1.802092	1.898299
12	1.511069	1.601032	1.695881	1.795856	1.901207	2.012196
13	1.563956	1.665074	1.772196	1.885649	2.005774	2.132928
14	1.618695	1.731676	1.851945	1.979932	2.116091	2.260904
15	1.675349	1.800944	1.935282	2.078928	2.232476	2.396558
16	1.733986	1.872981	2.022370	2.182875	2.355263	2.540352
17	1.794676	1.947901	2.113377	2.292018	2.484802	2.692773
18	1.857489	2.025817	2.208479	2.406619	2.621466	2.854339
19	1.922501	2.106849	2.307860	2.526950	2.765647	3.025600
20	1.989789	2.191123	2.411714	2.653298	2.917757	3.207135
21	2.059431	2.278768	2.520241	2.785963	3.078234	3.399564
22	2.131512	2.369919	2.633652	2.925261	3.247537	3.603537
23	2.206114	2.464716	2.752166	3.071524	3.426152	3.819750
24	2.283328	2.563304	2.876014	3.225100	3.614590	4.048935
25	2.363245	2.665836	3.005434	3.386355	3.813392	4.291871
26	2.445959	2.772470	3.140679	3.555673	4.023129	4.549383
27	2.531567	2.883369	3.282010	3.733456	4.244401	4.822346
28	2.620172	2.998703	3.429700	3.920129	4.477843	5.111687
29	2.711878	3.118651	3.584036	4.116136	4.724124	5.418388
30	2.806794	3.243398	3.745318	4.321942	4.983951	5.743491
31	2.905031	3.373133	3.913857	4.538039	5.258069	6.088101
32	3.006708	3.508059	4.089981	4.764941	5.547262	6.453387
33	3.111942	3.648381	4.274030	5.003189	5.852362	6.840590
34	3.220860	3.794316	4.466362	5.253348	6.174242	7.251025
35	3.333590	3.946089	4.667348	5.516015	6.513825	7.686087
36	3.450266	4.103933	4.877378	5.791816	6.872085	8.147252
37	3.571025	4.268090	5.096860	6.081407	7.250050	8.636087
38	3.696011	4.438813	5.326219	6.385477	7.648803	9.154252
39	3.825372	4.616366	5.565899	6.704751	8.069487	9.703507
40	3.959260	4.801021	5.816365	7.039989	8.513309	10.285718
41	4.097834	4.993061	6.078101	7.391988	8.981541	10.902861
42	4.241258	5.192784	6.351615	7.761588	9.475526	11.557033
43	4.389702	5.400495	6.637438	8.149667	9.996679	12.250455
44	4.543342	5.616515	6.936123	8.557150	10.546497	12.985482
45	4.702359	5.841176	7.248248	8.985008	11.126554	13.764611
46	4.866941	6.074823	7.574420	9.434258	11.738515	14.590487
47	5.037284	6.317816	7.915268	9.905971	12.384133	15.465917
48	5.213589	6.570528	8.271456	10.401270	13.065260	16.393872
49	5.396065	6.833349	8.643671	10.921333	13.783849	17.377504
50	5.584927	7.106683	9.032636	11.467400	14.541961	18.420154

Table 1 Future Amount of $1 (*continued*)

n	7%	8%	9%	10%	12%	15%
1	1.070000	1.080000	1.090000	1.100000	1.120000	1.150000
2	1.144900	1.166400	1.188100	1.210000	1.254400	1.322500
3	1.225043	1.259712	1.295029	1.331000	1.404928	1.520875
4	1.310796	1.360489	1.411582	1.464100	1.573519	1.749006
5	1.402552	1.469328	1.538624	1.610510	1.762342	2.011357
6	1.500730	1.586874	1.677100	1.771561	1.973823	2.313061
7	1.605781	1.713824	1.828039	1.948717	2.210681	2.660020
8	1.718186	1.850930	1.992563	2.143589	2.475963	3.059023
9	1.838459	1.999005	2.171893	2.357948	2.773079	3.517876
10	1.967151	2.158925	2.367364	2.593742	3.105848	4.045558
11	2.104852	2.331639	2.580426	2.853117	3.478550	4.652391
12	2.252192	2.518170	2.812665	3.138428	3.895976	5.350250
13	2.409845	2.719624	3.065805	3.452271	4.363493	6.152788
14	2.578534	2.937194	3.341727	3.797498	4.887112	7.075706
15	2.759032	3.172169	3.642482	4.177248	5.473566	8.137062
16	2.952164	3.425943	3.970306	4.594973	6.130394	9.357621
17	3.158815	3.700018	4.327633	5.054470	6.866041	10.761264
18	3.379932	3.996019	4.717120	5.559917	7.689966	12.375454
19	3.616528	4.315701	5.141661	6.115909	8.612762	14.231772
20	3.869684	4.660957	5.604411	6.727500	9.646293	16.366537
21	4.140562	5.033834	6.108808	7.400250	10.803848	18.821518
22	4.430402	5.436540	6.658600	8.140275	12.100310	21.644746
23	4.740530	5.871464	7.257874	8.954302	13.552347	24.891458
24	5.072367	6.341181	7.911083	9.849733	15.178629	28.625176
25	5.427433	6.848475	8.623081	10.834706	17.000064	32.918953
26	5.807353	7.396353	9.399158	11.918177	19.040072	37.856796
27	6.213868	7.988061	10.245082	13.109994	21.324881	43.535315
28	6.648838	8.627106	11.167140	14.420994	23.883866	50.065612
29	7.114257	9.317275	12.172182	15.863093	26.749930	57.575454
30	7.612255	10.062657	13.267678	17.449402	29.959922	66.211772
31	8.145113	10.867669	14.461770	19.194342	33.555113	76.143538
32	8.715271	11.737083	15.763329	21.113777	37.581726	87.565068
33	9.325340	12.676050	17.182028	23.225154	42.091533	100.699829
34	9.978114	13.690134	18.728411	25.547670	47.142517	115.804803
35	10.676581	14.785344	20.413968	28.102437	52.799620	133.175523
36	11.423942	15.968172	22.251225	30.912681	59.135574	153.151852
37	12.223618	17.245626	24.253835	34.003949	66.231843	176.124630
38	13.079271	18.625276	26.436680	37.404343	74.179664	202.543324
39	13.994820	20.115298	28.815982	41.144778	83.081224	232.924823
40	14.974458	21.724521	31.409420	45.259256	93.050970	267.863546
41	16.022670	23.462483	34.236268	49.785181	104.217087	308.043078
42	17.144257	25.339482	37.317532	54.763699	116.723137	354.249540
43	18.344355	27.366640	40.676110	60.240069	130.729914	407.386971
44	19.628460	29.555972	44.336960	66.264076	146.417503	468.495017
45	21.002452	31.920449	48.327286	72.890484	163.987604	538.769269
46	22.472623	34.474085	52.676742	80.179532	183.666116	619.584659
47	24.045707	37.232012	57.417649	88.197485	205.706050	712.522358
48	25.728907	40.210573	62.585237	97.017234	230.390776	819.400712
49	27.529930	43.427419	68.217908	106.718957	258.037669	942.310819
50	29.457025	46.901613	74.357520	117.390853	289.002190	1083.657442

TABLE 2 **633**

Table 2   Present Value of $1 at Compound Interest Due in n Periods: $p_{\overline{n}|i} = \dfrac{1}{(1 + i)^n}$

n \ i	$\frac{1}{2}\%$	1%	$1\frac{1}{2}\%$	2%	$2\frac{1}{2}\%$	3%
1	0.995025	0.990099	0.985222	0.980392	0.975610	0.970874
2	0.990075	0.980296	0.970662	0.961169	0.951814	0.942596
3	0.985149	0.970590	0.956317	0.942322	0.928599	0.915142
4	0.980248	0.960980	0.942184	0.923845	0.905951	0.888487
5	0.975371	0.951466	0.928260	0.905731	0.883854	0.862609
6	0.970518	0.942045	0.914542	0.887971	0.862297	0.837484
7	0.965690	0.932718	0.901027	0.870560	0.841265	0.813092
8	0.960885	0.923483	0.887711	0.853490	0.820747	0.789409
9	0.956105	0.914340	0.874592	0.836755	0.800728	0.766417
10	0.951348	0.905287	0.861667	0.820348	0.781198	0.744094
11	0.946615	0.896324	0.848933	0.804263	0.762145	0.722421
12	0.941905	0.887449	0.836387	0.788493	0.743556	0.701380
13	0.937219	0.878663	0.824027	0.773033	0.725420	0.680951
14	0.932556	0.869963	0.811849	0.757875	0.707727	0.661118
15	0.927917	0.861349	0.799852	0.743015	0.690466	0.641862
16	0.923300	0.852821	0.788031	0.728446	0.673625	0.623167
17	0.918707	0.844377	0.776385	0.714163	0.657195	0.605016
18	0.914136	0.836017	0.764912	0.700159	0.641166	0.587395
19	0.909588	0.827740	0.753607	0.686431	0.625528	0.570286
20	0.905063	0.819544	0.742470	0.672971	0.610271	0.553676
21	0.900560	0.811430	0.731498	0.659776	0.595386	0.537549
22	0.896080	0.803396	0.720688	0.646839	0.580865	0.521893
23	0.891622	0.795442	0.710037	0.634156	0.566697	0.506692
24	0.887186	0.787566	0.699544	0.621721	0.552875	0.491934
25	0.882772	0.779768	0.689206	0.609531	0.539391	0.477606
26	0.878380	0.772048	0.679021	0.597579	0.526235	0.463695
27	0.874010	0.764404	0.668986	0.585862	0.513400	0.450189
28	0.869662	0.756836	0.659099	0.574375	0.500878	0.437077
29	0.865335	0.749342	0.649359	0.563112	0.488661	0.424346
30	0.861030	0.741923	0.639762	0.552071	0.476743	0.411987
31	0.856746	0.734577	0.630308	0.541246	0.465115	0.399987
32	0.852484	0.727304	0.620993	0.530633	0.453771	0.388337
33	0.848242	0.720103	0.611816	0.520229	0.442703	0.377026
34	0.844022	0.712973	0.602774	0.510028	0.431905	0.366045
35	0.839823	0.705914	0.593866	0.500028	0.421371	0.355383
36	0.835645	0.698925	0.585090	0.490223	0.411094	0.345032
37	0.831487	0.692005	0.576443	0.480611	0.401067	0.334983
38	0.827351	0.685153	0.567924	0.471187	0.391285	0.325226
39	0.823235	0.678370	0.559531	0.461948	0.381741	0.315754
40	0.819139	0.671653	0.551262	0.452890	0.372431	0.306557
41	0.815064	0.665003	0.543116	0.444010	0.363347	0.297628
42	0.811009	0.658419	0.535089	0.435304	0.354485	0.288959
43	0.806974	0.651900	0.527182	0.426769	0.345839	0.280543
44	0.802959	0.645445	0.519391	0.418401	0.337404	0.272372
45	0.798964	0.639055	0.511715	0.410197	0.329174	0.264439
46	0.794989	0.632728	0.504153	0.402154	0.321146	0.256737
47	0.791034	0.626463	0.496702	0.394268	0.313313	0.249259
48	0.787098	0.620260	0.489362	0.386538	0.305671	0.241999
49	0.783183	0.614119	0.482130	0.378958	0.298216	0.234950
50	0.779286	0.608039	0.475005	0.371528	0.290942	0.228107

Table 2 Present Value of $1 (*continued*)

n \ i	3½%	4%	4½%	5%	5½%	6%
1	0.966184	0.961538	0.956938	0.952381	0.947867	0.943396
2	0.933511	0.924556	0.915730	0.907029	0.898452	0.889996
3	0.901943	0.888996	0.876297	0.863838	0.851614	0.839619
4	0.871442	0.854804	0.838561	0.822702	0.807217	0.792094
5	0.841973	0.821927	0.802451	0.783526	0.765134	0.747258
6	0.813501	0.790315	0.767896	0.746215	0.725246	0.704961
7	0.785991	0.759918	0.734828	0.710681	0.687437	0.665057
8	0.759412	0.730690	0.703185	0.676839	0.651599	0.627412
9	0.733731	0.702587	0.672904	0.644609	0.617629	0.591898
10	0.708919	0.675564	0.643928	0.613913	0.585431	0.558395
11	0.684946	0.649581	0.616199	0.584679	0.554911	0.526788
12	0.661783	0.624597	0.589664	0.556837	0.525982	0.496969
13	0.639404	0.600574	0.564272	0.530321	0.498561	0.468839
14	0.617782	0.577475	0.539973	0.505068	0.472569	0.442301
15	0.596891	0.555265	0.516720	0.481017	0.447933	0.417265
16	0.576706	0.533908	0.494469	0.458112	0.424581	0.393646
17	0.557204	0.513373	0.473176	0.436297	0.402447	0.371364
18	0.538361	0.493628	0.452800	0.415521	0.381466	0.350344
19	0.520156	0.474642	0.433302	0.395734	0.361579	0.330513
20	0.502566	0.456387	0.414643	0.376889	0.342729	0.311805
21	0.485571	0.438834	0.396787	0.358942	0.324862	0.294155
22	0.469151	0.421955	0.379701	0.341850	0.307926	0.277505
23	0.453286	0.405726	0.363350	0.325571	0.291873	0.261797
24	0.437957	0.390121	0.347703	0.310068	0.276657	0.246979
25	0.423147	0.375117	0.332731	0.295303	0.262234	0.232999
26	0.408838	0.360689	0.318402	0.281241	0.248563	0.219810
27	0.395012	0.346817	0.304691	0.267848	0.235605	0.207368
28	0.381654	0.333477	0.291571	0.255094	0.223322	0.195630
29	0.368748	0.320651	0.279015	0.242946	0.211679	0.184557
30	0.356278	0.308319	0.267000	0.231377	0.200644	0.174110
31	0.344230	0.296460	0.255502	0.220359	0.190184	0.164255
32	0.332590	0.285058	0.244500	0.209866	0.180269	0.154957
33	0.321343	0.274094	0.233971	0.199873	0.170871	0.146186
34	0.310476	0.263552	0.223896	0.190355	0.161963	0.137912
35	0.299977	0.253415	0.214254	0.181290	0.153520	0.130105
36	0.289833	0.243669	0.205028	0.172657	0.145516	0.122741
37	0.280032	0.234297	0.196199	0.164436	0.137930	0.115793
38	0.270562	0.225285	0.187750	0.156605	0.130739	0.109239
39	0.261413	0.216621	0.179665	0.149148	0.123924	0.103056
40	0.252572	0.208289	0.171929	0.142046	0.117463	0.097222
41	0.244031	0.200278	0.164525	0.135282	0.111339	0.091719
42	0.235779	0.192575	0.157440	0.128840	0.105535	0.086527
43	0.227806	0.185168	0.150661	0.122704	0.100033	0.081630
44	0.220102	0.178046	0.144173	0.116861	0.094818	0.077009
45	0.212659	0.171198	0.137964	0.111297	0.089875	0.072650
46	0.205468	0.164614	0.132023	0.105997	0.085190	0.068538
47	0.198520	0.158283	0.126338	0.100949	0.080748	0.064658
48	0.191806	0.152195	0.120898	0.096142	0.076539	0.060998
49	0.185320	0.146341	0.115692	0.091564	0.072549	0.057546
50	0.179053	0.140713	0.110710	0.087204	0.068767	0.054288

TABLE 2 **635**

Table 2 Present Value of $1 (*continued*)

n \ i	7%	8%	9%	10%	12%	15%
1	0.934580	0.925926	0.917431	0.909091	0.892857	0.869565
2	0.873439	0.857339	0.841680	0.826446	0.797194	0.756144
3	0.816298	0.793832	0.772183	0.751315	0.711780	0.657516
4	0.762895	0.735030	0.708425	0.683013	0.635518	0.571753
5	0.712986	0.680583	0.649931	0.620921	0.567427	0.497177
6	0.666342	0.630170	0.596267	0.564474	0.506631	0.432328
7	0.622750	0.583490	0.547034	0.513158	0.452349	0.375937
8	0.582009	0.540269	0.501866	0.466507	0.403883	0.326902
9	0.543934	0.500249	0.460428	0.424098	0.360610	0.284262
10	0.508349	0.463193	0.422411	0.385543	0.321973	0.247185
11	0.475093	0.428883	0.387533	0.350494	0.287476	0.214943
12	0.444012	0.397114	0.355535	0.318631	0.256675	0.186907
13	0.414964	0.367698	0.326179	0.289664	0.229174	0.162528
14	0.387817	0.340461	0.299246	0.263331	0.204620	0.141329
15	0.362446	0.315242	0.274538	0.239392	0.182696	0.122894
16	0.338735	0.291890	0.251870	0.217629	0.163122	0.106865
17	0.316574	0.270269	0.231073	0.197845	0.145644	0.092926
18	0.295864	0.250249	0.211994	0.179859	0.130040	0.080805
19	0.276508	0.231712	0.194490	0.163508	0.116107	0.070265
20	0.258419	0.214548	0.178431	0.148644	0.103667	0.061100
21	0.241513	0.198656	0.163698	0.135131	0.092560	0.053131
22	0.225713	0.183941	0.150182	0.122846	0.082643	0.046201
23	0.210947	0.170315	0.137781	0.111678	0.073788	0.040174
24	0.197147	0.157699	0.126405	0.101526	0.065882	0.034934
25	0.184249	0.146018	0.115968	0.092296	0.058823	0.030378
26	0.172195	0.135202	0.106393	0.083905	0.052521	0.026415
27	0.160930	0.125187	0.097608	0.076278	0.046894	0.022970
28	0.150402	0.115914	0.089548	0.069343	0.041869	0.019974
29	0.140563	0.107328	0.082155	0.063039	0.037383	0.017369
30	0.131367	0.099377	0.075371	0.057309	0.033378	0.015103
31	0.122773	0.092016	0.069148	0.052099	0.029802	0.013133
32	0.114741	0.085200	0.063438	0.047362	0.026609	0.011420
33	0.107235	0.078889	0.058200	0.043057	0.023758	0.009931
34	0.100219	0.073045	0.053395	0.039143	0.021212	0.008635
35	0.093663	0.067635	0.048986	0.035584	0.018940	0.007509
36	0.087535	0.062625	0.044941	0.032349	0.016910	0.006529
37	0.081809	0.057986	0.041231	0.029408	0.015098	0.005678
38	0.076457	0.053690	0.037826	0.026735	0.013481	0.004937
39	0.071455	0.049713	0.034703	0.024304	0.012036	0.004293
40	0.066780	0.046031	0.031838	0.022095	0.010747	0.003733
41	0.062412	0.042621	0.029209	0.020086	0.009595	0.003246
42	0.058329	0.039464	0.026797	0.018260	0.008567	0.002823
43	0.054513	0.036541	0.024584	0.016600	0.007649	0.002455
44	0.050946	0.033834	0.022555	0.015091	0.006830	0.002134
45	0.047613	0.031328	0.020692	0.013719	0.006098	0.001856
46	0.044499	0.029007	0.018984	0.012472	0.005445	0.001614
47	0.041587	0.026859	0.017416	0.011338	0.004861	0.001403
48	0.038867	0.024869	0.015978	0.010307	0.004340	0.001220
49	0.036324	0.023027	0.014659	0.009370	0.003875	0.001061
50	0.033948	0.021321	0.013449	0.008519	0.003460	0.000923

Table 3   Future Amount of an Ordinary Annuity of $1 per Period: $A_{\overline{n}|i} = \dfrac{(1 + i)^n - 1}{i}$

n	$\frac{1}{2}\%$	1%	$1\frac{1}{2}\%$	2%	$2\frac{1}{2}\%$	3%
1	1.000000	1.000000	1.000000	1.000000	1.000000	1.000000
2	2.005000	2.010000	2.015000	2.020000	2.025000	2.030000
3	3.015025	3.030100	3.045225	3.060400	3.075625	3.090900
4	4.030100	4.060401	4.090903	4.121608	4.152516	4.183627
5	5.050251	5.101005	5.152267	5.204040	5.256329	5.309136
6	6.075502	6.152015	6.229551	6.308121	6.387737	6.468410
7	7.105879	7.213535	7.322994	7.434283	7.547430	7.662462
8	8.141409	8.285671	8.432839	8.582969	8.736116	8.892336
9	9.182116	9.368527	9.559332	9.754628	9.954519	10.159106
10	10.228026	10.462213	10.702722	10.949721	11.203382	11.463879
11	11.279167	11.566835	11.863262	12.168715	12.483466	12.807796
12	12.335562	12.682503	13.041211	13.412090	13.795553	14.192030
13	13.397240	13.809328	14.236830	14.680332	15.140442	15.617790
14	14.464226	14.947421	15.450382	15.973938	16.518953	17.086324
15	15.536548	16.096896	16.682138	17.293417	17.931927	18.598914
16	16.614230	17.257864	17.932370	18.639285	19.380225	20.156881
17	17.697301	18.430443	19.201355	20.012071	20.864730	21.761588
18	18.785788	19.614748	20.489376	21.412312	22.386349	23.414435
19	19.879717	20.810895	21.796716	22.840559	23.946007	25.116868
20	20.979115	22.019004	23.123667	24.297370	25.544658	26.870374
21	22.084011	23.239194	24.470522	25.783317	27.183274	28.676486
22	23.194431	24.471586	25.837580	27.298984	28.862856	30.536780
23	24.310403	25.716302	27.225144	28.844963	30.584427	32.452884
24	25.431955	26.973465	28.633521	30.421862	32.349038	34.426470
25	26.559115	28.243200	30.063024	32.030300	34.157764	36.459264
26	27.691911	29.525632	31.513969	33.670906	36.011708	38.553042
27	28.830370	30.820888	32.986679	35.344324	37.912001	40.709634
28	29.974522	32.129097	34.481479	37.051210	39.859801	42.930923
29	31.124395	33.450388	35.998701	38.792235	41.856296	45.218850
30	32.280017	34.784892	37.538681	40.568079	43.902703	47.575416
31	33.441417	36.132740	39.101762	42.379441	46.000271	50.002678
32	34.608624	37.494068	40.688288	44.227030	48.150278	52.502759
33	35.781667	38.869009	42.298612	46.111570	50.354034	55.077841
34	36.960575	40.257699	43.933092	48.033802	52.612885	57.730177
35	38.145378	41.660276	45.592088	49.994478	54.928207	60.462082
36	39.336105	43.076878	47.275969	51.994367	57.301413	63.275944
37	40.532785	44.507647	48.985109	54.034255	59.733948	66.174223
38	41.735449	45.952724	50.719885	56.114940	62.227297	69.159449
39	42.944127	47.412251	52.480684	58.237238	64.782979	72.234233
40	44.158847	48.886373	54.267894	60.401983	67.402554	75.401260
41	45.379642	50.375237	56.081912	62.610023	70.087617	78.663298
42	46.606540	51.878989	57.923141	64.862223	72.839808	82.023196
43	47.839572	53.397779	59.791988	67.159468	75.660803	85.483892
44	49.078770	54.931757	61.688868	69.502657	78.552323	89.048409
45	50.324164	56.481075	63.614201	71.892710	81.516131	92.719861
46	51.575785	58.045885	65.568414	74.330564	84.554034	96.501457
47	52.833664	59.626344	67.551940	76.817176	87.667885	100.396501
48	54.097832	61.222608	69.565219	79.353519	90.859582	104.408396
49	55.368321	62.834834	71.608698	81.940590	94.131072	108.540648
50	56.645163	64.463182	73.682828	84.579401	97.484349	112.796867

TABLE 3 **637**

Table 3 Future Amount of an Ordinary Annuity of $1 (*continued*)

n \ i	3½%	4%	4½%	5%	5½%	6%
1	1.000000	1.000000	1.000000	1.000000	1.000000	1.000000
2	2.035000	2.040000	2.045000	2.050000	2.055000	2.060000
3	3.106225	3.121600	3.137025	3.152500	3.168025	3.183600
4	4.214943	4.246464	4.278191	4.310125	4.342266	4.374616
5	5.362466	5.416323	5.470710	5.525631	5.581091	5.637093
6	6.550152	6.632975	6.716892	6.801913	6.888051	6.975319
7	7.779408	7.898294	8.019152	8.142008	8.266894	8.393838
8	9.051687	9.214226	9.380014	9.549109	9.721573	9.897468
9	10.368496	10.582795	10.802114	11.026564	11.256260	11.491316
10	11.731393	12.006107	12.288209	12.577893	12.875354	13.180795
11	13.141992	13.486351	13.841179	14.206787	14.583498	14.971643
12	14.601962	15.025805	15.464032	15.917127	16.385591	16.869941
13	16.113030	16.626838	17.159913	17.712983	18.286798	18.882138
14	17.676986	18.291911	18.932109	19.598632	20.292572	21.015066
15	19.295681	20.023588	20.784054	21.578564	22.408664	23.275970
16	20.971030	21.824531	22.719337	23.657492	24.641140	25.672528
17	22.705016	23.697512	24.741707	25.840366	26.996403	28.212880
18	24.499691	25.645413	26.855084	28.132385	29.481205	30.905653
19	26.357181	27.671229	29.063562	30.539004	32.102671	33.759992
20	28.279682	29.778079	31.371423	33.065954	34.868318	36.785591
21	30.269471	31.969202	33.783137	35.719252	37.786076	39.992727
22	32.328902	34.247970	36.303378	38.505214	40.864310	43.392290
23	34.460414	36.617889	38.937030	41.430475	44.111847	46.995828
24	36.666528	39.082604	41.689196	44.501999	47.537998	50.815577
25	38.949857	41.645908	44.565210	47.727099	51.152588	54.864512
26	41.313102	44.311745	47.570645	51.113454	54.965981	59.156383
27	43.759060	47.084214	50.711324	54.669126	58.989109	63.705766
28	46.290627	49.967583	53.993333	58.402583	63.233510	68.528112
29	48.910799	52.966286	57.423033	62.322712	67.711354	73.629798
30	51.622677	56.084938	61.007070	66.438848	72.435478	79.058186
31	54.429471	59.328335	64.752388	70.760790	77.419429	84.801677
32	57.334502	62.701469	68.666245	75.298829	82.677498	90.889778
33	60.341210	66.209527	72.756226	80.063771	88.224760	97.343165
34	63.453152	69.857909	77.030256	85.066959	94.077122	104.183755
35	66.674013	73.652225	81.496618	90.320307	100.251364	111.434780
36	70.007603	77.598314	86.163966	95.836323	106.765189	119.120867
37	73.457869	81.702246	91.041344	101.628139	113.637274	127.268119
38	77.028895	85.970336	96.138205	107.709546	120.887324	135.904206
39	80.724906	90.409150	101.464424	114.095023	128.536127	145.058458
40	84.550278	95.025516	107.030323	120.799774	136.605614	154.761966
41	88.509537	99.826536	112.846688	127.839763	145.118923	165.047684
42	92.607371	104.819598	118.924789	135.231751	154.100464	175.950545
43	96.848629	110.012382	125.276404	142.993339	163.575989	187.507577
44	101.238331	115.412877	131.913842	151.143006	173.572669	199.758032
45	105.781673	121.029392	138.849965	159.700156	184.119165	212.743514
46	110.484031	126.870568	146.098214	168.685164	195.245719	226.508125
47	115.350973	132.945390	153.672633	178.119422	206.984234	241.098612
48	120.388257	139.263206	161.587902	188.025393	219.368367	256.564529
49	125.601846	145.833734	169.859357	198.426663	232.433627	272.958401
50	130.997910	152.667084	178.503028	209.347996	246.217476	290.335905

Table 3   Future Amount of an Ordinary Annuity of $1 (*continued*)

n \ i	7%	8%	9%	10%	12%	15%
1	1.000000	1.000000	1.000000	1.000000	1.000000	1.000000
2	2.070000	2.080000	2.090000	2.100000	2.120000	2.150000
3	3.214900	3.246400	3.278100	3.310000	3.374400	3.472500
4	4.439943	4.506112	4.573129	4.641000	4.779328	4.993375
5	5.750740	5.866601	5.984711	6.105100	6.352847	6.742381
6	7.153291	7.335929	7.523335	7.715610	8.115189	8.753738
7	8.654021	8.922803	9.200435	9.487171	10.089012	11.066799
8	10.259803	10.636628	11.028474	11.435888	12.299693	13.726819
9	11.977989	12.487558	13.021036	13.579477	14.775656	16.785842
10	13.816448	14.486562	15.192930	15.937425	17.548735	20.303718
11	15.783599	16.645487	17.560293	18.531167	20.654583	24.349276
12	17.888451	18.977126	20.140720	21.384284	24.133133	29.001667
13	20.140643	21.495297	22.953385	24.522712	28.029109	34.351917
14	22.550488	24.214920	26.019189	27.974983	32.392602	40.504705
15	25.129022	27.152114	29.360916	31.772482	37.279715	47.580411
16	27.888054	30.324283	33.003399	35.949730	42.753280	55.717472
17	30.840217	33.750226	36.973705	40.544703	48.883674	65.075093
18	33.999033	37.450244	41.301338	45.599173	55.749715	75.836357
19	37.378965	41.446263	46.018458	51.159090	63.439681	88.211811
20	40.995492	45.761964	51.160120	57.274999	72.052442	102.443583
21	44.865177	50.422921	56.764530	64.002499	81.698736	118.810120
22	49.005739	55.456755	62.873338	71.402749	92.502584	137.631638
23	53.436141	60.893296	69.531939	79.543024	104.602894	159.276384
24	58.176671	66.764759	76.789813	88.497327	118.155241	184.167841
25	63.249038	73.105940	84.700896	98.347059	133.333870	212.793017
26	68.676470	79.954415	93.323977	109.181765	150.333934	245.711970
27	74.483823	87.350768	102.723135	121.099942	169.374007	283.568766
28	80.697691	95.338830	112.968217	134.209936	190.698887	327.104080
29	87.346529	103.965936	124.135356	148.630930	214.582754	377.169693
30	94.460786	113.283211	136.307539	164.494023	241.332684	434.745146
31	102.073041	123.345868	149.575217	181.943425	271.292606	500.956918
32	110.218154	134.213537	164.036987	201.137767	304.847719	577.100456
33	118.933425	145.950620	179.800315	222.251544	342.429446	644.665525
34	128.258765	158.626670	196.982344	245.476699	384.520979	765.365353
35	138.236878	172.316804	215.710755	271.024368	431.663496	881.170156
36	148.913460	187.102148	236.124723	299.126905	484.463116	1014.345680
37	160.337402	203.070320	258.375948	330.039486	543.598690	1167.497532
38	172.561020	220.315945	282.629783	364.043434	609.830533	1343.622161
39	185.640292	238.941221	309.066463	401.447778	684.010197	1546.165485
40	199.635112	259.056519	337.882445	442.592556	767.091420	1779.090308
41	214.609570	280.781040	369.291865	487.851811	860.142391	2046.953854
42	230.632240	304.243523	403.528133	537.636992	964.359478	2354.996933
43	247.776497	329.583005	440.845665	592.400692	1081.082615	2709.246473
44	266.120851	356.949646	481.521775	652.640761	1211.812529	3116.633443
45	285.749311	386.505617	525.858734	718.904837	1358.230032	3585.128460
46	306.751763	418.426067	574.186021	791.795321	1522.217636	4123.897729
47	329.224386	452.900152	626.862762	871.974853	1705.883752	4743.482388
48	353.270093	490.132164	684.280411	960.172338	1911.589803	5466.004746
49	378.999000	530.342737	746.865648	1057.169572	2141.980579	6275.405458
50	406.528929	573.770156	815.083556	1163.908529	2400.018249	7217.716277

TABLE 4 **639**

Table 4 **Present Value of an Ordinary Annuity of $1 per Period:** $P_{\overline{n}|i} = \dfrac{1 - \dfrac{1}{(1+i)^n}}{i}$

n $\diagdown$ i	$\frac{1}{2}\%$	1%	$1\frac{1}{2}\%$	2%	$2\frac{1}{2}\%$	3%
1	0.995025	0.990099	0.985222	0.980392	0.975610	0.970874
2	1.985099	1.970395	1.955883	1.941561	1.927424	1.913470
3	2.970248	2.940985	2.912200	2.883883	2.856024	2.828611
4	3.950496	3.901966	3.854385	3.807729	3.761974	3.717098
5	4.925866	4.853431	4.782645	4.713460	4.645829	4.579707
6	5.896384	5.795476	5.697187	5.601431	5.508125	5.417191
7	6.862074	6.728195	6.598214	6.471991	6.349391	6.230283
8	7.822959	7.651678	7.485925	7.325481	7.170137	7.019692
9	8.779064	8.566018	8.360517	8.162237	7.970866	7.786109
10	9.730412	9.471305	9.222185	8.982585	8.752064	8.530203
11	10.677027	10.367628	10.071118	9.786848	9.514209	9.252624
12	11.618932	11.255077	10.907505	10.575341	10.257765	9.954004
13	12.556151	12.133740	11.731532	11.348374	10.983185	10.634955
14	13.488708	13.003703	12.543382	12.106249	11.690912	11.296073
15	14.416625	13.865053	13.343233	12.849264	12.381378	11.937935
16	15.339925	14.717874	14.131264	13.577709	13.055003	12.561102
17	16.258632	15.562251	14.907649	14.291872	13.712198	13.166118
18	17.172768	16.398269	15.672561	14.992031	14.353364	13.753513
19	18.082356	17.226009	16.426168	15.678462	14.978891	14.323799
20	18.987419	18.045553	17.168639	16.351433	15.589162	14.877475
21	19.887979	18.856983	17.900137	17.011209	16.184549	15.415024
22	20.784059	19.660379	18.620824	17.658048	16.765413	15.936917
23	21.675681	20.455821	19.330861	18.292204	17.332110	16.443608
24	22.562866	21.243387	20.030405	18.913926	17.884986	16.935542
25	23.445638	22.023156	20.719611	19.523456	18.424376	17.413148
26	24.324018	22.795204	21.398632	20.121036	18.950611	17.876842
27	25.198028	23.559608	22.067617	20.706898	19.464011	18.327031
28	26.067689	24.316443	22.726717	21.281272	19.964889	18.764108
29	26.933024	25.065785	23.376076	21.844385	20.453550	19.188455
30	27.794054	25.807708	24.015838	22.396456	20.930293	19.600441
31	28.650800	26.542285	24.646146	22.937702	21.395407	20.000428
32	29.503284	27.269589	25.267139	23.468335	21.849178	20.388766
33	30.351526	27.989693	25.878954	23.988564	22.291881	20.765792
34	31.195548	28.702666	26.481728	24.498592	22.723786	21.131837
35	32.035371	29.408580	27.075595	24.998619	23.145157	21.487220
36	32.871016	30.107505	27.660684	25.488842	23.556251	21.832253
37	33.702504	30.799510	28.237127	25.969453	23.957318	22.167235
38	34.529854	31.484663	28.805052	26.440641	24.348603	22.492462
39	35.353089	32.163033	29.364583	26.902589	24.730344	22.808215
40	36.172228	32.834686	29.915845	27.355479	25.102775	23.114772
41	36.987291	33.499689	30.458961	27.799489	25.466122	23.412400
42	37.798300	34.158108	30.994050	28.234794	25.820607	23.701359
43	38.605274	34.810008	31.521232	28.661562	26.166446	23.981902
44	39.408232	35.455454	32.040622	29.079963	26.503849	24.254274
45	40.207196	36.094508	32.552337	29.490160	26.833024	24.518713
46	41.002185	36.727236	33.056490	29.892314	27.154170	24.775449
47	41.793219	37.353699	33.553192	30.286582	27.467483	25.024708
48	42.580318	37.973959	34.042554	30.673120	27.773154	25.266707
49	43.363500	38.588079	34.524683	31.052078	28.071369	25.501657
50	44.142786	39.196118	34.999688	31.423606	28.362312	25.729764

Table 4 Present Value of an Ordinary Annuity of $1 (*continued*)

n \ i	3½%	4%	4½%	5%	5½%	6%
1	0.966184	0.961538	0.956938	0.952381	0.947867	0.943396
2	1.899694	1.886095	1.872668	1.859410	1.846320	1.833393
3	2.801637	2.775091	2.748964	2.723248	2.697933	2.673012
4	3.673079	3.629895	3.587526	3.545951	3.505150	3.465106
5	4.515052	4.451822	4.389977	4.329477	4.270284	4.212364
6	5.328553	5.242137	5.157872	5.075692	4.995530	4.917324
7	6.114544	6.002055	5.892701	5.786373	5.682967	5.582381
8	6.873956	6.732745	6.595886	6.463213	6.334566	6.209794
9	7.607687	7.435332	7.268791	7.107822	6.952195	6.801692
10	8.316605	8.110896	7.912718	7.721735	7.537626	7.360087
11	9.001551	8.760477	8.528917	8.306414	8.092536	7.886875
12	9.663334	9.385074	9.118581	8.863252	8.618518	8.383844
13	10.302738	9.985648	9.682852	9.393573	9.117079	8.852683
14	10.920520	10.563123	10.222825	9.898641	9.589648	9.294984
15	11.517411	11.118387	10.739546	10.379658	10.037581	9.712249
16	12.094117	11.652296	11.234015	10.837770	10.462162	10.105895
17	12.651321	12.165669	11.707191	11.274066	10.864609	10.477260
18	13.189682	12.659297	12.159992	11.689587	11.246074	10.827603
19	13.709837	13.133939	12.593294	12.085321	11.607654	11.158116
20	14.212403	13.590326	13.007936	12.462210	11.950382	11.469921
21	14.697974	14.029160	13.404724	12.821153	12.275244	11.764077
22	15.167125	14.451115	13.784425	13.163003	12.583170	12.041582
23	15.620410	14.856842	14.147775	13.488574	12.875042	12.303379
24	16.058368	15.246963	14.495478	13.798642	13.151699	12.550358
25	16.481515	15.622080	14.828209	14.093945	13.413933	12.783356
26	16.890352	15.982769	15.146611	14.375185	13.662495	13.003166
27	17.285365	16.329586	15.451303	14.643034	13.898100	13.210534
28	17.667019	16.663063	15.742874	14.898127	14.121422	13.406164
29	18.035767	16.983715	16.021889	15.141074	14.333101	13.590721
30	18.392045	17.292033	16.288889	15.372451	14.533745	13.764831
31	18.736276	17.588494	16.544391	15.592811	14.723929	13.929086
32	19.068865	17.873552	16.788891	15.802677	14.904198	14.084043
33	19.390208	18.147646	17.022862	16.002549	15.075069	14.230230
34	19.700684	18.411198	17.246758	16.192904	15.237033	14.368141
35	20.000661	18.664613	17.461012	16.374194	15.390552	14.498246
36	20.290494	18.908282	17.666041	16.546852	15.536068	14.620987
37	20.570525	19.142579	17.862240	16.711287	15.673999	14.736780
38	20.841087	19.367864	18.049990	16.867893	15.804738	14.846019
39	21.102500	19.584485	18.229656	17.017041	15.928662	14.949075
40	21.355072	19.792774	18.401584	17.159086	16.046125	15.046297
41	21.599104	19.993052	18.566109	17.294368	16.157464	15.138016
42	21.834883	20.185627	18.723550	17.423208	16.262999	15.224543
43	22.062689	20.370795	18.874210	17.545912	16.363032	15.306173
44	22.282791	20.548841	19.018383	17.662773	16.457851	15.383182
45	22.495450	20.720040	19.156347	17.774070	16.547726	15.455832
46	22.700918	20.884654	19.288371	17.880067	16.632915	15.524370
47	22.899438	21.042936	19.414709	17.981016	16.713664	15.589028
48	23.091244	21.195131	19.535607	18.077158	16.790203	15.650027
49	23.276565	21.341472	19.651298	18.168722	16.862751	15.707572
50	23.455618	21.482185	19.762008	18.255925	16.931518	15.761861

TABLE 4 **641**

Table 4 Present Value of an Ordinary Annuity of $1 (*continued*)

n \ i	7%	8%	9%	10%	12%	15%
1	0.934579	0.925926	0.917431	0.909091	0.892857	0.869565
2	1.808018	1.783265	1.759111	1.735537	1.690051	1.625709
3	2.624316	2.577097	2.531295	2.486852	2.401831	2.283225
4	3.387211	3.312127	3.239720	3.169865	3.037349	2.854978
5	4.100197	3.992710	3.889651	3.790787	3.604776	3.352155
6	4.766540	4.622880	4.485919	4.355261	4.111407	3.784483
7	5.389289	5.206370	5.032953	4.868419	4.563757	4.160420
8	5.971299	5.746639	5.534819	5.334926	4.967640	4.487322
9	6.515232	6.246888	5.995247	5.759024	5.328250	4.771584
10	7.023582	6.710081	6.417658	6.144567	5.650223	5.018769
11	7.498674	7.138964	6.805191	6.495061	5.937699	5.233712
12	7.942686	7.536078	7.160725	6.813692	6.194374	5.420619
13	8.357651	7.903776	7.486904	7.103356	6.423548	5.583147
14	8.745468	8.244237	7.786150	7.366687	6.628168	5.724476
15	9.107914	8.559479	8.060688	7.606080	6.810864	5.847370
16	9.446649	8.851369	8.312558	7.823709	6.973986	5.954235
17	9.763223	9.121638	8.543631	8.021553	7.119630	6.047161
18	10.059087	9.371887	8.755625	8.201412	7.249670	6.127966
19	10.335595	9.603599	8.950115	8.364920	7.365777	6.198231
20	10.594014	9.818147	9.128546	8.513564	7.469444	6.259331
21	10.835527	10.016803	9.292244	8.648694	7.562003	6.312462
22	11.061241	10.200744	9.442425	8.771540	7.644646	6.358663
23	11.272187	10.371059	9.580207	8.883218	7.718434	6.398837
24	11.469334	10.528758	9.706612	8.984744	7.784316	6.433771
25	11.653583	10.674776	9.822580	9.077040	7.843139	6.464149
26	11.825779	10.809978	9.928972	9.160945	7.895660	6.490564
27	11.986709	10.935165	10.026580	9.237223	7.942554	6.513534
28	12.137111	11.051078	10.116128	9.306567	7.984423	6.533508
29	12.277674	11.158406	10.198283	9.369606	8.021806	6.550877
30	12.409041	11.257783	10.273654	9.426914	8.055184	6.565980
31	12.531814	11.349799	10.342802	9.479013	8.084986	6.579113
32	12.646555	11.434999	10.406240	9.526376	8.111594	6.590533
33	12.753790	11.513888	10.464441	9.569432	8.135352	6.600463
34	12.854009	11.586934	10.517835	9.608575	8.156564	6.609099
35	12.947672	11.654568	10.566821	9.644159	8.175504	6.616607
36	13.035208	11.717193	10.611763	9.676508	8.192414	6.623137
37	13.117017	11.775179	10.652993	9.705917	8.207513	6.628815
38	13.193473	11.828869	10.690820	9.732651	8.220993	6.633752
39	13.264928	11.878582	10.725523	9.756956	8.233030	6.638045
40	13.331709	11.924613	10.757360	9.779051	8.243777	6.641778
41	13.394120	11.967235	10.786569	9.799137	8.253372	6.645025
42	13.452449	12.006699	10.813366	9.817397	8.261939	6.647848
43	13.506962	12.043240	10.837950	9.833998	8.269589	6.650302
44	13.557908	12.077074	10.860505	9.849089	8.276418	6.652437
45	13.605522	12.108402	10.881197	9.862808	8.282516	6.654293
46	13.650020	12.137409	10.900181	9.875280	8.287961	6.655907
47	13.691608	12.164267	10.917597	9.886618	8.292822	6.657310
48	13.730474	12.189136	10.933575	9.896926	8.297163	6.658531
49	13.766799	12.212163	10.948234	9.906296	8.301038	6.659592
50	13.800746	12.233485	10.961683	9.914814	8.304498	6.660515

APPENDIX **B**

Sample financial
statements

Financial statements are presented in this appendix for the following companies:

The financial statements of these companies were chosen because they provided realistic illustrations of many of the issues discussed in this book. Included, for example, are the following: a description of principles of consolidation, foreign operations and foreign currency translations, investment in net assets of unconsolidated subsidiaries, pooled company's stock dividends prior to business combinations, financial statements restated retroactively following a pooling of interests, and a set of separate financial statements for an unconsolidated subsidiary.

ARTHUR ANDERSEN & CO.

MARCH 31, 1974

Worldwide fees in fiscal 1974 were $315,728,000, an increase of $44,269,000 (16%) over 1973. This reflects a growth of almost 9% in hours of client service, a higher proportion of partner and manager time on client work, and higher billing rates in offices outside the United States to cover increased compensation levels.

The impact of worldwide inflation is particularly severe on our operations. For example, during both fiscal 1974 and 1973, almost 79¢ of every $1.00 of fees represented employee compensation and fringe benefits and partner earnings. Furthermore, with our large investment in net monetary assets (approximately $54,000,000 at March 31, 1974), partners' capital is being continuously eroded by the decrease in the purchasing power of the U.S. dollar.

During 1974, we invested $22,600,000 (including $8,417,000 of nonpayroll expenses) in direct training of our professional personnel. This amounts to over 7¢ of every $1.00 of fees and does not include over $8,000,000, or 3¢ of every $1.00 of fees, of related research and other professional development expenses incurred in 1974. Thus, the current partners continue an Arthur Andersen & Co. tradition of investing heavily to assure a well trained and well informed professional group to serve our clients and to enhance the future of our worldwide organization.

FEES *in Millions of Dollars*

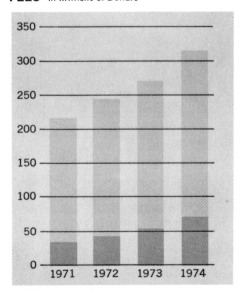

TOTAL PERSONNEL

at January 31 of Each Year   *in Thousands*

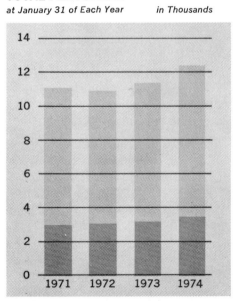

UNITED STATES & PUERTO RICO

OTHER COUNTRIES

Basis for Presentation of Financial Information

The following financial summaries present combined financial information of the legal entities which comprise the worldwide organization of Arthur Andersen & Co. The financial statements of each legal entity are prepared in local currency. Account balances for property outside the United States and Puerto Rico at March 31, 1974, were translated to U.S. dollars at exchange rates in effect when the property was acquired. All other assets and liabilities were translated to U.S. dollars at exchange rates in effect at March 31, 1974. Unrealized gains and losses from foreign currency translations, which were not significant in either 1974 or 1973, are included in income.

Working Capital

At March 31, 1974 and 1973, working capital consisted of the following:

	1974	1973
Cash and cash equivalents (excluding final year-end cash distributions made to partners in April and May—$10,585,000 in 1974 and $17,353,000 in 1973)	$ 16,415,000	$ 20,848,000
Receivables from clients and unbilled services, less reserves	92,491,000	78,951,000
Other current assets	5,033,000	3,565,000
Total current assets	$113,939,000	$103,364,000
Less—Current liabilities	32,475,000	27,899,000
Working capital	$ 81,464,000	$ 75,465,000

WORKING CAPITAL
PARTNERS CAPITAL
in Millions of Dollars

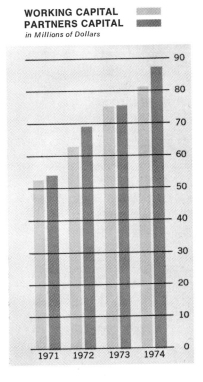

We avoid using short-term credit to finance working capital needs. Should temporary unforeseen conditions arise, we have a line of credit with a major non-client bank to cover such situations. We have also arranged credit lines with several international nonclient banks for use in countries outside the United States, principally to hedge against foreign exchange fluctuations. As of March 31, 1974, current liabilities included $583,000 of short-term bank loans (outside the United States) and the current portion ($1,303,000) of long-term debt.

Property

Property at March 31, 1974 and 1973 (less accumulated depreciation) consisted of the following:

	1974	1973
Center for Professional Development	$ 8,711,000	$ 6,965,000
Office buildings	4,015,000	3,993,000
Leasehold improvements	8,185,000	7,064,000
Office furniture and equipment	10,390,000	8,967,000
Property	$31,301,000	$26,989,000

Provisions for depreciation and amortization in fiscal 1974 and 1973 were $4,286,000 and $3,466,000, respectively. Net property additions during 1974 were $8,598,000 and during 1973 were $7,627,000. In May 1973, we completed a 160-room addition to the residence hall at our Center for Professional Development. Construction of an auditorium and expanded classroom and other facilities was well underway at March 31, 1974.

We currently lease 1,900,000 square feet of office and related space under agreements which expire on various dates to 2002. Rentals under such leases during fiscal 1974 totaled $11,028,000. As of March 31, 1974, commitments under these leases, excluding expense escalation provisions, aggregated $118,796,000. Amounts payable under these commitments for the five years ending March 31, 1979, average $10,651,000 annually.

Long-Term Debt

Long-term debt at March 31, 1974 and 1973, consisted of the following:

	1974	1973
Unsecured long-term note, payable $1,326,000 semiannually to 1985, including interest at 7¼%, to a major nonclient insurance company	$20,355,000	$21,471,000
Mortgage notes, payable $110,000 semiannually to 1985 and $1,436,000 semiannually in 1986, and approximately $20,000 annually to 1980 and $160,000 in 1981, including interest of 7¼% and 6%, respectively (secured by office buildings in Los Angeles and Milwaukee)	3,257,000	3,281,000
Purchase mortgage note, payable $406,000 annually to 1990, including interest (secured by Center for Professional Development)	3,257,000	3,330,000
	$26,869,000	$28,082,000
Less—Current portion	1,303,000	1,213,000
Long-term debt	$25,566,000	$26,869,000

Our long-term loan agreement with the insurance company has various re-strictive provisions, all of which have been complied with.

Partners' Capital

Partners' capital at March 31, 1974, was $87,200,000 compared with $75,585,000 at March 31, 1973, after deducting final year-end cash distributions made to part-ners in April and May. This includes capital contributed by partners and their share of unrealized income. It also includes $10,600,000 of capital that has not been allocated to specific partner accounts, a portion of which has been designated to cover uninsured risks. The average capital per active partner was $88,000 at March 31, 1974. The average capital for the twenty active partners with the highest capital interest was $262,000 at March 31, 1974.

Upon retirement, resignation or death of a partner, payments are made for the return of capital and other specified amounts. No amounts are paid in or returned to partners for goodwill; thus, partners do not realize any appreciation on their capital.

We carry professional indemnity insurance and, as noted above, have provided reserves to cover uninsured risks. A number of lawsuits and claims are pending; however, based on the opinions of counsel as to the disposition of these matters, we believe that the ultimate liability will not be material in relation to our finan-cial position.

Source and Disposition of Worldwide Income

In 1974, 67% of our fees was generated by our accounting and auditing practice, 18% by our tax practice, and 15% by our administrative services practice. Offices outside the United States and Puerto Rico contributed $70,046,000 or more than 22% of fiscal 1974 fees.

| | Year Ended March 31 | |
	1974	1973
SOURCE OF WORLDWIDE INCOME:		
Fees for professional services rendered to clients	$315,728,000	$271,459,000
DISPOSITION OF WORLDWIDE INCOME:		
Compensation and fringe benefits—		
Managers	$ 46,973,000	$ 41,107,000
Professional staff	99,493,000	87,680,000
Office support group	22,658,000	18,916,000
Retired and resigned partners and estates of		
deceased partners	4,855,000	2,766,000
	$173,979,000	$150,469,000
Active partners—		
Cash earnings	67,226,000	55,835,000
Unrealized income	6,497,000	7,918,000
Total compensation and fringe benefits	$247,702,000	$214,222,000

Nonpayroll operating expenses—		
Occupancy	$ 17,911,000	$ 15,218,000
Training and research	11,167,000	9,639,000
Insurance premiums and provision for uninsured risks	5,731,000	4,463,000
Interest (net)	1,809,000	1,850,000
Other	31,408,000	26,067,000
Total nonpayroll operating expenses	$ 68,026,000	$ 57,237,000
	$315,728,000	$271,459,000
Number of active partners	807	749
Average earnings per active partner (cash and unrealized)	$91,400	$85,100

Substantially all taxes on earnings are paid by the partners on the basis of their individual income tax returns. No provision for income taxes payable by the partners was made in the above financial summary.

There were 807 active partners and 90 retired, resigned and deceased partners who participated in worldwide income in fiscal 1974. Active partner earnings per unit (cash and unrealized) increased 7% in 1974 over 1973. Average earnings for the twenty active partners with the highest participation were $226,000 compared with $247,000 in 1973.

Partners' unrealized income for 1974 and 1973 consists of their share of the net change from the prior year in uncollected receivables from clients and unbilled services, less unpaid liabilities. This additional investment of partner capital is payable at various dates after a partner's retirement, resignation or death.

Significant changes in partners' income continuation and retirement benefit programs are under active consideration.

Partners' cash earnings and unrealized income are not comparable to compensation paid to corporate executives who usually receive fixed compensation plus bonuses, retirement and fringe benefits. Partners' earnings are not fixed; they depend upon current economic activity and profitability. Furthermore, from compensation received, each partner must personally pay for supplemental retirement and other fringe benefits. Over a period of time, partners' earnings must provide sufficient compensation and return on capital at risk to attract and retain top partner talent.

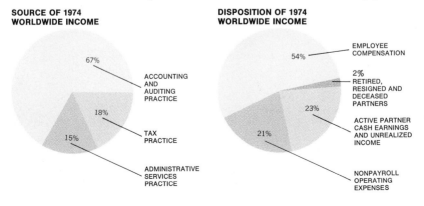

SOURCE OF 1974 WORLDWIDE INCOME

67% — ACCOUNTING AND AUDITING PRACTICE
18% — TAX PRACTICE
15% — ADMINISTRATIVE SERVICES PRACTICE

DISPOSITION OF 1974 WORLDWIDE INCOME

54% — EMPLOYEE COMPENSATION
2% — RETIRED, RESIGNED AND DECEASED PARTNERS
23% — ACTIVE PARTNER CASH EARNINGS AND UNREALIZED INCOME
21% — NONPAYROLL OPERATING EXPENSES

Textron Inc. Consolidated Statement of Income

Years Ended December 29, 1973 and December 30, 1972

	1973	1972*
Net sales .	$1,858,402,000	$1,678,422,000
Costs and expenses:		
Cost of sales .	1,333,037,000	1,209,012,000
Selling and administrative expense .	298,263,000	268,218,000
Depreciation	40,895,000	38,826,000
	1,672,195,000	1,516,056,000
	186,207,000	162,366,000
Equity in pretax income of companies not consolidated .	10,657,000	9,978,000
Operating income	196,864,000	172,344,000
Interest expense – net	15,327,000	10,571,000
Income before income taxes .	181,537,000	161,773,000
Provision for income taxes	80,700,000	73,150,000
Net income .	$100,837,000	$ 88,623,000
Net income per common share** .	$2.65	$2.30

*Restated for pooling of interests and reclassified to conform to 1973 presentation.
**Based on average shares outstanding during the year assuming full conversion of
preferred stock and exercise of warrants and stock options.

Textron Inc. Consolidated Statement of Retained Earnings

Years Ended December 29, 1973 and December 30, 1972

	1973	1972*
Balance at beginning of year .	$440,812,000	$397,169,000
Net income .	100,837,000	88,623,000
	541,649,000	485,792,000
Cash dividends declared:		
Textron:		
$2.08 preferred stock .	6,324,000	6,367,000
$1.40 preferred dividend stock .	6,441,000	6,538,000
Common stock ($.98 per share in 1973;		
$.93 per share in 1972) .	28,181,000	25,703,000
	40,946,000	38,608,000
Pooled company prior to acquisition	1,582,000	3,137,000
	42,528,000	41,745,000
Stock dividend of pooled company prior to acquisition .	—	2,221,000
Charges resulting from issuance of treasury shares		
upon exercise of stock options and warrants .	683,000	1,014,000
	43,211,000	44,980,000
Balance at end of year .	$498,438,000	$440,812,000

*Restated for pooling of interests.
See notes to financial statements.

Textron Inc. Consolidated Balance Sheet

Assets	December 29, 1973	December 30, 1972*
Current assets:		
Cash	$ 27,668,000	$ 30,234,000
Marketable securities, at cost (which		
approximates market)	13,474,000	42,477,000
Accounts receivable (less allowance for		
losses of $7,178,000 and $7,245,000)	313,502,000	255,366,000
Inventories, at lower of cost or market:		
Finished goods	159,114,000	138,632,000
Work in process (less progress payments of		
$78,181,000 and $64,677,000)	191,970,000	155,729,000
Raw materials and supplies	99,550,000	71,801,000
	450,634,000	366,162,000
Future income tax benefits	41,000,000	35,000,000
Prepaid expenses	8,558,000	6,527,000
Total current assets	854,836,000	735,766,000
Investments in companies not consolidated, at equity . . .	69,494,000	55,914,000
Investments of ARD, at cost	43,531,000	41,683,000
Property, plant and equipment, at cost:		
Land and buildings	149,443,000	131,827,000
Machinery and equipment	464,721,000	437,040,000
	614,164,000	568,867,000
Less accumulated depreciation	353,612,000	325,905,000
Net property, plant and equipment	260,552,000	242,962,000
Amount paid over value assigned to net assets		
of companies acquired, less amortization	50,585,000	51,335,000
Patents, at cost less amortization	12,850,000	12,516,000
Other assets	18,520,000	21,678,000
Total assets	$1,310,368,000	$1,161,854,000

*Restated for pooling of interests.

See notes to financial statements.

Liabilities and Shareholders' Equity	December 29, 1973	December 30, 1972*
Current liabilities:		
Notes payable	$ 39,261,000	$ 2,820,000
Accounts payable	93,165,000	72,349,000
Accrued expenses	116,718,000	90,145,000
Federal income taxes	61,524,000	61,281,000
Dividends payable	10,814,000	9,872,000
Current maturities of long term debt	1,026,000	3,745,000
Other current liabilities	68,322,000	64,941,000
Total current liabilities	390,830,000	305,153,000
Long term debt	225,561,000	217,100,000
Other liabilities	24,839,000	17,031,000
Shareholders' equity:		
Capital stock:		
$2.08 cumulative convertible preferred, Series A		
(Liquidation value — $153,340,000)	72,475,000	72,475,000
$1.40 convertible preferred dividend, Series B . . .	57,082,000	57,084,000
Common	7,873,000	8,219,000
Capital surplus	76,704,000	121,413,000
Retained earnings	498,438,000	440,812,000
	712,572,000	700,003,000
Less treasury stock, at cost	43,434,000	77,433,000
Total shareholders' equity	669,138,000	622,570,000
Total liabilities and shareholders' equity · ·	**$1,310,368,000**	**$1,161,854,000**

Textron Inc. Statement of Changes in Shares of Capital Stock

Years Ended December 29, 1973 and December 30, 1972

Shares issued (in thousands)	1973 Preferred Stock $2.08	1973 Preferred Stock $1.40	1973 Common Stock	1972* Preferred Stock $2.08	1972* Preferred Stock $1.40	1972* Common Stock
At beginning of year	3,067	4,831	32,877	3,067	4,834	30,891
Conversion of preferred stock	—	—	—	—	(3)	2
Issued for company acquired	—	—	—	—	—	1,842
Retirement of treasury shares	—	—	(1,387)	—	—	—
Pooled company prior to acquisition:						
Stock dividends	—	—	—	—	—	124
Exercise of stock options	—	—	—	—	—	18
At end of year	3,067	4,831	31,490	3,067	4,831	32,877

Treasury Shares (in thousands)	$2.08	$1.40	Common	$2.08	$1.40	Common
At beginning of year	19	199	2,365	1	127	1,163
Purchases	18˄	124	397	18	75	1,257
Issued in acquisition	—	—	—	—	—	(13)
Held by company acquired	—	—	—	—	—	44
Exercise of stock options	—	—	(55)	—	(3)	(29)
Exercise of warrants	—	—	(7)	—	—	(57)
Retirement of treasury shares	—	—	(1,387)	—	—	—
At end of year	37	323	1,313	19	199	2,365

*Restated for pooling of interests

Textron Inc. Consolidated Statement of Capital Surplus

Years Ended December 29, 1973 and December 30, 1972

	1973	1972*
Balance at beginning of year	$121,413,000	$ 61,535,000
Additions:		
Capital in excess of par value of shares issued upon conversion of preferred stock	1,000	32,000
Capital surplus resulting from acquisitions	—	57,417,000
Pooled company prior to acquisition:		
Stock dividends	—	2,221,000
Exercise of stock options	—	208,000
	121,414,000	121,413,000
Deductions:		
Charge resulting from retirement of treasury shares	44,710,000	—
Balance at end of year	$ 76,704,000	$121,413,000

*Restated for pooling of interests.
See notes to financial statements.

Textron Inc. Consolidated Statement of Changes in Financial Position
Years Ended December 29, 1973 and December 30, 1972

	1973	1972*
Sources of working capital:		
Net income.	$100,837,000	$ 88,623,000
Depreciation and other non-cash charges	42,177,000	42,057,000
Equity in net income of companies not consolidated	(7,646,000)	(7,356,000)
Total from operations	135,368,000	123,324,000
Long term borrowings	20,696,000	95,680,000
Common shares issued for ARD	—	57,793,000
Property, plant and equipment sold	8,049,000	8,505,000
Proceeds from exercise of options and warrants	1,142,000	1,320,000
Other	10,548,000	(834,000)
	175,803,000	285,788,000
Uses of working capital :		
Additions to property, plant and equipment	64,505,000	42,769,000
Dividends	40,946,000	38,608,000
Purchase of treasury shares	12,826,000	43,904,000
Purchase of treasury debentures.	7,869,000	2,329,000
Investments in non-consolidated subsidiaries	7,772,000	10,751,000
Reduction of long term debt	3,653,000	29,225,000
Purchase of businesses:		
Investments of ARD	—	46,241,000
Other non-current items – net	2,991,000	13,218,000
Increase (decrease) in ARD investments – net	1,848,000	(4,558,000)
	142,410,000	222,487,000
Increase in working capital during the year	33,393,000	63,301,000
Working capital at beginning of year	430,613,000	367,312,000
Working capital at end of year	$464,006,000	$430,613,000
Working capital changes – increase (decrease):		
Cash and marketable securities	$ (31,569,000)	$ 4,920,000
Accounts receivable	58,136,000	38,025,000
Inventories	84,472,000	34,376,000
Notes payable and current maturities of long term debt . .	(33,722,000)	(2,152,000)
Accounts payable, accrued expenses and dividends payable	(48,331,000)	(15,090,000)
Federal income taxes	(243,000)	6,284,000
Other	4,650,000	(3,062,000)
	$33,393,000	$ 63,301,000

Restated for pooling of interests.
See notes to financial statements.

Textron Inc. Notes to Financial Statements

1. Accounting Policies

Principles of Consolidation

The accompanying consolidated financial statements include the accounts of Textron Inc. and all wholly-owned subsidiaries except for an insurance group and a finance company, and a fifty-percent-owned foreign operating company, all of which are accounted for on the equity basis. Intercompany balances and transactions of the consolidated subsidiaries are eliminated in preparing the consolidated statements.

Translation of Foreign Currencies

Current assets and liabilities of consolidated subsidiaries outside the United States are translated into United States dollars at year-end rates of exchange. Long-term assets and long-term liabilities are translated at rates prevailing at dates when acquired or incurred. Income and expenses (other than depreciation) are translated at average rates prevailing during the year.

Net realized gains on foreign exchange during 1973 in the amount of $1,491,000 have been included in income. Net unrealized gains of $5,539,000 were not credited to income in 1973 but were used to establish a reserve for possible future exchange losses. The reserve is included in other current liabilities. In prior years exchange gains and losses, which were not material, were included in income.

Long term debt due in foreign currencies, if translated at rates in effect at December 29, 1973, would have increased $2,196,000.

Inventories

Inventories aggregating $380,435,000 at December 29, 1973 and $297,339,000 at December 30, 1972 were valued at the lowest of cost (generally first-in, first-out (FIFO) or average), replacement market, or estimated realizable value after allowance for selling and administrative expenses. The remaining inventories were valued at cost on the last-in, first-out (LIFO) basis (which was not in excess of market), and amounted to $70,199,000 and $68,823,000 at the respective dates. If such inventories had been valued on a FIFO basis they would have been higher than the LIFO basis by approximately $44,542,000 and $36,206,000 respectively.

Property, Plant and Equipment

Depreciation is provided at annual rates based on the estimated useful lives of the assets. Depreciation on additions of new property, plant and equipment is computed generally using accelerated methods. Depreciation calculated on this basis in 1973 amounted to $28,185,000 while the balance was calculated generally on the straight-line basis. Leasehold improvements are being written off over the period of the leases.

Amount Paid Over Value Assigned to Net Assets of Companies Acquired

This amount is being amortized on the straight-line method over 10 to 40 years.

Patents

Patents are amortized on the straight-line method over the period to expiration.

Government Contracts

Contracts currently in progress include firm fixed price, fixed price target incentive, cost plus fixed fee, cost plus incentive fee and cost plus award fee. Sales are recorded for firm fixed price and fixed price target incentive contracts as deliveries are made. Sales are recorded on cost plus contracts as work is performed and billed. Costs are accumulated by contract or groups of similar contracts and charged to cost of sales at rates based on periodic reviews of the relationship between the total estimated costs and sales. Provisions are made for prospective losses and anticipated cost overruns as the facts become known.

Research and Development

These expenses are charged directly to income or to the provisions for product development and are not deferred. In the Aerospace product group, new models and model changes involving substantial expenditures are frequently required, although not at a constant rate. Since these expenditures are necessary for continuance of the business, provisions for product development are charged to current income. Thus current business, which benefits from development expenditures made in prior periods, is charged for the cost of maintaining capability in these special product areas.

Income Taxes

Taxes are provided on the basis of income before income taxes regardless of the period in which items are reported for taxes. The principal differences between such provisions and taxes paid relate to those items which have been deducted from income but are not yet available as tax deductions, including provisions made for product development, possible adjustments or losses on contracts, self-insurance and litigation. As a result, taxes paid have exceeded the amounts charged to income, with the excess shown as future income tax benefits in the balance sheet.

Investment credits are included in income

over the average useful lives of the assets purchased or leased.

Details of the provision for income taxes are:

	1973	1972
Federal:		
Current . . .	$72,442,000	$61,017,000
Future benefits .	(5,000,000)	3,000,000
	67,442,000	64,017,000
State	6,800,000	5,528,000
Foreign	6,458,000	3,605,000
Total .	$80,700,000	$73,150,000

Total income tax expense was $6,437,000 and $4,501,000 less in 1973 and 1972, respectively, than the amount computed by applying the Federal income tax rate of 48% to income before income taxes. This condition was caused primarily by (1) the use of DISC corporations to lower taxes on exports ($2,826,000 in 1973 and $2,138,000 in 1972), (2) the amortization of investment tax credits ($1,585,000 in 1973 and $1,540,000 in 1972), (3) the 85% dividends received exclusion and tax exempt interest on bonds ($1,556,000 in 1973 and $1,317,000 in 1972), (4) the application of capital gains rates to net capital gains ($1,321,000 in 1973 and $490,000 in 1972), offset by (5) the impact of state income taxes, net of the related Federal income tax benefit, and lower foreign tax rates ($1,878,000 in 1973 and $2,793,000 in 1972).

Pension Costs

Textron has a number of pension plans covering 95% of its employees. The policy is to fund pension costs accrued. The total pension expense charged to income was approximately $23,000,000 and $20,000,000 in 1973 and 1972, respectively, which included amortization of unfunded prior service costs over periods ranging from 10 to 40 years. The unfunded past service costs were estimated at $119,000,000 at December 29, 1973. At that date the total of amounts funded with Trustees and accrued for all the plans exceeded Textron's actuarially determined liability for vested benefits.

Leases

As a general policy, Textron limits leasing to automobiles and trucks, data processing equipment, and occasionally land and buildings. Rental expense amounted to $18,728,000 in 1973 and $17,413,000 in 1972.

Minimum rentals under noncancelable leases for future years are as follows:

1974	$8,042,000
1975	6,690,000
1976	5,369,000
1977	4,444,000
1978	3,802,000
1979 to expiration	15,435,000
	$43,782,000

2. Mergers and Acquisitions

On July 6, 1973 The Security Corporation, the parent of five casualty insurance companies (see note 7), was merged into a wholly-owned Textron subsidiary. Textron issued 3,228,080 shares of common stock in exchange for all of the shares of Security common stock outstanding. This transaction was accounted for as a pooling of interests and accordingly, the consolidated financial statements for 1972 have been restated to include the investment in and earnings of Security, which is carried on an equity basis. Net income of Security included in the consolidated statement of income was $6,144,000 in 1973 ($3,074,000 for 6 months ended June 30, 1973) and $6,482,000 in 1972. Unrealized net gains on investments, net of applicable deferred federal income taxes, aggregating $3,008,000 at December 29, 1973 and $10,723,000 at December 30, 1972 which are included in Security's retained earnings have

been eliminated in recording Textron's equity in Security.

During 1973 Textron purchased two other companies for $4,907,000.

On May 18, 1972 American Research and Development Corporation was merged into Textron. In conjunction with the merger, which was accounted for as a purchase, Textron issued 1,842,000 shares of its common stock, which was recorded at $57,793,000, the approximate market value.

During 1972, Textron also purchased four other companies for $20,869,000 and 13,296 shares of treasury common stock valued at $432,000.

Operating results of all of the companies purchased have been included in the consolidated statement of income from the dates of acquisition. Inclusion of the operating results of these companies on a pro-forma basis for the full year would not have materially affected the net sales or net income for either year.

3. Long Term Debt

Exclusive of amounts due within one year, this debt consisted of:

	December 29, 1973	December 30, 1972
8.60% Notes due 1975	$50,000,000	$ 50,000,000
7¾% Eurodollar Sinking Fund Debentures due 1987	30,000,000	30,000,000
7½% Sinking Fund Debentures due 1997	50,000,000	50,000,000
6¾% Swiss Franc Notes due 1978	16,474,000	—
6¾% Dutch Guilder Notes due 1976 to 1979	9,285,000	9,285,000
6% Convertible Notes due 1982	6,250,000	6,250,000
5⅞% Sinking Fund Debentures due 1992	38,502,000	47,120,000
5% Subordinated Debentures due 1984	6,528,000	7,649,000
Other notes (4% to 8¼%)	18,522,000	16,796,000
	$225,561,000	$217,100,000

Sinking fund requirements for the debentures are: 7¾% Debentures–$1,200,000, annually 1978-1981 and increasing amounts thereafter; 7½% Debentures–$2,500,000, annually 1978-1996; 5⅞% Debentures–$2,250,000, annually 1978-1991; 5% Debentures–$100,000 and proceeds from warrants,quarterly.

The indentures relating to the 5% and 5⅞% Debentures contain restrictions on payment of cash dividends and the acquisition of treasury stock. Under the most restrictive of these provisions, none of the retained earnings were restricted at December 29, 1973 or at December 30, 1972.

At December 29, 1973 the amount of long term debt payable in 1975 is $57,382,000; in 1976, $4,305,000; in 1977, $4,890,000; and in 1978, $23,539,000.

4. Capital Stock

Authorized capital stock consists of 15,000,000 no par shares of preferred stock issuable in series and 75,000,000 shares of common stock, 25¢ par value.

Each share of the $2.08 preferred stock ($23.63 approximate stated value) is convertible into 1.1 shares of common stock and redeemable by the Company at prices ranging from $55 in 1974 to $50 in 1978 and thereafter. The $2.08 preferred stock may be redeemed only in its entirety through 1977 and thereafter in any amount. In the event of involuntary liquidation, the stock is entitled to $50 per share and accrued dividends. In the event of voluntary liquidation, each share is entitled to an amount equal to the prevailing redemption price.

Each share of $1.40 preferred dividend stock ($11.82 approximate stated value) is convertible into .9 share of common stock and starting in 1974 is redeemable at $45 per share. In the event of liquidation, holders of each share of $1.40 preferred dividend stock would receive accrued dividends and thereafter share ratably on a converted basis with holders of common stock, subject to prior rights of the $2.08 preferred stock.

Shares of common stock were reserved for conversion of preferred stock and notes and exercise of warrants and options at December 29, 1973 as follows:

$2.08 Cumulative Convertible Preferred Stock, Series A	3,373,483
$1.40 Convertible Preferred Dividend Stock, Series B (preferred only as to dividends)	4,348,016
Conversion of 6% Convertible Notes.	160,000
Warrants (exercisable at $8.75 per share until May 1, 1974 with $1.25 price increases each five years thereafter until expiration in 1984)	241,780
Options granted to employees	875,016
	8,998,295

5. Stock Options

Under the Stock Option Plan approved by stockholders in 1969, options for a maximum of 1,000,000 shares of common stock may be issued at prices not less than the fair market value at the date of grant. Options cannot be exercised for a period of 24 months after grant and may be made exercisable thereafter in cumulative installments of not more than 35% in each of the third and fourth years of the option and the balance in the fifth year. No option may be exercised later than five years from the date of grant.

At December 29, 1973 options for 310,965

shares of common stock were exercisable and 149,875 shares (408,675 shares at December 30, 1972) of common stock were available for the granting of future options.

Upon acquisition of The Security Corporation, Textron substituted options on shares of its stock for the outstanding options of Security. In 1973, options for 50,403 shares were exercised at prices ranging from $10.00 to $20.63. Options for 61,556 shares of common stock at prices ranging from $13.00 to $19.00 were outstanding at December 29, 1973. At that date all of these options were exercisable.

A summary of shares subject to options under the Textron Plan during 1972 and 1973 is shown below:

	Price per Share	Shares
Balance – January 1, 1972	$21.00 to $31.75	581,275
Add: Options granted	32.31 to 35.69	36,950
Deduct:		
Options exercised	21.00 to 31.75	29,000
Options cancelled	23.32 to 31.75	29,710
Balance – December 30, 1972	21.00 to 35.69	559,515
Add: Options granted	18.25 to 26.25	312,950
Deduct:		
Options exercised	23.32 to 24.25	4,855
Options cancelled	18.25 to 32.31	54,150
Balance – December 29, 1973	$18.25 to $35.69	813,460

6. American Research and Development

Investments of Textron's American Research and Development Division are carried at cost. In the case of those investments held by ARD at the date of acquisition by Textron (see note 2), such cost represents the allocated portion of the purchase price paid by Textron. The cost

method is utilized in recognition of the nature of the investments which are in venture capital businesses, over which Textron does not seek control. Consequently, portfolio income is recognized only to the extent of dividends and interest received and gain or loss upon disposition of investments.

Portfolio costs, values and income are as follows:

	1973	1972
Portfolio cost:		
Balance at December 30, 1972 and May 18, 1972	$41,683,000	$46,241,000
Investment additions	2,997,000	490,000
Investment reductions	(1,149,000)	(5,048,000)
Balance at end of year	$43,531,000	$41,683,000
Portfolio value at end of year (as determined by management based on market prices where available)	$44,570,000	$48,549,000

	1973	May 18 to December 30, 1972
Portfolio income:		
Dividends and interest	$426,000	$300,000
Realized gains	314,000	114,000
	$740,000	$414,000

7. *The Security Corporation Financial Statements*

Condensed consolidated financial statements for The Security Corporation, the parent of five casualty insurance companies (see note 2), for the years ended December 31, 1973 and 1972, are as follows:

Condensed Consolidated Statement of Income	1973	1972
Premiums earned	$ 79,084,000	$ 87,653,000
Losses and loss expenses	(54,913,000)	(57,229,000)
Underwriting expenses	(27,662,000)	(29,956,000)
Underwriting gain (loss)	(3,491,000)	468,000
Net investment income	7,848,000	7,466,000
Operating income before income taxes	4,357,000	7,934,000
Income taxes.	551,000	2,306,000
Income before realized investment gains	3,806,000	5,628,000
Net realized investment gains net of income taxes	2,338,000	854,000
Net income	$ 6,144,000	$ 6,482,000

Condensed Consolidated Balance Sheet	December 31, 1973	December 31, 1972
Cash	$ 1,802,000	$ 5,080,000
Investments	132,467,000	136,984,000
Premiums receivable	13,284,000	14,515,000
Deferred acquisition costs	9,418,000	9,547,000
Other assets	19,630,000	17,329,000
	$ 176,601,000	$183,455,000
Unearned premiums	$ 38,357,000	$ 39,070,000
Losses and loss expenses	70,575,000	73,178,000
Deferred federal income taxes	5,813,000	9,080,000
Other liabilities	10,016,000	12,126,000
	124,761,000	133,454,000
Stockholder's equity	51,840,000	50,001,000
	$ 176,601,000	$183,455,000

Condensed Consolidated Statement of Changes in Financial Position

	1973	1972
Funds provided:		
Net income	$ 6,144,000	$ 6,482,000
Non-cash charges (credits):		
Change in:		
Losses and loss expenses	(2,603,000)	(5,548,000)
Premiums receivable	1,231,000	1,846,000
Unearned premiums	(713,000)	(5,748,000)
Deferred acquisition costs	129,000	1,175,000
Deferred income taxes	85,000	2,306,000
Other, net	24,000	(33,000)
Less realized (gains) on sale of investments net of applicable tax	(2,338,000)	(854,000)
Total from (used in) operations	1,959,000	(374,000)
Proceeds from sale of investments net of applicable tax .	15,109,000	18,852,000
Capital contribution – Textron Inc.	5,000,000	—
	22,068,000	18,478,000
Funds used:		
Purchase of investments	19,600,000	17,969,000
Dividends	1,582,000	3,101,000
Advances to associations	2,107,000	1,219,000
Other – net	2,057,000	(368,000)
	25,346,000	21,921,000
Net decrease in cash	$ 3,278,000	$ 3,443,000

Accounting Policies for The Security Corporation

The financial statements have been prepared on the basis of generally accepted accounting principles for casualty insurance companies. Significant accounting policies are as follows:

Investments

Bonds eligible for amortization are stated at amortized cost. All other bonds and stocks are carried at values adopted by the National Association of Insurance Commissioners which approximate year-end market value. Realized gains and losses on sales of investments are reflected in the income statement net of applicable income taxes. Unrealized gains and losses are reflected in retained earnings, net of applicable deferred income taxes.

Premium Income

Premiums written are earned on a monthly prorata basis over the policy lives. Acquisition costs, principally commissions and premium taxes incurred at policy issuance, are deferred and amortized over the period of premium recognition. These costs are deducted as incurred for federal income tax purposes and deferred income taxes are provided.

Losses and Loss Expenses

Unpaid losses and loss expenses are estimates of losses on individual cases which have been reported to the Company and estimates of losses on cases which have occurred, but have not been reported to the Company.

Federal Income Taxes

Security is included in Textron's consolidated Federal income tax return. Taxes on Security's earnings are calculated as if Security were a separate entity. Effective income tax rates differ from statutory rates primarily due to the 85% dividends received exclusion and the tax exempt interest on certain bonds.

Report of Certified Public Accountants

ARTHUR YOUNG & COMPANY

The Board of Directors and Shareholders
Textron Inc.

277 Park Avenue
New York, N. Y. 10017

We have examined the accompanying consolidated balance sheet of Textron Inc. at December 29, 1973 and December 30, 1972 and the related consolidated statements of income, retained earnings, capital surplus, changes in shares of capital stock and changes in financial position for the years then ended. Our examination was made in accordance with generally accepted auditing standards, and accordingly included such tests of the accounting records and such other auditing procedures as we considered necessary in the circumstances.

In our opinion, the statements mentioned above present fairly the consolidated financial position of Textron Inc. at December 29, 1973 and December 30, 1972 and the consolidated results of operations and changes in financial position for the years then ended, in conformity with generally accepted accounting principles applied on a consistent basis during the period.

February 12, 1974

Arthur Young & Company

Transfer Agent and Registrar
Common and Preferred Stocks:
Rhode Island Hospital Trust National Bank
Providence, Rhode Island 02903

Sales and Income by Product Group

Dollars in millions

	Net Sales		Pretax Income		Net Income	
	1973	1972	**1973**	1972*	**1973**	1972*
Consumer	**$614.1**	$557.4	**$55.8**	$69.2	**$29.4**	$36.1
	33%	33%	**31%**	43%	**29%**	41%
Aerospace	**499.0**	505.9	**40.8**	47.9	**23.4**	27.2
	27%	30%	**22%**	29%	**23%**	31%
Industrial	**392.6**	335.9	**38.4**	19.6	**21.1**	10.3
	21%	20%	**21%**	12%	**21%**	11%
Metal Product	**352.7**	279.2	**38.2**	16.0	**20.3**	8.5
	19%	17%	**21%**	10%	**20%**	10%
Creative Capital	—	—	**8.3**	9.1	**6.6**	6.5
			5%	6%	**7%**	7%
Total Textron	**$1,858.4**	$1,678.4	**$181.5**	$161.8	**$100.8**	$88.6

*Restated for pooling of interests and reclassified to conform to 1973 presentation.

Ford Motor Company and Consolidated Subsidiaries
Consolidated Statement of Income
(in millions of dollars)

	1973	1972
Sales	$23,015.1	$20,194.4
Costs and Expenses		
Costs, excluding items listed below	19,069.3	16,280.2
Depreciation	485.1	455.0
Amortization of special tools	463.1	458.3
Selling and administrative	1,047.4	1,006.9
Employe retirement plans (Note 3)	335.9	312.1
Provision for supplemental compensation	60.5	64.0
	21,461.3	18,576.5
Operating income	1,553.8	1,617.9
Equity in Net Income of Unconsolidated Subsidiaries and Affiliates	48.5	60.9
Other Income (Deductions), Net (Note 4)	30.4	(16.2)
Income before income taxes	1,632.7	1,662.6
Provision for Income Taxes (Note 5)	702.1	773.3
Income before minority interests	930.6	889.3
Minority Interests in Net Income of Consolidated Subsidiaries	24.1	19.3
Net Income	$ 906.5	$ 870.0
Average number of shares of capital stock outstanding (in millions)	99.3	102.1
Net income a share (Note 6)	$9.13	$8.52
Net income a share assuming full dilution (Note 6)	$8.57	$8.17
Cash dividends a share	$3.20	$2.67½

The accompanying notes are part of the financial statements.

Ford Motor Company and Consolidated Subsidiaries
Consolidated Balance Sheet—December 31, 1973 and 1972
(in millions of dollars)

Assets	1973	1972
Current Assets		
Cash.	$ 434.4	$ 361.9
Marketable securities, at cost and accrued interest	647.8	1,107.3
Receivables—(including $139.2 million in 1973 and $99.4 million in 1972 from unconsolidated subsidiaries).	1,078.8	846.8
Inventories.	3,592.7	2,780.8
Income taxes allocable to the following year.	206.5	270.6
Other current assets.	229.3	177.1
Total current assets.	6,189.5	5,544.5
Investments and Other Assets		
Equities in net assets of unconsolidated subsidiaries and affiliates (Note 7).	1,069.1	913.9
Other investments, at cost, and other assets.	223.5	158.5
Total investments and other assets.	1,292.6	1,072.4
Property, Plant and Equipment		
Property, plant and equipment, at cost (Note 8)	8,836.7	8,212.2
Less accumulated depreciation.	4,460.1	4,159.2
	4,376.6	4,053.0
Unamortized special tools	816.1	684.9
Net property, plant and equipment.	5,192.7	4,737.9
Excess of Cost of Investments in Consolidated Subsidiaries over Equities in Net Assets	279.2	279.2
Total assets.	$12,954.0	$11,634.0

The accompanying notes are part of the financial statements.

Liabilities and Stockholders' Equity	1973	1972
Current Liabilities		
Accounts payable and accrued liabilities...	$ 3,537.1	$ 3,117.9
Income taxes..	158.9	348.6
Short-term debt of foreign subsidiaries (Note 9).......................................	651.8	355.4
Long-term debt payable within one year...	181.2	38.1
Total current liabilities..	4,529.0	3,860.0
Long-Term Debt (Note 9)	977.0	993.9
Other Liabilities and Reserves		
Accrued liabilities, noncurrent..	368.9	290.0
Supplemental compensation awards, deferred instalments.............................	43.5	31.2
Supplemental compensation reserve, unawarded balance.............................	61.6	65.3
Deferred income taxes..	284.9	194.8
Deferred investment tax credits..	98.9	75.8
Reserve for foreign operations (Note 2)..	60.0	55.0
Total other liabilities and reserves..	917.8	712.1
Minority Interests in Net Assets of Consolidated Subsidiaries	125.1	106.7
Stockholders' Equity		
Capital stock, par value $2.50 a share, 1973— 99,190,217 shares and 1972—101,485,442 shares (Notes 10 and 11).....................................	248.0	253.7
Capital account in excess of par value of stock.....................................	380.5	379.5
Earnings retained for use in the business...	5,776.6	5,328.1
Total stockholders' equity...	6,405.1	5,961.3
Total liabilities and stockholders' equity.......................................	$12,954.0	$11,634.0

Ford Motor Company and Consolidated Subsidiaries
Consolidated Statement of Stockholders' Equity
(in millions of dollars)

	Capital Stock		Capital Account in Excess of Par Value of Stock	Earnings Retained for Use in the Business	Total Stockholders' Equity
	Shares	Amount			
Balance, January 1, 1972..............	104,186,029	$260.5	$361.4	$4,925.3	$5,547.2
Net income............................				870.0	870.0
Cash dividends, $2.67½ a share...........				(272.9)	(272.9)
Common stock issued under certain employe stock plans....................	602,713	1.5	30.2		31.7
Capital stock retired....................	(3,303,300)	(8.3)	(12.1)	(194.3)	(214.7)
Balance, December 31, 1972..............	101,485,442	253.7	379.5	5,328.1	5,961.3
Net income............................				906.5	906.5
Cash dividends, $3.20 a share............				(317.1)	(317.1)
Common stock issued under certain employe stock plans....................	191,575	0.5	9.9		10.4
Conversion of debentures (Note 10)..........			0.6		0.6
Capital stock retired....................	(2,486,800)	(6.2)	(9.5)	(140.9)	(156.6)
Balance, December 31, 1973..............	99,190,217	$248.0	$380.5	$5,776.6	$6,405.1

The accompanying notes are part of the financial statements.

Ford Motor Company and Consolidated Subsidiaries
Consolidated Statement of Changes in Financial Position
(in millions of dollars)

	1973	1972
Working Capital, January 1	$1,684.5	$1,346.4
Additions to Working Capital		
From operations		
Net income	906.5	870.0
Depreciation	485.1	455.0
Amortization of special tools	463.1	458.3
Deferred income taxes and investment tax credits	113.2	41.5
Other	58.0	(19.0)
Total from operations	2,025.9	1,805.8
Issuance of long-term debt	186.7	401.4
Issuance of Common Stock	11.0	31.7
Increase in minority interests in net assets	18.4	5.3
Total additions	2,242.0	2,244.2
Dispositions of Working Capital		
Cash dividends paid	317.1	272.9
Net additions to property, plant and equipment	1,403.0	1,142.1
Additional investments in unconsolidated subsidiaries and affiliates	120.7	50.8
Reductions in long-term debt	203.6	209.7
Capital stock purchased	156.6	214.7
Increase in other investments	65.0	15.9
Total dispositions	2,266.0	1,906.1
Increase (Decrease) in Working Capital	(24.0)	338.1
Working Capital, December 31	$1,660.5	$1,684.5

Changes in the Components of Working Capital	Increase (Decrease) in Working Capital	
Cash and marketable securities	$ (387.0)	$ 384.6
Receivables	232.0	107.1
Inventories	811.9	241.3
Currently payable and deferred taxes on income	125.6	(51.4)
Accounts payable and accrued liabilities	(419.2)	(511.4)
Debt payable within one year	(439.5)	143.3
Other current assets	52.2	24.6
Net Change	$ (24.0)	$ 338.1

The accompanying notes are part of the financial statements.

Ford Motor Company and Consolidated Subsidiaries
Notes to Financial Statements

Note 1. Accounting Policies

The following is a summary of certain significant accounting policies followed in the preparation of these financial statements. The policies conform to generally accepted accounting principles and have been consistently applied.

Principles of Consolidation: The consolidated financial statements include the accounts of the Company and all of its domestic and foreign subsidiaries, except for the financing, insurance, real estate and dealership subsidiaries, all of which are included on an equity basis.

Foreign Currency Translation: The general policy followed in the translation of foreign currency items is to state assets (except net property, plant and equipment), liabilities and reserves at rates of exchange prevailing at the end of the period. Net property, plant and equipment is translated at the rates in effect on the dates of acquisition of the related assets. Earnings have been translated at rates of exchange in effect during the period, adjusted to reflect depreciation and amortization charges based on historical dollar costs. When more than one exchange rate for a particular currency exists, the rate applicable to remittance of dividends has been used in the translation of the foreign currency items. Normal gains and losses on exchange adjustments are included in current income; abnormal gains or losses may be charged or credited, as appropriate, to the reserve for foreign operations.

Depreciation and Tooling Amortization: Depreciation is computed principally by use of accelerated methods that result in accumulated depreciation of approximately two-thirds of asset cost during the first half of the assets' estimated useful lives.

The costs of special tools are amortized over periods of time representing the short productive use of such tools.

Pre-production operating costs in connection with new facilities are charged to expense as incurred.

Advertising and Sales Promotion: In general, advertising and sales promotion expenditures are charged to income as incurred.

Retirement Plan Costs: Current service costs are accrued and funded on a current basis. Prior service costs are amortized and funded over periods of not more than 30 years from the dates such costs were established.

Product Warranty Costs: Anticipated costs related to product warranty are recorded at the time of the sale of the products.

Product Development Costs: Costs associated with the development of new products and changes to existing products are charged to expense as incurred.

Investment Tax Credits: Investment tax credits are deferred and amortized over the useful lives of the related assets on a basis consistent with applicable depreciation policies.

Inventory Valuation: Inventories are stated at the lower of cost or market, with cost determined substantially on a first-in, first-out basis.

Excess of Cost of Investments Over Equities Acquired: The excess of cost of investments in consolidated subsidiaries over equities in net assets shown on the accompanying balance sheet, all of which originated prior to 1965, is not being amortized because, in the opinion of management, there has been no decrease in value.

Note 2. Foreign Operations

The contribution to sales and net income by operations outside the United States and Canada was as follows:

| | 1973 | | 1972 | |
	Amount (in millions)	Percent	Amount (in millions)	Percent
Sales	$5,925	26%	$5,099	25%
Net income	217	24	147	17

Net investments outside the United States and Canada included in the consolidated balance sheet were as follows (in millions):

	1973	1972
Equities of the Company in net assets:		
Europe	$1,166	$1,014
Latin America	273	224
All other, principally Asia-Pacific	349	305
Total equities in net assets	1,788	1,543
Excess of cost of investments over equities in net assets	252	252
Total investments	2,040	1,795
Less reserve for foreign operations	60	55
Net investments outside the United States and Canada	$1,980	$1,740

The reserve for foreign operations is provided by periodic charges to income and may be charged or credited, as appropriate, with abnormal foreign exchange adjustments and abnormal losses on foreign operations.

In 1973 and 1972, gains and losses on foreign exchange adjustments, all of which were included in current income, were not material.

Note 3. Retirement Plans

The Company has two principal retirement plans. The Ford-UAW Retirement Plan covers hourly employes represented by the UAW, and the General Retirement Plan covers substantially all other employes of the Company and certain consolidated and unconsolidated domestic subsidiaries. In addition to these two principal plans, certain other subsidiaries of the Company have separate plans covering their employes. The actuarially computed value of vested benefits under the various plans exceeded the market value of fund assets by approximately $620 million at December 31, 1973.

Amendments to the Ford-UAW Retirement Plan (which resulted from an agreement reached with the UAW on October 26, 1973) and the General Retirement Plan were adopted in 1973 and provide for substantial benefit increases over six years that will increase pension costs and the value of vested benefits in each of the years.

Note 4. Other Income (Deductions), Net

Other income and deductions consist of the following (in millions):

	1973	1972
Interest income	$ 189.9	$109.3
Interest on long-term debt	(74.7)	(62.7)
Other interest expense	(100.0)	(70.9)
All other, net	15.2	8.1
Net other income (deductions)	$ 30.4	$ (16.2)

Note 5. Provision for Income Taxes

The provision for income taxes consists of United States, foreign and state and local income taxes as follows (in millions):

	1973	1972
Federal		
Currently payable	$221.8	$473.9
Deferred	89.0	(7.7)
Deferred investment tax credits	23.1	5.6
Total federal	333.9	471.8
Foreign		
Currently payable	251.6	204.1
Deferred	65.2	24.0
Total foreign	316.8	228.1
State and local	51.4	73.4
Total	$702.1	$773.3

The provision includes estimated taxes payable on that portion of retained earnings of subsidiaries not consolidated for Federal income tax purposes which is expected to be remitted as dividends to the Company. No provision has been made with respect to the balance of such retained earnings, approximately $1,050 million at December 31, 1973. These retained earnings have been invested by the subsidiaries in facilities and other assets and have borne substantial foreign income taxes which would serve to offset in major part any tax liability resulting from their distribution.

Deferred income taxes result from timing differences in the recognition of revenues and expenses for financial statements and tax returns. The principal differences include depreciation, accrual of taxes on anticipated foreign dividend remittances, costs of certain employe benefit plans and provisions for product warranty.

The provision for income taxes was 43% of income before income taxes in 1973 compared with 46.5% in 1972 and a United States statutory tax rate of 48%. The lower rate in 1973 was caused by many factors, none of which was material.

Note 6. Net Income a Share

Net income a share is computed based upon the average number of shares of capital stock of all classes outstanding. Fully diluted net income a share is computed based upon the assumption of conversion of all outstanding convertible securities at the date of issuance, exercise of employe stock options where the exercise price was lower than the average market price (reduced by the shares that could have been purchased with the assumed proceeds) and payment of all contingently credited shares of Common Stock under the Supplemental Compensation Plan.

Note 7. Equities in Net Assets of Unconsolidated Subsidiaries and Affiliates

Equities in net assets of unconsolidated subsidiaries and affiliates at December 31, 1973 and 1972 were as follows (in millions):

	1973	1972
Ford Motor Credit Company	$ 823.8	$ 637.8
Retail dealerships	100.7	109.1
Ford Leasing Development Company	47.4	48.4
Ford Motor Land Development Corporation	35.5	26.7
All other	61.7	91.9
Total	$1,069.1	$ 913.9

Note 8. Property, Plant and Equipment

Property, plant and equipment at December 31, 1973 and 1972 are summarized as follows (in millions):

	1973	1972
Land	$ 173.6	$ 171.6
Buildings and land improvements	2,517.3	2,407.3
Machinery, equipment and office furniture	5,707.6	5,334.8
Construction in progress	438.2	298.5
Total	$8,836.7	$8,212.2

Note 9. Debt and Debt Guarantees

Long-term debt at December 31, 1973 and 1972, excluding amounts payable within one year, was as follows (in millions):

	1973	1972
Amounts payable in:		
United States dollars	$ 771.5	$ 747.6
British pounds	63.1	104.6
French francs	55.4	65.2
Belgian francs	32.5	32.9
German marks	23.8	20.0
Australian dollars	14.6	12.5
Other currencies	16.1	11.1
Total	$ 977.0	$ 993.9

The aggregate annual maturities and required prepayments of long-term debt are as follows (in millions) for the years ending December 31: 1974—$181; 1975—$62; 1976—$69; 1977—$199; 1978—$28.

On January 23, 1974, the Company issued $150 million principal amount of 7.4% Notes due January 15, 1980 and $80 million principal amount of 7.85% Sinking Fund Debentures due January 15, 1994, in exchange for 5,662,409 shares of Class A Stock owned by The Ford Foundation ("Foundation"). Such shares will be retired during 1974, resulting in a $230 million reduction in Stockholders' Equity.

Short-term debt at December 31, 1973, all of which was incurred by the Company's foreign subsidiaries, was $651.8 million, which is approximately $200 million more than the average short-term debt outstanding during the year.

At December 31, 1973, the Company and its consolidated subsidiaries had guaranteed $446 million of debt of unconsolidated subsidiaries of which $103 million was long term. The guaranteed amount included $399 million of unsecured debt of Ford Leasing Development Company, a wholly-owned unconsolidated subsidiary, which finances leased vehicles and owns and leases real estate properties. Substantially all of the real estate properties are leased or sub-leased to franchised Ford vehicle dealers. At December 31, 1973, the net investment in these properties was approximately $290 million and was financed principally by means of the unsecured debt of Ford Leasing Development Company guaranteed by the Company.

Note 10. Capital Stock

Authorized and issued shares of capital stock at December 31, 1973 were as follows:

	Authorized Shares	Issued Shares	Amount (in millions)
Class A Stock (Nonvoting)	101,420,960	6,709,363	$ 16.8
Class B Stock (Voting)	29,138,118	12,097,878	30.2
Common Stock (Voting)	250,000,000	80,382,976	201.0
	380,559,078	99,190,217	$248.0

All general voting power is vested exclusively in the holders of Common Stock and the holders of Class B Stock, voting together without regard to class. At December 31, 1973, the holders of Common Stock were entitled to one vote per share and in the aggregate had 60% of the general voting power, and the holders of Class B Stock were entitled to such number of votes per share as would give them in the aggregate the remaining 40% of the general voting power, as provided in the Company's Certificate of Incorporation. The Certificate provides that all shares of Common Stock, Class A Stock and Class B Stock share equally in the assets upon liquidation and in dividends, except that any stock dividends are payable in shares of Common Stock to holders of that class, Class A Stock to holders of that class and Class B Stock to holders of that class.

The Company has acquired a large portion of its requirements for Common Stock for the Company's Stock Option Plans by purchases of shares of Class A Stock of the Company from the Foundation pursuant to an agreement with the Foundation. These shares are retired following acquisition and shares of Common Stock are issued, as needed, to employes in connection with option exercises. During 1973, 265,950 shares of Class A Stock were acquired from the Foundation for this purpose at a cost of $17.1 million.

The Company has reserved 8,170,596 shares of Common Stock for conversion of outstanding convertible debentures issued by the Company's subsidiaries. These debentures mature from 1983 to 1998. Conversion prices of the debentures range from $63.09 to $81.90 a share. At December 31, 1973, the Company had acquired (principally by purchases from the Foundation) shares of its capital stock equal to the number of shares of Common Stock that may be required for the conversion of such debentures. All such shares have been retired and 30,435 shares of Common Stock have been issued upon conversion of debentures.

The Company has also purchased shares of Class A Stock from the Foundation for ultimate conversion, as needed, into an equal number of shares of Common Stock for issuance under the deferred payment provisions of the Company's Supplemental Compensation Plan. Such purchases were made pursuant to an agreement with the Foundation under which the Company acquired on a monthly basis substantially all of its requirements of stock for this purpose. A total of 405,075 shares of Class A Stock, with a cost of $21.1 million, acquired for purposes of the deferred payment provisions of the Supplemental Compensation Plan, are included with other investments in the accompanying balance sheet at December 31, 1973.

See Note 9 with respect to Class A Stock acquired from the Foundation in January 1974; it is expected that all remaining shares of Class A Stock held by the Foundation will be sold to the trustee under Ford's Savings and Stock Investment Plan during the first quarter of 1974.

Future requirements of Common Stock for the Supplemental Compensation Plan in excess of shares obtained upon conversion of the Class A Stock already held by the Company for purposes of the Plan, and future requirements of Common Stock for the Stock Option Plans, are expected to be provided by issuance of previously unissued but authorized shares of Common Stock.

Note 11. Stock Options

At December 31, 1973, options were outstanding to purchase 1,088,000 shares of Common Stock of the Company under the 1965 and 1970 employe Stock Option Plans of the Company (of which options on 635,250 shares were exercisable at that date) at prices ranging from $43.13 to $71.94 a share. Options granted under the 1965 and 1970 Plans may be exercised, in general, as to 50% of the shares after one year from the date of grant and in full after two years, and to the extent not exercised, expire five years from the date of grant for the 1965 Plan and ten years from the date of grant for the 1970 Plan. Each option outstanding was granted at an option price equal to the fair market value of the stock on the date of grant. No further options may be granted under the 1965 Plan. At December 31, 1973, there were 550,125 shares available under the 1970 Plan for future grants of options at any time prior to expiration of the Plan in 1975.

Changes during 1973 in options outstanding under the Stock Option Plans of the Company were as follows:

	Shares Subject to Option	Option Price Range Per Share
Outstanding January 1, 1973	992,930	$43.13 — $71.94
Granted	295,500	$65.81
Exercised	(190,680)	$43.13 — $60.38
Terminated	(9,750)	$43.13 — $71.94
Outstanding December 31, 1973	1,088,000	$43.13 — $71.94

Note 12. Litigation and Claims

Various legal actions, governmental proceedings and other claims are pending against the Company and certain of its subsidiaries, some of which purport to be class actions and seek damages in very large amounts, as well as other relief, which, if granted, would require very large expenditures. Although the amount of liability at December 31, 1973 with respect to such matters cannot be ascertained, in the opinion of counsel for the Company, any resulting liability will not materially affect the consolidated financial position or results of operations.

Note 13. Ford Motor Credit Company and Consolidated Subsidiaries

Ford Motor Credit Company is a wholly-owned unconsolidated subsidiary of the Company. The following condensed balance sheet includes the accounts of Ford Motor Credit Company and its subsidiaries, each of which is wholly owned. The balance sheet for 1972 has been restated to consolidate the insurance and claims service subsidiaries which were previously included on an equity basis.

Consolidated Balance Sheet—December 31, 1973 and 1972
(in millions of dollars)

Assets	1973	1972
Cash	$ 127.8	$ 115.8
Marketable securities	150.5	219.2
Finance receivables (including instalments due after one year)	6,604.1	5,627.7
Deduct:		
Unearned income	(377.3)	(297.3)
Allowance for credit losses	(111.8)	(99.5)
Finance receivables, net	6,115.0	5,230.9
Note receivable from affiliated company	113.1	80.4
Other assets	97.9	73.3
Total assets	$6,604.3	$5,719.6

Liabilities and Stockholder's Equity	1973	1972
Short-term debt, unsecured	$3,687.2	$3,553.3
Long-term debt payable within one year	64.8	57.3
Accounts payable and accrued liabilities	305.2	252.8
Long-term indebtedness		
Unsecured	1,723.3	1,218.4
Affiliated companies	170.0	156.6
Total liabilities	5,950.5	5,238.4
Stockholder's equity		
Capital stock	25.0	25.0
Paid-in surplus	476.8	341.0
Earnings retained for use in the business	152.0	115.2
Total stockholder's equity	653.8	481.2
Total liabilities and stockholder's equity	$6,604.3	$5,719.6

Auditors' Opinion

To the Board of Directors and Stockholders
of Ford Motor Company:

We have examined the consolidated balance sheet of Ford Motor Company and Consolidated Subsidiaries as of December 31, 1973 and the related consolidated statements of income, stockholders' equity and changes in financial position for the year then ended. Our examination was made in accordance with generally accepted auditing standards, and accordingly included such tests of the accounting records and such other auditing procedures as we considered necessary in the circumstances. We previously examined and reported upon the financial statements of Ford Motor Company and Consolidated Subsidiaries for the year ended December 31, 1972.

In our opinion, the aforementioned financial statements present fairly the consolidated financial position of Ford Motor Company and Consolidated Subsidiaries at December 31, 1973 and 1972, and the consolidated results of operations and the changes in financial position for the years then ended, in conformity with generally accepted accounting principles applied on a consistent basis.

Coopers & Lybrand

Coopers & Lybrand
211 West Fort Street, 23rd Floor
Detroit, Michigan 48226
February 8, 1974

Index